Charles Williams and C. S. Lewis

Charles Williams and C. S. Lewis

Friends in Co-inherence

PAUL S. FIDDES

OXFORD
UNIVERSITY PRESS

OXFORD
UNIVERSITY PRESS

Great Clarendon Street, Oxford, OX2 6DP,
United Kingdom

Oxford University Press is a department of the University of Oxford.
It furthers the University's objective of excellence in research, scholarship,
and education by publishing worldwide. Oxford is a registered trade mark of
Oxford University Press in the UK and in certain other countries

First Edition published in 2021

Impression: 1

Published in the United States of America by Oxford University Press
198 Madison Avenue, New York, NY 10016, United States of America

British Library Cataloguing in Publication Data
Data available

Library of Congress Control Number: 2021946953

ISBN 978–0–19–284546–7

DOI: 10.1093/oso/9780192845467.001.0001

Printed and bound by
CPI Group (UK) Ltd, Croydon, CR0 4YY

For Francis Warner
and Penelope Warner

Friends in the Co-inherence

Contents

PART III A COLLABORATION IN CO-INHERENCE

PART IV FURTHER STUDIES IN CO-INHERENCE

PART V THE THEOLOGY OF CO-INHERENCE

Preface and Acknowledgements

The genesis of this book lies in the children's section of my local library in 1955. There I discovered the *Chronicles of Narnia* by C. S. Lewis, and I must have been among their earliest readers; *The Magician's Nephew* was published that year, and I recall picking up *The Last Battle* from the new accessions tray in 1956. I made the discovery entirely for myself at the age of eight; nobody directed me to read the books, and nobody told me that C. S. Lewis was a 'Christian author'. Then, at the age of 11 or 12, I borrowed the novel *Many Dimensions* by Charles Williams from my school library, and found myself in the same kind of territory as I had with Lewis' Narnia, though it felt more wild and dangerous, and the impression continued as I eagerly consumed a couple more of his novels. Again, nobody mentioned Williams to me, and it was only much later that I learnt that Lewis and Williams had been friends. I have continued to read both C. S. Lewis and Charles Williams for the last sixty years, first through literary studies and then as a theologian. I have agreed (sometimes) and disagreed (sometimes) with both, but always admired.

I have aimed in this book essentially to read the two authors for myself, rather than to review secondary literature about them, although I have taken notice of some important scholarly work. I offer a close reading of texts, and there is one series of texts in particular that has been curiously neglected, even ignored. I mean the notebooks of Raymond Hunt, into which he transcribed, from shorthand notes, virtually all the lectures that Charles Williams gave to evening classes in London from 30 September 1932 to 23 June 1939, more than 300 of them. The notebooks also contain a wealth of other lecture notes, memoranda, addresses, and essays that Williams gave Hunt to copy, before and after 1939; but it is the lectures recorded and transcribed by Hunt as Williams' most faithful listener that give us Williams' voice—prophetic, sermonic, humorous, rambling, anecdotal, entertaining, and, above all, perceptive. I have drawn on these lectures for fresh material not previously commented upon, including Williams' reflections on Gerard Manley Hopkins, William Blake, and the theologian Karl Barth. It is these lectures that also provide us with the clues to Williams' discovery and development of the theme of co-inherence that is the focus of this book.

For access to the Hunt notebooks, the papers and letters of Charles Williams, and the manuscript archive of C. S. Lewis, I am deeply grateful to the Marion E. Wade Center at Wheaton College, Illinois. Especially I thank the Associate Director, Marjorie Lamp Mead, the Archivist Laura Schmidt, other members of the Wade staff, and the President of Wheaton College, Philip Ryken, for his hospitality. I also warmly thank the Center for awarding me a Clyde Kilby Research Grant in 2015, which made visiting the archive much easier. In

Oxford, I am much indebted to librarians and archivists of the Bodleian Library, who gave me access to several collections of papers of Charles Williams.

Extracts from the following published and unpublished writings of C. S. Lewis are copyright © CS Lewis Pte Ltd, and are reprinted by kind permission: *The Abolition of Man* © copyright CS Lewis Pte Ltd 1943, 1946, 1948; *A Grief Observed* © copyright CS Lewis Pte Ltd 1961; *Christian Reflections* © copyright CS Lewis Pte Ltd 1967, 1980; *Collected Letters*, Vols. I, II and III © copyright CS Lewis Pte Ltd 2000, 2004, 2006; *The Four Loves* © copyright CS Lewis Pte Ltd 1960; The Last Battle © copyright CS Lewis Pte Ltd 1956; *Letters to Malcolm: Chiefly on Prayer* © copyright CS Lewis Pte Ltd 1963, 1964; *The Lion, The Witch, and the Wardrobe* © copyright CS Lewis Pte Ltd 1950; *Mere Christianity* © copyright CS Lewis Pte Ltd 1942, 1943, 1944, 1952; *Miracles* © copyright CS Lewis Pte Ltd 1947, 1960; *Of This and Other Worlds* © copyright CS Lewis Pte Ltd 1982; *Out of the Silent Planet* © copyright CS Lewis Pte Ltd 1938; *Perelandra* © copyright CS Lewis Pte Ltd 1944; *The Pilgrim's Regress* © copyright CS Lewis Pte Ltd 1933; *Poems* © copyright CS Lewis Pte Ltd 1964; *Prince Caspian* © copyright CS Lewis Pte Ltd 1951; *The Problem of Pain* © copyright CS Lewis Pte Ltd 1940; *The Silver Chair* © copyright CS Lewis Pte Ltd 1953; *Surprised by Joy* © copyright CS Lewis Pte Ltd 1955; *That Hideous Strength* © copyright CS Lewis Pte Ltd 1945; *They Asked for a Paper* © copyright CS Lewis Pte Ltd 1962; *Till We Have Faces* © copyright CS Lewis Pte Ltd 1956; *Transposition and Other Addresses* © copyright CS Lewis Pte Ltd 1970; *Undeceptions: Essays on Theology and Ethics* © copyright CS Lewis Pte Ltd 1971; *The Voyage of the Dawn Treader* © copyright CS Lewis Pte Ltd 1952; *The World's Last Night and Other Essays* © copyright CS Lewis Pte Ltd 1960; the unpublished manuscript *Clivi Hamiltonis Summae Metaphysices Contra Anthroposophos* © copyright CS Lewis Pte Ltd; an unpublished letter to Michal Williams, 15 June 1948 © copyright CS Lewis Pte Ltd.

All extracts from the published and unpublished writings of Charles Williams and from the notebooks of Raymond Hunt are © Bruce Hunter and are printed by gracious and very generous permission of Bruce Hunter.

Lines from T. S. Eliot's poem 'Burnt Norton' are reprinted by kind permission of Faber and Faber Ltd © 2015, and the Houghton Mifflin Harcourt Publishing Company © 1942 and 1970. Extracts from C. S. Lewis, *A Grief Observed*, are also by kind permission of Faber and Faber, © 1961. Chapter 13 is a revised and expanded version of my essay '"For the Dance All Things Were Made": The Great Dance in C. S. Lewis's Perelandra', which originally appeared in *C. S. Lewis's Perelandra*, edited by Judith Wolfe and Brendan Wolfe (2013), and which is used by kind permission of the Kent State University Press.

Finally, I thank the members of the audiences of lectures I have given over the years to the Wade Center, the Charles Williams Society, the Oxford C. S. Lewis Society, and the Triennial Oxford Conference of the Inklings Society. Their responses have enriched my reading of Charles Williams and C. S. Lewis, and have ultimately found fruition in this book.

Abbreviations

Bod. MS	The manuscripts archive of the Bodleian Library, Oxford.
CLI	The City Literary Institute
Wade CWP	The Charles Williams Papers in the Marion E. Wade Center
Wade MS/CW	Manuscripts of the writings of Charles Williams in the Marion E. Wade Center
Wade RH Notebooks	Notebooks of Raymond Hunt in the Marion E. Wade Center
Wade CSL MS	Manuscripts of C. S. Lewis in the Marion E. Wade Center

Note

Where the lacuna...appears in transcriptions of manuscripts, this is original to the document.

Where a lacuna appears as [...], this has been inserted by the author.

PART I

THE 'SECRET ROAD' OF FRIENDSHIP

1

Two Lives Converge, 1936–1939

1.1 Friendship in Co-inherence

C. S. Lewis and Charles Williams first met each other through the *printed* page
and on the *written* page. The manner of their meeting seems altogether appropriate for the mutual debt in their writings that was to follow. In March 1936, they
wrote to each other to express admiration for a recent volume of each other's
work, and there began a nine-year literary and personal friendship that ended with
Williams' early death in May 1945. It was a relatively short segment of each of
their lives, and yet it was an extraordinarily productive time for both of them: they
were publishing the novels, literary criticism, and popular theology—and in
Williams' case, also volumes of poems—that were to define their particular
creativity. It was the period in which the word 'co-inherence' appears in
Williams' work, which critics of Williams have increasingly identified as his key
idea without—apparently—being aware that the word itself was a late arrival on
the scene, adopted by him only in early 1939.[1]

I suggest that Lewis and Williams might aptly be called 'friends in co-
inherence', since investigating the way that they treat the theme of co-inherence
(not always the precise term) shows up both affinities and differences between
them that could not otherwise be seen. A fuller exploration of what this co-
inherence might mean must wait for later chapters, but for those readers to
whom the unusual word in my subtitle is perplexing, I offer an initial explanation.
Co-inherence is—briefly—the conviction that human persons inhere or dwell in
each other so that they exist in a mutual interdependence, and that at the
foundation of this relational reality the 'Persons' of a triune God permeate one
another in love. Exploring the idea of a co-inherent world will throw light on a
wide range of theological and literary subjects that concerned our two authors—
for example, the poetry of William Blake and Thomas Traherne, the Arthurian
tradition, the nature of human and divine love, the theology of Karl Barth, and the
doctrine of the triune God.

In naming Williams and Lewis as '*Friends* in Co-inherence', the subtitle of this
book differentiates their relationship from that of the *companions* of the lay
religious order called 'The Company of the Co-inherence', which Williams

---

[1] This claim is substantiated in Chapter 4.

Charles Williams and C.S. Lewis: Friends in Co-inherence. Paul S. Fiddes, Oxford University Press. © Paul S. Fiddes 2021.
DOI: 10.1093/oso/9780192845467.003.0001

founded in 1939, shortly after alighting on the term 'co-inherence'. Lewis himself was never a member of that order, and nor were any of 'The Inklings', Lewis' name for the literary group in Oxford founded by himself and J. R. R. Tolkien, who shared conversation and friendship, and read their work in progress to each other. I also intend the subtitle to respect Lewis' own distinction of a 'friend' from a 'companion', which he explains in his late book *The Four Loves* (written in 1960), although Williams himself would not have made the distinction, and undoubtedly saw the 'companions' in 'The Company of the Co-inherence' as 'friends' in the sense that Lewis uses the word 'friend'.

Looking back on a life of significant friendships from the vantage point of a comparatively recent marriage, in *The Four Loves* Lewis characterizes the nature of friendship as a kind of co-inherence, though without using the term. Writing of the effect of the death of a friend named 'Charles', evidently Charles Williams, Lewis evokes the 'part' that each has in the other:[2]

> Lamb says somewhere that if, of three friends (A, B, and C), A should die, then B loses not only A but 'A's part in C', while C loses not only A but 'A's part in B'. In each of my friends there is something that only some other friend can fully bring out. [...] Now that Charles is dead, I shall never again see Ronald's reaction to a specifically Caroline joke. Far from having more of Ronald, having him 'to myself' now that Charles is away, I have less of Ronald.

There is something deeply poignant in this account of the friendship so alluded to between Lewis, Charles Williams, and 'Ronald'—John Ronald Reuel Tolkien. By 1960, Lewis did indeed 'have less of Ronald' than he had enjoyed in the 1930s when they had partnered to reform the syllabus of the Faculty of English Language and Literature at Oxford and together initiated the Inklings, but it is Lewis' own explanation that this was due to the loss through death of their mutual friend Charles. Tolkien's own view by this time was that their early close friendship had been undermined first by the advent of the mercurial Williams onto the scene, whom he regarded as having dazzled and fascinated Lewis to an unhealthy degree, and later by Lewis' 'very strange marriage'.[3] Nevertheless, beyond the specific example chosen, Lewis' vision of the particular kind of co-inherence there is in a friendship is surely valid, and it underlines his view of friendship as a level of intensity beyond companionship. Companions, he thinks, share interests in common, but friends 'will be doing something together more inward, less widely shared and less easily defined, still collaborating but in some work the world does not, or not yet, take account of; still travelling companions, but on a different kind

---

[2] Lewis, *Four Loves*, 73–4.
[3] Tolkien to Christopher Bretherton, 16 July 1964, in Tolkien, *Letters*, 349.

of journey'.[4] Friendship arises when 'two people [. . .] discover that they are on the same secret road'. It is, asserts Lewis, a form of love (*eros*)—and in the next chapter he quotes Williams on the theme of love: 'Love you? I am you.'[5] In the aftermath of Williams' death, Lewis simply called Williams 'my dearest friend'.[6]

In these opening three chapters, I will be attempting an overview of the 'secret road' shared by Williams and Lewis during the course of their friendship. It is not possible to understand their sense of co-inherence outside the context of this relationship, and so I intend to give an account of their friendship as a preparation for exploring at depth the place of co-inherence in their thinking in the remainder of this study. I do not aim to offer a biography of either of them, as that has been done very well by others—most effectively, and recently, by Alister McGrath in the case of Lewis and by Grevel Lindop in the case of Williams.[7] External events in their lives cannot and will not be ignored, but these will not be my main concern. Nor by looking more 'inward' am I venturing to offer any psychological assessment of either or both, as this seems largely a matter of speculation whenever it is attempted. My intention is to travel with them on their inward journey in a literary mode, as the road is marked out by their writings about each other, and by the way that in their written work each has been influenced by the other, or has resisted being influenced.

In the second part of the book, building on the foundation of the first, I will examine the development of the idea of co-inherence by Williams and Lewis, mainly separately, but with cross-references between them. The third part will firmly join the friends together again on the theme of co-inherence, presenting a dialogue and collaboration between them on an approach to Arthurian literature. The fourth part consists of the uses of co-inherence by Williams and Lewis in their separate ways, showing how it has made an impact in different genres of writing. Both Williams and Lewis produced a wide range of material—literary criticism, novels, poems, popular theology—and I aim to show the difference it makes to our reading of them all when we are alert to the idea of co-inherence. With regard to Williams, I show that it results in an original reading of the Swiss theologian Karl Barth and a change in the way he reads William Blake over the years. Further, attention to the development of the idea of co-inherence makes clear that there is a thematic progression in his novels, rather than the mere repetition of themes that some critics have supposed. With regard to Lewis, it clarifies the central place that one episode—the Great Dance of Perelandra—occupies in his science fiction novels, and suggests that Traherne plays a more significant part in his diverse work than would appear at first sight.

---

[4] Lewis, *Four Loves*, 79.

[5] Lewis, *Four Loves*, 111. Lewis is quoting from Williams, *Figure of Beatrice*, 204, and the context is Williams' discussion of Dante's 'in-theeing'.

[6] Lewis (CSL) to Sister Penelope, 28 May 1945, in Lewis, *Letters*, 2: 656.

[7] McGrath, *C. S. Lewis: A Life*; Lindop, *Charles Williams: The Third Inkling*.

Finally, at the conclusion of the book, I return to a comparison of the world views of Williams and Lewis, and—building on the history of the term 'co-inherence' in theology—I propose a common ground between these frameworks of reality, deriving from a co-inherence within the relations of the triune God. Here I step outside the role of a historical commentator on Williams and Lewis and into the mode of a constructive theologian, but I believe it is a transition of which they would have approved. In fact, they would have expected it.

1.2 A Meeting in 1936: Admiration and Dissent

The story has often been told of the moment that the lives of Lewis and Williams converged, or—we might say—began to co-inhere. In March 1936, Lewis sent a letter to Williams congratulating him on his novel *The Place of the Lion*, and Williams replied immediately, telling Lewis that he had himself been about to write to Lewis with admiration for his recent scholarly study *The Allegory of Love,* as yet provisionally called *The Allegorical Love Poem*.[8] As an editor with the Oxford University Press in London, Williams had the proofs of Lewis' book in front of him, and had been asked by the secretary of the Press, Humphrey Milford, to provide a cover blurb and publicity for the volume. If Lewis had waited one more day, he informed him, their letters would have crossed in the post. Lewis' letter invited Williams to visit him in Oxford and attend a meeting of 'a sort of informal club called the Inklings', the qualification for which was 'a tendency to write', and it seems that Williams took up the invitation on 18 May and then again at the beginning of November.[9] Lewis' own comment is that from that point 'our friendship rapidly grew inward to the bone'.[10] While Williams credited the apparent coincidence of their correspondence to 'the staff work of the Omnipotence',[11] there were human hands at work behind the scenes. Lewis himself tells us that R. W. Chapman, the Secretary to the Oxford branch of the Press—the Clarendon Press—had recommended Williams' novels to him several years earlier, although Lewis had only got round to reading one when a fellow English scholar, Neville Coghill, loaned him his copy of *The Place of the Lion*.[12] It seems that Chapman then encouraged Lewis to write to Williams,[13] and Humphrey Milford as Chapman's opposite number in London may well have deliberately assisted the acquaintance by asking Williams to deal with the final

---

[8] CSL to Charles Williams (CW), 11 March 1936, in Lewis, *Collected Letters* (henceforth *Letters*), 2: 183–4; CW to CSL, 12 March 1936, in Lewis, *Letters*, 2: 184–5.
[9] See letters of Charles Williams to Olive Willis and Phyllis Potter, in Lindop, *Charles Williams*, 259.
[10] Lewis, *Essays Presented to Charles Williams*, viii.
[11] CW to CSL, 12 March 1936, in Lewis, *Letters*, 2: 184.   [12] Lewis, *Essays*, viii.
[13] Lindop, *Charles Williams*, 258.

production of Lewis' Clarendon Press volume. It was to be Williams who finally came up with the familiar title *The Allegory of Love*.

However the epistolary meeting came to be, Lewis and Williams had recognized each other immediately as kindred spirits. Williams' novel was about the breaking through of Platonic archetypes into this world, a new twist on an ancient philosophical tradition with which Lewis had been familiar since undergraduate days, and which had assisted his conversion to Christianity five years earlier.[14] Lewis' study concerned the medieval tradition of courtly love and its association with the religious moods of the period, where Williams had long been absorbed by the relation between Christian theology and romantic love. Deservedly, the story of their literary encounter is told in all the biographies of Lewis and Williams and most accounts of the Inklings. However, what is usually omitted is the almost immediate difference of view on the nature of erotic love that was registered between them by Lewis, marked by a letter that he wrote some ten days after he received the enthusiastic reply to his initial letter, and in his view articulating a sufficiently serious dissent from Williams to make him wonder whether he had 'quenched all wish for a meeting', though he hoped for a 'pleasanter hypothesis'.[15] Almost all accounts of the exchange of letters omit any reference to this second letter of Lewis.[16] A noteworthy exception is Williams' biographer, Grevel Lindop, who with his usual exemplary attention to detail includes extracts from the second letter, rightly commenting that Lewis perceived, after reading Williams' letter and the volume of his poems (*Poems of Conformity*) that Williams had sent him, that 'caution was required'. Lindop deduces that at their first physical meeting, 'Lewis discerned what he most valued in a friend: enough agreement to make profound and affectionate communication possible, and enough disagreement to provide endless fodder for debate.'[17]

Lindop does not, however, comment further on Lewis' second letter, or clarify what the nature of the disagreement was, and we shall only be able to trace the complex way in which the paths of Lewis and Williams converge if we have a clear view of Lewis' initial dissent from Williams and how it remained until the end of Lewis' life. So let us revive the correspondence, beginning with parts of the generous letter from Lewis to Williams dated 11 March 1936:

> A book sometimes crosses ones path which is so like the sound of ones native
> language in a strange country that it feels almost uncivil not to wave some kind of

---

[14] See Chapter 6, section 2.   [15] CSL to CW, 23 March 1936, in Lewis, *Letters*, 2: 185–7.
[16] E.g. Carpenter, *Inklings*, 99; Green and Hooper, *C. S. Lewis*, 134–5; Hadfield, *Charles Williams: An Exploration*, 164; Wilson, *C. S. Lewis*, 150; Knight, *Magical World*, 25; McGrath, *C. S. Lewis*, 177; Duriez, *Oxford Inklings*, 25; Zaleski and Zaleski, *Fellowship*, 238. The second letter was, however, not available widely to writers until 2004, when Walter Hooper retrieved it from Williams' papers: see CWP 353.
[17] Lindop, *Charles Williams*, 259.

flag in answer. I have just read your *Place of the Lion* and it is to me one of the major literary events of my life – comparable to my first discovery of George Macdonald. G. K. Chesterton, or Wm. Morris. There are layers and layers – first the pleasure that any good fantasy gives me: then, what is rarely (tho' not so very rarely) combined with this, the pleasure of a real philosophical and theological stimulus: thirdly, characters: fourthly, what I neither expected nor desired, substantial edification. [...] Honestly, I didn't think there was anyone now alive in England who could do it.[18]

Williams replies by return of post, on 12 March 1936, enclosing one of his early collections of poems, *Poems of Conformity*:

I admit that I fell for the *Allegorical Love Poem* so heavily because it is an aspect of the subject with which my mind has always been playing; indeed I once wrote a little book called *An Essay in Romantic Theology*, which the Bishop of Oxford (between ourselves) shook his head over.[19] [...] I regard your book as practically the only one that I have ever come across, since Dante, that shows the slightest understanding of what this very peculiar identity of love and religion means. [...] [T]o write about your *Love Poem* and my *Lion* and both our Romantic Theology in one letter takes some paragraphs.

Response came from Lewis on 23 March, having received Williams' letter and volume of poems. Some ten days had been needed, perhaps to read the poems and—it seems—a second novel by Williams (*Many Dimensions*),[20] but also perhaps to mull over a suitable reply. With a little embarrassment, Lewis effectively dissociates himself from Williams' too-eager phrase 'both our Romantic Theology':

This is going to be a complicated matter. To make a clean breast of it, that species of romanticism which you found in my book and which is expressed in the poems you sent me, is not my kind at all. [...] I think you will find that I nowhere commit myself to a definite approval of this blend of erotic and religious feeling. I treat it with respect: I display: I don't venture very far. And this is perhaps what one ought to expect from a man who is native in a quite distinct, though neighbouring, province of the Romantic country, and who willingly believes well of all her provinces, for love of the country herself, though he dare not affirm except about his own. [...]

---

[18] Lewis, *Letters*, 2: 183.
[19] In fact, it seems to have been the Bishop of Ripon: see Lindop, *Charles Williams*, 110–11.
[20] Lewis remarks that he has read it 'with enormous enjoyment'; CSL to CW, 23 March 1936, in Lewis, *Letters*, 2: 187.

Put briefly, there is a romanticism which finds its revelation in love, which is yours, and another which finds it in mythology (and nature mythically apprehended) which is mine. Ladies, in the one: gods in the other – the bridal chamber, or the wood beyond the world – a service incensed with rich erotic perfume, a service smelling of heather, salt water etc.

But this distinction is a little complicated by two facts: 1. While writing about Courtly Love I have been so long a student of *your* province that I think, in a humble way, I am nearly naturalised. 2. In the book I am sending you (don't read it unless it interests you) you will find lots about the frontier between sexual and religious experience. But look to your feet here. It really has nothing to do with your province: it is simply about desire, longing, the impersonal thing: which oddly enough can be diverted from the wood beyond the world (are you still following me?) into lust just as quickly as 'love' can.[21]

In this reply, Lewis is taking up the geographical imagery he had employed in *A Pilgrim's Regress* for various states of mind and belief,[22] and he sends Williams a copy of that very book. His point is that, while he and Williams both live in 'the country of Romance', they dwell in 'quite distinct, though neighbouring' provinces. For Williams, Romance means finding an experience of God in sexual love within 'the bridal chamber', while for Lewis, Romance is the feeling of longing for an inexpressible and unreachable reality—'the wood beyond the world'—which ultimately finds its goal in God. Lewis recognizes that the sense of desire is thus common to both sexual and religious experience, but aims to hold the two experiences of desire apart rather than identifying them as does Williams. As a literary scholar, he has recognized a fusion of the erotic and the religious in some medieval writers such as Dante, but description does not mean approbation ('I display; I don't venture'). The 'inward' journey that he and Williams are to take together over the next nine years might then be mapped as negotiating a route between frontiers, involving some adjustment of the boundaries of adjoining districts within a larger country.

1.3 A Shared Journey through Romantic Territory

In his second letter to Williams, Lewis begins their journey by commenting on some of the poems in the collection sent him by the other. He writes that he 'embraces the opportunity of establishing the precedent of brutal frankness' by recording that he 'definitely disliked' the poems 'Orthodoxy' and 'Ecclesia

---

[21] Lewis, *Letters*, 2: 185–6.
[22] Lewis, *Pilgrim's Regress* includes such chapter headings as 'The Island', 'The Eastern Mountains', 'The Hill', 'The Grand Canyon', 'Furthest North', and 'The Main Road Again'.

Docens'. The titles of these poems is somewhat ironic: the 'orthodoxy' and the 'teaching church' that Williams celebrates are to be found in the body of his sexual partner, his wife Michal:

> Thy body's secret doctrines now
>   Are felt and proved and known:
> More wisdom on thy breast I learn
>   Than else upon my knees. ('Orthodoxy')[23]

Michal is eulogized in the same terms as the Virgin Mary, 'Immaculate in love, / As She', and as teaching 'New laws and sanctities' by her kisses. The same theme appears in 'Ecclesia Docens', but with an even more explicit identification of the beloved with the Christian church. All the traditional attributes of the church are transferred to her, for instance catholicity and sanctity:

> Thou lend'st the whole creation
>   An awful holiness,
> Till all things with new wonders
>   Do my affections bless.[24]

The poem ends with an intriguing anticipation of Williams' phrase in a much later poem, 'the heart-breaking manual acts of the Pope', referring to the use of priestly hands in the eucharistic ritual:[25]

> Their sacred dogmas colour
>   Thy sacerdotal eyes,
> Traditional, pontifical,
>   Thy hands, as theirs, are wise.
>   *And lo, in thee, O priestly fair,*
>   *Awhile I end my search,*
>   *Believing in the Catholic*
>   *And Apostolic Church.*
>   *In thee, in thee, revealèd fair,*
>   *I end awhile my search,*
>   *Thee, the One, Holy, Catholic,*
>   *And Apostolic Church!*[26]

One Roman Catholic critic, Theodore Maynard, had been at first scandalized by these poems, castigating them as 'Satanic' and a 'a deliberate attack upon the Christian faith and morality'. Maynard himself, however, gives an entertaining

---

[23] Williams, *Poems of Conformity*, 47.   [24] Williams, *Poems of Conformity*, 50.

[25] Charles Williams, 'The Vision of the Empire', in Williams, *Taliessin through Logres*, 9.

[26] Williams, *Poems of Conformity*, 51.

account of being charmed by meeting Williams, and of his wholly accepting Williams' explanation that 'he did not mean that physical passion was a more certain good than prayer, but only that there are many roads to faith, and that the road of human love has been the one followed by him'.[27] Certainly, Williams was not *substituting* human sexuality for church, dogmas, Eucharist, and God, but finding access to God *through* passion. In his letter, Lewis is not scandalized, but in effect is willing to accept only an analogy between sexual and religious experience, rather than the kind of identification (the 'blend of erotic and religious feeling') that Williams was affirming. Thus he offers a positive appreciation of 'Ascension', reading it in his own way:

> After this you will not be surprised to learn that I found your poems excessively *difficult*. I think I have followed *Ascension*. I take it this deals with the death of passion into matrimonial routine and the discovery that this death is also a birth – the birth of something which is to passion as the Church is to the earthly life of our Lord. Am I right? If so it is because we touch here: the death and re-birth motive being of the very essence of my kind of romanticism. If so, it is a good poem, specially stanzas 2 and 7.[28]

Without using the actual word 'analogy', Lewis considers that Williams has written a 'good poem' if it is about 'something which is to passion *as the Church is* to the earthly life of our Lord'. Williams himself, however, while presenting an analogy, finds identity also within the comparison, writing in this very poem of the ascended Christ, '. . . now my Fair / Flickered his presence in your hair', and:

> For in your face the Holy Ghost
> Kept—how long since!—his Pentecost.[29]

In his *Outlines of Romantic Theology*, written in 1924 but unpublished during his lifetime, Williams was to find several analogies between the stages of Jesus' life and the stages of married love. Thus, for example, the birth of love corresponds to Christ's birth, and the binding of one lover to another corresponds to Christ's being bound on the cross.[30] As in the poem 'Ascension', the departure of Jesus corresponds to a 'withdrawal of love into secret and heavenly places' and the coming of a grace that will sustain a happy marriage,[31] just as Lewis perceives. But these correspondences are precisely the basis for what Williams calls an '*identification* of love with Jesus',[32] which means that 'the presence of Love, that is of

---

[27] Maynard, 'Poetry of Charles Williams', 408–9.   [28] Lewis, *Letters*, 2: 186.
[29] Williams, *Poems of Conformity*, 78–9.
[30] Williams, *Outlines*, 15, 24. The idea is referred to much later in *Figure of Beatrice*, 188, n.1.
[31] Williams, *Outlines*, 25.   [32] Williams, *Outlines*, 14.

Christ, is sacramentally imparted by each to the other', and that 'the Christ of the Eucharist and the Love of the marriage-night are indeed not two but one'.[33] Much later, Williams is to find the term 'co-inherence' as a neat way of summing up this interpenetration of the divine and the human, but the sense of it is there already. In *Outlines*, Williams also provides a key for his naming of relation with the beloved as a 'church': he writes that 'if and in so far as Christ is to be identified with love and his life with marriage, then and to an equal degree two lovers stand for the disciples, and the whole company of the faithful, i.e. the Catholic Church'.[34]

It seems that Lewis, while 'definitely' disliking the poems that present an unambiguous identification of sexual with religious experience, is willing to accept those he can read as analogies. Thus he remarks that '*Churches* I didn't like, except *that dear duplicity of love and Love* – which I suppose is the thing we're talking about.' In this poem the speaker, addressing his 'madonna', finds no need to go to church, since he has found with her 'Worship in our own holy ground' and 'Love's epiphany'.[35] But the line singled out for approval, with its ambiguous word 'duplicity', hints at a possible separation, and even an acknowledgement of confusion, between human 'love' and divine 'Love' that would have been congenial to Lewis. Similarly, the 'orison of kisses' and the sword that 'shall pierce your hearts also' (Luke 2:35), in the poem 'Presentation',[36] can be read as analogy between love and religion, and it is not surprising that Lewis writes that he likes it. Significantly, Lewis discerns in 'Ascension' a pattern of death and rebirth, which he had long found to be at the heart of both pagan myth and the story of Jesus; the widespread myths of dying and rising gods had at first been a reason for his rejection of Christianity, but later substantiated the Christian gospel for him, in so far as 'myth became fact'.[37] In this declaration, there is an analogy between pagan myth and Christian fact, but no identity. He remarks that in the motif of death and rebirth the romanticism of Williams and himself 'touch'. Unknown to Lewis, Williams had in fact anticipated Lewis' discovery about myth; in his response to Theodore Maynard's criticism that he was drawing on pagan mythological figures such as Astarte alongside Christian figures such as Mary, Maynard reports Williams to the effect 'That Paganism was in many respects like Catholicism inclines him to believe in Catholicism. A myth demonstrates a mystery.'[38]

In his early study, *The Allegory of Love*, which was the occasion for Williams' letter to him, Lewis had identified a 'love-religion' in eleventh- and twelfth-century French poets that he saw as a 'mock-religion', a parody, rival, and even

---

[33] Williams, *Outlines*, 44.   [34] Williams, *Outlines*, 31.

[35] Williams, *Poems of Conformity*, 67, 68.   [36] Williams, *Poems of Conformity*, 45.

[37] See Lewis, *Surprised by Joy*, 222; CSL to Arthur Greeves, 18 October 1931, in Lewis, *Letters* 1: 976–7.

[38] Maynard, 'Poetry of Charles Williams', 407.

'escape' from what he calls 'real religion'.[39] The 'divorce' between religion and the 'imitated religion' of love is so complete, he writes, 'that analogies naturally arise between them'.[40] He recognizes, however, that in the poetry of Dante the 'religion' of courtly love 'find[s] a *modus vivendi* with Christianity and produce[s] a noble fusion of sexual and religious experience',[41] and even that 'When *Frauendienst* succeeds in fusing with religion, as in Dante, unity is restored to the mind.'[42] It is perhaps not surprising, in the light of these phrases, that Williams supposes that Lewis is espousing his own 'romantic theology'. In fact, Lewis seems personally to prefer the *divorce* between erotic love and 'true religion' that he finds in the Provençal poets, exemplified in Chrétien de Troyes and codified in the *De Arte Honeste Amandi* of Andreas Capellanus, rather than the 'fusion' in Dante.[43]

In his letter, Lewis nevertheless makes a concession to Williams that is borne out by his comments on the poems. While he and Williams occupy different districts of the same country of Romanticism, he must 'willingly believe [...] well of all her provinces'. Indeed, he goes on, 'while writing about Courtly love I have been so long a student of *your* province that I think, in a humble way, I am nearly naturalised'. In tracing the development of a 'love-religion' among poets of the twelfth century, Lewis' historical judgement had been that this was a 'parody' of the Christian religion, and so it is a little hard to see how by this study he could have been 'nearly naturalised' in Williams' province where sexual love and Christian faith mingled and fused. This expression seems to be a courtesy on Lewis' part, but it probably also indicates that Williams' poems have edged him towards a more positive view of the 'analogies' that (as he puts it) 'naturally arise' between the erotic and the spiritual.

Despite Tolkien's later complaint that Lewis had fallen under the 'dominant influence' of Williams,[44] Lewis seems to have maintained his qualification of Williams' 'romantic theology' throughout the course of their friendship. He continues to interpret Williams' erotic imagery in his own way, as we shall see. The story of the friendship of Williams and Lewis, I am suggesting, is a journey in which the two walked a boundary between their two provinces, while occasionally diverging into each other's territory, at least in sympathy or in order to review the scenery. The journey did not end with Williams' death. Though Lewis was left

---

[39] Lewis, *Allegory of Love*, 21. In modern literary scholarship, Lewis has come under severe criticism for placing the absolute origin of 'courtly love' in Languedoc at the end of the eleventh century, and for taking the ironic Andreas Capellanus too seriously; see Robertson, 'Myth', 154–63; Dronke, *Medieval Latin*, 1: 2–7. However, O'Donoghue, *Courtly Love Tradition*, 2–3, points out that this kind of love poetry was certainly more concentrated in the period Lewis identifies.

[40] Lewis, *Allegory of Love*, 42.   [41] Lewis, *Allegory of Love*, 21.

[42] Lewis, *Allegory of Love*, 42.   [43] Lewis, *Allegory of Love*, 29–35, 41.

[44] Tolkien to Christopher Bretherton, 16 July 1964, in Tolkien, *Letters*, 349.

apparently to walk alone, he once remarked to Michal Williams that 'I live on him almost every day.'[45]

1.4 Two Paths to a Meeting

In the epistolary meeting of 1936, two separate paths had converged into a shared journey. In their initial letters to each other, Williams and Lewis allude to the intellectual and spiritual route by which they have come to this point, and we can find both common features and different landscapes along the way. For Williams, what had come to matter was 'this very peculiar identity of love and religion', while for Lewis it was 'longing' and 'the wood beyond the world'.

At the time of their meeting, Lewis had been Fellow and Tutor in English Language and Literature at Magdalen College, Oxford for 11 years. Williams had been a senior editor at Amen House, the London branch of the Oxford University Press, for some 16 years, having begun work at the Press in 1908 and progressively increased in seniority since that time.[46] In fact, he had a similar length of experience in teaching literature as Lewis, since he had been offering regular classes in English Literature for London City Council's Evening Institutes since 1923, to enthusiastic and devoted audiences. Earlier, he had only been able to spend one year at University College London, unable to continue through his family's lack of money, and had completed his education through evening classes and his own voracious reading. Lewis, by contrast, had spent four years at Oxford reading two Final Honour Schools, in Greats (Classics and Philosophy) and English, supported by his father, though this had been interrupted by serving on the front line in the Great War. Williams had been declared medically unfit for war, mainly owing to his poor eyesight.

Both Lewis and Williams had started their respective careers with the aim of becoming poets: Lewis had published two volumes of poetry—*Spirits in Bondage* in 1919 and *Dymer* in 1926—and Williams had published five: *The Silver Stair* in 1910, *Poems of Conformity* in 1917, *Divorce* in 1920, *Windows of Night* in 1925, and *Heroes and Kings* in 1930. None of these volumes by either writer was a success with the general public, and few copies were sold. While Williams continued to think of himself first and foremost as a poet—and was to publish two more collections of poems after 1936—Lewis was becoming reconciled to making his reputation as a prose-writer, and to publishing only occasional verses in various journals. While *The Allegory of Love* was Lewis' first major venture into

---

[45] CSL to Michal Williams, 15 June 1948, in uncatalogued list of Wade MSS. Cited by Lindop, *Charles Williams*, 468, n.1525.

[46] He was employed at first as an assistant proofreader, but was soon advanced to the status of a junior editor, becoming a full editor in 1920.

literary criticism, Williams had already published three volumes in this genre: *Poetry at Present* (1930), *The English Poetic Mind* (1932), and *Reason and Beauty in the Poetic Mind* (1933). Deeply original in approach, none of these made an impact on the literary scene, and the brilliance of the second in particular has had to wait until recent years to be recognized;[47] in any case, Lewis, as a don in Oxford teaching English literature, appeared unaware of them at the point of their meeting, and knew only of the novels—by then five in number.

Both writers were Anglican Christians, though Williams had continued in unwavering Christian faith since early childhood, while Lewis had come to an adult belief in God only in 1930, and to belief in the divinity of Christ in 1931.[48] Not long after his conversion, in 1933, Lewis had published an allegorical account of his journey to Christian faith in *The Pilgrim's Regress* (ironically echoing John Bunyan's *The Pilgrim's Progress*). In 1924, Williams had written an account of his own particular approach to faith in his *Outlines of Romantic Theology*, but had failed to find a publisher. Parts of the intended book would eventually find a place in other publications by Williams, such as the book *He Came Down from Heaven* (1938) and the booklet *Religion and Love in Dante: The Theology of Romantic Love* (1942). The term 'romantic' or 'romanticism' is linked with religious faith in the titles of both Lewis' *Pilgrim's Regress* and Williams' *Outlines of Romantic Theology*, Lewis' volume bearing the subtitle 'An Allegorical Apology for Christianity, Reason, and Romanticism'. I have already suggested that 'romanticism' was the larger country through which the writers were to take their subsequent joint journey of friendship, and their respective volumes of 1924 and 1933 also make clear the particular character of their single journeys to the point of their meeting.

Williams' phrase 'this peculiar identity of love and religion' has its background in his early reading (from 1908) of the Victorian poet Coventry Patmore, whom he discussed intensively with a fellow editor at the Press, Fred Page, who was himself 'obsessed' by Patmore.[49] Lewis detects this influence even in Williams' short letter of 12 March 1936, writing that Williams may have been led astray by Lewis' own 'apparently tell-tale familiarity with Coventry Patmore' evidenced in *The Allegory of Love*.[50] The authority of Patmore is stamped rather clearly on Williams' *Outlines of Romantic Theology*, as for example in Williams' reflections on 'The Mass in Romantic Theology':

"The Blessed Sacrament," said Patmore, "is first of all a symbol of the beloved; afterwards the beloved is a symbol of the Blessed Sacrament." Such a pregnant saying has conceived within it the whole of Romantic Theology [...] In the

[47] Hill, *Collected Critical Writings*, 562–3, hails it as a 'critical masterpiece'.
[48] For this chronology, see McGrath, *C. S. Lewis*, 142, supported by Wolfe, 'Note', 68–9.
[49] Lindop, *Charles Williams*, 30.   [50] See Lewis, *Allegory of Love*, 123, 184, 225, 276.

intense experience of the birth of love [...] the Sacrament which he accepts mentally to be that of the Divine Humanity, the Body and Blood of the Saviour, should appear to the lover to be closely related to that glorious body of his lady through which he apprehends divine things.[51]

Williams' biographer Grevel Lindop has convincingly shown that, from reading Patmore, Williams gleaned two patterns of thought that remained with him throughout his life. In some respects, the two are bound to be in tension, even in conflict, and Patmore himself never seems to have resolved them. First, Patmore suggests through his poetry that sexual union between man and woman can be a spiritual path to God, since God's love for humanity is of the same nature as the erotic desire of lovers for each other.[52] This is the pattern of thought that shapes *Outlines*, which Lewis rejects in his letter of March 1936 as 'not my kind [of romanticism] at all', and with which he finally makes some accommodation in *The Four Loves*. But there is a second strand in Patmore: certain poems suggest that a mystical experience of God can be attained by combining sexual desire with *chastity*—that is, giving desire its full rein, cultivating its intensity towards another person, but stopping short of intercourse and consummation.[53] In his prose *Magna Moralia*, Patmore reflects that 'Every true Lover has perceived, at least in a few moments of his life, that the fullest fruition of love is without the loss of virginity.'[54] This is the kind of relationship with a beloved that Williams commends in his first volume of poems and addresses to the young woman he is courting, Florence Sarah Conway. While the poems express a total identification between Love and Christ ('All lives of lovers are His song of love'),[55] the sequence climaxes with an acclamation of 'the Solemn Feast of Love's Virginity'.[56]

I suggest that it is the tangle of these two patterns of love that lies at the heart of the ambiguities and complexities in Williams' personal and artistic life. When Williams married Florence in 1917, now always to be named Michal,[57] she took the place of the beloved within the first strand of Patmore's thought about love and religion, at the centre of a sacramental understanding of sexual union. The fruit of this is seen in *Poems of Conformity*. The second strand of (so-called) 'chaste' sexual desire was to find its outlet after his marriage in a series of

---

[51] Williams, *Outlines*, 36-7.

[52] See 'To the Body', in Patmore, *Unknown Eros*, 2: 72-3: 'Little, sequester'd pleasure house / For God and for His Spouse.'

[53] E.g. 'The Contract', *Unknown Eros*, 2: 59, depicting the 'virgin spousals' of Adam and Eve; 'Deliciae Sapientiae de Amore', *Unknown Eros*, 2: 77: 'praeternuptial ecstasy and fear'.

[54] Coventry Patmore, *Magna Moralia*, V, 150, portraying the relationship between Joseph and the Virgin Mary.

[55] Williams, Sonnet 67, *The Silver Stair*, 75.   [56] Williams, Sonnet 80, *Silver Stair*, 88.

[57] After 2 Samuel 6:14-16, in view of her embarrassment at Williams' exuberant mannerisms; see Lindop, *Charles Williams*, 34.

relationships that Williams developed with female 'muses', beginning with Phyllis Jones, a young librarian at Amen House. Williams' reading of Dante confirmed the two patterns acquired from Patmore, since Dante's adoration of Beatrice was both a vision of the divine glory within her and a desire for a Beloved with whom he never consummated a sexual union. Calling Phyllis by the mythical name of Celia, in the poems of *Heroes and Kings* Williams celebrated a 'Celian moment' of the disclosure of the glory of the beloved, later to become the 'Beatrician moment' as he developed his study of Dante. It seems clear, however, that the moment could occur within either of the two patterns of love.

Williams, going beyond Patmore (or Dante), added a dark depth to the second kind of love: it seems that the element of sexual arousal within it was intensified by the playing of games in which Williams threatened and inflicted small punishments for failures to carry out the tasks he had assigned to his 'pupils', often characterized by (usually, but not invariably light) strokes on the hand, and even the buttocks, with a ruler. The fantasy character of the 'game' was accompanied by a more ritual formality, the ceremonial manner (but not the sexuality) perhaps deriving from Williams' membership in the esoteric circle of the Fellowship of the Rosy Cross (from 1917 to 1927).[58] Increasingly, these sexually charged acts of control and submission also became a way of actualizing his own myth of the ancient Welsh poet Taliessin and his relations with his household, as celebrated in his Arthurian poems. Williams was well aware of the nature of these games, writing to Phyllis in 1930 about the publication of *Heroes and Kings* that 'I suspect that I am a mild masochist as well as a mild sadist.'[59] Lindop has thoroughly demonstrated, from the text of Williams' own letters and books, that he saw these practices of awakening and restraining sexual desire as a means of transforming the 'sex energy' into the drive of poetic creativity, so becoming what he regarded as a channel of grace.[60] Lindop calls this process a 'transmutation of energy', which he appears to derive from the use of this phrase by Williams' character Considine in his novel *Shadows of Ecstasy*, dating from 1925, although oddly Lindop does not explicitly make the connection between the theories of Williams and his creation, Considine.[61]

I want to be clear that I regard Williams' sexual games with his various muses as inexcusable. Things could be said in an attempt at mitigation: these were acts between consenting adults; Williams always ceased the games when the young women concerned no longer felt comfortable with them; Williams sustained long-term relations with some women in which the games never played a part at all

---

[58] This order, a faction split from the Order of the Golden Dawn, was led by A. E. Waite and was mystical and Christian in essence.

[59] CW to Phyllis Jones, Bod. MS Eng. Res. c. 320, box 3, letter 146a. Inaccessible, transcribed by Lindop, *Charles Williams*, 160.

[60] Lindop, *Charles Williams*, 241, 290, 348, 369, 388.   [61] Lindop, *Charles Williams*, 116–19.

(with, for example, Anne Bradby—later Anne Ridler—Thelma Mills, and Alice Mary Hadfield); and Williams welcomed criticism of his poetry from all the women to whom he related, treating them as equals in the discussion of literature and acknowledging their part in his creative work. But no excuse can be offered for behaviour in which he was controlling the situation as a male with an authority that derived from being respected by the women concerned as a spiritual advisor, an inspiring teacher, and a published author. Whether or not this behaviour amounted to what is now legally defined as abuse or harassment, it was unethical. He was exploiting his position and so exerting psychological pressure on the women concerned to collaborate with what appeared to become an increasing dependency. In one well-publicized instance, a relationship with Lois Lang-Sims (whom he dubbed 'Lalage'), he seems to have *presumed* consent to the physical game before any was actually given—and indeed it was subsequently withdrawn.[62] Nor can the situation be called anything other than unfaithfulness to Michal. Phyllis Jones made a shrewd point in pointing out to him that it would be incongruous for Williams to make efforts to publish his intended book on love in marriage (*Outlines* of *Romantic Theology*) unless 'the circumstances' of his relation with her were to be 'altered'.[63] She makes the fairly damning comment that 'It is better that the practice of public men should coincide with their theories.' She had, it seems, felt the tension between the two patterns of love even if Williams thought he could live with both at once.

I have already stressed that the present study is a literary one, concerned not essentially with biography or psychology, but with a relationship between C. S. Lewis and Charles Williams as revealed by written texts, published and unpublished; more specifically, it compares and contrasts their use of the notion of co-inherence. But the 'mildly' sadistic aspect of Williams' complex personality can no longer be escaped by anyone venturing to write about his work, and especially about his version of the 'Theology of Romantic Love'. There can be little doubt that all this was in Williams' mind when he writes to Lewis about 'this very peculiar identity of love and religion'. Williams' theory of the 'transmutation' of spiritual energy through sexual restraint appears plentifully in his writings up to this point, not least in *Shadows of Ecstasy*, and in his own life this practice seems to have been inseparable from games of sexual control. Rowan Williams, sensitive to the damage done by Williams' actions, nevertheless concludes that 'his reflections on co-inherence, the single most accessible and most dangerous element in his theology, depend on one way of handling the interface of desire and pain', even as manifested in his abusive behaviour.[64]

---

[62] See Lang-Sims, ed., *Letters to Lalage*, 47–8, 68, 79–80.

[63] Phyllis Jones to CW, undated, Bod. MS Res. c. 321. Inaccessible, transcribed by Lindop, *Charles Williams*, 143.

[64] Rowan Williams, 'Charles Williams', 163.

What then might justify a specialist study of Charles Williams, given the priority rightly given in our own age to the safety, dignity, and integrity of women? Here I venture to dissent a little from Rowan Williams' comment. I judge that, while Charles Williams' highly original ideas of exchange, substitution, and co-inherence have arisen partly in the *context* of inexcusable behaviour, they are valid—and even beautiful—in their own right, and do not *depend* on the theory of 'transmutation of energy' to make them work. Admittedly, with the advantage of a hindsight that Williams' friend Lewis did not have, this must be a less positive assessment of Williams' social life than that which Lewis gave in his preface to the essays presented to Charles Williams after his death. There Lewis writes that Williams 'was extremely attractive to young women and (what is rare) none of his male friends ever wondered why: nor did it ever do a young woman anything but immense good to be attracted by Charles Williams'.[65]

1.5 The Allegory and Sacrament of Love

It seems even-handed at this point to observe that Lewis commends his own version of games of sexual domination in *The Four Loves*. Although making this point requires us to leap forward some thirty years or so in our story, it is revealing to find him still maintaining there his early insistence on an 'analogy' between the erotic and the religious. He writes about 'a certain attitude which Venus, in her intensity, evokes from most (I believe, not all) pairs of lovers', and goes on to explain:

> This act can invite the man to an extreme, though short-lived, masterfulness, to the dominance of a conqueror or a captor, and the woman to a correspondingly extreme abjection and surrender. Hence the roughness, even the fierceness, of some erotic play; the 'lover's pinch which hurts and is desired.'[66]

Lewis thinks this behaviour is 'harmless and wholesome' for a Christian couple—presumably a married couple, though he does not make this quite clear—as long as the two are aware that they are playing parts in something 'comparable to a mystery-play or ritual [...] and to a masque or even a charade'.[67] This approach seems quite close to Williams' own ritualized games, although Lewis has a reason for (in his words) 'giving full value to the word play', which Williams would not own from his perspective of 'romantic theology'. For Lewis, the game of domination and submission is an acting out of a 'pagan sacrament' in sex, where in the

---

[65] Lewis, *Essays*, x.
[66] Lewis, *Four Loves*, 118–19, quoting from Shakespeare, *Anthony and Cleopatra*, 5.2.294–5.
[67] Lewis, *Four Loves*, 119.

lovers 'all the masculinity and femininity of the world, all that is assailant and responsive, are momentarily focused'. The man is playing the part of the 'Sky-Father' and the woman the 'Earth-Mother'; he elaborates, in more Platonic terms, that the man is playing the role of 'Form' and the woman 'Matter'. Once again, then, Lewis is urging an *analogy* between the 'pagan sacrament' of erotic love and true Christian sacramentality; they are not to be confused. Just how much Lewis is ascribing to a traditional sexual polarization in Western culture according to which men and women are typecast as the active and passive elements respectively becomes even more clear when he remarks: 'The Sky-Father himself is only a Pagan dream of One far greater than Zeus and far more masculine than the male.'[68]

It is rather startling that Lewis thinks this sexual game of male 'masterfulness' (which he calls 'extreme' twice) is played by 'most pairs of lovers'. On his conversion to Christianity, Lewis had put behind him the sadistic tendencies that he recognized in himself as a young man, and about which he had written freely to his close friend Arthur Greeves at the time.[69] In *The Problem of Pain*, he clearly rejects sadism and masochism as 'perversions', but when he writes that 'Sadism and Masochism respectively isolate, and then exaggerate, a "moment" or "aspect" in *normal* sexual passion',[70] he seems to be anticipating his later proposal in *The Four Loves*.

From these late references of Lewis to sexual union as a 'pagan sacrament', which remain in contrast to Williams' association of erotic love with imagery of the Christian sacrament, we may return to Lewis' earlier view of allegory, as expressed in his *Allegory of Love*. This anticipates the later development of thought, since in the earlier book Lewis sharply distinguishes allegory from 'symbol' or 'sacrament'. In allegory, immaterial *fact*, such as the passions we experience, is expressed in *invented* visible things. As Lewis puts it, 'The allegorist leaves the given—his own passions—to talk of that which is confessedly less real, which is a fiction.' For example, 'anger', 'patience', or 'nature' will appear as personifications. On the other hand, Lewis maintains that in symbolism or sacramentalism, visible things in the material world are discerned as being mere shadows of the immaterial world, so that 'the archetype is seen through the copy'. So, Lewis explains, 'The symbolist leaves the given to find that which is *more real*.'[71] According to Lewis, the poetry of the medieval period, such as the poetry of

---

[68] Lewis, *Four Loves*, 120–1. Hilder, *Surprised by the Feminine*, 91–100, has argued that Lewis regards the Christian ethos of obedience to the divine as the supreme human act, and so privileges feminine receptivity over male 'heroism'. But this defence of Lewis as 'feminist' soft-pedals the general pattern of male aggression and female submission he identifies in human relations.

[69] CSL to Arthur Greeves, 28 January 1917, in Lewis, *Letters*, 1: 269; 31 January 1917, in Lewis, *Letters*, 1: 270–1, 271–2; 7 February 1917, in Lewis, *Letters*, 1: 274; 15 February 1917, in Lewis, *Letters*, 1: 278; 3 June 1919, in Lewis, *Letters* 1: 313; 10 June 1917, in Lewis, *Letters*, 1: 319–20. On this issue see McGrath, *C. S. Lewis*, 61; Poe, *Becoming C. S. Lewis*, 234–6.

[70] Lewis, *Problem of Pain*, 80 (my italics).   [71] Lewis, *Allegory of Love*, 45.

courtly love, is essentially allegorical, and is not to be mistaken for symbolist. *Amor* in Dante's *Vita Nuova* is 'only a personification'; there is nothing 'mystical' or 'mysterious' about medieval allegory; Lewis insists that the poets, including Dante, are well aware that the figures they present to us are fictions.[72] This does seem slightly at odds with Lewis' assertion that Dante offers a 'noble fusion' of love and (true) religion,[73] and it is not surprising that Williams gets the wrong impression, but Lewis' own general stance in the matter is clear.

The love poetry offers an 'allegory of love', and so there is, for Lewis, no identity between the religion of love and the reality of God; there is not even the route offered by sacrament between the copy and the Real. In this early book, the two modes of expression are held firmly apart, allegory opposed to sacrament. While this 'divorce',[74] between the two, is to be mitigated in the later book on love, where the love-religion is allowed to be a *'pagan* sacrament', it is still not a Christian sacrament as Williams portrays it. In his *Allegory of Love*, Lewis finds that symbolism made its first effective appearance in the *Dialogues* of Plato, where 'visible things exist insofar as they imitate the transcendent Forms'.[75] The diffused Platonism, or Neoplatonism ('if there is a difference') of Augustine, Pseudo-Dionysius, and Boethius 'provided the very atmosphere in which the new world awoke'. Lewis had in fact come to this point in his journey in 1936 through immersion in the philosophy first of Subjective Idealism and then Absolute Idealism, before embracing theism and finally a Neoplatonist Christianity.[76] Through the last three phases, his world view remains essentially dualistic, as the New Testament scholar N. T. Wright discerns and notably regrets;[77] Lewis constantly stresses the difference between the temporal materials of a world of 'becoming' and the eternal Ideas of the world of 'being', or between the Absolute and its relative forms in the contingent world. His conversion had taken the shape of believing first that the Absolute Idea was a personal God, and afterwards that Christ was the Son of this God.[78] After conversion, he interpreted the 'longing' or *Sehnsucht* that he had experienced since boyhood as traces of a divine realm beyond the world, more real and a more enticingly 'home' than anything we experience in our daily lives, and essentially unattainable here and now. It is a 'joy' that leaves us unsatisfied.

This is the story that is told in the allegory (*The Pilgrim's Regress*) with which Lewis had furnished Williams in reply to his letter. Allegory, as Lewis wrote of the account of another pilgrim's journey, is not a 'cryptogram to be translated',[79] but a

---

[72] Lewis, *Allegory of Love*, 47–8.   [73] Lewis, *Allegory of Love*, 21.

[74] Lewis, *Allegory of Love*, 42.   [75] Lewis, *Allegory of Love*, 45–6.

[76] For a careful analysis of Lewis' stages of thought, see Feinendegen, 'Philosopher's Progress', 105–13. Feinendegen maintains, however, that the Absolute Idealist phase was followed by a return to Subjective Idealism, albeit in Lewis' own modified version. See Chapter 6, section 2.

[77] Wright, 'Simply Lewis', 30–1.   [78] Lewis, *Surprised by Joy*, 203–15.

[79] Lewis, 'Vision of John Bunyan', 149.

making visible of invisible desires, aims, and passions. His pilgrim, John, travels a road from which he is always tempted to diverge, to the North or to the South, to the extremes of the reason or the imagination. North lies a region where rational thought excludes any notion of the transcendent as a goal for human longing, which insists that every kind of feeling is suspect, and that the sense of desire needs to be explained and analysed away as part of a human mechanism. South of the road there is the territory of subjective ways based purely on emotion, an imagination undisciplined by reason, where desires are simply indulged with the satisfactions of this world. As McGrath summarizes the landscape, 'The rationalist philosophy of the Enlightenment, romantic art, modern art, Freudianism, asceticism, nihilism, hedonism, classical humanism and religious liberalism are all located on this map, only to be tried and found wanting.'[80] Though Lewis seems not to be certain about the trajectory of a road that integrates reason and imagination, his map is orientated to a certain compass bearing: the transcendent world is real, but the Pilgrim always finds it elusive until death: 'whatever there is beyond the brook, it cannot be the same [. . .] It is a real brook.'[81]

We are bound to wonder what impression Lewis expected his allegory to have on Williams in sending it to him. He may have wanted Williams to realize the danger of the far Southern 'provinces', but in fact Williams had always stressed the necessary place of reason in his romanticism, as exemplified in his book *Reason and Beauty in the Poetic Mind*.[82] The difference of their route to this point is perhaps summed up in the image of the wood, which is the place where Dante finds himself 'Midway this way of life'.[83] For Lewis, as he writes in his initial letter to Williams, there is 'the wood beyond the world', an object of longing, ultimate form. For Williams it is 'Broceliande' in the poetry he is writing at the time, the 'sea-wood' that is part-forest and part-water, image of the formless that is still penetrated in everyday life by the numinous. The spiritual interweaves with material, and the region is ambiguous: it joins the Antipodean Sea, which is the way both to Sarras (the Land of the Trinity, where Christ says mass in the chapel) and to P'o-Lu, where the headless Emperor walks backwards, and octopus tentacles fill the sea around. No one enters it without being changed. In Williams' path to this point, we can detect hints of what he is later to identify as co-inherence.[84]

While Lewis' path so far appears to be more shaped by dualism, we can also find an openness to another way. He is enthusiastic about Williams' novel *The Place of the Lion*. This might be expected in so far as the plot of the novel is based on the Platonic scheme of shadows and copies in this world of eternal archetypes or

---

[80] McGrath, *C. S. Lewis*, 172.
[81] Lewis, *Pilgrim's Regress*, 197, © copyright C. S. Lewis Pte Ltd, 1933.
[82] Williams, *Reason and Beauty*, 17–35, 124–8.
[83] Dante, *Divine Comedy*, *Hell*, 1.71. One translator, Dorothy Sayers, was prompted by reading Williams' *Figure of Beatrice* to begin her study of Dante: see Reynolds, *Dorothy L. Sayers*, 353–4.
[84] See Williams, 'Taliessin's Return to Logres' and 'Vision of the Empire', *Taliessin*, 4, 12.

Ideas. But the archetypes do not behave as Plato thought they should: for Plato, copies participate (upward, as it were) in Ideas or Forms, but the Ideas do not participate (downwards, as it were) in the copies. The changing world of becoming, and especially its created souls, engages in the world of unchanging being, but being does not participate in becoming. There is, we might say, no true co-inherence between the spiritual and the material. In Christian Platonism, there is an exception to the rule: Christ, as world-soul and Logos, mediates between two worlds through the co-inherence of his human and divine natures, and is incarnate in the 'lower' world. In the Narnia stories, Lewis is to embody this mediator in the great lion, Aslan. But in Williams' story, it is not only the archetype of strength, in the form of the Lion, who appears in the world; he is only one of a series of archetypes or 'Celestials' who break through into the world unmediated and actively absorb their finite copies. Beauty, for example, takes the form of a butterfly and draws all created butterflies into itself.[85] While Williams is depicting an apocalyptic scenario, in which a magical procedure has caused a tear in the fabric of time and space, and the world is facing the threat of becoming uncreated, the novel raises the possibility of a mutual participation between eternal energies and created things, a clue that Lewis will take up in a future novel of his own.[86]

1.6 Lewis' Appreciation of Williams, 1936–1939

In the way so far described, Williams and Lewis first 'met' over an admiration for one book of the other, aspects of which actually presented a challenge to each of them; then, to explain the intellectual and spiritual paths they had taken to that point, they sent each other *another* of their books. From here onwards, they were to take what Lewis calls the 'secret road' of friendship. From 1936 until 1939, their friendship had to subsist on occasional meetings both in Lewis' rooms at Magdalen and 'in Williams' tiny office at Amen House'. But, writes Lewis in reminiscence, 'even thus, he had already become as dear to all my Oxford friends as he was to me'.[87] Poignantly, Lewis goes on to reflect after Williams' death that 'I am afraid that in our pride we half-imagined that we must be the friends whom he had been in search of all his life. Only since his death have we fully realized what a small and late addition we were to the company of those who loved him, and whom he loved.'[88] It may be that Lewis had transferred to the other Inklings the *depth* of the friendship that he himself felt with Williams, real enough though the mutual affection and general delight in Williams' company was at the time.[89] It seems Lewis cast himself as the particular friend for whom Williams had been seeking 'all his life', and reciprocated in due measure.

---

[85] Williams, *Place of the Lion*, 34–46.   [86] See Chapter 8, section 6.   [87] Lewis, *Essays*, viii.
[88] Lewis, *Essays*, ix.   [89] See Lindop, *Charles Williams*, 309–10.

We only have evidence (at the present time of writing) of *Lewis'* appreciation of *Williams* with regard to their books published during this period of 1936–9, apart from *The Allegory of Love*. No letters or records of conversations so far identified tell us about Williams' view of Lewis' first book in his science fiction trilogy, *Out of the Silent Planet* (1938), although we know that Lewis urged Williams to attend an Inklings' meeting in Oxford on 20 or 27 October 1937 to discuss the forthcoming novel, writing that 'I have written a thriller about a journey to Mars on which I urgently want your opinion.'[90] There are no opinions yet discovered by Williams on Lewis' collected essays in *Rehabilitations* or Lewis' contribution to *The Personal Heresy* (a dialogue with E. M. W. Tillyard about the nature of poetic creation), both of which books Williams saw through the Oxford University Press in 1939.[91] All this may be simply failure to find evidence, but it seems to reflect a trajectory in which Williams is appreciative of the company and conversation of Lewis but refrains from commendation of his written work—the exception being a continued expressed enthusiasm for *The Allegory of Love*.

Williams strongly commends Lewis' book in a lecture on 'Courtly Love', which he gave on 29 January 1937; extant are both a (rather fragmentary) transcription of the lecture by Raymond Hunt,[92] and four pages of notes that Williams made in preparation for it.[93] As transcribed, Williams tells his audience that Lewis' book is 'one of those very few books produced in a generation...that are really intelligent'. He acknowledges 'a tremendous scholastic background, and a very definite creative capacity'. However, he adds that 'He is not altogether right on all points', and tells of a conversation he had with Lewis 'about Romantic Love'—presumably disputing these points—'which lasted to 3.0 o'clock in the morning'.[94] Hunt has failed to transcribe the date that Williams had apparently given,[95] but we might assume this was the meeting Lewis and Williams had arranged for September 1936. In this lecture, Williams agrees with Lewis that courtly love, which is basically adulterous, arose in reaction to the teaching of the church that ruled out passion from sex in marriage as sinful. However, he still wants to name courtly love as 'romantic love', and moderates Lewis' view that it is simply a parody of religion. That 'there is in real passion something illuminating', he comments, 'is a notion of which St Thomas hadn't heard'.[96]

While it is not an essential part of Williams' basic thesis about the theology of romantic love that it *must* be exemplified by the medieval love poets earlier than

---

[90] CSL to CW, 23 September 1937, Lewis, *Letters* 2: 219–20.

[91] CSL to CW, 22 February 1939, Lewis, *Letters* 2: 249.

[92] 'Courtly Love', in CLI series 'Poetry and The Pattern of Life I: The Idea of Salvation' 15, Wade RH Notebooks 12: 2153–9. The transcription contains many gaps and is unintelligible at points.

[93] Wade CW/MS-496 'Courtly Love' (4 pages). Hunt appends a copy of these preparatory notes to the lecture transcription, RH Notebooks, vol. 12: 2159–61.

[94] Wade RH Notebooks 12: 2154.

[95] Hunt transcribes 'I had conversation with Mr. Lewis last...at...about Romantic Love.'

[96] Wade RH Notebooks 12: 2156.

Dante, it would be congruent with his view that it should be so. He tells his audience that 'In discussing the past, we do expect people to be definitely one thing or the other... either he must be passionately A, or passionately B... and so, Courtly Love is looked upon as being either a complete parody, a fantastic [imitation] of religion, or a solemn, serious [affair]... the answer is, it is neither'.[97] Here he has come, we might say, part-way onto Lewis' territory by finding an *element* of parody in the poets' love-religion, but he remains at home in his own province when he finds this only 'semi-profane' and mixed with 'truth'. He continues in the same vein:

> You get spring up in the middle of this metaphysical period... this semi-serious, semi-profane, almost at times blasphemous chat. I am very pleased to see that Mr. Lewis doesn't think it derives from the worship of the Blessed Virgin; in fact, I suspect the worship of the Blessed Virgin got a kick out of it... Courtly love, this odd fantastic development of idea and fact which grew up... After Dante's time it remains for us a perfectly definite matter of choice—a new sentiment. We have learned a new way of looking at things. [...] Humility, courtesy, Adultery, and the Religion of Love... and this is where things linked up... Half parody, half t[ruth], half symbolical[.][98]

With Dante, too, he comes to some degree onto Lewis' ground, admitting that 'we tend to mix [allegory] up with symbolism. I realise here, Mr. Lewis does check my own tendency to introduce symbolism into Dante.'[99] Presumably he means 'everywhere in Dante', since he defends the earlier medieval love poetry as '*half symbolical*'. Altogether, Williams' partial accommodation to Lewis is summed up in a comment he inserted into the margin of his notes for the lecture: 'I depend on Mr. Lewis, but partly because I recognize the truth of my own view expounded.'[100]

In September 1937, Lewis wrote to Williams about his newly published novel *Descent into Hell*, calling it 'a thundering good book and a real purgation to read'. He judges that Williams has presented evil as 'the real thing', and considers that 'in sheer writing [...] you have gone up, as we examiners say, a whole class'.[101] But he has trenchant criticisms to make. He warns against a 'representative style' in which 'the writer writes as if *he* were in the predicament he describes'; the conversation of the novelist Peter Stanhope with the heroine of the piece, Pauline Anstruther, is—he admits—very like the way that Williams himself speaks when 'most serious and most sincere', but most people would not sound like this. In particular, Lewis dislikes the 'interchange of formulae like "Under the Mercy"' that might 'sound like a game to people who don't know you'. The phrase was, in

---

[97] Wade RH Notebooks 12: 2154.   [98] Wade RH Notebooks 12: 2157.
[99] Wade RH Notebooks 12: 2154.   [100] Wade CW/MS-496: 3.
[101] CSL to CW, 23 September 1937, Lewis, *Letters* 2: 218–20.

fact, a ritualized blessing or farewell, associated with the esoteric ceremonies of the Order of the Rosy Cross;[102] it seems that Williams was habitually using the phrase with close acquaintances by 1936, and it was to become the mantra of his Company of the Co-inherence from 1939 onwards.

Lewis adds that 'I fancy the rift between us is here pretty wide.' The gulf seems to relate again to inhabiting different 'provinces' of romanticism. Williams is prone to the romantic projection of the 'Ego' and emotions of the artist into his novels and his poetry, while Lewis had already rejected any approach to poetry that expects to find an expression—or 'representation', to use Lewis' word to Williams in this letter,[103] of the artist's own personality there, and we can presume that the same prohibition applies to novels. In a series of papers begun in 1934 with an article by Lewis on 'The Personal Heresy in Criticism',[104] Lewis enters into debate with Professor E. M. W. Tillyard on the function of the personality and experience of the poet in the meaning of a poem. In his response to Lewis' essays on the theme, Tillyard discerns that Lewis is making an attack on those Romantics who—in his view—'concentrat[e] on the poet rather than on the activity of poetry'.[105] Lewis' own idea of 'romance' is to allow a poem or piece of prose to give us an experience that is 'a new kind of consciousness, but [...] not the consciousness of a single individual'.[106] Correspondingly, in Lewis' advice to Williams about his new novel in his letter of September, 1937, he urges him: 'I would rather see you becoming or remaining rigidly sober and classic as you describe [...]' In fact, this critical judgement, and Lewis' dispute about it with Tillyard, was the basis of the very book, *The Personal Heresy: A Controversy*, that Williams was later to steer through the Press.

The most significant part of the conversation between Stanhope and Pauline in *Descent into Hell* concerns the spiritual practice of 'substitution', Williams' belief that a person can, out of love, carry the anxieties and pain of another, and can bear them more easily than the other because they are not his or her own. For Williams, this act had arisen out of the more general theology of romantic love and was to find its fulfilment in the later idea of 'co-inherence'; it was to become a regular practice of the 'Companions', and he had already suggested it to two of his female 'muses',[107] in much the same terms as Stanhope proposes it here.[108] Stanhope offers to carry the burden of Pauline's fear about her strange experience of meeting a duplicate version (*Doppelgänger*) of herself, and she herself in turn is to bear the

---

[102] Williams reached at least the grade of Adeptus Exemptus, belonging to the sphere of *Chesed*, the Divine Mercy: see Lindop, *Charles Williams*, 93 and my Chapter 8 n.108.

[103] Compare Tillyard and Lewis, *Personal Heresy*, 4.

[104] Lewis and Tillyard, 'Personal Heresy in Criticism', 7–28.

[105] Tillyard and Lewis, *Personal Heresy*, 125.

[106] Tillyard and Lewis, *Personal Heresy*, 15, cf. 50, 'my romantic bias'.

[107] Perhaps the first instance is Williams' request to Thelma Mills in 1929 (see Lindop, *Charles Williams*, 483–4), and this is repeated with Ann Bradby in 1931 (Lindop, *Charles Williams*, 444, n.591).

[108] Williams, *Descent into Hell*, 96–102.

fear of an ancestor, John Anstruther, facing being burnt at the stake during religious persecution. As Lindop observes, Lewis does not mention this central theme at all in his comments on the novel, and I suggest that it may well be because it fell into his suspicion of the artist's self-'representation'. If so, there is an interesting development of Lewis' handling of Williams' poetic self-expression a year later, as we shall see. Williams does notice that none of the reviewers of the novel in print had picked up what he felt to be its original idea; ironically, he writes: 'I presume that the whole reviewing world is absolutely acquainted with the general idea of substituted love.'[109]

The next book Williams published was a book of popular theology, *He Came Down from Heaven*, appearing in May 1938, which contained an exposition of both the 'theology of romantic love' and 'the practice of substituted love'. Lewis wrote immediately to Williams on 7 June, calling it 'a really great book'. He continued, tongue in cheek, but with an adulatory tone:

> Damn you, you go on steadily getting better even since you first crossed my path: how do you do it? I begin to suspect that we are living in the 'age of Williams' and our friendship with you will be our only passport to fame. I've a good mind to punch your head when next we meet.[110]

There is no use of the term 'co-inherence' in the book, and I will be giving evidence later that Williams had not yet discovered it. However, the whole book is permeated by the vision of a great web of 'exchange' in which all creatures are held. Early on in the book, Williams considers an intimate 'connection', later he says 'exchange',[111] between 'events in the human soul' and 'events in history', and asserts that neither could exist without the other. His conclusion is that if we could be certain that the historical events upon which Christendom reposes had not happened, 'all that could be said would be that they had not *yet* happened'.[112] Lewis seizes upon this last phrase and declares it to be a 'patin of bright gold'; indeed, he thinks somewhat extravagantly that 'this may become one of the sentences that straddle across ages like the great dicta of Plato, Augustine, or Pascal'. Williams' declaration, that with love-in-heaven 'every point of the circumference is at the centre',[113] is to reappear in the Great Dance of Lewis' *Perelandra* some five years later,[114] and by that time Lewis is thoroughly aware of the continual emphasis of Williams on co-inherence.

Lewis offers no dissent from the vision of a 'theology of romantic love' in this book, as he had done in his initial letter to Williams, but it may be that he is by

---

[109] CW to Phyllis Potter, 11 October 1937, Bod. MS 16124/1.
[110] CSL to CW, 7 June 1938, in Lewis, *Letters*, 227–8.   [111] Williams, *He Came Down*, 84.
[112] Williams, *He Came Down*, 6.   [113] Williams, *He Came Down*, 106.
[114] Lewis, *Perelandra*, 249. See my Chapter 13, section 2.

now simply reinterpreting it in his own way. I suggest that his perspective is similar to that expressed in his series of three essays in the journal *Theology* during 1940 on the theme of spirituality and culture,[115] where he refers to both his own and Williams' genres of romanticism—*Sehnsucht* and romantic love—as 'sub-Christian values' with some limited usefulness as a vehicle for bringing their adherents to Christ. Of his own province in romanticism, he writes that 'I have not (or not yet) reached a point at which I can honestly repent of my early experiences of romantic *Sehnsucht* [...] Without them my conversion would have been more difficult.'[116] With regard to romantic love, he explicitly cites Williams' *He Came Down from Heaven* as an exemplification,[117] and comments: 'The road described by Dante and Patmore is a dangerous one. But [...] for some souls romantic love also has proved a schoolmaster.'[118] However, Lewis is emphatic at this point that these 'sub-Christian values' are not spiritual virtues, and that 'Cultural activities do not in themselves improve our spiritual condition.'[119]

Williams, for his part, chooses in *He Came Down from Heaven* to read and commend Lewis' *Allegory of Love* from his own perspective, as in his lecture the previous year. He compliments Lewis on having written 'one of the most important critical books of our time', in describing the decisive 'change' in human imagination that resulted in the mood of romantic love.[120] But, somewhat more emphatically than before, he does not follow Lewis in finding the religious element within the verses of eleventh-century poets to be a 'parody' of true religion; though he admits the love-religion could *become* a 'superstition', in itself it was 'a thing not of superstition and indulgence, but of doctrine and duty'.[121] He treats Dante's blend of religion and love, seeing and adoring the beloved in the glory of her eternal state with God (the 'Beatrician encounter'), as if it were in continuity with the earlier poetry. Despite what must then have been divergences between Williams and Lewis, the appearance of the book was marked by what was effectively a London meeting of the Inklings, including Lewis' brother 'Warnie' and Hugo Dyson. They all lunched at Shirreffs, Williams' favourite wine bar, on 4 July 1938, Lewis recalling that nobody would 'forget a certain immortal lunch [...] Nor the almost Platonic discussion which followed for about two hours in St Paul's churchyard'.[122] One can only speculate on the content of the long conversation.

[115] Lewis, 'Christianity and Culture', 'Christianity and Culture (a letter)', and 'Peace Proposals', all reprinted in Lewis, *Christian Reflections*, 12–36, omitting the responsive essays by S. L. Bethell, E. F. Carritt, and George Every.
[116] Lewis, 'Christianity and Culture', in Lewis, *Christian Reflections*, 23.
[117] Lewis, 'Christianity and Culture', 22.
[118] Quoting from the Apostle Paul, Galatians 3:4–5 on the law, 'a schoolmaster to bring us to Christ'.
[119] Lewis, 'Christianity and Culture', 25.   [120] Williams, *He Came Down*, 86.
[121] Williams, *He Came Down*, 87.   [122] Lewis, *Essays*, viii.

Six months later, in December 1938, Williams published his *Taliessin through Logres*. In a cycle of poems, three 'landscapes' merge together in a modernist way—the Christian empire of Byzantium, the Britain of Arthurian mythology (Logres), and the features of the human body.[123] In this palimpsest of realities, the central figure is Arthur's court-poet, Taliessin, whom Williams finds in ancient Welsh epic. Lewis reviewed the book for the journal *Theology*, and judged that Williams had written 'a great poem', praising lavishly its prevailing 'quality of Glory',[124] and 'the fresh, harsh energy of its unstaled diction and the headlight sharpness of its vision'.[125] He is negatively critical about only one poem, 'The Coming of Galahad', in which he finds that 'the obscurities are to me impenetrable and the style is dangerously near a mannerism'. This is in fact the poem in which Williams portrays his poet Taliessin as discussing the nature of romanticism, urging a 'fitting together' of the 'stone' with the 'shell', or reason with imagination.[126] At this stage, it seems that Lewis could not entirely comprehend Williams' romantic approach, though by the time of *Arthurian Torso*, he is able to give seven pages to an appreciative exposition of the poem, defending its admitted difficulty against any accusation of poetic failure.[127]

Despite some incomprehension in 1938, Lewis testifies in his review to the experience of being drawn into Williams' own province of the poetic landscape, writing that 'as I went on I found bit after bit of my "real world" falling into its place within the poem'. What had seemed to be a 'deliciously private universe' was, he affirms, 'the common universe after all', and 'this apparently romantic and even wilful poem was 'really "classic" and central'.[128] When Lewis reviewed the book for a second time, in 1945 for the *Oxford Magazine*, he takes up again the same image of a territory to be inhabited; now it seems he is not quite so sure that it is a 'common universe', and he distances himself rather more from Williams' province, but he still bears witness to being enticed into it. One of his reasons for 'anticipating that it will finally take its place among our great poems' is that:

> The world into which this poem carries me is emphatically not mine. My admiration is not based on the secret affinity which makes even the first reading of some books feel like a home-coming. It is therefore, in my opinion, more likely to be a just admiration. Taliessin takes me where I never wanted to go and where I remain a foreigner, but it takes me. *Ecce deus fortior me.*'[129]

In tracing the journey of Williams and Lewis through the landscape of romanticism, it seems that Lewis continually shifts in mood about how much he is at

---

[123] For this layering, see Higgins, 'Double Affirmation', 73–9.
[124] Lewis, 'Sacred Poem', in Lewis, *Image and Imagination*, 135.
[125] Lewis, 'Sacred Poem', 134.   [126] Williams, 'The Coming of Galahad', *Taliessin*, 71.
[127] Lewis, 'Williams and the Arthuriad', 166–72.   [128] Lewis, 'Sacred Poem', 135.
[129] Lewis, 'Charles Williams', in Lewis, *Image and Imagination*, 141.

'home' in Williams' own part of the territory, even up to the *Four Loves* of 1960. Sometimes, as we have seen, he can feel more at home by reinterpreting the scenery—as Williams reinterprets Lewis' own environs. But he is always willing to be drawn away from his natural path into Williams' own province, confessing that he is under a strange compulsion, echoing the words of Dante: *Ecce deus fortior me*, 'Behold, a god more powerful than I.'[130]

Lewis' comments on the themes of the Taliessin poems in 1938 show how much he is willing at that moment to recognize a 'common universe'. With regard to the theology of romantic love, he remains somewhat non-committal, but is not overtly negative, judging that 'Mr Williams reaffirms the amatory doctrine of the *Vita Nuova* with complete conviction.'[131] While he had not referred to the idea of substituted love in his letter to Williams about *Descent Into Hell*, here he is much more forthcoming: '"Substitution or "exchange" [. . . is] the most familiar thing in the world, a fact of daily experience. What some thought most fantastic in the author's greatest romance (*Descent into Hell*) is serious.'[132] It seems that Lewis is not as troubled now by the self-'representation' of the poet as he was earlier, as he cannot have missed that Taliessin is essentially a projection of Williams, especially in his promotion of this favourite doctrine.[133] Lewis is also commendatory of the presentation of the Fall in these poems, as the disaster of capitulating to the temptation to 'experience good as evil'. Williams had already offered this explanation as to how beings living in communion with the Good could nevertheless fall away from it in *He Came Down from Heaven*,[134] and Lewis was himself to adopt it a couple of years later in *Perelandra*. There, the 'Lady' is tempted to regard the evil of disobedience to God's command not to remain on the 'fixed land' as the 'good' of becoming mature.[135]

But the most significant indication that Lewis is at least partly inhabiting Williams' own world is his comment that 'The greatest, but also the most legitimate of Taliessin's difficulties lies in its symbolism.' In symbolism, as distinct from allegory, according to Lewis here the images stand 'for something the poet has experienced which he has not reduced, perhaps cannot reduce, to a concept'.[136] Read as an allegory, Lewis thinks we can say that 'Byzantium' stands for the total embodied person, for human order and civilization, and for divine order, but he finds that 'Byzantium' is also a symbol that evokes an 'experience which has no name', but which we can recognize in our own lives.[137] Lewis had insisted that medieval love poetry was 'allegorical', but here he perceives a love

---

[130] Dante, *La Vita Nuova*, 29–30. Dante means the god of love; Lewis perhaps means love as encountered through Williams.

[131] Lewis, 'Sacred Poem', 127.   [132] Lewis, 'Sacred Poem', 127.

[133] In publishing his earlier essays in the book *Personal Heresy*, Lewis moderates somewhat his earlier critique of romantic projection in the light of Tillyard's criticism: 148–50.

[134] Williams, *He Came Down*, 16–18.

[135] For a longer exposition, see Fiddes, 'Charles Williams', 66–9.

[136] Lewis, 'Sacred Poem', 128.   [137] Lewis, 'Sacred Poem', 129, 131.

that is a symbolic 'celebration of the human body'. The difference seems to be that this kind of love-religion is not 'unmediated feeling', but a 'doctrine of Euclidean love', a love that has order and mathematical proportion within it, expressed in the image of the hazel rod that is used both for measurement and for keeping order.[138] Doubtless Lewis is taking his own way to recognize a 'common universe' that he and Williams inhabit; it may well be that he thinks of Williams' poetry as symbolic of the depths only of *human* experience, since he makes such a strong distinction (at this point) between nature and spirit. But a certain ambiguity hovers around the idea of an experience that 'has no name', and we seem to be at least pointing in the direction of experiencing, through romantic love, the final reality of the spiritual realm associated with the nameless Absolute.

If we had comments by Lewis on Williams' next theological book, *The Descent of the Dove*, subtitled *A Short History of the Holy Spirit in the Church*, published in late October 1939, we might be able better to assess just how far Lewis had been drawn into Williams' own territory. This is, significantly, the first published work of Williams in which the term 'co-inherence' appears, and the idea forms a major theme of the book, which ends with a kind of manifesto for the Companions of the Co-inherence, proposing the need for an Order within the church whose purpose would be to affirm the 'pattern' of co-inherence and the 'substitutions in love' and 'exchanges in love' that are a part of co-inherence.[139] Although Williams quotes from Lewis' *Allegory of Love* to the effect that the love-religion of the medieval poets expressed 'an antagonism between their amatory and their religious ideals',[140] he immediately follows this with the assertion that 'In certain states of romantic love the Holy Spirit has deigned to reveal, as it were, the Christ-hood of two individuals each to other.' As in the Taliessin poems, passion has divine order and divine geometry within it: 'the discovery of a supernatural justice between two lovers was passion's justification, and [. . .] its very cause'. This was 'the Christian diagram of universal good-will'; it was a 'vision' of the Glory, and it was also— now—a 'co-inherence'.[141]

We do not know what Lewis thought of all this. We have only two letters, from ten years later, in which he simply commends the book, without comment, to a correspondent.[142] The month before its publication, however, Williams had moved to work in Oxford as part of the transplanting of Amen House into that city for the period of the Second World War, and the 'inward journey' of Williams and Lewis was to enter a new phase.

---

[138] There is a hint of sadism both in Williams' portrayals of whipping with the hazel rod in his poems, and in Lewis' apparent agreement that these punishments are 'good rods for barbarian backs', and that 'stocks and the rod are a good – the appearance of law'; Lewis, 'Sacred Poem', 129–30, 131.
[139] Williams, *Descent of the Dove*, 236.   [140] Williams, *Descent of the Dove*, 130
[141] Williams, *Descent of the Dove*, 131.
[142] CSL to Rhona Bodle, 24 October 1949 and 3 November 1949, in Lewis, *Letters*, 2: 988, 993.

2

Together in Oxford, 1939–1945

2.1 The Weaving of Lives Together

When the London branch of the Oxford University Press moved to Oxford in September 1939 for the duration of the ensuing war, Williams was established at its offices at Southfield House, and as a lodger at the capacious home of the Spalding family at 9 South Parks Road.[1] There began a period when Williams could be absorbed more intimately into the life of the Inklings, and in particular had the opportunity to deepen his friendship with Lewis.

As Grevel Lindop observes, 'Lewis' appetite for [William's] company was boundless.'[2] He lent his college rooms to Williams over the weekend so that he could escape the hectic atmosphere of the Spaldings' house,[3] lunched with him routinely on Tuesdays and Thursdays in a pub, and made him part of the meetings of the Inklings on—usually—two evenings of the week. It seemed that Lewis' friends appreciated the volcanic eruption of Williams onto the scene as much as Lewis did, and it was only when Tolkien was looking back, in the 1960s, that a different tone emerged, as Tolkien wrote with regret: 'Yes, CSL was my closest friend from about 1927 to 1940, and remained very dear to me. His death was a grievous blow. But in fact we saw less and less of one another after he came under the dominant influence of Charles Williams.'[4] In another letter he writes about his own friendship with Williams: 'We liked one another and enjoyed talking (mainly in jest) but we had nothing to say to one another at deeper (or higher) levels [. . .] I remained entirely unmoved. Lewis was bowled over.'[5] Little or nothing of this negativity appeared at the time, Tolkien, for example, lauding 'Our dear Charles Williams' in a long poem written during the war; while mocking the mythology of the Taliessin poems in a friendly way, the poem hails him as 'beloved Druid poet' and celebrates him as being able to 'soaring, race / up to the threshold of Eternal Grace'.[6]

---

[1] Ruth Spalding was a producer with the Religious Drama Society, and had become a friend after contacting Williams about directing one of his plays, *Seed of Adam*.

[2] Lindop. *Charles Williams*, 307.

[3] CW to Michal Williams, 'Monday' 1939, in Williams, *To Michal*, 15; CW to Michal Williams, 17 September 1939, in Williams, *To Michal*, 18.

[4] Tolkien to Christopher Bretherton, 16 July 1964, in Tolkien, *Letters*, 349.

[5] Tolkien to Dick Plotz, 12 September 1965, in Tolkien, *Letters*, 362.

[6] Carpenter, *Inklings*, 123–6.

Charles Williams and C.S. Lewis: Friends in Co-inherence. Paul S. Fiddes, Oxford University Press. © Paul S. Fiddes 2021.
DOI: 10.1093/oso/9780192845467.003.0002

'Warnie' Lewis records that Williams was 'the most constant attendant' at the Inklings, and that he therefore knew him better than any other of the members.[7] When Williams joined the group, C. S. Lewis was reading aloud weekly from the *Problem of Pain* and Tolkien from his drafts for *The Lord of the Rings*. Williams read them a new play, *The House by the Stable*, in November 1939, and Lewis reports that it was 'approved by all', while his comment that it was 'unusually intelligible for him' shows that he may not have been so entirely 'bowled over' by Williams as Tolkien was later to judge.[8] Lewis, however, seems to have recognized without rancour that he now had a rival for being the social centre of the group, recollecting later that 'I had passed for our best conduit of quotations but he easily outstripped me [...] he excelled at showing you the little grain of truth or felicity in some passage generally quoted for ridicule.'[9] For his part, Williams began his period in Oxford with an appreciation of Lewis' lectures. In a letter to his wife Michal in October 1939, he writes of hearing Lewis lecture on Tasso and Milton, judging it to be 'very good' and reflecting that 'it is years since I have heard anyone talk intelligently on poetry'.[10] It seems in fact that Williams regularly attended Lewis' lectures; Anne Renwick, an undergraduate who was to become a pupil of Williams and one of his female 'muses', recalls that she first caught sight of him as 'the odd-looking man who always sits in the same place at Lewis' lectures and laughs at all the jokes'.[11]

However, in the same month, October 1939, there is an early indication that Williams was never to feel properly understood by his Oxford friends. Writing to Anne Ridler, he complains that 'There is no-one (NO-ONE) in Oxford to whom I can talk about Taliessin. This is a serious blow...'[12] We recall that this was written *after* Lewis' published review of *Taliessin through Logres*. Despite the emphatic 'NO-ONE', Williams does indeed later make a partial exception for Lewis, but the sense of reserve still remains. Writing to Michal in 1941, Williams feels that Lewis is 'perhaps' the only person in Oxford who understands the symbolism of the Taliessin poems: 'if you think ANY human creature in Oxford—except perhaps C.S.L.—would understand me there, you are *wrong*'.[13] Again, he writes to Anne Ridler in 1942, telling her that he misses her badly as a critic of his poems: 'No-one of a vivid brain ever talks to me about them [...] CSL admires them and alludes to them, but—'[14] But what? We would like to know, but

---

[7] Warren Lewis, diary entry for 15 May 1945 (the day of Williams' death), in Kilby and Mead, eds., *Brothers and Friends*, 182.

[8] CSL to W. H. Lewis, 11 November 1939, in Lewis, *Letters*, 2: 289.   [9] Lewis, *Essays*, xi.

[10] CW to Michal Williams, 25 October 1939, in Williams, *To Michal*, 27.

[11] Scott (Renwick), 'Charles Williams', 6.

[12] CW to Anne Ridler, 6 October 1939, Bodleian Anne Ridler Papers, uncatalogued; transcribed by Lindop, *Charles Williams*, 315.

[13] CW to Michal Williams, 7 August 1941, in Williams, *To Michal*, 124.

[14] CW to Anne Ridler, 30 September 1942, Bodleian Anne Ridler Papers, uncatalogued; transcribed by Lindop, *Charles Williams*, 361.

the rest is silence. The mood of complaint continues as the years go by. In 1943, he is writing to Michal, 'what else happens here? Nothing except in my mind: and the creative energies of my mind (as once they were!) I do not otherwise discuss— O well, with C.S.L. a little.'[15] At about the same time he is writing to another female 'muse', Joan Wallis, that: 'I do not know what I need: yes, I do. C.S.L. *et hoc genus omne* are admirable, but (in a way) useless. You have done, in your time, more towards the creation of great verse than all the Great.'[16]

We must be cautious in assessing this evidence of apparent disaffection. Williams is evidently aiming to cultivate the sympathy of the women to whom he is writing, and to make them feel their value to him. He also believed that to produce his best work he needed the female muse and a 'transmutation of energy' through a restrained sexuality,[17] and this certainly lies behind his comment to Joan Wallis about what he 'needs'. Williams seems to have swung in mood about his literary acquaintances in Oxford—on the one hand feeling that his friendships failed to generate the poetic energy he craved, but on the other hand referring to them as 'brothers of our energy'. He writes to Michal on 5 March 1940 complimenting her on being 'the Origin of all' his work: 'Am I only to be followed by the feminine? You will be attended—you—by the masculine minds: great minds, strong males, brothers of our energy—those who know our work—Lewis & Eliot & Raymond [Hunt] & Tolkien & the young males...'[18] This is testimony of a sort to the impulse given to his creativity by literary friends, and especially by Lewis, though we cannot miss the tone of felt superiority in the phrase 'those who know our work' (another similar phrase he often uses is 'our people').[19] From his youth, Williams had always enjoyed discussion with male groups;[20] in fact, concurrent with his attendance at the Inklings, he set up a kind of second literary group that met at the Eastgate for lunchtime meetings, consisting of himself, the bookseller Basil Blackwell, the playwright Christopher Fry, and his colleague at the press Gerard Hopkins.[21]

In his apostrophe to Michal as 'the Origin', Williams links together 'Lewis & [T.S.] Eliot', and he was perhaps unique in being on equally good terms with both of them. He was pleased that both admired his work; Eliot, for instance, had recently reviewed *The Descent of the Dove* warmly, at the same time commending his poetry and novels.[22] Williams played with the idea of bringing Lewis and Eliot

---

[15] CW to Michal Williams, 23 September 1943, in Williams, *To Michal*, 170.

[16] CW to Joan Wallis, 20 August 1943, Wade CWP 86.   [17] See Chapter 1, section 4.

[18] CW to Michal Williams, 5 March 1940, in Williams, *To Michal*, 50–1.

[19] E.g. CW to Raymond Hunt, 21 December 1942, Wade CWP 38.

[20] Early instances are the 'Theological Smokers' in St Albans, and the discussion group gathered by the Revd Arthur ('Hugh') Lee at his vicarage in St John's Wood, London.

[21] See Lindop, *Charles Williams*, 310.

[22] Eliot, 'Lay Theologian'. Ricks and McCue, *Poems of T. S. Eliot*, I: 1038, compare Williams, *Descent of the Dove*, 3, with Eliot's 'The dove descending breaks the air' in 'Little Gidding' IV. See Barber, 'Charles Williams', 8.

together with him, perhaps for a radio broadcast; writing to Phyllis Potter in 1941, he muses that 'I do think that three or four of us—Lewis, and perhaps Eliot and so on let loose on the question of what love is for twenty minutes each would be amusing.'[23] He did finally bring them together for tea at The Mitre in Oxford in the spring of 1945, and although it was a social disaster, he nevertheless seems to have enjoyed it personally.[24]

Yet despite Williams listing a number of 'males' as 'brothers of our energy', Lewis was surely right to feel that there was a friendship between him and Williams like none other of his circle; it is revealing that each time Williams complains about not being understood, he makes—if cautiously—an exception for Lewis. The 'inward journey' we are tracing between Lewis and Williams is complicated on both sides, freighted with reservations, qualifications, and courteous dissent. We have already seen in the matter of romantic love how Lewis put clear space between the two of them in 1936, moved a little onto Williams' ground in reviewing *Taliessin* in 1938, and distanced himself more (though sympathetically) in his second review of 1945. We are going to see how Lewis finally seems to have come to share some common territory in *The Four Loves* of 1960 and some other writing of his late period. This is evidence that Lewis was not simply 'bowled over' by Williams, as is—more anecdotally—a passage in a letter by Lewis to his brother Warnie about one of the first Inklings meetings Williams attended after moving to Oxford.[25] The discussion that evening was about whether 'one really could believe in a universe where the majority were damned and also in the goodness of God'. One can deduce from the letter that Williams, unlike C. L. Wrenn,[26] who was present, thought there *was* some problem with divine goodness in this case, and expressed himself so vigorously that Wrenn 'maintained that conversation with Williams enabled him to understand how inquisitors had felt it right to burn people'. Lewis' jocular comment was that 'Tolkien and I agreed afterwards that [...] as some people at school [...] are eminently kickable, so Williams is eminently combustible.' Despite the levity (and just a hint of sadism), a serious difference between Williams and Lewis about theodicy was emerging that would come more fully to light—as we shall see—in Williams' response to Lewis' book *The Problem of Pain*.

In a letter to his brother two weeks after the previous one, Lewis writes about hearing Williams read a paper to students in the Junior Common Room of St Hilda's College—'or rather not "read" but "spout"—i.e. deliver without a single note a perfectly coherent and impassioned meditation, variegated with quotations in his incantatory manner'.[27] He writes that 'this most wonderful performance

[23] CW to Phyllis Potter, 6 February 1941, Bodley MS 16124/1.
[24] Green and Hooper, *C. S. Lewis*, 223–4.
[25] CSL to W. H. Lewis, 5 November 1939, in Lewis, *Letters*, 2: 283.
[26] A scholar of Old English like Tolkien, and Fellow of Pembroke.
[27] CSL to W. H. Lewis, 19 November 1939, in Lewis, *Letters*, 2: 293.

impressed ... the young women', and it certainly impressed him. Lindop suggests that it was this experience that made him determined to 'smuggle him onto the Oxford lecture list',[28] and with Tolkien's help, Lewis pressed Williams' case for filling the gap caused by a wartime shortage of lecturers, despite Williams' lack of a degree.

The result of this scheming was that Williams began lecturing in the University on Milton in January 1940, with Lewis present along with Tolkien and Gerard Hopkins from the Press.[29] The Milton series was accompanied by a lecture course on Wordsworth the same year, and by lectures on Shakespeare from 1943. The second lecture in his course on Milton, on 5 February 1940, was on *Comus*, and Lewis and Tolkien were again present. Lewis' often-quoted account of this occasion was given in a letter to Warnie:[30]

> On Monday C.W. lectured nominally on Comus, but really on Chastity. Simply as criticism it was superb—because here was a man who really started from the same point of view as Milton and really cared with every fibre of his being about the 'sage and serious doctrine of virginity' [...] It was a beautiful sight to see a whole room full of very modern young men and women sitting in that absolute silence which can *not* be faked, very puzzled, but spell-bound [... ;] that beautiful carved room had probably not witnessed anything so important since some of the great medieval or Renaissance lectures. I have at last, if only for once, seen a university doing what it was founded to do: teaching Wisdom.

The final word, Wisdom, is to be echoed in Lewis' later critical verdict on Williams' Arthurian poems, which he judges to be 'a book of wisdom—a book that makes consciousness'.[31]

We can reconstruct the 'wisdom' that Lewis detected on that day in 1940 from a fragment on *Comus*, probably notes for a lecture somewhere, which is to be found among Williams' manuscripts.[32] He writes that the Greeks and Romans, succeeded by Shakespeare, Dante, Spenser, and Milton, all 'imagined chastity as a positive and transmuting thing. It is, in fact, power.' When he poses the question, 'power to what?', he replies, 'Milton told us', and then gives a reference to *Comus*, lines 453–63. In these lines we read that chastity casts a beam on 'The unpolluted temple of the mind', so turning it 'to the soul's essence / Till all be made immortal.' Williams' argument is that in the ancient world, chastity was not merely

---

[28] CSL to W. H. Lewis, 28 January 1940, in Lewis, *Letters*, 2: 335; see Lindop, *Charles Williams*, 314.
[29] CW to Michal Williams, 29 January, in Williams, *To Michal*, 42; CSL to W. H. Lewis, 3 February 1940, in Lewis, *Letters*, 2: 339.
[30] CSL to W. H. Lewis, 11 February 1940, in Lewis, *Letters*, 2: 345–6.
[31] Lewis, 'Williams and the Arthuriad', 190–1.
[32] Fragment on Comus, Bod. MS 16125/2, folder 4; cf. Wade CW/MS-356 (Milton Lectures, January–March 1945).

abstinence but spiritual power, and the finding of such 'transmutation' of the flesh in *Comus* is attested in several of Williams' published works.[33] Writing that to understand this aspect of *Comus* 'you must give yourself up to imagination', he cites Patmore as one place where that imagination can be found. Although we cannot be certain that this fragment is part of the momentous lecture of 1940,[34] Lindop's perceptive comments on it throw light on the whole progress of Williams' mind and sexual behaviour:

> For Williams, Milton's masque was less about physical virginity than about transmutation, about the changing of sexual energy into spiritual power. It justified what he had undergone with Phyllis, and what he still believed to be a path to poetic inspiration. His discussion of Comus was fired with a fervour derived from the long efforts and sufferings of his personal history.[35]

No interpretation of Williams in the future can neglect this brilliant insight. I wonder, however, whether he is quite right when he goes on to say that Lewis 'probably understood nothing about this'. It is just as likely that Lewis was 'overwhelmed' (Lindop's word) precisely because he *did* understand the personal import of what Williams was saying about transmutation, even if he did not know all the intense details of the story of Phyllis, and that he had some sympathy with it. Though I speculate here, it is not impossible that Lewis' sympathy came from his own experience.[36] Lewis must have been aware of Williams' argument, at least because Williams had made the general theory part of his published work. In addition to the fictional figure of Considine he had, for instance, spent several pages of his *Descent of the Dove* on the historical case of the *subintroductae*, women in the early church who had taken a vow of celibacy but lived in spiritual marriage with male ascetics, and 'apparently slept with their companions without intercourse'.[37] When Williams writes approvingly that 'the use of sex, in this experiment, might have been to pass below itself and release the dark gods of D.H. Lawrence into the kingdom of Messias', Lindop is surely right to propose that Williams 'clearly saw this as a parallel to his own experiences of "transmutation of energy" with Phyllis Jones and other women'.[38] Significantly, Williams saw the practice of *subintroductae* as part of the greater pattern of 'exchange' and now of 'co-inherence'; it was an 'energy of effort [. . .] towards a work of exchange

---

[33] See Williams, *English Poetic Mind*, 114; Williams, 'John Milton', in *Image*, 27–9.

[34] In reconstructing the content of the lecture, Lindop, *Charles Williams*, 319–20, appears to draw on the Bodleian Comus fragment and on 'John Milton', 28–9.

[35] Lindop, *Charles Williams*, 320.

[36] Lewis' relations with Mrs Jane Moore in their earlier days remain a matter of speculation among writers of Lewis' biography: see McGrath, *C. S. Lewis*, 73–6, 86; Sayer, *Jack*, xvii–xviii; Wilson, *C. S. Lewis*, 58–9. McGrath points to Lewis' sonnet 'Reason', written in the early 1920s, which expresses a longing for someone who could 'reconcile in me both maid and mother': Lewis, *Poems*, 81.

[37] Williams, *Descent of the Dove*, 13.   [38] Lindop, *Charles Williams*, 312.

and substitution', a union between love on earth and in heaven, an 'experience of life from others'.[39]

Lewis found the lecture in the University Divinity School to be a momentous event in the entire history of the University and in his own life; he supposed it to have the same impact in the lives of others whom he describes as 'spell-bound'. Lindop dramatizes the occasion in a most effective prologue to his biography of Williams, describing graphically how Williams left his audience 'dazed, exhilarated, inspired' and using the incident as introduction to 'this extraordinary man who changed so many people's lives'.[40] But of course we have no record of the event except that of Lewis; Tolkien says nothing about it in his letters. A. N. Wilson in his acerbic biography of Lewis tells us that 'some of those who attended the lecture have implied to me that not everyone took it particularly seriously. There were even giggles...'[41] There is no doubt that Williams came to be regarded as an inspiring, even sensational, lecturer,[42] drawing a good student audience (voluntary at Oxford) and prompting requests from undergraduates to their colleges to receive tutorials from him.[43] Following the Comus lecture, Wilson himself records, the lectures had to move to a larger lecture room at the Taylorian Institute.[44] But it is possible that it was Lewis alone who found this lecture so *very* astonishing. When Williams writes to Michal with the news that 'Lewis says that my last Monday's address on the Comus-Chastity was "the most important thing that has happened in the Divinity Schools for a hundred years, or is likely to happen for the next hundred"',[45] he seems surprised, though pleased, adding: 'I tell you for love's sake & laughter's.'[46]

In March 1940, Lewis and Williams separately reviewed the same book— *Passion and Society* by Denis de Rougement—and their reviews offer a window onto the road of their 'inward journey' at this point. They agree that the book has two aspects, historical and moral. The first part, they explain, argues that the 'passion myth' that begins with the 'courtly love' of the medieval period was not really an expression of sexual passion at all, but the symbolic expression of a wish for death and pain, the product of a widespread eros-mysticism that continues into nineteenth-century romanticism. Lewis and Williams agree that this historical analysis is tendentious and totally untenable.[47] The second part distinguishes Christian marriage from a kind of love that is intensely emotional and non-rational, as the modern form of the 'passion myth'. Lewis and Williams both

---

[39] Williams, *Descent of the Dove*, 14. 'Co-inherence' appears on p. 10.
[40] Lindop, *Charles Williams*, 2–3.   [41] Wilson, *C. S. Lewis*, 170.
[42] See McGrath, *C. S. Lewis*, 194.   [43] Lindop, *Charles Williams*, 389–91.
[44] Wilson, *C. S. Lewis*, 170.
[45] CW to Michal Williams, 9 February 1940, in Williams, *To Michal*, 44.
[46] He writes similarly to Phyllis Potter, in 'half-amusement and half-shame': CW to Phyllis Potter, 18 February 1940, Bod. MS 16124/1, folder 4.
[47] Williams, 'One Way of Love', in *Image*, 159–61; Lewis, 'Denis de Rougement', in *Image and Imagination*, 59–62.

judge that this ethical section is a valuable account of true marriage. Williams, however, takes care here to introduce another 'great tradition' of romantic love that he believes Rougement has ignored: 'when the lover sees the beloved in light, when he or she (in the proper sense) adores [...] [and] the Divine Child spiritually lives in the two gay lovers'.[48] Lewis' affirmation of the section on marriage is somewhat ambiguous. On the one hand, he may be referring obliquely and not unfavourably to Williams' version of romantic theology when he remarks: 'An English reader, bred on Patmore, Chesterton, and *Mr Charles Williams*, may sometimes wonder whether Romanticism has not a greater internal power of shedding its own errors than M. de Rougement supposes.'[49] On the other hand, he shows a far greater enthusiasm for this part of the book than does Williams, proposing that it makes the book 'indispensable', and that it is 'one of the most cleansing and penetrating sermons I have read for a long time'.[50] His somewhat remarkable encomium perhaps demonstrates his suspicion about *any* espousal of the medieval love-religion at all, however interpreted, quoting Rougement to the effect that 'all of us need to learn, every day that Eros ceases to be a demon only when he ceases to be a god'. Lewis, then, appears to be most comfortable on his own ground, while being prepared at this point to look with interest on the kind of theology of romantic love developed by Williams, as he had shown in his review of *Taliessin* in the previous year.

I have already suggested that the *way* that Lewis is prepared to enter the 'province' of romanticism indwelt by Williams is marked out by the parameters of his three papers on Christianity and culture, written for the journal *Theology* between March and December 1940, in conversation with S. L. Bethell, E. F. Carritt, and George Every. There he argues that 'sub-Christian values' expressed in literature and other cultural artefacts have only a limited use for Christian believers. A culture that is characterized by such values as honour, romantic love, pantheistic reverence for nature, and romantic *Sehnsucht* is 'innocent and pleasant', might be a vocation for some (teachers of literature like himself for instance), is helpful in bringing certain persons to Christ, and can be pursued to 'the glory of God'. However, it is not 'meritorious' and cannot be 'elevated into a spiritual value'.[51] Following his general approach of analogy, Lewis remarks that culture is about human striving for ends that, 'though not the true end of man (the fruition of God), have nevertheless some degree of similarity to it',[52] so that cultural values are 'dim antepasts and ectypes of the truth'.[53] Given the theological

[48] Williams, 'One Way of Love', 61. 'Gay' at this time, of course, meant 'light-hearted' or 'mirthful' and had not acquired its present meaning of 'same sex'.

[49] Lewis, 'Denis de Rougement', 61–2. My italics.   [50] Lewis, 'Denis de Rougement', 61.

[51] Lewis, *Christian Reflections*, 28.

[52] Lewis, *Christian Reflections*, 26; cf. 23, 'Some reflection of spiritual values'.

[53] Lewis, *Christian Reflections*, 24.

significance for both Lewis and Williams of the word 'glory', it is interesting that Lewis qualifies what pursuing culture 'to the glory of God' might mean; he insists that culture is not 'per se' an act of glorifying, but that the *offering* of it to God will be to God's glory. By contrast, Williams would certainly see romantic love as per se an opening to glory. Lewis has Williams in mind here, both because he cites his *He Came Down from Heaven* as an example of the affirmation of romantic love in religion,[54] and because an example of a 'sub-Christian value' he selects outside literature as something 'good in itself' but not (in his view) a 'spiritual good' is the very act of 'conjugal *eros*'.[55]

We do not know whether Williams read these articles, although he was a regular reader (and writer for) *Theology*. However, perhaps by chance, an explosive address by Williams to the sixteenth Annual Church Union School of Sociology, meeting at St Hilda's College on 2 October 1940, touched directly on an expression used by Lewis in his article of March 1940. Lewis had written that some sub-Christian values in literature could be an innocent source of pleasure for Christians who lived by higher, spiritual values: 'Since we must rest and play, where can we do so better than here—in the suburbs of Jerusalem?'[56] Invited to speak on the theme, 'The Recovery of Spiritual Initiative', Williams insists that the church must learn to listen, with 'humility of recognition',[57] to those outside the church who delight in literature—and those are not the upper-class undergraduates of Oxford, or what Williams calls 'this provincial centre',[58] but those from the lower middle-classes who get their education by attending the evening classes of the London County Council Institutes. These are the true explorers of culture, and Williams insists that we must attend to them 'if we are really thinking of the re-energizing of all values by spiritual grace'.[59] And now he uses the metaphor of 'play' that Lewis had used for the pleasures of secular culture, but with a withering scorn against those who set the 'spiritual' against nature:

> The way in which people talk normally about matter and the body,—I mean Christians—very often has about it a slightly derogatory sense. There is always a slight feeling that the body has fallen further than the soul,—that it is a poor thing. And we may say 'Of course God likes you to enjoy things.' As though you said 'Of course your father likes you to play in the garden—don't make too much noise, and don't tread on the flower-beds, but yes, father likes to see you happy.'

---

[54] Lewis, *Christian Reflections*, 22. He refers to the path of Dante and Patmore as 'dangerous', and is ambivalent in reference to Williams.

[55] Lewis, *Christian Reflections*, 33–6.   [56] Lewis, *Christian Reflections*, 24.

[57] Typescript in Bod. MS 16125/5, folder 4 (wrongly dated in catalogue 1939, owing to pencilled note on MS, not in Williams' hand), 9. Another copy of the typescript was published by Horne, 'From the Archives', 12–24.

[58] Williams, 'Recovery of Spiritual Initiative', 5.

[59] Williams, 'Recovery of Spiritual Initiative', 6

There is something of this sort in the way that matter and the 'holy and glorious body' are talked about.[60]

Lewis assures us that God wants us to 'rest and play' in the suburbs of culture, as long as we do not think that there is any spiritual value in this activity. For Williams, the play is of the utmost import if the 'spiritual initiative' is to be 'recovered'.

2.2 The Problem of Pain: A Difference

Another insight into the shared journey of these friends is provided by the moment when, in January 1941, Williams reviewed Lewis' new book, *The Problem of Pain*, for *Theology*.[61] In this, his first popular theological book, Lewis adopts a version of what is often called a 'free-will' approach to maintaining that God is both almighty and good despite the suffering in the world. Pain is due to our being a 'spoiled species' through our own free rebellion against God, a situation that God turns into good. Lewis argues that in the very moment of creation God knew that the freedom and self-will of creatures would inevitably result in their suffering, and so composed a 'dance', 'drama', or 'symphony' of goodness in which God's own assuming of suffering in the human nature of Christ and in his crucifixion would result in a more 'complex' good than that of creation itself; this was the possibility of sharing in the relation of the divine Son to God the Father.[62] Lewis writes:

> The world is a dance in which good, descending from God, is disturbed by evil arising from the creatures, and the resulting conflict is resolved by God's own assumption of the suffering nature which evil produces. The doctrine of the free Fall asserts that the evil which thus makes the fuel or raw material for the second and more complex kind of good is not God's contribution but man's.[63]

Lewis continues that human beings need to be awoken to their state, and to the rightful retribution that they have incurred, and that pain itself can be a good when God uses it for the purposes of putting an end to our illusions. In this context, he writes in what has become a famous sentence: 'God whispers to us in our pleasures, speaks in our conscience, but shouts in our pains: it is His megaphone to rouse a deaf world.'[64] The whole human situation is thus good as

---

[60] Williams, 'Recovery of Spiritual Initiative', 7.   [61] Williams, 'Problem of Pain', 62–3.
[62] Lewis, *Problem of Pain*, 79.   [63] Lewis, *Problem of Pain*, 72.
[64] Lewis, *Problem of Pain*, 81. This is only in an attenuated sense an 'instrumental' argument for the existence of suffering. Cf. Brian Williams, 'C. S. Lewis & John Hick', 3–28.

a product of the love of God, which Lewis underlines is not the same as mere 'kindness'.[65] In this love, God is the active lover, and—in a gender polarization reminiscent of the later *Four Loves*—'our role must be that of patient to agent, female to male, mirror to light, echo to voice. Our highest activity must be response, not initiative.'[66]

Williams' review is a curious one, and has the prevailing tone of a back-handed compliment. He begins by lauding Lewis' style as 'goodness working on goodness, a lucid and sincere intelligence at work', and by commenting that 'to add that the wise reader will generally find himself learning is, with Mr. Lewis, to be platitudinous'. He then draws a contrast between his reason and his emotion in reading the book:

> Reason is a living power, not dependent on immediate personal emotion. All my own emotions rebel against the pattern of this book. I do not want to be shown that pain is, or may be, a good, that (given our present state) its inevitability is a good.[67]

Williams 'want[s] to disagree' with Lewis that it is better for a 'really bad man' to suffer the pains of eternal damnation than to continue in the 'ghastly illusion' of being contented in his state of evil. But he admits that what he 'dare question' is only Lewis' raising 'such half-speculative questions' as this. On the whole, 'The great pattern of the book is wrought too deeply into Christian dogma and the nature of man [...] for one to disagree.' The impression he gives is that he is forced by his reason and orthodoxy to agree with Lewis that 'pain is, or may be, a good', but that his emotions remain in rebellion. We are left by this review to experience the conflict and to decide the outcome for ourselves.

This impression is confirmed by subsequent writings and events. Two years later, in his essay for the collection *What the Cross Means to Me* (1943), Williams raises again the conflict between reason and emotion about the problem of pain, and resolves them in an understanding of the cross that is significantly different from Lewis'. He writes that it is 'revolting to our sense of justice' that 'We are instructed that [God] contemplates from His infinite felicity, the agonies of His creation, and deliberately maintains them in it.' Williams finds it 'credible' (in reason) that God should deign to create beings with free will in order to increase their joy, but he does not find it 'tolerable' (emotionally) that the Creator should deliberately 'sustain His created universe in a state of infinite distress as a result of

---

[65] Lewis, *Problem of Pain*, 28. Beversluis, *C. S. Lewis*, 232–4, 237–9, 250, 263–4, identifies this distinction as a first step to 'Ockhamism', or Divine Command Theory, whereby God determines what is good; he views this as a moving away from the Platonic understanding of the Good that Lewis espouses elsewhere in the book. On Lewis' supposed Ockhamism, see my Chapter 3, section 3, and Chapter 6, section 2.

[66] Lewis, *Problem of Pain*, 39.   [67] Williams, 'Problem of Pain', 63.

this choice'.[68] Unlike Lewis, Williams does not delight in the drama that God allows to develop, but asserts that 'it need not have been', since 'He could have willed us not to be after the Fall'.[69] Only in the cross of Jesus can Williams find a partial resolution of what is credible and intolerable:

> The Cross justifies it to this extent at least—that just as he submitted us to His inexorable will, so He submitted Himself to our wills (and therefore to His). He made us; He maintained us in our pain. At least, however, on the Christian showing, He consented to be Himself subject to it [. . .] He deigned to endure the justice He decreed. [. . .] God therefore becomes tolerable as well as credible. Our justice condemned the innocent, but the innocent it condemned was one who was fundamentally responsible for the existence of all injustice—its existence in the mere, but necessary, sense of time, which His will created and prolonged.[70]

Both Lewis and Williams believe that on the cross God endured the pains of suffering humanity. Lewis, indeed, writes in anticipation of Karl Barth that the impassible God can choose to suffer passion, that 'the immutable heart' can choose to be 'grieved' by creatures of its own making.[71] But for Lewis at this stage, the cross is part of a planned divine 'dance' that brings about a 'more complex good' in face of the Fall. For Williams, it is the only thing that (partially) justifies the whole unjust situation of a God who allows pain. For Lewis, the cross is an act of substitution consistent with a love of God that is displayed in the goodness of creation; *we* are responsible finally for all the pain. Williams had earlier made his view clear, in *He Came Down From Heaven*, that God as First Cause 'cannot escape' responsibility for pain, and Christ, as the union of God and humanity, 'accepted responsibility'.[72] Only thus is the cross the 'central substitution' that energizes and reaffirms all our substitutions and exchanges, and especially those of love. And living in love means that 'our experiences of good need not be separated from our experiences of evil', an evil for which God is after all partly responsible (despite our own choices) because God chooses to make us with free will and then to sustain us in its misuse.[73] For Lewis, the relation between Creator and created is the pattern of the dance. Williams had also himself much earlier used the image of the cosmic dance,[74] but for him the pain in the dance needs to be justified and atoned for. Already, in 1938, Williams had expressed his

---

[68] Williams, 'Cross', in *Image*, 131. Similarly, in 'Percivale at Carbonek', *Taliessin*, 82, Galahad in divine identity asks forgiveness of Lancelot, representing humankind; in 'The Last Voyage', *Taliessin*, 87, Galahad sings *Judica te* to God in the ship to Sarras; so King, *Pattern in the Web*, 112, 119.
[69] Williams, 'Cross', 132.   [70] Williams, 'Cross', 132, 133-4.
[71] Lewis, *Problem of Pain*, 38-9; cf. Barth, *Church Dogmatics*, IV/1, 187 cf. II/1, 313.
[72] Williams, *He Came Down*, 140-1. Also Williams, *Forgiveness of Sins*, 32.
[73] Williams never resolves the question as to whether evil is part of the divine Necessity: see Chapter 11, section 1.
[74] In his novel, *The Greater Trumps* (1932); see my Chapter 11, section 4.

sense of the intolerable state of creation, remarking 'if Creator created N.L. [Natural Law] and had full omniscience, he knew all that would happen, and why should we not be very angry indeed?'.[75]

A second confirmation of the ambiguity in Williams' review comes from Lewis himself, who tells a story against himself. After Williams' death, he recounts a discussion in the Inklings (undated) in which Williams had been vigorously recalling that Job had not been condemned by God for his protests against suffering, but that 'his apparent blasphemies had been accepted'. Lewis goes on to remember that in Williams' view,

> The weight of the divine displeasure had been reserved for the 'comforters', the self-appointed advocates on God's side, the people who tried to show that all was well—'the sort of people', he said, immeasurably dropping his lower jaw and fixing me with his eyes—'the sort of people who write books on the Problem of Pain.'[76]

It says a lot for Lewis that he was able to recount this anecdote with good grace, but choosing to tell this particular story may also show that Williams' review had stuck in his mind, and perhaps rankled there. One wonders whether the force of Williams's criticism remained with him and had some influence on his reaction to his wife Joy's death in 1960, when he himself—in his book *A Grief Observed*— becomes a Job in protest against God, finding comforters intolerable.

Williams, then, was critical of an excessive appeal to reason over emotion and feeling in Lewis' treatment of the problem of pain. In this context he makes a significant critique of Lewis' *Broadcast Talks*, observing 'how even CSL has to omit (because of time) points of some seriousness' in the process of popular broadcasting. His example is that Lewis makes play with 'this business of trusting reason', urging opponents of Christianity to follow their own prescription, and take Christian arguments seriously—saying 'If you trust reason'. Williams points out that agnostics may not be entirely relying on reason: 'I reminded him of the pure agnostic answer: "But I do not trust reason, not so far".' He concludes that 'if I had been a listener I should have lost all real interest when I realised that he had just left [this] out'.[77]

Did Williams' review of *The Problem of Pain* prompt Lewis' suggestion that they should not review each other's work any more? Williams tells Michal in a letter of 23 September 1942 that 'oddly enough' Lewis had telephoned him about a request from *Time and Tide* to review his recent booklet on *Religion and Love in Dante*, subtitled *The Theology of Romantic Love*. Lewis advised that 'he and I had

---

[75] Notes on the Doctrine Commission of the Church of England, dictated to Alice Mary Miller [Hadfield] from April 1938: Bod MS. 16123/5, folder 4 (envelope 36).

[76] Lewis, *Essays*, xiii.   [77] CW to Hunt, 31 July 1942, Wade CWP 36.

better not review each other's work any more', and suggested Anne Ridler as a reviewer.[78] It was indeed an 'odd' proposal, since Lewis had reviewed in print only one of Williams' books (*Taliessin through Logres*), and Williams had reviewed only two of Lewis' books; in addition to *The Problem of Pain*, he had offered a witty but uncontroversial review of *Screwtape Letters* in *Time and Tide* in March 1942,[79] his review consisting of letters from a senior devil threatening to 'see after Lewis'. There could hardly have been the danger of creating the appearance of a mutual admiration club. Grevel Lindop suggests that it was Lewis' disagreement with Williams over the subject of 'romantic theology' that made him reluctant to review the booklet on Dante;[80] this divergence, we have already noted, had been flagged up at the beginning of their relationship in his second letter to Williams of March 1936, and at this stage Lewis seems to have been moving away from a momentary accommodation to Williams' 'territory'.

However, it may be that Lewis also wanted to avoid any more disputes in print such as had been at least hinted at in the *Problem of Pain* review. At any rate, he did not review the more substantial book on Dante that Williams was to publish the following year (June 1943), *The Figure of Beatrice*, this also being reviewed for *Time and Tide* by Anne Ridler. We can catch a glimpse of how Lewis might have written when we read his view in a letter of 1959 that this was 'a book every student of Dante must reckon with', dubbing Williams as 'an amateur of genius' in Dantean studies. While judging that Williams 'knows less' than the 'narrow experts' about Florentine politics and the history of the language, he affirms that he knows 'a great deal more about poetry and love'.[81] In this neat form of words, we still do not know what Lewis actually thought of Williams' exposition of the theology of romantic love he found in Dante.

2.3 The Weight of Glory: A Common Conversation

About the same time as Williams' review of Lewis' book on suffering, we can find another window on their relationship in their respective treatment of the theme of 'the weight of glory', a phrase of the Apostle Paul from 2 Corinthians 4:17: 'For our light affliction, which is but for a moment, worketh for us a far more exceeding and eternal weight of glory.'[82] This is the text on which Lewis preached a University Sermon at the University Church of St Mary the Virgin, Oxford, on Sunday 8 June 1941, which his biographers Roger Lancelyn Green and Walter

---

[78] CW to Michal, 23 September 1942, in William, *To Michal*, 143.
[79] Williams, 'Letters in Hell', 245–6. Williams was to publish a second review, 'The Screwtape Letters', later that year in the *Dublin Review*.
[80] Lindop, *Charles Williams*, 360.
[81] CSL to Barbara Reynolds, 19 March 1959, in Lewis, *Letters*, 3: 1031.
[82] King James Version, evidently used by both Lewis and Williams.

Hooper have deservedly called 'perhaps the most sublime piece of prose to come from his pen'.[83] There is evidence that I will present—I believe for the first time—that there was some common thinking going on between Williams and Lewis on this image of the 'weight' of glory. It seems very likely that it was a topic of their conversation together (though we have no direct record of this), but I am not attempting or presuming to determine any direction of influence from one to the other. The comparison itself is illuminating, without judging indebtedness.

Central to Lewis' sermon is the yearning he detects in all human beings for eternity, a 'desire for our own far-off country',[84] and his concern that we should be motivated in our behaviour not by the reward of immortality but by the vision of God. This is the true promise of future 'glory', the state of being pleasing to God, or being noticed by God. This might be called a 'weight', Lewis supposes, because being delighted in by God 'seems impossible, a weight or burden of glory which our thoughts can hardly sustain. But so it is.'[85] The sermon ends with Lewis urging his hearers not to be preoccupied with 'our own potential glory hereafter'. Rather, we should think about the glory of our neighbour:

> The load, or weight, or burden of my neighbour's glory should be laid daily on my back, a load so heavy that only humility can carry it, and the backs of the proud will be broken. It is a serious thing to live in a society of possible gods and goddesses [...] There are no ordinary people. You have never talked to a mere mortal [...] Next to the Blessed Sacrament itself, your neighbour is the holiest object presented to your senses [...] for in him also Christ *vere latitat*—the glorifier and the glorified, Glory Himself, is truly hidden.[86]

We notice immediately a reuse of two of Williams' themes, which are brought together in a striking way with a new twist of meaning. First, there is the central idea of Williams' theology of romantic love, that the lover sees the Beloved in her eternal state of glory ('the glory that Love had with the Father before the world was'),[87] and that this is nothing less than an incarnation of the glory of Christ in her, since Christ is love:

> The beloved (male or female) is seen in the light of a Paradisial knowledge and experience of good. Christ exists in the soul, in joy, in terror, in a miracle of newness. *Ecce, omnia nova facio.* He who is the mystical child of the lovers sustains and supports them.[88]

[83] Green and Hooper, *C. S. Lewis*, 203.
[84] Lewis, 'Weight of Glory', in Lewis, *They Asked for a Paper*, 200.
[85] Lewis, 'Weight of Glory', 206.   [86] Lewis, 'Weight of Glory', 210–11.
[87] Williams, *Outlines*, 17.   [88] Williams, *He Came Down*, 107.

So Williams writes (1938), 'The glory is apt to dazzle the beholder unless he already has a mind disposed to examine the pattern of the glory.'[89] Later, Lewis himself was to comment that for Williams, 'The essence of the glory is that it appears in the flesh...'[90] Significantly, this experience of seeing the glory of the other is associated by Lewis in his sermon with the sacrament in which Christ is also hidden, just as in Williams' love-theology. But in Lewis' peroration, this vision of the other as a 'god' or 'goddess' in the making is widened from intense love between partners to a universal neighbour-love, as Lewis reinterprets and defuses Williams' theology of romantic love. Nevertheless, on one occasion Williams is recorded as having himself extended the range of this seeing of glory in the other; in a lecture of 1933 on William Blake, he addressed his audience in a manner much like that of Lewis' later sermon:

> You cannot see...the celestial glories in this room!—For how can you see your fellow creatures blazing with the eternal splendour of the original order of things, when you cannot even see clearly even the littlest flaws in everyday life?[91]

Usually, however, Williams reserves the vision of glory in the other to the beloved. There is another important difference between Lewis and Williams, which relates to their vision of the relation between God and the world. For Williams, the glory belongs both to an 'original' state, to a kind of pre-existence of the loved one in eternity, and to the incarnation of Christ in love here and now, as the 'mystical child' of lovers. For Lewis the glory is eschatological, a glory that is *promised* to daughters and sons of God, and we must see each other as '*possible* gods and goddesses', in 'potential glory hereafter'. Christ is 'hidden' in the neighbour as 'glorifier and glorified', in the sense that we cannot yet see properly what we shall be:

> In the end that Face which is the delight or the terror of the universe must be turned upon each of us either with one expression or with the other, either conferring glory inexpressible or inflicting shame [...] The promise of glory is the promise, almost incredible and only possible by the work of Christ, that some of us, that any of us who really chooses, shall actually survive that examination, shall find approval, shall please God. To please God [...] to be a real ingredient in the divine happiness [...] to be loved by God, not merely pitied, but delighted in as an artist delights in his work or a father in a son—it seems impossible, a weight or burden of glory which our thoughts can hardly sustain. But so it is.[92]

---

[89] Williams, *He Came Down*, 95. This refers in its immediate context to Dante and Beatrice, but is transferable to all lovers.
[90] Lewis, 'Williams and the Arthuriad', 116, 119.
[91] Wade RH Notebooks, 1: 179, 'Blake', in series 'Poetry and Philosophy', 12 May 1933 (174–80).
[92] Lewis, 'Weight of Glory', 205–6.

For Williams, it is possible here and now to 'see your fellow creatures blazing with the eternal splendour of the original order of things'.

This theme of 'seeing the glory', either in actuality or potentiality, is then woven with a second—Williams' favourite idea of 'bearing one another's burdens', or substitution in love. As Williams puts it, 'If A is to carry B's burden he must be willing to do it to the full.'[93] But again there is a twist: for Lewis, the 'heavy' burden of the other is not his or her fear, anxiety or pain, but the burden—the 'weight'—of his or her glory. It is a burden for the reason Lewis has given earlier, the heavy responsibility of being delighted in by God, but it can be carried by another. Yet again, however, the Lewisian twist of meaning is not unanticipated in Williams. In his book *The Descent of the Dove*, Williams had already appealed to this very text from Paul in association with the idea of substitution and—now since early 1939—'co-inherence':

> 'He hath made him to be sin for us, who knew no sin; that we might be made the righteousness of God in him' — 'an exceeding and eternal weight of glory.' In such words there was defined the new state of being, a state of redemption, of co-inherence, made actual by that divine substitution, 'He in us and we in him.'[94]

This is, of course, a little different from Lewis' point. For Williams in *The Descent of the Dove*, the weight of glory is ours through *divine* substitution; for Lewis, we can *ourselves* act as substitutes for the glory of others. But within two months of Lewis' sermon, Williams was to send to the publishers a small book, *The Forgiveness of Sins*, which *does* contain the idea of our bearing the burden or weight of another's glory. In considering forgiveness as a practical virtue, Williams suggests that 'admiring' the divine glory in another person is sharing in their labour for God and so carrying the grace of a 'weight of glory' that is not ours. The advocacy of humility here has echoes of Lewis' concluding appeal:

> We must not cease from our own labour because the glory is seen free in another; but neither must we cease to admire the glory because the labour is all that we can feel in ourselves. Nevertheless we might unconsciously learn to carry even grace with an air; it is not ours, and so we may; we have nothing to be proud of; another has laboured and we are entered into his labour. An unconscious magnificence of any virtue is only to be attained by the practice of that virtue combined with humility [...] in itself the grace of 'the weight of glory' is precisely its lightness.[95]

---

[93] Williams, *He Came Down*, 126.   [94] Williams, *Descent of the Dove*, 9–10.
[95] Williams, *Forgiveness of Sins*, 69–70.

William's own summary of the book is that forgiveness is 'a Mutual Act: and is a great exchange of hearts'.[96] It is clear from Williams' letters to Michal that he was working feverishly on writing the text of this book from June to the end of July 1941, the period in which Lewis preached his sermon.[97] In an essay published in *The Dublin Review* in October 1941 on 'The Redeemed City', the key phrase appears again; in this life the exchange of mutual forgiveness may require forgetting, Williams suggests, because 'the weight of our memories is too intense a weight of glory for us to bear'.[98] He appears to mean that they are heavy with glory because they carry the intensity of the other person's forgiving love. In all this there is surely an ethos of a shared conversation, a mutual interchange of ideas, in which Williams and Lewis were sparking off each other.

In any case, Williams evidently decided to deliver his own sermon on the theme of 'The Weight of Glory', and took the opportunity when invited to preach at a service for students in Cambridge at Great St Andrew's on 25 October 1942. He had actually been given the title 'The Individual for Christ', but chose 2 Corinthians 4:17 as his text and concentrated on the words 'The Weight of Glory'. From his very brief notes for the sermon, it is apparent that he was well aware of the fame of C. S. Lewis' sermon in Oxford (by now printed in *Theology*), as he began with the words, 'A borrowed text'.[99] His friend and scribe, Raymond Hunt, also began his transcription of Williams' sermon notes (which Williams had given him) into his notebook with a reference to Lewis' sermon and its publication.[100]

As with the larger part of Lewis' own sermon, Williams does not approach the issue at first with the idea of bearing the burden of another's glory, but rather considers what it means to have one's *own* burden of glory. From the mere twelve lines or so of notes—the sermon must have been preached virtually extempore—it seems that Williams' challenge to his hearers is that it is up to each person 'to say whether the "weight" he or she endures in life is, or might become, a "weight of glory"'. This is in accord with the given title, 'The Individual for Christ'. Christ himself, he affirms, carried the burden of glory in the cross. The notes can be read as asserting that that the burden or weight we carry daily is the impossibility of doing good in the world without adding to the sum total of evil. Caiaphas and Pilate both intended good, he argues, but 'the good destroys the good', and so we must pray for God's will to be done (and God's glory to be seen) 'directly in the good; indirectly in our evil'. He returns, that is, to the theodicy in 'What the Cross means to Me'; for Williams, the 'weight of glory' links directly to 'the problem of pain'. Referring to the text, 'ought not Christ to have suffered?', Williams declares

---

[96] CW to Michal Williams, 6 August 1941, in Williams, *To Michal*, 122.

[97] It was sent to the publisher on 5 or 6 August 1941: see Williams, *To Michal*, 122.

[98] Williams, 'Redeemed City', in Williams, *Image*, 109.   [99] Wade CW/MS-347, 36–7.

[100] 'The Weight of Glory', Wade RH Notebooks, 21: 4144–5. The title is provided by Hunt.

in a gnomic sentence: 'He created Necessity; he underwent Necessity; he was Necessity.' We may presume that he means that in this world, evil appears to be part of the 'necessity' God intends, since God 'maintains' the world in the fallen state it is in.[101] One tantalizing line reads: 'He created; he maintains. Life—and Hell.' This weight of affliction (2 Corinthians 4:17), Williams appears to be saying, can be experienced as ('transferred' into, he notes) a weight of glory. 'Weight', he explains at the beginning, is 'something carried with difficulty', but can be 'the weight of love' Wordsworth felt in nature as 'a bright visual impression of awe and joy'.

While Williams does not appear to speak of substitution and exchange in the sermon (unless he introduced these ideas extemporarily), the sermon was planned as the third in a series of addresses in Cambridge on successive days, the first one of which was on the topic 'Love and Exchange', and which explained the increasing depth of intensity of love from exchange to substitution and finally to co-inherence.[102] In personal terms, Williams believed he scored a 'triumph' in preaching the sermon because Raymond Hunt agreed to carry the burden of nervousness for him, and Hunt's notes include a poem that Williams wrote for him in thanks, containing the words: 'You went; you suffered; and I / triumph, if I did, because of you.' It ends with the declaration that his voice issued from 'the Mount of our co-inherence'.[103] It would have been easy, with all this in his mind, to follow Lewis' ingenious notion of carrying one another's weight of glory, but he seems to have resisted it, following his own path.

The same appears to be the case in a series of three Passiontide addresses that Williams gave in Lincoln to theological students on 21–2 March 1945, just two months before his death.[104] The substance of the first two addresses is familiar: the movement between exchange (a 'vast principle', including 'civil life'), substitution ('bearing one another's burdens'), and co-inherence ('in the Trinity, & in us').[105] In the third, he turns to 'the weight of glory', and affirms the burden that we live under in the world in all its complexity. After a heading 'The *weight* [underlined] of glory', he continues with a fuller account than in the notes for the sermon three years earlier:

> He ascended into heaven; he ascended into his glory. The weight of that glory had been—dare one say?—all but too much for him, as it certainly is for us. We faint under a destiny he will not relax. We use the word often to mean a blur; it is not a blur; it is a precise pattern. There is no glory but the facts. Unless these facts, here

---

[101] On Williams' failure to resolve the issue of whether evil is part of the divine Necessity, see Chapter 11, section 1.
[102] Wade CW/MS-347, 19–32; the section on co-inherence occupies pp. 31–2. The second address was on 'Shakespeare and Religion', Wade CW/MS-347, 33–5.
[103] Wade RH Notebooks, 21: 4145.   [104] Wade CW/MS-347, 38–49.
[105] 'Three Passiontide Addresses', Wade CW/MS-347, 45–6.

and now, are that glory, I fail to see how there can be any [...]. Refuse the co-inherence, and you are left (in the old jest) to your own incoherence.[106]

The brief notes for the Cambridge sermon, however, contain the same point—that 'glory' need not mean a 'a blur of numinousness', but 'rather a pattern, a diagram'.[107] This is the theme of the Taliessin poems, where the diagram of divine order is laid across the body of the 'Empire' (Byzantium) and glory becomes visible in 'the facts'. In the poem 'The Calling of Taliessin', Taliessin as a young poet is journeying from his home among the Welsh tribes to explore the Empire of which he has heard rumours, and Williams describes his immature state with the lines:

> The weight of poetry could not then sink
> into the full depth of *the weight of glory*.[108]

Lewis comments on these lines that 'He is even only a pagan, druidical poet; and the Druids, as I learn from one of Williams' own notes, represent "a kind of ancient earthly poetry—say, like Wordsworth". He has not yet been to Byzantium.'[109] His poetry has not yet been immersed into 'the weight of glory' that characterizes the Empire—that is, into the daily facts of life that are carrying the weight of the divine organization of reality. Williams goes on to repeat the idea within a few lines:

> ...the city and the light
> lay beyond the sun and beyond his dream,
> nor could the weight of poetry sink so far
> as *the weight of glory*; on the brink of the last depth
> the glory clouded to its own covering...[110]

What the phrase 'the weight of glory' contributes for both Williams and Lewis is that this pattern of glory in which we live is also a burden. For Lewis it is the burden of feeling unworthy to be delighted in by God as the fulfilment of human desire, while for Williams it is the burden of an ambiguous world where good and evil cohabitate in the facts; Williams writes that 'we faint under a destiny',[111] or under 'necessity'.[112] Both Williams and Lewis stress that to live under the weight is a matter of humility: for Lewis, it is 'a load so heavy that only humility can carry

---

[106] 'Three Passiontide Addresses', Wade CW/MS-347, 49.
[107] 'Weight of Glory', Wade CW/MS-347, 36.   [108] Williams, *Region*, 15. My italics.
[109] Lewis, 'Williams and the Arthuriad', 103.   [110] Williams, *Region*, 15–16. My italics.
[111] 'Three Passiontide Addresses', Wade CW/MS-347, 49.
[112] Williams, 'Weight of Glory', Wade CW/MS-347, 36; cf. Williams, *Descent of the Dove*, 175–6.

it',[113] and for Williams, it means 'Humility—a fact; to be personally "put up with".'[114] In the Apostle Paul's own thought, it is unlikely that he means 'burden' by the word 'weight', but is rather emphasizing the sheer worth, reality, and 'abundance' of a glory that is both present now and will come later after an affliction that seems 'light' in comparison.[115] This also seems the obvious meaning to a reader of the text. Neither Lewis nor Williams probably knew that the consonants of 'weight' and 'glory' in Hebrew are the same, which may be leading Paul to make a pun on the spur of the moment.[116] While Williams is following his own path, the fact that both—rather unexpectedly—understand the word 'weight' as a 'burden' to be humbly carried seems to betray a common conversation.

2.4 Debts and Obligations

During this period, the friendship between Williams and Lewis was overshadowed a little, but not spoilt, by Williams' conviction that Lewis was indebted to him for various ideas for which he was not receiving sufficient credit, and by Williams' consequent worries about establishing his own reputation.

In May 1942, Williams listened to Lewis reading from a draft of his 'new novel' at a meeting of the Inklings, and wrote in some agitation to Anne Renwick:

> Lewis is becoming a mere disciple; he is now collecting the doctrine of exchange in the last chapter of the new novel. 'That,' he says, 'is all yours'—I do not deny it, but no-one else will think so. I shall be thought his follower everywhere. 'Rejoice always; again I say, Rejoice!'[117]

Lindop names the novel, which is unidentified in the letter, as *That Hideous Strength*, but this cannot be right.[118] The first mention of the third novel in the space trilogy occurs in a letter from Lewis at the end of December 1942,[119] and his increasing dissatisfaction with it ('all rubbish', 'all bosh', April–May 1943),[120]

---

[113] Lewis, 'Weight of Glory', 210, referring to the weight of glory of the neighbour.
[114] 'Three Passiontide Addresses', Wade CW/MS-347, 47: the note runs: 'Humility—a fact; to be personally "put up with" and enjoy it "the *weight* [underlined] of glory".'
[115] The translation of 'weight' as 'abundance' is made by Barrett, *Commentary*, 148.
[116] Moule, *Idiom Book*, 186.
[117] CW to Anne Renwick, 13 May 1942; Bod. MS Eng. Lett. d. 452/4. I am obliged to Grevel Lindop for alerting me to this letter, though I draw a different conclusion from it.
[118] Lindop has generously conceded my point in a personal email of 11 September 2018.
[119] CSL to E. R. Eddison, 29 December 1942, in Lewis, *Letters*, 2: 543–4, written jokingly in a pastiche of sixteenth-century English, mentioning 'I haue brought in a beare in the book I now write and it shal to bedde in the end with the other' (Mr Bultitude in *That Hideous Strength*).
[120] CSL to E. R. Eddison, 29 April 1943, in Lewis, *Letters*, 2: 571; CSL to Owen Barfield, 17? May 1943, in Lewis, *Letters*, 2: 574.

meant that he did not finally declare it finished until September 1944,[121] with publication only in July 1945. On the other hand, on 20 January 1942, he mentions in a letter that 'Ransom is having a grand time on Venus at present',[122] and on 11 May 1942, he writes to Sister Penelope, at the Wantage convent,[123] that 'the Venus book [Perelandra] is just finished, except that I now find the two first chapters need re-writing';[124] on 29 July 1942, he sends her the completed type-script, to seek the permission of the Mother Superior to dedicate it to the sisters there.[125] The 'new novel' to which Williams refers in his letter to Anne as being read to the Inklings in May 1942 must have been Perelandra.

This raises the important question of where Williams detected, and Lewis acknowledged, the theme of 'exchange' in the final chapter of Perelandra. I suggest later that the vision of the Great Dance, with its many exchanges (its 'enamoured and inter-interanimated circlings'), is influenced by Williams' image of the dance, and we have already seen Lewis taking up the same image in his Problem of Pain.[126] Elsewhere, I also propose that the image of the Great Dance is a pictorial display of the idea of co-inherence, but it is intriguing that neither the actual words 'exchange' or 'co-inherence' appear in Lewis' chapter, where Williams constantly uses them in his writings (the latter term after early 1939). Lewis has absorbed the basic metaphysic of Williams into his mythological imagination and made it his own without slavish imitation; in this context it serves the end of imagining an unfallen world, a venture on which Williams never embarked. In this he seems to have been over-generous in apparently telling Williams: 'That is all yours.'[127]

However, from another angle, it is 'all Williams'. The debt to Williams here makes the last chapter of Perelandra an exception, even an erratic block, in Lewis' general approach to analogy between spiritual and natural realities. Following Williams' affirmation (adapting Bonaventure) that 'every point of the circumfer-ence is at the centre',[128] Lewis develops the dance of God in creation to the point where God ('Maleldil' in this mythology) is not just reflected in natural things but dwells within them: 'He dwells (all of him dwells) within the seed of a single flower

---

[121] CSL to Sister Penelope CSMV, 6 September 1944, in Lewis, Letters, 2: 624. He had previously declared it finished in a letter to Arthur Greeves, 20 December 1943, in Lewis, Letters, 2: 596, but he evidently went on tinkering with it for another nine months.

[122] CSL to Mary Neylan, 4 January 1942 [corrected], in Lewis, Letters, 2: 508.

[123] Lewis dedicates Perelandra to 'Some Ladies at Wantage', being the Anglican Community of St Mary the Virgin.

[124] CSL to Sister Penelope CSMV, 11 May 1942, in Lewis, Letters, 2: 520.

[125] CSL to Sister Penelope, CSMOV, 29 July 1942, in Lewis, Letters, 2: 527.

[126] Lewis, Problem of Pain, 72; see also 141, and my Chapter 13.

[127] The reported words stand against the statement of Brian Horne, 'A Peculiar Debt', 93, that the first two novels of Lewis' science-fiction trilogy 'owe nothing to Williams'. The reported admission is also incompatible with Lewis' later declaration that 'I have never been consciously influenced by Williams', although he acknowledges that 'there may have been a great deal of unconscious influence going on': Green and Hooper, C. S. Lewis, 184.

[128] Williams, He Came Down, 106; Lewis, Perelandra, 249; see my Chapter 10, section 1.

and is not cramped [...] He is in every place. Not some of Him in one place and some in another, but in each place the whole Maleldil.'[129] The omnipresence of God is of course a standard element of Christian orthodoxy to which Lewis would have subscribed. But the image of the dance is used to portray a mutual *indwelling* in which the natural is everywhere transfigured by the divine glory: 'He has immeasurable use for each thing that is made, that his love and splendour may flow forth ... '[130] Even where one nature has no 'similitude' (analogy) to another, the edges 'border' so that they are in some way deeply and bodily connected to the triune God: 'Of many points one line; of many lines one shape; of many shapes one solid body; of many senses and thoughts one person; of three persons, Himself.'[131] There is going to be nothing like this movement of Lewis onto Williams' ground in the country of romanticism until Lewis' final work in the 1960s. Perhaps it was the genre of fiction that allowed him to experiment in a way that he declined to do in his deliberately theological work. As I suggest later, Lewis was always inclined to be carried by an image further than perhaps he intended to go.

Nevertheless, despite Lewis' admission 'That is all yours', Tolkien is wrong to attribute too much derivation from Williams in Lewis' mythology, though right in perceiving the influence, when he writes in 1965:

> C. S. Lewis was one of only three persons who have so far read all or a considerable part of my 'mythology' of the First and Second Ages, which had already been in the main lines constructed before we met. [...] But his own mythology (incipient and never fully realized) was quite different. It was at any rate broken to bits before it became coherent by contact with C. S. [*sic*] Williams and his 'Arthurian stuff'—which happened between *Perelandra* and *That Hideous Strength*. A pity, I think. But then I was and remain wholly unsympathetic to Williams' mind [...]. But Lewis was a very impressionable man, and this was abetted by his great generosity and capacity for friendship.[132]

Tolkien misses any connection with Williams in *Perelandra*, as have all modern commentators, but his singling out of *That Hideous Strength* for debt to Williams has been reiterated in most studies of Lewis' work. Perhaps Williams need not have worried in the long run. The Zaleskis write, for example: '*That Hideous Strength* is the Lewis novel most clearly indebted to Charles Williams.'[133] A. N. Wilson asserts that 'It is above all a book drenched in admiration for Charles Williams.'[134] Green and Hooper record that it 'has been described as a

---

[129] Lewis, *Perelandra*, 247, 249. © copyright C. S. Lewis Pte Ltd, 1944.
[130] Lewis, *Perelandra*, 250.   [131] Lewis, *Perelandra*, 247.
[132] Tolkien to Dick Plotz, 12 September 1965, in Tolkien, *Letters*, 361–2.
[133] Zaleski and Zaleski, *Fellowship*, 126.   [134] Wilson, *C. S. Lewis*, 189.

Charles Williams novel written by C.S. Lewis', and add that while this is a 'wild exaggeration', nevertheless 'it bears the seeds of critical truth'.[135] The debt was, it is true, not noticed by reviewers at the time, who consistently disliked it for its mixture of the realistic and the supernatural, which Lewis regarded as 'a pity, because (a) it's just the mixture I like, and (b) We have to put up with it in real life'.[136] It was, of course, exactly the tone that Williams himself conveyed in his own novels, and makes Lewis' book characteristically 'Williams-ish': 'What could be more Williams-ish', exclaims Wilson, 'than the sudden swoop from a depiction of ordinary, provincial, middle-class English life in the first chapter to the discovery that in a wood adjacent to a twentieth-century college, Merlin's uncorrupted, undead body has been sleeping since the close of the Dark Ages?'[137] Broadcasting a talk on 'The Novels of Charles Williams' in 1949, Lewis prefers to call this blend of the ordinary and the supernatural a mixture of 'the Probable and the Marvellous', and characterizes Williams' novels as a 'violation of frontier' between the two.[138]

The hero of the previous two novels, Ransom, has become director of a small company similar to Williams' Company of the Co-inherence, and is revealed to be the Pendragon, successor to King Arthur and ruler over the spiritual, Arthurian kingdom of Logres. Although Lewis was familiar with the name 'Logres' some years before he met Williams,[139] that this is essentially Williams' Logres is made clear when one of the characters quotes lines from Williams' *Taliessin Through Logres*.[140] The heroine, Jane Studdock, is a female academic, writing a literary thesis, very much like Damaris Tighe in *The Place of the Lion*, and is similarly to be persuaded not to allow academic work to prevent her from giving proper attention to her male partner on the grounds that this is about 'reality'.[141] Both Damaris and Jane are to learn to recognize the active principle of the 'masculine' in Anthony and Mark respectively, and to find their place as the more passive feminine— though adored and courteously respected by the male. Of Damaris before Anthony, Williams writes: 'there was in him something which shook her with a fear [...;] this was power and intelligence; this was command.'[142] Ransom tells Jane that 'You are offended by the masculine itself; the loud, irruptive, possessive thing—the gold lion, the bearded bull—which [...] scatters the little kingdom of your primness.' As he is later to do in *The Four Loves*, Lewis has Ransom direct us to 'the masculine none of us can escape'. 'What is above and beyond all things', he assures Jane, 'is so masculine that we are all feminine in relation to it.'[143] The

[135] Green and Hooper, *C. S. Lewis*, 174.
[136] CSL to Dorothy Sayers, 6 December 1945, in Lewis, *Letters*, 2: 682.
[137] Wilson, *C. S. Lewis*, 189.   [138] Lewis, 'Novels of Charles Williams', 46–7.
[139] Gleaned from his reading of Chrétien de Troyes: see Barkman, *C. S. Lewis & Philosophy*, 249, n.126.
[140] Lewis, *That Hideous Strength*, 237; quotation from 'Mount Badon', *Taliessen*, 17.
[141] See Lewis, 'Novels of Charles Williams', 50.   [142] Williams, *Place of the Lion*, 135.
[143] Lewis, *That Hideous Strength*, 390–1.

conclusion is the idea, which seems at first 'nonsensical' to Jane, of Ransom's 'comparison between Mark's love and God's'.[144]

In his presentation of the thoughts of Jane, Lewis seems to be wavering between Williams' territory of romantic theology and his own preferred ground of analogy between human and divine love. While Jane reflects on a 'comparison' between human and divine love, a little earlier she had been wondering whether 'the invasion of her own being in marriage from which she had recoiled' had not after all been 'the lowest, the first, and the easiest form of some shocking contact with reality [. . .] on the highest levels of all'.[145] We are clearly meant to approve of this train of thought, which seems 'Williams-ish' in the idea expressed in the word 'contact'.

As with *Perelandra*, however, Lewis is absorbing Williams' Arthurian mythology into his own concerns, which are quite distinctive. The Company of the Pendragon is marshalling its forces—which will include a descent of angelic powers and the possession of a reawakened Merlin by Saturn—in order to overthrow an insidious experiment in social engineering which is using animal vivisection. A. N. Wilson rightly comments that 'Reading the book today, one is struck by how much Lewis, paradoxically by the very fact that he is a conservative, anticipates many of the modern "environmentalist" objections to scientific development.'[146] The novel seems to have had at its very inception the image of a bear,[147] liberated from the violent hands of NICE (National Institute of Co-ordinated Experiments) and destined for a mating with a tame bear from the household of the Pendragon. 'Take her, Bultitude,' commands Ransom, 'But not in the house.'[148] There is nothing like this in *The Place of the Lion*, where the animals are Platonic archetypes. As Sanford Schwartz argues, throughout his space trilogy Lewis is developing his own distinctive approach to the blend of the 'Probable' and the 'Marvellous', based on his concern for the nature of human development and the danger of 'conspiring with demonic powers to seize control of evolutionary development'.[149]

Unlike Williams' reaction to *Perelandra*, we cannot know what he would have made of *That Hideous Strength*, and how he would have assessed its borrowings from him, since it was of course published after his death. But another grievance that Williams *does* seem to have nursed against Lewis concerned Milton, the focal point of his own Oxford lecture courses, and the subject of the Introduction he had recently written for the Oxford World's Classics edition of the Poems of Milton, published in 1940. When Lewis' *A Preface to Paradise Lost* appeared in 1942, Williams felt that the reviewers were praising Lewis for what were his own

---

[144] Lewis, *That Hideous Strength*, 393.   [145] Lewis, *That Hideous Strength*, 390.
[146] Wilson, *C. S. Lewis*, 190.
[147] CSL to E. R. Eddison, 29 December 1942, in Lewis, *Letters*, 2: 543–4.
[148] Lewis, *That Hideous Strength*, 470.   [149] Schwartz, 'Perelandra', 59–63.

original thoughts, and his reaction in mentioning this to Lewis shows that he felt Lewis bore some responsibility for the reviewers' ignorance. Writing to Raymond Hunt, he complains:

> You will not think me reluctant to acknowledge the great value of the book, but I have seen so many reviews of it all treating it as the real original exploration & instruction that I was driven to say lightly even to [Lewis] the other day that our people—yours & mine—were reading M[ilton] so while his undergraduates were still in comparative outer darkness [...] I have a faint feeling that the same thing is going to happen—with him or another—about Dante. It's extraordinary how an adult can still hanker—hanker? No; perhaps not so much as that—for [...] being called chief.[150]

In dedicating his *Preface* to him, Lewis had praised Williams in fulsome terms for his Oxford lectures and for his 'Introduction'—Lewis calls it a 'Preface'—to the World's Classics edition of Milton, acknowledging that they were 'the recovery of a true critical tradition after more than a hundred years of laborious misunderstanding'.[151] Moreover, Lewis continues this praise of Williams' Introduction as a 'remarkable piece of criticism' in a number of places in the ensuing chapters.[152] In a typically felicitous image, he ends the dedication with the words, 'Apparently, the door of the prison was really unlocked all the time; but it was only you who thought of trying the handle.' However, Lindop has perceptively pointed out that some of Lewis' wording in the dedication undermines its general tone.[153] Lewis writes that in his lectures Williams had 'partly anticipated, partly confirmed, and most of all clarified and matured, *what I had long been thinking about Milton*' (my italics). Perhaps it was the claim that Lewis had long been thinking the same thoughts as Williams that led Williams to say that, while his own students in his London evening classes were reading Milton in the way that Lewis now commends, 'his undergraduates were still in comparative outer darkness'. There is an echo here of the contrast between upper-class Oxford students and his own lower middle-class students in Williams' polemical paper at St Hilda's in 1940.[154]

The nub of the 'true' way of reading Milton is offered by Lewis in the same dedication—'that when the old poets made some virtue their theme they were not teaching but adoring'—and as an example of such exegesis he refers to Williams' Oxford lecture on chastity in Milton's *Comus*, which had so powerfully affected him. Lewis is in accord with Williams in insisting that Milton should be read according to his own intentions, and that these should be perceived in the context

---

[150] CW to Raymond Hunt, 21 December 1942, Wade CWP 38.
[151] C. S. Lewis, *Preface to Paradise Lost*, v.   [152] Lewis, *Preface*, 129; cf. 93, 94, 95.
[153] Lindop, *Charles Williams*, 360.   [154] See the end of section 2.1.

of the thought and theology of his age rather than with the meaning we bring to it from either a romantic or modernist angle. Thus (in opposition to much contemporary criticism), the poem really does commend a hierarchy of obedience from inferior to superior in the cosmos, the sin of Eve really is pride in disobeying the heavenly order of things, and Satan is not a hero but the chief exemplar of disobedience who has the illusion of self-existence.[155] Milton may have failed in his depiction of God, but this does not undermine his intention to set out a cosmic pattern of which God is the centre, and which is marred by rebellious self-love. All 'shape of virtue' is finally directed towards adoration of God.[156]

With all this, Lewis is on common ground with Williams. Lewis also seems to have gained from Williams the insight that there is a pervasive air of comedy and laughter in *Paradise Lost* that others have missed.[157] Nevertheless, there is a notable difference between the tone of Lewis' 'Preface' and Williams' 'Introduction'. With regard to the cosmic hierarchy of obedience, which both scholars not only register as Miltonic but appear to commend as a Christian world view,[158] it is obedience that Lewis stresses; in his view, 'Milton loved from his heart the principle of obedience', and 'everything that he cares about demands order, proportion, measure and *control*'.[159] Williams, on the other hand, always *qualifies* obedience by love, which he envisages as being deeply woven into the hierarchy, with a continuity between passionate human love and adoration of God. For Williams, Milton's celebration of divine order is the 'law of self-abnegation *in love*',[160] and the derived existence of the creatures, created by only one self-existent reality, is a 'derivation in love'.[161] This is what Satan denies in his ludicrous claim to aseity, and the reaction of heaven is that 'Love laughs at anti-love.'[162] The overthrow of the rebel angels in the war in heaven is 'the overthrow, spiritually, of all in whom that deriving and nourishing love is dead'.[163] It is not that Lewis is blind to the place of love in the created order. He cites Renaissance Platonic doctrine to the effect that lower realities turn to the higher in eros-love, the higher to the lower in agape-love.[164] But throughout he is keeping in mind that for Milton (in his view), 'sexual love provided an *analogy* for, or was even a real ectype of, celestial and Divine Love'.[165] For Williams, as he explains in an earlier essay on Milton, the 'new universe' of the poem is summed up in Raphael's definition of free will—'We freely love'.[166] In a 'Dialogue on Hierarchy', written in 1943, the

---

[155] On Satan, see Lewis, *Preface*, 95–6; Williams, 'John Milton', in Williams, *Image*, 31; cf. Williams, *English Poetic Mind*, 122.
[156] Lewis, *Preface*, 80; Williams, 'John Milton', 32.
[157] Lewis, *Preface*, 93; Williams, 'John Milton, 28, 30.
[158] See explicitly Lewis, *Preface*, 64, 'I actually do believe'.   [159] Lewis, *Preface*, 79–80.
[160] Williams, 'John Milton', 29.   [161] Williams, 'John Milton', 31, 36.
[162] Williams, 'John Milton', 30.   [163] Williams, 'John Milton', 32.
[164] Lewis, *Preface*, 75. My italics.   [165] Lewis, *Preface*, 73.
[166] Williams, *English Poetic Mind*, 133.

hierarchy of obedience in the cosmos is to be placed in the context of 'co-inherence', when (according to 'Celia'), 'by grace, one is free and in love'.[167]

The basic homogeneity of that love at all levels of the universe for Williams may be seen in a comparison of his and Lewis' view of Adam's love for Eve. Lewis draws attention to Milton's account that Adam in Paradise smiles with 'superior love' on Eve's 'submissive charms'. That this echoes Lewis' own view of the relation between the sexes becomes clear when he adds gratuitously 'like the great Sky-Father smiling on the Earth-Mother', an image that he reuses, as we have seen, in *The Four Loves* twenty years later. When Adam then falls, following Eve's example of disobedience because he wants to share her fate, this is—for Lewis—sheer 'uxoriousness' for which Adam is to be severely blamed.[168] Williams has a similar view of the relation of command and submission between Adam and Eve, but takes a different view of the passion for Eve, which leads Adam to follow her in the fatal act lest he be parted from her; it is 'almost' an exemplification of Raphael's great saying, 'We freely love'.[169] Williams admits that Milton denounced Adam's action, but—he writes winsomely—'it was, after all, Milton who imagined his passion so intensely as to make us almost wish that it could be approved'.[170] It is this approval of human love within the whole cosmic scheme, not its depreciation, that leads Williams to the celebration of chastity in *Comus*, as 'that great miracle of the transmutation of the flesh'.[171]

Williams, then, was probably over-sensitive in seeing Lewis' *Preface* simply as a restatement of his own ideas. For Lewis, Milton is writing an 'epic' poem designed to display the 'objective pattern of things',[172] and Lewis offers a dazzling analysis of the literary category of 'epic' to demonstrate this.[173] Lewis is interested in the *intentions* of Milton as a poet, particularly his religious intentions, and takes them much more seriously than other modern commentators; but he believes that reading the poem as an expression of the poet's 'consciousness' behind (and sometimes in conflict with) his intentions, as Tillyard does, is a totally false move.[174] Williams agrees, but he is more interested than Lewis in the ability of Milton, through his distinctive mind and emotions, to enhance our own consciousness, so that 'the whole of our visibility, metaphysical, psychological, actual, has been increased by him'.[175] The poem portrays states of personal 'being',[176] and

---

[167] Williams, 'Dialogue on Hierarchy', in Williams, *Image*, 128.   [168] Lewis, *Preface*, 122–3.
[169] Williams, *English Poetic Mind*, 133.   [170] Williams, 'John Milton', 32.
[171] Williams, 'John Milton', 27; cf. Williams, *English Poetic Mind*, 110–11.
[172] Lewis, *Preface*, 128.   [173] See Fleming, 'Literary Critic', 20–1.
[174] Tillyard, *Milton*, 237–9. In his personal copy of Tillyard's book, Lewis has written 'arch error' and 'fatal' in the margins of these pages. A short critical piece by Lewis written, presumably in the early 1930s, inside the front pages of the book, as well as his critique of Tillyard's *Milton* in *The Personal Heresy*, 2, goes some way to justifying his claim that he had 'long been thinking' about the points raised by Williams. Lewis' copy is held in the Lewis collection at Azusa Pacific University, and I am grateful to Christine Murphy and Roger White for informing me about these annotations. See also Lewis' criticism of Tillyard in *Preface*, 70.
[175] Williams, 'John Milton', 34.   [176] Williams, 'John Milton', 32.

especially the state of love and joy. Lewis will always be suspicious that this kind of approach is simply a romantic projection of a poet's state of mind. We are not only back in the area of Lewis' dispute with Tillyard about the relation between the poet and the poem; we are also treading the ground of Lewis' complex 'inward journey' of Romanticism with Williams.

2.5 The Figure of the Magus

In May 1943, Williams reports in a letter to Anne Renwick that Lewis had disliked one of the poems that was later to appear in his collection *The Region of the Summer Stars*.[177] About 'The Founding of the Company', he writes to her:

> I have also written a poem on the Founding of the Company which C.S.L. says is *not* very good. But I think he a little has decided what kind of stuff I ought to do, or anyhow I think I shall keep it. When you get a day off & can come to Oxford I will read it to you.[178]

Fortunately, we know why Lewis thought it 'not very good', as we have his commentary on the poem in *Arthurian Torso* to guide us, although by that time he seems to have modified his judgement to expressing perplexities. This is in fact a key poem for Charles Williams' vision not just of the household of Taliessin, but of the Company of the Co-inherence, the lay 'Order' he had created, with himself as Taliessin, living his own myth. At the end of the new 'Promulgation' of the Company of the Co-inherence made by Williams in September 1943, revising the clauses first set out in 1939, Williams signs it as 'given, as it were from Caerleon, by the permission of Almighty God, at the will of the Companions, and in the hand of Taliessin'.[179] This is a long-held identity with Taliessin, as witnessed in an unpublished poem sent to Anne Ridler in June 1935:

> Mocking I sang while she lay and listened:
> "Mock'st thou, Ianthe, the word of Taliessin?
> I am Taliessin, I have told, I have sung:
> All is in the glory; naught is the person
> but in the form, the order of the glory[.]"[180]

---

[177] Published October 1944 by Poetry Editions, London, as a pamphlet.
[178] CW to Ann Renwick, 4 May 1943, Bod. MS Eng. Lett. d. 452/6, 66.
[179] 'The Order of the Co-inherence', Bod. MS 16125/5, folder 1.
[180] Bod. MS 16125/1, folder 3.

There are lines in 'The Founding of the Company' that refer directly to the promulgation of the Company of the Co-inherence, such as 'having no decision, no vote or admission',[181] and 'its cult was the Trinity and the Flesh-taking'.[182] Further, there is among the donation of Williams papers by Anne Ridler a poem headed 'The Founding of the *Companionship*',[183] which contains some of the same lines as in 'The Founding of the Company', but which also gives more explicit identification of Williams as Taliessin, locating the household of the king's poet somewhere between St Paul's Cathedral and Camelot, the court of Arthur—the latter being Amen House in William's personal mythology. It also contains more material from the 'promulgation', such as the celebration by the company of four major feasts of the church year:[184]

> Grounded therefore in that household of Taliessin
> there grew in Logres a new Companionship, founded
> by none, known by no name—his own
> least; it held, four times a year, on the Feast
> of the Trinity, the Transfiguration, the Annunciation,
> and the lofty Commemoration of All Souls,
> its secret recollection [.]

Another version in the same papers includes the straightforward reference that 'all promulgated the co-inherence'. It is likely, I suggest, that this 'Companionship' poem was written for the Companions themselves in 1939 before the 'Company' poem was written for the public (and shown to Lewis) in 1943, especially since the former portrays Williams-Taliessin as still living in London, with his sentences 'sealing the soul through the whole of Logres/by the mouth of London in Logres'.[185]

It appears from Lewis' commentary that he understood the background to 'The Founding of the Company' very well. He remarks that 'It is [...] I suspect, the most autobiographical element in the cycle. Something like the company probably came into existence wherever Williams had lived and worked.'[186] The first of two perplexities he expresses about the poem in this later reflection is the difficulty of understanding the 'third and highest degree' of the company, namely the 'co-inherence', a point I shall be returning to in Chapter 5.[187] With the second

---

[181] Cf. 'Order', clause 1.   [182] Cf. 'Order', clause 5.   [183] Bod. MS 16125/2, folder 2.

[184] 'Order', clause 7.

[185] Further, it was contained originally in an envelope in which Ridler also kept the draft of a liturgy that Williams had written, in 1939 and before his removal to Oxford, for a service in St Paul's Cathedral at the commission of the Bishop of Chichester.

[186] Lewis, 'Williams and the Arthuriad', 142.

[187] Lewis, 'Williams and the Arthuriad', 143. See my Chapter 5, section 2.

query we come to the biographical issue, and what is evidently Lewis' assessment of Williams' own place in the company of those (almost entirely women) who had recognized him as their spiritual leader. Lewis raises the question as to 'what leadership or lordship can properly mean among redeemed souls, and how... they can be exercised without disobeying the words "Be not called Rabbi"'.[188] Lewis discerns the answer given in the poem to be that, while Taliessin at first recoils from being called 'lieutenant of God's new grace', he accepts the title ruefully, on the basis that in God's eyes such pre-eminence is a celestial joke, since nobody is actually necessary to God. Nothing is left, comments Lewis, but 'to thank God for the "excellent absurdity" which enables us [...] to play great parts without pride'.[189]

> Unvowed, they allowed the lieutenancy in Camelot, but on feasts
> served it in Caerleon with such a delicate smile,
> such joyous and high-restrained obeisance of laughter
> as (more than in all households of the great lords)
> ordained through all degrees an equality of being.[190]

Lewis here compliments Williams, writing that 'Williams' answer, to anyone who had it from his own lips, and his own life, is as lucid as the sun and (I think) of the deepest moment.' Presumably his answer in life is the same as that in the poem, and Lewis' words catch something of the extraordinary combination people noticed in Williams of both an air of authority and deference to the other, both sovereignty of manner and courtesy in manners. However, it is evident that Lewis is uneasy, even after Williams' death and the dissolution of the Company, since he adds about the 'answer': 'Yet I can find hardly any words of my own to express it.'[191]

   If Lewis did feel any unease at the time about Williams' role as spiritual leader (guru is perhaps the only word) in his own Company, and if this was a reason why he felt the poem was 'not very good', he must have been reassured by hearing Williams read to the Inklings from his last novel, All Hallows' Eve. Unlike the ambiguity that surrounds the earlier Considine, the Clerk Simon (recalling the Simon Magus of Acts 13) is clearly condemned by the story for his spiritual pride of wanting to rule in the kingdoms of the living and the dead, and his manipulation of the members of his company is exposed for the manipulation and exploitation that it is, though they adore him for the miraculous healing he has brought them. Williams read the draft of the novel to Lewis and Tolkien as he wrote it in the last months of 1944 and early 1945, and Tolkien records in a letter

---

[188] Lewis, 'Williams and the Arthuriad', 144.   [189] Lewis, 'Williams and the Arthuriad', 145.
[190] Williams, Region, 41.   [191] Lewis, 'Williams and the Arthuriad', 144. My italics.

years later that Williams altered it considerably in response to Lewis' comments: 'the very great changes made to it were I think mainly due to C.S.L.'.[192]

We may wonder whether the complete lack of ambiguity from the beginning of the novel about the magician, Simon, with his insidious rituals, was thanks to Lewis' clear view of the matter, but we have no original drafts from which to make the judgement. Williams himself only writes to Michal (12 January 1944) that 'I have read some of it to CSL & Tolkien [...] who admire and approve.'[193] If there is just a slight tinge of something Simon-like in that report, this seems amplified in another comment at about the same time when Williams writes to Michal about his hopes of receiving a readership at Oxford following his retirement from the Press: 'CSL and Tolkien are only human, and are likely to take more trouble over a project that would enable them to see a good deal more of me than over anything that didn't.'[194] But we must remember that he is under huge strain of work at this time,[195] and is desperately wanting to reassure Michal that they have the prospects of a good future together despite the financial worries that have troubled them all their marriage.

All Hallows' Eve was sent to the publisher (T. S. Eliot) in May 1944, to be published in January 1945.The reading matter of the Inklings over the subsequent summer months of 1944 then included Lewis' new story *The Great Divorce*, or—as it was called at the time—*Who Goes Home*? As a theological fantasy set in the afterlife, exploring post-mortem experience of the dead, it seems—as Lindop comments—to be 'not unlike *All Hallows' Eve*'.[196] Other critics have been more vociferous, such as Charles Moorman who earned the scorn of Warnie for suggesting in 1966 that Lewis had 'borrowed' the framework of his story from Williams' novel:[197] 'just as if', Warnie wrote, 'this speculation about a transitional state must not have occurred to hundreds of Christians who didn't even know of each other's existence [...] Yes, on the whole a silly book.'[198] But, of course, Lewis and Williams did know of each other's existence, and were reading their work on the afterlife to each other in the very same year. If Lewis helped to shape *All Hallows' Eve*, as Tolkien believes, there was surely some mutual influence, some striking off from each other, and these two books may aptly mark what was to be the end of the earthly phase of their journey together.

---

[192] Tolkien to Anne Barrett, 7 August 1964), in Tolkien, *Letters*, 349; cf. Carpenter, *Inklings*, 194.

[193] CW to Michal Williams, 12 January 1944, in Williams, *To Michal*, 186.

[194] CW to Michal Williams, 5 February 1944, in Williams, *To Michael*, 189. It seems he would have been disappointed about this prospect if he had lived; Lewis, *Essays*, vi, remarks in passing that Williams' Oxford friends had planned his *Festschrift* for when 'peace would recall him from Oxford to London'.

[195] On Williams' workload, see Zaleski and Zaleski, *Fellowship*, 336–7; Lindop, *Charles Williams*, 346–7.

[196] Lindop, *Charles Williams*, 410; cf. Carpenter, *Inklings*, 194.

[197] Moorman, *Precincts of Felicity*.

[198] Kilby and Meade, *Brothers and Friends*, 268. For Warnie, it seemed especially 'silly' that Charles Moorman had identified a 'group mind' among the group, whom he dubbed 'the Oxford Christians'.

There is some undeniable affinity between the two stories, both set in the streets of a town or city in people's post-mortem state. For Williams, the streets duplicate those of London, and so retain something of the Glory and the Acts of the living city; but Lester, a young woman recently killed in an air raid, has the sense that 'everything was but a façade, with nothing at all behind it'. The streets are empty.[199] For Lewis, the streets are those of a drab town with mean streets, but there is the same vacuity: 'I never met anyone,' recounts the narrator, 'the whole town seemed to be empty.'[200] The differences between the scenes, however, are substantial. For Williams the city is on the borderlands of the living and the dead, and overlaps are continually possible. The emptiness contrasts with a fulness of life that is being lived just over the frontier, or that can be reached anew by setting out to go deeper into the City with love in one's heart, as Lester finally does.[201] Lewis is describing hell and makes one of his characters offer an explanation of the emptiness: people have moved further and further out from the civic centre because they quarrel with their neighbours, and as they 'think' houses into existence, they leave more and more empty streets behind them.[202] The bus stop for a 'trip' to heaven is located far away from the centre of town, many miles away from the place of arrival. There is some affinity, however, with his ghosts and Williams' character Evelyn, who refuses grace offered by Lester, and 'was gone into that other City, there to wait and wander and mutter . . .'[203]

The image of a town with empty streets may well have come from listening to Williams read his novel;[204] Lewis was susceptible to images (as I intend to show later),[205] but Lewis' development is quite different from Williams'. Indeed, as early as April 1933, 'Warnie' Lewis records in his diary that his brother has had an idea for a story of 'a sort of an infernal day excursion to Paradise',[206] based on the Patristic idea of intermittent respite granted to the damned. It was possibly some recollection of this intention that had made Warnie so severe on Moorman in the 1960s. Lewis had apparently come upon this idea of the *refrigerium* in 1931, in the work of Jeremy Taylor.[207] But a long-germinating idea needed a catalyst, and Williams' image and general theme seems to have provided this.

Yet the influence was not only one way. In 1945, not long before his death, Williams proposed to Anne Ridler a future novel he wanted to write that would be more completely in the realm of the dead, rather than about the borderland

---

[199] Williams, *All Hallows' Eve*, 15, 13.   [200] Lewis, *Great Divorce*, 13.

[201] Williams, *All Hallows' Eve*, 237.   [202] Lewis, *Great Divorce*, 19–20.

[203] Williams. *All Hallows' Eve*, 236.

[204] Green and Hooper, *C. S. Lewis*, 222, suggest that the image comes from Valdemar Adolph Thisted's *Letters from Hell* (1885, Preface by George MacDonald) which he owned in translation. There is no reason why the influence should not have been multiple.

[205] See Chapter 7, section 1.

[206] W. H. Lewis, Diary entry for Sunday 16 April 1933, in Kilby and Meade, *Brothers and Friends*, 102.

[207] Hooper and Green, *C. S. Lewis*, 220–1.

between living and dead. It would, he writes, deal with the theme of assumption of the soul into 'the Omnipotence'. A major theme of all his work had been the need to integrate the 'positive way' of reaching God through the 'affirmation of images', and the 'negative' way through rejection of any images. He planned, it seems, to show how the two ways work together when participating finally in the divine after death: 'the Rejection aims at this, the Affirmation endures it'.[208] It might be said that this is a reworking of Lewis' own scenario, set entirely in the world of the dead, since Lewis portrays the way that souls resist being transmuted into Glory by hanging onto the positive images that give them a sense of security, and being unwilling to endure the negation that will cause pain but cleanse them. The ghost who wants to steal the golden apples of heaven symbolizes this.[209]

Perhaps Williams had gleaned an idea from Lewis, as Lewis had received an image from him, but if he been given the opportunity he would doubtless have worked it out quite differently. Lewis is a master of analysing the moods, grudges, self-pity, and self-concern that we must let go if we are to be transformed into glorious creatures,[210] whereas Williams—it seems—intended to take another angle, showing that 'the essentials of one way' of union with God 'are the accidents of the other'.[211] Williams was, however, to be denied the opportunity to write a new novel, or to complete other projects he had in mind,[212] such as a third volume of his Taliessin poems. The death about which he had been fantasizing came to claim him.

---

[208] CW to Anne Ridler, 6 March 1945, Bod. Anne Ridler Papers, inaccessible, cit. Lindop, *Charles Williams*, 414.

[209] Lewis, *Great Divorce*, 48.   [210] Lewis, *Great Divorce*, 94.

[211] CW to Anne Ridler, 6 March 1945; see note 208.

[212] He planned two further 'Figure' books to complement *The Figure of Beatrice*: the book on the Arthurian legend, *The 'Figure of Arthur'*, and a book on Wordsworth, *The Figure of Power*. An outline of the latter can be found in Williams' hand in Bod. MS 16125/2, folder 4.

3

Life after Death, 1945–1963

3.1 Two Reflections on the Journey: Essays and a Torso

Charles Williams died unexpectedly in the Radcliffe Infirmary, Oxford, on 15 May 1945, the morning after the day he had entered hospital. Complications had developed from what was an old problem of adhesions in his intestines, and an operation failed to resolve them. Lewis learned the news on arrival at the hospital with a book he wanted to loan Williams, on the way to an Inklings lunch at their usual venue of the Eagle and Child a little further down the road.[1] For Lewis, the death of Williams was 'the first really severe loss I have suffered',[2] but he wrote to Michal that 'My friendship is not ended. His death has had the very unexpected effect of making death itself look quite different. I believe in the next life ten times more strongly than I did.'[3]

This is a conviction that CSL also confesses in letters to Owen Barfield and to Sister Penelope. To the former, he writes that 'what the idea of death has done to him is nothing to what he has done to the idea of death. Hit it for six[.]',[4] and to the latter that his death had 'made the next world more real and palpable'.[5] Later, he relates the impression again in his memoir prefaced to the *Essays Presented to Charles Williams*: 'No event has so corroborated my faith in the next world as Williams did simply by dying. When the idea of death and the idea of Williams thus met in my mind, it was the idea of death that was changed.'[6] Lewis also bears witness in his memoir to experiencing, as—he claims—other friends have also, 'the ubiquitous presence of a dead man, as if he had ceased to meet us in particular places in order to meet us everywhere'. In his letter to Michal Williams, he recounts some words of Hugo Dyson:

> Mr. Dyson, on the day of the funeral, summed up what many of us felt, 'It is not blasphemous', he said, 'To believe that what was true of Our Lord is, in its less degree, true of all who are in Him. They go away in order to be with us in a new way, even closer than before'. A month ago I wd. have considered this silly sentiment. Now I know better. He seems, in some indefinable way, to be all

---

[1] Lewis, *Essays*, xiii–xiv.　　[2] CSL to Owen Barfield, 18 May 1945, Lewis, *Letters*, 2: 651.
[3] CSL to Michal Williams, 22 May 1945, Lewis, *Letters*, 2: 653.
[4] CSL to Owen Barfield, 18 May 1945, Lewis, *Letters*, 2: 652.
[5] CSL to Sister Penelope CSMV, 28 May 1945, Lewis, *Letters*, 2: 656.　　[6] Lewis, *Essays*, xiv.

Charles Williams and C.S. Lewis: Friends in Co-inherence. Paul S. Fiddes, Oxford University Press. © Paul S. Fiddes 2021.
DOI: 10.1093/oso/9780192845467.003.0003

around us now. I do not doubt that he is doing and will do for us all sorts of things he could not have done while in the body.[7]

He repeats Dyson's words in his preface to the *Essays*, this time adding to them another phrase from Dyson: 'Our Lord told the disciples it was expedient for them that He should go away for otherwise the Comforter would not come to them.'[8] The 'expedience', referred from Christ to Williams, reappears in his letter to Barfield, and in his letter to Sister Penelope where he asks 'May one accept this?' It is a common phenomenon in bereavement to experience for a while the presence of the one who has died, but with Lewis the feeling seems to have persisted a long time; in 1948, when Lewis writes to Michal assuring her that 'I live on [Charles] almost every day', he recounts a dream in which he has met Charles, and adds that 'Sometimes I have felt he was just beside me and almost heard him say, "You know, the only reason I don't appear is that it would be . . . well, bad manners." '[9]

One practical way that Lewis could continue his journey with Williams, and to experience what he called 'doing for us all sorts of things', was to hand. I have already mentioned in several places the volume of *Essays Presented to Charles Williams*, edited by Lewis and published in 1947. He and Williams' friends had been preparing a volume of essays in his honour before he died, and now it was to become a tribute in his memory. The preface by Lewis contained reflections on their friendship, recollections of Williams' charismatic personality, and a judgement on Williams' distinctive achievements from which I have already drawn. While Lewis wrote that 'he gave to every circle the whole man', expanding this to mean that 'all his attention, knowledge, courtesy, charity, were placed at your disposal', Tolkien scribbled in the margin of his copy—to which he had contributed his seminal essay 'On Fairy-Stories'—'No. I think not.'[10] In his preface, Lewis indeed admits that some of Williams' friends found him to be 'reserved, one in whom, after years of friendship, there remained something elusive and incalculable', but he explains this by saying that 'a selfless character, perhaps, always has this mysteriousness'.[11]

A significant insight into their journey together comes in Lewis' account in his preface of what Williams considered 'romantic theology' to be. We have already seen how both Williams and Lewis tend to reinterpret each other's particular ground in the territory of romanticism, and here is a startling example by Lewis, offering a distinctly enervated account of Williams' own theory:

[7] CSL to Michal Williams, 22 May 1945, Lewis, *Letters*, 2: 653–4.   [8] John 16:7.
[9] CSL to Michal Williams, 15 June 1948; in uncatalogued list of Wade Williams MSS, cit. Lindop, *Charles Williams*, 468n1525.
[10] Zaleski and Zaleski, *Fellowship*, 269.   [11] Lewis, *Essays*, x.

He was [...] a 'romantic theologian' in the technical sense which he himself invented for those words. A romantic theologian does not mean one who is romantic about theology but one who is theological about romance, one who considers the theological implications of those experiences which are called romantic. The belief that the most serious and ecstatic experiences either of human love or of imaginative literature have such theological implications, and that they can be healthy and fruitful only if the implications are diligently lived out and severely lived, is the root principle of all his work.[12]

One cannot escape the impression that Lewis is rewriting Williams, by proposing his definition of romantic theology to be 'considering the theological implications of those experiences which are called romantic'. Such a generalized account drifts away from what Williams had called in his very first letter to Lewis 'the identity of love and religion'. But, while too minimal for Williams in particular, it does offer a generic description that might cover the romanticism of both Williams and Lewis, together with that of Tolkien and another Inkling close to the three, Owen Barfield. It might describe the *whole country* through which Williams and Lewis are making their 'inward' journey, a territory of which the four friends represent distinct 'provinces' within a terrain not simply of romanticism, but of 'theological romanticism'. It was some such mapping as this that Barfield seems to have had in mind when looking back in 1969. He relates that when the idea was first put forward that the Inklings could be classified as a group of 'Oxford Christians' with common concerns, he had been inclined to dismiss the idea, but now he thinks he can discern a shared movement of 'romantic theology' that might be 'a kind of christening' of the 'heritage of the Romantic Impulse'.[13]

A further, more imaginative, stage on his shared journey with Williams also came to Lewis' mind fairly immediately. The letters of Williams to Michal from Oxford show that a major desire had been to finish and publish his study of the myths, the cultural development and religious significance of King Arthur, titled *The Figure of Arthur*, on which he had been at work in odd periods of time from February 1944.[14] On 15 February 1945, Williams writes to Michal that T. S. Eliot, on behalf of Faber, 'does not wish to press me but would like to know when Arthur is likely to be ready'. He continues, in a confessional mood, that 'There being only 3000 words done out of 90,000, it doesn't seem as if the answer was *Soon*.'[15] Nevertheless, Williams had read the first two completed chapters of the book to Tolkien and Lewis on a couple of Monday mornings over Easter 1945, one of

---

[12] Lewis, *Essays*, vi.
[13] Owen Barfield, lecture 'C. S. Lewis and His Friends', given at Redlands University in the spring of 1969, as recalled by Rand Kuhl, 'Owen Barfield', 8. Thus Barfield was less dismissive of Charles Moorman's designation 'Oxford Christians' than was Warnie Lewis: see my Chapter 2, section 5.
[14] See e.g. Williams, *To Michal*, 190, 200, 237, 244–5, 254, 255.
[15] CW to Michael Williams, 15 February 1945, Williams, *To Michal*, 248.

which Tolkien recalled as a 'bright morning' with the mulberry tree outside the window shining 'like fallow gold' outside Lewis' rooms at Magdalen.[16] Lewis vividly describes what appears to be the same scene. Though it is the best visual account of an Inklings' meeting we have, and often-quoted, it was of course a meeting of only three and was not on the usual Thursday evening:

> Picture to yourself, then, an upstairs sitting-room with windows looking north into the 'grove' of Magdalen College on a sunshiny Monday Morning in vacation at about ten o'clock. The Professor and I, both on the chesterfield, lit our pipes and stretched out our legs. Williams in the armchair opposite to us threw his cigarette into the grate, took up a pile of the extremely small, loose sheets on which he habitually wrote—they came, I think, from a twopenny pad for memoranda, and began as follows :—[17]

Lewis now determined to publish these chapters, together with three others retrieved in draft from Williams's friends, as a fragment, and to complete the book with his own commentary on the 'Taliessin' poems. It was not to be the whole 'figure' of Arthur as Williams had composed the figure of Beatrice, but it could be at least a 'torso' of the figure if it could not be a full-length sculpture.

Lewis' section had been given as a series of lectures at Oxford as early as the Michaelmas Term of 1945, the very next term after Williams had died.[18] This seems to have been an unusual decision, since the Oxford English syllabus, devised by Lewis and Tolkien, stopped at the end of the Victorian period,[19] and lectures were not customarily given on modern writers. Lewis had been greatly assisted in his exposition by a long explanation that Williams had sent him earlier, in reply to his questions that he had sent in preparation for his review of *Taliessin* in 1939.[20] He confesses in the introduction to *Arthurian Torso* (which was finally published in 1948) that he had failed to preserve the document, but that fortunately he had 'copied large extracts from it into the margin of my copy of *Taliessin* at the relevant passages'.[21] We are now in the happy position of being able to read Williams' original paper, in his own hand,[22] as well as the typewritten transcript made by Margaret Douglas.[23] I shall draw on these documents, evidently a fuller account than Lewis had before him, when I comment in detail on *Arthurian Torso* in Chapter 8. There I intend to show that Williams' section shows a slight shift towards Lewis' view of the medieval love poems before Dante. For his part, in presenting Williams' understanding of romantic love, Lewis is much more specific

---

[16] According to Carpenter, *Inklings*, 197.   [17] Williams and Lewis, *Arthurian Torso*, 2.
[18] See CSL to Herbert Palmer, 15 December 1945, Lewis, *Letters*, 2: 684: Lewis describes himself as having been 'immersed' for the previous six months in Williams' poems.
[19] See Duriez, *Oxford Inklings*, 102–3, 264, n.13.   [20] See Wade RH Notebooks 19: 3597.
[21] Williams and Lewis, *Arthurian Torso*, 1.   [22] Bod. MS. 16125/2, folder 4.
[23] Wade CW/MS-2/X.

than in his Preface to the *Essays*, but he still omits a large amount of what Williams wants to affirm:

> The Beatrician experience may be defined as the recovery (in respect to one human being) of that vision of reality which would have been common to all men in respect to all things if Man had never fallen. [...] The 'light' in which the beloved appears to be clothed is true light; the intense significance which she appears to have is not an illusion; in her (at that moment) Paradise is actually revealed, and in the lover Nature is renovated. [...] There is no question here of the so-called 'Platonic solution'; of loving the lady's soul instead of her person. The distinction of soul and body is forever impossible in the Beatrician experience: that is the very schism which the experience momentarily heals. The essence of the glory is that it appears in the flesh[.][24]

In other words, Lewis is explaining, with fidelity, the lover's vision of the glory of the beloved in her eternal state, but saying nothing about the glory that breaks from the incarnation of Christ in the relation of the two lovers, including their sexual union. Lewis is not here, of course, actually adopting the Beatrician vision, even in the moderated form in which he presents it, but we shall later see evidence that he may, in future writings, be edging towards it.

3.2 Analogy of Love and Approach to God

During the eighteen years in which Lewis lived on after Williams' death, we can trace other phases of their journey, at least from Lewis' point of view in his work. Tolkien makes the fascinating observation that 'Williams' influence [over Lewis] actually only appeared with his death.'[25] In context, he seems to have been referring to the publication of *That Hideous Strength*, but I believe his words have a much wider application. We can tease out the way that Lewis continued his journey with Williams by exploring the further development of Lewis' interest in the linked ideas of exchange, substitution, and co-inherence.[26] Moreover, a cluster of writings in Lewis' last years between 1960 and 1963 shows, I believe, that Lewis finally moved further into Williams' 'province' of romanticism than he had ever occupied before. We can catch a first glimpse of this shift in the late book to which I have already referred, *The Four Loves*, and which, we might say, holds a kind of map to the route of the 'secret road' shared by Lewis and Williams.

---

[24] Lewis, 'Williams and the Arthuriad', 116, 119.
[25] Tolkien to Michael Tolkien (draft), undated, but November or December 1963, in Tolkien, *Letters*, 342.
[26] See especially Chapter 5.

In his chapter on 'Eros', in which he directly quotes Williams to the effect that to love is to say 'I am you', Lewis explains the phrase as an expression of the lover's desire for the beloved, which has such intensity that it is like Milton's vision of 'angelic creatures with bodies made of light who can achieve total interpenetration instead of our mere embraces'.[27] 'Interpenetration' is, of course, a synonym for co-inherence. Such an Eros, he informs us, may involve the sexual element of Venus, but she is not to be taken too seriously. As an example of being too serious about sex, he gently mocks an (unnamed) author who writes that 'Venus should recur through the married life in "a solemn, sacramental rhythm"'; Lewis' verdict is that 'We have reached the stage at which nothing is more needed than a roar of old-fashioned laughter.'[28] Lewis is unlikely to have Williams in mind as the author, especially since in *Arthurian Torso* he had written that Williams 'thought nothing more ridiculous than any attempted subjection of the natural playfulness of Caucasia [i.e. sex] to some kind of quasi-sacramental gravity'.[29] But Lewis, at that stage, was still reinterpreting Williams' theology of romantic love in a way with which he felt most comfortable, and Williams himself did certainly think of sexual union as a sacrament.[30] He *could* have written the phrase that Lewis wants to laugh away, whether or not Lewis was thinking of him. Identity of love and religion is still, it seems, to be rejected, a quarter of a century after Lewis' first exchange of letters with Williams.

Yet Lewis recognizes that Venus, while a mischievous spirit, and not to be taken too seriously, is to be taken seriously enough. Sex is serious, Lewis assures us, because it is 'the body's share in marriage which, by God's choice, is the mystical image of the union between God and Man'. So it is an 'image' of divine love, but not it seems a Christian sacrament; in fact, Lewis now regards sex as a 'pagan' or 'natural' sacrament, which is 'our human participation in, and exposition of, the natural forces of life and fertility'. Mythologically expressed, this is a sharing in 'the marriage of the Sky-Father and the Earth-Mother'.[31] In Chapter 1, we saw how Lewis understood this 'marriage' of natural forces as basis for the dominant, even 'playfully' violent, role of the male lover in sexual congress. In a sermon preached in the chapel of Mansfield College in 1944, Lewis had already ventured the idea of a 'sacrament' within nature, as a sign that marks the 'transposition' of some higher level of reality within nature into a lower;[32] now he coins the phrase 'pagan sacrament' for the participation of the sexual act within larger principles of fertility in the world. Lewis is not thinking of participation in the life of God; he is still clearly working with his early idea of analogy between sexual and religious experience. This is confirmed when he goes on to write that there is a 'god-like'

---

[27] Lewis, *Four Loves*, 110–11.   [28] Lewis, *Four Loves*, 113.
[29] Lewis, 'Williams and the Arthuriad', 167.   [30] See Williams, *Outlines*, 36–48.
[31] Lewis, *Four Loves*, 114.
[32] Lewis, 'Transposition. A Sermon', in *Transposition and Other Addresses*, 15, © copyright C. S. Lewis Pte Ltd, 1970.

quality in Eros as suffused by Venus: this love is 'really and truly *like* Love Himself'.[33]

It is at this point, however, that Lewis takes what seems like a step into the province of Williams:

> In [Eros] there is a real nearness to God (by Resemblance); but not, therefore and necessarily, a nearness of Approach. Eros, honoured so far as love of God and charity to our fellows will allow, may become for us a means of Approach. His total commitment is a paradigm or example, built into our natures, of the love we ought to exercise towards God and Man.[34]

This is a declaration full of tensions, and uncharacteristically unclear. The words 'by resemblance', 'paradigm', and 'example' continue Lewis' theme of 'likeness' or analogy between sex and experience of God's love. But then we have the notion of 'real nearness to God' in the sexual act, immediately qualified by 'not *necessarily* a nearness of Approach', leading to the assurance that eros 'may *become* for us a means of Approach'. If sexual union may become a means of grace, it seems that after all it *is* sacramental, as Williams had always maintained. The denial that it is 'necessarily' or automatically a means of approach does not rule out its sacramental nature (as perhaps Lewis supposes), since any good sacramental theologian knows that there is nothing mechanical about a sacrament that depends on the gracious and free activity of God as well as reception in faith.[35] Though Lewis is writing in a guarded manner, it may be that towards the end of their 'secret journey', these two friends are treading the ground of the same district as well as the same country.

Lewis, of course, wants to rule out *worship* of Eros, which is only 'like' a god. He deliberately recalls his earlier *Allegory of Love*, and remarks that now (probably in the light of his marriage to Joy) he recognizes that the tendency to turn love into a religion is not just a 'literary phenomenon' of 'make-believe', but happens in everyday life. Eros invites worship because 'he is, at his height, most god-like'. Of himself, 'he always tends to turn 'being in love' into a sort of religion.[36] Lewis remains as opposed to this love-religion as he was in 1936, but now perhaps has come to realize that Eros *can* be sacramental and a 'means of approach' to God without becoming an idol or a demon.

---

[33] Lewis, *Four Loves*, 124.   [34] Lewis, *Four Loves*, 126.

[35] The Roman Catholic doctrine of *ex opere operato* affirms that the grace of the sacrament is not dependent on the spiritual state of the human administrator, not that it happens automatically, regardless of the faith of the recipient: see *Catechism of the Catholic Church*, 1992 (available www.vatican.va/archive/catechism), 1127–8. Christ is *auctor* of the sacraments, the 'author' and 'actor': Ambrose, *De sacramentis* IV.4.13; Augustine, *Contra Litteras Petitiani* 2.24.57.

[36] Lewis, *Four Loves*, 127.

In the same year as *The Four Loves* appeared, Lewis prepared a paper for the twelfth Symposium of the Colston Research Society,[37] entitled 'The Language of Religion', although he was not able to deliver it personally because of ill health. He proposes that 'Ordinary Language' is developed or 'improved' into Scientific language on the one hand, and Poetic language on the other.[38] Theology is a kind of Scientific language, and religious language is a form of language that 'ranges between the Ordinary and the Poetical',[39] but he is anxious to stress that neither poetic nor religious languages are a mere expression or stimulant of emotion, but a 'real medium of information'.[40] The evoking of emotion by these sorts of language is in order to show us the *object* to which emotion would be the appropriate response. Lewis is still, that is, rejecting what he called as early as 1934 'the personal heresy' in reading poetry, whereby a poem supposedly tells us about the state of mind and emotions of the poet. Analogy in theology belongs to the 'scientific' kind of language, and will be carefully qualified by negatives. Thus an affirmation such as 'Jesus is the Son of God' could be read theologically as analogy, in which the human father–son relationship stands for the relation between Jesus and God, or it could be read religiously with the feeling-tone of what it is like for us to be a good son and a good father.[41]

The real point of the paper, however, is to claim that both scientific and poetic language are inadequate to the actual experience of the reality to which religion points. Lewis admits that he may be 'getting into deep water' here, but he believes that on the one hand, imagining (in poetic language) is something more than the images used, and on the other hand, thinking (in scientific language) is something more than the succession of linked concepts in an argument. Imagination and conceptualization are always 'a sort of translation of a prior activity'. It is the 'very essence of our life as conscious beings' that images and concepts are the by-product of a prior act of 'attending to' or 'looking towards something'.[42] We catch a hint of this in Job's exclamation that 'now my eye hath seen thee'. Although Lewis does not put it this way, we might say that while all language about God as ultimate reality must be analogical, there is a *participation* in God that underlies all concepts and images; the word Lewis uses in *The Four Loves* is 'approach' to God.

If we apply this perception to Lewis' previous insistence that the human sexual union is only an analogy for the love and glory of God, then it seems that Lewis is getting discontented with this purely 'scientific' way of thinking. There must be 'something' in the very essence of life to which we are 'attending' that transcends analogy. That this is in Lewis' mind is confirmed by the final sentences of the paper, proposing that beyond concepts or images of God, there is an 'experienced

---

[37] Held at the University of Bristol, March 1960.   [38] Lewis, 'Language', 129.
[39] Lewis, 'Language', 135.   [40] Lewis, 'Language', 134.   [41] Lewis, 'Language', 137.
[42] Lewis, 'Language', 139.

glory'. Reflecting on the so-called 'Ontological Argument' for the existence of God, he concludes:[43]

> I don't think we can initially argue from the *concept* of Perfect Being to its existence. But did they really, inside, argue from the experienced glory that it could not be generated subjectively?

Although there is a passing reference to the statement 'God is love', the paper does not explicitly deal with the experience of *eros*. By its reference to the 'very essence of our life as conscious being', its scope *does* seem to include what Lewis elsewhere calls 'nature'. He is more explicit about sexual love in natural life in a revision that he made for the publication about this same time of the sermon, titled 'Transposition', that he had preached in Mansfield College in 1944.[44] When Lewis includes the sermon in the 1962 collection *They Asked for a Paper*, he notes that, in comparison with its first publication in *Transposition and Other Addresses* (1949), it is 'now slightly augmented'.[45] The epithet 'slightly' might cause us to miss what is actually a significant addition to the original argument, extending over some three pages.[46] The revision has a good deal to tell us about the shift Lewis was obviously making in his thought, from about 1960, away from mere analogy to symbol, and a consequent closing of the gap between spirit and nature that he had opened somewhat widely in his three essays on 'Christianity and Culture' in 1940.[47]

To begin with the original sermon, preached on Pentecost Sunday, Lewis is intrigued by the phenomenon of *glossolalia* ('speaking in tongues'), where the Holy Spirit appears to be at work in the physical senses. Using the musical metaphor of 'transposing' from one key to another, Lewis argues that a value from a 'higher' system or medium can be truly represented on a 'lower' level of sensation without exact correspondence: it adapts and accommodates itself to the lower. By 'higher', Lewis means a level of life that is richer, more varied, more subtle, and this may be a higher level in nature or a level outside nature altogether (in Lewis' view, the 'supernatural'). An example he gives of transposition within nature is Pepys' observation that the intense aesthetic delight he felt in wind music was like a sick sensation in the stomach or making love to his wife. Lewis comments that an aesthetic value on a high level is being transposed into three

---

[43] Lewis, 'Language', 141.   [44] On 28 May, Pentecost Sunday, 1944.

[45] The 1962 version will be referenced as 'Transposition (revised)'. The sermon in its 'augmented form' was also published in Lewis, *Screwtape Proposes a Toast and Other Pieces*, a volume assembled by Lewis but published posthumously; the editor, in 'Preface', notes that the sermon as published is 'a slightly fuller version' than the original. Yet another version, translated into Italian, had been published in *Rivista giornale* (Milan) between 1944 and 1949, but its contents do not affect my present argument.

[46] From the paragraph beginning 'I believe' (176) to the paragraph ending 'too transitory, too phantasmal' (179).

[47] See Chapter 2, section 1.

different physical phenomena—the sound of physical instruments, a 'flutter' in the stomach, and married love.[48] As an example of a natural phenomenon into which a 'supernatural' reality is transposed, Lewis gives 'the erotic language and imagery we find in the mystics' and 'the language of human lovers'.[49]

All this is consistent with Lewis' theory of analogy between human passion and divine love. Transposition is, we might say, the reverse movement of analogy: as we make an analogy, a higher reality is transposing itself to be *represented* within it. Lewis' closing peroration in the original sermon draws attention to the way that a picture can represent what it depicts so well that 'we shall almost feel cold while we look at the paper snow and almost warm our hands at the paper fire'. So, he continues:

> May we not, by a reasonable analogy, suppose likewise that there is no experience of the spirit so transcendent and supernatural, no vision of Deity Himself so close and so far beyond all images and emotions, that to itself also there cannot be a correspondence on the sensory level? Not by a new sense but by the incredible flooding of those very sensations we now have with a meaning, a transvaluation, of which we have here no faintest guess?[50]

In transposition from the world of spirit to body, there is a 'correspondence' on the level of the senses—say, in erotic love—a 'transvaluation of meaning'. Thus it stands in the original sermon of 1944; Lewis has not transgressed the limits of analogy. But in that sermon, Lewis also notes that something more can happen *within the orders of nature*: a sign of a higher reality can be the place where 'the thing signified is really in a certain mode *present*'. Within nature, 'the emotion descends bodily, as it were, into the sensation and digests, transforms, transubstantiates it'; aesthetic joy, for instance, transubstantiates Pepys' making love to his wife. This is a 'sacrament' in nature, not just a symbol, and through transposition the 'lower reality can actually be *drawn into* the higher and become part of it'.[51]

For this action, Lewis can only use the word 'incarnation'. He writes that, 'The sensation which accompanies joy becomes itself joy: we can hardly choose but say "incarnates joy".' Thus, Lewis finds a 'real analogy' between transposition in nature and the incarnation of God in Christ. In Christ, 'humanity, still remaining itself is [...] veritably drawn into deity', and this, writes Lewis, 'seems to me *like* what happens when a sensation [...] is drawn into the joy it accompanies.'[52] What Lewis is careful *not* to say is that a natural sensation, such as erotic love, can itself be drawn into God. Elsewhere, he makes it clear that human passion is not a 'Christian sacrament'; at this point, Lewis is restricting a sacrament that makes the

---

[48] Lewis, 'Transposition', 11–14.   [49] Lewis, 'Transposition', 10, 11.
[50] Lewis, 'Transposition', 20.   [51] Lewis, 'Transposition', 15–16, 18–19.
[52] Lewis, 'Transposition', 19. My italics.

life of *God* present in physical matter to the person of Christ, and (presumably) to the bread and wine of a church Eucharist. There is no extension from the sacraments of the church to sacramentality in the world of nature.

Now, it is this boundary that Lewis remarkably transgresses in his addition to the sermon in 1962. It is as if Williams' theology of romantic love has taken possession of him at this latest point of life. The divine glory does not just 'revalue' the meaning of the senses through analogy; it 'descends bodily' into sensual life, and the senses are 'drawn into' it. Lewis offers two ways of putting this:

> You can put it whichever way you please. You can say that by Transposition our humanity, senses and all, can be made the vehicle of beatitude. Or you can say that the heavenly bounties by Transposition are embodied during this life in our temporal experience. But the second way is the better.[53]

Williams would have 'put' this kind of transposition in the first sense. Lewis, it seems, prefers the second because it seems to him to indicate better that the realities of the spiritual life are more solid than temporal things, which are not more dense than 'heavenly bounties' but 'too flimsy, too transitory, too phantasmal' to inherit the Kingdom of God. In his added section he rewrites Plato's parable of the cave and the sun to make this point.[54] But both ways of expression are contesting the kind of separation of nature and spirit that he was previously anxious to maintain. The additional material also contains, correspondingly, an urging of the same kind of affirmation of images as Williams advocated, to balance the negative way: 'We must believe—and therefore in some degree imagine—that every negation will be only the reverse side of a fulfilling.'[55]

3.3 Suffering: The Reasonable and the Tolerable

Perhaps the most startling instance of this late ongoing engagement with Williams' thought occurred in the sequence of the illness, temporary recovery, and finally death of Lewis' wife Joy. When Joy entered the Churchill Hospital, Oxford, in March 1957 in the expectation of an imminent death, hands were laid on her for healing by a young priest, the Revd Peter Bide, at the request of Lewis, and at the same time Bide—also at Lewis' urging—conducted a Christian marriage

---

[53] Lewis, 'Transposition (revised)', in *They Asked for a Paper*, 179.
[54] Lewis, 'Transposition (revised)', 177–9. Lewis offers a parable of an imprisoned woman in a dungeon, making drawings of the outside world for her son, who had never seen it. Lewis had in fact already expressed the same conviction in *Great Divorce*, 27–8, where the ghosts from hell find the grass of heaven so substantial that it does not even bend under their feet.
[55] Lewis, 'Transposition (revised)', 177. See Lewis, 'Novels', 52, and my Chapter 8, section 7.

between him and Joy.[56] After Joy returned home to The Kilns, expecting her life soon to end, she received a remission of her cancer, while Lewis was now himself suffering from osteoporosis. In a letter to Sheldon Vanauken, Lewis hesitantly raised the possibility that he and Joy had experienced the kind of substitution Williams had practised and encouraged, in which for love one can carry the pain of another:

> The intriguing thing is that while I (for no discoverable reason) was losing the chalcium from my bones, Joy, who needed it much more, was gaining it in hers. One dreams of a Charles Williams substitution! Well, never was a gift more gladly given: but one must not be fanciful.[57]

Lewis is being rather imprecise in referring to 'a Charles Williams substitution'. Usually in his writings, Williams only conceives of substitution between human persons as the exchange of states of consciousness and emotion (grief, fear, anxiety), not of physical conditions. In his book *He Came Down From Heaven*, he does, however, tentatively raise the possibility of the kind of substitution Lewis has in mind, and it is firmly tied to the theology of romantic love:[58]

> The body is probably the last place where such interchange is possible [...] In some states of romantic love it is felt that the power of healing exists, if only it could be brought into action, and on the basis of Romantic Theology it could so be brought into action. We habitually expect too little of ourselves.

Williams gives 'paralysis or consumption' as examples of burdens that might in principle be carried by another in love, though he admits that in practice 'it remains at present an achievement of which our "faith" is not yet capable'.[59] In *A Grief Observed*, following the death of Joy, Lewis raises the notion again only to dismiss it more firmly than Williams does, except in the unique case of the death of Christ.[60] But we should note that his view of the issue is not entirely out of line with that of Williams. Lewis is not rejecting the practice of substitution altogether, but only of substitution in physical healing, about which Williams himself has reservations.

---

[56] The date was 21 March 1957. Bide recounted the event in a talk given to the Oxford C. S. Lewis Society in 1995, printed as 'Marrying C. S. Lewis' in 2015; he also told me the story personally in the early 1980s.

[57] CSL to Sheldon Vanauken, 27 November 1957, Lewis, *Letters*, 2: 901. Green and Hooper, *C. S. Lewis*, 268, record from personal conversation Lewis' reaction to 'the nearest thing to a miracle he had ever experienced', but do not mention substitution. Coghill, 'Approach to English', 63, recalls Lewis' telling him that he had been 'allowed to accept [Joy's] pain'. On prayer and healing in general, see Lewis, 'Efficacy of Prayer', 3–4.

[58] Williams, *He Came Down*, 123.   [59] Williams, *He Came Down*, 124.

[60] Lewis (as N. W. Clerk), *A Grief Observed*, 36–7.

In this final phase of considering the problem of pain, nothing has changed in Lewis' *theology* of creation and fall since 1941. Lewis continues with his belief that God allows or inflicts pain on creatures in divine goodness: 'what you are up against is a surgeon whose intentions are wholly good. The kinder and more conscientious he is, the more inexorably he will go on cutting.'[61] The reasoned case is the same, but what has changed is the emotional reaction; he has discovered the tension that Williams knew and wrote about, that excessive pain in the world may be 'reasonable' and 'credible', but not 'tolerable'.[62] While writing *The Problem of Pain*, he had explained, in a letter to his brother Warnie, that he was being careful to detach his theory from the experience of pain in 'actual life', believing this would be a distraction—'quite unconnected and irrelevant'.[63] Now he discovers how connected it is. He knows with his mind that God is not 'the Cosmic Sadist, the spiteful imbecile', but his emotions bear a different witness. At one point he wonders: 'What do people mean when they say, 'I am not afraid of God because I know He is good? Have they never even been to a dentist?'[64]

This is the same theology as earlier, but the feeling-tone is different. Recalling the sequence of 'H's' (Joy's) illness, with moments of soon-frustrated hope, he remembers: 'Time after time, when He seemed most gracious He was really preparing the next torture.'[65] Indeed, in his sense of the intolerable he even exceeds Williams. He takes up a phrase from Williams himself about God's maintaining of the cosmic order and inverts it: 'Someone said, I believe, "God always geometrizes".[66] Supposing the truth were "God always vivisects"?' Lewis knows well who the 'someone' is; he had quoted the phrase approvingly from Williams' *He Came Down from Heaven* in *Arthurian Torso*.[67] But now Lewis complains, 'Meanwhile, where is God? [...] go to Him when your need is desperate, when all help is vain, and what do you find? A door slammed in your face, and a sound of bolting and double bolting on the inside.'[68] A page later he recalls Williams again, and the conviction he had experienced when he died about his overcoming of death:[69] 'After the death of a friend, years ago, I had for some time a most vivid feeling of certainty about his continued life; even his enhanced life.' Now, he testifies, 'I have begged to be given even one hundredth part of the same assurance about H.' But there is 'no answer. Only the locked door, the iron curtain, the vacuum, absolute zero.'[70]

A turning point comes when he is prepared to think again about the cross of Jesus. Thinking evidently of the 'Williams-substitution' in physical healing he had

---

[61] Lewis/Clerk, *Grief Observed*, 36.   [62] See Chapter 2, section 2.
[63] CSL to W. H. Lewis, 3 December 1939, Lewis, *Letters*, 2: 302.
[64] Lewis/Clerk, *Grief Observed*, 36.   [65] Lewis/Clerk, *Grief Observed*, 27.
[66] Lewis/Clerk, *Grief Observed*, 26. See Williams, *He Came Down*, 40.
[67] Lewis, 'Williams and the Arthuriad', 106. While Williams attributes the phrase to Plato in *He Came Down from Heaven*, the English form is Williams'.
[68] Lewis/Clerk, *Grief Observed*, 9.   [69] See the beginning of this chapter.
[70] Lewis/Clerk, *Grief Observed*, 10.

written to Vanauken about, he writes: 'And then one babbles—"if only I could bear it, or the worst of it, or any of it, instead of her".' Then he adds:

> But is it ever allowed? It was allowed to One, we are told, and I find I can now believe again, that He has done vicariously whatever can be so done. He replies to our babble, 'You cannot and you dare not. I could and I dared.'[71]

It has been argued that, in order to retain his faith in the goodness of God, Lewis capitulates in the second half of his book to an extreme 'Ockhamism', or radical voluntarism, according to which something is good simply because God commands it, wills it, or does it. The protest against the 'Cosmic Sadist' in parts 1 and 2 is thus replaced by submission in parts 3 and 4 to the 'Divine Iconoclast', who breaks all our images and destroys the illusions of faith.[72] The contrary argument has been put (effectively in my view) that Lewis continues to hold to a 'modified Platonism' in which the supreme Good must be in accord with our own moral intuitions, but that there may be elements within it that we find difficult or perplexing.[73] I intend to return to this issue later (Chapter 6, section 2) in considering Lewis' kind of Platonism, but for the moment I want to observe that the pivot in his reflections is not a philosophical argument about the Good at all, but an appeal to the crucifixion of Jesus. It is immediately after this that Lewis records 'Something quite unexpected has happened [...] For various reasons, not in themselves at all mysterious, my heart was lighter than it had been for many weeks.'[74] McGrath, with good theological instincts, perceives the significance of this sequence in his account of Lewis' experience.[75]

Here I suggest that we should read Lewis' movement into a state of living with his grief from a standpoint of a continuing journey with Williams. Having now experienced for himself the conflict between reason and emotion, between the credible and the intolerable, as Williams had expressed it acutely twenty years before, it is possible that he has also taken into himself something of Williams' view of the cross as a kind of theodicy. There is a strong indication that he had come to do so in an earlier reflection in the book: 'Sometimes it is hard not to say "God forgive God". Sometimes it is hard to say so much. But if our faith is true, He didn't. He crucified Him.'[76] This need not be taken to imply a 'penal substitutionary' view of atonement, which Lewis was reluctant earlier on to endorse.[77] Lewis can be read in an exaggerated, rhetorical mood, rather like the theologian Jürgen Moltmann's provocative saying that 'God gave up his own Son, abandoned

[71] Lewis/Clerk, *Grief Observed*, 36-7.
[72] See the interpretation of pages 32-3 by Beversluis, *C. S. Lewis*, 279-91.
[73] Baggett, 'Divine Iconoclast', 124-9.   [74] Lewis/Clerk, *Grief Observed*, 37.
[75] McGrath, *C. S. Lewis*, 347.   [76] Lewis/Clerk, *Grief Observed*, 25.
[77] Lewis, *Mere Christianity*, 44-6.

him, cast him out.'[78] He may well be affirming with Williams that God stands in need of forgiveness ('God forgive God') for maintaining a suffering world in being with its inflexible laws, and this is only possible because God endures in God's own self the pains of crucifixion. As Williams wrote, 'This was the best law, the clearest justice man could find, and [God] did well to accept it.'[79] Williams continues: 'They crucified Him; let it be said, they did well. But then let it be said also, that the Sublimity itself had done well.' Referring to Christ's vicarious act, Lewis puts into Christ's mouth the words 'I could, and dared.'[80] This is not a conceptual answer to the problem of pain, but it can be a 'theodicy of consolation', of the presence of a vulnerable God in the deepest human suffering.

A Grief Observed thus contains several echoes of Williams' thought, and Williams still appears to be present in Lewis' mind. He continues to affirm that Williams' death had given him a stronger belief in immortality, but says nothing about the sense of the actual presence of Williams with him which had persisted for a long period. In his letter to Vanauken in 1957, Lewis uses virtually the same words as he had done in 1945 about its being 'expedient' for a loved one, like Christ, to go away, but this time he does not apply the expression to an experience of the dead person's presence. He cites the scriptural text with a different application—in order to confirm the experience of what Vanauken calls a 'second bereavement', or the passing of poignant grief and 'the fading of the beloved as-she-was'.[81] Perhaps it is this second stage of bereavement he had, by that time, reached with Williams.

It was a complicated 'secret' and 'inward' journey on which Lewis had embarked with Williams in 1936. Their assessment of each other did not always chime with that of themselves. In the last year of his life, for example, Williams movingly writes to his wife on several occasions to explain what he has tried to achieve in the past, and to set out the goals he is setting before himself in the future. He judges that 'after poetry, criticism is my real work'.[82] This differs strikingly from Lewis' final judgement in his Preface to Essays in Williams' honour, when he writes that Williams' criticism is 'probably the least valuable part of his work' and implies that, after the poetry, he finds the most value in the novels.[83] Earlier, in March 1943, Lewis had written to Eliot: 'I agree, as you know, about C.W.—but only, if he cd. be induced to write more fiction and less criticism! The last novel, in which he had begun to chasten the exuberance of style ought to have been the beginning of a great new development.'[84]

The image I have been offering of their relationship is of a shared journey along a boundary between adjacent 'provinces', in which each was prepared to

---

[78] Moltmann, Crucified God, 242. On Moltmann's phrase, see Clarke, Cry in the Darkness, 87–9.
[79] Williams, 'The Cross', 133.   [80] Lewis/Clerk, Grief Observed, 37.
[81] CSL to Sheldon Vanauken, 27 November 1957, Lewis, Letters, 3: 901.
[82] CW to Michal Williams, 7 Sept. 1944, Williams, To Michal, 223.   [83] Lewis, Essays, vii.
[84] CSL to T. S. Eliot, 10 March 1943, Lewis, Letters 2: 562.

experience the view from the territory the other preferred and in which he naturally dwelt. At times it seemed as though Lewis had crossed over more decisively onto Williams' ground than Williams had onto his, but a reserve remained. Until the latest phase of his life—with the extraordinary exception of the last chapter of *Perelandra*—Lewis tended to reinterpret Williams in a way that he was comfortable with. In his 1945 review of the Taliessin poems, he writes that he has been drawn into a world that 'is emphatically not mine', and there is an echo of this experience in his later BBC broadcast (1949) on 'The Novels of Charles Williams':

> I am convinced that both the content and the quality of his experience differed from mine and differed in ways that oblige me to say that he saw further, that he knew what I do not know. His writing, so to speak, brings me where I have never gone on my own sail or steam; and yet that strange place is so attached to realms we do know that I cannot believe it is mere dreamland.[85]

This tribute is in the context of discussing the 'different world' that invades the 'mundane scene' in Williams' novels,[86] and seems to relate to the way that Williams understands natural and physical life to be transfigured by a greater reality. But the examples that Lewis gives (Lester in *All Hallows' Eve*, Margaret in *Descent into Hell*) concern characters who glimpse something of life after death and eternity, and that is ground that is more Lewis' native land:

> I am not suggesting that he knows in one sense—that he is giving me factual details about the world beyond death or on the brink of death, What I am quite sure of is that he is describing something he knows which I should not have known unless he had described it; and something that matters.[87]

In this passage, there is just a hint that the 'strange place' of Williams can become a route to Lewis' own land of heart's desire. It was the longing for this 'home' that Lewis felt all his life, and was the defining character of his own romantic province. Lewis' most personal testimony, *A Grief Observed*, closes with his attributing this same desire to Joy, as she turns away from him towards 'the eternal fountain' in the moment of her death:

> How wicked it would be, if we could, to call the dead back! She said not to me but to the chaplain, 'I am at peace with God.' She smiled, but not at me. *Poi si tornò all' eterna fontana.*

---

[85] Lewis, 'The Novels of Charles Williams', 52.   [86] Lewis, 'Novels', 47.
[87] Lewis, 'Novels', 52.

We are thus left at the end with a question about just how much Lewis has come to share Williams' vision of romantic theology on their journey together. For when Williams invokes the same phrase in his description of Beatrice's own turning away from Dante 'to the eternal fountain',[88] he adds that 'In what sense, if ever, Beatrice looks at him again is a thing for consideration only in a more detailed study of the *Comedy*, from the other end of the Paradise.'[89] When Williams does that study, in *The Figure of Beatrice*, her turning is—contrasting with Lewis' phrase 'not at me'—to underline the unity between human passion and the eternal love of God:

> It is so she is, in her passion, last seen. She turns, and though that turning is now her proper function, yet it has a minor function; it is to live again *for him* the vicarious life of heaven.[90]

---

[88] Dante, *Divine Comedy, Paradise*, 31.93.   [89] Williams, *He Came Down*, 100.
[90] Williams, *Figure of Beatrice*, 221. My italics.

PART II
WAYS OF EXCHANGE

4

Charles Williams and the Word
of Co-inherence

4.1 'Co-inherence': A Late Arrival on the Scene

It has become a commonplace in studies of Charles Williams to declare that the
theme of co-inherence runs through all his literary output. It is usually identified
as the 'golden thread' that binds together his mass of poetry, plays, critical essays,
and theological writing.[1] Williams and co-inherence seem inseparable. For him, it
is generally the concept that all human beings are connected with each other and
with God, and that all persons are dependent on each other. More exactly, it can
express the interweaving of three Persons in one divine substance in God, two
natures in one person in Christ, many human persons in the one Body of Christ,
flesh and spirit in the Eucharist, and human lovers in each other. In much
theology of the present day, the notion of co-inherence is expressed in the
Greek words *koinonia* and *perichoresis*, even where the English word 'co-
inherence' is not used, and these indicate a mutual 'indwelling' of human persons
in each other, in Christ, in the church, and in the triune God.[2]

All these recent theological usages of indwelling and interpenetration—with the
exception of one—are indeed already pervasive throughout the whole of Williams'
work. The exception is significant, and I am going to come to it in due course.
However, this is not to say that the *word* 'co-inherence' in itself was similarly
present throughout. Williams' friend and former colleague Alice Mary Hadfield,
who paid him the compliment of writing his biography twice, states confidently
that 'coinherence unifies everything',[3] and she uses the idea to illuminate much of
his early writing, from the poetry of 1918 onwards.[4] C. S. Lewis bids a correspondent find the notion of co-inherence in his favourite Williams' novel, *Descent*

---

[1] E.g. Newman, 'Charles Williams and the Companions of the Co-inherence', 6.
[2] See Chapter 15.
[3] Hadfield, *Introduction to Charles Williams*, 55; she spells the word as 'coinherence', without the
hyphen, unlike Williams' consistent practice.
[4] For instance, in her *Introduction*, 136, she wrongly finds the term in Williams, *He Came Down
from Heaven*. Similar anachronisms are committed by e.g. Walter Hooper in Lewis, *Letters*, 2: 232,
n.207; Howard, *Novels of Charles Williams*, 269; Cavaliero, *Charles Williams, Poet of Theology*, viii, 19,
32, 79, 98; Roukema, 'A Veil that Reveals: Charles Williams and the Fellowship of the Rosy Cross', 68;
Wendling, 'Charles Williams: Priest of the Co-inherence'; Newman, 'Charles Williams', 10.

Charles Williams and C.S. Lewis: Friends in Co-inherence. Paul S. Fiddes, Oxford University Press. © Paul S. Fiddes 2021.
DOI: 10.1093/oso/9780192845467.003.0004

into Hell (1936).[5] It may then come as a surprise to observe that the term itself does not actually appear in Williams' published writing until his book *The Descent of the Dove* in 1939. It also appears earlier that same year in two lectures and in personal letters and papers about the founding of his lay religious order, The Company of the Co-inherence,[6] to whom *The Descent of the Dove* is dedicated and whose founding is introduced at the end of the book.

The term appears, that is, only six or seven years before his death in 1945, though on the eve of the marvellous flowering of his creativity in this late period. It appears many times in *The Descent of the Dove*, it is important for his little book on *The Forgiveness of Sins* (1942), it is pivotal to his essay on 'The Way of Exchange' (1943), and it appears more than a dozen times in his book about Dante, *The Figure of Beatrice* (1943). It occurs in three poems in *The Region of the Summer Stars* (1944), one of them significantly called 'The Founding of the Company',[7] recalling his own Company of the Co-inherence. However, those poems had been submitted to the publisher, *Poetry London*, in mid-1943, and the term is absent from his play *The House of the Octopus* (1945), where *themes* of co-inherence are certainly present.[8] Finally, it only crops up once in his final novel, *All Hallows' Eve* (1945). Possibly Williams went through a peak period of enthusiasm for using the actual term 'co-inherence' in the years 1939–43, associated with his spiritual leadership in the order of Companions. After that, he could assume the ethos and context of a co-inherent existence without feeling he must continually repeat the word. However, in all his work after 1939, the term 'exchange' remains constant and ever-present.

It is my contention that Williams took this unusual term 'co-inherence' from a book on the Church Fathers by G. L. Prestige, *God in Patristic Thought*, published in 1936, where Prestige uses it extensively to translate the Greek *perichoresis*.[9] Williams tells us in a footnote in *The Figure of Beatrice* that the clearest exposition of co-inherence in the 'Divine Life' he knows is in the chapter of Prestige's book headed simply 'Co-inherence', spelt with a hyphen as Williams always wrote it.[10] He continues that 'Humanly, the word stands for the idea of the "in-othering" and "in-Godding" of men which appears in Dante.' On the same page as the footnote, we have a short account of what Williams himself means by the term, implying that it is already being used by someone else ('is said to be . . .'):

---

[5]   CSL to Rona Bodle, 24 October 1949, Lewis, *Letters* 2: 988.
[6]   For an account of a participant, see Hadfield, *Charles Williams*, 173–4, 232–3.
[7]   The other two poems are 'The Calling of Taliessin' and 'The Prayers of the Pope'.
[8]   For example, the term 'conjunction' in *House of the Octopus* serves a comparable function: Williams, *Collected Plays*, 250, 297.
[9]   G. L. Prestige, *God in Patristic Thought*, 280–1, 284–9. Prestige had earlier used the term in his article 'ΠΕΡΙΧΩΡΕΩ and ΠΕΡΙΧΩΡΗΣΙΣ (*Perichoreo and Perichoresis*)', 248–51.
[10]   Williams, *Figure of Beatrice*, 92n.

[Human] likeness to the divine unity [. . .] consists in a likeness to the manner by which it exists. That manner *is said to be* by the 'co-inherence' of the Divine Persons in each other, and *it has been held* that the unity of mankind consists in an analogical co-inherence of men with each other. (Italics mine)

I suggest Williams thinks Prestige's account of co-inherence to be the best he has come across because he is indebted to it for the very term itself. Before Prestige, there were only occasional usages of the word in the nineteenth century, where it appears as a new coinage in English as there is no verb *coinhaereo* in Latin.[11] Coleridge,[12] and J. S. Mill,[13] used it to express an interpenetration of faculties in the human consciousness, and significantly John Henry Cardinal Newman employed it to translate the Greek *perichoresis* in relation to the doctrine of 'the divine unity' in the Church Fathers.[14] It may be Newman's use that Prestige is picking up, although Newman's spelling was 'coinherence', without a hyphen. In any case, it is unlikely that Williams knew Newman's work, and the very fact that he starts using the word in the period in which we know he has been reading Prestige is surely indicative of direct debt to him.[15] I will be drawing attention to other connections with Prestige's text that confirm this. Clearly, the technical term *does* serve to sum up key themes in Williams' thought that he had been developing over the years, especially the three ideas of exchange, substitution, and the theology of romantic love. He must have pounced upon it as remarkably confirming all that meant most to him. It does not yet appear where one might expect it in his theological book of 1938, *He Came Down from Heaven*, where he discusses substituted love, exchange, and romantic love at length, and so we can be fairly sure that he came across it sometime between mid-1938 and early 1939.

The story of the emergence of the term begins, I suggest, with a lecture by Williams on 'The Epistles of St. Paul' on 7 October 1938.[16] According to Hunt's transcription, Williams draws attention to Paul's 'very remarkable phrase about the fellowship of the Mystery', but there is no mention of co-inherence. In discussing the nature of faith, Williams cites a phrase of Dante, which he translates 'the in-meing of me, the in-theeing of thee', which he is later to associate closely

---

[11] There is *inhaereo*, with the meaning 'stick in', or 'adhere to'.

[12] Coleridge, *Biographia Literia*, 1: 187; Coleridge, *Hints*, 54, 67, 69; cf. Coleridge, *Aids to Reflection*, 'Aphorisms on Spiritual Religion' II, 180: 'co-inherence of act and being'.

[13] Mill, *System*, 129–30.   [14] Newman, *Arians*, 168.

[15] In addition to the reference to Prestige in *Figure of Beatrice* in 1943, Williams had reviewed Prestige's book *Fathers and Heretics* some three years earlier in *Time and Tide*, 21.46 (16 November 1940), although the review makes no reference to Prestige's earlier book. It is not impossible that Williams had read the word 'co-inherent' in Coleridge, although he refers only to Coleridge's poetry in his critical works.

[16] CLI series 'The Christian Idea in Literature' 2, Wade RH Notebooks, 19: 3363–81.

with co-inherence,[17] and he explains this by the phrase 'cohere in': 'Origen, I think, first used the word "*cohere*" [underlined]. Something coheres in you, something of you coheres in something else.'[18] To this 'cohering in' he adds the word 'consubstantiation', 'consubstantiate yourself in faith',[19] by which he means participating 'by will and belief' in the substance of Christ, notably through the Eucharist. Williams had urged his hearers in a previous series of lectures on Dante to search for the substance of faith (referring to Hebrews 11.1), which in his preparatory notes for this lecture he calls 'substantifying',[20] but in the lecture as delivered he adds the 'co(n)' prefix: 'by faith is meant the consubstantiation of everything'.[21] We seem to be hovering in the air of co-inherence without actually naming it, and it is likely that by now he has read Prestige's book.

The key word was to appear suddenly and for the first time in Williams' work at the beginning of a lecture on Friday, 20 January 1939. The lecture as transcribed in Hunt's Notebook is headed 'Coinherence. The Middle Ages & the Great Schism (Luther, etc.)'.[22] In the original typescript of the syllabus issued to students,[23] the title of the lecture is simply 'Luther'. It is likely that Hunt has provided the heading himself (coinherence is spelled without the hyphen that Williams invariably uses), probably writing up the lecture later at a time when it had become clear how significant the term 'co-inherence' was becoming. Hunt records Williams as beginning thus, his transcript unfortunately broken, probably by his failure to hear words:

> It occurred to me...as a single-word epigram...co-inherence [underlined]. The dictionary defines it as...[24] But...the development of Christendom. You have the notion of coinherence in almost all the doctrines. It had been co-inherence which had been the solution of the difficulties about the definition of the Divine Trinity. The Persons of the Trinity coinhered in each other; the Son was coinhered in by the Father, the Father was coinhered in by the Son, and...It was certainly with the whole process of things which Christendom discovered for itself;...not impossible that co-inherence was the real fact underlying all social order.[25]

---

[17] Dante, *Paradise*, 9.81: *s'io m'intuassi, come tu t'immii*. Associated with co-inherence in Williams, *Figure of Beatrice*, 204; in Cambridge address I (1942), Wade CW/MS-347, 31; and in Lincoln Passiontide Address II (1945), Wade CW/MS-347, 46.

[18] Wade RH Notebooks, 19: 3369.   [19] Wade RH Notebooks, 19: 3375.

[20] Williams' notes for lecture, copied into RH Notebooks 19 (3380–1): 'In the Vulgate [Hebrews] 11:1 [...] we may perhaps take the word "substance" as effective, or at least as a substitute [...] it is the substantifying, by will and belief, in Christ Jesus' (3381).

[21] Wade RH Notebooks, 19: 3375.

[22] Wade RH Notebooks, 19: 3545–3551, CLI series 'The Christian Idea in Literature', 14.

[23] Wade RH Notebooks, 19: 3348.

[24] Williams probably used the *Oxford English Dictionary* (12 volumes, 1933), which defines 'co-inhere' as 'to inhere together', offering citations from Coleridge, Mill, and William Hamilton.

[25] Wade RH Notebooks, 19: 3545. Breaks as in the transcription.

In Williams' own preparatory notes for the lecture (copied into his notebook by
Hunt, to whom Williams gave them), he begins differently:

> I remind you of a few of the great phrases, maxims of the Way: 'Another is in-
> me', 'lay down our lives for the brethren', 'Your life and death are with your
> neighbour', and I add one more p. 100 [ ]
>
> And before them, 'My yearning is crucified'.[26]

Williams here does not in fact 'add one more' to the first three sayings, leaving
instead empty square brackets and a page reference; we shall be able to fill the gap
shortly, and we shall see that it was not occupied in his mind by any reference to
co-inherence. It does not seem that Williams originally intended to begin the
lecture with an affirmation of co-inherence at all, though the word does appear
once, without explanation, in a later list of subjects to be considered in the
lecture.[27] It appears that he has only decided on co-inherence as the key concept
when he comes to deliver the lecture orally, where he deploys the term quite freely
in the opening paragraphs. His appeal to the word is a way of introducing the
breaking down of a vision of unity in Christendom, first in the Great Schism
between East and West, and then in the Reformation, lamenting a loss of co-
inherence.[28] There are all the signs here of Williams' having made a new discovery, marked by the opening words, 'It occurred to me', and the elevation of the
term from one word in a list two-thirds of the way through his notes to the
opening gambit of the whole lecture. It is obviously a new word to Hunt, as he
alternates between spelling it with a hyphen and without.

Having begun with the word 'co-inherence' in the lecture as delivered, he then
turns to the three 'maxims of the Way' with which his notes actually begin, and
places them all in relation to 'co-inherence' as 'exhibiting' and 'advancing' the
'point of view' expressed by the term. The 'central fact of Christendom' is that the
same order exists in the spiritual and in the social realm: from the doctrine of
Christ to 'the basis of the social order, co-inherence was the real statement of the
whole thing'. In the delivered lecture, we now discover the fourth 'maxim' missing
at the beginning of the notes: alongside the sayings that Williams now identifies as
being from the Martyrdom of Felicitas, Clement of Alexandria, and 'Anthony the
Solitary', he places an extended passage from 'A certain brother' as recounted in
The Paradise of the Fathers translated by Wallace Budge. It is from this edition,
extensively used in his *New Christian Year*, that the mysterious page number (100)
comes. The whole passage from *The Paradise* is contained in the lecture notes, and
is reproduced, without attribution, in *The Descent of the Dove*.[29] The passage
includes the words, 'to put his own soul in the place of that of his neighbour and to

---

[26] Wade RH Notebooks, 19: 3563.   [27] Wade RH Notebooks, 19: 3564.
[28] See Wade RH Notebooks, 19: 3549.   [29] Williams, *Descent of the Dove*, 55.

become, if it were possible, a double man', and we can select the last phrase as a suitable maxim to place alongside the others.[30]

Williams now adds that 'Beatrice and Dante in a sense co-inhere', and celebrates 'this terrific development, this notion reaching from the most secret places of the Uncreated Being, this relationship... right out to the most casual ordinary action'.[31] The whole history of the doctrine of the medieval church and reaction against it can, Williams thinks, be understood in the light of co-inherence: there was 'co-inherence or exchange' between the Church Militant on earth, the Church Triumphant in heaven, and its members in purgatory, not least in prayer, exemplifying the maxim 'Your life and your death is with your neighbour'.[32] It seems clear that Williams' material for his lecture, as laid out in his notes, has been reorganized in its delivery from the perspective of co-inherence.

The context of this lecture is significant. Williams was writing The Descent of the Dove from August 1938 to May 1939,[33] while searching for a publisher (it was eventually published by Longmans in August 1939), and he seems to have been writing most intensively from January to May 1939. The book was to be the first place where he used the word 'co-inherence' in print, and it remained his most extended exploration of the idea. At the same time he was delivering a lecture series at the City Literary Institute nominally billed as 'The Christian Idea in Literature', which—despite its title—was a history of the church and its thinkers that increasingly ran parallel to the contents of the book. Into his lectures, delivered in a mainly extempore fashion and based on only brief notes, he seems to have been pouring his current ideas and his passions. It may be that he came across Prestige's God in Patristic Thought while consulting scholarly sources for his book. Perhaps the word 'co-inherence' was somewhere in his mind from August 1938 until it suddenly surfaced as 'the real statement of the whole thing' in late January. Over the next few months, he was clearly trying it out, as it has a significant place in a lecture on Karl Barth, as delivered in March 1939, while it does not appear at all in the preparatory notes for that lecture.[34] It appears in no more lectures in the series, but in late April there came his proposal for the founding of 'The Company of the Co-inherence,' as heralded also in The Descent of the Dove.

Williams appears to echo, in various places, Prestige's argument about the evolution of the term 'co-inherence'. This turns on the difference between 'perichoresis to' and 'perichoresis in'. Prestige translates the Greek term perichoresis as co-inherence, and locates a development in its use in a supposed theologian traditionally dubbed 'pseudo-Cyril' in the seventh century. Prestige maintains

---

[30] W. H. Auden was deeply influenced by the idea of the 'double man' which he read in Descent of the Dove: see Mendelson, Later Auden, 124–5.

[31] Wade RH Notebooks, 19: 3546. As I shall observe later, the idea of 'co-inherence' thus transgresses any kind of Platonist hierarchy of being.

[32] Wade RH Notebooks, 19: 3550. So also Williams, Descent of the Dove, 163.

[33] See Lindop, Charles Williams, 283.   [34] See Chapter 10.

that when the term was used earlier by other theologians for Christology, it was to describe the divine nature as being in *perichoresis* with the human nature in the sense of an 'interchange' or 'reciprocity' between the operations of the two natures. Thus it was *perichoresis* of one 'to' another; it was never a *perichoresis* 'in' one another or 'through' one another in the sense of an interpenetration. By contrast, when pseudo-Cyril uses the term for the union of two nature in Christ, he speaks of a 'permeation or co-inherence' of natures that is 'interpenetrative'. Pseudo-Cyril, proposes Prestige, then extends the same image of *perichoresis* to the Trinity for the first time, and similarly envisages the persons as being 'in' one another. Prestige writes of this shift of thought: [35]

> [He says] we call the holy Trinity one God. He continues by explaining the consistency of this doctrine with the fact of the hypostaseis; they are united, he says, not so as to be confounded, but so as to adhere to (*exesthai*) one another, and they possess co-inherence in one another without any coalescence or commixture. [. . .] it is even more important to observe how subtly and silently the phraseology of perichoresis has been changed. It is no longer perichoresis 'to' one another, but perichoresis 'in' one another. The former was the traditional form, when the term was used for Christology and in its original sense. It is sometimes retained by pseudo-Cyril for Christology, from sheer habit, and sometimes altered. But in relation to the Trinity it is never used, either by him or by John of Damascus, who took over the term from him and employed it frequently.

Scholars now know that the writing attributed here to a postulated 'pseudo-Cyril' was not just *adopted* by John of Damascus in the eighth century, as Prestige thought, but was in fact authored *by* the Damascene himself.[36] But the point still stands that, when applied to the Trinity, *perichoresis* means actually being 'in' each other, and not simply being 'to' each other in the sense of interchanging actions and attributes. This very point seems to be made by Williams in his lecture on 'The Epistles of St. Paul', when he maintains that 'something coheres in you, something of you coheres in something else'. In an article in *Time and Tide* for 7 March 1942, Williams makes the point even more clearly by distinguishing between mere 'coherence' (we might say, *perichoresis* 'to') and 'co-inherence' (as, we might say, *perichoresis* 'in'), insisting that the need for national unity in time of war can only be met by the 'co-inherence' of the officers of the state in each other and in the people, while 'coherence' is insufficient. The difference is between 'sticking to' and 'abiding in'. So he writes:

> We must conceive these high officers as working not certainly *against* each other, but also not merely *with* each other. The first, we know does sometimes happen,

---

[35] Prestige, *God*, 298.   [36] See further Chapter 15.

but we passionately hope that, here and now, it will not. The second is the common way of expressing what we hope will happen, and yet the phrase is inadequate; as lovers we might feel that it was inadequate to our own intense feelings. [...] We do not so much want them to cohere, to 'stick to' each other, as (if I may press the word again) to co-inhere, to 'abide in' each other [...] the difference between the idea of cohering and the idea of co-inhering is precisely the distinction between two [...] habits. The first is a decision of the will, necessary for civilized life; the second is a discovery, by means of that decision, of the very manner of all human life, call it (if we must) natural or arch-natural; therefore of national life.

He then draws an analogy with the Trinity; the three persons are 'abiding in each other', and 'we are all made in that image'.[37]

The likelihood that Williams has gleaned this argument from Prestige's account about the difference between *perichoresis* 'to' and *perichoresis* 'in' is supported by Williams' first address at Cambridge (1942) on 'Love and Exchange'. There he uses, to exemplify co-inherence, the same phrase from Dante—'if thou in meest'— as in his October 1938 lecture on St Paul, remarking that Dante 'uses the prefix "in-" with admirable effect'; he then quotes a phrase from the same page in Prestige (298) on which the argument about '*perichoresis* in' is advanced:

> I have read—Dr. Prestige's *God in P.T.* [underlined] is the best statement I have come across—that the doctrine of the life of the Blessed Trinity is called pericoresis [sic] or circumincessio or co-inherence. 'They possess co-inherence in one another without any coalescence or commixture'. This doctrine, Dr. Prestige adds, stands 'as a monument of inspired Christian rationalism'.[38]

Of course, it is clear that by 1942 Williams has read Prestige. My argument is that in his lecture of October 1938, stressing a 'cohering in', he already appears to echo Prestige's argument as set out on the very page (i.e. p. 298) that he later chooses to quote.

4.2   Companions of the Co-inherence

Within three or four months after 'it has occurred' to Williams that the idea of co-inherence was central both to the history of Christian thought and to his own vision of reality, he outlined the principles of his new Order of the Co-Inherence, sending the promulgation to a number of close friends (whom he called 'the

---

[37] Williams, 'Notes on the Way', 194–5.
[38] Wade CW/MS-347, 31–2; copied into Wade RH Notebooks, 21: 4141–2.

household'),[39] among them Alice Mary Miller [Hadfield], Anne Ridler, Thelma Shuttleworth, and Richard and Joan Wallis.[40] As Raymond Hunt records, he also personally presented a copy to him on Friday, 21 April at King's Cross railway station.[41] An accompanying note records that he had begun writing the promulgation on the 'Feast of the Annunciation' that year, which was 25 March (the day after his lecture on Karl Barth, which employs the term 'co-inherence'). For some time, it seems from at least 1934,[42] his friends had been urging him to set up some kind of organization or lay religious order in which they could be encouraged to practise 'substituted love', but he had not actively pursued the idea before. Now, with the looming threat of war, and a new need for mutual support, he decided to make 'this small step towards the Order'.[43] Perhaps too, the discovery of the word 'co-inherence' gave him the 'single-word epigram',[44] as a focus for such a group and the consolidating of his 'household'. The clauses of the document are studded with his favourite quotations, including two of the 'maxims of the way' with which he had begun his lecture of January that year. As in the lecture, the 'maxims' are all now seen as exemplifications of the principle of co-inherence. The original version of the promulgation of the 'Order'—later to be re-named by him as the 'Company'—, as circulated in April 1939, ran as follows (with original underlining in the typescript replaced by italics):[45]

The Order of the Co-inherence

1. The Order has no constitution except in its members. As it was said: *Others he saved, himself he cannot save.*
2. It recommends nevertheless that its members shall make a formal act of union with it and of recognition of their own nature. As it was said: *Am I my brother's keeper?*
3. Its concern is the practice of the apprehension of the Co-inherence both as a natural and as a supernatural principle. As it was said: *Let us make man in Our image.*

---

[39] Hadfield, *Charles Williams*, 173.   [40] Lindop, *Charles Williams*, 292.

[41] Wade CW/MS-77; transcribed into Wade RH Notebooks, 20: 3777. Hunt adds: 'CW now on the last chapter of his *History of Christendom*.'

[42] Lindop, *Charles Williams*, 291.

[43] Hadfield, *Charles Williams*, 173; she is however anachronistic when she records that his friends had been pressing him to form an Order 'concerned with his ideas of co-inherence', as well as substitution and exchange. In his piece 'Society of Jesus', in Williams, *Image*, 163–5, Williams compares his Order to the Jesuits, but as a Company 'working along the lines of the indirect' rather than the 'direct' love of God.

[44] See section 4.1 for this phrase in his lecture of January 1939.

[45] Wade CW/MS-77 (4 typescript copies); transcribed into Wade RH Hunt Notebooks, 20: 3777–8. Bod. MS. 16125/5, folder 1 has: (a) typescript copy of 'Order' dated April 1939; (b) undated typescript emending 'Order' to 'Company'; (c) MS, in CW's hand, of revision of 'Company' dated 20 September 1943; (d) typescript copy of 1943 revision.

4. It is therefore, *per necessitatem*, Christian. As it was said: *And whoever says There was when this was not, let him be anathema.*

5. It recommends therefore the study, on the contemplative side, of the Co-inherence of the Holy and Blessed Trinity, of the Two Natures in the Single Person, of the Mother and Son, of the communicated Eucharist, and of the whole Catholic Church. As it was said: *figlia del tuo figlio.* And on the active side, of methods of exchange, in the State, in all forms of love, and in all natural things, such as child-birth. As it was said: *Bear ye one another's burdens.*

6. It concludes in the Divine Substitution of Messias all forms of exchange and substitution, and it invokes this Act as the root of all. As it was said: *He must become, as it were, a double man.*

7. The Order will associate itself primarily with four feasts: the Feast of the Annunciation, the Feast of the Blessed Trinity, the Feast of the Transfiguration, and the Commemoration of All Souls. As it was said: *Another will be in me and I in him.*

The significance of *figlia del tuo figlio* (article 5) requires a knowledge of Williams' use of the term in his exposition of Dante in *The Descent of the Dove*, and later in *The Figure of Beatrice*.[46] Dante places the phrase—'The daughter of your son'—in the mouth of Bernard of Clairvaux near the end of the *Paradiso*,[47] and Williams takes this phrase as archetypal of exchange and co-inherence. Applied in the first place to the Virgin Mary, who is the (spiritual) daughter of her son, Christ, Williams maintains that the title belongs second to Beatrice as 'Mother of love' and third to all human beings; all are offspring of love (Christ) and in turn love is conceived in them and born from them. All are daughters of their Son, who is Love Itself. As Williams puts it in *The Figure of Beatrice*, the 'Beatrician experience' is the lover's knowledge of 'the quality of love off-springing from the quality of Beatrice, and the quality of Beatrice off-springing from the quality of love ("figlia del tuo figlio")'.[48] That this is the love of God is clear from a passage earlier in *The Descent of the Dove*, when—after recalling Dante's image of 'in-meing and in-theeing'—Williams writes:[49]

It is these great doctrines of matter, of exchange, or perfect love, which are made apparent in the paradox of the line "Verge Madre, figlia del tuo Figlio." This is the secret of the universe, the mortal maternity of Godhead.

[46] He also quotes the phrase in his first Cambridge address of 1942, Wade CW/MS-347, 31; transcribed in Wade RH Notebooks, 21: 4141–2.

[47] Dante, *Divine Comedy, Paradise*, 33.1.   [48] Williams, *Figure of Beatrice*, 47; also 222–3.

[49] Williams, *Descent of the Dove*, 138.

Williams has already written that 'the holy vision of co-inherence through the Salvation' embraces 'the martyrs, the saints and the Mother of God', then immediately quoting *figlia del tuo figlio*.[50] Later, in *The Figure of Beatrice*, Williams refers to the phrase as 'the great maxim of exchange', indicating 'in-othering [...] in-Godding and the infleshing',[51] and remarks that 'co-inherence [...] is an idea similar to that carried by the Beatrician and Marian title: "figlia del tuo figlio"'.[52] However, the phrase *figlia del tuo figlio* makes clear that there is no mere analogy between two areas of co-inherence—that of Christ in his church, and that of people among themselves. Although the author of the Letter to the Ephesians develops an analogy between Christ and his church on the one hand, and a married couple on the other,[53] Williams transgresses the borders of analogy. Mary, symbol of the Church in Christian tradition, physically gives birth to Christ and remains his spiritual offspring. So all members of the church, and all human lovers, give birth to that Love that is actually Christ—as 'mothers' of love—while being born anew from Love. They are all 'sons and daughters of their son'. Christ is incarnate in Mary as Mother of God, and is incarnated again in all who live in the co-inherence of love. One of Williams' favourite poets, Gerard Manley Hopkins, expresses a similar idea in a poem to the Virgin Mary:[54]

> [She] makes, O marvellous!
> New Nazareths in us,
> Where she shall yet conceive
> Him, morning, noon and eve[.]

On the same page of *The Figure of Beatrice* where Williams offers a definition of 'co-inherence' with reference to Prestige's book, he writes about Dante's phrase 'daughter of your son' that: 'The Incarnation, or rather the motherhood of the Incarnation, is the function for which *we* were created.'[55] I intend to return to some implications of this breaking open of analogy later.

4.3 Exchange and Substitution

Williams thus only begins using the term 'co-inherence' in January 1939, despite the often-made assumption that it lies at the centre of his work over many years. But my interest in this chapter extends further than correcting an error of fact. I want to ask whether the term 'co-inherence', once he *had* discovered it, offered

---

[50] Williams, *Descent of the Dove*, 103.   [51] Williams, *Figure of Beatrice*, 158, cf. 231–2.
[52] Williams, *Figure of Beatrice*, 92; so also 172.
[53] Ephesians 5:25–33. The writer is probably a disciple of St Paul, drawing on his thoughts and sayings.
[54] Hopkins, *Poems*, 95.   [55] Williams, *Figure of Beatrice*, 92 (my italics).

him any more than his previous notions of exchange, substitution, and romantic love. Was there a dimension that it added to the constellation of ideas he had already been putting together? Even more ambitiously, I want to ask in Chapter 6 whether C. S. Lewis added anything further to Williams' use of it. To answer, in this chapter, the question about what 'co-inherence' might have added to the store of Williams' imaginative ideas, we need to backtrack somewhat. We shall only reach an answer by exploring what he intends by the images of exchange and substitution, together with their place in the theology of romantic love, which are rooted deeply throughout his work.

The notion of 'exchange' or 'the way of exchange' is perhaps the most widespread of themes in Williams' work. It denotes relations in everyday life between inhabitants of the City of the world that all the time is being transfigured by the bright outlines of the City of God. At any moment, the City of London or the Byzantium of the Arthurian poems can become the eternal Jerusalem with its Acts of love. For Williams, we all live by exchange and interchange, a mutual dependence that is the law of the City, sharing tasks and responsibilities. Coins, for instance, are media of economic exchange that can create flourishing within the City, or can be abused into weapons of power.[56] In the Arthurian poem 'Bors to Elayne; On the King's Coins', the king's steward Kay welcomes the 'traffic' of the new coinage, affirming 'Money is the medium of exchange.' But the king's poet Taliessin is doubtful about this new medium, comparing the potential damage to the city to the dangers of the unchecked use of words as tokens of exchange:

> 'Sir, if you made verse you would doubt symbols.
> I am afraid of the little loosed dragons.
> When the means are autonomous they are deadly; when words
> escape from verse they hurry to rape souls[.]'

Yet the archbishop is more hopeful, citing from Heracleitus what is one of Williams' own favourite quotations about exchange:

> '... for the wealth of the self is the health of the self exchanged.
> What saith Heracleitus?—and what is the City's breath?—
> *dying each other's life, living each other's death.*
> Money is a medium of exchange.'[57]

The poet concludes: 'pray for the coins'. In Williams' vision, even conventional uses of the word 'exchange' become freighted with meaning, as in sinister smiles of

---

[56] See Williams, 'Way of Exchange', in Williams, *Image*, 149. Lewis, 'Sacred Poem', 128, is thus wrong to regard coinage in Williams' thought as a mere 'parody' of exchange and substitution.
[57] Williams, *Taliessin*, 44–5.

complicity in evil 'exchanged' between Simon the magician and the dead girl Evelyn in *All Hallows' Eve*, which to the observer, Richard, seemed an 'outrage' and a 'breach of spiritual law'.[58] By contrast, when the dead Lester meets Richard, 'she seemed to recall her body in the joy they exchanged'.[59]

Exchange, while not ceasing to be exchange, is intensified into a second Act of the City, which is substitution. This is a process of making a *deliberate* and intentional exchange, in which the mental suffering, anxiety, or fear of one can be carried by another, fulfilling the command of St Paul to 'bear one another's burdens, and so fulfil the law of Christ'.[60] Williams believed that this imaginative offering of oneself to be a substitute had ontological reality, and that because the pain or fear assumed was not one's own it could be carried more easily than by the owner, though still at great cost to the bearer.[61] Substitution or 'substituted love' was a spiritual practice Williams encouraged and even requested among the participants in his group of close friends, first called the 'household', and then the Companions of the Co-inherence, or simply the Company; the instruction to 'bear one another's burdens' is the maxim at the heart of the fifth article of the promulgation of the Order. The process had already been dramatically depicted in two of the novels.

As early as 1932, in *The Greater Trumps*, Sybil is allowed to heal by an act of substitution the gypsy patriarch, Aaron, who has sprained his ankle. We read:

> Her hand closed round the ankle; her mind went inwards into the consciousness of the Power which contained them both; she loved it and adored it: with her own thought of Aaron in his immediate need, his fear, his pain, she adored. Her own ankle ached and throbbed in sympathy, not the sympathy of an easy proffer of mild regret, but that of a life habituated to such intercession. [. . .] Their eyes exchanged news. She throbbed for an instant not with pain but with fear as his own fear passed through her being. It did but pass through; it was dispelled within her, dying away in the unnourishing atmosphere of her soul, and with the fear went the pain.[62]

In *Descent into Hell* (1936), Pauline Anstruther has since childhood been haunted by a Doppelgänger, a duplicate figure of herself whom she often sees on the road in the distance, and whom she has an extreme fear of meeting face to face. She is released from her crippling anxiety by the offer of Peter Stanhope to carry her burden of fear for her, described in a chapter called 'The Doctrine of Substituted Love':

---

[58] Williams, *All Hallows' Eve*, 106.   [59] Williams, *All Hallows' Eve*, 152.
[60] See 'Order', article 5; Williams, *He Came Down*, 123; Galatians 6:2, cf. Matthew 11:30.
[61] Williams, 'Way of Exchange', 151–2.   [62] Williams, *Greater Trumps*, 219.

The body of his flesh received her alien terror, his mind carried the burden of her world. The burden was inevitably lighter for him than for her, for the rage of a personal resentment was lacking. He endured her sensitiveness, but not her sin; the substitution there, if indeed there is a substitution, is hidden in the central mystery of Christendom which Christendom itself has never understood, nor can.[63]

Pauline has an ancestor who was burned at the stake as a Protestant martyr, and who is described in the history books as going to his death in an ecstasy of joy, shouting in the midst of the fire, 'I have seen the salvation of my God.' She discovers *how* he did this when at the climax of the book she is transported back through time to the martyr's condemned cell. She finds him in trembling of the coming fire. She sees herself, full of joy, appearing to the condemned man, offering to carry his fear for him: she hears her own voice saying, 'Give it to me, give it to me, John Struther.' He does so in thanksgiving, and at that moment Pauline understands why she has been so afraid of her Doppelgänger, which she now realizes is a counterpart of herself created by her journey back in time; in fact, the fear she was carrying was not her fear of her other self at all, but John's fear of the fire. We read: 'she had all her life carried a fear which was not hers but another's, until it had become for her in turn not hers but another's'.[64] She carries John's burden and Peter Stanhope carries hers. This is the way of exchange that makes it possible to embrace even the fire.

Finally, in Williams' last novel of 1945, *All Hallows' Eve*, there is 'an exchange of redeeming love' between the dead woman, Lester, and a living woman, Betty. Saying 'Let me...',[65] Lester experiences the suffering inflicted by the magician Simon's attempt at a magical sacrifice of Betty by use of the reversed tetragrammaton.[66] More exposition of all these novels will be provided in Chapters 11 and 12.

Williams grounds these principles of exchange and substitution theologically. In the first place, they are rooted in creation itself, in 'the one great natural fact involving exchange—childbirth'. As expressed in his pamphlet 'The Way of Exchange' (1941), Williams' argument here is threefold, appealing to both exchange and substitution. In the first place, producing a child is a mutual act of a man and a woman, but when it comes to actually bearing the child the women acts both for herself and as a substitute for the man: 'the woman carries, literally, the burden'.[67] Second, each generation 'inheres' in the one before it, so that 'we carry the burden of others'. Third, 'our natural life begins by being borne in another; our mothers have to carry us'.[68] Williams understands this process as not

---

[63] Williams, *Descent into Hell*, 101.   [64] Williams, *Descent into Hell*, 171–2.
[65] Williams, *All Hallows' Eve*, 139.   [66] Williams, *All Hallows' Eve*, 142–4.
[67] Williams, 'Way of Exchange', 150.   [68] Williams, 'Way of Exchange', 150–1.

just a matter of biology but of theology: from childbirth to those 'adult in love' there is only 'one Nature', and this nature 'is not divided from grace'. It is indeed, affirms Williams, 'with submission to the theologians, the nature of grace'. Indeed, 'from childbirth to the Divine Trinity itself the single nature thrives; there is here no difference between that natural and that super-natural'.[69] It is thus appropriate that in his 1939 version of the promulgation of his 'Order', childbirth is included in 'all methods of exchange' (clause 5).

These 'methods' are rooted theologically, not only in the grace of creation, but also in the person of Christ, in his incarnation, and in his cross. We are 'in' our neighbour only because we exist 'in Christ'. Williams has taken the insight of St Paul that human beings can live 'in Christ',[70] along with the correlation that 'Christ lives in me', and interpreted it in terms of exchange and substitution. Christ has made the greatest exchange in becoming human so that we can become divine, and he has made the 'central substitution' at Calvary, taking our state of sin and separation upon himself. Williams writes that:

In the last reaches of that living death to which we are exposed He substituted himself for us. He submitted in our stead to the full results of the Law which is He [. . .] By that central substitution, which was the thing added by the Cross to the Incarnation, he became everywhere the centre of, and everywhere He energized and affirmed, all our substitutions and exchanges.[71]

While this lapidary declaration comes from the essay 'What the Cross Means to Me' in 1943, its ideas are anticipated in the period when Williams is not yet using the term 'co-inherence', but only 'exchange' and 'substitution'. In *He Came Down From Heaven*, for example, he writes that before Christ the old law that answered yes to the question 'Am I my brother's keeper?' was felt as a mere 'burden'; but this bearing of another's burden was 'borne by heaven in the form of the Holy Thing that came down from heaven', so that 'the new law of the kingdom made that substitution a principle of universal exchange'.[72] The direct concern of the new kingdom was 'with the love that had substituted itself for men',[73] not least in the cross where Christ was mocked with the words 'He saved others; himself he cannot save.' This taunt, declares Williams, was in fact 'an exact definition of the kingdom of heaven in operation, and of the great discovery of substitution which was then made by earth'.[74] The 'taunt' and the 'rhetorical question' 'Am

---

[69] Williams, 'Way of Exchange', 153.
[70] Schweitzer, *Mysticism*, 1–3, takes an eschatological view of 'Christ-mysticism'; but see Best, *One Body*, 14–19.
[71] Williams, 'Cross', 137.   [72] Williams, *He Came Down*, 116.
[73] Williams, *He Came Down*, 117.   [74] Williams, *He Came Down*, 115.

I my brother's keeper?' were to find their place as maxims in the first and second articles of the promulgation of the Order of the Co-inherence in 1939.

Williams precedes this discussion of exchange and substitution in *He Came Down From Heaven* with a quotation from St Paul about being 'in' Christ: 'It is no more I that live but Christ that liveth in me.'[75] Before finding the term 'co-inherence', Williams was thus stressing the reality of 'being in' that he found both in Paul's 'in Christ' and in Dante's 'me in thee-ing' and 'thee in me-ing'.[76] It is not surprising that he brings the Apostle and the poet together in his lecture on the Epistles of St Paul, which—I have suggested—marked the dawning of co-inherence in his mind.

4.4 Being 'in' Love

It is also a 'being in' that links exchange and substitution with romantic love, or the state of being 'in love'.[77] As Mary says to Joseph in the nativity play, *Seed of Adam*, when she has received Christ in a miraculous conception:

> Dearest, to be in love is to be in love,
> no more, no less. Love is only itself,
> everywhere, at all times, and to all objects.
> My soul has magnified that Lord[.][78]

Beyond being in love with a particular someone, there is being in love itself, or in Christ's-self. Later, Williams is to write that 'one no longer merely loves an object; one has a sense of loving precisely from the great web in which the object and we are both combined. There is, if only transitorily, a flicker of living within the beloved.'[79] By this point (1941), Williams has a vision of 'the great co-inherence of all life', but already in *He Came Down from Heaven*, exchange and substitution are strongly linked with romantic love: substitution is 'substituted love'. Indeed, more generally, the idea of being 'in Christ' is basic to Williams' *Outlines of Romantic Theology*, written in 1924, which pre-dates even the formative stages of his thoughts about exchange and substitution in the early 1930s. In that book, unpublished in his lifetime, Williams writes of the way that 'the body of the Beloved seems to [the lover] transfused with the Divine Body, how Christ Incarnate is almost visibly made one with her'.[80] With this thought there occurs

---

[75] Gal 2:20, KJV; Williams, *He Came Down*, 115.
[76] Wade RH Notebooks, 19: 3369. In *Figure of Beatrice*, 204, Williams draws attention to other in-prefixes in Dante, *The Divine Comedy*: the life of the blessed virgin 'in-heavens' her—*inciela* (*Paradise* 3.97); each seraph 'in-Gods' himself—*india* (*Paradise* 4.28); joy 'in-poured'—*infonda* (*Paradise* 8.86).
[77] Williams, *Religion and Love*, 9.   [78] Williams, *Collected Plays*, 159.
[79] Williams, 'Way of Exchange', 153.   [80] Williams, *Outlines*, 43.

an early instance of the word 'exchange': dwelling in the Body of Christ, both church and lovers are preserved from sin 'in the mutual exchange of contemplative delight which we call love'.[81] Williams urges:

'If the lovers abide in him at the beginning as Man and God, human and divine, how easy, how natural should be their growth with Him into the full consciousness of Divinity and its full possession [...] since Love and Christ are one.'[82]

Through the beloved, the lover is thus brought to the consciousness of Christ; the conversion that takes place is 'the New Birth', or the nativity of both Love in the lover and of the lover himself to a new life.[83] In this early work, Williams stresses that all those who love are 'in' the Body of Christ, and the normal medium of this participation is the Eucharist, through which Christ as Love draws lovers into himself:

The Sacrament [...] should appear to the lover to be closely related to the glorious body of his lady through which he apprehends divine things. To identify them [however] would be too much; it is Love, and not the mother of Love [i.e. the beloved woman], who draws the world into Himself in mass and communion.[84]

It is being 'in love/ Love' like this that is at the centre of substitution. The first recorded instance of Williams' broaching the idea of *substitution* to a friend was to Thelma Mills, probably in June 1929, requesting that she might carry the burden of his anxiety about the visit of an inspector to his evening classes. Lindop speculates that he may have already discussed the idea and perhaps experimented with it in conjunction with the hermetic group gathered around the Revd Henry Lee, who led the *Stella Matutina* offshoot of the Hermetic Order of the Golden Dawn.[85] At any rate, in his letter to Thelma Williams, he envisages substitution as an act of love, though he is still finding his way with some hesitation:

I have a point to discuss with you: which has made me wonder whether the New Testament may not be merely true in some of its advice. All about 'bearing one another's burdens'. I have an awful (full of awe) feeling that one can. The older

---

[81] Williams, *Outlines*, 33.   [82] Williams, *Outlines*, 46.   [83] Williams, *Outlines*, 32.
[84] Williams, *Outlines*, 37.
[85] Lindop, *Charles Williams*, 156. This group had more 'magical' interests than A. E. Waite's offshoot from the Golden Dawn (at first The Independent and Rectified Rite of the Golden Dawn, and then after 1914 The Fellowship of the Rosy Cross), which was more mystical in its orientation, and through whose ranks Williams had risen to become *Adeptus Exemptus*. Williams appears to have belonged to both groups.

I get the more amazed I become at the pure convenience of—what we call Love. It is not merely beautiful; it is useful.[86]

By the time of a letter to Phyllis Jones in 1934, the phrase 'substituted love' is established, as it is to appear as a chapter heading in *He Came Down from Heaven*: 'And now, inseparable comrade, what do we do about substituted love? Might it be useful?'[87] The burden is to be carried out of love for the other, and directed towards love for God, 'fulfilling the law of Christ'. In 1940, Williams wrote to one of the Companions of the Co-inherence, Olive Speake, asking her to carry the burden of anxiety of an Italian woman who was feeling suicidal, appealing to her on the grounds of love and being in Christ: 'your experience is part of the mystical life of our Lord—of Love, of *Caritas*'.[88]

The links between love, substitution, and exchange are firmly set out in *He Came Down From Heaven*. Indeed, they are the focus successively of the final three chapters, in that order. Chapter VI on 'The Theology of Romantic Love' begins by setting the scene for the development in society of a new 'religious idea' of love: 'The grand substitution had been carried out and society was to be organized on the basis of a belief in substitution and salvation.'[89] Williams finds the quintessence of the theology of romantic love in Dante's vision of Beatrice, the young Florentine girl he met glancingly one day in the streets of the city,[90] and at the heart of this encounter is a being 'in' love because of being 'in Christ'; this in turn is based on Christ's being 'in us' because of the incarnation. In the 'Beatrician moment', the lover sees the 'light that enlightens every man' made visible through the beloved;[91] he certainly sees her in the light of her own eternal state in heaven as a created being, but this is because divine light radiates from her, which is the light of Christ. This glory has the power to renovate nature, and so through her and her beauty the new life comes into existence. Williams sums up this moment: 'they are "in love"'.[92] Beatrice is not Love itself (or Himself), but is 'Mother of Love in the soul', Mother of grace, and even Mother of the hidden God there. This, comments Williams, is the result of the incarnation that has opened up matter to carry 'all the potentialities of the knowledge of the kingdom of heaven' in and through it. Stressing the 'in' particle again, he quotes, 'my covenant shall be *in* your flesh',[93]

---

[86] Cited by Hadfield, *Introduction*, 139–40, without attribution. Lindop, *Charles Williams*, 155, identifies the recipient as Thelma Mills from the letter in Bod. MS Eng. Lett. E. 136, f95, dated simply '26 June', which he implies in his narrative was 1929. Hadfield dates the letter as August 1930, but Lindop (171) draws attention to another letter written to Thelma in August 1930, again requesting an act of substitution (over his worry about the safety of Phyllis Jones who was horse-riding), and Hadfield may have confused the two.

[87] Cited by Hadfield in her 'Sequel' in Williams, *Outlines*, 76.

[88] CW to Olive Speake, 22 February1940, Wade CWP, 78.   [89] Williams, *He Came Down*, 84.

[90] Williams, *He Came Down*, 98.   [91] Williams, *He Came Down*, 93.

[92] Williams, *He Came Down*, 97.

[93] Williams, *He Came Down*, 101. The text is Genesis 17:13, which in context refers to the sign of the covenant in circumcision. Williams seems to associate the phrase with John 1:14.

which he uses as an epigram for the incarnation of love/Love,[94] either in the body of Christ or in that of the lover. Romantic love is thus in the *Paradiso* 'seen to mirror the Humanity and Divinity of the Redeemer', the two natures of Christ reflected in the two eyes of Beatrice.[95]

Williams concedes that love in Dante's *Vita Nuova* is not initially an allegory of Christ, but he thinks Dante develops it in this way as he continues. At any rate, love is 'in the centre', and Williams associates this with Bonaventure's great statement that 'God is a circle whose centre is everywhere and circumference nowhere.'[96] In this view, Dante would be inhabiting the circumference, but Williams adds a twist: if, according to the *New Life*, love is at the centre, then to this centre 'all parts of the circumference, all times, all experiences, have this equal relation', and 'every point of the circumference is at the centre, for the circumference itself is *caritas*'. This is the cosmic perspective that C. S. Lewis is going to adopt in the Great Dance of the last chapter of his *Perelandra*: 'because we are with Him, each of us is at the centre'.[97] This is what it means to be 'in love', and Williams concludes, echoing Dante, that 'this is love-in-heaven'.[98]

Having set the trajectory of romantic love as being 'in love' and loving 'in Christ' (without as yet any mention of 'co-inherence'), Williams continues in the next two chapters to explore substitution and exchange. Love between human beings, he states near the beginning of his chapter on 'The Practice of Substituted Love', 'forms itself after the manner of that original love' that had 'substituted itself for men'.[99] The phrase 'substituted love' thus seems to be a shorthand for 'love that substitutes itself for others': acts of substitution are signs of 'the old self on the new way', and Williams comments that this degree of consciousness is 'the frequent result of romantic love'.[100] To love is 'to die and live again', and part of the experience of romantic love, as he has shown, is the experience of being made new, or the 'renovation of nature'.[101] We love each other, affirms Williams by acts of substitution; 'we are to be substituted and to bear substitution'. So 'all life is to be vicarious' and this kind of life is simply 'love-in-substitution'.[102] In fact, the experience of 'the Beatrician state' of romantic love can prompt a 'desire to make any contract of the kind mutual', so that each lover performs acts of substitution for the other.[103] That the context of substituted love is being 'in love' is made clear when the chapter ends with the same citation of Bonaventure as in the previous

---

[94] Also in *Figure of Beatrice*, 188, with a footnote to the way that 'the Life of our Lord as enacted in the love-relationship [...] is the heart of Romantic Theology'. So Williams, *Outlines*, 15–25.

[95] Williams, *He Came Down*, 104.

[96] Bonaventure, *Itinerarium Mentis In Deum*, 5.8; Williams, *He Came Down*, 105.

[97] Lewis, *Perelandra*, 149.

[98] Williams, *He Came Down*, 106. Cf. *Figure of Beatrice*, 27: Dante sees the glory of Beatrice as she is 'in heaven'; in *Figure of Beatrice*, 204, the life of the Blessed Virgin 'in-heavens' her.

[99] Williams, *He Came Down*, 117.   [100] Williams, *He Came Down*, 119.

[101] Williams, *He Came Down*, 120.   [102] Williams, *He Came Down*, 121.

[103] Williams, *He Came Down*, 128.

one, to which Williams now adds two other scriptural verses, the first an ironic saying about Christ as a substitute for others, and the second the vision of mutual indwelling in God from the prayer of Christ in the Fourth Gospel:[104]

> ... it may be possible to be astonished at the self as at everything else, when that which is God is known as the circle whose centre is everywhere and the circumference nowhere. 'He saved others; himself he cannot save.' 'The glory which thou gavest me I have given them, that they may be one, even as we are one; I in them, and thou in me, that they may be made perfect in one.'[105]

The final chapter ('The City') is a chapter about the way of exchange, and is again an extension of the trajectory launched from the chapter on romantic love. From the 'fact' of the great substitution in Christ, where God has 'accepted responsibility' for human suffering, the City 'descends to Patmos and the world'. Williams characterizes the City of God, to be found in the streets of our world, as a 'web of exchanged glory'. The glory is 'the web, and the operation down all the threads of the web, and the eternal splendour of threads and web at once'.[106] While the City contains myriad exchanges of human love as well as commerce, Williams stresses that in the vision of the City as God wants it to be, everything is loved 'because God loves it' and is to be loved 'for my [Christ's] sake'. 'Beatrice [...] is no longer to be loved for the gratification of the lover, in however pure or passionate a sense. She is no longer to be loved for herself alone.'[107] The earlier note of being 'in love' because the lovers are 'in Christ' is intensified: the 'law of exchange' means exchanging a love of created things for God, and receiving back, in exchange, 'its equivalent multitudinously restored'.[108]

Williams now adds another link between love and exchange: in this City, the 'law of interchange' is 'the ardent interchange of pardon'—those who love practise mutual forgiveness.[109] Further, all 'sharers of exchange' on earth are held in 'the organic word of prayer' for each other.[110] What could be said about love and about substitution can also be said about the way of exchange; taking up the image from Bonaventure that Williams has used (and adapted) before, in this City 'the centre is everywhere and the circumference nowhere'. In a parallel to his earlier statement that 'everything is at the centre' (because it is in Christ), Williams writes that 'everything and everyone is unique and is the subject of due adoration'.[111] In this

---

[104] The first, Mark 15:31 = Matthew 27:42, later appears in the 'Order', article 1, to underline that 'The Order has no constitution except in its members.' The second is John 17:22–3, and continues with a phrase about unity in love; the whole prayer of Jesus is a classic expression of what is to be called 'co-inherence'.

[105] Williams, *He Came Down*, 132–3.   [106] Williams, *He Came Down*, 146.

[107] Williams, *He Came Down*, 141.   [108] Williams, *He Came Down*, 142.

[109] Williams, *He Came Down*, 145. Williams is to develop the nature of forgiveness as co-inherence as well as exchange: see section 4.5.

[110] Williams, *He Came Down*, 144.   [111] Williams, *He Came Down*, 138–9.

'web of exchange' in which we all live, the glory of God is manifest and yet also hidden: we must always confess both 'This also is thou', and 'neither is this Thou'.

We may take a phrase from a later article by Williams as a comment on this chapter: 'The more intense the element of love between two or more persons, the more clear, generally, that exchange of activities is.'[112] By that time, however, Williams had discovered the word 'co-inherence'. In this book we are hovering on the edge of the discovery, with a vision of the 'web of glory' and the centrality of 'being in' Christ and each other for both exchange and substitution.

4.5 Co-inherence, Christology, and Trinity

When the term 'co-inherence' finally appears, it fits smoothly, as 'a single-word epigram',[113] into the twofold trajectory that Williams has been developing, namely that of being 'in love' and 'in Love (Christ)'. The major idea as Williams develops the term from 1939 to 1943 is a co-inherence 'in Christ', through the incarnation, cross, and Eucharist—and working further back, in the very act of creation through Christ. This co-inherence embraces what he has been calling 'substitution' and 'exchange', together with the romantic experience of union 'in love'. There is a neat summary of this Christological co-inherence in his essay of 1941, 'The Way of Exchange':

> The doctrine of the Christian Church has declared that the mystery of the Christian religion is a doctrine of co-inherence and substitution. The Divine Word co-inheres in God the Father (as the Father in Him and the Spirit in Both), but also He has substituted His Manhood for ours in the secrets of the Incarnation and the Atonement. The Principle of the Passion is that He gave His life 'for'—that is, instead of and on behalf of ours. In that sense he lives in us and we in Him, He and we co-inhere.[114]

This co-inherence is the basis for all acts of substitution we make in 'fulfilling the law of Christ', either by deliberate compact or by 'the operation of an instinctive love; a wife for a husband, a lover for a lover, a friend for a friend'.[115] Thus, 'to love God and to love one's neighbour are but two movements of the same principle', and 'the principle is the Word [Christ] through whom all things were made'. As Williams puts it in his little book *The Forgiveness of Sins* (1942), there is an original co-inherence of all created beings in Christ, a corporate solidarity or 'web of humanity'; in a striking play on words (which appears elsewhere), the

---

[112] Williams, 'Way of Exchange', 149.
[113] Lecture, 'Coinherence' [sic], Wade RH Notebooks, 19: 3545.
[114] Williams, 'Way of Exchange', 152.   [115] Williams, 'Way of Exchange', 151.

web becomes 'in-coherent' through sin and is restored to a new 'co-inherence' of glory.[116]

It is hardly surprising that when the term 'co-inherence' first appears in print in *The Descent of the Dove*, where it is most prominent in all Williams' work, nearly all his uses of the term simply underline the themes of exchange, substitution, and community that he had been developing without the help of the word. The largest group of usages refer to the co-inherence of believers in the church, including several about 'co-inhering in love'.[117] Then come references to the co-inherence of human persons in Christ, either directly or through the Eucharist, and correspondingly the co-inherence of the eternal Christ in the sensuality of human flesh.[118] This is the note struck by the very first printed use of the word by Williams, apart from the dedication of the book to 'The Companions of the Co-inherence'; after a number of scriptural texts about reconciliation 'in' Christ, Williams comments that 'In such words there was defined the new state of being, a state of redemption, of co-inherence, made actual by that divine substitution, 'He in us and we in him.'[119] In frequency after the co-inherence of the church and co-inherence in Christ, there are a number of references to the natural co-inherence of humanity,[120] either in God's original intention or in a present sinful state. Three references relating co-inherence to the triunity of God, and three more simply to 'God', I will return to in a moment. A few instances refer to the co-inherence of time and eternity,[121] the co-inherence of freedom and necessity,[122] the co-inherence of belief and unbelief,[123] and the co-inherence of communism.[124] The book is subtitled 'the history of the Holy Spirit in the Church', but it could equally be called 'the history of co-inherence in the Church', ending with a couple of summary pages about co-inherence in a whole range of relations, and presenting a kind of apology or manifesto for the Order or Company to whose members the book is dedicated.

There continue to be many references to 'exchange' and 'substitution', as well as to the 'web' of human life (as in 'the vibrant web of universal and supernatural co-inherence'),[125] and the themes of exchange and interchange appear in a number of quotations that also appear abundantly elsewhere in Williams' writings. Among them are the following epigrams: 'I live, and yet not I, Christ liveth in me' (St Paul),[126] 'your life and death are with your neighbour' (St Anthony, as

---

[116] Williams, *Forgiveness of Sins*, 22, 26, 30–2.

[117] Williams, *Descent of the Dove*, 87, 91, 100, 103, 106, 117, 120, 124, 163, 166, 174, 177, 202, 205, 217, 218, 231, 235.

[118] Williams, *Descent of the Dove*, 9–10, 79, 103, 115, 117, 131, 162, 168, 192, 224, 225, 234–5.

[119] Williams, *Descent of the Dove*, 9–10.

[120] Williams, *Descent of the Dove*, 69, 132, 142, 162, 196, 225, 234.

[121] Williams, *Descent of the Dove*, 84, 103.   [122] Williams, *Descent of the Dove*, 174.

[123] Williams, *Descent of the Dove*, 192.   [124] Williams, *Descent of the Dove*, 229, 231, 235.

[125] Williams, *Descent of the Dove*, 87.   [126] Williams, *Descent of the Dove*, 62.

cited by Athanasius),[127] 'another will be in me who will suffer for me as I will for him', or simply 'another is in me' (the martyr St Felicitas),[128] 'This is also is thou; neither is this thou' (source unknown),[129] 'my eros is crucified' (St Ignatius),[130] 'they in Me and I in them' (Jesus in the Fourth Gospel),[131] *figlia del tuo Figlio* ('the daughter of your son'—Dante),[132] and 'you must become a double man' (an unknown monk).[133] Several of these quotations reappear in the promulgation that Williams wrote for the Companions of the Co-inherence. Apparently missing from *The Descent of the Dove* is the Pauline maxim often cited by Williams, 'Bear ye one another's burdens', but the passage about 'the double man' begins 'It is right for a man to take up the burden for them who are near to him.'

In these ways, *The Descent of the Dove* continues the earlier twofold trajectory of co-inherence: 'in Christ' and 'in love'. Typical is Williams' comment about the establishment of Christianity in the West, that vernacular languages were needed to declare that 'Love could love, that love could be loved, that our Yearning was crucified, that Another co-inhered in us and us in each other.'[134] In all, there are about sixty instances of the word 'co-inherence' in *The Descent of the Dove*, but it is remarkable that of these only three relate co-inherence to the mutual relations of the persons of the Trinity, respectively dealing with the theology of Origen, of Nicaea, and of baptism.[135] There are three other incidental references to 'the co-inherent God',[136] and one other passing reference to Trinity (without co-inherence) outside the three noted.[137] This, I suggest, is remarkable, both because of the centrality of the doctrine of the Trinity within the history of ideas of the Christian Church, and because the chapter on co-inherence in Prestige's book—which Williams considers the 'clearest' exposition of the term—is actually all about the development of the term within trinitarian the-ology. I mean the mutual indwelling of the three Persons of the Trinity in each other—Father, Son, and Spirit in *perichoresis*, interweaving and interpenetrating in one divine essence. Admittedly, the word *perichoresis*, translated by Prestige as 'co-inherence', does not appear as a concept for Trinity until the eighth century—though Prestige dates it to the seventh (with the fictional pseudo-Cyril). This does not prevent Williams applying the English word 'co-inherence', in his own account of their thought, to Origen and the Nicene Fathers, but there—apart from the concluding 'Postscript'—Williams stops. Nothing is said about the great

---

[127] Williams, *Descent of the Dove*, 46, 57.

[128] Williams, *Descent of the Dove*, 28, 37, 46, 49, 52, 161.

[129] Williams, *Descent of the Dove*, viii; Williams confesses he first thought it came from Augustine, but now does not know its source.

[130] Williams, *Descent of the Dove*, 46, 49, 62, 76, 80, 89, 110, 115, 173.

[131] Williams, *Descent of the Dove*; cf. Dante's phrase: 'in-meing', 138.

[132] Williams, *Descent of the Dove*, 103, 138.   [133] Williams, *Descent of the Dove*, 55, 192–5.

[134] Williams, *Descent of the Dove*, 79.   [135] Williams, *Descent of the Dove*, 39–40, 52, 234.

[136] Williams, *Descent of the Dove*, 87, 92, 199.   [137] Williams, *Descent of the Dove*, 113.

expositions of trinitarian *perichoresis* in the theology of the medieval theologians and the Reformers, let alone in Eastern Orthodox theology.

The second of Williams' three references to co-inherence in the Trinity seems indicative of what is going on in his thought. Commenting on the Council of Nicaea, Williams writes:[138]

> Was there, in the most Secret, in the only Adored—was there that which can be described only by such infelicitous mortal words as an equal relation, an equal goodwill, an equal love? Was this in its very essence? Was the Son co-eternal with the Father? If there had been no creation, would Love have practised love? And would Love have had an adequate object to love? Nicaea answered yes. It confirmed, beyond all creation, in the incomprehensible Alone, the cry of Felicitas: 'Another is in Me.' The Godhead itself was in Co-inherence.

'The Godhead *itself* was in Co-inherence.' This phrasing implies that the co-inherence already perceived in the church and in Christology was now being affirmed in the Godhead—perhaps being found there for the first time. There is an air of discovery here not just for the early theologians at Nicaea but for Williams himself. It is as if an existing doctrine of exchange and substitution ('Another is in me') is now being *extended* into a trinitarian vision. This is the answer to the question as to what Williams gains from the addition of the term 'co-inherence'; he seems to have had no notion of 'exchange' or interchange within the persons of the divine Trinity before he found the word.

We can then distinguish between a 'weaker' and 'stronger' way that 'co-inherence' takes Williams beyond 'exchange' and 'substitution'. In a weaker sense, co-inherence intensifies the meaning of the two former terms, making them more universal, summing up their content in an epigram, and neatly making a connection between them and the theology of romantic love. In a stronger sense, 'co-inherence' has a trinitarian context in view. When Williams uses it, he has the Trinity in mind, even if only in the background. And yet the question remains as to how *deeply* exchange is being rooted in the Trinity, and what *difference* a vision of a co-inherent Trinity makes to the doctrine of exchange in Christ and in human life, which has already been formulated as being 'in love' and 'in Love'.

Williams' new discovery is essentially that there is an analogy between exchange and substitution in human relations on the one hand, and the eternal relations of love between Persons of the Trinity on the other. We have already seen that when Williams defines 'co-inherence' in *The Figure of Beatrice*, making reference to Prestige's exposition, he affirms an 'analogy' between co-inherence in human life and the Trinity; he notes an 'analogical co-inherence' and a 'likeness'

---

[138] Williams, *Descent of the Dove*, 52.

of human life to the 'manner by which [the triune God] exists'.[139] He goes on to write that 'it is with the *image* of the co-inherent Godhead which is in mankind that we have to deal' (my italics). Not much is made of this discovery in *The Descent of the Dove*, which retains an essentially Christological trajectory, and later Williams is to make more of the analogy. However, as a theologian, I want to suggest what *would* make a substantial difference to the idea of exchange and substitution in human life: we need to exceed a mere analogy, a sublime likeness, between co-inherence in the Trinity and in human life. I mean, with much Protestant and Catholic trinitarian theology of the last forty years,[140] the step of affirming a participation of human relationships *within* the interweaving relations of the Trinity, and an indwelling of those divine relations within human community—what we might call a co-inherence of human co-inherence and trinitarian co-inherence. Williams stops short of any explicit statement of this kind of co-inherence, though we shall see that his theology does hold the promise of it.

There seems to be an irony here: Williams has asserted from the beginning of his work (against all the instincts of C. S. Lewis) that there is more than an analogy between divine love and human passion. The point of the theology of romantic love is that the two are fused, identified with each other, although divine love is of course always excessive and cannot be exhausted by human love. But when it comes to the co-inherence of love in the Trinity and in human relations, he urges ostensibly an analogy and not an identity. In accord with this approach, Williams draws a distinction in the fifth article of his original promulgation of the Order of the Co-inherence (1939) between a 'contemplation' of the 'Co-inherence of the Holy and Blessed Trinity' on the one hand, and the 'active side' of practising many kinds of exchanges on the other. Daily exchanges and substitutions in human community do not apparently participate in God's co-inherent relations.

In 'The Way of Exchange' (1941), there is an appeal to a co-inherent Trinity by analogy, which is more definite and thought out than in *The Descent of the Dove* (1939):

> Our Lord promised to the members of His Church a particular and intense union with each other through Himself. He defined that union as being of the same nature as that which He had with His Father. The later definitions of the inspired Church went further; they declared not merely that the Father and the Son existed co-equally but that they existed co-inherently—that is, that the Son existed *in* the Father and that the Father existed *in* the Son. The exact meaning

---

[139] Williams, *Figure of Beatrice*, 92.
[140] Examples are: Balthasar, *Theo-Drama*, II: 262–84; Jüngel, *God's Being is in Becoming*, 37–53; Moltmann, *Trinity*, 108–14; Johnson, *She Who Is*, 227–33; Fiddes, *Participating in God*, 34–56. See also Chapter 15.

of the preposition [in] there may be obscure. But no other word could satisfy the intellect of the Church. The same preposition was used to define our Lord's relations with his Church: 'we in him and he in us.'[141]

The analogy here (a union 'of the same nature') is not only between the Trinity and relations in the church, but between the Trinity and the relations of *Christ* with the church ('a particular and intense union with each other *through* Himself'). Here Williams appeals to the words of Jesus in John 17, 'we in him and he in us', but he fails to get beyond analogy to the mutual indwelling in the life of God that the Johannine Christ actually promises to his disciples in this passage. However, as we saw with the paradoxical phrase *figlia del tuo figlio*, the relation of Christ to the church exceeds a mere *analogy* with the relations between the members of the church: it is a matter of 'a particular and intense union'. Here we may find one of the notes in Williams' work in which we can catch overtones of a real participation in the co-inherence of the Trinity. And there are still more signs of promise to which we need to attend, as the next chapter will show.

---

[141] Williams, 'Way of Exchange', 149.

5

Charles Williams and the Promise
of Co-inherence

At the very beginning of his friendship with Charles Williams, C. S. Lewis offered the image of a common country through which they were journeying, with distinct 'provinces' for their particular concerns.[1] In his *Region of the Summer Stars*, Williams names one such province that intrigues him, and draws him to it by its mystery. It is 'the land of the Trinity', an area in his spiritual geography of Byzantium. It is a land full of promise, and not least because the image holds the potential for a further development of co-inherence than he actually seems to achieve in his work after the discovery of co-inherence in 1939. I suggested in Chapter 4 that in its stronger sense, co-inherence always has a trinitarian context, but that Williams falters in developing a theology of human *dwelling* in the co-inherent Trinity. There is much in his work that promises this kind of co-inherence, and on the way to the 'land of the Trinity' we should explore the potential within his long-standing theology of Romantic Love.

5.1 Romantic Love and Participation in God

The content of the 'paradoxical' phrase from Dante,[2] on which Williams seizes, from 1939, as expressive of co-inherence—*figlia del tuo figlio*—was already contained in his earlier love-theology. There, of course, it was without the word 'co-inherence'. In its earliest form, Williams' love-theology sets out two 'principles': that love is to be identified with Jesus Christ, and that the progress of love in marriage can be identified with the various stages of Christ's life.[3] Thus, the conception and birth of Christ through the Virgin Mary has its actualization in the appearance of the human beloved to the lover as 'Mother of Love' and so 'Mother of Divine Grace' and 'Mother of our Saviour'. Through her, love is born in the one who loves her and 'the Divine Presence that accompanies her [...] is born of her'. Yet, Williams adds, it is this Presence, who is 'helpless as a child in her power', who also 'created her'. Though Williams does not at this stage use the Dantean line, she is thus 'daughter of her son' (*figlia del tuo figlio*). She is both

---

[1] See Chapter 1, section 'A shared journey through romantic territory'.
[2] Williams, *Descent of the Dove*, 138.   [3] Williams, *Outlines*, 14.

Charles Williams and C.S. Lewis: Friends in Co-inherence. Paul S. Fiddes, Oxford University Press. © Paul S. Fiddes 2021.
DOI: 10.1093/oso/9780192845467.003.0005

'Theotokos, Mother of God',[4] and also the offspring of God. Correspondingly, as the lover is brought to the consciousness of love, 'conversion takes place, or the New Birth, a nativity of the lover as well as love'. Not only is *love* born in the relationship, but the *lover* is born from love. If, as Williams does later, we apply these roles either to the man or the woman, then both can be 'daughter of their son'—that is, giving birth to love and being born of love, that Love being Christ. This duality of birthing and being born is carried through into Williams' later work, though he appears to drop the other parallels with the life of Christ. In *He Came Down from Heaven*, Beatrice and any beloved person are the 'Mother of Love',[5] while lovers also experience a new birth, or a 'renovation'.[6]

Next to the truth of *figlia del tuo figlio* we can set another central idea of Williams' love-theology. In the 'Beatrician moment', the lover sees the beloved in the glory that she (or he) has in heaven in an unfallen state. She is seen in her own created glory, but from his earliest work Williams wants to identify this glory with the uncreated Light—not simply the same, but inseparable and so indistinguishable by the human reason. If Christ who is Love is born in the human soul, then this union with Christ can be extended back from his incarnate life to his eternal life. According to *Outlines of Romantic Theology*, in the new state of consciousness love brings, the lover sees the human beloved as 'the perfection of living things':

> She appears to him, as it were, archetypal, the alpha and omega of creation; without father or mother, without human ties of any sort, for she is before humanity, the first-created of God [...] she recovers her glory, which is the glory that Love had with the Father before the world was.[7]

In this passage, Williams moves from the beloved as 'first-created' (i.e. a creature) to having the glory of the first-born (Christ)—'the glory that Love had with the Father' before creation. The title 'alpha and omega' is traditionally applied to Christ, and here is transferred to the archetypal creature. So the beloved can be identified not only with the incarnate Christ, but with the Christ who is the eternal image of the Father. That same Christic glory is seen in the lover's smile: Williams writes here that 'love is bestowed by her smile; she is its source and its mother', and much later he quotes Dante as seeing 'the sacred smile [of Beatrice], and how deep and clear it made the sacred countenance'.[8] What Dante is doing, he states, 'is to identify the power which reposed in Beatrice with the nature of our Lord', and he is 'Almighty Love'.[9] Williams comments on the appearance of Beatrice in Paradise:

---

[4] Williams, *Outlines*, 17.   [5] Williams, *He Came Down*, 97, 101, 113.
[6] Williams, *He Came Down*, 120.   [7] Williams, *Outlines*, 16–17.
[8] Williams, *Figure of Beatrice*, 215.   [9] Williams, *Religion and Love*, 11.

'[Dante] turns, he gazes. Her love and Love itself ray out on him—rather, Love rays on Beatrice and thence on him, with derived aspect; this is the 'isplendor'. He gazes, she smiles... "Turn and listen, not only in my eyes is Paradise".'[10]

She commands us: 'Open your eyes, see what I am. You have seen things by which you are able to endure my smile' (23.46–8).[11] She and Christ look into each other's eyes, and, as Williams puts it in his *Religion and Love in Dante*, 'she is seen mirroring the Incarnate Splendour, as in Florence its light had been about her'.[12] But the splendour is not confined to the glory of the incarnation. Williams relates the moment when Dante sees Christ as 'the shining Substance', and comments that as the 'Bearer of [this] Substance' Beatrice is 'the primal motion in substance, the motion being an exchange in unity–"figlia del tuo figlio"'.[13] Whatever Dante means by 'substance' (*la lucente sustanzia*), Williams seems to have in mind the 'one substance' of the triune Godhead, or the credal affirmation of Christ as being 'one in substance' with the Father,[14] since he writes:

> He had seen Christ flashing in the cross of courage [i.e. in the incarnation]; he now sees him as 'substance'. They have come to the heaven where that substance begins to appear in itself, and all the redeemed sustained and lit by it [...] It is 'Substance' as well as 'Christ' which Dante is seeing, and Substance dominating in everything.[15]

In accord with this sense that Beatrice (and every beloved) is 'lit' by the eternal Substance of God, in *He Came Down From Heaven*, Williams describes the sight of Beatrice as arousing a sense of intense significance, an awareness that 'an explanation of the whole universe is being offered',[16] a conviction that she is 'the perfect centre and norm of humanity',[17] and that from her radiates 'that portion of the divine light which, in the eternal creation of her in heaven, possesses her'.[18] Every person who is loved bids us, like Beatrice, 'See who I am.' So the poetry communicates 'the "in-Godding" of the self, the taking of the self into God'.[19]

As with William's developed ideas of exchange and substitution, the focus of this theology of love is Christological. But if we combine Williams' two insights that the lover is both bearer and born of a love that is Christ, and that the lover shares in the eternal glory of Christ, which he has in one 'substance' with the

---

[10] Williams, *Figure of Beatrice*, 209. *Isplendor* (*Paradiso* 31.139) means 'splendour'.
[11] Williams, *Figure of Beatrice*, 215.   [12] Williams, *Religion and Love*, 30.
[13] Williams, *Figure of Beatrice*, 216, 231.
[14] Creed of Nicaea-Constantinople: Christ is *homoousios to patri*, or *consubstantialis patri*.
[15] Williams, *Figure of Beatrice*, 214.   [16] Williams, *He Came Down*, 92.
[17] Williams, *He Came Down*, 93.   [18] Williams, *He Came Down*, 93.
[19] Williams, *Religion and Love*, 32–3.

Father and in the fellowship of the Holy Spirit, we are surely brought to the idea that the one who loves participates in eternal relations within the Trinity. As born of love, we may say that we can share in an eternal movement of love that is like a son being begotten by a father. This has been an insight of Christian mystics such as the fourteenth-century Jan van Ruusbroec (quoted by Williams in his *New Christian Year*),[20] who writes that created beings share in 'an eternal going-out, this eternal life which we have and are within God', as part of 'an eternal out-flowing through the birth of the Son into an otherness with distinction'.[21] Correspondingly, as bearer or mother of love, we share in an eternal movement that is like a father begetting a son, participating in a movement of creativity, a role that has been given traditionally to the *Theotokos* as mother of the incarnate Christ who is both human and divine.

Such a vision of participating in the personal relations of the triune God (without being confused with God) is not a direction that Williams seems to have taken explicitly, despite his enigmatic comment that Beatrice is 'the primal motion in substance'.[22] He does not seem to understand the general 'in-Godding' as being specifically 'in the Trinity'. Being 'in love' does not mean being in the love of the Trinity, but 'in Christ' who is Love itself. But he does offer a useful corrective if we are inclined to think of this participation in an individualistic way. He draws attention to the eagle in Paradise, which is formed of a multitude of sacred spirits, whom Dante calls 'burning lights of the Holy Spirit'. Observing that Dante describes them as speaking in one voice—'I am exalted in this glory'— Williams comments that the eagle *thinks* 'we', but *says* 'I', so that 'the [singular] pronoun is an intense image of the way of life which this affirming justice involves'. It is not an image of reduction to an individual, but rather of 'co-inherent justice': 'it does not talk about this co-inherence, but only shows it'.[23] Williams also notes that co-inherence is here associated with the Third Person of the Trinity; this scene might, he curiously comments, 'encourage those who would associate the whole idea of the co-inherence with the Third Person'. It is doubtful whether he counts himself among 'those', since his emphasis elsewhere is on

---

[20] Williams, *New Christian Year*, 110. The quotation does not reflect the doctrine to which I refer, but appropriately it does affirm that 'Christ was common to all in love'. No reference given, but it is from Ruusbroec, *Spiritual Espousals*, 86.b1097–1108.

[21] Ruusbroec, *Spiritual Espousals*, 116–17.c100–60; cf. 113.b2213–16.

[22] The 'first motion' presumably refers to the *primum mobile*, or 'first mover' in the Aristotelian-Ptolemaic universe, the sphere that moves all other physical objects and beings. If Beatrice is being identified with the *primum mobile*, then 'in substance' either means (a) being enclosed within the mind of God, or the Empyrean (in Christian terms, the 'one substance' of God), where it/she is moved by divine love; or (b) 'first mover among physical substances'. In the first case, Beatrice is being conceived as 'in God', but one might expect Williams to use an upper case initial for Substance. The final sonnet of Dante's *Vita Nuova* appears to associate Beatrice with the love that *moves the primum mobile*, which Williams quotes in *Figure of Beatrice*, 43. See further on the *primum mobile* in Chapter 13, section 1.

[23] Williams, *Figure of Beatrice*, 209–10.

co-inherence in Christ. In his last sermon, prepared but never delivered, he describes Pentecost as the moment when human beings were 'intimately' united with their own humanity in Christ.[24] But we shall see that in two later plays he does also portray co-inherence in the Spirit, or in the 'flames' (energies) of the Spirit.

This is not the only ambiguity we find in Williams about co-inherence. In places he appears to hold apart a 'natural' or 'material' co-inherence received in creation, from a 'supernatural' co-inherence received in faith and baptism.[25] But these spheres of co-inherence must interact, since he places Christ as the centre of both of them, Christ being active in creation as well as redemption. Basic to his theology of romantic love is the insistence that Christ is born in the soul of everyone who truly loves, and that the beloved is seen in a light that is infused with the Christ-light 'that lightens everyone who comes into the world'.[26] This, he has been affirming since 1924, is the ordinary and yet extraordinary experience of *everyone* who falls in love.[27] It is not just a literary convention of love poetry, but it really happens; any young man (like Dante) can meet his Beatrice; any young woman (like Eve) can meet her Adam. His Christology thus unites the spheres of the 'natural' and the 'supernatural', and this might well prompt us to consider whether it is helpful to distinguish between two spheres of reality at all.[28] As early as his *Outlines of Romantic Theology*, Williams himself queried the distinction; quoting Patmore that, with regard to love, it was 'First the natural, afterwards the supernatural', he adds that the question that remains to be decided by the church is 'whether, in the end, even that division can be, save for the purposes of morality, maintained'.[29]

Williams, however (like Lewis), persists with the dualism, though it gets him into inconsistencies. Some attempt to reconcile the ambiguity is to be found in *Forgiveness of Sins*, where he affirms that humanity was created in a state of 'intense' co-inherence in 'the body' of Christ, and that this body was 'dissolved as far as it could be' by the primal sin, but that the 'great co-inherent web of humanity' could not actually break 'unless its maker consented that it should'. What 'as far as it could be' is left open, though Williams affirms that the Maker 'still loved it'.[30] Thus, Williams formulates the concern of the Order [subsequently, 'Company'] of the Co-inherence somewhat equivocally to be (article 3): 'the practice of the apprehension of the Co-inherence both as a natural and as a supernatural principle. As it was said: *Let us make man in Our image.*'

---

[24] Wade RH Papers 1–24, File b (loose pages intended for notebook, Vol. 22).
[25] Williams, *Descent of the Dove*, 87, 234.   [26] Williams, *He Came Down*, 93.
[27] Williams, *Outlines*, 15–16, 50.   [28] See Chapter 15, section 5.
[29] Williams, *Outlines*, 65; the quotation is from Patmore, 'Aurea Dicta' XXIV, *The Rod, the Root and the Flower*, 9.
[30] Williams, *Forgiveness of Sins*, 22–3, 26–7.

5.2 The Land of the Trinity

There is, I am suggesting, a potential within the theology of romantic love for what could be a deeper trinitarian dimension to co-inherence—that is, a sharing of human beings in the loving relations between the God the Father, the Son, and the Spirit through the glory of Christ that is manifest in them. There is, however, no obvious sign of such a theology in the place where Williams comes closest to formulating a place for Trinity in co-inherence. The Arthurian poem, 'The Founding of the Company' (in *The Region of the Summer Stars*, 1944), describing the poet Taliessin's establishing and arranging of his 'household', is related in some way to an earlier poem describing the creation of Williams' Order of the Co-inherence, and is perhaps based on it.[31] Whereas 'Exchange' was placed after 'Substitution' in the order of thought articulated in the sequence of chapters of *He Came Down From Heaven* (1938), in the poem published in 1944, the inclusion of the term 'co-inherence' has led to a progress of 'stages', 'stations', or 'modes' in the Company in the order: first exchange, second substitution, and finally co-inherence.

The poem describes these three as modes of 'largesse',[32] or generous self-giving, a term that Williams had previously discussed in a review article in 1941, and associated with the Trinity. The word, he had claimed, was 'used originally of the Black Prince, who was said also to have a peculiar devotion to the Holy and Undivided Trinity'. Indeed, he goes on: 'The doctrine of the Trinity is a doctrine of largesse; the doctrine of Atonement is a doctrine of largesse; the doctrine of church is a doctrine of largesse[.]'[33] The 'cult' of Taliessin's Company was thus 'the Trinity and the Flesh-taking' (the Incarnation). The structure of three stages of largesse appears to constitute three degrees of membership in the Company, probably an echo of the three levels of spiritual achievement within the Order of the Rosy Cross through which Williams progressed,[34] though we have no evidence of such grades of enlightenment within his own Order of the Co-inherence. Any ranking of members seems to have been in Williams' own mind, although C. S. Lewis neglects some significant differences when he judges that the degrees are 'separable only by an abstraction'.[35] At the first station,

> were those who lived by a frankness of honourable exchange,
> labour in the kingdom, devotion in the Church, the need

---

[31] See Chapter 2, section 5.   [32] Williams, *Region*, 37.

[33] Williams, 'Doctrine of Largesse', in Williams, *Image*, 141.

[34] Roukema, 'Veil that Reveals', 42–4, points out that there were four orders, but that Waite had collapsed the third and fourth into one, new 'inner order'. King, *Pattern*, 155, indicates a parallel with three levels of achievement of the Sephirotic Tree.

[35] Lewis, 'Williams and the Arthuriad', 142. This is not quite what Williams means by 'no wisdom separate but for convenience of naming' (*Region*, 37); while the wisdom was unified in a 'common union', there were 'parts' distinguishable by the 'intellect' within it.

each had of other; this was the measurement and motion
of process—the seed of all civil polity[.]

All societies, whether 'Esquimaux or Hottentots', depend on an exchange of 'taking and giving,' so we may presume that this mode of largesse is to be found widely outside the Company, as well as being a 'living of largesse' within it. The second mode of the Company:

> ...exchanged the proper self
> and wherever need was drew breath daily
> in another's place, according to the grace of the Spirit,
> 'dying each other's life, living each other's death'.
> Terrible and lovely is the general substitution of souls[.][36]

The incarnation of Christ ('the Flesh-taking') established this 'decree of substitution' in creation generally ('in its first creation'), but it reached a new level when the incarnate One 'deigned to be dead in the stead of each man'. The Company is a community where the decree is never forgotten, and where it is practised deliberately and regularly: 'they claimed and were claimed at once'. Few, however, enter on the third station:

> ...where the full salvation of all souls
> is seen, and their co-inhering, as when the Trinity
> first made man in Their image, and now restored
> by the one adored substitution; there men
> were known, each alone, and none alone,
> bearing and borne, as the Flesh-taking sufficed
> the God-bearer to make her a sharer in Itself.[37]

This third mode concerns human fellowship ('their co-inhering') as an analogy or image of the Trinity, 'each alone and none alone', but we notice that no actual *dwelling* in the Trinity is portrayed. There is an echo of *figlia del tuo figlio*, as the 'God-bearer' is both 'bearing and borne (born)', and this is a state not confined to the Virgin Mary, though exemplified by her. 'Men'—or people—whose lives are 'restored' through the central substitution in the death of Christ become 'sharers' along with Mary in the Christ who takes flesh. They are not said to be sharers in the relations of the *Trinity*. It is a little puzzling, however, that co-inherence appears to be limited to 'Few—and that hardly', since the lines also seem to echo the familiar theme that *all* those who truly love ('bearing and borne') are

---

[36] Williams, *Region*, 38.   [37] Williams, *Region*, 39.

theotokos. C. S. Lewis aptly comments that 'The third and highest degree is harder to understand.'[38]

The clue, I suggest, lies in the fifth article of the Order of the Co-Inherence, that members of the Order are devoted to the 'contemplation' of 'the Co-inherence of the Holy and Blessed Trinity, of the Two Natures in the Single Person, of the Mother and Son, of the communicated Eucharist, and of the whole Catholic Church'. So people generally participate in the 'web' of co-inherence established by creation through Christ and his incarnation, and will experience it intensely in moments of romantic love; but the 'few' make trinitarian co-inherence an object of contemplation. Lewis cannot be interpreting Williams correctly when he suggests that only the few 'experience' it.[39] This distinction corresponds to what I have earlier called a 'weaker' and 'stronger' meaning of co-inherence. In its weaker sense, co-inherence is an intensification of exchange, substitution, and romantic love. In its stronger sense, there is a deliberate placing of co-inherence in the context of a triune God. Williams' failure, however, to carry through his theology into a mutual *indwelling* of God and humanity in the relations of the Trinity is exemplified in this very article of the Order when 'contemplation' of the Trinity is distinguished from 'methods of exchange', which are placed on the 'active side' and accompanied by the words 'Bear ye one another's burdens.' This misses, I suggest, the potential for making a whole realm of *practices* in the Christian life an actual participation in the co-inherence of the Trinity.

In 1943, at about the time when Williams was completing the compilation of *The Region of the Summer Stars*, he proposed a revision of the articles of the Order,[40] now called 'Company', which unfortunately seems to drive contemplation and activity even further apart. The 1939 version of the fifth article reads:

> It recommends therefore the study, on the contemplative side of the Co-inherence of the Holy and Blessed Trinity, of the Two Natures in the Single Person, of the Mother and Son, of the communicated Eucharist, of the whole Catholic Church. As it was said: *figlia del tuo figlio.* And on the active side, of methods of exchange, in the State, in all forms of love, and in all natural things, such as child-birth. As it was said: *Bear ye one another's burdens.*

The 1943 revision reads:

> It intends the study, on the contemplative side, of the Co-inherence of the Holy and Blessed Trinity, of the Union of the Two Natures in one Person, of the

---

[38] Lewis, 'Williams and the Arthuriad', 142.   [39] Lewis, 'Williams and the Arthuriad', 143.
[40] Wade CW/MS-78 carries the note by Raymond Hunt: 'Revised Draft of the Promulgation. Composition 19 September 1943. Received with Margaret Douglas' Letter of 22 September 1943. Transcribed into Lectures Vol. 21 pp. 4197–8.'

relation of the God-bearer and the Flesh-taker, of the exchange of offerings in the Eucharist, and of the whole Catholic Church; on the intellectual, of the co-inherence of opposite ideas in each other; on the active, of methods of exchange and substitution in all the many forms of love and in all operations of the State. As it was said: *Figlia del tuo figlio*; and again: *Bear ye one another's burdens.*[41]

In the 1939 version, the words *figlia del tuo figlio* ('daughter of your son'), which can have an ambiguous applicability both to Mary and to all lovers who bear love and are born from love, has a significant placing; it stands at the boundary between contemplation of the Trinity and 'methods of exchange, in all forms of love, and in all natural things, such as child-birth'. Its location implies application in both contemplative and active areas. However, in the revision dated 19 September 1943, the phrase *figlia del tuo figlio* is placed at the end of the article, reaffirming its general relevance to all life but not so clearly yoking together the active and contemplative spheres. The reference to 'Mother and Son' in the area of contemplation, which could be read generally as the experience of being a child of love (*figlia del tuo figlio*), so making a bridge across to the active side of 'all forms of love', has been replaced by 'the relation of the God-bearer and the Flesh-taker' (simply Mary and Christ). Childbirth, which can be an everyday analogy of the spiritual 'mother and son' relationship of love, is removed from the 'active' section altogether. Moreover, the 'contemplative' and the 'active' are separated even further by a new, third area in between—an 'intellectual' co-inherence. We have the impression that there is something here about co-inherence that is not settled in Williams' mind.

We should also notice the deepening of the connection between the articles of the promulgation and the imaginative 'Company' of Taliessin in Williams' poem, 'The Founding of the Company'. The Order is formally renamed as The Company of the Co-inherence, and the word 'Order' is replaced by 'Company' throughout (although there is evidence that this change may have been made informally earlier).[42] There is also a note attached to the manuscript of the 1943 revision, in Williams' hand, identifying his own 'Company' with that of Taliessin, whose household was situated in 'Caerleon':

Given, as it were from Caerleon, at the midnight preceding the twentieth of September, at the midnight preceding the Fructiferous Incarnation 1943, by

---

[41] The 1943 revision, both in Williams' own hand and in a typescript version, is in Bod. MS 16125/5. 137/1, Folder 1, together with the 1939 version. The copy in Wade CW MS-78 is typescript (see previous note). A further substantial revision in the 1943 version is article 2, where there is a less formal approach: the previous gathering of the Order by a 'formal act' is replaced by 'a private act of union with the other Companions and with all men', and the Company now 'leaves to Holy Luck communication between its members and any enlargement of the Companionship'. After Christ 'all luck is good', *Death of Good Fortune*, in *Collected Plays*, 179; cf. *He Came Down*, 85, 122; Williams, *Witchcraft*, 90.

[42] See Chapter 4, section 2, n.45.

the permission of Almighty God, at the will of the Companions, and in the hand of Taliessin.[43]

Whether or not Williams intends the effect I have analysed, the revision of the promulgation makes it even less likely that Williams thought naturally and easily of human relations ('on the active side') as participating in the co-inherence of 'the Holy and Blessed Trinity'. Yet Williams does in fact have a potentially effective metaphor to hand for indwelling the Trinity, since his poem continues by referring to an area in the Empire as 'the *land* of the Trinity, the land of the perichoresis'.[44] So we reach the image from which I launched my own chapter here: a land is a place in which one can dwell. Once, from the high deck of a ship, Taliessin caught a glimpse of this country, as an island where light 'thrice charged' glances from one mass of granite to another, 'each in turn the Holder and the held'. This last phrase echoes 'the bearer and the borne', and the viewer's eyes 'altered and faltered' as they followed the shifting glory. The very landscape thus evokes the interweaving relations of the Trinity, and the phrase 'the land of the Trinity' recurs a number of other times in the poems (eight times altogether), associated both with 'largesse' and with co-inherence.[45]

The land is also named as Sarras,[46] and in the 1938 *Taliessin Through Logres*, this is the place where Galahad achieves the Grail; three characters 'dwell', if only temporarily, in Sarras, and in Malory it is much more densely inhabited with a very different character.[47] However, while there are a number of references to 'exchange',[48] as well as 'substitution',[49] in these earlier poems, neither co-inherence nor Trinity appear there. In *The Region of the Summer Stars* the symbol of 'Sarras' appears to work differently. As the 'land of the Trinity', or 'the world of the three-in-one',[50] it is the place where the Holy Ghost 'works creation and sanctification of flesh and blood',[51] and where one can know 'the deep impassable Trinity [...] uttering unsearchable bliss'.[52] The metaphor of 'dwelling' is not, however, applied to Sarras or the land of the Trinity in this 1944 volume. The mutual confession of the 'Company' is said to be 'of the indwelling, of the mansion and session of each in each', but this applies in context to the indwelling of the persons of the Trinity in each other ('its cult was the Trinity'), actually quoting 'mansion and session' from Prestige's *God in Patristic Thought*.[53] Human dwelling in the land is not raised as a possibility since the country is portrayed in terms of

---

[43] Bod. MS. 16125/5, folder 1.   [44] Williams, *Region*, 39.

[45] In addition to p. 39, see also instances on pp. 6, 14, 17, 45, 55, 58, 60.

[46] Williams, 'Calling of Taliessin', *Region*, 14.

[47] Malory, 'The Quest of the Holy Grail', *Works*, 605–6.   [48] Williams, *Taliessin*, 55, 69, 85.

[49] Williams, *Taliessin*, 47, 87, 89.   [50] Williams, 'Calling of Taliessin', *Region*, 8.

[51] Williams, 'The Queen's Servant', *Region*, 45.

[52] Williams, 'The Prayers of the Pope', *Region*, 60.

[53] Williams, 'The Founding of the Company', *Region*, 37; Prestige, *God*, 299, where Prestige is quoting from John of Damascus.

the negative rather than the positive way, as an area that is contracted to a point, 'deep beyond or deep within Logres', beyond body and spirit, 'inturned to its disappearing':

> The entire point of the thrice co-inherent Trinity
> where every crown and every choir is vanished,
> and all sight and hearing is nothing else.[54]

The co-inherence of human creatures is thus not in the Trinity, but (as we read in another poem) the 'bodies and souls of the dead' are 'co-inherent all in Adam and in Christ'.[55] Williams' apparent reluctance to consider 'dwelling' in the land of the Trinity may well be prompted by the 'diagram' of his poetic vision that he finds in the ancient Kabbalistic symbol of the Sephirotic Tree, according to which the mystic who sees the imageless world of the 'supernals' through a 'portal' always returns to the world of images.[56] This context must await exploration later.[57] We should note here, however, that the use of the technical word *perichoresis* ('land of the perichoresis') does not issue from hermetic sources, but is likely to have come simply from Williams's reading of G. L. Prestige's account of the development of trinitarian theology,[58] another confirmation of his debt to it.

Of the three clear references to a co-inherence of divine persons in the Trinity in *The Descent of the Dove*,[59] the third *does* hint at a co-inherence of human persons in the triune God, beyond a dwelling in the person of Christ alone. This comes in the 'Postscript' in which Williams summarizes a range of co-inherent relationships in human life, and makes a case for the establishing of the Order of the Co-inherence. Williams writes about the 'about-to-be-born' child, declaring that it 'already co-inheres in an ancestral and contemporary guilt', and so:

> It has been the habit of the church to baptize it, as soon as it has emerged, by the formula of the Trinity-in-Unity. As it passes from the most material co-inherence it is received into the supernatural [co-inherence]; and it is received by a deliberate act. The godparents present themselves as substitutes.[60]

In the context of substitution, the child is received into a new kind of co-inherence that is, apparently, that of the 'Trinity-in-Unity'. This co-inherence is immediately identified Christologically, however, as being made 'partaker of death and

---

[54] Williams, 'Calling of Taliessin', *Region*, 16–17.
[55] Williams, 'Prayers of the Pope', *Region*, 60.
[56] Unless, like Chloe in *Many Dimensions*, she remains in a coma and finally dies.
[57] See Chapter 8, section 3.
[58] King, *Pattern*, 155, defends the use of this technical term, but does not notice that it actually comes from Prestige's account.
[59] Williams, *Descent of the Dove*, 39–40, 52, 234; also see my Chapter 4, section 5.
[60] Williams, *Descent of the Dove*, 234.

resurrection', and it is *this* co-inherence that the child is to confess and ratify at the later point of confirmation.[61] Williams goes on to emphasize the Christological perspective, referring to the co-inherence of the divine nature with material substance in Christ, and declaring that 'within *that* sublime co-inherence all our lesser co-inherences cohere'.[62] Williams thus falters at developing the co-inherence of human persons, in their materiality, in the Trinity, in any 'land' or space opened up by God in God's own interweaving movements of relationships.

Another hint of participation in the triune God, again undeveloped, comes in *The Forgiveness of Sins* (1942). Williams here analyses forgiveness as a mutual act, depending on two or more 'dispositions' towards forgiving, and in this context he draws an analogy with the Trinity:

> He who will claim the supernatural must claim it wholly; its validity cannot be divided; like the Blessed Trinity Itself it lives according to its proper complex method, but it altogether lives as a unity [...] we are part of [the repentant offender] and he of us; that is the centre; by his death there—his death in that repentance—we live, and he by ours: 'dying each other's life, living each other's death'.[63]

Thus far, Williams is drawing only an analogy between triune and human relations. But then he goes on to speak of a person's refusal of forgiveness as 'shut[ting] himself out of the mortal co-inherence [...] out of the act in which, more than any other, the mortal co-inheres with the divine'.[64] In the context of likeness with 'the Blessed Trinity', this is at least a hint that in forgiveness we co-inhere in the Trinity, not only in Christ. But elsewhere in this book he does not associate co-inherence with the Trinity. He tends to envisage forgiveness as essentially a matter of 'exchange', 'interchange', and 'substitution', rooted in the incarnation and atonement of Christ.[65] Dramatically, he envisages Christ as forgiving those who were crucifying him, and—since all things are created through him—ironically maintaining them in existence at the very moments when they were inflicting suffering upon him, 'as he had maintained the tree that made the wood and the metal that made the nails'. This is the depth of the exchange by which he lived: 'he exchanged his love for man's loss'.[66] Human beings co-inhere in the Christ who makes this great exchange of forgiveness, and this leads to a new state of co-inherence among themselves.

Instances, few though they are, of bringing co-inherence together with Trinity, hinting at a participating in God, prompt us to ask for more about dwelling in 'the

---

[61] Williams, *Descent of the Dove*, 235.   [62] Williams, *Descent of the Dove*, 213.
[63] Williams, *Forgiveness of Sins*, 120–1.   [64] Williams, *Forgiveness of Sins*, 122.
[65] E.g. Williams, *Forgiveness of Sins*, 2, 61, 64, 88, 101, 112.
[66] Williams, *Forgiveness of Sins*, 64.

land of the Trinity'. But little is forthcoming. One reason seems to be Williams' established Christological trajectory, focusing on a 'being in love' as equivalent to 'being in Christ', and another is his treatment of Trinity as a subject for contemplation rather than the location of human action. Yet another is his adherence to the classical doctrine of the self-sufficiency of God.[67] Further, his doctrine of atonement is characterized by exchange and substitution, and the desolation of the cross is not for Williams situated within the life of the Trinity—as it has been in modern exponents of 'theology of the cross'.[68] There is no idea of receiving the salvific exchange Christ offers through co-inhering in the relations of the Trinity. This is a point to which I intend to return in Chapter 15.

5.3 The Idea without the Word: Showing Co-inherence

Once Williams had found the word 'co-inherence', the idea could appear without the word. As Williams himself writes about Dante's portrayal of the 'eagle of just souls' in the *Paradiso*, 'it does not talk about this co-inherence, but only shows it'.[69] Moreover, in this 'showing', the promise of a more trinitarian theology of co-inherence can also be traced, though not fulfilled.

This is the case in a prose play, *Terror of Light*, written not long after the foundation of the Company of the Co-inherence, in April 1940, and featuring the Twelve Apostles who are significantly named 'Companions'.[70] Williams read it to the Inklings on 2 May 1940, and Lewis records in a letter to Warnie that he thought this 'Whitsun play' to be 'a mixture of very good stuff and some deplorable errors in taste'.[71] The 'errors' probably refer to the conversation on love between Mary Magdalene and the Apostle John, an imaginary relationship that Williams ingeniously blends with other events: primarily the coming of the Holy Spirit at Pentecost to the waiting disciples of Jesus (Acts 2), but also their encounter with the magician Simon Magus and the young woman—here named Luna—whose psychic gifts he is exploiting (Acts 8:9–24), an early glimpse of St Paul in his orthodox, Jewish phase, and the death ('dormition') of Mary the Mother of Jesus. The play was first performed later in the month in the University Church, Oxford, by a band of players directed by Ruth Spalding.[72] After some severe criticism by Michal Williams on the opening night, Williams

---

[67] See Williams, 'St Anselm's Rabbit', 828, a review of E. L. Mascall's book *He Who Is*, where he writes of the 'almost physical delight' that the doctrine gave him. Mascall reciprocates in appreciation of Williams in 'Charles Williams as I Knew Him', 1–5.

[68] As a distinct movement, *Kreuzestheologie* first appeared in Germany in the late 1960s. See Link, 'Zur Kreuzestheologie', 337–45; Jüngel, 'Vom Tod des lebendigen Gottes', 93–116; Moltmann, *Crucified God*, 200–48; Fiddes, *Creative Suffering of God*, 12–13, 112–43.

[69] Williams, *Figure of Beatrice*, 209–10; Dante, *Divine Comedy, Paradise*, 18–19.

[70] Williams, *The Terror of Light*, in Williams, *Collected Plays*, 344, 350, 366, 371, 372.

[71] CSL to W. H. Lewis, 4 May 1940, Lewis, *Letters*, 2: 410.   [72] Lindop, *Charles Williams*, 326.

revised the play for a subsequent performance a couple of days later.[73] This revised version is the text first published in the *Collected Plays*, but Williams had determined to rewrite it entirely in verse,[74] a project on which it is possible that he was still engaged at the time of his death, as Hadfield oddly refers to it as 'his last play'.[75] There are certainly interesting similarities between the Simon Magus of this play and Simon the Clerk in *All Hallows' Eve* (1945), and the play seems to have been actively present in Williams' mind in writing the novel.

Exchange and substitution are abundantly promulgated and practised by these Companions. 'Others he saved, himself he could not save' is the 'formula of the Kingdom' that Peter gives freely to Simon, and when Simon offers to buy the spiritual power that the Apostles are exercising, Peter laments that money can be abused to become a means of domination over others; echoing the positive view of the archbishop in the poem 'Bors to Elayne',[76] he affirms that in itself 'Money is a means of exchange, and exchange is a kind of little love and a medium of greater love. It is a way of losing the self.'[77] Mary Magdalene offers herself as a substitute for the slave girl who is Simon's medium, and who has become trapped in a kind of hell 'at the bottom of the light', declaring: 'There is no magic, Simon; there is only exchange.' She rescues Luna, risking herself with the words 'I will die for you or live for you in the Lord.'[78] The dead Judas Iscariot, brought up from 'beyond the light' by Simon's necromancy, finally agrees that Matthias shall be his substitute in the seat of the Apostles, so that through love even Judas is brought into the circle of exchange: 'his exclusion shall be his inclusion'.[79] The romantic love between John and Mary Magdalene is presented as an exchange, and the light in which they see each other is both the glory of their eternal state, and the divine light:

JOHN.   [...] We have been together all this time; and it is only today that I have seen you—only since the light was in you and you in the light. MARY. He has exchanged us with each other. I have begun to live in him through you ever since that morning in the garden [...] You will love other people for themselves, the selves that the light loves. But you will have to love me for myself—even then. JOHN. [...] You are to be loved because He loves you—and everyone is to be loved because He loves them.[80]

---

[73] On 9 May 1940, CW writes to Michal Williams that 'I loved your comments about *T. of L.*' Williams, *To Michal*, 60.

[74] According to Roma King in Williams, *To Michal*, 279 n.23.

[75] Hadfield, *Charles Williams*, 295; but she records the 1940 performance in her *Introduction*, 191. The editor of his *Collected Plays*, John Heath-Stubbs, places it chronologically after *The House of the Octopus* (published 1945), printing sections of the original, unrevised text in footnotes. He appears to be incorrect in claiming that Williams died shortly after the prose revisions, which were probably made not in 1945 but in 1940.

[76] Williams, *Taliessin*, 45.   [77] Williams, *Terror*, 354–5.   [78] Williams, *Terror*, 357.

[79] Williams, *Terror*, 370.   [80] Williams, *Terror*, 365, 367, 368.

For John, his love is an analogy with divine love, but for Mary it is identical: 'I must love only because God loves, but you love as God loves.'

There is also an echo of the command to 'become a double man' when Mother Mary exclaims that those who 'love the other and rejoice in the other' know that 'the heavens are doubled'.[81] Although John refers to the love of 'God', the place of 'exchange' is clearly the love of *Christ*, who has 'exchanged us with each other', and who 'lights every one who comes into the world'.[82] This dual theme of being 'in love' and 'in Love (Christ)' is a familiar one, sounded many times by Williams before his discovery of 'co-inherence'. However, without using the word co-inherence, the established image of seeing 'light' in the one loved is used in a new way, to portray an interplay, a 'twisting' and 'mingling' of divine light, fire, and wind within the bodies of those who are 'hidden in God',[83] and who are open to the heavenly light. When Simon claims to be 'the standing Pillar, the union of the worlds', Luna—seeing the descent of the Spirit in the Apostles at Pentecost in a trance—makes her riposte to Simon:

You are not the Pillar of the world. Each of them is a pillar, and the wind blows round and round them. There are millions of pillars, in the air, within the air [...] Every pillar is opening into the fire: there are flames playing in the wind, and tongues singing. The pillars are crowned with flame, and there is a light beyond and below them [...] The light is within the air and breaking out of the air. The edge of the light, where it mingles with the air, is a company of twisting flames. The flames sit upon their heads. The edge of the light is in the air, and the edge of the air is in the earth; the edge of the earth is in the air; and the edge of the air is in the light. Their bodies are compacted of what is beyond the light: their voices are flame in the mingling of the light and the air.

We can only call this a vision of co-inherence, embracing not only the twelve Apostles but myriad others ('millions of pillars'). It recalls Dante's vision of the eagle of just souls, all of whom are flames of the Spirit, and is a kind of *perichoresis* of human beings in the Spirit of God. Luna reports that she enters this 'mingling'—'I have gone into the edge of the light. I am going down into it, among the shapes and the images'—though for her this becomes an experience of judgement. This interweaving of light, fire, and air could be a portrayal of *perichoresis* in the whole Trinity, hinted at, for example, in the phrase 'The light is within the air and breaking out of the air.' But the image only hovers on the borders of trinitarian co-inherence, and so holding only the promise of being developed into a human dwelling in the triune life of God ('I am going

---

[81] Williams, *Terror*, 368–9.   [82] Williams, *Terror*, 365, 367–8.
[83] Williams, *Terror*, 332; cf. Col. 3:3, 'Your life is hidden with Christ in God.'

down into it'). It is a 'Union', in which—as Williams is to repeat in *Forgiveness of Sins*—forgiveness is fostered. As Mary Magdalene says to Judas,

'If there is a Union, I see now that the only way to it is to obey the Union. If you are doing that, will you do it more, and forgive me for being so angry?'[84]

'Union' has been a key term also in *The Descent of the Dove*, and there it is definitely Christological, a union of humanity with the Christ who is in himself a union of human with divine natures. There Williams writes of the existence in the early church of 'the work of exchange and substitution, which is a union on earth and in heaven of that love which was now understood to be capable of loving and of being loved.'[85] In this play the 'Companions' are thus united with Christ and with the Spirit, being named 'Companions of the Spirit' and 'Companions of your [Mary's] Son'.[86]

Towards the end of the play the idea of co-inherence in the Holy Spirit—though not the word itself—appears again. Mother Mary declares before her death that on this day of Pentecost, the Spirit who had been until today secluded in her own flesh (since, presumably, the annunciation when she was 'overshadowed' by the Spirit),[87] 'has now given of himself in a thousand places'.[88] She continues enigmatically that 'The glory has issued out of Themselves', and when John queries the word 'Themselves' explains 'Themselves, who are He; and you shall go out with it.' The pronoun 'Themselves' could refer to the Persons of the Trinity, in which case John's following comment that 'I knew then that the light had always been intertwined with your body' would imply a participation in a co-inherent Trinity. But in context, 'Themselves' could be the multiple flames of the Spirit, energies of God such as were manifest at Pentecost, now scattered into the world to empower the mission of the church which will 'go out with them'. Mary indeed goes on to speak about 'when the Companions begin their journeys'.[89] The identification of the many flames with 'He' would then be with 'our Lord the Spirit' mentioned just before. Perhaps Williams intends to be ambiguous.

It is with the myriad flames of the Holy Ghost that Williams' *The House of the Octopus*, a missionary play, begins four years later.[90] It opens with a soliloquy of the 'Flame', who declares himself to be one of those who first came into being when the Holy Spirit 'measured the angle of creation', and were then 'dropped from his rushing flame-scattering wind' at Pentecost.[91] They are, declares the flame, 'seeds of conjunction',[92] another of Williams' 'co-' words. The play was written, in the second half of 1944, for the drama group of the United Council for

---

[84] Williams, *Terror*, 352, cf. Williams, *Forgiveness of Sins*, 108.
[85] Williams, *Descent of the Dove*, 12.   [86] Williams, *Terror*, 344, 371.
[87] Luke 1:35, cf. Matthew 1:20.   [88] Williams, *Terror*, 370.   [89] Williams, *Terror*, 372.
[90] Williams, *House*, 245–324.   [91] Williams, *House*, 249.   [92] Williams, *House*, 250.

Missionary Education, who gave Williams the commission to write something relating to the persecution of Christians by the Japanese in the Pacific. Williams explores this theme by identifying the persecutors with the evil realm of P'o-l'u from his Arthurian mythology, whose 'infinite and nameless' Emperor enforces his domination by using ferocious octopuses (or cephalopods) which strangle victims with their tentacles.[93] The Empire here also aims to wrap more insidious mental tentacles into people's minds, to achieve 'spiritual absorption'.[94] Themes of exchange and substitution run throughout the play, but despite the language being the most trinitarian in all Williams' plays—in the sense of giving attention to all three Persons—a 'co-inherence' in the Trinity is only implied, and human participation within it remains as a hint or promise.

Co-inherence in Christ is implicitly presented in terms of living in each other through living in Christ.[95] The chorus of Christians, young in the faith, declares that 'We take refuge in the Maker of all and the Flesh-Taker [...] we believe that we are in him and he in us.'[96] Against the shocked orthodoxy of their priest, Anthony, they insist that even though the young woman Alayu has denied the faith before being killed, 'Because of her death we live more strong.'[97] Being in Christ through baptism has not been cancelled out by her recantation in the face of persecution by the forces of P'o-l'u, and the general social principle of exchange cannot be obliterated:

> We in these isles
> live in our people—no man's life his own—
> from birth and initiation. When our salvation
> came to us it showed us no new mode—
> sir, dare you say so?—of living to ourselves.
> The Church is not many but the life of many
> in ways of relation.

Alayu, now dead, consents to the call of the Flame, one of the 'masters of exchange', to engage in an act of substitution, taking Anthony's fear in the face of execution while he takes her place in a true martyr's death. So 'the dead [shall save] the living, and the living the dead'.[98] This contrasts with Assantu's attempt to kill Anthony to provide himself with a substitute in face of what he believes to be the desire of his 'hungry' ancestral God to devour him. When thwarted, he cries

---

[93] See Williams, 'The Vision of the Empire', *Taliessin*, 12, 13; 'The Departure of Merlin', *Taliessin*, 76; 'The Prayers of the Pope', *Region*, 60.

[94] Williams, *House*, 275.

[95] Cavaliero, 'Charles Williams and Twentieth Century Verse Drama', 204, judges that the play succeeds in uniting 'the vision of divine-human co-inherence that is the master meaning of his work in theology'.

[96] Williams, *House*, 262.   [97] Williams, *House*, 299.   [98] Williams, *House*, 319, 310.

out, 'I wanted a substitution / I wanted salvation', and is given the reply: 'But you had it; here it is'—that is, in Christ and the Eucharist.[99] While the Marshal of Po'-l'u adores the Emperor as only consuming, and never consumed by others,[100] and Assantu affirms the same of the bloodthirsty tribal deity of the islands to whom he has apostasized, only the Christians worship a God who both 'consumes and is consumed'—in cross and Eucharist—in a divine exchange.[101] They too are to 'consume' (Christ in the Eucharist) and to be willing to be 'consumed' in giving their lives.

The theological point of the play turns upon the Marshall's urbane proposal that the Christians should be allowed to live and worship the way they want, as long as Anthony on their behalf recognizes that the same word—'God'—can be used, as matter of mere civil convention, of the Emperor as well as of the Christians' deity.[102] His argument is that there is the same 'Fatherhood' in both—and indeed Assantu also claims that his all-devouring God is a 'Father', while Anthony himself claims to be a 'Father' to his flock. The question is whether this is not all the same thing, and differences a mere matter of words. Is not social 'exchange', queries the Marshall, better than dogma? Though he wavers, Anthony finally refuses to accept the compromise, on—in effect—two grounds. The first is that the Christian God is unique in consenting to be 'consumed', and the second is that 'Father' in a Christian sense is not just a general ascription (Father of all), but specifically the Father of Jesus Christ: 'the only image of the Father is the blessed Son'.[103] This latter point echoes the argument powerfully being made by the theologian Karl Barth in this period,[104] and once again reminiscent of Barth is Anthony's reply that in other circumstances there might be something to consider in the Marshall's argument, but that this is a time of crisis when only 'no' will do: 'it must not be'.[105]

Despite what may seem an incongruous, and biologically inaccurate, appeal to the habits of cephalopods (as Auden gently pointed out),[106] this play has thus some astute trinitarian theology at its heart. There is, further, just a slight hint of human dwelling in this triune God when the Flame declares:

> Our Father retracts himself in his own nature—
> for his Son in himself and on earth for every creature;

---

[99] Williams, *House*, 316.

[100] There is an affinity here with Lewis' *Screwtape Letters*, in which the aim of the devils is to consume the weaker; see Lewis, *Screwtape*, 156.

[101] Williams, *House*, 314, 320.   [102] Williams, *House*, 283–4, 318.

[103] Williams, *House*, 282.   [104] Barth, *Church Dogmatics*, 1/1, 386–90.

[105] Williams, *House*, 319. Cf. Barth, *No!* 67–9; Barth, *How I Changed My Mind*, 46–7.

[106] W. H. Auden to CW, 11 January 1945, in a letter generally expressing admiration of *The Region of the Summer Stars*, but evidently recalling *Taliessin*: 'I'm not quite happy about P'o-l'u and the octopi. The latter are of course for us a nightmare image, but I suppose God created them for other purposes as well.' Wade CWP 163.

> this is the good of fatherhood—to be food,
> and an equal friend in the end[.][107]

The picture seems to be that the Father limits himself ('retracts himself') or allows himself to be consumed, to make room 'in himself' for the Son, and perhaps 'for every creature' alongside the Son. This may recall the Lurianic Kabbalistic doctrine of the *zim-zum*, according to which—since God fills all space—God retracts into God's self in order to make room for creation.[108] Williams knew much of the Kabbala through his earlier membership of the Fellowship of the Rosy Cross,[109] and these lines might be an indication that Williams could conceive of a co-inherence of 'equal friends' within God. But the Kabbalistic image is not in itself, of course, trinitarian,[110] and it is also ambiguous; it is not clear whether God makes room for creation inside or outside the divine being.

At the end of the play, Williams offers a vision of eternal co-inherence in the Spirit for the martyred and confessing Christians:

> Happy they whose first sight in heaven
> is the flight or the stillness of the flames of the Holy Ghost [...]
> The skies and the earth open, and there are we.
> Well, well, and again well at last![111]
> Fast is our sphere fixed, and fast it moves,
> All loves circling in exchange of loves.[112]

Thus, this play affirms the formula of the Trinity, or in the words of the new Christians of the island: 'We know that the Father is a true power of good, and his Son our food and not we his, and there is but one Ghost, and that holy.'[113] Without the actual word, we have seen that there is a portrayal of some kind of co-inherence between created beings and each of the three persons of the Trinity *separately*. The 'circling' of all loves 'in exchange of loves' holds the potential of an indwelling in the co-inherence of the *whole* Trinity, but the promise is not yet fulfilled.

In his last novel, *All Hallows' Eve*, written also in 1944, husband and dead wife Richard and Lester are able to recapture a sight of each other in their glory as they exchange joy, but Williams does not use the term 'co-inherence' to describe this. The term only occurs once in the novel—the *only* time it occurs in any of his

---

[107] Williams, *House*, 298.   [108] See Scholem *Kabbalah,* 129–35.

[109] Roukema, 'Veil that Reveals', 57–9; Ashenden, *Charles Williams*, 44–55.

[110] The image is used in a trinitarian way by several Christian theologians: Solovyov, *Russia,* 250, 257; Moltmann, *Trinity,* 59–60, 108–11.

[111] This is a reference to the phrase of the Lady Julian, *Revelations,* ch. 27 (79), 'All shall be well, and all shall be well, and all manner of things shall be well'; it is also cited by T. S. Eliot at the end of 'Little Gidding'.

[112] Williams, *House,* 323.   [113] Williams, *House,* 264.

novels—not to describe the mutuality of love but to relate the way that Lester and her dead friend, Evelyn, occupy an artificial body created by the magician Simon: 'The magical form which united them also separated; through it they co-hered to each other but could not co-inhere.'[114] This recalls the distinction between 'adhering to' and 'adhering in' that Williams—I have suggested—culled from Prestige's chapter on co-inherence.[115] Though the reference seems incidental, it carries considerable significance; it enables us to learn that an evil will that designs to manipulate others cannot achieve co-inherence 'in', but can only 'stick' things together. Such a will simply wants to absorb others. It cannot say: 'This also is Thou. Neither is this Thou.' When first used in the earlier theology of romantic love, this epigram was about the affirmation of images, the positive way to God: things and persons in the world such as the beloved could be identified in image with divine realities. When Williams uses it again in *He Came Down from Heaven* it fuses this affirmation of images with the way of exchange:[116] when we substitute for another, she is both me and 'not me'. Such exchange, as we learned already from the pretensions of Simon Magus in *Terror of Light*, is denied by the Simons of this world.

The themes of exchange and substitution run through the novel, and there are a number of portrayals of co-inherence without the word.[117] The last of these has strong resonances with the Pentecost scene in *Terror of Light*, and the 'circling' of the martyrs and saints around the Flame at the end of *The House of the Octopus*:

> [Lester] stood, quiet and very real, before them; almost she shone on then; then the brightness quivered in the air, a gleam of brighter light than day, and in a flash traversed all the hall; the approach of all the hallows possessed her, and she too, into the separations and unions which are indeed its approach, and into the end to which it is itself an approach, was wholly gone. The tremor of brightness received her.[118]

Much could be built on the 'separations and unions' that are an 'approach' to 'the end', or the goal of the hallows' (saints') co-inherence. It is not an end point that we reach in Williams, and to explore what that destination might be we must— and *will* in the next chapter—read C. S. Lewis.

---

[114] Williams, *All Hallows' Eve*, 196.
[115] See Chapter 4, '"Co-inherence": a late arrival on the scene'.
[116] Williams, *He Came Down*, 146.   [117] See Chapter 12, section 3.
[118] Williams, *All Hallows' Eve*, 237.

6

C. S. Lewis and the Idea of Co-inherence

In a letter of October 1949, C. S. Lewis replied to a correspondent who had told him that she feared 'spiritual pride when people asked you to pray for them'. In his typically robust manner he responds, 'Pish! There's nothing to be proud about', and then continues:

> [...] looked at another way, the really efficacious intercession is Christ's, and yours is *in* His, as you are in Him, since you became part of His 'body', the Church. Read Charles Williams on Co-inherence in almost any of his later books or plays (*Descent of the Dove, Descent into Hell, The House of the Octopus.*)[1]

The appeal to Williams, slight though it is, is of considerable interest for our theme for several reasons. In the first place, it is not accurate, at least if Lewis' correspondent hoped to find the *word* 'Co-inherence' after reading Lewis' letter. Though Lewis is correct that it appears in Williams' 'later' books or plays, it actually does not occur in two of the three works he mentions. *Descent into Hell* is too early for Williams' use of the word, but then Lewis later admitted to another correspondent, the author Charles Moorman, that he did not know when Williams first met 'the doctrines of Coinherence [*sic*] and Substitution'.[2] In this book, I have attempted to fill in the blanks—the first written evidence we have of substitution is in 1929,[3] and the first reference to co-inherence in early 1939,[4] although the related word 'exchange' in something like Williams' special sense appears as early as 1924.[5] It seems that Lewis is discerning the *idea* of co-inherence to be present in Williams' books, probably through references to exchange and substitution. In the second place, we notice that Lewis echoes Williams in himself relating co-inherence closely to being 'in Christ'.

More substantially, the almost casual appeal to the notion of co-inherence is curious. It appears to be at the forefront of Lewis' mind, at least in thinking about prayer, and Neville Coghill, one of the Inklings, recalls that 'it was Charles Williams who expounded to him the doctrine of co-inherence'.[6] Yet the word is missing from almost the whole of the Lewis corpus, despite his debt to Williams in

---

[1] CSL to Rhona Bodle, 24 October 1949, Lewis, *Letters*, 2: 988.
[2] CSL to Charles Moorman, 2 October 1952, Lewis, *Letters*, 3: 232.
[3] See Chapter 4, section 4, n.86.   [4] See Chapter 4, section 1.   [5] Williams, *Outlines*, 33.
[6] Coghill, 'Approach to English', 63.

Charles Williams and C.S. Lewis: Friends in Co-inherence. Paul S. Fiddes, Oxford University Press. © Paul S. Fiddes 2021.
DOI: 10.1093/oso/9780192845467.003.0006

many ways.[7] It appears twice in his vast mass of letters, at the moments I have already mentioned. It appears—as would be expected—in Lewis' account of Williams' Arthurian poems in *Arthurian Torso*, and in fact he uses it in exposition of the poems (as we shall see) even where it is not present in the original text. However, it seems to be absent from all the rest of Lewis' varied literary and theological output. We might suggest two explanations for this, and I am going to argue that they are both valid and indeed intertwined. One is that, like Williams himself, he 'shows' the idea where the word is not mentioned.[8] The idea is implied in a whole constellation of other metaphors and technical terms Lewis employs: among them, as I intend to demonstrate, are substitution, dance, participation, co-existence, union, and presence. In using these, I want to argue that Lewis adds the very dimension to co-inherence that seems lacking in Williams—that is, something like an 'indwelling' of finite beings in the infinite Trinity. Another explanation, however, is that there was a certain resistance to the word itself in Lewis' mind, and the use of other terms enabled him to qualify and finesse the idea in line with his own metaphysic and general world view. Why there should be this hesitation I shall consider later.

A final point of interest about this almost passing reference to co-inherence in Lewis' letter is that it is related to prayer, and here again he is echoing Williams.[9] Lewis' recalling of the experience of prayer is also a good place to begin in exploring his 'showing' of co-inherence.

6.1 Metaphors of Co-inherence

In his broadcast on 'The Three-Personal God', published in *Beyond Personality* in 1944, Lewis supposes a listener asking, 'If we cannot imagine a three-personal Being, what is the good of talking about Him?' and responds that 'there isn't any good in *talking* about Him. The thing that matters is being actually *drawn into* that three-personal life.'[10] This happens, he affirms, every time a simple Christian kneels down to say his prayers, when

---

[7] Duriez, *Oxford Inklings*, 227, judges that Lewis 'was influenced by the ideas of Charles Williams, particularly his concept of "Co-inherence"', but offers no evidence of this. Conversely Brian Horne, 'Peculiar Debt', 89–90, judges that 'the concept of co-inherence along with the notions of exchange and substituted love' was not incorporated by Lewis into his own work 'except in a few and interesting cases', but he surely underestimates their presence.

[8] See Williams' comment on Dante's eagle: 'it does not talk about this co-inherence, but only shows it'. *Figure of Beatrice*, 209–10.

[9] In *He Came Down*, 129, Williams associates prayer with substituted love; in *Descent of the Dove*, 163, prayer is linked to exchange.

[10] Lewis, *Beyond Personality*, 16–17; repr. in Lewis, *Mere Christianity*, 129. My italics.

the whole threefold life of the three-personal Being is actually going on in that ordinary little bedroom where an ordinary man is saying his prayers. The man is being caught up into the higher kind of life—what I call Zoe or spiritual life: he is being pulled into God, by God, while still remaining himself.

Lewis has perhaps, then, been over-generous in pointing his correspondent to Williams. He is himself giving us the idea of co-inherence as being 'caught up into' the triune relations of God—an idea scarcely present in Williams—as is clear when he adds:

'The whole dance, or drama, or pattern of this three-Personal life is to be played out in each one of us: or (putting it the other way round) each one of us has got to enter that pattern, take his place in that dance.'[11]

What it means for the 'dance' to be played out in each of us is that 'God is the thing to which [a Christian] is praying—the goal he is trying to reach. God is also the thing inside him which is pushing him on—the motive power. God is also the road or bridge alongside which he is being pushed to that goal.'[12]

In taking up this image of dance at the end of *Perelandra* (1943), the actual word 'co-inhere' is once again not used in portraying the Great Dance of the cosmos, but the idea is there with words such as 'intertwining undulations', 'mutually embracing', 'entangled', and 'interanimated circlings'.[13] In this context, Lewis places a direct reference to the Trinity: 'of many senses and thoughts one person;[14] of three persons, Himself,'[15] and associates it with a mutual indwelling. 'He dwells within the seed of the smallest flower' runs the hymn accompanying the dance, 'Deep heaven [is] inside Him who is inside the seed and does not distend him',[16] thus reflecting an original association of trinitarian *perichoresis* with 'containing'. G. L. Prestige stresses that the verb *chorein*, lying at the root of *perichoresis* ('co-inherence'), is applied by early theologians to each person of the Trinity as *containing* the other;[17] this, he suggests, is an 'extension' of the affirmation that God 'contains' all things,[18] but Prestige does not conclude this must mean that created beings are therefore contained within the interweaving relations of the three Persons. Something like this is being conveyed by the image of the dance; in any case, Lewis is taking a large step beyond his *Preface to Paradise Lost*,

[11] Lewis, *Mere Christianity*, 139.   [12] Lewis, *Mere Christianity*, 129.
[13] Lewis, *Perelandra*, 251–2.
[14] In context, this refers to an individual, created person, not to the one nature of God.
[15] Lewis, *Perelandra*, 247. Here I gladly revise my early view that there is no hint of participation in the triune God in *Perelandra*; see Fiddes, 'Lewis the Myth-Maker', 142–3.
[16] Lewis, *Perelandra*, 247.
[17] Prestige, *God*, 289–91, citing Gregory of Nyssa and Cyril of Alexandria, at a time when the actual term *perichoresis* had not been developed.
[18] Hilary, *de Trinitate* 3.2, cf. 2.6.

where he allowed that one could say only that God 'virtually' contains matter, 'as the poet the poem or the feet swiftness'.[19]

Now we can see the extraordinary place that the last chapter of *Perelandra* plays in Lewis' imagination. While Williams finds an *identity* between bodily passion and the incarnation of Christ—Christ actually born in lovers—we have seen that he generally finds an *analogy* between human relations and relations in the Trinity. By contrast, until his late work, Lewis finds an *analogy* between human passion and divine love, and this remains a profound difference between himself and Williams from 1936 onwards. But once a human nature has become 'super-natural' through union with Christ, the Christian *participates* spiritually in the relations of the Trinity in a way that Williams does not express. This is the point of Lewis' image of the dance in *Beyond Personality*. Yet the Great Dance of *Perelandra* is an erratic block, an anomaly on the landscape, in this general picture: the impression given is that everybody, and every *body*, in the world participates in the Trinity. Lewis will not try to justify this picture in terms of theology and metaphysics for another twenty years, and he will not repeat anything like it during this period. It may be that, for a moment, a metaphor ran away with him.

In *Beyond Personality*, there is also a resonance with Williams' vision of the co-inherence of all humanity, which Williams describes as beginning for each individual in the exchange, substitution, and co-inherence of childbirth, writing that:

> That new life exists literally within the mother; it inheres in its mother. The value of the sexual act itself is a kind of co-inherence [...] with conception comes the physical inherence of the child. And this is renewed through all the generations; each generation has inhered in that before it.'[20]

Lewis seems to echo this picture:

> Human beings are not [separate]. They look separate because you see them walking about separately. But then, we are so made that we can see only the present moment. If we could see the past, then of course it would look different. For there was a time when every man was part of his mother, and (earlier still) part of his father as well: and when they were part of their grandparents. If you could see humanity spread out in time as God sees it, it would [...] look like one single growing thing—rather like a very complicated tree. And not only that. Individuals are not really separate from God any more than from one another.

---

[19] Lewis, *Preface*, 88, commenting on Milton's sentence that 'the more excellent substance virtually and essentially contains within itself the inferior one' (*De Doctrina* 1.7.).

[20] Williams, 'Way of Exchange', 150.

Every man, woman, and child all over the world is feeling and breathing at this moment only because God, so to speak, is 'keeping him going.'[21]

Lewis goes on to argue, from this vision of human participation in others, that when Christ becomes man, 'it is as if something which is always affecting the whole human mass begins, at one point, to affect that whole human mass in a new way'. But as Lewis proceeds, it becomes clear that the incarnation has 'affected' people only 'in principle', so that 'we individuals have to appropriate that salvation' by 'laying ourselves open' to Christ. We notice that while Lewis affirms that each person has been 'part' of their parents, he does not say that by nature every person is 'part' of God (or has a part in God). Every man, woman, and child is not separated from God only in the sense of God's 'keeping him going'. An engagement in God that exceeds being sustained in existence requires a deliberate movement of will and the receiving of a new nature.

Lewis' conviction in this passage from *Beyond Personality* about a participation of people in each other's lives that transgresses the borders of time is marked in *Arthurian Torso* by his own use of the word 'co-inherence'. Commenting on the poem 'Taliessin on the Death of Virgil', Lewis explains that 'such is the co-inherence of all souls that they are not even limited by time'.[22] Williams presents Virgil as being saved from the Inferno and given a place in Purgatory as a virtuous pagan by the intercession of his many readers through the ages, for not even Virgil could be saved by his poetry alone. The first part of the poem graphically describes the dissolving of his consciousness in death, and the second part tells of how helpers rushed to catch him as he was about to perish in 'perpetual falling, perpetual burying'. They were those who had lived 'by his hexameters', and they rushed back through the 'infinity of time' to offer 'what salvation may reign here by us [. . .] in this net of obedient loves'.[23] Lewis finds in this poem the theme of 'co-inherence', even though the collection (*Taliessin Through Logres*) is too early for Williams' use of the actual word, and Lewis further implies in his exegesis that the idea is to be found in the novel *Descent into Hell*, where the heroine similarly takes upon herself the terror of someone in the past—in this case her ancestor. Williams certainly uses the word 'exchange' to interpret the event of this poem: Virgil was 'set on the marble of exchange', and the novel does illustrate both exchange and substitution. But it is Lewis who invokes the term 'co-inherence', and he is anxious, it seems, to make clear that the co-inherence in Virgil's case is in Christ, writing 'As they in Christ, so he in the Christ in them, tasted the "largesse" of "the land of the Trinity".' None of this is in the poem, and the phrases quoted come from later poems in *The Region of the Summer Stars*. Williams does apply to Virgil the great maxim of exchange that applies pre-eminently to Christ—"Others

[21] Lewis, *Mere Christianity*, 142–3.   [22] Lewis, 'Williams and the Arthuriad', 123.
[23] Williams, *Taliessin*, 31–2.

he saved; himself he could not save"—but the reference to Christ remains unspoken. Lewis at this point, as earlier in *Beyond Personality*, appears hesitant to regard co-inherence as a phenomenon of nature in general.[24]

Just how far Lewis goes beyond Williams in envisaging something like human 'co-inherence' within the relations of the Trinity is shown by a range of metaphors. One of the most significant is that of 'person' itself, which is—as he recognizes in *Miracles*—a metaphor for God, although it is more accurate to say that our own 'physical and psychic energies' are 'mere metaphors' of the Life that is God.[25] In *Beyond Personality* he remarks:

> 'At the beginning I said there were Personalities in God. Well, I'll go further now. There are no real personalities anywhere else. Until you have given up your self to Him you will not have a real self.'[26]

The title of the book, *Beyond Personality*, is a deliberately ambiguous phrase, applying both to God and to human beings. *God* is infinitely personal, and so 'beyond' any human personality we know. With the vision of God as Trinity, says Lewis, Christians offer an idea of what a God who is 'beyond personality' might be like. Indeed, he claims, 'the Christian idea is the only one on the market'.[27] Human beings in turn become truly personal only in this God, going 'beyond' the personalities they have been given by nature. A supremely personal God is a trinitarian God, a God who begets God, and so this is a vision of the Trinity as a deeply 'practical' doctrine, concerned with human transformation. 'I warned you that theology is practical. The whole purpose for which we exist is to be thus taken into the life of God.'[28] It is by being 'drawn' into God's trinitarian life—by co-inherence in the Trinity, if Lewis had used the word—that we become truly persons or, as Lewis puts it, become real selves.

Here Lewis has anticipated a great deal of modern Christian doctrine, which has stressed the making of persons through participation in the triune God; I need mention in passing only Wolfhart Pannenberg, John Zizioulas, and Hans Urs Von Balthasar as representative theologians.[29] Moreover, like them he does not consider this personal engagement in God to be mere individualism. Using the image of a telescope for seeing something that will otherwise be unknown, he proposes that the instrument through which we see God is the whole Christian community: 'Christian brotherhood is, so to speak, the technical equipment for this science.'[30]

---

[24] For Lewis' later reflections on the way that prayer breaches the sequence of time, see *Letters to Malcolm*, 67, 142.

[25] Lewis, *Miracles*, 111.   [26] Lewis, *Mere Christianity*, 177.

[27] Lewis, *Mere Christianity*, 127.   [28] Lewis, *Mere Christianity*, 128.

[29] Pannenberg, *Systematic Theology*, 2: 196–292; cf. Pannenberg, *Anthropology*, 224–42; Zizioulas, *Being as Communion*, 49–65; Balthasar, *Theo-Drama*, II: 382–410.

[30] Lewis, *Mere Christianity*, 131.

Lewis does not explicitly take the step that recent theology has done, to affirm that we are involved in a God of communion *through* human community, that we are immersed into a God of relations through being persons in relation; however, he might be thought to imply it since he follows his introduction to the doctrine of the Trinity immediately by his thoughts about Christian believers as one body, united in love.[31] The Christian concept of a tri-personal God is, he admits, complicated, but then 'we cannot compete, in simplicity, with people who are inventing religions [...] of course anyone can be simple if he has no facts to bother about'.[32]

Fundamental to the concept of the Trinity is the belief that the Father eternally generates the Son; the Son is 'begotten, not made', as the Creed of Nicaea affirms. This offers a further metaphor for indwelling the triune God. Since human beings are to become truly persons by being drawn into the Trinity, it seems that the generation of the Son must also be relevant to this becoming personal of created beings. Lewis thus draws the conclusion that, since Christ is begotten and not made, human beings can themselves move on from the state of being 'made' to that of being 'begotten'. If the Son in the Trinity is begotten and not made, then by entering the Trinity we cease in effect to be 'made' and become 'begotten', as sons and daughters of God. This is the 'next step' in human history, which Lewis generously allows us to call 'evolution' if we want to; it is 'a change from being creatures of God to being sons of God'.[33]

Lewis' proposal here is essentially in accord with the Christian tradition. The New Testament shows several variations on the theme of becoming 'sons' of God. The Apostle Paul regards this as a kind of adoption, where we are accepted into God's family alongside the true Son, Jesus.[34] The Fourth Gospel pictures regeneration as being 'born from above', a second birth after our natural birth.[35] Athanasius explains salvation as *theosis*, or divinization, in which 'Christ became man so that we might become gods', and he understands this transformation (following Hebrews 2:10) as 'bringing many sons to glory'.[36] Lewis seems to have acquired a closer acquaintance with Athanasius shortly before preparing this third series of *Broadcast Talks*, through reading Sister Penelope's translation of *De Incarnatione* and writing an introduction to it.[37] He had already spoken of becoming 'gods and goddesses' in, for example, his sermon 'The Weight of Glory' (June 1941),[38] perhaps deriving this theme from his earlier reading of Augustine. Lewis, however, draws the ideas of 'becoming a son' more closely into relation

---

[31] Lewis, *Mere Christianity*, 130. In this period, he is also critical of Martin Buber's 'I-Thou' personalism for what he discerns as an excessive individualism: see his letter to Sister Penelope, 29 July 1942, in Lewis, *Letters*, 2: 526.

[32] Lewis, *Mere Christianity*, 131.   [33] Lewis, *Mere Christianity*, 172.

[34] Galatians 4:5, Romans 8:15, 23, cf. Ephesians 1:5.   [35] John 3:3–6.

[36] Athanasius, *De Incarnatione*, 10.   [37] 'Sister Penelope' was Penelope Lawson.

[38] Lewis, 'The Weight of Glory', 210.

with the movement of sonship within the Trinity than these earlier authors. He describes Christ as 'someone standing at your side, helping you to pray, trying to turn you into another son' in the context of a 'spirit of love', which is 'a love going on between the Father and the Son'.[39] Being drawn into Christ as a son is to 'become part of that wonderful present which the young Prince of the universe wants to offer to His Father—that present which is Himself and therefore us in Him'.[40] Before modern theology (much of it influenced by Hegel),[41] we would have to turn to a medieval mystic, such as Jan van Ruusbroec,[42] to find the same insights about being 'begotten in God along with the Son'.

In fact, Lewis in this period is careful to restrict the notion of human beings begotten by God, and so received into a kind of co-inherence with God; this is a condition limited to union with God through faith in Christ through his cross. He insists that human beings are first created and only subsequently become begotten. He sees the objection that God might as well have begotten many sons 'before all worlds' rather than first making them and then 'bringing them to life by such a difficult and painful process', but replies that if there were many from the outset they could not have been distinguished individually from each other, since space and matter—and so a created universe or 'Nature'—are necessary to differentiate spirits.[43] The idea of the part played by a material world in giving spirits individuality (as well as a meeting point) is taken from his earlier Idealist phase— ironically, because it is probably to distance himself from Idealism that he is cautious about calling the 'begetting' of creatures by God a co-inherence (as we shall see in a moment). However, the concise formulation that becoming sons and daughters of God means transferring from a state of being 'made' to one of being 'begotten' by God is not frequently found in the Christian tradition. It *can* be found, as in another work of Athanasius, who comments that 'we are not begotten first, but made',[44] but it can hardly be called 'mere' or 'common' Christianity. Further, Lewis' contrast between two sorts of *life*, a life that is 'made' and a life that is 'begotten',[45] appears to be without precedent, though arguably an extension of the same idea. His somewhat uncommon, though not unorthodox, definitions are perhaps indicative of a theological struggle that engages Lewis throughout his writings and of which he was very well aware; that is, how to discern the proper continuities and discontinuities between a 'natural' state and a 'spiritual' state, or between 'nature' and 'super-nature'. To this we shall return.

Two other images belong with the general ethos of 'co-inherence,' without the word's appearing. In thinking about the incarnation, where Williams continually appealed to the 'co-inherence' of divine and human natures, Lewis prefers a metaphor. First, the image of the 'descent' of God into the world has a long history in Christian tradition, and while it *can* be pictured as something like an invasion (as Lewis does elsewhere),[46] he also pictures it as an immersion, like someone diving 'down through increasing pressure into the death-like region of ooze and clime and old decay; then up again, back to colour and light'.[47] Second, in *Broadcast Talks*, Lewis enquires how the new life can be 'put into us',[48] and later, in *Beyond Personality*, he answers that the new life is to be caught as we catch an 'infection'. This new life is not carried on, he writes, by sexual reproduction and heredity as in the process of evolution.[49] Christ transmits the new life by 'good infection'. We are infected by being in the company of Christ, and by other people who are 'carriers' of Christ to other people, sometimes without being infected themselves.[50] 'People who were not Christians themselves helped me to Christianity', recalls Lewis. We catch the good infection from the presence of the invisible Christ alongside us, helping us. The images of immersion and infection are allied in tone to the image of the dance. As we take our place in it, we come close to a 'great fountain of energy and beauty spurting up at the very centre of reality', and we are bound to become wet with its spray.[51] It is not surprising then that, in describing the effect of the Grand Miracle—the resurrection of Jesus—on nature, Lewis returns to the image of the dance:

> 'The partner who bows to man in one movement of the dance receives Man's reverences in another. To be high or central means to abdicate continually: to be low means to be raised: all good masters are servants: God washes the feet of Men.'[52]

We get into the dance, according to Lewis in *Beyond Personality*, by sharing in Christ's life,[53] which Lewis explains in the activist terms of 'laying ourselves open' or 'handing over our whole self to Christ', or 'shoving back' all our own wishes and hopes at the beginning of each day, in order to let the new life 'rush in'. But is it possible to say more about the act of God in drawing us in or 'infecting' us? Many modern theologians will want to affirm that all human beings are by their creation *already* immersed into the triune life, already participating in the dance of the threefold personal God. Even the human rebellion against God is within God,[54] a distortion and a breaking of the steps of the dance. Through that engagement in God's dynamic life, persons are enabled to trust in Christ and so make their participation in God *deeper* and more transforming. They can move, in the title of the penultimate chapter of *The Last Battle*, Lewis' last chronicle of Narnia, 'farther

---

[46] In *Broadcast Talks*, incorporated into *Mere Christianity*, 33–7.   [47] Lewis, *Miracles*, 135.
[48] Lewis, *Mere Christianity*, 48.   [49] Lewis, *Mere Christianity*, 173.
[50] Lewis, *Mere Christianity*, 150.   [51] Lewis, *Mere Christianity*, 139–40.
[52] Lewis, *Miracles*, 150.   [53] Lewis, *Mere Christianity*, 139.
[54] See Balthasar, *Theo-Drama*, IV: 330.

up and farther in'. But this is not an answer that Lewis wants to give until his very last period. To that we shall come, but not for a while.

6.2 Co-inherence and Participation

In addition to using various metaphors—dance, begetting, immersion, and infection—to 'show' co-inherence, Lewis also adopts some technical terms. A word that Lewis uses occasionally, but always with significance, is 'participation', echoing the Platonic *methexis*. It is this term that he employs in his spiritual autobiography, *Surprised by Joy*, when he recalls the time before he was a Christian, inhabiting the air of Idealism suffused by an enduring Platonism.[55] He remembers that he was happy to think of the 'participation' of the human mind in 'a cosmic logos',[56] and how 'as Reasoners, we participated in a timeless and deathless world';[57] now, looking back, he believes he was self-deceived in maintaining that this was an entirely different thing from theism. He had come to see that 'Joy' would fit into his idealist philosophy only if a personal God (a form of the Absolute Idea) were the source and the goal of the desire he had known all his life.[58] From this conversion to theism, he then experienced a further conversion to believing that Jesus Christ was the Son of this God.

But this new world view now raises questions about the 'participation' of created beings in the Absolutely Real, or God. In his autobiography, Lewis describes how, as an atheistic idealist, he had believed that he could participate in the world of Absolute Reality simply by recalling that his spirit really belonged there: 'All my acts, desires and thoughts were to be brought into harmony with the universal Spirit.'[59] In his earlier phase of Subjective Idealism (following Berkeley), he had thought that most of the ideas in human minds came from a single omnipotent Spirit who was known as immediately as a mind knows other minds.[60] When he moved into Absolute Idealism, he thought of his mind or spirit as an autonomous splinter or relative form of the Absolute Mind, with which he was thus unified by nature. This 'pantheist' spirit was nothing less than the totality of all finite souls.[61] However, he recounts that, when he attempted to harmonize with this infinite and eternal Spirit, he was appalled to discover that his human condition ('a zoo of lusts, a bedlam of ambitions, a nursery of fears') prevented it, and that he needed to pray to a personal God and obey him to achieve this

---

[55] McGrath, *Intellectual World*, 39, maintains that Lewis' own Idealism was shaped by the Cambridge Neoplatonism of Henry More that he was studying in 1924.

[56] Lewis, *Surprised by Joy*, 169.   [57] Lewis, *Surprised by Joy*, 203.

[58] Lewis, *Surprised by Joy*, 208.   [59] Lewis, *Surprised by Joy*, 213.

[60] That is, known by 'notions', not by ideas: see Lewis, unpublished lecture notes 1924–5, 'The Moral Good—Its Place among the Values', Wade CSL MS/X–76, 36.

[61] Lewis, *Clivi Hamiltonis Summae Metaphysices Contra Anthroposophos Libri II*, 40, unpublished document from the 'Great War' with Owen Barfield, Wade CSL/MS-29/X.

union.[62] This was a central experience in his conversion to theism when, as he put it in memorable words, 'I gave in and admitted that God was God'.[63] After conversion to Christ, he came to believe that—as he explains in his essay 'Membership'—it was only through 'participation' in the Body of Christ that an individual soul could gain immortality and outlive the physical universe: only 'everything that is joined to the immortal head will share his immortality'.[64] The further implication in the essay is clear, that membership of Christ requires faith.

Lewis' reaction against Idealism may well account—at least partly—for his curious hesitation about the word 'co-inherence', which could too easily be given an idealist meaning. There are further possible reasons in the metaphysical framework that he adopted on becoming a Christian; we can call this Christian Neoplatonism,[65] the modification of Neoplatonic thought that was typical of Augustine and Boethius,[66] to both of whom Lewis continually confesses his debt. It was, for Lewis, a congenial element of this kind of Platonism to insist on a strong distinction between God and creation,[67] and a hierarchy in which lower realities find their fulfilment in obedience to those higher than they.[68] Plato himself had envisaged all human souls as participating in a higher world-soul that constituted a mediation between the eternal world of Being and the transient world of Becoming. He had also thought that particular, empirical objects in the world participated in the universal Forms or Ideas of which they were copies or shadows, and which the world-soul contemplated.[69] While his thought was fragmentary and ambiguous, and he recognized there were problems about the relation between sensible objects and Ideas,[70] it is probable that Plato envisaged the transcendent Forms as participating in turn in the supreme 'Form of the Good'. There was thus unlimited participation 'up' the hierarchy of Being, but not downwards; the Ideas were present to the sensible objects in the world, but did not participate in them (in the sense of being dependent on them or deriving any properties from them, or being 'in' them).

In the tidier scheme of Neoplatonism, however, as pioneered by Plotinus, there was felt to be a greater problem about the 'participation' of lower realities in the highest Reality, since this Reality, or the One, was absolutely transcendent. The One overflows into the many, and in first place into mind, proceeding as the radiance of light from light. The human goal is to become fully *nous* (mind) and so

---

[62] Lewis, *Surprised by Joy*, 213.   [63] Lewis, *Surprised by Joy*, 215.
[64] Lewis, 'Membership', 41.
[65] Barkman, *C. S. Lewis*, 63, opts for 'Neoplatonic Christianity', rather than the 'Christian Platonism' identified by Rose, 'Christian Platonism', 203.
[66] For Lewis' selective use of Boethius and Augustine, see Edwards, 'C.S. Lewis', 24–5, 28–31.
[67] See CSL to Owen Barfield, 19 August [1948?], Lewis, *Letters*, 2: 870–1.
[68] Lewis, *Preface*, 72–80.
[69] Plato, *Parmenides*, 132E-133a; cf. 131A-E. He also recognized some puzzles about the nature of this participation: *Phaedo* 100d. See Lewis, *Studies in Words*, 296–7, on the Platonic *eidos*.
[70] See Plato, *Parmenides* 131b–c, 132c–d.

finally to achieve union with—and absorption into—the One.[71] But sensible objects in the world do not by their *nature* participate in the One, which is ineffable, inexpressible, and inactive. This contrasts with Plato's likely view that objects known by the senses can participate in the Supreme principle, the Form of the Good. Plotinus certainly affirmed the participation of bodily objects in eternal *ideas*, but these are at a lower level in the hierarchy of Being from the One. Plotinus also considered that this participation must mean that objects are immediately *present* to the ideas in order to gain properties from them; particular things can thus be said to be 'in' the eternal forms.[72] But this presence is not reciprocal; here Plotinus agrees with Plato and works out more exactly than his predecessor why this is so. Though ideas are present to sensible things, they are not 'in' them;[73] objects only acquire properties from the idea as an 'appearance' rather than a possession; thus, immanent forms and images of Ideas only 'appear' in sensible things.[74] The result of this metaphysic is to emphasize that 'participation' means that there is a resemblance or analogy between transcendental forms and their particulars in the world, but no reception of the Ideas into the substance of this-worldly objects. Lewis diagnoses the medieval world view in the same way, writing that the movement of the heavenly spheres was believed to derive from a 'love or appetite for God', which was a 'desire to *participate* as much as possible in His nature, i.e. to *imitate* it'.[75]

Lewis seems to have adopted a Christianized form of this later 'widely-diffused' Platonism,[76] after his conversion in place of his earlier Idealism—having found by personal experiment that notion of general human participation [unity] in the Absolute failed to deliver its promise. It is more accurate to call Lewis' philosophy 'Neoplatonic Christianity' rather than simply 'Platonist Christianity', since his romantic sense of 'desire' and 'yearning' fitted in more with the Neoplatonist view of 'spiritual eros',[77] as a desire for *union* with God, than the Platonic view of eros, as desire for *knowledge* of God (the beauty of truth).[78] His thought is also typically Neoplatonic in finding analogies between natural life and that which is ultimately real, rather than an ontological continuity, as we have already seen in his reaction to Williams' theology of romantic love from 1936 onwards. The goal of the human soul is union with God—for a Christian, available through Christ—but this is not the present condition of general human nature in its material environment. Rather, Lewis thought, 'the secular community, since it exists for our natural

---

[71] Plotinus, *Enneads*, 6.9.8, 33–4; 6.9.11. See Rist, 'Forms', 30–1.

[72] Plotinus, *Enneads*, 6.4.10, 1–22.

[73] Plotinus, *Enneads* 6.4.2, 25–7; 6.5.3, 12. So Strange, 'Plotinus' Account', 491.

[74] Strange, 'Plotinus' Account', 493–4.   [75] Lewis, 'Imagination and Thought' 51. My italics.

[76] However, Lewis calls this simply 'Platonism', reserving 'Neo-platonism' for the 'theosophy' developed by such as Ficino or Pico: see Lewis, 'Neoplatonism', 149.

[77] See Lewis, *Spenser's Images of Life*, 133.

[78] For a Christian Neoplatonic desire for union with the one, see Boethius, *Philosophiae Consolationis* 3.11.104–23.

good and not for our supernatural, has no higher end than to facilitate [...] natural values', and among these Lewis names 'nothing half so good as a household laughing together over a meal, or two friends talking over a pint of beer, or a man alone reading a book that interests him'—the goods of family, friendship, and solitude.[79] We have already read Lewis as affirming that human culture fosters only its own values which are not 'spiritual values',[80] and that human passion offers only 'participation in natural forces of life and fertility'.[81]

For Lewis, the analogy between the good we 'recognize' in natural life generally and the 'supernatural' goodness of God is thus real, but not exact. This is then a modification of Plato's (presumed) preferred view that the gods love what is holy 'because it is [intrinsically] holy'.[82] Though Lewis has been accused of moving towards an 'Ockhamism' where what is good is simply established by the will of God,[83] it is better to see him—as a Christian Neoplatonist—as refusing to take the view of Plato himself without qualification. What it means to affirm the goodness of God must have *continuity* with a human moral intuition of what is good, but will also have some *discontinuities* and surprises, as Lewis already makes clear in *The Problem of Pain*,[84] and as he much later appears to experience for himself in his personal agony of *A Grief Observed*. There is no need to doubt that, at the same time, Lewis continues to reject the alternative of Ockhamism as portraying an 'omnipotent fiend'.[85]

As with Aquinas, for Lewis the uncreated God thus 'participates' in creation in the limited sense of *causing* analogies of God's self, and especially producing reflections of the divine light in the light of the human intellect.[86] Williams, we have seen, finds the light of Christ not simply reflected in, but actually *embodied* in, the person who is loved by another.[87] Lewis writes in his essay 'Membership' about participation in the Body of Christ, asserting that 'the head of this Body is so unlike the inferior members that they share no predicate with him save by analogy'.[88] By contrast, when Williams writes that for early Christendom 'the other world certainly co-inhered in this, and this co-inhered in the other',[89] he shows a kind of dualism, but he is far from being a Neoplatonist, with his vision of mutual indwelling in 'a vibrant web of universal and supernatural co-inherence'.[90]

---

[79] Lewis, 'Membership', 36.   [80] Lewis, *Christian Reflections*, 28.

[81] Lewis, *Four Loves*, 114.   [82] Plato, *Euthyphro*, 12.

[83] So Beversluis, *C. S. Lewis*, 232–40, 263–5.

[84] See Lewis, *Problem of Pain*, 27–8; also Lewis, 'Obstinacy in Belief', in *They Asked for a Paper*, 192.

[85] Lewis, *Problem of Pain*, 25–6.

[86] Aquinas, *Summa Theologica* Ia.6.4, reply; Ia. 44.1.1; I.a.3.3.2 and reply; *Summa Contra Gentiles* III.97.3. On the importance of the image of light in Lewis, see McGrath, *Intellectual World*, 90, 92–5, 136.

[87] Williams, *He Came Down*, 93–4.   [88] Lewis, 'Membership', 38.

[89] Williams, *Descent of the Dove*, 84.

[90] Williams, *Descent of the Dove*, 87. It is thus an error to classify Williams as a Christian Platonist alongside Lewis, as in Rose, 'Christian Platonism', 206–8.

Lewis' Christianized Neoplatonism does, of course, differ from Neoplatonism proper. As with the early church Fathers who first modified the scheme, the eternal ideas of Plato and Plotinus are ideas in the mind of a personal God. The highest triad of Plotinus (the One, the Mind, and the Soul) is replaced by a co-equal Trinity.[91] The movement from the One to the Many is not a matter of determinism but shaped by the free will of God and creatures.[92] Matter is inferior to Spirit but not evil. Christ as the eternal mind of God has taken bodily form in Christ, so scandalously transgressing the rule that higher realities do not partici-pate in lower. Most notably for our theme, the Neoplatonist goal of absorption into the One is replaced by a union with God, or 'blessed participation' in God,[93] in which the created being retains its identity and distinction from God:

> We all once existed potentially in Him and in that sense were not other than He [...] To what end was creation except to separate us in order that that we may be reunited to Him in that unity of love wh[ich] is utterly different from mere numerical unity and indeed presupposes that lover & beloved be distinct? [...] If mere unity (as opposed to union) is the aim all Creation seems otiose.[94]

So each thing must find its good in 'that kind and degree of the fruition of God which is proper to its nature', and for human beings the summons is 'to a reflection of the Divine life, a creaturely participation in the Divine attributes which is far beyond our present desires'.[95] That participation is only through Christ, as Lewis goes on to make clear: 'We are bidden to "put on Christ", to become like God.' 'Putting on Christ' is a daily summons, and so, while fullness of participation awaits us in the future, union with the Supreme Good can be achieved to some degree in this life.

Summing up Lewis' spiritual and intellectual 'pilgrimage' to the point when he begins writing popular theology (about 1940), we find that he has adapted for Christian purposes a tradition of philosophy in which human life in its natural state has only limited 'participation' in what is most real—the Good and the One. It is restricted to participation by analogy, in which there are both continuities and discontinuities between the 'natural' and the 'spiritual'. The participation in the relational life of the Trinity that Lewis celebrates in *Beyond Personality*, and which marks a step beyond Williams' 'co-inherence', only becomes available on faith in Christ, or in a pure kind of faith in other divine figures that might be counted, in God's generosity, as equivalent.[96] In this respect (with the remarkable exception of

---

[91] For an early example of this process, see Clark, 'Neoplatonic Commentary', 28–31.
[92] See Lewis, *Problem of Pain*, 23.   [93] Lewis, *Miracles*, 187.
[94] CSL to Bede Griffiths, 27 September 1948, Lewis, *Letters*, 2: 880.
[95] Lewis, *Problem of Pain*, 41–2.
[96] See Lewis, *Last Battle*, 166. © C. S. Lewis Pte Ltd, 1956. Cf. CSL to Chad Walsh, 23 May 1960, Lewis, *Letters*, 3: 1154: 'addressing Christ *sub specie Apollinis* [sic]'.

the Great Dance of *Perelandra*, which Lewis told Williams 'is all yours'),[97] participation in God according to Lewis is very different from participation according to Williams, which might not be so trinitarian but is part of the very nature of human beings. For instance, according to Williams, Christ is born into the souls of all lovers who love truly. It is as objectively true as the incarnation: indeed, it *is* an incarnation. Thus Lewis' Christian Neoplatonism accounts, I suggest, for the otherwise odd situation that he both seems to show a hesitation about Williams' idea of co-inherence, and yet also shows a development of it when exploring the pattern of Christian life. There is, however, one further complication of this analysis; at the same time as depreciating natural values as less than Christian virtues, Lewis wants to maintain that humans exist in an environment that in some way includes God, even if most people are unaware of God's existence.[98] God is separate but not separated from the world.

This kind of idea occurs in *The Abolition of Man*, related explicitly to 'participation' when he writes approvingly that in early Hinduism, good conduct 'consists in conforming to, or almost participation in [...] that great ritual or pattern of nature *and supernature*'.[99] Lewis then associates this 'pattern' or 'order' with the *Tao*, or 'Way' of life in Chinese philosophy, 'which every man should tread in imitation of that cosmic and supercosmic progression' of the universe. Though he is hesitant here in speaking about an '*almos*t participation', and an 'imitation', later he is more confident about walking in this Way: 'as long as we remain within it, we find the concrete reality in which to participate is to be truly human'.[100] Adam Barkman proposes that Lewis had come across the idea of the 'Tao' in the theologian Charles Gore's book *The Philosophy of the Good Life*, which he had certainly read in 1940 and went on recommending, and Barkman also suggests that Lewis used the word 'Tao' instead of 'Natural Law' in order to demonstrate 'that Goodness and Truth do not belong exclusively to the West'.[101] Gore maintains that the Tao is 'closely akin to what the Stoics described as Nature, to which all things in heaven and on earth must conform, and to which human nature is akin'.[102] Lewis presents the *Tao* as a pattern of life that belongs essentially within the realm of nature, but the manner in which he speaks of it just hints at introducing a divine immanence into what is otherwise a Neoplatonist universe of hierarchy. He uses the phrases 'pattern of nature and supernature', 'cosmic and supercosmic progression', and—referring to Plato—a Good 'beyond existence'.[103] In *Surprised by Joy*, Lewis recounts an occasion when he 'happened to refer to philosophy as "a subject", and Owen Barfield quickly corrected him: "It wasn't a subject to Plato [...] it was a way."' This rebuke was one prompt, Lewis records,

---

[97] See Chapter 2, section 4.   [98] Lewis, *Problem of Pain*, 19.
[99] Lewis, *Abolition of Man*, 16 (Italics mine).   [100] Lewis, *Abolition of Man*, 51.
[101] Barkman, *C. S. Lewis*, 175.   [102] Gore, *Philosophy*, 87.   [103] Lewis, *Abolition*, 15–16.

that brought him to theism.[104] Lewis' affirming of 'the Way' is one more trace of a tension in Lewis' thought that will be finally resolved only in his final writings.

6.3 Co-inherence and Co-existence

Another term that seems close to 'Co-inherence' is 'co-existence',[105] an idea that runs throughout *The Problem of Pain*. Free spirits, maintains Lewis, co-exist with each other and they need an external, material environment in which to do so:

> People often talk as if nothing were easier than for two naked minds to 'meet' or become aware of each other. But I see no possibility of their doing so except in a common medium which forms their 'external world' or environment . Even our vague attempt to imagine such a meeting between disembodied spirits usually slips in surreptitiously the idea of, at least, a common space and common time, to give the *co-* in *co-existence* a meaning: and space and time are already an environment.[106]

Lewis goes on to explain that a material environment is not only required as a meeting-place, but is the means for the individual identity of each subject within it: 'If your thoughts and passions were directly present to me, like my own, without any mark of externality or otherness, how should I distinguish them from mine?' For this argument, Lewis is, strangely, indebted to his Idealist past.[107] In Subjective Idealism, an external world of 'sensible ideas' (impinging on and perceived by the senses) is necessary for the identity and encounter of spirits, and in Absolute Idealism an emanated, external material world of nature plays the same part; in both, a stronger and more universal Spirit than the individual spirit is needed to sustain such worlds. Moreover, spirits co-exist in this context in connection to the greater Spirit: in Subjective Idealism they require a theistic Spirit in order to have any contact with each other,[108] while in Absolute Idealism spirits have this contact because they are all part of, and present in, a pantheistic Spirit that is therefore 'personal and more'.[109] While Idealism gave Lewis the basic notion of co-existence, a conviction that persisted into his Christian thinking, it took a form in Idealism that he strongly reacted against in becoming a Christian, and the actual term 'co-inherence' may have seemed to him to be in danger of evoking what he had rejected. He makes clear that the situation of co-existence of 'many independent things' that are 'mutually necessary' to each other is the result,

---

[104] Lewis, *Surprised by Joy*, 212.
[105] See Williams, *Descent of the Dove*, 57: 'to co-exist; one might almost say, to co-inhere'.
[106] Lewis, *Problem of Pain*, 18.   [107] See Lewis, *Clivi Hamiltonis Summae Metaphysices*, 29.
[108] See Berkeley, *Three Dialogues*, 220–5, 229–31.
[109] Bradley, *Appearance and Reality*, 529–33.

not of the diversification of Spirit, but of 'a single, utterly self-consistent act of creation'.[110]

This kind of co-existence gives us hope that animals—or at least domestic ones—can attain redemption in the resurrection of the dead by being included 'in' the life and community of the redeemed human beings who care for them. Thus, co-existence of humans and animals is not 'a mere contingent result of interacting biological facts'.[111] Lewis here appeals to the 'mysterious force' of the word 'in', and illustrates it by the mutual indwelling of the human believer in Christ, God, the Holy Spirit, and the church. Here there is at least an implicit trinitarian *perichoresis*—Christ, God, Spirit. We notice that it is not a general or universal 'being in' God, and is confined to the life of faith, and yet with the combination of 'co-existence' and 'in' we are surely hovering on the borders of 'co-inherence':

> I have already noted the mysterious force of the word 'in'. I do not take all the senses of it in the New Testament to be identical, so that man is in Christ and Christ in God and the Holy Spirit in the Church and also in the individual believer in exactly the same sense. They may be senses that rhyme or correspond rather than a single sense. I am now going to suggest—though with great readiness to be set right by real theologians—that there may be a sense, corresponding, though not identical, with these, in which those beasts that attain a real self are in their masters. That is to say, you must not think of a beast by itself, and call that a personality and then inquire whether God will raise and bless that. You must take the whole context in which the beast acquires its selfhood.[112]

That context is the whole 'body' of 'The goodman - and - the - goodwife - ruling - their - children - and - their - beasts - in - the - good - home-stead.' Lewis suggests that this is a body in the Pauline sense, but since he does not want to suggest that it is simply the 'body of Christ', he adds 'or a closely sub-Pauline' sense. Another reason perhaps now appears for why Lewis does not call this 'co-inherence': the body for Lewis is strictly hierarchical in character. If God is the centre of the universe, man is 'the subordinate centre' of terrestrial nature, and the beasts 'are not co-ordinate with man, but subordinate to him'.[113] The domestic animal, such as the dog, has an identity that resides not only 'in its relation to the Body', but especially 'to the master who is the head of that Body'. So man and the animals are 'co-existent', and 'in' each other but not 'co-ordinate'. As long as 'being in' is controlled by a fixed hierarchy between the lower and the higher, there will be difficulties with the word 'co-inherence'. Absolute Idealism does have room for hierarchy, but this is of different levels of spirit, which are finally co-present and

---

[110] Lewis, *Problem of Pain*, 22–3.   [111] Lewis, *Problem of Pain*, 126.
[112] Lewis, *Problem of Pain*, 127.   [113] Lewis, *Problem of Pain*, 129.

constitutive of the one, all-embracing Spirit. By becoming a Neoplatonist Christian, Lewis has accentuated the hierarchy, the differences between the uncreated reality and creatures, and between the creatures among themselves.

In line with Augustine, Lewis thinks that loving God means serving God obediently in the place assigned for every person in the hierarchy, and that justice means loving every thing according to its place and worth as given by God.[114] By contrast, Williams has a similar regard for hierarchy, but love has a different effect on the situation. In a Platonic dialogue, he explores 'hierarchies of love', and proposes that 'if each creature is unique, he owes discreet obedience to all others and all others to him'.[115] There is a change, or 'exchange' of hierarchical position according to the context, at one moment someone being 'hierarchically ascendant' to another, and at the next moment the other taking the higher position instead. In this 'classless Republic of hierarchies', there is 'exchange of duty', and equality is 'the name we give to the whole sum of such changes'. It is not difficult to recognize when the change happens, asserts Williams' Celia, 'when, by grace, one is free and in love'.[116] Williams' character Eugenio recognizes that the relation between hierarchy and equality might be called 'dialectical', but prefers another word, which he hopes has not become 'tiresome' by repetition: 'the important things about these two principles is their co-inherence'. Dialectic promises a future resolution of a tension, but co-inherence is about 'union' here and now. In the very moment, he exclaims, of 'looking down on the ranks below, the whole order is happily changed and one finds oneself looking up at the astonishing blaze of those same ranks now high and high above'.[117] With his more fixed concept of hierarchy and roles within it (which rules out, for example, women priests),[118] it seems that it is more difficult for Lewis to use the word 'co-inherence'.

Yet Lewis leaves room in the system, allowing him to depict something like co-inherence in God elsewhere in his writing. Lewis is appealing to the redemption of animals that have become part of the human community in order to meet the challenge to theodicy of animal pain; animals, he is arguing, have sentience but not consciousness, and so those who acquire a 'real self' or soul attain this through co-existence with, and relation to, their human masters. For all that, when the philosopher C. E. M. Joad objected that Lewis' theodicy 'does not cover the case of the higher animals who do not know man',[119] Lewis replied that he had only given one 'illustration' of animals attaining resurrection in order to 'liberate the imagin-ation'. He draws attention to his earlier statement that 'if our previous assertion of divine goodness was sound, we might be sure that *in some way or other* "all would be well and all manner of things would be well"'.[120] Perhaps Lewis would have

---

[114] Lewis, *Preface*, 75–80; Augustine, *City of God*, 12.5.
[115] Williams, 'Dialogue on Hierarchy', 129.   [116] Williams, 'Dialogue on Hierarchy', 128.
[117] Williams, 'Dialogue on Hierarchy', 130.
[118] Lewis, 'Priestesses', in Lewis, *Undeceptions*, 195–6.
[119] Lewis, 'Pains of Animals', in *Undeceptions*, 131.   [120] Lewis, 'Pains of Animals', 135.

given more 'illustrations' had he not been trying to avoid his Idealist past, in which he had supposed that all animals have souls on the grounds that there is a behaviour in animals similar to that which we 'recognize as flowing from our souls', and all souls are held together in one Spirit.[121]

Hierarchy and the need for a material environment come together in Lewis' hopes for resurrection of the body. Human spirits, he affirms, 'participate' to some degree in God through Christ, and they need bodies in order to differentiate and identify them. If they are to participate fully in God in life after death, they cannot be disembodied. In *Miracles*, he thus proposes that there must be an 'intermediate floor' between the two spheres of the unconditioned reality of God 'beyond all worlds' and our present finite existence, in which embodied beings can exist in the 'glory' of union with God. 'Heaven' is consequently an ambivalent word; it may mean the state of participating in the life of God, or it may mean 'The whole Nature or system of conditions in which redeemed human spirits, still remaining human, can enjoy such *participation* fully and for ever.'[122] This is the 'new Nature' that the resurrection of Jesus began to create, and Christ has now gone to 'prepare' a place for us to dwell on that 'floor' of existence: 'A new Nature is being made out of an old one [. . .] Something is being pulled down and something is going up in its place.'[123]

A rather different picture of the resurrection of the body is, however, offered in the late *Letters to Malcolm*. There he envisages the sensuous life as being inside the soul, so that a new world can be created out of the spirit alone, which carries the sensations created by matter within it. Vividly, he writes, 'I can now communicate to you the vanished fields of my boyhood—they are building sites today—only imperfectly by words. Perhaps the day is coming when I can take you for a walk through them.'[124] This new creation is not apparently being prepared for us by the ascended Christ, but it is 'in the sense-bodies of the redeemed' that 'the whole new earth will arise'.

There are evident resonances in this account with Lewis' earlier Subjective Idealism, in which the external, material world consisted of 'sensible ideas' conceived by spirit; as Lewis once wrote in his idealist days, 'matter exists, together with souls, inside Spirit'.[125] However, Lewis is now envisaging something like this to be the case only for the 'world' of resurrection. During this life, matter has been objectively distinct from spirit, and has delivered sense impressions to the mind, which has—much as Kant proposed—associated these into perceptions of the world ('out of these I build myself a neat little box stage').[126] Then, after death, rather like the 'image-body' of the philosopher H. H. Price,[127] there will be a

---

[121] Lewis, *Clivi Hamiltonis Summae Metaphysices*, 32.   [122] Lewis, *Miracles*, 187. My italics.
[123] Lewis, *Miracles*, 185.   [124] Lewis, *Letters to Malcolm*, 155.
[125] Lewis, *Clivi Hamiltonis Summae Metaphysices*, 35.   [126] Lewis, *Letters to Malcolm*, 108.
[127] Price, 'Survival', 176–95. Price was a life-long colleague of Lewis at Magdalen College, and a frequent speaker at the Socratic Club with which Lewis was closely associated.

survival of 'the sensuous life', and a continuity between nature and spirit in the redemption of sensations or sense-memories. Despite the difference from earlier Idealism, there is some similarity in a process of what we might aptly call a co-inherence between body and spirit, to which Lewis had not subscribed earlier. It is the view of James Patrick that in Lewis' later writings he 'returned to the old idealistic strains',[128] and Barkman concurs with this judgement, though he finds the return 'more figurative', that is, a matter of language rather 'than literal'. My own view is that on the question of divine and human presence in the world *Letters to Malcolm* shows a 'return' (or at least a closer alignment) to Charles Williams, not to Idealism. My reasons for this will occupy some of the next chapter.

---

[128] Patrick, 'Reason', 355.

7

C. S. Lewis and a New Turn
to Charles Williams

'It all began with a picture' runs the heading to a short piece that C. S. Lewis wrote
for the *Radio Times* of 15 July 1960. Writing for the children who were listening to a
dramatization of the *Narnia* tales, Lewis reflected on the genesis of his storytelling:

> All my seven Narnian books, and my three science fiction books, began with
> seeing pictures in my head. At first they were not a story, just pictures. The *Lion*
> all began with a picture of a Faun carrying an umbrella and parcels in a snowy
> wood [...] At first I had very little idea how the story would go on. But then
> suddenly Aslan came bounding into it.[1]

Lewis' words about the Faun have been often cited in commentary on the
Chronicles of Narnia. But Lewis' very last sentence in this piece has usually not
been noticed. Suddenly, he turns from story to idea, asking his young readers:
'When you "have an idea" could you tell anyone exactly how you have thought of
it?' The movement of Lewis' own thought here betrays something about his
method of composition. Pictures, images, certainly drive the story. But for Lewis
they also drive the ideas and the argument of his theological reflections. This is
what makes his prose a delight to read, even when we might be taking issue with
the content. In Chapter 6, I suggested that a series of images or metaphors—dance,
drama, begetting, and immersion—supported by the concepts of 'participation'
and 'co-existence' are 'showing' a situation that we can only call co-inherence. The
picture prompts a train of thought that takes us to a destination one step further
than even Charles Williams travelled, to an indwelling in the triune God.
How easily a picture can lead to such a concept in Lewis' mind is illustrated by
his rather extraordinary comment to a schoolgirl, that the three replies of Aslan
to Shasta (in *The Horse and His Boy*), repeating 'Myself' three times to the
question 'Who are you?', 'suggest the Trinity'.[2] This, as he repeats many times,

---

[1] Reprinted in Lewis, *Of This and Other Worlds*, 78–9. See also Hooper, 'It All Began with a Picture',
152–4.
[2] CSL to Sophia Storr, 24 December 1959, Lewis, *Letters*, 3: 1113. See Lewis, *Horse and His Boy*, 147;
cf. Ware, 'C. S. Lewis', 146–7.

Charles Williams and C.S. Lewis: Friends in Co-inherence. Paul S. Fiddes, Oxford University Press. © Paul S. Fiddes 2021.
DOI: 10.1093/oso/9780192845467.003.0007

is not allegory,[3] but following through where a picture might take you, perhaps unexpectedly.

But at the same time, there seems to be a counter-movement of thought going on, which may explain why Lewis hesitates about using the actual word 'co-inherence'. I have suggested that this belongs to his philosophical commitments: he has inherited general Neoplatonist qualifications of 'participation', he is in reaction against an idealist pantheism, and he is faithful to a hierarchy of obedience. There appears to be a tension here between metaphor and concept. Now I want to suggest that a picture in Lewis may hold such a tension within itself, both fostering and inhibiting the showing of the co-inherence of all things. Then, through the creation of myths, including Narnia, there comes another way of 'showing' co-inherence, until with Lewis' final work there is a return to Williams' kind of thinking about the relation of God and the world. Writing to an American scholar in 1959 who was enquiring about common ground between the Inklings, Lewis judges that 'Charles Williams certainly influenced me, and I perhaps influenced him. But after that I think you would draw a blank.'[4] By that time, I want to show, Lewis is showing even stronger traces of Williams' thought than in the days when they talked together in his rooms at Magdalen. There is a 'return' to Williams, and thus to his particular vision of co-inherence.

7.1 Tensions within Images of Co-inherence

Underlying Lewis' philosophical commitments is a conviction I have already touched upon several times and which now deserves fuller exploration—that is, the inferior position of what Lewis variously refers to as 'material', the physical 'body', and 'Nature'. For Lewis, matter was not in itself an evil, as it was in the classical Neoplatonist metaphysic, but it occupied a subordinate status in the great hierarchy of being.

I have suggested that Lewis imaginatively reuses the biblical image of the 'begetting' of sons and daughters of God in order to 'show' co-inherence of human beings in God. But this very image can lead Lewis in another direction, into a severance from natural life. This becomes clear in *Mere Christianity* when Lewis places it alongside another image.[5] This is the picture of statues coming to life, derived from the Pygmalion myth, and drawn upon by Shakespeare in *The Winter's Tale*. In the Pygmalion myth, the sculptor falls in love with the statue of a beautiful woman he has made, and the gods bring her to life for him.

---

[3] See also CSL to Mrs Hook, 29 December 1958, Lewis, *Letters*, 3: 1004–5; CSL to Anne Jenkins, 5 March 1961, Lewis, *Letters*, 3: 1244–5.

[4] CSL to Charles Moorman, 15 May 1959, Lewis, *Letters*, 3: 1049.

[5] In the following pages, I reuse material from my article 'On Theology', 93–9.

In *The Winter's Tale*, Hermione who has been thought to be dead for twenty years pretends to be a statue and apparently comes miraculously to life for Leontes. Elsewhere, Lewis makes reference to both these sources.[6] So he proposes that human beings can similarly come to life, and be changed from being mere statues to being children of God. The progression of his thought is this: 'What God begets is God [...] what God creates is not God.'[7] So God has *begotten* Christ, and only *made* human beings. They may be like God in certain respects, but they are not things of the same kind. They are, says Lewis, 'more like statues or pictures of God'.[8] If we are to become *gods*, then like Christ we shall have to be *begotten* not made. When we become sons in this true sense, we are like statues that have come alive: 'This world is a great sculptor's shop. We are the statues and there is a rumour going round the shop that some of us are some day going to come to life.'[9]

For Lewis, all human beings are created in the image of God, but in their natural life—which he calls *Bios*—they are mere statues of the divine. As created, they are lifeless as far as spiritual life—*Zoe*—is concerned. Christ gives us this *Zoe* life, which, Lewis says, is 'the spiritual life which is in God from all eternity and which made the whole world'.[10] It is as if we are the creatures in the White Witch's courtyard in *The Lion, the Witch and the Wardrobe*, turned by her magic into stone statues;[11] like them, we need the breath of Aslan to come to life. So we become *begotten* and not just *created* 'sons', coming to spiritual life just as Christ is alive. Christ is made incarnate and dies to natural life in order to make it possible for human beings to come alive as sons. Lewis sums up:

> We are not begotten by God, we are only made by him: in our natural state we are not sons of God, only (so to speak) statues. We have not got *Zoe* or spiritual life: only *Bios* or biological life which is presently going to run down or die. The whole offer which Christianity makes is this: that we can, if we let God have his way, come to share in the life of Christ. If we do, we shall then be sharing a life which was begotten, not made, which always has existed and always will exist.[12]

Perhaps, as in the ribbons of light and love in the vision of *Perelandra*, Lewis thinks of this *Zoe* life as the very pattern of the dance of the Trinity. By being taken into this 'life which is begotten' and not made we—mere statues—come to life as sons, or as gods. This is touching doctrine with the glow of imagination. Lewis' fundamental insight is that, by entering the dance or drama of the Trinity, we truly become sons and daughters of God; we truly become persons. This is, we may say, co-inherence. The supplementary image of statues coming to life is a vivid one,

---

[6] See CSL to Arthur Greaves, 5 September 1931, Lewis, *Letters*, 1: 968; also Lewis, 'William Morris', 224.

[7] Lewis, *Mere Christianity*, 124.   [8] Lewis, *Mere Christianity*, 124.

[9] Lewis, *Mere Christianity*, 126.   [10] Lewis, *Mere Christianity*, 125–6.

[11] Lewis, *Lion, the Witch and the Wardrobe*, 88–91.   [12] Lewis, *Mere Christianity*, 140.

and effective in a particular literary context. But there always remains the danger of opening up too large a gulf between a life that is created (*Bios*) and a life that is begotten (*Zoe*). The image has captured his imagination and shaped the doctrinal concept, and this is now underlined by another image—that of tin soldiers or toy soldiers:

> Did you ever think, when you were a child, what fun it would be if your toys could come to life? Well suppose you could really have brought them to life. Imagine turning a tin soldier into a real little man. It would involve turning the tin into flesh. And suppose the tin soldier did not like it. He is not interested in flesh; all he sees is that the tin is being spoilt. He thinks you are killing him.[13]

This image inevitably magnifies the difference between being created and re-created, opening an ontological gap, and so depreciating the state of natural existence. There can be no continuity between tin and flesh, no basis for the one in the other. The simile presents nature as a phase to be superseded by something else, which can only come into nature wholly 'from outside.'[14] It also leaves nature as a space that can be occupied by the Dark Power, and in which Christ is an invader. Here is another potent image, drawn from the contemporary experience of war in Europe, that of invasion. The rightful king has landed in enemy-occupied territory in disguise and is calling us all to take part in a great campaign of sabotage.[15] Dualism, states Lewis, is closer to Christianity than people think: Christianity agrees that the universe is at war, but it is occupied by a Dark Power that was created by God and has rebelled. The image of a secret invasion here is telling. For theologians such as Gustaf Aulén and Karl Barth, the decisive grand battle against evil has been already won in the cross of Jesus, and all that is left is a mere mopping-up operation.[16] For Lewis, the last battle has not yet happened, but there are soldiers of the resistance dotted all over the world. Perhaps Lewis' sense of the power of evil is truer to its reality as we experience it, but the image again tends to relegate nature to something less than real.

Of course, a Christian theologian must agree with Lewis that we can only attain *full* personality in Christ. We must be summoned to go 'beyond personality', transcending our human beingness in the life of God. But our biological personality is liable to be undermined as a creation of God when Lewis writes: 'what I so proudly call myself [is] merely the meeting-place for trains of events which I never started and I cannot stop', a matter of 'heredity and upbringing and surroundings', and with desires 'thrown up by my physical organism or pumped into me by other

---

[13] Lewis, *Mere Christianity*, 141.   [14] Lewis, *Mere Christianity*, 172–3.
[15] Lewis, *Mere Christianity*, 37.
[16] Aulén, *Christus Victor*, 58–60; Karl Barth, *Church Dogmatics*, III/3, 366–7. Lewis had read Aulén, with approval: see letter to H. Morland, 19 August 1942, Lewis, *Letters*, 2: 529.

men's thoughts or even suggested to me by devils'.[17] In his broadcast version of *Beyond Personality*, Lewis glosses the phrase 'there are no real personalities anywhere else' than in God with the phrase 'I mean no *full, complete* personalities', which gives the respect to human nature that he certainly intends.[18] In the printed version, this phrase is unfortunately omitted, leaving only the qualifier 'real', implying that our *Bios* life is somehow unreal.

When thinking more philosophically about the status of nature, Lewis defends himself here against the process theologian Norman Pittenger,[19] who criticizes Lewis for supposedly regarding miracles as a 'violation of the laws of nature'. Lewis points to his study on *Miracles*, which makes clear that supernatural events 'interrupt nature' but do not break the laws of nature, since nature always has the capacity to adjust to new events.[20] Nature, he affirms, is through a fall from God, partly good and partly evil, and will be redeemed.[21] Lewis tells us that he had never wanted to be 'interfered' with,[22] and so when he yielded and confessed that 'God was God'—that the Absolute Spirit of idealism was a personal God to whom he could relate—it seems apt that he came to conceive of this God as an 'invader' of the world. Nature *must* suffer an invasion or interference (or 'interruption') by its creator.

Strictly speaking, for Lewis only God is entirely 'supernatural', beyond *all* created natures whatsoever. But higher stages in the hierarchy of creation are 'supernatural' to the lower, exceeding their own particular nature, when God empowers them to be so.[23] Thus, for Lewis, even the rational spirit of human beings has a 'super-natural' element to it, as 'something which *invades* the great interlocked event in space and time, instead of merely arising from it',[24] although this sort of spirit is actually created and so is still another kind of nature. How much more, argues Lewis, will the 'absolutely supernatural' invade the natural world.[25] So the Incarnation for Lewis is the Grand Miracle; it is the supreme invasion of nature to which all other invasions are related, and because of which they are not just 'arbitrary raids'. Statues and tin soldiers can become persons because their world has been invaded.

Lewis thus argues that we begin to see how God can become a man at all when we see that every human being is already the site of an invasion: a supernatural creature—the mind—is united with a natural creature—the physical organism.[26] In Jesus, not a supernatural *creature* but the supernatural *Creator* himself becomes united with a natural creature. So, as Lewis puts it, 'our own composite existence is

---

[17] Lewis, *Mere Christianity*, 176.

[18] Lewis, *Mere Christianity*, 177. The original phrase can be heard on the BBC recording of this broadcast, unusually preserved.

[19] Lewis, 'Rejoinder to Dr Pittenger', 143–8.   [20] Lewis, *Miracles*, 72–3.

[21] Lewis, *Miracles*, 80–1.   [22] Lewis, *Surprised by* Joy, 198–214.

[23] Lewis, *Studies in Words*, 64–6.

[24] Lewis, *Miracles*, 203. Cf. *Letters to Malcolm*, 96, 'God injects a person into the realm of Nature'.

[25] Lewis, *Miracles*, 204.   [26] Lewis, *Miracles*, 133.

a faint image of the divine Incarnation itself—the same theme in a very minor key'. In Christ, the divine spirit dwells within a human spirit just as the human spirit dwells within any human body.[27] We need not explore here the similarity of this Christology to the 'Logos–Sarx' (Word–Body) Christology of fourth-century Alexandria, in which the divine Logos either replaces the human mind or (as in the doctrine of Athanasius) effectively replaces its functions as director of the body.[28] The kind of mind–body dualism this relies upon derives from a Platonic world view, as it does in Lewis.

For Lewis, the essential location of the supernatural invasion of our natural world is thus the human spirit or mind itself. The human being can acquire the new *Zoe* life through the transformation of the rational mind, not through the body or even a synthesis between mind and body. For Lewis, in our natural state and because of an ancient Fall from communion with God, rational mind and physical body are at war with each other. A natural organism is 'tenanted' by 'a supernatural spirit', and is attacking its superior and rightful occupant.[29] This idea of a *warfare* between the body and mind in every human being, and the conquering of his own body by the mind of Christ, is surprisingly like the Christology of an Alexandrian—Apollinaris—whom the church finally decided was heretical.[30] For Lewis, the original blessed state of humanity, and its hoped-for goal in the resurrection, is for the spirit to be 'fully "at home" with its organism, like a king in his own country or a rider on his own horse'. He adds that in the pre-Fall condition, 'where spirit's power over the organism was complete and unresisted, death would never occur'.[31] And in the resurrection, he exults in *Miracles*, the human spirit will be finally in full control of its body like a rider on an obedient horse, riding 'bareback, confident and rejoicing, those greater mounts, those winged, shining and world-shaking horses' that await us in the stables of the King.[32]

This kind of dualism between mind and body, as the basis for a greater dualism between spirit and nature, thus inhibits a co-inherence between God and the world in its 'natural' state. But as everywhere in Lewis, one image tends to counterbalance another. Alongside these pictures of a conquering of body by the spirit Lewis also gives us the term 'symbiosis' for the relation between them.[33] At the very same time as he gives us the dualistic image of horse and its rider, he offers another that implies some kind of co-inherence: 'better still, as the human part of a Centaur was "at home" with the equine part'.[34] What such a union might look like we can glean from the Narnia novels, where the Centaurs are noble and fully integrated beings, appearing to be very far from someone

[27] Lewis, *Miracles*, 134.   [28] see Kelly, *Early Christian Doctrines*, 153–8, 284–95.
[29] Lewis, *Miracles*, 152–3.   [30] See Norris, *Manhood and Christ*, 112–22.
[31] Lewis, *Miracles* 152.   [32] Lewis, *Miracles*, 194–5.   [33] Lewis, *Miracles*, 152.
[34] Lewis, *Miracles*, 152.

riding 'bareback'. But the dualistic metaphysic, if held rigidly (which Lewis' readers might do), evidently resists a co-inherence of the spiritual with the natural. Here we may contrast Williams's approach, where the body is an 'index' to all the Virtues, displaying 'heavenly qualities, incarnated influences',[35] every natural body formed in accord with the Body of Christ:

> The Sacred Body is the plan upon which physical human creation was built, for it is the centre of physical human creation [...] As His, so ours; the body, in this sense of an index, is also a pattern. We carry about with us an operative synthesis of the Virtues, and it may be that when we fall in love (for example), we fall in love precisely with the operative synthesis [...] The 'index' of our bodies, the incarnate qualities of the moral universe, receive the Archetype of all moralities truly incarnated.

Williams recognizes (like Lewis) that 'we cannot properly direct and control our sensations and emotions', but this is not a situation of warfare between mind and body: 'the greatness of man is written even in this incapacity, and when he sins he sins because of a vision which, even though clouded, is great and ultimate'. To say this means rejecting the Platonic dualism of mind and body, and Williams immediately goes on to affirm 'that unity' that we 'under the influence of our Greek culture, divide into soul and body.' He then goes on to approve the judgement of a philosopher (William Ellis) that we are wrongly dominated by 'the concept of the two fold nature of man, as man as a union of the active, or spiritual, with the inactive, or corporeal'.[36] We have, he affirms, 'a complete self-consciousness, and not a self-consciousness in schism'. That spirit and matter are regarded as divided is, he reflects in an article for *Theology* (1941), 'due perhaps to that lack of intellectual clarity produced by the Fall'. In the same piece he proposes that incarnation, the embodiment of God is the 'divine reason' for creation, but that God would have taken a body even if there had been no creation of 'other flesh'; he hesitantly attributes this doctrine to Duns Scotus, although Scotus' point is that incarnation would have taken place even if there had been no human *fall*.[37] Williams here seems to have intensified the stress on God's 'union of Himself with matter in flesh'.

Williams thus affirms that the 'radiant interchange' of love is 'part of the heavenly vision [...] because it is a physical as well as a spiritual vision'.[38] It is sacramental, but not in the sense of 'the spiritual *using* the physical'; rather it is

---

[35] Williams, 'Index of the Body', in Williams, *Image*, 87.   [36] Williams, 'Index', 86.

[37] Williams, 'Natural Goodness', in Williams, *Image*, 76. For authority, Ridler in *Image*, xxxviii suggests Scotus, *Opus Oxoniense* iii. Dist. 19. Gerard Manley Hopkins, whose poetry influenced Williams deeply, also follows Scotus: see Hopkins, *Sermons and Spiritual Writings*, 358–61, citing Hopkins' retreat notes for 8 November 1881.

[38] Williams, 'Index', 85.

'a common—say, a single—operation'. With this we may compare Lewis, who writes that 'Spirit and Nature have quarrelled in us', and that we only have 'faints hints' of a healing in 'the Sacraments, in the use made of sensuous imagery by the great poets, in the best instances of sexual love, or in experiences of the earth's beauty'.[39] In another essay in *Theology* (1939), Williams quotes the Lady Julian of Norwich, that 'our Substance is in God', and 'in our sensualite God is'. Affirming that the 'sensuality' God indwells must mean 'our whole physical nature', Williams goes on to expand this with a further phrase from Julian: 'our soul with our body, and our body with our soul, either of them taking help of other'.[40] While not entirely rejecting the Platonic dictum that 'soul is form and doth the body make', he immediately ripostes: 'but soul ought not to be allowed to reduce the body to its own shadow'.[41]

Of course, Lewis also sees the danger of 'reduction' of nature. He stresses that the invasion—whether in the many miracles of the Old and New Testaments, or in the incarnation itself—is not the invasion of an alien power.[42] Nature is being invaded by her own king, and so her laws are not being broken. Nature is not an illusion, though she is infected with evil and depraved by the fall of humanity. She 'has the air of a good thing spoilt'.[43] We can thus still see within her some poor reflections of God's own patterns of activity,[44] and, for Lewis, one is the pattern of God's descent into death and reascent to life. As expressed in myths of the dying and rising corn-king, the process of death and rebirth is written large into all levels of the natural world. In Christ this myth becomes fact; he is the reality to which all myths of a dying and rising god refer.[45] Lewis does not write, as Williams does, that the 'patterns' of the human body are the plan of the Sacred Body; for Lewis, the patterns of nature are only 'transpositions of the Divine theme into a minor key', but there is unquestionably some overlap of thought.

It is with the pattern of dying and rising, 'a thing written all over the world', that Lewis introduces the image of 'immersion' and 'diving' that I have already suggested evokes the ethos of co-inherence. God goes down, says Lewis, 'to come up again and bring the whole ruined world up with him'.[46] I suggest that this image of immersion into the depths is a more potent metaphor than 'invasion', and that it avoids opening a gap between nature and spirit. Lewis affirms the resurrection of the body, as we have seen; he also celebrates the value of the human senses in his poem 'On Being Human', again with a striking image—the lack of nerves and sense-organs in an angel:

---

[39] Lewis, *Miracles*, 190.
[40] Williams, 'Sensuality and Substance', in Williams, *Image*, 68. The quotations are from Julian of Norwich, *Revelations*, chapter 55. See further Chapter 8, section 4.
[41] Williams, 'Sensuality and Substance', 69.   [42] Lewis, *Miracles*, 159.
[43] Lewis, *Miracles*, 147.   [44] Lewis, *Miracles*, 136.   [45] Lewis, *Miracles*, 135–40.
[46] Lewis, *Miracles*, 135.

> The tremor on the rippled pool of memory
> That from each smell in widening circles goes,
> The pleasure and the pang—can angels measure it?
> An angel has no nose.[47]

In *Mere Christianity*, reflecting on the sacraments, he rejoices that 'God likes matter. He invented it.'[48] In *Miracles*, he insists that God is the God of wheat and wine and oil; he is Bacchus, Venus, and Ceres all rolled into one.[49] In *The Allegory of Love*, he writes that he distrusts 'that species of respect for the spiritual order which bases itself on contempt for the natural'.[50]

With his metaphors of dance, drama, begetting, and immersion, with the concepts of 'participation' and 'co-existence', and with his apparently approving uses of the term 'co-inherence' in his commentary on Williams' poems, Lewis appears to have an intuitive leaning towards co-inherence. The Neoplatonist framework of his metaphysic works against it, especially in his reaction against idealism. 'I have stressed the transcendence of God more than His immanence', explains Lewis, since 'the present situation demands this.'[51] But Lewis is always prepared to treat metaphysics with a certain lightness of touch, and especially to let metaphors and verbal pictures—even that of the noble centaurs who inhabit Narnia—lead him into strange regions. The very metaphor of the dance, about which I shall have more to say in Chapter 13, shows this willingness to adapt as well as adopt. One source for this image seems to have been the fifth-century Christian Platonist Chalcidius, whom Lewis names as portraying the celestial dance (*caelestis chorea*);[52] but Chalcidius' dance of love and justice is one in which all things participate which are created—God as creator does not move in the dance in the way that Lewis himself depicts when he calls the Trinity a dance in which we can participate. His final work, in which we shall see that he comes to an accommodation with Williams, is therefore not entirely at odds with his earlier, though it places the stress differently.

7.2 Exchange, Substitution, and Myth

As in Williams (after 1939), so in Lewis, 'co-inherence' is often implied by the associated words 'substitution' and 'exchange'. Lewis comments that Williams understood Christ's act of substitution in his death not as a forensic 'transaction' or 'legal fiction' but as 'the most familiar thing in the world, a fact of daily

---

[47] Lewis, *Poems*, 35.   [48] Lewis, *Mere Christianity*, 51.   [49] Lewis, *Miracles*, 138.
[50] Lewis, *Allegory of Love*, 267.   [51] Lewis, 'Rejoinder', 146.
[52] See Lewis, *Discarded Image*, 55; Lewis, *Spenser's Images of Life*, 96.

experience'.[53] This 'daily' process of exchange runs through Lewis' famous sermon on 'The Weight of Glory', as we have already seen, and it also comes to light in the mysterious moment in Lewis' own life when he felt he *might* have carried by exchange the burden of his wife Joy's illness.

Exchanges and substitutions occur in Lewis' works of fiction, which exhibit his art as a myth-maker. While Lewis' use of metaphors in his prose works of popular theology often carry a tension with his philosophical framework, and even a tension within themselves, the creation of myth allows him to show a co-inherence imaginatively, in a less contested way. Given his view of the Christian story as 'myth become fact', we can classify his fiction as myths made 'after the fact', 'alongside the fact' and 'before the fact',[54] and in each case there is a notable exchange that echoes the great 'exchange' between Christ and humanity in his incarnation and passion. Each event is also placed in a context of meaning that we can appropriately call co-inherence.

First, in his trilogy of novels written in the genre of science-fiction, Lewis creates a myth that explicitly refers back to the incarnation. In the novel set on Venus, *Perelandra*, Christ is spoken about under the name of Maleldil, his redemptive visit to earth (Thulcandra) is recalled, and the hero, Ransom, affirms that he is a 'Christian'. The mythical action is thus 'after the fact'. True to his name, the hero is called to be a 'ransom' in imitation of Christ, being prepared to give his life and suffering a wound that, like the wounds of Christ on the cross, remains permanently.[55] He hears a voice saying 'It is not for nothing that you are named Ransom,' and 'My name also is Ransom.'[56] But since this event is 'after the fact' of incarnation, it takes a form appropriate to that sequence. Christ suffered a passion without making any violent resistance, but Ransom is being called to act as a member of the body of Christ; through his death Christ has made members of this body through whom 'henceforward He would save and suffer'. The hero is to make a ransom of himself in order to prevent a repetition of the fall in this unfallen world, and so to 'save Perelandra not through Himself [Christ] but through Himself in Ransom'.[57] The appropriate saving action of a member of Christ's body, in this situation, is—for Lewis—a physical conflict, unarmed combat, with the 'Un-man' who used to be a fellow-scientist on earth but is now occupied by Satan, and who is tempting the Eve of Perelandra to disobey God.

There is a whole web of exchange here—the exchange between Christ and Ransom, and the exchange of Ransom's safety for the preservation of the 'Eve' and

---

[53] Lewis, 'A Sacred Poem', 127.

[54] I work out this classification in greater detail in Fiddes, 'Lewis the Myth-Maker', 132–55.

[55] Ramson is wounded in his heel, which brings together the prophecy of Genesis 3:15, the Arthurian myth of the Fisher King who suffers from the 'dolorous stroke', and the wounds of Christ that remain for eternity (John 20:20; Revelation 5: 6; 13:8).

[56] Lewis, *Perelandra*, 168.   [57] Lewis, *Perelandra*, 165.

so the 'Adam' of Perelandra, of all their successors, and of Perelandra's very future. When the battle is over, the new Adam reflects that 'Maleldil always goes above' mere justice:

> All is gift. I am Oyarsa [ruler] not by His gift alone but by our foster mother's [the Angel of Perelandra], not by hers alone but by yours, not by yours alone but by my wife's—nay, in some sort, by gift of the very beasts and birds. Through many hands, enriched with many different kinds of love and labour, the gift comes to me, It is the Law. The best fruits are picked for each by some hand that is not his own.[58]

In Ransom's case, his gift is not just exchange but—in Williams' terms—a substitution in love, because it is a deliberate and willing bearing of the burden of another. So the new 'Adam' makes a comparison between the blood from Ransom's wounded heel, where the Evil One bit him, and the blood of Christ: 'I have never seen such a fluid before. And this is the substance wherewith Maleldil remade the worlds before any world was made.'[59]

The larger context of this exchange and substitution is a universal network of relations that embraces any particular loving action, and can aptly be called 'co-inherence', though the word is not used. In the course of the struggle with the 'Un-man', Ransom is nearly brought to despair by a vision of non-co-inherence (or incoherence), as the Un-man depicts a vast universe in which life is a mere shallow 'rind' on the surface of a few disconnected worlds. Under the rind, he stresses, there is the dark interior to which all life is destined to sink, and if God exists, he remains outside: 'as we pass into the interior we pass out of his ken. He doesn't follow us in.'[60] This anti-vision is to be matched in the closing pages of the book by the vision of the Great Dance, in which 'each of us is at the centre' because 'Where Maleldil is, there is the centre. He is in every place.'[61]

Lewis' *Chronicles of Narnia* are myths made 'alongside the fact' of incarnation. The adventures of the children in the magical land of Narnia take place, formally speaking, after the time of the incarnation. The children belong to the nineteenth and twentieth centuries, and they come and go between Narnia and the modern world, which exist in parallel but with differently elapsing time scales. The whole history of Narnia from creation to apocalypse takes place within the span of the human children's lives. However, there is no intention of giving any thematic importance to the fact that incarnation has already happened in this world; the turning of 'time's corner',[62] in Judaea, has seemingly no effect upon this other world. The stories are not allegories; it is as if Christ in this world and the great Lion Aslan in Narnia are parallel incarnations of the divine Logos, resulting in

---

[58] Lewis, *Perelandra*, 241.   [59] Lewis, *Perelandra*, 254.   [60] Lewis, *Perelandra*, 193.
[61] Lewis, *Perelandra*, 249.   [62] Lewis, *Perelandra*, 69.

events and patterns of experience that are naturally similar, but by no means identical.[63] Readers, living in the world of this myth will become sensitive to recognizing similar patterns of love and courtesy when they meet them in the Fact. When Aslan, at the end of *The Voyage of the Dawn Treader* promises to meet the children in their own world, he voices the intention of Lewis himself in writing the stories:

> 'Are—are you there too, Sir?' said Edmund. 'I am,' said Aslan. 'But there I have another name. You must learn to know me by that name. This was the very reason why you were brought to Narnia, that by knowing me here for a little, you may know me better there.'[64]

In this land of Narnia there occurs, in *The Lion, the Witch and the Wardrobe*, a central exchange or substitution. Aslan allows himself to be sacrificed on a great Stone Table, the tables of law coming immediately to mind,[65] by the White Witch, in exchange for the life of Edmund, who has committed the sin of betrayal. The Witch knows the 'Deep Magic' inscribed on the Table, that 'every traitor belongs to me as my lawful prey and that for every treachery I have a right to a kill',[66] but— as Aslan declares when he has risen to new life—she did not know the 'Deeper Magic' from before the dawn of time, that 'when a willing victim who had committed no treachery was killed in a traitor's stead, the Table would crack and Death itself would start working backwards'.[67] Echoes of the 'Latin theory' of the atonement in Christ are evident in this act of substitution, but we notice that Lewis does not include a 'penal' kind of substitution in his Narnian version: there is nothing said about 'satisfying' the Law or the 'Emperor' who made the law,[68] only a kind of *Christus Victor* account of the overcoming of death.[69] We recall Lewis' comment that Williams' treatment of the atoning substitution of Christ was not formulaic, but related to the 'daily experience' of exchanges in the world.[70] Just as the substitution by Ransom in *Perelandra* is followed by the Great Dance, so the substitution by Aslan is followed by a dance between Aslan and the children: 'it was such a romp as no one has ever had except in Narnia; and whether it was more

---

[63] Walter Hooper, *Past Watchful Dragons*, 100–4, nevertheless cautions against the idea of a *literal* incarnation in Aslan. Schakel, 'Elusive Birds', 125–8, stresses that Lewis' use of myth carries us 'to a new range of experience'.

[64] Lewis, *Voyage of the Dawn Treader*, 222. © copyright C. S. Lewis Pte Ltd, 1952.

[65] 2 Corinthians 3:3–7. Lewis makes the association in CSL to William L. Kinter, 30 July 1954, Lewis, *Letters*, 3: 497.

[66] Lewis, *Lion, the Witch and the Wardrobe*, 130.

[67] Lewis, *Lion, the Witch and the Wardrobe*, 150.

[68] Lewis, *Lion, the Witch and the Wardrobe*, 131.   [69] Aulén, *Christus Victor*, 20–31.

[70] See Lewis' own resistance to explanations of the atonement in *Mere Christianity*, 43–5.

like playing with a thunderstorm or playing with a kitten Lucy could never make up her mind'.[71]

The dance by itself would hardly offer a context of co-inherence, though the image of dance in Lewis consistently evokes more than the surface meaning, but Aslan is always bringing with him the ethos of wider relations, other connections. He comes, mysteriously and uncontrollable, from a world that is larger than Narnia, called 'the Mountain of Aslan'. It is on this mountain that King Caspian is raised to new life when, in another exchange in a later story, Aslan bids Eustace pluck a long thorn from a thicket and drive it into his paw; a great drop of blood falls into the stream on whose bed lies the dead body of the king, and he leaps up to a life after death.[72] Reference to 'the Mountain' or 'Aslan's country' comes with the implication that Aslan has other business to do in other places, and that he links Narnia with them in himself. In fact, the two worlds of England and Narnia may be parallel and quite distinct, but at the same time they interpenetrate each other through the person of Aslan who has 'another name' elsewhere. A 'son of Adam and daughter of Eve' from our own era of time have been the first King and Queen of Narnia,[73] and human beings must sit upon the thrones of Cair Paravel if the land of Narnia is to be restored to harmony after the ravages of evil.

We are not surprised that *The Last Battle* finally makes explicit what has been implicit all along, that (as Tumnus says), 'That country [England] and this country [Narnia]—all the real countries—are only spurs jutting out from the great mountains of Aslan.' Aslan is at the centre of 'world within world', and Aslan's country is 'part of a great chain of mountains which ringed round the whole world'.[74] We have moved here, in this apocalyptic vision from myth to fact, since what are joined are the 'real' England and the 'real' Narnia. As the Faun declares. 'You are now looking at the England within England, the real England just as this is the real Narnia.' The chapter is called 'Farewell to Shadowlands', and the Platonic underpinning is finally exposed: England and Narnia are both shadowy images of a transcendent Idea of the Good. We can believe in the archetype of Narnia, though we can only suspend disbelief in its shadow. This 'co-inherence' of worlds, which embraces all the exchanges and substitutions of daily life, is remarkably like Lester's vision of the intersection and interpenetration of all cities, those of the living and the dead, in Williams' novel *All Hallows' Eve* ('coincident yet each distinct; or else, in another mode, lying by each other as the districts of one city lie'),[75] except that in Williams there is no Platonic framework.

Lewis' fiction thus demonstrates particularly well a continuity with Williams' ideas of exchange and substitution, progressing towards a vision of co-inherence.

---

[71] Lewis, *Lion, the Witch and the Wardrobe*, 151. Williams, *Lion's World*, 57, cites this dance as an example of the 'physicality' of the children's experience of the divine.
[72] Lewis, *Silver Chair*, 213–14.   [73] Lewis, *Magician's Nephew*, 164–5.
[74] Lewis, *Last Battle*, 181–2.   [75] Williams, *All Hallows' Eve*, 168.

For most of his writing career in the genre of popular theology, participation in God takes a more trinitarian form than in Williams, but—unlike Williams—it is a so-called 'spiritual' state restricted to those who identify with the form of the Body of Christ in the church. He is a Christian Neoplatonist in a way that Williams is not, but he is always ready to let dogma be coloured—and so modified—by metaphor, and a mythical mode of writing gives scope for this freedom. In a final phase of religious and devotional writing, Lewis will begin to express that participation in a form that is grounded in human experience more generally, and so come closer to Williams' idea of co-inherence. On the way to that point, another type of myth-making allows him to hint at a universal immersion into a movement of divine life.

In Lewis' final novel, *Till We Have Faces* (1956), he adopts the method of myth-making that seems most obvious: to imitate the sequence of the dreams among the pagans, setting his myth in the period before the incarnation. It is myth before the Fact, and the myth created is Lewis' own version of the Greek Cupid and Psyche story. This appears to anticipate the incarnation in both its main characters. Psyche is an example of the 'dying and rising god' that is sown through all the pagan myths; it is fitting that the priest of her shrine should mix her story with the vegetation myth of the renewal of nature. In her dying as a substitute to heal the nation, half-drugged, naked, and desolate, Psyche is evidently a 'dream' of Christ. As Lewis himself points out in commenting on the part of Psyche in the story, many good people who follow the pattern of sacrifice are like Christ: 'what else could they be like?'.[76] Though in an unpromising form, the temple of Ungit represents the sacrifice that appears in a much more refined form in Ancient Israel, and defeats the intellect of the Greeks (represented by The Fox), who can only ask in their wise foolishness: 'How can the victim be both the Accursed and the best?'[77]

It is not only Psyche who is a dream of Christ. Eros/Cupid in his tremendous final coming wears the lineaments of Someone greater than he: 'The earth and stars and sun, all that was or will be, existed for his sake. And he was coming [...] the only dread and beauty there is was coming.'[78] The mythical dream of the love of gods for human beings (Psyche represents the human soul) will come to an awakening in the self-giving love of God at the cross, and metamorphosis becomes real in the raising of humanity to share in the fellowship of the divine life (*theosis*).[79] The sacrificial love that fosters personal relationships is not characteristic of the gods in Greek myths; but Lewis stresses it in this half-awakening from the Cupid-Psyche myth.

---

[76] CSL to Clyde S. Kilby, 10 February 1957, Lewis, *Letters*, 3: 830.
[77] Lewis, *Till We Have Faces*, 57.   [78] Lewis, *Till We Have Faces*, 318–19.
[79] See Athanasius, *De Incarnatione*, 54. In his introduction to the translation by Sister Penelope, 9, Lewis refers to the work as 'a picture of the Tree of Life'.

What is even more surprising in Lewis' retelling of the myth is the exchange and substitution he attributes to Psyche's elder sister, Orual. As in the original myth she is the cause of Psyche's disobedience to Cupid, but here it is because she is jealous that the gods have stolen her object of love. In a dream state, she then bears the burden of Psyche's fear as Psyche wanders the world achieving the tasks set her as a punishment by the gods. When Orual looks at pictures shown her of the tasks undertaken by Psyche, she exclaims, 'How could she [...] do such things and go to such places—and not...? [...] She was almost happy.' She is told 'Another bore all the anguish.' She asks, 'I? Is it possible?' and the reply is: 'Don't you remember? We're all limbs, parts of one Whole. Hence, of each other. Men, and gods, flow in and out and mingle.'[80] The final judgement of the God upon her is 'You are also Psyche,'[81] recalling Williams' epigram 'This also is Thou.'

Orual is not an anticipation of Christ in the way that both Psyche and Cupid are, but through becoming a substitution for Psyche she also becomes, as Lewis says about Psyche, 'like Christ'. Her assuming of a permanent veil throughout her reign in Glome is an outward sign that she is veiling herself to the gods and others. She has no face for them to see. When Orual, in her judgement before the gods, at last realizes her self-centredness and possessive love, she is stripped naked. The veil is removed and she is barefaced at last. As Lewis writes later in *Letters to Malcolm*, 'By unveiling we assume the high rank of persons before Him. And He, descending [...] reveals himself as Person.'[82] To be unveiled is to be aware that God sees us, so that Orual echoes Job in confessing 'Before your face questions die away.'

It is thus Orual who, in her substitution, takes us furthest into co-inherence. As she is told, in the life of exchange, where all are parts of one Whole, 'Men and gods flow in and out and mingle.' Already, in the Great Dance of *Perelandra*, an angelic voice had affirmed that 'Each grain is at the centre [...] The worlds are at the centre [...] The race that sinned is there [...] The gods are there also.'[83] In *Perelandra*, as a post-incarnation myth, it may be that Lewis has in mind 'the gods' of Psalm 82, heavenly beings who are only semi-divine.[84] But in *Till We Have Faces*, by setting the myth before the fact of incarnation, and by using the language of pagan myth (gods), a universal affirmation can be made about the immersion of all persons in the life of the God who is to be finally revealed in Christ. All can see and be seen by God. There is of course no place for an invocation of Trinity (the doctrine of Trinity is anyway not about three 'gods'), but there is an image of co-inherence that expresses exactly the dynamic indwelling that Williams is reaching towards but never quite seems to achieve: 'men and gods flow in and out and mingle'.

---

[80] Lewis, *Till We Have Faces*, 311–12.   [81] Lewis, *Till We Have Faces*, 319.
[82] Lewis, *Letters to Malcolm*, 33–4.   [83] Lewis, *Perelandra*, 249.
[84] Psalm 82:6, John 10: 34–5; see Emerton, 'Interpretation of Psalm lxxxii', 329–34.

7.3 A Presence of God like Co-inherence

There is a first move towards the vision of a 'flowing in and out' of God in a paper written at the same time (1943) as Lewis was developing the argument about 'the way' in *The Abolition of Man*. In this paper,[85] Lewis asserts that the *Tao* is neither a law created arbitrarily by the will of God, nor a rule external to God to which God is bound to conform.[86] Reflecting on the issue of the relation of the 'good' to God (with the shades of Ockhamism threatening), Lewis asserts that 'God neither obeys nor creates the moral law.' Rather, he declares, this 'way' is uncreated, issuing from the existence of God as Trinity, from 'a begetting love, a love begotten, and the love which, being between these two, is also imminent [*sic*] in all those who are caught up to share the unity of that self-caused life'. Employing the significant metaphor of 'begetting', Lewis might well be confining 'those caught up' into the Trinity to Christian believers who have experienced 'new birth', but in context Lewis also appears to be discussing all those who follow the 'way'.

In Lewis' final book, *Letters to Malcolm* (completed in May 1963, when Lewis was already very ill), I suggest that we find a resolution of this tension in Lewis' earlier thought, and an accommodation to the vision of Williams about co-inherence. Though Williams' actual word does not appear, Williams is present in the book, not least in Lewis' quotation twice of his favourite maxim, 'This also is Thou: neither is this Thou.'[87] Williams himself considered this to be both a summary of the whole history of the Christian church, and the experience of every single created thing. So Lewis now affirms, 'Of each creature we can say, "This also is Thou: neither is this Thou."' Here, however, Lewis typically achieves a more analytical point of view than Williams. Williams had used the saying poetically to bring together the positive way of knowing God ('the affirmation of images', or 'kataphatic' theology) and the negative way (a rejection of all images, or 'apophatic' theology), but Lewis perceives a logical means of asserting this truth while retaining the essential theological insight that 'all creatures are other than God, with an otherness to which there is no parallel: incommensurable'.[88] The key now for Lewis is that: 'God is present in each thing, but *not necessarily in the same mode.*'[89]

Lewis (as we have seen) had raised this idea in *The Problem of Pain* over twenty years earlier, but there it was limited to different ways in which the *believer*, Christ, the Holy Spirit and the *church* are 'in' each other.[90] Now the principle of varied

---

[85] Lewis, 'The Poison of Subjectivism', in Lewis, *Christian Reflections*, 72–81.
[86] Lewis, 'Poison of Subjectivism', 80. Beversluis, *C. S. Lewis*, 266–7, identifies these two options as Ockhamism and Platonism.
[87] E.g. Williams, *Descent of the Dove* viii; Lewis, *Letters to Malcolm*, 99, cf. 34.
[88] Lewis, *Letters to Malcolm*, 98–9.   [89] Lewis, *Letters to Malcolm*, 100. Italics mine.
[90] Lewis, *Problem of Pain*, 41–2.

participation is being extended universally: God gives God's self by indwelling every created thing, but—differing from pantheism—God is not 'all', but desires to be 'all *in* all'.[91] Among Pantheists, writes Lewis in his brisk style, one must emphasize the 'distinctness and relative independence' of creatures from God, but among Deists 'one must emphasize the divine presence in my neighbour, my dog, my cabbage-patch'.[92] This is a greater deviation than Lewis has made before from the Neoplatonist tradition that he has been following in a Christianized form; in fact, it comes close to a contradiction. Lewis seems to have arrived finally at a way of conceptualizing the kind of divine indwelling he had envisioned in the Great Dance of Perelandra, and from which he had then retreated with an apparent sense of entering dangerous territory, not even invoking it when writing about 'transposition'.[93] Now, God is present in *all*, but not in the same way:

> ...not in a man as in the consecrated bread and wine, not in a bad man as in a good one, not in a beast as in a man, nor in a tree as in a beast, nor in inanimate matter as in a tree. I take it there is a paradox here. The higher the creature, the more and also the less God is in it; the more present by grace, and the less present (by a sort of abdication) as mere power.[94]

If Lewis had come to this theology of the diversity of divine indwelling in 1940, he would surely not have made the statement he did that a thing could be 'good' but could not be 'elevated into a spiritual value'.[95] Lewis still has a somewhat dualistic view of God as 'injecting' the human personality into the realm of Nature,[96] but when the eternal Son of God assumes the body and human soul of Jesus into 'His own Being', this is now not only a *potential* that can be realized for all persons when they come to faith; by that very act, Lewis now affirms, as does Williams, he also objectively takes 'the whole environment of Nature into His own being'. Lewis also appears now to think that since this is an eternal intention of God, God not only performs *acts* 'through the things He has made' but determines his own *being* through them, willing 'on varying levels to *be* Himself'.[97] Writing as a theologian, and acclaiming Lewis' perception that God dwells in all created things and beings not homogeneously but in different ways, I must add that the resolution of a universal with a particular participation in the triune God by creatures will only finally be attained if the dualistic 'two-world' metaphysic of a natural and a supernatural realm is totally abandoned. But an exposition of this claim must wait for the final chapter of this book. Significantly, Lewis does here return to an

---

[91] Lewis, *Letters to Malcolm*, 97.   [92] Lewis, *Letters to Malcolm*, 99.
[93] See Chapter 3, section 2.   [94] Lewis, *Letters to Malcolm*, 100.
[95] Lewis, 'Christianity and Culture', 28.   [96] Lewis, *Letters to Malcolm*, 96.
[97] Lewis, *Letters to Malcolm*, 96. My italics.

earlier image that has the capacity to transgress the boundaries, that of the 'play or dance' of Heaven.[98]

Another place where Lewis quotes the phrase 'This also is Thou, neither is this Thou', explicitly attributing its use by Charles Williams, is in his late Cambridge lectures on the poet Edmund Spenser.[99] He recalls that Arthur in *The Faerie Queene* wishes that beloved Florimell were Gloriana, who is an emanation or image of the transcendent One of the Neoplatonist hierarchy of reality. Lewis remarks that the 'Platonic' Arthur is 'easily syncretized' in the reader's imagination with the Christian, who prays in the affirmative tradition of theology, 'This also is Thou, neither is this Thou.'[100] Plotinus, Lewis reminds us, had written that 'those to whom the divine *eros* is unknown may guess at it by the passions of earth, if they remember how great a joy the possession of a beloved person is'.[101] But, continues Lewis, Plotinus had also bidden us remember that love of earthly beloveds is only a 'wooing of images', and Spenser had blundered as a 'doctrinal poet' in failing to emphasize this. Emphasizing this caution had, in fact, been Lewis' own approach to earthly passion throughout his shared journey with Williams. Lewis comments that Spenser's Arthur transgresses this way of analogy when he prays 'O that this *were* Thou, O that Thou *were* this.'[102] This, thinks Lewis, as he always had done,[103] is a 'dangerous sentiment', but he now suggests an alternative that would not have occurred to him earlier: 'Unless Arthur only means, "O that I were now really finding Thee".' The divine *eros* is not its earthly image, but neither is the relation simply a matter of analogy: the divine, implies Lewis now, can be 'found' in the earthly image. This implies a world view of the indwelling of creation by God, or precisely what Williams had called 'co-inherence'.

To hold such a view of co-inherence between God and the world requires a rethinking, and a redefinition, of the traditional divine attribute of impassibility, which must be strongly upheld in a Neoplatonized Christianity. In *Letters to Malcolm*, C. S. Lewis evidently believes he *should* hold to this tradition, but confesses that he has come to have doubts about it, and wants to interpret it in a modified way. In God's forgiveness, for example, he notes that 'the Divine action is consequent upon, conditioned by, elicited by, our behaviour'. He supposes that you could therefore say that we can 'act upon' God, though he prefers the formulation that God takes our acts, and especially our prayers 'into account'.[104] He comments, accurately, that 'you must admit that Scripture doesn't take the slightest pains to guard the doctrine of Divine Impassibility [...] We are constantly represented as exciting the Divine wrath or pity—even as grieving God.'

---

[98]   Lewis, *Letters to Malcolm*, 121.   [99]   Lewis, *Spenser's Images of Life*, 134.
[100]   Lewis calls Neoplatonism of a general kind simply 'Platonism'.
[101]   Plotinus, *Enneads*, 6.9.9; Lewis' own translation.   [102]   Spenser, *The Faerie Queene*, 3.4.54.
[103]   See, for example, *Problem of Pain*, 33–4.   [104]   Lewis, *Letters to Malcolm*, 72–5.

Lewis had, in fact, already anticipated much earlier the view he records here that, for rational creatures, 'to be created also means "to be made agents"' over against God and not just passive 'receptacles':

> Then again, is the contrast between Agape (God active coming to man passive) and Eros (man by desire ascending to God qua passive object of desire) really so sharp? [...] Can the thing really be conceived in one way or the other? In real life it feels like both, and both, I suspect, are the same.[105]

This is a 'both'/'and' that bends the rigidity of a Neoplatonic Christianity, expressed as early as 1935, long before Lewis' restatement of divine impassibility in *Letters to Malcolm*. From his picture of praying 'in God' in *Beyond Personality*, we may deduce that he has been driven to the position of understanding prayer as exerting a causal impact on God precisely because he understands prayer as co-inherence, or a participation in the life (the dance) of the Trinity. His depiction of the same situation of a man praying in his room in *Letters to Malcolm* is, admittedly, less trinitarian, but it does expand his vision of the 'operation' more obviously into the natural world:

> Here is the actual meeting of God's activity and man's—not some imaginary meeting that might occur if I were an angel or if God incarnate entered the room. There is no question of a God 'up there' or 'out there'; rather, the present operation of God 'in here', as the ground of my own being, and God 'in there', as the ground of the matter that surrounds me, and God embracing and uniting both in the daily miracle of finite consciousness.[106]

The God in whom Lewis is praying is 'embracing' the ground of Lewis' own being and the ground of matter at the same time. Put Christologically, Lewis looks at the material world, and says, '*That* and I grow from one root' because 'the Word, coming forth from the Father, has made both, and brought them together in this subject-object embrace'.[107] If one were to think that this late work shows a return of Lewis to Idealism, then a parallel might be found with the Absolute Spirit from which both matter and mind have emanated, and with which (unlike the Neoplatonist view of emanation from the One) they remain in continuity. I am suggesting, however, that this thought is a 'return' not to Idealism but to Williams, who finds, like Gerard Manley Hopkins,[108] Christ incarnate everywhere in the physical world. In *Letters to Malcolm*, there is thus a closer alignment with

---

[105] CSL to Janet Spens, 8 January 1935, Lewis, *Letters*, 2: 153. Lewis is criticizing the disjunction of *agape* from *eros* in Anders Nygren's book, *Agape and Eros*.

[106] Lewis, *Letters to Malcolm*, 106.   [107] Lewis, *Letters to Malcolm*, 106. My italics.

[108] See Hopkins' poems, 'The Windhover', 'The Starlight Night', 'Hurrahing in Harvest', 'As kingfishers catch fire.'

Williams' understanding of the relation between God and the world, just as in *The Four Loves* we can see a growing approximation to Williams' theology of romantic love.[109]

If his life had not come to an end when it did, it may be that Lewis would have developed this general participation in God into a trinitarian form, perhaps elaborating the idea of the whole of nature caught within the flow of a relational divine life, but in different ways and at its different levels. Then indeed the potential of his earlier vision of the Great Dance of Perelandra would have been fulfilled.

---

[109] See Chapter 3, section 2.

PART III
A COLLABORATION IN CO-INHERENCE

8

Romantic Love and the Arthurian Myth

Divergence and Convergence in Charles Williams and C. S. Lewis

In the year after Charles Williams died, C. S. Lewis set to work to preserve and—if not to complete—at least to complement Williams' unfinished book on the legend of King Arthur. T. S. Eliot at Faber had been anxious for Williams to provide them with the finished manuscript, to develop a series begun with Williams' *Figure of Beatrice*, but *The Figure of Arthur* remained a fragment of five chapters, of which Lewis himself had seen only three before Williams' death. Alice Mary Hadfield fortunately had a typed copy of the remaining two that she could supply to Lewis. The plan that Lewis devised to make a satisfactory book out of *Arthur* was to follow Williams' fragment with his own commentary on Williams' cycle of Arthurian poems in *Taliessin Through Logres* and *The Region of the Summer Stars*, though it was the Oxford University Press and not Faber that was ultimately to publish the consequent *Arthurian Torso* in 1948. The two parts of the book were linked by the fact that Williams had supplied Lewis with a quite systematic exposition of *Taliessin through Logres*, in response to Lewis' plea for assistance before he reviewed the book for the journal *Theology*. Although Lewis himself had to rely on large extracts from the notes he had copied into the margin of his *Taliessin*, having lost the original, we are now in the happy position of having both handwritten and typed copies of Williams' explanations.[1]

8.1 Approach to the Arthuriad

The purpose of this section is not to duplicate the wide range of studies now available on the Arthurian poems of Charles Williams,[2] but rather to explore a 'collaboration' between Williams and Lewis on the Arthurian theme—staged, of course, by the survivor, Lewis—as an opportunity to view from this particular

---

[1] See note 27.
[2] For example, Moorman, *Arthurian Triptych*; McClatchey, 'Charles Williams and the Arthurian Tradition', 51–62; Göller, 'From Logres to Carbonek', 121–73; Curtis, 'Byzantium and the Matter of Britain' 28–54; King, *Pattern in the Web*; Cavaliero, 'Charles Williams and the Arthuriad', 7–17; Schneider, 'A Comparison of the Treatment of the Grail Legend', 8–22; Bradbury, 'Charles Williams' Arthuriad', 33–46; Peirano, *Under the Mercy*; Higgins, *The Inklings and King Arthur*.

Charles Williams and C.S. Lewis: Friends in Co-inherence. Paul S. Fiddes, Oxford University Press. © Paul S. Fiddes 2021.
DOI: 10.1093/oso/9780192845467.003.0008

angle their mutual journey through the landscape of romanticism that we surveyed in Chapters 1–3. It should also enable us to detect more of the similarity and the differences in their approach to a vision of co-inherence that we have considered in Part II. In addition to Lewis' part in *Arthurian Torso*, we should count into this 'collaboration' Lewis' treatment of the Arthurian theme in his third science-fiction novel, *That Hideous Strength*. It is illuminating to place alongside his critical commentary on Williams' Arthurian poems his own imaginative drawing on the myth, highly indebted to Williams as it is.

It should be established right at the beginning of discussion that for Williams, the matters of Arthur and romantic love are—as indicated in my chapter heading—bound up together. Where ideas of exchange and substitution appear, even before the use of the word 'co-inherence', they are naturally associated with love. But the myth of Arthur as conceived by Williams is itself shaped by affairs of love. Both Lewis, in his *Allegory of Love*, and Williams, in his 'Figure of Arthur', give prominence to the legend of Lancelot's love for Arthur's Queen, Guinevere.[3] Telling this story had been the centre of Chrétien de Troyes' poetry of courtly love, which Lewis had considered to be a parody of true religion, and which Williams had earlier seen as a precursor to Dante's theology of romantic love. The story was also pivotal to Malory's version of the *Morte D'Arthur*; although Williams is clear that there it does not at all exemplify 'Dantean romantic love', he notes of the couple that 'they are still passionately and permanently in love'.[4] Lewis, however, in a late essay (1961, published in 1963), thinks that Malory deals more harshly with the relationship and that Malory himself declines to 'rehabilitate' Lancelot.[5]

Other love stories in the Arthurian cycle had further supplied Williams with images with which to develop his understanding of romantic love—notably the love of Bors for Elaine, the frustrated love of Palomides for Iseult, the reciprocated love of Tristram for Iseult, the obsessive love of Lamoracke for Morgause, and the ambiguous love of Percival for his 'sister' Blanchefleur. In three erotic poems in his collection *Heroes and Kings* (1930), the last three took the form in Williams' mind of an intense but chaste sexual love (chaste, at any rate, in the sense of stopping short of intercourse), a practice of 'transmutation' which he himself conceived as giving him poetic energy.[6] In this small collection of Arthurian poems within the book, Williams assumes the figures of Tristram, Lamoracke, and Percival into himself—along with Taliessin, King Arthur's court poet, and, to a much lesser degree, Palomides. In their 'Songs', Tristram and Lamoracke hold back—but only on the particular occasion depicted—from sexual consummation. Tristram covers the body of Iseult with the inscription of a poem, and Lamoracke ties the naked body of Morgause to a bed ('bound and prisoned for love's good laws') while

---

[3] Lewis, *Allegory of Love*, 23–32, 113–15; Williams, 'Figure of Arthur', 45–59.
[4] Williams, 'Malory and the Grail Legend', in Williams, *Image*, 188.
[5] Lewis, 'English Prose Morte', 15, 17.   [6] See Chapter 1, section 4.

singing a song of 'the joy and grief that come by her'.[7] Percival's love for Blanchefleur is perpetually chaste; Williams had noted in his commonplace book that Blanchefleur was 'called "sister" only as a kind of name to describe their virginal love'.[8] In his 'Song to Blanchefleur', Percival celebrates the parts of her body as representing the whole caste of chivalric characters in Camelot, with the Grail as her vagina.[9]

Further in *Heroes and Kings*, Taliessin, in a 'Song of the Princess of Byzantion' (Byzantium),[10] sings to King Arthur about a maiden he knew in Byzantion who had been assumed into heaven. There none of the virtues her soul possesses are sufficient to identify her, until God names her as 'Love-in-Caelia'. Into her Williams pours the essence of his theology of romantic love: she exhibits 'excelling Godhead', and she stands in 'perfect union' with God:

> Even as the Revelation sank to rest,
> she stood in perfect union manifest:
> heaven opened from her; from her inmost soul
> The Centre issued in the unchanging Whole.[11]

As we have already seen, Williams is going to play with the idea of Christ at 'the Centre' in future writing.[12] The Princess, together with Iseult, Morgause, and Blanchefleur, are all intended by Williams to be identified with the one whom he called 'Celia' in daily life, Phyllis Jones.[13]

All these pairs of lovers reappear in the next cycle of Arthurian poems, *Taliessin Through Logres*, where Williams' dominant self-identity has become Taliessin, the king's poet who is destined never to consummate love with *any* woman. He is the 'quick panting unicorn' who comes, as in the traditional legend, to lay his head in a maiden's lap, but 'no way to rejoice / in released satiation', the horn only to be 'polished, its rifling rubbed between breasts'.[14] In another poem a line about

---

[7] Williams, 'Lamoracke's Song to Morgause', *Heroes and Kings*, 49.

[8] Williams, *Image*, 170–1. Short extracts from Williams' Commonplace Book, compiled 1912–16 and containing a mass of material about Arthur, are reproduced by Anne Ridler in *Image* 170–5 from the MS in her possession; the entire book in now in Bod. MS. Eng.e.2012.

[9] Williams, *Heroes and Kings*, 61.

[10] This was originally, in draft, called 'The Assumption of Caelia'. On the Princess, see Williams, 'Notes on the Arthurian Myth', in Williams, *Image*, 178. Ridler dates these 'Notes' (her title: in *Image*, 175–9), which are printed from a typescript in her possession, as 'late twenties or early thirties', and identifies them as written as an introduction to the never-published cycle of Arthurian poems, *The Coming of Galahad* (Ridler, in *Image*, 168). This copy of the typescript is now in Bod. MS. 16123/5, folder 5 (typescript unlisted in catalogue), with another copy in Wade CW/MS-2/X.

[11] Williams, *Heroes and Kings*, 68.

[12] See Williams, *He Came Down*, 105–6, 132–3; 'Cross', 157. The emergence of the 'centre' may also correspond to the emanation of the Mystery called Tiphereth on the sephirotic tree: see end of section 3.

[13] For letters of Williams to Phyllis Jones explaining her role in the poems, now deposited in the Bodleian (not accessible), see Lindop, *Charles Williams*, 157–61.

[14] 'Taliessin's Song of the Unicorn', *Taliessin*, 22.

Taliessin is repeated from the Welsh epic, the Mabinogion, that 'it is a doubt whether my body is flesh or fish', and Williams interprets, 'therefore no woman will ever wish to bed me'.[15] The frustrated Palomides appears, and Taliessin acknowledges some affinity with him, but Tristram and Lamoracke only have minor roles.[16] The love of another couple, Bors and Elaine, is more celebrated, but it is of a different kind from Taliessin's unconsummated loves. Percivale plays a significant part in the achievement of the Holy Grail, while it is Taliessin who has a profound—though chaste—love for Percivale's 'sister', Blanchefleur, who is also called 'Princess' Dindrane (a name taken from French Romance).[17] The identity of Blanchefleur/the Princess with Phyllis has by now ebbed away, but there are other female muses whom no doubt Williams had in mind.

Thus, from *Heroes and Kings* onwards, Williams' distinctive notion of romantic love is intertwined with the Arthurian themes, and the dark thread of his theory of transmutation of energy is present in the weave. It is also distinctive of Williams' handling of the Arthurian legend that the matter of Arthur is intimately bound up from its inception with the associated legend of the achieving of the Holy Grail. In approaching Williams' Arthuriad, we can thus discern a triangulation in Williams' appropriation of the Arthurian legends: woven together are the Grail (including mystical union with God), romantic love (including transmutation), and exchange—the last to become, in the *Region of the Summer Stars*, co-inherence.

In his commentary in *Arthurian Torso*, Lewis integrates the poems of *Taliessin Through Logres* and *The Region of the Summer Stars* to provide what he considers to be a 'chronological sequence' of events.[18] While making a consecutive story for the reader, this unfortunately obscures the fact that 'co-inherence' is developed only in the second volume, where the word is entirely absent in the first—which does of course celebrate the exchange and substitutions of love. It also obscures the fact that the word 'Trinity' does not appear once in *Taliessin*, but seventeen times in *Region*. The two phenomena are related, as I have already suggested; the concept of co-inherence emerges for Williams only in the context of a trinitarian doctrine of God, at the time of the writing of *The Descent of the Dove*. Lewis is not the only critic who has failed to perceive this: the more recent study of the Arthurian poems by Roma King, *The Pattern in the Web*, carefully nuanced as it is, applies the notion of co-inherence indiscriminately to exegesis of all poems in both volumes.

---

[15] 'The Calling of Taliessin', *Taliessin*, 7, 10.

[16] Williams comments that, in Malory, 'Tristram was superfluous': so 'Chances and Changes of Myth', in Williams, *Image*, 183, cf. 169.

[17] Lewis, 'Williams and the Arthuriad', 138, explains what he regards as an 'unfortunate' confusion, but he misses the advantage for Williams that Blanchefleur is therefore a 'princess'.

[18] Lewis, 'Williams and the Arthuriad', 96.

8.2 A Spiritual Geography of Exchange

The world that Williams depicts in his two cycles of poems overlays the Christian Byzantine Empire of history with the mythical kingdom of Arthur (Logres), and superimposes on this double geography the form of the human body.[19] It is in fact a spiritual geography, or 'geography breathing geometry, the double-fledged Logos'.[20] The world bears the form of a diagram, which is shaped throughout by the double nature of the incarnate Logos, Spirit united with flesh. A similar term Williams uses is 'trigonometrical',[21] and Lewis rightly invokes a phrase in explanation that Williams uses elsewhere: 'God always geometrizes.'[22] This geography exhibits the order, the 'pattern of the glory', that God brings to an otherwise chaotic world, symbolized in these poems by the 'cut hazel' that appears everywhere as both a measuring rod and an instrument of correction. But this is a special kind of ordering, which Lewis again rightly identifies as 'co-inherence' (though the word itself only strictly applies to *Region*), and which he brings into conjunction with his own abiding conviction that this present world is one in which desire for God is felt as a sense of joy:

'Other modern myths depict a dialectical world. Keats' Titans and Wagner's Gods beget their opposites and are transcended by them. Williams paints a Co-inherent world: "joy remembers joylessness".'[23]

It is no small insight that Lewis has singled out the word 'co-inherent' to describe Williams' world of imagination. It does not appear in the first cycle, *Taliessin Through Logres* (since Williams has not started using it anywhere at this point), and naturally does not occur in the extensive notes on *Taliessin* that Williams gave Lewis. It only appears in three poems in the second cycle, *The Region of the Summer Stars*, and of those it has a substantial presence only in 'The Founding of the Company', which reflects Williams' own founding of his Order or Company of the Co-inherence.

Once alerted to the importance of the word, the reader can, however, find continual demonstrations of its truth in the poems, and here Lewis seems to have exercised a considerable influence on commentators who have followed him, while Williams himself is quite economical in deploying it. In his commentary on a number of the poems, Lewis introduces the word where it is not in fact present, as we shall see. In this book, I have already reviewed some of the reasons

---

[19] See Higgins, 'Double Affirmation', 73–81.   [20] Williams, 'Prelude', *Taliessin*, 1.
[21] Williams, 'The Vision of the Empire', *Taliessin*, 8; 'The Coming of Palomides', *Taliessin*, 33.
[22] Lewis, 'Williams and the Arthuriad', 106; Williams, *He Came Down*, 40; Lewis, *Grief Observed*, 26. Plutarch attributed the verb to Plato, writing that 'Plato said god geometrizes continually': Plutarch, *Convivialium disputationum*, 8.2.
[23] Lewis, 'Williams and the Arthuriad', 193.

why Lewis is especially sensitive to the idea, as well as partly resistant to it. In his final chapter of *Arthurian Torso*, assessing the value of the poems, from which the quotation above comes, Lewis seems on the whole to be approving of word and concept. Shortly before remarking that Williams 'paints a Co-inherent world', he judges that 'wisdom is the mark of a great poem', and that we shall grow in wisdom by contemplating Williams' symbols as different forms 'under which the Divine appears'. Weighing the possible accusation that Williams' poetry is obscure because it is a 'private' language, he retorts that this would destroy 'Co-inherence', and that Williams is certainly not guilty of this 'discourtesy'.[24] However, we shall discover that Lewis does not use the word 'co-inherence' entirely with the meaning that Williams himself puts into it. Incidentally, the published text of Lewis' contribution to *Arthurian Torso* wavers between spelling the word in a hyphenated form (co-inherence) as Williams always does—deriving, I have suggested, from G. L. Prestige's use—and the un-hyphenated 'coinherence'. I will reflect this diversity in my own references to Lewis' discussion.

The main features of Williams' spiritual geography are set out in 'The Vision of the Empire' in the first cycle of poems, and are further explored in the second cycle in 'The Calling of Taliessin', from the angle of Taliessin's early journeys. Eastwards from Arthur's Logres, 'Britain and more than Britain',[25] is the Empire of Byzantium, of which Logres is a province, while westwards there is the land of Broceliande, which is a kind of sea-wood, part-forest, part-water. As Williams expresses its position, Logres thus lies between an area of 'doctrine and history' on the one hand, and a zone of 'myth' on the other.[26] Broceliande is the place of the numinous in all its ambiguities, and it represents a formlessness from which the particularities of creation emerge: 'huge shapes emerge from Broceliande, and the whole matter of the form of the Empire'.[27] Williams notes that it is 'one of the great forests of myth',[28] and Lewis adds that 'indeed Broceliande is what most romantics are enamoured of; into it good mystics and bad mystics go'. He remarks that those who have gone even a little way into the wood 'are changed when they come out again'.[29] On its far borders, but before reaching the open sea is Carbonek, the 'Castle of the Hallows' (holy things), which is the dwelling-place of Pelles, the Fisher-King and guardian of the Grail. Its chapel houses the Grail—the vessel used at the Last Supper of Christ—together with the Spear that wounded the heart of Christ, but the Grail is present in a mysterious way, not normally visible to human eyes or tangible to human hands. Broceliande joins the Antipodean Sea, which is the way both to Sarras (called in *Region*, 'the Land of

---

[24] Lewis, 'Williams and the Arthuriad', 189.   [25] Williams, 'Figure of Arthur', 80.
[26] Williams, 'Figure of Arthur', 80.
[27] Williams, 'Notes for C. S. Lewis', typescript (made by Margaret Douglas), Wade MS CW/MS-486, 3. Hunt copied this typescript into RH Notebook 19: 3597–606. The handwritten original by Williams is in Bod. MS. 16125/2, folder 4.
[28] Williams, 'Figure of Arthur', 81.   [29] Lewis, 'Williams and the Arthuriad', 100–1.

the Trinity'), where Christ himself offers mass in its chapel, and P'o-lu, where a headless Emperor walks backwards, and octopus tentacles fill the sea around as an evil force strangling life. The state of Broceliande is thus the route to either destination.

The Empire is also to be pictured as an organic body. Its mind lies in Logres, while its breasts are Gaul, sustaining its children with the milk of theology and philosophy. In Italy are the hands, the means of transforming bread and wine into sacraments, place of 'the heart-breaking manual acts of the Pope',[30] and Jerusalem is the location of the generative organs, giving birth to three major religions. The area of Caucasia is the buttocks, not to be despised as representing the senses and the natural and pleasurable life of the body. Williams claims that this identification of the Empire with the human organism was not a piece of ingenious allegory he devised, but that it simply 'happened' to him.[31] He had in fact already employed the body as an index to the society of Camelot in his earlier poem, 'Percivale's Song to Blanchefleur', but more significantly it allows him to associate his spiritual geography with another powerful image with which he had been familiar since his initiation into the Order of the Rosy Cross, the Sephirotic Tree of the Kabbala. This presents ten gateways of the glory and grace of God, diverse channels through which the ineffable 'One' emanates and is manifest in creation, forming a sacred tree that can be ascended towards the 'One' by the initiate. In several diagrams of the tree, a human body is superimposed over the network of 'stations' of the *sephiroth* (see Figure 1),[32] so that for Williams the body becomes the means by which the various regions of the Empire can be—loosely and imaginatively, not dogmatically—seen as functioning like the *sephiroth* as mediations of the divine light of wisdom (Sophia):

> Carbonek, Camelot, Caucasia,
>   were gates and containers, intermediations of light;
>   geography breathing geometry, the double-fledged Logos.[33]

If this interweaving web of life were not complex enough, Williams adds in the map of astrology, again as an imaginative image rather than a strict system. In his essay on 'The Index of the Body', Williams writes that the houses of the Zodiac are 'not unworthy fables', since they 'direct attention to the principles at work both in the spatial heavens and in the structure of man's body'.[34] The body of the Empire

---

[30] 'Vision of the Empire', *Taliessin*, 9; cf. 'Calling of Taliessin', *Region*, 15, 'the hands of the Pope are precise in the white sacrifice'.
[31] Williams, 'Making of Taliessin', 181.
[32] Frontispiece to Waite, *Secret Doctrine in Israel*, titled 'The Sacred Tree of the Sephiroth'.
[33] Williams, 'Prelude', *Taliessin*, 1.   [34] Williams, 'Index', 83.

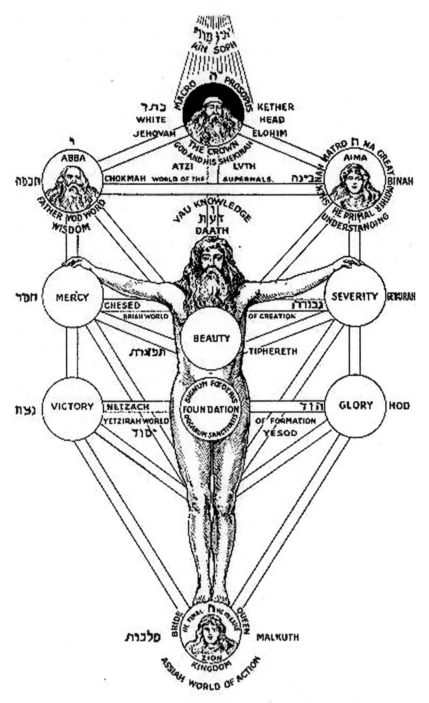

THE SACRED TREE OF THE SEPHIROTH

Figure 1 Frontispiece to A. E. Waite, *The Secret Doctrine in Israel* (1913).

is seen as divided into the various zodiacal 'houses', with the Emperor holding rule in all of them like the sun passing through the star signs:

> The Acts of Identity issued from the Throne; there
> twelve images were shown in a mystery, twelve
> zodiacal houses; the sun of the operative Emperor
> wended through them, attended by the spiritual planets . . . [35]

The Emperor is, however, not directly God, but 'God-in-operation' or 'God-as-known-by man' (so 'the operative Emperor').[36] In a lecture that William gave on the Arthuriad in 1939, Williams expresses some frustration that, despite his note for Lewis to this effect, Lewis had, in his review of *Taliessin*, still identified the Emperor as simply God.[37] In *Arthurian Torso* Lewis continues to write that 'the Emperor symbolizes God'.[38] We can see evidence here that Lewis' mind works with a more strict hierarchy of Being than does Williams', a point to which we must return.

Now, the point of portraying this complex interplay between regions of the Empire, members of the body, sephirotic 'gates', and zodiacal houses is to lament that the web is fractured, the links broken. The state of human life is fallenness, expressed by a double wound. King Pelles, according to the Arthurian legends, is bleeding continuously from the Dolorous Blow, having been wounded (at the hands of Balin Le Sauvage) by a thrust from the sacred spear that pierced Christ. For Williams, the counterpart to Pelles is Arthur, wounded by his unwitting incestuous union with his sister, Morgause, which is to result in Mordred who will finally give him a fatal blow. In both cases, 'man wounds himself'.[39] Williams had made an imaginative move as early as his Commonplace Book (1912–16) in seeing the two kings as two categories of the same reality, the fallen state, and this idea was to be repeated in later notes on the myth and his lecture of 1939.[40] In that lecture, he explains that reading Malory, 'It occurred to me that in fact Arthur and Pelles could be regarded as the same person, the same identity in two categories.'[41] Identifying Pelles, the Keeper of the Grail, with Arthur himself was Williams' own original contribution to the Arthurian myths; Lewis oddly does not mention this essential part of Williams' scheme in *Arthurian Torso*, but the fact that he understands this identification is shown by his making Ransom in *That Hideous Strength* both the Fisher-King (suffering from an ever-bleeding wound) and the

[35] Williams, 'Taliessin in the Rose-Garden', *Region*, 23–4.
[36] Williams, 'Notes for C. S. Lewis', Wade MS CW/MS-486, 1.
[37] Williams, 'Arthurian Myth', Wade RH Notebooks 20: 3882, 23 June 1939, CLI series 'The Christian Idea in Literature 34.
[38] Lewis, 'Williams and the Arthuriad', 104.   [39] Williams, 'Figure of Arthur', 85.
[40] So Williams, 'Commonplace Book', extracts in Williams, *Image*, 171; Williams, 'Notes on the Arthurian Myth', 175, 177; Wade RH Notebooks, 20: 3874.
[41] See note 40 above.

successor to Arthur (the Pendragon in line of descent). This identification of Arthur and Pelles leads Williams in turn to integrate the legends of Arthur and the Grail Quest more closely than in any previous accounts, though he interprets Malory as taking us some considerable way in this direction. Much later, Lewis offers the same critical judgement on Malory.[42] Williams thus reads the Arthurian stories as showing that 'Logres, then, must be meant for the Grail.'[43]

Along with disunity, then, comes the theme of restored unity. The aim of the Empire is to achieve a union between Logres and Broceliande through the quest for the Grail and its achievement, thereby uniting the Empire itself with Broceliande through the mediation of Logres. The active, bodily life of the Empire in history is to be unified with the contemplative life of the Spirit. With the achieving of the Grail by Galahad, son of Lancelot and 'High Prince', the union is made and the wounded king is healed. Williams celebrates this moment by a kind of fusion between Arthur and Pelles. In the poem 'Taliessin at Lancelot's Mass', the now repentant Guinevere in her nun's cell makes an act of substitution, taking upon her the responsibility of mothering Lancelot ('the mystical milk rose in the mother of Logres' child'), and the result is that the two kings become one in serving the Grail:[44]

> Out of the Queen's substitution the wounded and dead king
> entered into salvation to serve the holy Thing;
> singly seen in the Mass, owning the double Crown,
> going to the altar Pelles, and Arthur moving down.

Williams then comments that 'Lancelot and Arthur wove the web'. The place of substitution in this network of spiritual geography is underlined by the role given here to Guinevere, who has previously played a part in tearing the web. Exchange is at the centre of the pattern of the web, and exchange will be finally achieved between Byzantium and Broceliande through Logres. In the disruption of the unity of the Empire, 'all exchange [was] stilled',[45] and the commission of the king's poet Taliessin is to stand by Arthur until 'The land of the Trinity' (Sarras) comes to the 'stair' of the king.[46] This 'stair' is perhaps the ladder of ascent to the divine Glory, as in the Tree of the Sephiroth, whose stations correspond to the regions of the Empire, since Williams continues that Taliessin is to be faithful until:

> Sarras is free to Carbonek, Carbonek to Camelot;
> in all categories holds the largesse of exchange,
> and the sea of Broceliande enfolds the Empire.

---

[42] Lewis, 'English Prose *Morte*', 19–20.   [43] Williams, 'Figure of Arthur', 83.
[44] Williams, 'Taliessin at Lancelot's Mass', *Taliessin*, 89.
[45] Williams, 'Calling of Taliessin', *Region*, 9.   [46] Williams, 'Calling of Taliessin', *Region*, 17.

There is to be 'largesse of exchange' between all the parts of human life, repairing the brokenness of the Fall. The part played in this by Galahad, who symbolizes the human capacity for Christ,[47] is accentuated by another novel idea of Williams that he adds to the Arthurian themes: in Galahad there is the union or exchange of the 'two ways' of approaching God, the positive and the negative, the ways of affirmation and denial of images.

We might say, in the language of co-inherence that Williams adopts from 1939, the aim of the Emperor is for a co-inherent world, while the tragic situation is one of incoherence. While employing the terms 'substitution' and 'exchange', Williams himself, however, does not apply the word 'co-inherence' to the intricate web of his spiritual geography until almost the very end of the last poem of the second cycle, when the pope invokes peace on the dead and living, 'co-inherent all in Adam and all in Christ'.[48] Even this only hints at the co-inherence of the parts of the body of the Empire, an idea that is not present at all in Williams' only two previous references to co-inherence in *The Region of the Summer Stars*.[49] Lewis, by contrast uses the word freely in his exegesis of 'The Prayers of the Pope'.[50] Exploring the vision of a disintegrating world that troubles the mind of the pope, Lewis comments that 'All over the world the principle of co-inherence is lost', while 'co-inherence is the one grand secret,' and 'the Pope reaffirms the co-inherence'. He cites the reflection of the pope that people are 'frantic with fear of others', and that the difference of his household from them is that 'we declare' and 'they deny'

> that we derive from them and they from us,
> and alive are they in us and we are in them.

This is a situation of mutual indwelling that Lewis then names as 'co-inherence': he writes that 'The difference lies, and must always be made to lie, only in this, that we confess and declare our co-inherence in them while they deny their co-inherence in us.' They live 'under the primal curse' still, and a symptom, according to Lewis, is that they 'deny the co-inherence of Deity and flesh in Christ'. The idea of exchange and co-inherence certainly appears to underlie Williams' text, such as in the pope's reflection that 'the doctrine of largesse teaches' that 'what recovers / lovers in love is love', recalling Williams' earlier assertions that what matters for lovers is to be dwelling 'in love' as a state of being.[51] But Lewis has brought the idea to the surface, and it seems to him to be the more necessary to affirm it in light of 'the situation which Williams

---

[47] Williams, 'Notes on the Arthurian Myth', 176.
[48] Williams, 'Prayers of the Pope', Region, 60.
[49] In 'The Calling of Taliessin' and 'The Founding of the Company'.
[50] For the following quotations, see Lewis, 'Williams and the Arthuriad', 182–4.
[51] See Chapter 4, section 4.

contemplated in 1944 and which we still contemplate in 1946', namely a world torn by division, a scenario that is interfused with the world of the poem, evoking as it does the division of Christendom that culminated in the breach between pope and patriarch in 1054. In fact, elsewhere Williams does call precisely for 'co-inherence' in Britain in face of the current crisis, and empathy with Germans.[52] Lewis aptly sums up: 'we are in the enemy and he in us'.

Lewis then clearly perceives the centrality of 'co-inherence' if the world is to be healed, and his reading of the word into Williams' text was to be followed by generations of interpreters, even more widely and extensively than he did. His practice supports, I suggest, my claim in Chapter 7 that the idea is important for Lewis, although he offers a somewhat different philosophical framework for it than Williams. This can be seen in his understanding of the relation between different parts of Williams' 'co-inherent world', and the means of their unification, based on the duality of the active and the passive. It is true that the Emperor is depicted by Williams as an active principle, like the life-giving sun, or Wordsworth's 'feeling intellect',[53] and that there is a formlessness about Broceliande, as a kind of receptacle of possibilities. Lewis writes that 'it is [...] what the Greeks called the *apeiron*—the unlimited, formless origin of forms'.[54] The presiding genius of Broceliande is Nimue, Malory's Lady of the Lake transformed; she is mother of Merlin (representing Time) and Brisen (representing Space), and they are the energies that have the potential to bring about the creation that Taliessin sees in a vision. Lewis, however, then imposes a fairly rigid Aristotelian scheme of active principle and passive recipient on the relation between Byzantium and Broceliande, form shaping formlessness. Williams, he proposes, has in mind

> 'Divine Order as a flawless and mathematic precision imposing itself on the formless flux of natural moods and passions, the shape of virtue, courtesy, intelligence, ritual. Thus the *Peras* (limit) met the *Apeiron*, the Empire met Broceliande.'[55]

Lewis thus reads the phrase 'wildness formalized' in 'The Crowning of Arthur' as the union of Byzantium and Broceliande.[56] Stephen Medcalf is surely right to object that this is too doctrinaire an identification of the Empire and Broceliande with active and passive principles. He comments that 'the difference is *like* that of form and matter, but not I think nearly so opposed, more like [...] the same

---

[52] See Williams, 'Notes on the Way', 194–5.
[53] Williams, 'Calling of Taliessin', *Region*, 14; cf. Wordsworth *Prelude*, 14.226; for the 'feeling intellect' see Chapter 9, section 3.
[54] Lewis, 'Williams and the Arthuriad', 101.   [55] Lewis, 'Williams and the Arthuriad', 106.
[56] Lewis, 'Williams and the Arthuriad', 111.

person waking and dreaming'.[57] Williams' own note to Lewis was that Nimue 'is almost the same state represented by the Emperor's court, but more vast, dim and aboriginal'.[58] Lewis' contrast misses all the nuances of the way that the two regions balance and interweave. In short, we may say, it misses Williams' own understanding of co-inherence.

One more point should be made about the spiritual geography of Williams' poems. It is certainly the setting for a story in apparently chronological order—the establishing of Logres, the achieving of the Grail, and the dissolution of the kingdom—in which the adventures of the Grail, as in Malory, strike a 'double note' of both the redemption of Logres and ruinous judgement 'whereby Logres sinks into mere Britain'.[59] But at the same time, it is also a portrayal of concurrent human states that cannot be limited by sequence. Williams draws attention to this, when he observes that the identification of the wounds of Pelles and Arthur 'is difficult because of the time scheme [...] Arthur does not begin to be till Pelleas is wounded'. However, Williams points out that, though the Fall *was* once, it is 'repeated in each one of us'.[60] In his early Commonplace Book, he notes that in his mythology 'time and space are only modes of thought', and that his aim is to 'make everything happen at once (if it were possible in poetry!)'.[61] Anne Ridler aptly points out that in 'The Prayers of the Pope', Williams is expressing, 'in the sequential form of poetry, happenings which require to be held simultaneously in the mind'. So the pope's Christmas Eucharist gives us 'the *happening* of the division and the reconciliation which have been the subject of the whole cycle'.[62]

The hope with which the poem ends, feeling the Empire 'revive in a live hope of the Sacred City', is thus not only an eschatological expectation (so Roma King),[63] but an experience that is available in the present for those who embrace the way of love (so Lewis).[64] Above all, perhaps, the achieving of the Grail is accessible to everyone who truly desires it, since this is to become as conscious of Christ as of oneself. It is 'knowing how God comes into the sacrament',[65] the practical knowledge of living in a world where sacrament and incarnation happen. This is a consciousness that can be gained by romantic love, poetry, and religious contemplation. Carbonek, and even Sarras, are 'gates' by which one can know the Glory of God here and now.

---

[57] Medcalf, 'Objections', 212.   [58] Williams, 'Notes for C. S. Lewis', Wade MS CW/MS-486, 3.
[59] Lewis, 'Williams and the Arthuriad', 157.   [60] Williams, 'Notes on the Arthurian Myth', 175.
[61] Williams, Commonplace Book, extracts in Williams, *Image*, 171.
[62] Ridler, in Williams, *Image*, lxvi; cf. Williams, *Reason and Beauty*, 14, on the (unattainable) ideal of writing poetry which 'shall include all experiences of time'.
[63] King, *Pattern*, 38.   [64] Lewis, 'Williams and the Arthuriad', 184.
[65] Williams, *'Figure of Arthur'*, 78–9.

8.3 Co-inherence and Hierarchy: Divergences

As we have seen, Lewis sympathizes with Williams in his concern for an integrated universe, bound by the bonds of exchange. To this, he applies the term 'co-inherent' even where Williams does not. In 'Taliessin on the Death of Virgil', for example, where Williams presents Virgil's future readers as rushing to save him from falling to oblivion, Lewis explains that 'such is the co-inherence of all souls that they are not even limited by time'.[66] There is another significant instance of this in Lewis' commentary on 'Taliessin in the Rose-Garden' from *The Region of the Summer Stars*. In this poem, Taliessin is musing on the need for Queen Guinevere to exercise properly her 'feminine headship' in Logres, so that through the energies of her body the kingdom may flourish and with it the Empire to which it is connected. The dark undercurrent of implication is that she is failing to do so by maintaining her affair with Lancelot, although this is not directly stated. Guinevere through her female ministry *could* do much to heal an empire that is suffering from the impact of the Dolorous Blow, and where the zodiacal houses which mark the various regions of the web of the Empire are 'split'. Taliessin recalls that:

> Out of the pit and split zodiac I came
> to the level above the magnanimous stair, and saw
> the Empire dark with the *incoherence* of the houses.[67]

By this time, Williams was making elsewhere the play on words between 'inco-herence' and 'co-inherence',[68] and so it is appropriate for Lewis to read the word 'co-inherence' into his comment here, even placing it in quotation marks as if he is actually quoting Williams:

> 'In the state of innocence all the Houses of the Zodiac are 'co-inherent': each is all in all; whichever you go into, you will find yourself at the centre. But since the Fall, instead of Co-inherence there is Incoherence.'[69]

Lewis exceeds the intention of Williams, however, when he suggests that the co-inherence has been fractured by Guinevere's failure to respect her function as a woman and as a wife:

> 'Had all gone well in Logres, Guinevere would have summed up in herself and exhibited to perfection the element of matter, of the feminine, of the sensuous,

---

[66] Lewis, *Williams and the Arthuriad*, 123. For exegesis, see Chapter 6, section 1.
[67] Williams, 'Taliessin in the Rose-Garden', *Region*, 26. My emphasis.
[68] See Chapter 9, section 1.   [69] Lewis, 'Williams and the Arthuriad', 149.

and Arthur would have done the same for form, for the masculine, for intelligence.'[70]

That this kind of pairing is Lewis' own view of true marriage is shown by his next sentence: 'Their marriage would have been the holy wedding of Sun and Earth, *as every true marriage is*.' We have already observed that as late as *The Four Loves*, Lewis is still writing of the union of 'Sky Father and Earth mother'.[71] Lewis places co-inherence then within a strict hierarchy, in which there are active principles and passive recipients, and in his commentary in this poem, he identifies these functions with the masculine and feminine genders. Earth or matter is the feminine recipient of God's (supremely masculine) act of creation; Lewis writes that 'consciously or not Williams is here recalling the Greek doctrine that Form is masculine and matter feminine', and he finds the same relation in several pairings that Williams sets out in the poem: the Empire to the Emperor—who moves through the zodiacal houses like the sun—the slaves to masters or mistresses, Caucasia to Carbonek (Broceliande) and the queen to the king:

> I saw how the City
> was based, faced square to the Emperor as the queen to the king,
> slaves to lords, and all Caucasia to Carbonek.[72]

Here Lewis draws particular attention to the identification of the queen with the earth; as with all women she is seen in a 'flash' of revelation 'in the world's base', which Lewis understands as the feminine principle that is given form by the masculine. However, I suggest that, just as Lewis has made the passive relation of Broceliande to the Empire too dogmatic, so he has imposed a philosophical scheme on Williams' portrayal of the vocation of the queen. This is not what Williams means by 'incoherence' and an implied co-inherence.[73] He does indeed give instances of the relation between active and passive elements within the 'web', but these are better understood in the context of what he describes elsewhere as a situation where 'one hierarchy suddenly changes to another',[74] with the possibility of exchanging roles in appropriate circumstances. As he puts it in his 'Dialogue on Hierarchy', the feminine may at times be 'hierarchically ascendant',[75] taking the lead and the initiative. This is what he identifies as a 'co-inherence' of the two principles of 'hierarchy' and 'equality' in the City.[76] In this poem Williams

---

[70] Lewis, 'Williams and the Arthuriad', 148.
[71] Lewis, *Four Loves*, 114, 119–20; cf. Lewis, *Preface*, 122–3.
[72] Williams, 'Taliessin in the Rose-Garden', *Region*, 23.
[73] Brewer, 'Women', 102, emphasizes that the women in the poems are 'not simply the passive objects of male adoration'.
[74] Williams, 'Dialogue on Hierarchy', 128.   [75] Williams, 'Dialogue on Hierarchy', 127.
[76] Williams, 'Dialogue on Hierarchy', 129.

counterpoints 'the articled form / of the Eve in the Adam' with 'the Adam known in the Eve'. While Carbonek/Broceliande can play a passive part to the Empire, in the quotation above it is active towards Caucasia. While slaves are 'to lords' as the City is to the Emperor, when Taliessin sees three women in the rose garden—the queen, Princess Dindranee, and a maid hard at work among the roses—he reflects that 'what was even Dindrane but an eidolon [a reflection, an image] of the slaves?'.[77] There is an implicit challenge to conventional language of male 'head-ship' in the repeated reference to the queen's 'feminine headship' in Logres: while her body has its base in the earth, this is a 'base in Libra'—with the earth as the location of justice, symbolized by the astrological sign of the scales—and Logres lives under her headship, just as it also defers to Sarras, the 'land of the Trinity':

> Glorious over Logres, let the headship of the queen
> be seen, as Caucasia to Carbonek, as Logres to Sarras.[78]

Behind this difference between Lewis and Williams about the framework for co-inherence—and so its very meaning—there lies a difference between different views of the emanation of ultimate divine reality into creation. Lewis, as I have shown in Chapters 6 and 7, is for most of his intellectual career working with a Neoplatonism modified and corrected by Christianity. God is operative as active cause in the world, but—except in the Grand Miracle of the incarnation of the eternal Logos in Christ—does not strictly 'participate' in the bodies of the world. This metaphysic allows Lewis to have the romance of the 'joy' of longing for the unattainable. Williams has a different picture in mind, which is a great network or web of life in which there are multiple places where God participates in creation. The Tree of Life in the Kabbala, with its various 'stations' or 'gateways' (*sephiroth*) of the divine presence has, it seems, given him an image for this suffusion of the world by the Glory of God. Despite the strong influence of Neoplatonism on the Kabbala, especially the concept of God as the ineffable One that diversifies into the many, its picture of the relation between God and the world is not simply the same, giving far more scope for mutual interaction between the divine realities and the world. Williams' early membership of the Order of the Rosy Cross, a society that aimed to lead its initiates through the various gradations of the *sephiroth*, offers him a range of images associated with the sacred tree, which he uses in an eclectic rather than a doctrinaire way. Such sephirotic images abound in his poems, the interplay of the 'gateways' with each other and the two-way 'paths' between them giving a context for a world of exchange.

Indeed, as the notable Zohar scholar Isaiah Tishby points out, the ten *sephiroth* in Jewish mysticism were not 'static points on the ladder of ascent' to the hidden

---

[77] Williams, 'Taliessin in the Rose-Garden', *Region*, 21.
[78] Williams, 'Taliessin in the Rose-Garden', *Region*, 24.

God, but were 'in continuous motion, ascending and descending, involved in innumerable processes of interweaving and interlinking'. Though they had a basic ordering to each other, this order 'could change as a result of their internal movement'.[79] Significantly, in his essay on 'hierarchy', Williams compares the 'co-inherence' of hierarchy and equality to the way that in the Zohar the apple tree has two colours, and the 'Cup of Blessing is offered with two hands'.[80] That is, two hands work together, as do hierarchy and equality.

In the poem 'The Death of Palomides', the Saracen knight Palomides stumbles early on upon the divine blessing that comes not in the highest but in one of the lower stations of the tree. He encounters *Netzach*, meaning 'Victory', through meeting with some Jewish mystics, but it is only on the brink of death that he is able fully to know its meaning, to know that 'Netzach is the name of the Victory in the Blessing', and to embrace the formula 'The Lord created all things by means of his Blessing.'[81] For much of his life, traversing the paths between the points of divine light in the tree, seeking 'the power and the glory', has been a weary exercise:

> The paths open between.
> Once the paths were interminable; paths were stations.
> Unangelical speed loitered upon them.

In the poem we are considering, Taliessin is a skilled traveller in the tree. In his vision he climbs the tree of life like a stairway, and at the 'level above the magnanimous stair' looks down to survey the 'stretched' and 'incoherent' Empire; standing at the top of the way that 'wove [...] about the City and the body', he lets his eyes follow the parts of the body downward until:

> Under the flashes, down a steep stair, I came
> to a deep figure; I came to the house of Libra.
> Libra in the category of the flesh is the theme of Caucasia,
> the mesh of the net of the imperially bottomed glory;
> and the frame of justice and balance set in the body .... [82]

This is the lowest sephirotic station, *malkuth*, meaning 'the kingdom' at the 'base' of the tree which is the earth, and it is this gateway of the divine glory ('the bottomed glory') of which the queen is a supreme representative in Logres. This position is far from being a merely passive receptacle to an active force, as envisaged by Lewis. In the Neoplatonist hierarchy of emanations, matter is at

---

[79] Tishby, *La Kabbale*, 'La Divinite', section IV(3).   [80] Williams, 'Dialogue on Hierarchy', 129.
[81] Williams, 'The Death of Palomides', *Taliessin*, 79.
[82] Williams, 'Taliessin in the Rose-Garden', *Region*, 25.

the furthest remove from the One, as a kind of absence of being, and while in Christian Neoplatonism it is more honoured, it remains inferior to Spirit. In Kabbalistic lore, while it is uniquely passive in itself, the light of all the other *sephiroth* drains into *malkuth*, so that it contains them in itself and becomes the 'architect of creation' and even the Word of God.[83] This lowest station on the tree is thus contained in the highest, *kether*, meaning the head or crown,[84] a union that Williams may well intend to reflect in his startling phrase 'feminine headship'.

The matching piece to this poem in the earlier cycle is 'Taliessin in the School of the Poets', where the new poets of the Arthurian age are exploring the image of the body, 'the diagram of the style of the Logos'.[85] Again we have the image of the stair leading to the throne of the Emperor, and this time it rises between the 'right and left newel', which Roma King convincingly identifies as being the pillars on the right and left of the sephirotic tree, the two opposing forces in God and creation, each containing three stations and characterized respectively as male and female.[86] Williams' mentor in kabbalistic lore, A. E. Waite, had cultivated the 'middle path' between these pillars, three central gateways leading from *malkuth* directly to the 'head' (*kether*),[87] and Williams here is concerned to discern the 'centre', whether of the path or of the body, orientated to 'the straight absolute spine'. In measuring the human body poetically, Williams explains in his notes for Lewis, the 'centre line is given, obviously, and never is quite given'.[88] We may understand the body best 'by the living beauty of love' when we make our ascent to the 'eternity' of God, where 'each moment there is the midmost':

> From the indulged Byzantine floor
>   between right and left newel
> floats the magnanimous path of the stair
> to a tangle of compensations,
> every joint a centre,
>   and every centre a jewel.[89]

On the Byzantine 'floor' of the Empire in Logres, 'the willows of the brook sway'. In his notes written for Lewis, Williams comments that 'the willows of the brook' is the name given to 'the lower parts of the Sephirotic tree', but he minimizes the

---

[83] Cordovero, *Palm Tree of Devorah*, 202.

[84] The relation of the bottom to the head of the tree is expressed in the *Sepher Yetzirah*, the oldest book of Kabbalistic mysticism, printed in Edersheim, *Life and Times*, Appendix V, § 4: 'There are Ten Intangible Sefiroth whose end is fixed in their beginning (and beginning fixed in their end), as the flame is bound to the coal' (chapter 1.7).

[85] Williams, *Taliessin*, 30.   [86] King, *Pattern*, 59.

[87] Roukema, 'Veil that Reveals', 52–4. See Waite, *Secret Doctrine*, 255.

[88] Williams, 'Notes for C. S. Lewis', Wade MS CW/MS-486, 4.

[89] Williams, 'Taliessin in the School of the Poets', *Taliessin*, 29.

significance of this identity ('of no importance').[90] Indeed, Williams is not interested in imparting esoteric kabbalistic doctrine through the use of these images; Lewis is right to interpret the 'centre' more generally, affirming that in the human body, as in the Empire, 'Everything turns out to be equally central when we see it in the full light of the Unity', and 'at the Centre, all things here that are remote and diverse from one other, and all in infinite strength [...] come together, drawn from the far blue distances'.[91] This is the insight about the omnipresent 'centre' on which Lewis draws in the Great Dance of Perelandra, and it can be easily detached from any kabbalistic connections.[92] But we do feel that Lewis' realization that 'everything turns out to be equally central' ought to have modified the strict hierarchy that he applies to the relation of Guinevere and Arthur, or of any wife and any husband, and by the preservation of which he estimates gain or loss of co-inherence.[93]

Returning to 'Taliessin in the Rose-Garden', Williams in fact places the emphasis differently here when exploring 'incoherence', and the possibility of overcoming it. Taliessin in the garden sees 'a rush of crimson'—the centifoliae roses ('hearts folded strong in a hundred meanings') and the 'deep-rose-royal' ruby ring of the queen. The path of the garden thus becomes a way 'into the wound,' which has multiple forms: the blood of King Pelles, suffering from the Dolorous Blow, the 'bloodletting' that afflicts the Empire, the sacrifice of Christ on the cross, and the 'victimization of blood' that women in their menstrual cycle share with Christ, so that 'women's flesh lives the quest of the Grail.' Jupiter, the 'red-pierced planet', stands as a symbol of all this blood within the web of the zodiac. Dissolution in the created world will be healed, not by obedience of women to the active force of the male (as Lewis proposes), but by a woman's vocation to open her body to the promise of Galahad—to a human consciousness of Christ (for which Galahad stands), who has himself taken body:

> her flesh bright in Carbonek with Christ,
> in the turn of her body, in the turn of her flesh, in the turn
> of the Heart that heals itself for the healing of others...[94]

It may be objected that the contrast I am suggesting between two possible pictures of a 'co-inherent world', a strict hierarchy and an interactive web—one inspired by Neoplatonism and the other (at least partly) by Kabbalism—is undermined by the fact that the source for both is an emanation of the many from the ineffable One

[90] Williams, 'Notes for C. S. Lewis', Wade MS CW/MS-486, 4.

[91] Lewis, 'Williams and the Arthuriad', 120.

[92] As Williams himself detaches it in He Came Down, 105–6, 132–3.

[93] It should also have modified Williams' own depiction of female–male relations in such characters as Damaris and Chloe in his early novels: see Chapter 11.

[94] Williams, 'Taliessin in the Rose-Garden', Region, 27.

(*en soph*). The presence of God in the many 'gateways' and 'stations' of the tree of life is thus, it seems, only by emanation, and so is a distant image of the One. But the sources are modified by Christian doctrine: the One is also Trinity, and one hypostasis of this triune God has actually become incarnate in the material of the world. I now want to argue that this Christianization has a considerable effect on the kind of world of exchange (and later co-inherence) that Williams has in mind.

Since the time of Pico della Mirandola, among the Christian kabbalists of the Renaissance there was a tradition of identifying the three highest *sephiroth* or 'supernals' in the tree—*kether* (head), *chokmah* (wisdom), and *binah* (understanding)—as representations of the Trinity, respectively Father, Son, and Holy Spirit.[95] This was the pattern of thought followed by Williams' mentor, A. E. Waite, in his book *The Secret Doctrine in Israel*, which Williams deeply admired.[96] The only other 'gateway' treated with any thoroughness by Renaissance Christian thinkers was the sixth of the sephiroth, *tiphereth* (beauty), which was conceived as the representation of the incarnate Son of God.[97] Williams' multiple references in his second cycle to a 'land of the Trinity', named Sarras, in which the Grail is finally achieved, seems to fit in with this scheme, in that the image of 'land' can be read as making 'Sarras' an area demarcated by the upper three *sephiroth*, just as Caucasia appears to be approximately the area of the lower *sephiroth* and Camelot occupies the middle region. To Carbonek (and Broceliande) we will return. This, of course, is a very different Sarras from that portrayed in Malory, which is a place of violence and corruption as well as spiritual vision.[98]

Leon Blau makes the perceptive point that the Renaissance identification of the upper three *sephiroth* with the Trinity, at the same time as identifying God with the *En Soph*, actually weakened Trinitarianism, since an ineffable Unity was being postulated behind the Trinity known by human beings.[99] Pico della Mirandola, for instance, distinguishes between God's 'extreme, profound and solitary retraction in the remotest recess of his divinity' from the 'ten garments' (the ten *sephiroth*) in which God manifests himself in the world.[100] While it might be argued that the *En Soph* was equivalent to the abstract unity of essence of God described in scholastic thinking,[101] to be in line with the tradition of trinitarian theology this would have to be complemented by an 'essential Trinity', or movements of the generation of

[95] Blau, *Christian Interpretation of the Cabala*, 15, 92; cf. 20–1 (on Pico), 27–8 (on Archangelus), 91–2 (on Jean Thenaud). See Pico della Mirandola, 'Seventy-One Cabalistic Conclusions' 11.6, 11.39, 11.58, 11.62 (Farmer: 523, 537, 545, 546–7).

[96] Waite, *Secret Doctrine*, 41–2, 192, 217–18, 315. For Williams' admiration of this book, see Ridler, in Williams, *Image*, xxv, and Lindop, *Charles Williams*, 93–4.

[97] Blau, *Christian Interpretation of the Cabala*, 15, 51 (on Johannes Reuchlin). See e.g. Pico, 'Seventy-One Cabalistic Conclusions', 11.65 (Farmer: 549).

[98] See Malory, 'Quest of the Holy Grail', 605–6.

[99] Blau, *Christian Interpretation of the Cabala*, 16.

[100] Pico, 'Seventy-One Cabalistic Conclusions', 11. 35 (Farmer: 535), cf. 11.4 (Farmer: 521).

[101] So Farmer, *Syncretism in the West*, 521n.

the Son and procession of the Spirit from the Father *within* the inner being of God, which are identical with the one essence. In modern trinitarian theology, this is often referred to as the 'immanent Trinity', as distinct from—though entirely corresponding to—the 'economic Trinity', or God as revealed and at work in the *oikonomia* (household) of creation.[102] In Renaissance Christian Kabbalism, the three highest 'supernals' are 'numerations' or 'manifestations' of the one divine nature and thus approximate to what may be called the 'economic' Trinity; but in orthodox Christian theology there must also be a Trinity immanent in the essence of God, as scholastics such as Aquinas emphasize.[103] Such an immanent Trinity appears absent from the speculations of the Christian kabbalists.

In Williams, however, there is no hint anywhere of a distant and absolute One *beyond* the Trinity; he affirms an orthodox Three in One, and seeing 'the land of the Trinity' simply appears to be an image for a mystical vision of God. Williams portrays Taliessin as contemplating the 'thrice co-inherent Trinity' at a point 'deep beyond or deep within Logres' where 'every crown and every choir is vanished' and all the usual senses are 'nothing'.[104] Taliessin also climbs the porphyry stairway to the Emperor, whom Williams identifies simply as 'God-in-operation'.[105] But nowhere is the relation of the Emperor to the Trinity explained; he is not, for example, equated with the 'head' or 'crown' (*Kether*) among the 'supernals' in the sephirotic tree, and here Williams is in tune with the orthodox formulation of God as three in one, not the highest of a triad. Given what Williams says about 'God-in-operation', it is not impossible that he might have in mind a distinction between an 'operative' or 'economic' Trinity (the Trinity in action in the world) within the sephirotic web, and an immanent Trinity beyond the web. But Williams is not enough of a systematic theologian to explore or resolve such issues. The Emperor is presented neither as one Person among three, nor a unity beyond the Three. The 'Emperor' and 'The land of the Trinity' are, it seems, simply alternative ways of talking about a glimpse of the divine.

Whether portrayed as having a sight of the Emperor on his throne, or as granted a vision of the land of the Trinity, Taliessin finds words to communicate what is disclosed to him, creating correspondence between 'the word of the heart and the word of the voice'.[106] Earlier, in 'The Vision of the Empire', Williams portrays Taliessin as walking 'through the hither angels / from the exposition of grace to the place of images.' Williams explains in his notes for Lewis that 'he has gone out of the direct presence of the Emperor into the outer world, which is precisely a place of images; from the Sacred Palace [...] from God *in Himself* to 'God in his creatures'.[107] In the rites of the Rosy Cross in which Williams

---

[102] Rahner, *Trinity*, 21–4, 99–103.   [103] Aquinas, *Summa Theologiae* 1a.27.1–3.
[104] Williams, 'Calling of Taliessin', *Region*, 16.
[105] Williams, 'Notes for C. S. Lewis', Wade MS CW/MS-486, 1.
[106] Williams, 'Calling of Taliessin', *Region*, 11.
[107] My italics. 'Notes for C. S. Lewis', Wade MS CW/MS-486, 2.

participated, this point of mystical contemplation appears to be the 'invisible station' or 'non-sephirah' of *Daath* (knowledge) at the portal of entry into the area of the three highest *sephiroth*. According to Aren Roukema, Williams was admitted to this grade—called *Adeptus Exaltatus* in the Fourth Order of the Rosicrucian Fellowship—on 10 July 1924, and he participated in several ceremonies of contemplation at 'the threshold of the Holy Supernals' in July 1925.[108] Roukema also observes that adepts of the Fourth Order had the responsibility of returning from their mystical illumination to express, in symbols and images suitable for non-initiates, the knowledge they had gained. This, she suggests, is the vocation that Williams was fulfilling in his writing of novels.[109] It also seems to be close to the calling received by Taliessin as a poet, to put 'the word of the heart' into the voice. In terms of Williams' spiritual geography, perhaps the 'dark' sephirah of *daath* is equivalent to the chapel of Carbonek, in the land of Broceliande, on the borders between Camelot and Sarras.

Nevertheless, it seems that Williams sat loose to the rituals and doctrines of the Rosy Cross after he left the Order in 1927, as shown by his expectation that Companions of his own Order of the Co-inherence could attain to contemplation of the 'Co-inherence of the Holy and Blessed Trinity' without esoteric initiation into a grade of a hermetic order.[110] These actual companions are reflected poetically in the members of the 'company' of Taliessin who pass through the two 'modes' of exchange and substitution, and attain to the 'third station' where they can see the 'co-inhering of all souls' by analogy with the Trinity ('as when the Trinity / first made man in Their image').[111] I argued in Chapter 4 that the idea of a human 'dwelling' within the relations of the Trinity is missing from Williams' account of co-inherence. Perhaps this is because of the stress on *contemplating*, as if from a doorway, the three highest sephiroth within quasi-kabbalistic rituals. But in the sephirotic tree, there are also flowing paths and shifting identities between the three supernals and the lower sephiroth, which makes the failure to take up imaginatively the Gospel image of dwelling in the persons of the Trinity (John 17:20–4) rather odd. The best explanation, I have suggested, is that he is focusing the image of 'co-inherence' on a dwelling in Christ.[112] In variance from the Hebrew kabbalistic tradition of 'numerations' of an unknown Unity, Williams is clear that the incarnation of the eternal Son is not a mere emanation of God ('nor only an image'), but God's substantial union with human nature:

---

[108] Roukema, 'Veil that Reveals', 44–6. Roukema had access to the minutes of the Order, and so is to be preferred to Lindop's account that Williams was not formally admitted to the grade, but was *deemed* to have reached it on 27 July 1925 (Lindop, *Charles Williams*, 117). In Lindop's view, the highest grade to which Williams was actually admitted was *Adeptus Exemptus*, at the sephirotic station of Chesed.

[109] Roukema, 'Veil that Reveals', 48.

[110] Promulgation of the 'Company' (formerly 'Order'), article 5: Bod. MS. 16125/5, folder 1.

[111] Williams, 'Founding of the Company', *Region*, 39: see Chapter 5, section 2.

[112] See Chapter 4, section 5.

> ...the total Birth intending the total Death,
> [...] the Love that lost itself, nor only an image
> nor only all the images but wholly Itself.[113]

This is what happens according to Christian kabbalists at the gateway of *tiphereth*, and it is worth recording that when Williams attained this grade (Adeptus Minor) in the Fellowship of the Rosy Cross in August 1919, he was symbolically bound to a cross as a sign of being 'crucified with Christ'.[114]

Williams seems to emerge from his Rosicrucian period with a set of kabbalistic images that he uses, as a poet, to give a ritual and mysterious depth to what is essentially an Anglican Christian faith—or rather to explore the depths of a mystery that is there. The effect of his distinctive Christianization of Kabbala is nevertheless far-reaching in terms of a doctrinal understanding of the relation of God to the world, about which Christian theologians will differ. In a Christian Neoplatonist scheme, the incarnation of Christ is a miraculous exception to the hierarchy produced by the differentiation of the One into the many. Otherwise God is not immanent in the world. In the Kabbala, the *sephiroth* interact with one other and mutually indwell each other, so that in a Christian kabbala the incarnation of the second Person of the Trinity at one particular location—*tiphereth*—will be experienced *everywhere* in the tree of life. Everything is 'at the centre', *tiphereth* holding the central position in the central pathway. The scheme of a web or network of life, later to be called co-inherence, is thus the framework for the incarnation of Christ in the bodies of lovers that we have already seen to be key to Williams' theology of romantic love. Moreover, because Williams moves easily between the vision of 'God' and the vision of 'Trinity', the glory that is manifested in love is not simply the glory of the incarnation but an eternal weight of glory. There is no reality 'beyond' this love and glory, though there are many different places of its actualization.[115] It is, then, to love in the Arthurian poems that we now turn.

8.4 The Exchange of Love

In the poem 'Bors to Elayne: the Fish of Broceliande', King Arthur's knight Bors, while administering the farms on the borders of Logres, plucks a fish from a stream in Broceliande, and envisages it entering the bloodstream of his beloved wife Elayne through the 'channel of your arm'.[116] Williams explains in his note for

---

[113] Williams, 'Prayers of the Pope', *Region*, 50.   [114] Lindop, *Charles Williams*, 77.
[115] Mahan, *Unexpected Light*, 50–8, stresses that in Williams' poetry the 'proper habitation' of the divine glory is the natural order of the world.
[116] Williams, 'Bors to Elayne: the Fish of Broceliande', *Taliessin*, 24.

Lewis that 'the Fish is the strange quality in R[omantic] Love which comes from B[roceliande] originally and seems to flash through the beloved'.[117] In other poems too, the arm of a woman becomes a kind of flashpoint, a place where the glory of the beloved is suddenly revealed to the one who loves her. Palomides, for example, recalls the moment when he first saw Iseult, and 'down her arm a ruddy bolt / fired the tinder of my brain'.[118] In this poem, Williams intends the symbol of the fish to recall the early Christian symbol of Christ, writing in his note that 'the Fish is not exactly Christ, but the early Church symbolized Christ by a Fish; so the light of R[omantic] love is of Christ'. The fish can only be summoned from the stream that runs in Broceliande, the land of creative potencies, by the voice of a 'twy-nature'. Williams explains that this 'two-fold nature' is 'two lovers (and, more extremely, Christ).' C. S. Lewis expands on this terse note by commenting that

> when the two lovers become 'a twy-nature' (one organism in two sexes) they are a living symbol of the grand Twy-Nature, Christ (the union of God and Man in one Person) who alone can utter celestial, as they utter earthly, love.[119]

This seems such a lucid exegesis that we may miss Lewis' subtle reshaping of Williams' vision. In the state of romantic love, the lovers, Lewis declares, are a 'symbol' of Christ and their 'earthly' love is only analogous to the 'celestial' love of Christ ('celestial, as [...] earthly'). Williams' theology of romantic love exceeds symbol and analogy, however. The light that 'through the great leaves is blown' is 'of Christ', not just like Christ. As he points out in his note, the life of Caucasia, or the senses, is in its way 'as deep as Broceliande', and 'the divine *anthropos* is there'.[120] What it means for the divine man to be 'there' in sensual love is explained elsewhere by Williams, when he writes that 'when the lover sees the beloved in light' and adores her, 'the divine child lives spiritually in the two lovers'.[121] Earlier, he had written that 'the body of the lover is transfused with the divine body' and 'Christ incarnate is almost invisibly made one with her'.[122] The Christ who is incarnate at the 'centre' of the web of life (at *tiphereth*, in terms of the *sephiroth*) is incarnate in the love between the lovers and in the lovers themselves.

Lewis, however, understands the light that breaks from the arm of Elayne, and with which every lover sees his or her beloved clothed, as simply the glory that the loved one had in a paradisial state before the Fall: 'the lover sees the Lady as the Adam saw all things before they foolishly chose to experience good as evil'. This is indeed *one* of the meanings that Williams gives to the 'Beatrician experience', the

---

[117]   Williams, 'Notes for C. S. Lewis', Wade MS CW/MS-486, 3.
[118]   Williams, 'The Coming of Palomides', *Taliessin*, 34.
[119]   Lewis, 'Williams and the Arthuriad', 116.
[120]   Williams, 'Notes for C. S. Lewis', Wade MS CW/MS-486, 3.
[121]   Williams, 'One Way of Love', 161.   [122]   Williams, *Outlines*, 43.

moment when Dante saw Beatrice 'as she (and all things) will be seen to be, and always to have been' (Lewis),[123] an experience that can be shared by all lovers. But, as we have already seen many times in this study, there is a second meaning that Williams gives to the Glory: this is the manifestation in human love of the Glory that the Son had with the Father from eternity within the triune life of love.[124] The birth of love within the lovers must mean the birth of Christ within them as 'the mystical child of the lovers',[125] since Christ is love.

The clearest statements of this second aspect come from Williams' early, unpublished, *Outlines of Romantic Theology*, where he declares that the sacrament of the body of Christ 'should appear to the lover to be closely related to the glorious body of his lady'.[126] However, three manuscripts from the period 1940–1 continue the same duality of the glory that appears in love. One manuscript consists of notes for the first of four addresses given to clergy of the Diocese of Chelmsford at a retreat house in Pleshey, on the overall subject of 'The Church and Young People in Love'.[127] Among the notes is a kind of manifesto:

[T]he Christian religion makes 3 statements:
(i) the sacred significance of the body.
(ii) the offering of the 'New Birth' of Christ in the soul.
(iii) the union of one living creature with another.
And I say that at this time of falling in love there are two things communicated.
(i) the vision of the beloved in the perfection he (or she) had in Christ before the world was; the perfection of the individual image of God.
(ii) the birth of Love—mystically, & of course emotionally—in consciousness.
[...] I allow, of course, that we must say of it, as of so much, 'this also is He; neither is this He.'

The last statement is in line with Williams' holding together of what he calls in these notes 'the Affirmative and Negative' ways, which is echoed in his note to Lewis on 'Bors to Elayne', that the fish 'is not exactly Christ [...] [but] of Christ'. Of the Love that is born in the consciousness of lovers, we *may* say affirmatively 'this also is He', since it is 'the New Birth of Christ in the soul'. In another manuscript, a brief essay on romantic theology,[128] Williams invokes the experience whereby 'the beloved appears, as it were, "in glory", disseminating light,

[123] Lewis, 'Williams and the Arthuriad', 117.   [124] Williams, *Outlines*, 16–17.
[125] Cf. Williams, *He Came Down*, 107.   [126] Williams, *Outlines*, 37.
[127] Wade, RH Notebooks, vol. 21: 4057–62: first Address at Chelmsford, headed 'Romantic Theology', 17 June 1941, a transcription of CW's notes for the occasion, given directly to Hunt by Williams. Hunt notes that 17 clergy were present.
[128] Wade CW/MS-455, 'An Essay on Romantic Theology' (typescript). Undated, but it has similarities to the piece on Romantic Love in Wade CW/MS-72.

fulfilled with virtue, an exposition of sanctity', and he claims that 'this experience is justified and this vision actual, because it is the operation of Christ, and because romantic love is, in some sense, identifiable with Christ'. He then continues with reference to the first aspect of the glory disclosed in love: 'The beloved is seen in the glory which is properly hers (or his) in eternity.' In a third manuscript from this period, notes written for an address (location unknown) in 1940,[129] Williams describes the experience of falling in love as 'a vision of Light, of unity, of authority, of virtue', and asks rhetorically 'Vision of the beloved in Christ or not?'

Lewis writes that 'The essence of the glory is that it appears in the flesh',[130] but he understands the 'pattern of the glory' as a glory *given* by God, not (as actually in Williams), the glory *of* God. Behind this difference is the difference between two world views, as I have been arguing: those of hierarchy and web, of glory *caused by* God and glory *shared with* God. We must not miss, however, a certain accommodation going on between Lewis and Williams, from both sides. Even in his understanding of seeing the beloved in 'paradisial glory', Lewis has moved on from his first resistance to the association of romantic love with religion to occupy more of Williams' ground. The fact that Lewis approves of this aspect of the theology of romantic love, beyond interpreting Williams, emerges in his comments on the poem 'The Star of Percivale'. The scene is that of Taliessin's hearing music played by Percivale on his harp, and 'borrowing' it to play and sing himself. A slave-girl is entranced by the sound, and she and Taliessin experience a mutual 'Beatrician moment' as she touches him with her hands: 'the cords of their arms were bands of glory'—again the arm is the channel of light.[131] Her face is so flushed with 'the mere speed of adoration' that Archbishop Dubric on the way to mass enquires: 'Hast thou seen so soon, bright lass, the light of Christ's glory?'

> She answered: The light of another, if aught, I bear,
> as he the song of another; he said: I obey.
> And Dubric: Also thy joy I wear; shall we fail
> from Percivale's world's orbit, we there once hurled?

Lewis perceives that there is a complex process of exchange here: the girl bears the light of Taliessin as he bears the song of Percival, and all three are turning to obey Another (Christ) whose glory and joy is worn on their faces. In turn the archbishop wears the joy of the girl. Lewis aptly comments that 'She is converted, saved in a labyrinth of vicariousness.'[132] The essence of Byzantium is 'sweet joy given / and its fusion with a new heaven, indirect joy of substitution.' This is a joy that

---

[129]   CW MS-72, 'Romantic Love' (handwritten). Top note in pencil, '?incomplete. Added number 21, dated 29.11.40.' This seems to refer to RH's Notebook 21, and appears to be RH's note, relating it probably to the Pleshey address in June 1941.

[130]   Lewis, 'Williams and the Arthuriad', 119.   [131]   Williams, 'Star of Percivale', *Taliessin*, 46.

[132]   Lewis, 'Williams and the Arthuriad', 136.

comes 'indirectly' through exchange with another. It is ironic that at mass some of the worshippers know nothing of this way of substitution in love: Balin is moved only by anger, the king loves only 'himself crowned', and Lancelot sees only 'the ghost of the Queen in the elevated host'. This way of exchange in love need not be sexual: in this poem Williams celebrates the unconsummated love that he believed was the spring of poetic energy, as Percivale is ever-virginal, and Taliessin refuses the invitation of the girl, 'Take me for thine.'

Lewis' comment that the girl 'receives divine grace' is glossed by 'paradise being momentarily revealed to the girl'—that is, the glory is of her and Taliessin's origin and destiny in an unfallen state. He writes that 'Taliessin shows her paradise', that 'they have adored together [...] they have been in Paradise', and that 'she had, for a moment, and with full understanding, seen him with unfallen vision'.[133] It is 'that light' that Taliessin sees continually, 'resting on innumerable faces'. These comments have little foundation in the text, but they are in accord with Lewis' understanding of the nature of the 'glory' revealed in the state of human love, whereas Williams himself lays stress on 'the light of *Christ's* glory' that brightens the girl's face, just as in the next poem the girl's face is 'suffused with [Christ's] brilliant blood'.[134] The fact that Lewis agrees that paradisial splendour is disclosed in such moments is shown when Lewis steps outside the role of a neutral exegete and comments that Williams telescopes into a matter of minutes what 'in real life [...] would, I suppose (but Williams knew better than I) take a few weeks'.

We can see this same attenuation of Williams' concept of the 'glory' in Lewis' comments on other poems. In 'The Sister of Percivale', Taliessin watches a slave-girl drawing water from a well, exposing scars on her bent back, and at the same time, Blanchefleur (also called Dindrane) arrives in the court at the call of a trumpet. Taliessin experiences a 'Beatrician moment' in seeing *both* women: 'a trumpet's sound from the gate leapt level with the arm [of the girl]',[135] and 'the stress of the scar ran level with the star of Percivale'.[136] Williams comments in his note for Lewis that 'He sees her and Blanchefleur together, as sisters, twins, categories', and 'Blanchefleur could hardly be perfect to understanding without the slave.'[137] The poem works out this twinning in geometrical terms: Taliessin sees the slave's arm and bent spine as the radius of a half-circle, representing the eastern body of the Empire (Caucasia, the life of the senses):

> Taliessin saw the curved bottom of the world [...]
> she steadied the handle, the strain ceased; her arm
> balanced the line of the spine and reached for the gain.
> Taliessin, watching, played with a line: 'O

[133] Lewis, 'Williams and the Arthuriad', 137.   [134] Williams, 'Ascent of the Spear', *Taliessin*, 50.
[135] Williams, *Taliessin*, 52.   [136] Williams, *Taliessin*, 53.
[137] Williams, 'Notes for C. S. Lewis', Wade MS CW/MS-486, 5–6.

> Logres centre, can we know what proportion
> bear the radii so to the full circumference everywhere?'

The question raised in Taliessin's mind is where the circle might be completed. Williams comments in his note to Lewis: 'What is the *full* circle? how do we find it? It must be everywhere, yet . . . And this kind of thing is felt at such moments as seeing someone drawing water.' The curve of the back of the slave now merges into the curve of the face of Blanchefleur, completing the circle in this moment of vision:

> . . . the circle closed;
> the face of Blanchefleur was the grace of the Back in the Mount.

Williams' own explanation of these difficult lines is that 'the back of sensation changes into the face of exchange-in-love'. What is disclosed in this full circle is the grace of God that was given when Moses saw the 'back' of God on Mount Sinai, which is described in the Book of Exodus as the moment when 'my [God's] glory passes by' (Exodus 33:22). Williams' idea is that in the experience of Moses God's face of love is seen only as God's 'back', which is nevertheless still a revelation of glory,[138] just as the two women have exchanged their back and face, and that this is the kind of experience that Taliessin is having now. Through the two women, and their 'exchange-in-love', Taliessin is seeing a 'front of glory' (which is not just the description of Blanchefleur's dress, though it is this too). Percivale thus sees Taliessin 'rapt on the just glory of the sacred Throne', a glory that is 'patterned in the blast and bone'.[139]

Lewis, however, interprets the poem differently. His idea of the exchange is that 'Substitution which shows its heavenly face in heaven can show little more than its scarred back in the world.'[140] He has read the reference to the 'back' of God to mean that the divine glory is obscured and dimmed in the world, and he thereby loses any sense that Taliessin is seeing the glory of God in either the back of the slave or the face of Blanchefleur. We are not surprised at Lewis' comment that, although Blanchefleur is the 'Beatrice *par excellence*' of Taliessin's whole life, 'Taliessin is living on that rung of the Platonic ladder whence the soul sees the beauty in all beautiful bodies to be one.'[141] Lewis perceives that Taliessin is seeing beauty in both the slave and Blanchefleur, but he relegates this to a mere 'rung' on the ladder of ascent to God. In a Neoplatonic hierarchy, the image of a 'back' is

---

[138] Here Williams appears, intuitively, to be in agreement with scholars of the Hebrew Bible: see Noth, *Exodus*, 258: 'the back of the glory'.
[139] Williams, *Taliessin*, 53.   [140] Lewis, 'Williams and the Arthuriad', 140.
[141] Lewis, 'Williams and the Arthuriad', 137, 138.

appropriate—except in the case of Christ—for all we can see of God in a material world.

But Williams is working with a different world view, a web in which Christ is incarnate everywhere in love. In his notes he comments that when Blanchefleur finally speaks to Taliessin ('and sang in one note the infinite decimal'), 'B's greeting (like Beatrice's) is the always-approaching, never reaching relation of the divine part to the divine whole.'[142]

Williams adds the exclamation 'Coo!' to underline that this is a challenging thought, and he seems to mean that Blanchefleur's smile and greeting are a segment of the circle whose diameter is nowhere, which Taliessin describes as the 'proportion of circle to diameter'. If Williams also has in mind the phrase that 'its centre is everywhere', then Christ as the centre is present in such revelations as Taliessin has with the slave-girl and Blanchefleur. Williams (as Lewis records) inscribed Lewis' own copy of the book on this page with the words 'The perfect union of sensuality and substance is seen for a moment'. Lewis responds that, while he realizes that the terms sensuality and substance are borrowed from *Lady Julian's Revelations of Divine Love*, they 'do not help me very much since I know neither what Lady Julian meant by them not what Williams understands her to have meant'.[143] This frank disavowal is made despite Lewis' going on to write that:

> He found the key to her [Julian's] meaning (as another of his notes tells me) in the passage where she says that the City is built at the meeting place of Sensuality and Substance—at that very border line where the supersensible joins the sensible, where incarnation or embodiment occurs, where the Word (in some degree or on some level) becomes flesh.

Lewis' bafflement appears to derive from his inability to conceive that the Word 'becomes flesh' in the bodies of *human* lovers and not only in Christ, although his qualification in parenthesis 'in some degree or on some level' might open up this possibility. He might have been helped by reading Williams' essay on 'Sensuality and Substance' in *Theology* for May 1939, which begins with an extended quotation from the Lady Julian, ending that 'our kindly Substance is enclosed in Jesus'.[144] The point of the essay is that our 'substance' or essential being (or 'soul') is intimately united with the 'sensuality' of our bodies, and the two cannot be torn apart. It follows that if our substance is united with Christ, so are our bodies, and here Williams cites the words of Beatrice to Dante in the *Purgatorio*, 'You should have been faithful to my buried flesh', commenting that 'in her actual

---

[142] Williams, 'Notes for C. S. Lewis', Wade MS CW/MS-486, 6.
[143] Lewis, 'Williams and the Arthuriad', 140.
[144] Williams, 'Sensuality and Substance', 68. The quotations are from Julian of Norwich, *Revelations*, chapter 55.

eyes he sees reflected the two-natured Gryphon of Christ'.[145] In a lecture on 'Juliana of Norwich' in December 1938, the rather broken transcription by Raymond Hunt runs as follows:

> And there is one phrase: (Methuen ed. pp. 130–1) 'I saw no difference between God and our substance... that we are in God and God is in us.' but the point is, this notion of the double form in man, one substance, one sensuality.—at the point at which the soul enters sensuality, the City [of God] is made.[146] It is the old notion: Man is the only means by which matter could be made divine and lovely to the Godhead. All went well; the only trouble was that the movement onward of sensuality was blocked, delayed, by man wanting to be God.[147]

Williams' thought is moving between the earthly City made in the body of Christ incarnate and the City built in all human life. In an earlier section of the lecture (again in a fragmented transcription), quoting from the eleventh 'Showing', he makes clear that Christ ('She') as love can be born from every soul, which is therefore *Theotokos*, mother of God:

> 'And for the high, marvellous, singular, love [. . .] that I have in Her and she in me'.—and she sees Her, as it were, all mankind —'Wilt thou see in her how thou art loved?'
> — and there you come to the old idea. Every soul in its degree is a Theotokos. The business of every soul is so to exist in Love that the fullness of Love which is God may exist from it: 'For thy love I made her so high, so noble and so worthy.'[148]

In his poem 'Taliessin's Song of the Unicorn', Williams gives us an image for every human soul as *Theotokos*. I have already drawn attention to the self-identification of Taliessin (and behind him Williams) as a chaste unicorn, and other instances of unicorns in these poems are Percivale and his 'sister', Blanchefleur. This is, of course, a selective choice of an image; there are many instances in the tradition of art and literature of the unicorn as a beast of strong sexuality, even lasciviousness.[149] In this poem, Williams tells the legend of the catching of the unicorn—the placing of the virgin under the tree, the unicorn's laying of his head in her lap, and then the capture and killing of the entranced

---

[145] Williams, 'Sensuality and Substance', 74.

[146] Williams also paraphrases the Lady Julian in this way in his paper 'Recovery of Spiritual Initiative', Bod. MS 16125/5, folder 4, 8–9: 'when the soul becomes sensual, there the City of God is set up'.

[147] 'Juliana of Norwich', Wade RH Notebooks, 19: 3486, Friday 2 December 1938, CLI series 'The Christian Idea in Literature' 10 (3475–88).

[148] Wade RH Notebooks, 19: 3480.   [149] See Shepard, *Lore*, 47–8.

unicorn by the hidden hunters. The unicorn-poet can only polish his horn between the maiden's breasts, while the hunter can offer the 'satiation' of 'his spear flesh-hued'.[150] Yet, the poet continues, if only the maiden will allow the unicorn to pierce through her hands holding his horn, and on through her breast, pinning her to the tree, she will become 'Mother of the Unicorn's Voice,' and her son will be 'the new sound that goes / surrounding the City's reach'. She will give birth to new poetry and to new love that can never come to a close:

> Horn-sharp, blood-deep, ocean and lightning wide,
> in her paramour's song, by intellectual nuptials unclosed.[151]

Commentators, including first Lewis, have, however, ignored the significance of the line 'O twy-fount, crystal in crimson, of the Word's side', and the stress on 'one giant tree':

> ... twisting from the least
> to feel the sharper impress, for the thrust to stun
> her arteries into channels of tears beyond blood
> (O twy-fount, crystal in crimson, of the Word's side),
> and she to a background of dark bark, where the wood
> becomes one giant tree[.]

There is an extensive tradition of religious art and texts in which the virgin maid under the tree is a symbol for the Virgin Mary,[152] pierced through the heart by the horn of Christ the eternal unicorn in fulfilment of the Gospel text 'a sword shall pierce through your own heart also', and foreshadowing the piercing of Christ's side at the tree of crucifixion. From this piercing, she gives birth to the Word incarnate, and so—as Williams puts it—is 'Mother of the Unicorn's voice'. This poem, however, is not specific to the Virgin Mary. Any woman—and surely any man—can allow themselves to be pierced by the unicorn's horn of poetry and love, and so become *Theotokos*, 'God-bearer'. Williams' somewhat gnomic note to Lewis ends: 'And *so with all*, including the B.V.M. [Blessed Virgin Mary].'[153] Lewis, however, is out of tune with this 'paramour's song'.

---

[150] The phallic significance of these images is evident.
[151] Williams, 'Taliessin's Song of the Unicorn', *Taliessin*, 23.
[152] See Shepard, *Lore*, 58–61; Cavallo, *Unicorn Tapestries*, 45–51.
[153] Williams, 'Notes for C. S. Lewis', Wade MS CW/MS-486, 3.

8.5 A Growing Convergence

Despite his inability to follow Williams into his kind of unity between 'sensuality and substance', Lewis has been willing to adopt one strand of the theology of romantic love, the vision of the beloved in a paradisial glory. This appears to take him one step beyond the 'potential' or eschatological glory envisaged in his famous sermon 'The Weight of Glory'. On the other hand, in his *Figure of Arthur*, Williams seems to have made a concession to Lewis, finally taking account of Lewis' argument that the courtly love of the medieval French poets is only a parody of religion, and that Williams' own kind of romantic theology, 'a noble fusion of sexual and religious experience',[154] does not appear until Dante. In his lecture on 'Courtly Love' in 1937, Williams was still maintaining that the love-religion in the French poets was 'semi-serious, semi-profane [...] half-parody, half t[truth], half-symbolical, half-growing up'.[155] In his notes for the lecture, he describes 'some new note which appealed at once to those new worlds of Christian, Catholic, and fantastic belief. It was pushed to a serious extreme. Chretien de Troyes took it up.'[156] Now, in his *Figure of Arthur*, he is much less sure. Surveying 'love', as it appeared to the court of Troyes and as it was exemplified in Chrétien's poem *Lancelot*, Williams judges that his lovers Lancelot and Guinevere

> do not very much go into the soul; there is nothing of Dante here, and nothing of what, after Dante finished with it, has been meant by romantic love. This is the early style, and not yet mature.[157]

Considering the scene, also related by Lewis,[158] where Chrétien's Lancelot kneels to the queen, 'for in no holy body had he such belief', Williams now calls this an 'exaggeration of what was at best only one element in human experience', behaviour prompted 'by what the code told him he ought to feel and in any case how he ought to behave'.[159] Again, he judges that in Lancelot's genuflection:

> The two elements of a proper worship and (*pace* the adultery) a proper sensuality are too close together for our taste. The maxim for any love affair is 'Play and pray: but on the whole do not pray when you are playing and do not play when you are praying'. We cannot yet manage such simultaneities, and it is difficult for us to believe that the early Middle Ages could.[160]

---

[154] Lewis, *Allegory of Love*, 21.   [155] Wade, Wade RH Notebooks 12: 2157.
[156] 'Courtly Love', Wade CW MS-496, 4.   [157] Williams, 'Figure of Arthur', 50.
[158] Lewis, *Allegory of Love*, 29.   [159] Williams, 'Figure of Arthur', 54.
[160] Williams, 'Figure of Arthur', 58–9.

This sentiment is, of course, quite consistent with the theology of romantic love, since Williams had always warned against the idolatry of treating the beloved's body as an object of worship in itself, rather than adoring it as a revelation of the divine glory. But the passage in its emphasis does read as some kind of placation of Lewis. In summary, he admits that 'I am not sure that [...] the great love-tale comes properly now under the heading of Romantic Love, either in the historic or the metaphysical sense.'[161]

Williams' position 'now' is that religious experience within romantic love— seeing the glory of the beloved *and* the glory of Christ in her/him—is authentic, but that it just does not appear as early as the versions of the Arthurian myths in the French Romances or as reflected later in Malory.[162] However, this does not rule out making it appear in his own poetic Arthuriad. Embodied in the first cycle (1938) in such figures as Bors, Taliessin, and anonymous slave-girls,[163] it is still apparent in the second cycle in 1944.[164] Moreover, his later view that it fails to appear in early Arthurian romances except in parody form is consistent with his depiction of *false* Beatrician visions. He writes that even the instinct behind genuflecting to a beloved's body is 'natural', but in the case of Lancelot's Chrétien it has been distorted and falsified by a 'code' of behaviour.[165] In Williams' own poetry, Palomides begins with a true vision of Iseult as his Beatrice, but it develops into sheer lust, symbolized by his pursuit of the 'questing beast' when 'the queen's arm lay [...] empty of glory'.[166] That this is essentially a failure in perceiving Christ is expressed by Palomides' confusion between the 'scratching' around of the beast in its cave and the 'scratching' of the Chi-Ro sign (the first two letters of Christos) on the walls of early Christian tombs:

> The Chi-Ro is only a scratching like other scratchings;
> but in the turn of the sky the only scratching—[167]

Lewis judges that this is an 'ill-judged' borrowing from the manner of T. S. Eliot,[168] and the reader has the impression that this is a critique not only of style but content. He does not seem convinced by this Christological element within a human love story.

The roster of failures to hold the Beatrician vision continues with Lamorack. While his visionary love for Morgause was celebrated in Williams' earlier poem in *Heroes and Kings*, here his love has become a joyless obsession with someone who

---

[161] Williams, 'Figure of Arthur', 88.   [162] Williams, 'Malory and the Grail Legend', 188.
[163] See Williams' poems 'Bors to Elayne' (both), 'The Sister of Percivale' and 'The Star of Percivale' in *Taliessin*.
[164] See 'The Queen's Servant', in *Region*.   [165] Williams, 'Figure of Arthur', 55.
[166] Williams, 'The Coming of Palomides', *Taliessin*, 36.
[167] Williams, 'Palomides before his Christening', *Taliessin*, 67.
[168] Lewis, 'Williams and the Arthuriad', 163.

is hard as 'primeval rock', rejecting, as Lewis puts it—'all exchange'.[169] This is the sister that Arthur has unwittingly committed incest with, intending only adultery, and now she bears in her body not the son of love, but a child—Mordred—who will betray and kill him, weaving a different web from that of the gateways of glory: 'unformed in his brain is the web of all our doom'.[170] Lewis perceives well that, in the cumulative imagery of the poem, stone has become 'fully incarnate' in Morgause like a 'giant inhuman form', so that in the Fall evil is 'not so much an imperfection [...] as miscreation'.[171] By contrast, Lewis does not see so readily the fleshly incarnation of *Christ* in properly loving relationships. For Williams, Lancelot has failed to find this kind of incarnation in his love for Guinevere, so that this too falls short of the genuine vision; when the host is elevated, Lancelot finds 'only a ghost of the Queen'.[172] The point is not, as Lewis supposes, that 'Lancelot worships only the Queen'[173]—here he is reading in the idolatry of Lancelot from Chrétien's account of his genuflection to Guinevere. The point is that Lancelot sees only a 'ghost of the Queen' in the sense that he did not see her solid flesh united gloriously with the body of the sacrament. Again, Lewis' underlying view of the relation between God and world is different.

To some extent, Lewis is in tune with Williams when he considers the disturbing 'reappearing' of the glory in a different person from the one in whom it was at first manifested. Like Williams, he distinguishes this from an illusory Beatrician vision, either in its first or second or consequent appearances. He quotes Williams with apparent approval (from *The Figure of Beatrice*) that the second image is not to be denied, or its worth diminished.[174] Indeed Lewis suggests that if the first appearance of the glory *does* reveal someone 'as beings really and eternally are', then we ought to expect that this glory may return 'to reveal similar transcendental truth about another being'.[175] He adds that 'the way to which the glory invites us may run through marriage or it may not'—the important thing, he again agrees with Williams, is that the second or subsequent appearing of the glory should not be met with concupiscence. We are uncertain, reading this comment, whether Lewis realized that Williams had found subsequent appearances of the glory *after* his marriage with Michal, and that he thought it right to 'adore' other women for the glory within them. Moreover, for Williams, the imperative to take notice of the glory wherever it appeared was not just—as Lewis mentions—that it revealed someone's heavenly state where it 'will clothe every woman and every man, every beast, blade of grass, rock'. For Williams, there is also a summons to see the glory of *Christ*. Once again Lewis either fails, or refuses, to acknowledge this more theological dimension of glory in the vision of the lover. Significantly, Lewis ends

---

[169] Lewis, 'Williams and the Arthuriad', 130.
[170] Williams, 'Lamorack and the Queen Morgause of Orkney', *Taliessin*, 41.
[171] Lewis, 'Williams and the Arthuriad', 131–2.   [172] Williams, 'Star of Percivale', *Taliessin*, 47.
[173] Lewis, 'Williams and the Arthuriad', 136.   [174] Williams, *Figure of Beatrice*, 49.
[175] Lewis, 'Williams and the Arthuriad', 118.

his quotation from *The Figure of Beatrice* with Williams' words that both the first and second appearances are movements 'alike intense towards most noble love', and fails to go on to the next phrase: 'that is, towards the work of the *primal Love* in the creation,' leading on to Williams' following comment that 'to observe and adore the glory' is a gift of 'the largesse of our Lord'.[176]

Williams' own accommodation to Lewis over courtly love was already beginning—some while before writing 'The Figure of Arthur'—in a review of 1942,[177] in which he attempts a classification of different 'ways of love', as embodied in three lovers: Tristan, Lancelot and Dante. In the light of Dante, who represents truly Christian romantic love, Tristan in the legends may be seen as pagan carnal love, while Lancelot's passion for Guinevere in the French romance of Tristan is a carnal passion that is 'Christian' only in the sense of being capable of being redeemed. In itself it is 'not of the kind of Dante and Beatrice'. Williams' comment that 'there is no celestial significance about Guinevere' makes clear that their love is not even halfway (a 'half-truth') towards the bonding of love and spirituality in Dante. We must, however, 'allow too the mysterious redemption, through the sorrow of loyalty and the loyalty of sorrow, of the flesh of Lancelot and Guinevere, in the begetting of Galahad'.[178] While Williams is commenting in the first place on the French 'Tristan', his remarks seem to be a more general picture of the Lancelot of the romances.

An earlier typology of love appears in Williams' notes on the Arthurian myth, which he probably wrote at least ten years earlier. Here he presents a triad of lovers consisting of Galahad, Percivale, and Bors, the three knights who are present at the achieving of the Grail in Carbonek. Their three 'capacities' are different: Bors is 'the ordinary man, married', and is 'the spiritual intellect concerned with earthly things'; Percivale is the 'virginal' lover who is simply 'spiritual intellect'; Galahad is aware only of the 'End' of the spiritual quest, and is finally assumed into Christ.[179] So Williams writes in *Taliessin* about the voyage to Sarras, 'by three ways of exchange the City sped to the City'.[180] As Williams remarks in an essay of 1941, there seems to be a hierarchy here, and 'yet the hierarchy was one',[181] since all three reach Sarras, carrying the body of Blanchefleur in the ship, who has given her life's blood in substitution to save a sick woman. Lancelot is not part of the threefold typology, but at this phase in his thinking, Williams affirms that he 'has his heart mostly on pure love' and is 'illuminated' by Guinevere, and that (despite his being tricked by magic into intercourse with Helayne) Galahad is born of 'pure passion and pure law'. Lancelot is 'eighth in succession from Christ', and is

---

[176] Williams, *Figure of Beatrice*, 49–50 (my italics).
[177] Williams, 'The Chances and Changes of Myth', 183–5.
[178] Williams, 'The Chances and Changes of Myth', 185.
[179] Williams, 'Notes on the Arthurian Myth', 177.
[180] Williams, 'The Last Voyage', *Taliessin*, 85.   [181] Williams, 'The Making of Taliessin', 180.

concerned with love as 'a thing of dolour and labour and vision'.[182] Lancelot thus appears, implicitly, as an exemplar of the type assigned to Bors.[183] There is no idea that Galahad's birth is a 'redemption' of a 'carnal passion'.

Much later, in an essay of 1944, Williams returns to the earlier typology that he reads as being present in Malory, 'exhibiting three degrees of love':[184] Bors returns to the outer world of Camelot where his wife and children await, Percivale remains in contemplation as a hermit, and Galahad is assumed into the Grail. 'The High Prince is at the deep centre,' writes Williams, 'but he also operates in [the others] towards the world.'[185] Lancelot, however, is presented much as in the review-essay of 1942. Clearly, Williams has agreed with Lewis in renouncing the view that the Lancelot of either the romances or Malory demonstrates a Dantean kind of love. Language about the 'vision' of love in Lancelot has been dropped; Malory was not concerned with 'the greater passion and truer vision of the Dantean Romantic love' and 'Lancelot and Guinevere do not develop that'.[186] Admittedly, Williams remarks that in Malory 'the whole question of Courtly Love may be ruled out at once', and so it is possible that he is still hankering after at least the 'half-truth' of spiritual vision that he had once found in courtly, romantic love before Dante, but his review of 1942 and his treatment of Chrétien in the *Figure of Arthur* seem to rule this out.

8.6 Convergence in the Wood of the World

While Williams comes somewhat onto Lewis' ground about courtly love, Lewis appears to have entered Williams' Arthurian terrain in the third of his science-fiction trilogy, *That Hideous Strength*. The Arthurian elements are evident. Ransom holds the office of Pendragon in the seat of Arthur, as well as being identified with the Fisher-King, by way of a bequest from a sister in Australia that he should take her name of Fisher-King in exchange for her large fortune, and in order to thwart a pressing danger to the world. Finally Ransom is to be carried away to 'the House of the Kings' beyond the seas of Perelandra as Arthur was taken to the lake isle of Avalon.[187] The noxious research institute, N.I.C.E., which is running experiments to recondition the human race through sinister programmes of genetic engineering, biochemical control of the brain,

---

[182] Williams, 'Notes on the Arthurian Myth', 166–7.
[183] In 'The Song of the Riding of Galahad', *Heroes and Kings*, 69–74, Galahad's repeated refrain is 'I also am Lancelot', which appears commendatory.
[184] Williams, 'Malory and the Grail Legend', 193.
[185] Williams, 'Malory and the Grail Legend', 193.
[186] Williams, 'Malory and the Grail Legend', 188.
[187] Williams recounts the passing of Arthur to 'Avilion' only in 'Notes on the Arthurian Myth', 178, and not in the two Taliessin cycles. But the dead body of Nigel Considine in Williams, *Shadows*, 223, is carried away by submarine to an unknown place, perhaps to return.

and sterilization, has set itself up on the edge of Bragdon Wood, near 'Merlin's Well' where the legendary magician is said to lie asleep. Bragdon is obviously a version of Broceliande in Williams' myth, and to oppose N.I.C.E. Ransom has founded a Christian community nearby in St Anne's, which resembles the company of Taliessin: 'you may call it a company' says one person.[188] Merlin, Taliessin/Ransom,[189] and the wood of primal generation are thus brought together as in Williams' poem 'The Calling of Taliessin'. But the common ground with Williams is more than circumstantial; it is also ritual. Merlin, woken for the time of crisis that is befalling humanity, is convinced of Ransom's credentials through the solving of a series of occult riddles that seem to have been lifted directly from the pages of Williams' novels. In the second riddle, for example, Merlin asks, 'Where is the ring of Arthur the King? What Lord has such a treasure in his house?'

> 'The ring of the King,' said Ransom, 'is on Arthur's finger where he sits in the House of Kings in the cup-shaped land of Abhalljin, beyond the seas of Lur in Perelandra. For Arthur did not die; but Our Lord took him, to be in the body till the end of time and the shattering of Sulva, with Enoch and Elias and Moses and Melchisedec the King. Melchisedec is he in whose hall the steep-stoned ring sparkles on the fore-finger of the Pendragon.'[190]

Ransom and Merlin later present themselves to the company respectively in magicians' robes of blue and red. The robes depict a hierarchy: the blue stands for the cosmic, angelic powers (*eldila*) of which Ransom is the channel, after his abode in the deep heavens, while the red evokes the earthly powers of nature of which Merlin is the master. The question for us, arising from *Arthurian Torso*, is what kind of hierarchy of power and grace they might be portraying, and which one Lewis is subscribing to as a world view behind the symbols of his mythical story. The title of Ransom as 'the Head' of his household (alongside being named 'The Director') has obvious resonances with Christ as 'head' of the church, but is this to be read in the context of a Christian Neoplatonism or a kind of Christian Kabbalism? As I have observed in section 3, there is no question of either Lewis or Williams holding to a doctrinaire form of either kind of Christianized philosophy; it is a matter of the general pattern of reality with which they are working—either a graded ascent to glory or an interactive web of manifested glory.

Despite the occult trappings, with Lewis we seem to be in the ethos of a Neoplatonic hierarchy, with those on each rung of the spiritual ladder in strict

---

[188] Lewis, *That Hideous Strength*, 57. Rowan Williams, 'That Hideous Strength', 97–9, finds St Anne's to be an unsuccessful reflection of Williams' own 'Company', with an 'esoteric lure'.

[189] And therefore also Charles Williams: for an uncritical picture of Williams as a spiritual teacher see Lewis to 'A Friend', undated, *c.* 1945–6, *Letters* ed. W. H. Lewis, 208.

[190] Williams, *That Hideous Strength*, 337.

obedience to those above. As Denniston explains, 'He is really a Head, you see. We have all agreed to take his orders.' Jane Studdock, a young academic who has clairvoyant visions of what N.I.C.E is up to, can only join the community of Ransom if she owns obedience first as a wife to her husband, Mark (who has been lured into N.I.C.E.), and then to Ransom as Head. We are meant to read her horrified reaction as a matter of spiritual immaturity that she needs to grow beyond:

> All this talk of promises and obedience to an unknown Mr Fisher-King had already repelled her. But the idea of this same person sending her back to get Mark's permission—as if she were a child asking leave to go to a party—was the climax.[191]

There is little here of the 'excellent absurdity' of headship that Taliessin sees himself as allowing.[192] Perhaps significantly, there is also no sense of seeing radiance or glory in the loved one. When Venus descends into the community at St Anne's it is with a burning fire of celestial love, and even though the damaged marriage of Jane and Mark is to be repaired through these events,[193] none of this 'translunary virtue' is evidently transferred from the 'incarnation' to the acts of human, sexual love:

> it was Charity, not as mortals imagine it, not even as it has been humanised for them since the Incarnation of the Word, but the translunary virtue, fallen upon them direct from the Third Heaven, unmitigated. They were blinded, scorched, deafened. They thought it would burn their bones. They could not bear that it should continue. They could not bear that it should cease.[194]

Oddly, glory is only ascribed to earthly creatures in the person of the bear, rampant both in battle and in mating: 'The pride and insolent glory of the beast.'[195]

Similarly, the 'magic' of Merlin, which works in sympathy with the forces of nature, is presented as a neutral virtue, not filled with any kind of divine grace. His magic belongs to the age of easy converse between human beings and the 'gods, elves, dwarfs, water-people, *fate, longaevi*' of the natural world, energies neutral towards human beings and with which an 'innocent' art could communicate that

---

[191] Williams, *That Hideous Strength*, 40–1. Schwartz, *C. S. Lewis*, 97, suggests that Jane's initial repulsion by, and then attraction to, Ransom echoes the myth of Cupid and Psyche, which Lewis would reuse in *Till We Have Faces*.

[192] Williams, 'Founding of the Company', *Region*, 41.

[193] Ward, *Planet Narnia*, 174, emphasizes that Venus 'lingers to preside over Mark and Jane's bed'.

[194] Lewis, *That Hideous Strength*, 400.   [195] Lewis, *That Hideous Strength*, 434.

had not yet been conscripted for either good or evil.[196] When Dimble explains that Merlin is the last vestige of an old order in which 'matter and spirit were, from our modern point of view, confused,' by 'spirit' he means a created soul or personality, not the divine Spirit. He is recollecting an ideal picture of nature in itself, a union of the material and the personal or 'soul-ish'. But it is not a means of access *in itself* either to the divine or the demonic. N.I.C.E. has built its institute near Merlin's Well because it wants to make use of this natural magic, to enlist Merlin in its cause for evil, just as Ransom and his company plan to employ him for good, in the service of the cosmic powers, the Oyéresu who bear the characteristics of the planets. This mythological scheme fits generally into Lewis' conception that 'natural' values are not in themselves 'spiritual',[197] and he gives Merlin a more central place than he has in Williams' poems precisely because he is a symbol of the natural.[198] One of the purposes of his awakening, Ransom tells him, 'was that your own soul should be saved'.[199]

All this—a strict obedience, a distinction between human love and divine glory, and a realm of nature that has to be redeemed through being assumed into Christ—belongs naturally within a Christian Neoplatonist hierarchy. But at the same time, there are hints of another pattern of how things are. The heavenly and the earthly powers, the blue and red, could be connected in a more interactive and interwoven way, with the base station of the 'tree of life' (*malkuth*, the earth) contained in the 'head' (*kether*). This would be a kabbalistic kind of web, of which Taliessin has a vision,[200] and there may be a clue that Lewis has been consulting Williams when the direction of N.I.C.E. is given to a demonic version of the Head. The N.I.C.E. Head is actually the severed head of a criminal kept alive and speaking by a perverted science as a conduit for evil powers who are really directing the business of the institute. In Kabbalism, there is an inverted form of the tree of life, a tree of death called Klipot (*Kliphoth*) or the realm of 'the shells', mere empty husks of the true *sephiroth*.[201] Here there is a counterpart/counterfeit Head. Gareth Knight comments that 'Here again we have an example of Lewis picking intuitively or deliberately from arcane tradition.'[202] In his vision of the Empire, Williams depicts an antitype to Byzantium:

---

[196] Lewis, *That Hideous Strength*, 351–2, 356–7. Lewis, *English Literature*, 11–12, mentions the 'middle spirits' that appear in Apuleius, Bernardus Sylvestris and Layamon, which create the possibility of 'an innocent traffic with unseen and therefore of high magic or *magia*.' Hannay, 'Arthurian and Cosmic Myth', comments that Merlin's magic according to Lewis 'had been more effective and less wrong than Renaissance magic.'

[197] Lewis, *Christian Reflections*, 24–8.

[198] Williams also saw Merlin as 'natural man' and 'the natural body': see Williams' Commonplace Book, in Williams, *Image*, 172.

[199] Lewis, *That Hideous Strength*, 357.

[200] Williams, 'Taliessin in the Rose-Garden', *Region*, 24–5.

[201] Waite, *Secret Doctrine*, 255, 303.   [202] Knight, *Magical World*, 70.

> Inarticulate always on an inarticulate sea
> Beyond P'o-lu the headless Emperor moves,
> the octopuses round him; lost are the Roman hands;
> lost are the substantial instruments of being.

The counterfeit Emperor is 'headless' in that he is without the proper Head (*kether*) that belongs to the stations of life and glory ('the substantial instruments of being'). His head is a mere empty 'shell'.

It is a glimpse of this web of life that we have in the climactic chapter of *That Hideous Strength* when the heavenly powers of the planets descend onto earth, bringing all their virtues into the world, and pouring into the body of Merlin to make an irresistible weapon to overcome evil. This manifestation of the glory of the celestial powers in the places (stations) of earthly life is much more kabbalistic than Neoplatonic, and it is here that Lewis stands at least momentarily on Williams' own ground.[203] Yet, significantly, he still wants to maintain that it is not the everyday occurrence that Williams can see it as being. Merlin protests that such an event has been forbidden by Maleldil (God-in-Christ) until the end of the world: 'Has not our Fair Lord made it a law for Himself that He will not send down the Powers to mend or mar in this Earth until the end of all things? Or is this the end that is even now coming to pass?' Ransom replies:

> It may be the beginning of the end,' said Ransom. 'But I know nothing of that. Maleldil may have made it a law not to send down the Powers. But if men by enginry and natural philosophy learn to fly into the Heavens, and come, in the flesh, among the heavenly powers and trouble them, He has not forbidden the Powers to react. For all this is within the natural order.[204]

Here then is another qualification. It is not only unprecedented and unique, but 'within the natural order'. In Williams, working with a more kabbalistic pattern, the natural is suffused continuously with the glory of the Shekinah, which is nothing less than an extension of the divine Being. Lewis, however, is careful to differentiate between the celestial powers of the planets and the presence of God.[205] The presence of God is available for the Christian community at St Anne's, and is promised to Jane as a Christian believer and to those who deliberately open themselves to God:

---

[203] Horne, 'Peculiar Debt', 94, aptly compares this scene to Williams' *Place of the Lion*.

[204] Lewis, *That Hideous Strength*, 358.

[205] Schwartz, *C. S. Lewis*, 96, does not notice this distinction in writing of 'the triumph of a divinely enchanted world of traditional romance'.

A boundary had been crossed. She had come into a world, or into a Person, or into the presence of a Person. Something expectant, patient, inexorable, met her with no veil or protection between. [...] This demand which now pressed upon her was not, even by analogy, like any other demand. It was the origin of all right demands and contained them. In its light you could understand them; but from them you could know nothing of it.[206]

Lewis, as narrator, is quite clear that from the 'right' demand of—say—love for the neighbour, one can know 'nothing' of the ultimate Demand, such as he had felt fall upon himself in his rooms at Magdalen in 1930, when he had become 'perhaps, that night, the most dejected and reluctant convert in all England'.[207] The difference even of the angelic planetary powers descending on Bragdon Wood from the practice of the presence of God is demonstrated when Ransom stops Merlin from kneeling to the incoming glorious beings: 'See thou do it not! Have you forgotten that they are our fellow servants?'[208] For Williams, the glory that permeates creation, and especially the created love of two people, is not just that of the angels but of 'God-in-operation'. With these qualifications, there is, nevertheless, a partial convergence between Lewis and Williams on the ground of Bragdon Wood/Broceliande, where both Taliessin and Ransom meet Merlin.

8.7 The Co-inherence of the Two Ways

In Lewis' commentary on Williams' Arthurian poems, it is in the person of Galahad that we find further convergence between the two friends. What is distinctive about Galahad emerges in a poem in which he appears almost incidentally, and which is another where Lewis introduces, in his commentary, the term 'co-inherence' where it does not actually appear in the text. 'The Departure of Dindrane' presents the opposite vocations of Taliessin and Dindrane (or Blanchefleur) whom Taliessin loves deeply, though chastely. Dindrane is leaving Camelot to take up her life as a nun in the convent of Almesbury, and Taliessin is accompanying her part way there on horseback. Dindrane as a recluse represents the 'negative way' of knowing God, as Taliessin as a poet represents the positive way of the affirmation of images, and yet the two ways mingle and interact. On the 'highroad of the hazel' between city and convent, there is exhibited in the two travellers:

---

[206] Lewis, *That Hideous Strength*, 394.   [207] Lewis, *Surprised by Joy*, 215.
[208] Lewis, *That Hideous Strength*, 396. However, Ward, *Planet Narnia*, 171, claims that Aslan incarnates the characteristics of the planets in the Chronicles of Narnia, including the female Intelligence of Venus in *Magician's Nephew*.

> the two great vocations,
> the Rejection of all images before the unimaged,
> the Affirmation of all images before the all-imaged,
> the Rejection affirming, the Affirmation rejecting, the king's poet
> riding through a cloud with a vowed novice,
> and either no less than the other the doctrine of largesse[.][209]

In their final words to each other, they speak of the way that the two ways intertwine; she pledges, 'I will affirm, my beloved, all that I should,' and he replies, 'I will reject all that I should.' Lewis comments: 'The co-inherence of their opposite vocations is expressed in their parting words.'[210] The depth of Lewis' sympathy with Williams is shown at this point, where he uses the exact word that is no doubt in Williams' mind. Though he does not use it himself here, Williams had previously written in *The Descent of the Dove* about fourth-century Christianity that:

> Both methods, the Affirmative Way and the Negative Way, were to co-exist; *one might almost say, to co-inhere,* since each was to be the key of the other: in intellect as in emotion, in morals as in doctrine. [...] No Affirmation could be so complete as not to need definition, disciplines and refusal; no Rejection so absolute as not leave necessary [...] the divine imagery of matter.[211]

Had Lewis recalled this passage from his reading of *The Descent of the Dove*, and made the 'almost saying' definite? Now Galahad makes his entrance in the poem, as the one in whom the two ways are united. He does not actually appear, as he is not yet born, but he is foreshadowed in the riding together of the representatives of the two ways, one of whom is to be his foster-mother:

> So, over the galloping household, sang
> in the third heaven, overheard above the hooves,
> the foster-ward of Dindrane before his birth:
> 'Fair Lord, salute me to my lord Sir Lancelot my father,
> and bid him remember of this unstable world.'
> The grand Rejection sang to the grand Affirmation:
> itself affirming, itself honouring its peer:
> Salute me, salute me, to my Lord Sir Lancelot my father.'[212]

The twice-repeated phrase beginning 'Salute me' is given to Galahad by Malory just as he is about to achieve the Grail and leave the world,[213] and it seems to have

---

[209] Williams, 'The Departure of Dindrane', *Region*, 32.
[210] Lewis, 'Williams and the Arthuriad', 151.
[211] Williams, *Descent of the Dove*, 57. My emphasis.
[212] Williams, 'The Departure of Dindrane', *Region*, 33.
[213] Malory, 'The Quest of the Holy Grail', 607.

struck Williams with the force of a revelation.[214] From the beginning of his reading of Arthurian myths, Williams had been convinced that Galahad was the key to the whole; as the one who achieved the Grail, he represents 'man's capacity for Christ', so that 'In Sarras all things are assumed to Galahad and he is assumed to Christ.'[215] At some time between 1938 and 1939, Williams conceived this assumption as a unity of the 'two ways' that he had been frequently invoking in the phrase 'This also is Thou; neither is this Thou.' Williams read the farewell words of Galahad to his father as a message to one who had had all his life affirmed the images of love, reminding him of the alternative way which realized that the world was 'unstable', and yet still honouring the path he had taken ('Salute me...'). Galahad could unite the two ways in himself because, according to the myth, he was conceived in Carbonek by the lying of Lancelot with Helayne, daughter of Pelles and Princess of the Grail. In Williams' mind, these two people represented respectively the positive and the negative ways. Lancelot had been tricked into this congress and conception by a magic potion administered by Brisen, and so was acting under the deception that Helayne was Guinevere. The result was to drive Lancelot mad with remorse for nine months, reducing him to the condition of a wild wolf, but was also to produce Galahad, a man in whom was combined uniquely both the affirmation and rejection of images.

This reading of the nature of Galahad appears first in *The Descent of the Dove*; there is no hint of it in the Galahad poems of *Taliessin Through Logres*, nor in the notes on the poems that Williams gave Lewis. The account in *Descent* includes the farewell words of Galahad, as well as a comparison of the dark chamber of the union of Galahad with Helayne (in Malory's version) with the Dark Night of the Soul,

> where the princess of the Grail abandoned her virginity, and Lancelot was defrauded of his fidelity, so that the two great Ways might exchange themselves for the begetting of Galahad. The High Prince has remained as an intense symbol of the two Ways; he is not on them, but they are both in him. He is flesh and blood in union with the Flesh and the Blood.[216]

Williams makes clear that Galahad himself is following the path of the rejection of images, but the other way is *within* him because 'he is the child and climax of the greatest of mortal affirmations, of a passionate, devout,[217] and tragic double love', and he recalls this positive way with respect in addressing his father. All these

---

[214] It appears as the climax of both Williams' pieces, 'The Chances and Changes of Myth' and 'Malory and the Grail Legend.'

[215] Williams, 'Notes on the Arthurian Myth', 176–7.

[216] Williams, *Descent of the Dove*, 116–17.

[217] At this point it seems that Williams wants still to attribute a genuine religious romantic love to the Lancelot of the French romances.

ideas are repeated in Williams' lecture of June 1939 on 'The Arthurian Myth', underlining the Dark Night of the Soul as the place where the two ways are united, and leading to an appeal to the experience of his audience:

> ...the dark chamber of that state is so like the dark night of the soul—in which the Way of the Affirmation and the Way of the Rejection come together; and it is from that moment that the begetting of the High Prince who is both emerges [...]
>
> and yet the High Prince must know images. He knows them in his father; he knows the whole sex business as in Pelles; as in Bors; as in Lancelot. For after all, all the images of the beloved, of our friends... what are they to us in a way but those things that propagate in us [...] unless the soul is born of those things. [...] All that kind of recognition of the incredible value of images, of the incredible worth of images, occurs in the sensation of the last words of Galahad: Fair Lord, Sir Lancelot, my father,
>
> —bid him remember of this unstable world.[218]

Williams thus concludes that 'the High Prince is that state which does seize on the moments of Affirmation and the moments of Rejection with equal power, and with equal intensity'. The 'coming together' or 'exchange' of the two ways in Galahad is not actually called a 'co-inherence' either in this lecture, or in *The Descent of the Dove*, although more generally (as we have seen) Williams refers earlier in *Descent* to the 'co-existence' of the two ways as being—'one might almost say'—a co-inherence. However, in the fragment of another lecture, the manuscript of which Williams gave Raymond Hunt in 1941, Williams does apply the term to the interchange between rejection and affirmation of images in Galahad himself:

> if she [Helayne] rejects images, she yet has to submit to them; and if Lancelot has accepted them, he is yet cheated of them: and in that closed chamber an awful substitution is doubly accomplished, and the High Prince, who is both, is born. But how his synthesis is expressed, I haven't an idea. So that on the one hand we have (i) co-inherence and (ii) women: and at the other the terrible magical operation, in the dark chamber, which is the Dark Night of the Soul.[219]

How much the idea was running in Williams' mind in early 1939, at the time he was developing the concept of co-inherence, is demonstrated by a lecture on a different subject altogether, the early English poem *The Dream of the Rood*, delivered in April 1939. The poem alternates between the experiences of the suffering tree (the cross) and the hero who ascends it (the Christ),[220] and

---

[218]   Wade RH Notebooks 20: 3883.   [219]   Wade CW/MS-2, 8–11, headed 'Taliessin'.
[220]   See Woolf, 'Doctrinal Influences on The Dream of the Rood', 29–48.

Williams suggests that it offers us two separate 'poetic' states of mind, drawn together in one overall conception, claiming that 'the thing got more and more complicated until in fact when you come to the conception of the high prince of the Sangreal, and the whole sophistication of the culture are [*sic*] brought together, and you get that conscious conception of Lancelot as the father of Galahad'.[221]

This is the development of thought that lies behind the lines on Galahad in 'The Departure of Dindrane', and it confirms the appropriateness of Lewis' phrase for Taliessin and Dindrane: 'the co-inherence of their opposite vocations'. As a matter of fact, however, Lewis has no comment to make on the particular lines about Galahad. Perhaps this is because of the interpretation that he has of the line in Malory that struck Williams with such force; while Williams asserts that it is 'one of the greatest phrases in Malory',[222] Lewis reads it as a simple reproof of his father by Galahad.[223] Lewis does nevertheless direct our attention to another aspect of the co-inherence of the two ways, taking us in a different direction from Galahad. There is a second major theme in the action of the poem, alongside the interplay between Taliessin and Dindrane—a comparison between the vocations of two women, for 'love and a live heart' lay in both the princess and a slave.

While Dindrane is on the point of departing Camelot for the convent, a slave-girl who is due her freedom under the seven-year law of release has to decide on *her* vocation—whether to take freedom and leave the household of Taliessin, or bind herself to her master voluntarily. She is impressed by the resolve with which Dindrane has accepted 'bondage' in her cell and, in a moment of felt exchange with Dindrane, she sees suddenly that 'servitude and freedom were one and interchangeable', and that she can 'follow the household's heart / in a twin freedom and servitude'. Lewis perceives rightly that the two themes of the poem are woven together, the two ways of life and the relation of serving to freedom. Both servitude and freedom are forms of obedience, but—as Lewis summarizes the matter—'servitude obeys an 'imaged' and freedom an 'unimaged' law.[224] The problem with this dialectic is that the way of the 'affirmation of images' might then lead to mere obedience to a fixed hierarchy—master and slave. Williams in fact offers a slightly different perspective:

> Servitude is a will that obeys an imaged law;
> freedom an unimaged—or makes choice of images.[225]

The last phrase (ignored by Lewis) throws new light on the interchangeability of freedom and servitude. Freedom consists in either following the way of the

---

[221] 'The Dream of the Rood', Wade RH Notebooks 20: 3767–78, 21 April 1939, CLI series 'The Christian Idea in Literature' 25. Williams lists 'Dream of the Rood, Transl by Cook. OUP' in a list of miscellaneous books, Wade MS/CW-95, 6.

[222] Williams, 'Malory and the Grail Legend', 194.   [223] Lewis, 'English Prose Morte', 17.

[224] Lewis, 'Williams and the Arthuriad', 153.

[225] Williams, 'The Departure of Dindrane', *Region*, 33.

negation of images—where only the unimaged God remains as the goal of obedience—or, in the 'choice of images' exercised, as Roma King puts it, 'by those who see in every image a valid expression of some aspect of the godhead but refuse to regard any one as definitive'. In this case when images of law 'become ends in themselves, they are enslaving'.[226] The outcome, as King has underlined,[227] is that the girl understands her final decision as being more to bind herself to 'the household and its future' than to Taliessin; that is also how King interprets the final lines:

> They only can do it with my lord who can do it without him,
> and I know that he will have about him only those.

Lewis, by contrast, understands the lines to mean that the slave-girl has come to her decision on her own, without any direct guidance from Taliessin. King's interpretation has interesting implications for the way that Williams saw his own position among the 'companions' around him. Lewis has put his finger on the centrality of co-inherence in this poem, despite the absence of the actual word and his lack of interest in Galahad's last message, and King follows him in judging that 'the slave girl is being initiated into the great mystery of co-inherence'. But we find that Lewis tends to place it in a hierarchical context, the slave-girl finding an inner freedom in willingly taking up the position of servitude to her master.

When Williams regards the 'two ways' to God as co-inherent, he also intends that this mutual intertwining of the affirmation and rejection of images should provide a context for the incarnation of Christ in human lives and in human consciousness of love. Taliessin and Dindrane ride together to Almesbury,

> ... close-handed, oath-bonded,
> *word-in-the-flesh-branded*, each seconded
> to the other, each in the crowd of Camelot vowed
> to the other, the two Ways, the Ways passing ... [228]

Their love participates in the enfleshment of the divine word, which Williams associates with receiving the sacrament of the Eucharist. Galahad, perfectly combining the two ways, is to be assumed into God during the eucharistic celebration of the body of Christ.

There is no reason to doubt that Lewis generally approves Williams' notion of the co-inherence of the two ways; on this he is not just a neutral commentator. In his book *Miracles*, which he was writing at the same time as *Arthurian Torso*, and which offers the most extended study he made of images of God, he explains that

---

[226] King, *Pattern*, 148.   [227] King, *Pattern*, 151.
[228] Williams, 'The Departure of Dindrane', *Region*, 32–3. My italics.

the two ways need each other. Positive mental images of God need to be modified and corrected by the negative way of thinking them away. While it is inevitable that positive images should come to our minds, we should make them as adequate as possible by employing negative tactics.[229] Conversely, he observes that if we try to use negatives for God ('infinite, immaterial, impassible, immutable, etc.'), 'unchecked by any positive intuition', we end up with a merely 'intellectual religion' since 'In St Paul's language, the purpose of all this unclothing is not that our idea of God should reach nakedness but that it should be re-clothed.'[230] This is a conviction Lewis takes up much later, in his revisions to the sermon 'Transposition', when he writes that our notion of heaven 'involves perpetual negations' against which we should set the positive image of the Beatific vision, even if this conception is 'a difficult, precarious and fugitive extrapolation from a few and ambiguous moments in our earthly experience'. We must believe, he urges, that 'every negation will be the reverse side of a fulfilling'.[231]

Nevertheless, this complementarity of the positive and negative ways, regarded by Lewis himself as a 'co-inherence', does not lead Lewis—for almost all his writing career—to follow Williams into his vision of an unlimited incarnation of the glory of Christ in human life and love. We have seen that in his commentary on Williams' Arthuriad, Lewis recognizes (even where Williams does not use the term) that the world Williams presents is a 'co-inherent' one, and that our present-day world needs a similar co-inherence. But he passes over in silence Williams' idea that Christ is 'born' in the consciousness of those who love, and doubts whether meaning can be given to the 'union of substance and sensuality'.[232] There is thus a tendency for Lewis to use the idea of the co-inherence of human beings in each other and in God to confirm a rather fixed hierarchical world view, characteristic of a Christian Neoplatonism. Yet there are hints in Lewis that he *could* move more in Williams' direction.

For instance, there is Lewis' commentary on the poem 'The Founding of the Company', which follows 'The Departure of Dindrane' in *The Region of the Summer Stars*, portraying the 'company' that gradually spread out from the very 'household' of Taliessin that the slave-girl in the previous poem had determined to stay within. As we have seen, the participants in the company inhabit one of three modes—exchange, substitution, or co-inherence—and those in the last are described as 'bearing and being borne'; like the pre-eminent 'God-bearer', Mary, they live in the image of the perichoretic Trinity where 'the Basis is in the Image, and the Image in the Gift.'[233] Lewis explains that:

---

[229] Lewis, *Miracles*, 90–6.   [230] Lewis, *Miracles*, 109.
[231] Lewis, 'Transposition' (revised), 177.   [232] See towards the end of section 4.
[233] Williams, 'The Founding of the Company', *Region*, 39. See Chapter 5, section 2.

What this co-inherence means is best seen in the instance of the Blessed Virgin. Christ is born (and borne) of her: she is born (and borne) of Christ. So in humanity as a whole there is not merely an interchange of symmetrical relations [...] but of those unsymmetrical relations which seen incompatible on the level of 'rational virtue'. Each is mother and child, confessor and penitent, teacher and pupil, lord and slave to the other.[234]

These relations, admit Lewis, seem incompatible from a standpoint of rationality. In face of them, that is, Lewis' own hierarchy of virtues breaks down. Here he is, of course, exegeting Williams, but he does so in a way that takes more account of Williams' vision than his previous exposition of male–female and master–slave relations in the previous two poems ('Taliessin in the Rose Garden' and 'The Departure of Dindrane'). It is another matter whether he is willing to adopt this vision himself. He still misses seeing, we notice, the implication of this co-inherence that 'bearing and being borne' means that—like Mary—all human beings can bear the son of love, or the Christ.

In his final period, Lewis seems to have moved even more towards Williams' view of the affirmation of images, as I have already aimed to demonstrate. In *The Four Loves*, there is yet another consideration of positive images of divine life. Lewis cautions that while 'the created glory may be expected to give us hints of the uncreated' since the one reflects the other, there can be 'no direct path from an image of glory to increasing knowledge of God'.[235] We recall the narrator in *That Hideous Strength* stating that 'right demands' upon us can tell us 'nothing' of the ultimate Demand of God, although that 'contains' all other proper demands.[236] The negative way qualifies any simple identification. However, Lewis' anxiety seems to be that of avoiding the idolatry of a nature-religion. At the same time he now thinks that, as human loves (and especially 'gift-love') can be glorious images of divine love, they can act as 'proximities of likeness' that can help or hinder 'proximities of approach' to God.[237] Here he exceeds a 'nearness' to God that derives from image or likeness, envisaging a 'nearness' in the sense of actual access to God or a 'proximity of approach'. The very possibility that the first can become the second takes us closer onto the ground that Williams occupied, and by now Lewis has an idea that allows him to take this step—that there are different *kinds* of presence of God in the world.[238]

The very word 'proximity' opens up a connection with the spiritual geography of Williams' Arthuriad. The radiance that shines out in Bragdon Wood now opens up a way into the world of a Byzantium studded everywhere with gateways or stations of light, which lead us to God's glory and wisdom.

---

[234] Lewis, 'Williams and the Arthuriad', 143.
[235] Lewis, *Four Loves*, 30–1.
[236] See Chapter 8, conclusion of section 6.
[237] Lewis, *Four Loves*, 12–13, 145.
[238] See Chapter 7, section 3.

PART IV
FURTHER STUDIES IN CO-INHERENCE

9

The Web of the World

Charles Williams and William Blake

Throughout his adult life, Williams returned constantly to reading and talking about William Blake. Williams seems to have felt an affinity with the earlier poet, and they might both be called 'poets of prophecy', adepts of a hieratic style that cuts beneath the surface of everyday life with protest and challenge. In notes for a lecture from about 1928, Williams exclaims:

> Blake—he comes on us like a revelation. [It is] only, as we get older, and then reluctantly, that we admit he is not a final revelation; that other things have to be brought in. And even then we are haunted by a fear—was he right after all? Have we lost something more than Blake and our own youth? Some freshness, some capacity of ardour and love we shall never find again?[1]

From the manuscript archive, as well as from published work, we can trace Williams' preoccupation with Blake through the years, and this—I suggest—is intertwined with his absorption in the idea of 'co-inherence', both before and after the discovery of the actual term. In the series of chapters in Part IV, I intend to explore the difference that the term or concept of co-inherence makes to examples from the wide range of genres in which Williams and Lewis write or speak—literary criticism, fantasy novels, and theology. Having traced the development of 'co-inherence' in their thought, and considered how they interact with each other on the theme of co-inherence in their approach to Arthur, I now consider further the way that, separately, the notion of co-inherence shapes their wide range of interests. First, with Williams, it is possible to detect that his thought about Blake has been influenced by adoption of the word 'co-inherence' in 1939, despite his affirmation of much of its *implicit* content earlier. This leads him, I want to suggest, to say something quite distinctive about the Blake with whom he has been fascinated since the 'freshness [. . .] ardour and love' of his youth, something that also contributes an original insight to the plethora of Blake studies.

For material to work with, we have what appear to be two sets of lecture notes preserved among Williams' papers, and in addition the transcriptions of three

---

[1] Lecture Notes on Blake (n.d.), Wade CW/MS-190, 14.

Charles Williams and C.S. Lewis: Friends in Co-inherence. Paul S. Fiddes, Oxford University Press. © Paul S. Fiddes 2021.
DOI: 10.1093/oso/9780192845467.003.0009

lectures made by Raymond Hunt. None, as far as I can trace, have been drawn on in published work on Williams, and so it will be convenient to list them. The first notes (= Lecture[1]) seem, by internal evidence, to be written for a lecture given in 1928 and are complete.[2] The second set of notes (= Lecture[2]) shows what appears to be a later handwriting,[3] but it does not correspond to any of the lectures transcribed by Raymond Hunt, who began his attendance and recording of evening lectures in 1932. It might well have been written for another occasion after 1932 when Hunt was not present, but from its contents I judge that in any case it belongs to the period before Williams' discovery of term 'co-inherence' in 1939. It appears to be incomplete, concluding abruptly. Then we have a transcribed lecture of May 1933, headed 'Blake' (= Lecture[3]),[4] and another of December 1933 with the title 'Blake and the "Lyrical Ballads"' (= Lecture[4]).[5] The final lecture for which there is a transcription, titled 'Blake', was given on Friday 3 March 1939 (= Lecture[5]).[6] Hunt's transcription concludes with a copy of two pages of notes made by Williams, supposedly for this lecture, and supplied to him by Williams himself, as was Williams' custom with his amanuensis;[7] however, these hardly seem to correspond to the lecture as actually given.

There are two further sources for this chapter, more widely known than the previous ones. The first is an article, *Blake and Wordsworth*, published by Williams in the *Dublin Review* in April 1941.[8] It is in this final piece that he uses the actual term 'co-inherence', based on the observation that the whole attraction of Blake's Prophetic Books is that 'there is an element of co-inherence in them as well as incoherence'.[9] By the time of the fifth lecture, Williams had just begun using the word (first in January 1939 in a lecture on Luther, and then in a lecture on Karl Barth three weeks later than the Blake lecture), but it was apparently still new to him, and so it is not surprising that it fails to appear there. Finally, there are a few pages on Blake in Williams' *The English Poetic Mind*,[10] published in 1932, and so belonging to the period between the first and third lectures.

---

[2] Wade CW/MS-190, 14–21. My dating is derived from his comment, 'in 1827 – a hundred years ago last August – he died, working, singing, shouting, loving' (15).

[3] Lecture Notes on Blake (n.d.), Wade CW/MS-190, 30–6.

[4] 'Blake', Wade RH Notebooks 1: 174–80, Friday 12 May 1933, CLI series 'Poetry and Philosophy' 28.

[5] 'Blake and the "Lyrical Ballads"', Wade RH Notebooks 2: 322–7, Wednesday 3 December 1933, CLI Tooting series 'Poetry' 12.

[6] 'Blake', Wade RH Notebooks 20: 3673–88, Friday 3 March 1939, CLI series 'The Christian Idea in Literature' 20.

[7] 'Blake: C.W.'s Notes', Wade RH Notebooks, 20: 3689–90. Hunt divides these into two sections, the first 'written for this lecture' and the second 'apparently another set of notes'.

[8] Williams, 'Blake and Wordsworth', in Williams, *Image*, 59–67. The manuscript for this piece is preserved in Wade CW/MW-191, but does not differ from the published version.

[9] Williams, 'Blake and Wordsworth', 59.   [10] Williams, *English Poetic Mind*, 185–7.

9.1 An Incoherent and Co-inherent World

While Williams does not use the term 'co-inherence' in writing about Blake until 1941, many of the ideas that it expresses appear in the earlier five lectures, where Williams' exposition of Blake's vision of the world contains features that he would later identify as 'co-inherence'.

From the first lecture notes onwards, Williams celebrates a 'freshness' in Blake's approach to the world around him, which he finds marks Blake off from the previous writings of the eighteenth century, and which is characterized by a sympathy with all things. Having remarked that Blake's poetry is 'full of children & angels & animals', Williams continues that:

> It is not his own joys and sorrows but those of others he is lamenting. There is no personal pleasure, but impersonal delight. And then the animals are so wonderful.[11]

For Blake, he judges, 'Real existence is passionate and one with all things; it is unity as opposed to division; it is love as opposed to hate or even detachment.'[12] Recalling Blake's infant visions of God's face at the window and Isaiah in the garden, he remarks that children might not seem strangers to us if we knew them 'with much more sympathetic understanding'.[13] And it is not only children to whom we should reach out with sympathy. He quotes Blake's couplet:

> A Robin Red breast in a Cage
> Puts all Heaven in a Rage.[14]

and suggests this means that 'when you do these things you antagonize the whole of living creation'.[15] Summing up this sense of the interrelatedness of living things, human and animal, and playing on the words 'whole' and 'holy', Williams pronounces in his lecture of March 1939 that:

> The nature of that creation is a kind of creation in which everything that lives is holy—physically, mentally, whatever kind—everything that lives is holy because it is entirely related to the whole. It is this unity that Los is aware of: that is why he builds this great city.[16]

[11] Williams, Lecture[1], Wade CW/MS-190, 15–16.
[12] Williams, Lecture[1], Wade CW/MS-190, 20.
[13] Williams, Lecture[3], Wade RH Notebooks 1: 175.
[14] Blake, 'Auguries of Innocence', K.431. I am quoting from the Oxford Keynes' edition (K), though Williams himself used the early Nonesuch Keynes' edition of Blake, of which there were three editions between 1927 and 1932.
[15] Williams, Lecture[3], Wade RH Notebooks 1: 180.
[16] Williams, Lecture[5], Wade RH Notebooks 20: 3684.

We will come back to Los, one of Blake's mythological figures, who represents the imagination. While Williams is not yet using the word 'co-inherence' (though it was available to him by March 1939), we notice that the lecture uses the metaphor of a 'web' to express the wholeness of creation that is built by the imagination. Blake believed, Williams asserts, that it was 'an ultimate demand that your business is to create':

> You will remember how William Law said it was necessary for everybody to be in their soul the Mother of Christ; and it is true that Christianity involves the notion of every human being the centre. If indeed every soul must be the mother of God, if you regard every soul as the source of the web, then from every soul the whole web of creation springs.[17]

Williams' conviction that lovers are the 'mother' of the Christ-child, who is love,[18] is here extended to a universal creative mothering, and so to a universal centrality. We recall the vision of the Great Dance in C. S. Lewis' *Perelandra*, of which Lewis assured Williams '[it] is all yours':[19] there an angelic voice affirmed, 'each of us is at the centre'.[20] Later, in his book *The Forgiveness of Sins* (1942), the image of the web is to be joined with the word that is implied here, when Williams writes about 'the great *co-inherent web* of humanity'.[21]

The word 'co-inherence' *does* appear in William's account of Blake's universe in his article on 'Blake and Wordsworth' for the *Dublin Review* (1941). Using it allows Williams to pair 'co-inherence' with 'incoherence', thus denoting Blake's picture of the reintegration of a disintegrating world. In *Jerusalem*, notes Williams, the figure of 'Albion', the giant man, represents universal humanity as well as England, and as a symbol of the 'incoherent' state of things Albion is split from his feminine counterpart, or 'emanation', named Jerusalem. Williams claims here that Wordsworth uses the term 'Albion' in a similar way in *The Prelude*, symbolizing in that case the division of England from France through the effect of the French Revolution.[22] Williams begins the article by quoting Yeats' assertion that in myth—including Blake's—there are 'certain glowing or shining images of con-centrated force' that the human being uses to 'brag of its triumph over its own incoherence'.[23] Williams comments that this applies remarkably well to Blake's use of the 'great figures' who inhabit his *Prophetic Books*, although in fact 'incoherence can only be solved by being reduced to co-inherence', and we have no cause to brag about that since the solution is 'not ours'. Despite Blake's

---

[17] Williams, Lecture[5], Wade RH Notebooks 20: 3682.   [18] Williams, 'One Way of Love', 161.
[19] CW to Anne Renwick, 13 May 1942; Bod. MS. Eng. Lett. d. 452/4.
[20] Lewis, *Perelandra*, 241.   [21] Williams, *Forgiveness of Sins*, 26. My italics.
[22] Williams, 'Blake and Wordsworth', 63, 67. My italics.
[23] W. B. Yeats, on the sixteenth phase of the moon, in *A Vision* (1937), 138–9; Williams offers no reference.

'bragging', he suggests he is aware of the true situation, since 'The whole attraction of the Prophetic Books is that there is an element of *co-inherence* in them as well as of incoherence.'[24]

It is Yeats' quotation, using the term 'incoherence' that seems to have prompted Williams' play on words, though he also finds the word in Blake; he draws attention to Blake's phrase the 'struggles of intanglement with incoherent roots' that have caused Christians 'to leave the Divine Harvest to the Enemy'.[25] The pairing between 'incoherence' and 'co-inherence' was also to appear in the book *Forgiveness of Sins*, which Williams began to write in May 1941, close to the publication of the *Dublin Review* essay. Human beings, he writes, have 'refused the co-inherence of the original creation and become incoherent in their suffering. [Christ] proposed to make those sufferings themselves co-inherent in him.'[26]

In the preceding lectures, Williams had analysed the nature of the 'incoherence' as he thought Blake conceived it. In the first lecture he remarks that the *Songs of Innocence* arose from 'a state conceived in Blake's mind which remained perman-ently there and could re-appear at any moment... it was the archetypal world'.[27] However, while 'this place of innocence and joy is in our minds... all around it are tempests and darkness'.[28] The description 'all around it' could mean *in* the mind, or it could mean *outside*, in the external world. In lecture[3], Williams at first suggests that this contrary state to innocence, what Blake calls 'experience', refers to a state within himself.[29] It was a desire to shut oneself away from the world in which 'everything that lives is holy', and Blake explored its depths under the heading of 'selfhood'. As the Blake critic Katherine Raine puts it, 'Experience is the antithesis of life. Life may be impeded and denied.'[30] For this divided self, Williams paraphrases St Paul, 'When I would do good, evil is with me!' (Romans 7:19). The two states, Williams discerns, 'go on existing in the soul'. But on the next page of the lecture, Williams presents Blake as finding 'experience' to be that of an external darkness, a pressure from outside that limits love. Williams tells us that 'Blake was confronted with this fact *internally* and *exter-nally*; the world was a cruel place, people did not want beauty.'[31] Raine has a similar perception into Blake, detecting the influence of Jacob Boehme that 'No psychic energy, or the mood of the soul, is merely good or merely evil; the face turned depends upon [external] circumstances.'[32] Williams comments that

---

[24] Williams, 'Blake and Wordsworth', 59.

[25] Blake, 'Jerusalem', K.716; Williams, 'Blake and Wordsworth', 66.

[26] Williams, *Forgiveness of Sins*, 32. Cf. W. H. Auden, 'That from our incoherence we / May learn to put our trust in Thee', *For The Time Being*, V. Chorale, in Auden, *Collected Poems*, 374. Auden wrote to Williams, 'I've never told you what a beautiful little book I found *The Forgiveness of Sins*.' Auden to Williams, 11 January 1945, CWP 163.

[27] Williams, Lecture[1], Wade MS/CW-190, 16.

[28] Williams, Lecture[1], Wade MS/CW-190, 17.

[29] Williams, Lecture[3], Wade RH Notebooks 1: 176.

[30] Raine, *William Blake*, 58.

[31] Williams, Lecture[3], Wade RH Notebooks 1: 177.

[32] Raine, *William Blake*, 56.

Blake in fact inclined to find the incoherence more *outside* him than within, remarking that 'he did not so much realise as Shelley sombrely did that the evil was in himself'.

From his first lecture on Blake onwards, Williams suggests that all the Romantic poets felt themselves to be faced by the problem of being 'face to face with the world, the apparent present world'. Using images from Blake's lyrics, Williams exclaims:

> 'Everything that lives is holy'. Well, is it and we don't understand it? What about Hayly? What about the black slaves, or the chimney-sweepers' masters, or armies spreading desolation, or thwarted love? All these poets of perfection had to deal with that.[33]

In several of the lectures Williams puts the question: 'what was to be done?'.[34] In the 'Blake and Wordsworth' article, he poses the question as: 'by what means we may [...] reduce the incoherence to co-inherence'.[35] In Hunt's transcription of lecture[4], we can hear Williams speaking in an extempore way, diagnosing both external and internal incoherence, in a voice passionately trying to get the point across to his young audience:

> Blake is an image, a synopsis of the whole Romantic movement [...] The Romantic poets found themselves firmly down to the question of what is to be done. In youth it seems that the Kings and priests must be destroyed, and then they realized that awful fact that man does not want to be just, man does not want beauty; that evil is not in the Kings and the priests but in the secret heart of yourself and your friends!—And what are you going to do about it? And Wordsworth was the only one who tried to do something about it; he closed the *Excursion* with suggestions of the education of the young. Coleridge was beaten another way. Shelley was just up against it when he died.[36] And then there is Blake's answer; part of it is clear and part of it unintelligible[.][37]

What Williams means by the 'unintelligible' answer is, in his view, the mythology Blake develops in the *Prophetic Books*. He is sceptical that 'co-inherence' can be achieved and 'incoherence' can be defeated by the effect of the 'great figures' who inhabit the landscape of the myth, as Yeats seems to suggest. This is mere 'bragging'. In lecture[5], Williams remarks that:

---

[33] Williams, Lecture[1], Wade MS/CW-190, 16.

[34] Williams, Lecture [2], Wade CW/MS-190, 36; lecture [4], Wade RH Notebooks 2: 325.

[35] Williams, 'Blake and Wordsworth', 60.

[36] In his first lecture, Williams tells us that it was Keats who died and Shelley who was 'looking forward to miracles': CW/MS-190, 17.

[37] Williams, Lecture[4], Wade RH Notebooks 2: 325.

[Blake] could think of a lot of names, and he could think of a great system to put them in [...] I can myself find a certain interest in Los, though I am never quite certain what he is; but apart from Los it is quite impossible for any one to get excited about the others; they are always charging about this indescribable universe...[38]

Little more, he thinks, is being said than was said already in the early lyrics about the tiger and the lamb: 'here you get the same kind of [division].' He is equally scathing in his 'Blake and Wordsworth' article:

The great figures do indeed sit about, in those commentaries, chained in a frozen land: Urizen rules over them [...] Blake depended on his myths being exciting; and alas, the sound itself is too monotonous. We are defeated by the sameness of the rhythms, the unintelligibility of the tale.[39]

Certainly, there is a rhetorical exaggeration here. Williams shows by his comments that he does not find the tale completely 'unintelligible', and we shall see that he makes highly perceptive comments on Urizen as well as Los. He is more excited than he professes to be. But his complaint, from early on, is that the mythical figures do not connect emotionally with the daily lives of readers. In lecture[3], his criticism is that Blake may be depicting 'an original catastrophe in eternity, where...there has been a terrific division' but that 'he did not see things as they really are *here* in the body of the imagination... [for example] a man parting from a woman is another statement of the tragic crisis and of the reconciliation'.[40] In this lecture, Williams concludes that 'his was the effort to relate innocence and experience',[41] but in the pages on Blake in *The English Poetic Mind*, he judges that Blake lacked a 'convincing single figure' to express the union between innocence and experience, and that 'he will not stop to make his mythical figures important'.[42] Here Blake is compared to Wordsworth to the detriment of Blake, but in the 'Blake and Wordsworth' essay the two poets are brought together, as Williams turns his attention to what he earlier described as Blake's 'clear' answer. As he declares, 'the myth may be dim to us; the morals are not'.[43]

For Blake, the power to 'do something about it' in overcoming incoherence is first of all the imagination, which Williams notes is represented by 'The [Divine] Lamb, who is also the "Human Imagination" and the "Divine Body"'.[44] In his very first lecture on Blake, Williams had referred to Blake's answer to the Romantic

---

[38] Williams, Lecture [5], Wade RH Notebooks 20: 3680.
[39] Williams, 'Blake and Wordsworth', 59–60.
[40] Williams, Lecture[3], Wade RH Notebooks 1: 178.
[41] Williams, Lecture[3], Wade RH Notebooks 1: 180.
[42] Williams, *English Poetic Mind*, 186–7.   [43] Williams, 'Blake and Wordsworth', 60.
[44] Williams, 'Blake and Wordsworth', 65.

problem as 'something much more difficult but perhaps less unsatisfactory' than the other attempts by the Romantic poets.[45] Innocence and experience are states of mind, but '"The imagination", [Blake] said, "is not a state, it is the human existence itself. Affection or love becomes a state when divided from imagination".' In lecture[4], Williams concludes that Blake 'was in the state of this "holy imagination"; and it is in this state that Blake saw the redemption that Wordsworth and other Romantics had looked for'.[46] In Williams' mind the solution to the Romantic 'problem' is not, however, imagination alone; he thinks that that imagination is effective in overcoming incoherence for Blake because it is the driver for a practical act, that of forgiveness. This is what 'can be done'.

In his very first lecture, Williams had identified Blake's 'sympathies' with all things, which would find fuller expression in Williams' later vision of 'co-inherence'. It is the discovery of 'co-inherence' that will give new depth and focus to the sympathetic act of forgiveness. In the face of the 'incoherence', within and outside the mind, Williams is going to use the idea of 'co-inherence' to show something important about forgiveness in Blake that we might otherwise miss.

9.2 Forgiveness in a Co-inherent World

Williams discerns the significance of forgiveness in Blake from his earliest commentary. Already in Lecture[1] he found Blake affirming that we should act 'from the holy imagination . . . act in love', and this meant abandoning revenge. 'He bore no grudge, he desired no vengeance. Against possession, against vengeance, he lifted up his voice.'[47] In lecture[3], forgiveness becomes explicit, as Williams emphasizes that for Blake forgiveness is 'part of that Divine Imagination'. Here Williams draws attention to what he considers to be one of 'the finest bits in *Jerusalem*', the dialogue in Chapter 3 between the Divine Voice and Jerusalem herself, the despised and rejected emanation of Albion.[48] He is to repeat this judgement and recall the passage again in his 'Blake and Wordsworth' article nine years later. The Lamb of God shows Jerusalem 'in the visions of Elohim Jehovah' the scene of Joseph and Mary in Nazareth, and tells it from the perspective of the verse in Matthew's Gospel that Joseph, learning of Mary's pregnancy, 'planned to dismiss her quietly'. Joseph denounces Mary, who answers with an appeal to 'the forgiveness of sins'. Here, Williams in his lecture quotes almost the whole of Plate 61, which begins:

[45] Williams, Lecture[1], Wade CW/MS-190, 17.
[46] Williams, Lecture[4], Wade RH Notebooks 2: 327.
[47] Williams, Lecture[1], Wade CW/MS-190, 21.
[48] Williams, Lecture[3], Wade RH Notebooks 1: 179.

She looked & saw Joseph the Carpenter in Nazareth & Mary
His espoused Wife. And Mary said, 'If thou put me away from thee
"Dost thou not murder me?' Joseph spoke in anger & fury, 'Should I
"Marry a Harlot & an Adulteress?' Mary answer'd, 'Art thou more pure
"Than thy Maker who forgiveth Sins & calls again Her that is lost? . . .
            if I were pure, never could I taste the sweets
Of the Forgive[ne]ss of Sins; if I were holy, I never could behold the tears
Of love, of him who loves me in the midst of his anger in furnace of fire.

Joseph answers her appeal by embracing her with love and tears, and this leads to
his reflection on the nature of forgiveness as practised by God:

"I heard his voice in my sleep & his angel in my dream,
"Saying, 'Doth Jehovah Forgive a Debt only on condition that it shall
"'Be Pay'd? Doth he Forgive Pollution only on conditions of Purity?
"'That Debt is not Forgiven! That Pollution is not Forgiven!
"'Such is the Forgiveness of the Gods, the Moral Virtues of the
"'Heathen whose tender Mercies are Cruelty. But Jehovah's Salvation
"'Is without Money & without Price, in the Continual Forgiveness of
     Sins . . .
"'In the Perpetual Mutual Sacrifice in Great Eternity.'"[49]

In this lecture of 1933, Williams contents himself with taking up the implications
of the word 'continual', commenting that 'forgiveness is not telling the fellow not
to do it again'. In 'Blake and Wordsworth', as we shall see, he expands his
exposition with the aid of the word 'co-inherence'.[50]

In lecture[4] the same year, Williams refers to the problem of the Romantics—
what to do about the world, how to reconcile innocence and experience—and then
continues that Blake 'arranged all the phenomenal world according to his own
ideas. But he also put down one perfectly lucid idea: when you are hurt you must
forgive entirely and absolutely—not [the "Don't do it again" or "I'll forgive you
this once".]'[51] As illustration, he quotes again from the Joseph and Mary passage
on the 'continual Forgiveness of Sins'. It is in lecture[5] that a new idea appears,
prompted by the image of a worldwide web, though without as yet the new word
'co-inherence'. The web is composed of 'passionate relationship', founded on the

[49] Blake, *Jerusalem*, 3.61, K.694.

[50] In neither place, incidentally, does Williams comment directly on Blake's implication that the
birth of Jesus was natural and illegitimate. In 'Blake and Wordsworth', 65, he does comment that Mary
does not choose to 'justify herself', which could imply that there was a justification available, namely
claiming a virgin birth.

[51] Williams, Lecture [4], Wade RH Notebooks 2: 327. The square brackets here are supplied by RH,
probably showing that he is paraphrasing or summarizing Williams, having failed to record his exact
words.

'whole business of the universe...between the absolute sublime inconceivable mind and the conceivable matter.'[52] In discussion following the lecture, Williams makes clear that he is talking about a web that originates in God's continuous relation with the world, 'the sacrifice of Love knowing love'.[53] But then, reframing the Romantic question, Williams comments that 'you come back to the old thing: how can man get into it?'. He replies, 'the only way is by forgiveness', then proceeding to quote at length once more from the Joseph and Mary passage in *Jerusalem*, Chapter 3.

Forgiveness, then, is the 'way in' to the web of passionate relationship. Here he expands a little (though not as much as in 'Blake and Wordsworth') on the dialogue between Joseph and Mary:

> Mary is in fact a name used not of the Blessed Virgin, [but] of some kind of image which in effect does express the motherhood of this enormous triumph and salvation. She is in a way the image of a pollution which is utterly destroyed by mere forgiveness.[54]

'Mary' is a name for a universal experience of forgiveness. Williams thus follows this exposition by his *own version* of the final line of Jerusalem. Blake had written, 'And I heard the Name of their Emanations: they are named Jerusalem.'[55] Williams quotes it as: 'And I heard the name: and their name was Jerusalem',[56] concluding with the comment, 'all gathered up in this absolute identification of each through the state of self-annihilation'. The 'their' in Blake's final line refers back to the first line of the plate, 'all Human Forms identified', and Williams appears to be indicating that all can be Mary, all can be Jerusalem. He has universalized the 'name' of Jerusalem by omitting Blake's qualification 'of their Emanations', perhaps feeling this is too limited. It is not just the 'emanations'— female counterparts—of all human forms that are Jerusalem and can know forgiveness. The pollution of all is forgiven; all can enter the web of relations. But as yet, Williams is not really explaining how forgiveness achieves this entrance. A little earlier, he had repeated from earlier lectures that 'you must not take vengeance',[57] but now he hints at something approximating to co-inherence when he speaks of all being 'gathered up' in 'identification of each' through loss of the selfhood. But we feel that something is not being fully spelt out if the Romantic problem is to be solved.

---

[52] Williams, Lecture[5], Wade RH Notebooks 20: 3686.

[53] Williams, Lecture[5], Discussion, Wade RH Notebooks 20: 3688.

[54] Williams, Lecture[5], Wade RH Notebooks 20: 3687.

[55] Blake, *Jerusalem*, 4.99, line 5, K.747.

[56] This quotation is, of course, in Hunt's transcription, but the modification fits in with the surrounding argument.

[57] Williams, Lecture[5], Wade RH Notebooks 20: 3686.

Outside Williams' exposition of Blake, and not long before the lecture of March 1939, he had been developing the relationship between forgiveness and the web of life. In his book *He Came Down from Heaven*, forgiveness is presented as a mutual and 'ardent exchange' of pardon.[58] There Williams wrote that the prayer 'forgive us as we forgive' was 'the assent to the law of interchange, the accommodation of heaven to our intention upon earth'. It invoked 'the web and the operation down all the threads of the web, and the eternal splendour of threads and web at once'. It was to know the divine glory, and yet to realize that it can never be known in itself: 'This also is Thou ... neither is this Thou.'[59] At that point (1938),Williams had not discovered the word 'co-inherence' for this web between human beings and God. It is when he does adopt the word 'co-inherence' that he begins to apply this developing insight to exegesis of Blake. Returning to the Joseph and Mary passage in *Jerusalem*, supplied now in the 'Blake and Wordsworth' essay with the exact term 'co-inherence',[60] he once more quotes the lines:

> But Jehovah's Salvation
> Is without Money and without Price, in the Continual Forgiveness of Sins,
> In the Perpetual Mutual Sacrifice in Great Eternity.

This time, however, Williams dwells on the words 'mutual sacrifice'. Pardon without condition, without the 'condition of non-repetition' of the offence, involves sacrifice, and this means a costly 'exchange of pardon' to which Williams now gives the word 'co-inherence':

> 'every sacrifice for others is a little death';[61] and the exchange of pardon between all men and women is the nature of the co-inherence which is eternal life.

Thus we enter the web, which is an exchange of relations, through the exchange of forgiveness, each forgiving the other. This is perhaps what was about to be articulated in the lecture of 1939 but was never quite voiced, and the idea of 'co-inherence' has triggered this new way of reading Blake. The 'state of self-annihilation' mentioned at the end of the lecture is now clearly spelt out as a mutual offering of self, not preferring one's own selfhood to the other and, in consequence, noticing how another is offered instead of oneself. 'It is as necessary to accept this sacrifice as to make it' declares Williams, then quoting Blake:[62]

---

[58] Williams, *He Came Down*, 145.   [59] Williams, *He Came Down*, 146.
[60] Williams, 'Blake and Wordsworth', 65.
[61] Williams is apparently misquoting from Blake, *Jerusalem* 4.96, line 27, K.743, where Blake has 'every *kindness* to another is a little Death'.
[62] Williams, 'Blake and Wordsworth', 66; *Jerusalem* 4.96, line18, K.743.

> Thus do Men in eternity,
> One for another to put off by forgiveness every sin.

Williams had already begun to associate the exchange of forgiveness with engaging in the whole web of exchanges, but now this becomes a lens through which to read Blake. The forgiveness of sins in Blake is understood to be not only important, but also the very nature of all the interweaving relations of Blake's cosmos, the 'nature of the co-inherence'. Williams seizes on the word 'covenant' as summing up this reality of 'offering oneself for the other'.[63] It is a covenant at the same time between human beings and between humanity and God. Williams points out that Blake defines the command 'forgive as you are forgiven' as 'the Covenant' of humanity with God. The 'law of interchange' about which he had written earlier could now be recognized as Blake's 'covenant'. Again we read in the Mary and Joseph passage:

> ' "And this is the Covenant
> Of Jehovah: If you Forgive one-another, so shall Jehovah Forgive You
> That He Himself may dwell among You. Fear not then to take
> To thee Mary thy Wife, for she is with Child by the Holy Ghost." '[64]

Living in the covenant through the imagination means nothing less than living in the body of Christ, and Christ's living in our bodies. Towards the end of the poem, Blake similarly writes of:

> Driving outward the Body of Death in an Eternal Death & Resurrection,
> Awaking it to Life among the Flowers of Beulah, rejoicing in Unity
> In the Four Senses, in the Outline, the Circumference & Form, for ever
> In Forgiveness of Sins which is Self Annihilation; it is the Covenant of
> Jehovah.[65]

Quoting these lines in another essay of the same year, Williams insists that forgiveness requires two persons to 'co-inhere' in a mutual act of pardon.[66] The association of the exchange of forgiveness with co-inherence that appears in this essay on Blake and Wordsworth was to be repeated in his book *The Forgiveness of Sins* a year later, when Williams asks what the 'inventor' of both the 'word' and the 'thing' of forgiveness meant by it, and answered that it was the bringing of 'the incoherence into the co-inherence'.[67] In this essay, the pairing of 'co-inherence' with 'incoherence' is not only prompting Williams' exegesis of Blake, but bringing

---

[63] Williams, 'Blake and Wordsworth', 66.   [64] Blake, *Jerusalem*, 3.61, lines 24–7, K.694–5.
[65] Blake, *Jerusalem*, 4.98, lines 19–23.   [66] Williams, 'Redeemed City', 109–10.
[67] Williams, *Forgiveness of Sins*, 33.

him to think that Blake is closer to Wordsworth than he had previously supposed. The 'exchange of pardon' between people (as 'co-inherence') is precisely the kind of particular human, emotional situation that Williams valued in Wordsworth and had missed in Blake in his reading of him up until this point. Blake writes in *Jerusalem* that 'General Forms have their vitality in Particulars',[68] and Williams now judges that Blake's grasp of this principle, both 'emotionally and intellectually', is like Wordsworth's 'feeling intellect'.[69] To this kinship I intend to return. With the mutuality of forgiveness, he thinks that Blake 'ceases to "brag of his triumph over his own incoherence"'.

However, as I have suggested in Chapter 5 (section 2), while the idea of 'co-inherence' accentuated Williams' sense of the relation—here the covenant—between God and humanity, it did not result in a vision of a human inhabiting of the loving relations in the triune God. Following Blake, Williams has a good deal to say about being in the body of Christ, occupying the realm of the holy imagination. But living in the Divine Body does not extend for Williams to dwelling in the relations that are represented symbolically in the Christian faith as the 'persons' of the Trinity. There is a Reformed tradition in Christian theology of envisaging this inner-divine web of relations as a divine covenant, each person bound in covenant love to the other,[70] but Williams does not envisage this kind of covenant, and certainly not one in which room is made for human beings. The Blake scholar Susanne Sklar judges that 'In Blake, the Father, Son and Holy Spirit certainly coinhere with one another', and that 'they also coinhere with universal humanity: trees, animals, rivers and angels are all part of universal humanity'.[71] This might then have given Williams a symbol for dwelling in the Trinity. But the image for this mutual relationality—which Sklar significantly calls 'coinhering'—is the Divine Family, which is also simply identified with Jesus in plates 37 to 45 of *Jerusalem*. The 'Saviour', for instance, proclaims:

> We live as One Man; for contracting our infinite senses
> We behold multitude, or expanding, we behold as one,
> As One Man all the Universal Family, and that One Man
> We call Jesus the Christ; and he in us and we in him
> Live in perfect harmony in Eden, the land of life[.][72]

However, if Sklar is correct that 'the Universal Family' is embraced impartially by God as Trinity and by the inclusive person of Jesus, the result appears to be a loss of distinct identity between the 'persons' of the Father and the Son in the Trinity, such as Williams himself certainly wants to maintain. In the discussion following

---

[68] Blake, *Jerusalem*, 91.30. See Damon, *Blake Dictionary*, 281, on 'particulars' in Blake.
[69] Williams, 'Blake and Wordsworth', 66.   [70] See Lillback, *Binding of God*, 212–14.
[71] Sklar, *Blake's Jerusalem*, 115.   [72] Blake, *Jerusalem*, 2.38, 17–21, K.664–5.

lecture[5], he speaks of 'the happy astonishment of the Divine Father that the Divine Son is'.[73] The indwelling in the triune God that I have argued for in previous chapters, and which C. S. Lewis envisions,[74] does not simply identify the triune God with the multiplicity of the world.

9.3 Reason in a Co-inherent World

The introduction of the term 'co-inherence' into Williams' exegesis of Blake has an effect not only on the idea of forgiveness, but on that of reason. When Williams brought Blake and Wordsworth into opposition in his lectures on Blake, another cause of dissension was Blake's handling of the idea of reason. Observing the image of Urizen, sitting bound, Williams exclaims that 'Blake hated that horrible use of reason as a means of dividing joy and life', and compares the rationalizing of Shakespeare's Iago and Regan. By contrast, 'in Wordsworth, Reason is the *business* of immediate perception; it is that which sees things and has to harmonise them'.[75]

While Williams professes that he finds the tale of the Prophetic Books 'unintelligible', he understands well enough that Urizen's usurping of power in the universe represents the domination of reason that was characteristic of the Enlightenment and the Industrial Revolution, and that Los is a Christic figure who represents the imagination that brings life, love, and forgiveness. When Blake writes of the 'dark Satanic mills', he is thinking of something even more funda-mental than the evil of machines: he is pointing to an inner state of mind that has been expressed outwardly in this dehumanizing technology. There are mills of the mind. For Blake, this was the rationalism of the eighteenth-century Enlightenment period, the scientific calculations of Newton, and the mechanistic philosophy of Locke. In Blake's view, the age of Reason was the age of Law that had imprisoned and stifled the free creative imagination: humanity has made its machines in the image of its own rationalizing mind. Williams understands all this, and demurs a little: Blake, he judges, 'was a little unfair to the period that preceded him. He denounced everything that seemed to limit some energy.'[76]

It is not quite so apparent whether Williams gathers that Blake intends the four key 'giant figures' of the *Prophetic Books* to represent four faculties in the human person. Blake depicts the building of Jerusalem through developing the drama of consciousness, as that which is begun in *The Book of Urizen* with Los, Urizen, and Urizen's revolutionary child 'red Orc', is expanded in *The Four Zoas*. The cast of characters is completed, and we are given a complete map of the human spirit. Orc (revolutionary desire) is accompanied by a less extreme form of himself in Luvah

---

[73] Lecture[5], Discussion, Wade RH Notebooks 20: 3688.
[74] See, for example, Chapter 4, section 5 and Chapter 5, section 2; for Lewis, see Chapter 6, section 2.
[75] Lecture[3], Wade RH Notebooks 1: 178.   [76] Lecture[5], Wade RH Notebooks 20: 3682.

(the emotions), and to make up a quartet of major faculties Blake adds Tharmas, or sensual, instinctive life: 'Four Mighty Ones are in every Man'.[77] The four faculties or 'Zoas' (life-forms) are contained within the consciousness of the eternal Man, or the Giant Albion, whose internal dislocation is represented by his being asleep. Human life has suffered division, or in Williams' word, 'incoherence', and this is mainly through Urizen's (reason's) forcible replacing of Los (imagination) by himself as the leading faculty within the quaternity. To further complicate the schism within the consciousness, these characters all have their female counterparts or emanations from whom they are alienated. Blake sets these figures in spinning motion, and involves them in conflicts and adventures, until he achieves a vision of unity through the death, resurrection, and final coming of Christ. This Gospel story represents the re-establishing of the imagination in its proper place through the overcoming of selfhood. The human imagination is the link with divine life; Los is the prophet of the imagination, and so when Jesus comes and Albion awakes, 'the Divine Appearance was the likeness & similitude of Los'.[78]

Los (or Urthona, Los' heavenly form), Urizen, Luvah and Tharmas are thus the Imagination, Reason, Emotion, and Instincts, and following the imagery of a city they are also located geographically; they should occupy the places of North, South, East, and West respectively, but their locations have been disturbed. In the poem *Jerusalem*, they are associated first with different areas of London, and are then superimposed upon the whole map of England by being identified with various cathedral cities.[79]

It is difficult to glean from his lectures and other writings on Blake how much Williams is interested in this mythology, beyond the Urizen-Los dialectic. As we have seen, he tends to dismiss it as an abstract scheme that is detached from actual human emotions. In lecture[5], he judges that: 'The trouble about the *Prophetic Books* is that Blake invented a "my theology" all for himself.'[80] However, the lectures give us a distinct sense that Williams is often playing to the gallery, intending to amuse the audience. Williams himself is actually doing something rather similar in what I have called the 'spiritual geography of exchange' in his Arthurian poems (see Chapter 8), in which he overlays the Christian Byzantine Empire of history with the mythical kingdom of Arthur (Logres), and superimposes on this double geography the form of the human body with its various parts and faculties. He never draws any comparison between himself and Blake, but there are hints that his interest has been more quickened than he acknowledges. In Lecture[1], he tells us that the mythical figures are 'parts of England and parts of the world'. Though he adds 'They seem to be saying something and no-one is quite sure what', he goes on to offer an interpretation, that 'there is always this

---

[77] Blake, *The Four Zoas*, 1.9, K.264.
[78] Blake, *Jerusalem*, 96.7, K.743.
[79] Blake, *Jerusalem*, 74.2–4, K.714.
[80] Williams, Lecture[5], Wade RH Notebooks 20: 3680.

schism; an attempt to express on the cosmic side what was so obviously true on the microcosmic'.[81] Williams is drawing on some of the same esoteric and mystical sources as Blake does to find the human being as 'the measure of all things'; [82] in Lecture[5], reflecting on the mythology, he comments that 'man is the image of all things—not so much man's soul as man's actual physical form [...] The limit of contraction is man.'[83] In his essay on 'Blake and Wordsworth', he is enthusiastic about the spiritual geography of Jerusalem:

> The Prophetic Books are strewn with a kind of mystical geography of Britain; some of their best passages are catalogues of Cities. In the fallen state of Albion these cities are also fallen, images of the Emanation Jerusalem; London is a stone of her ruins. Oxford is the dust of her walls. It is the union of the strange mythical figures with the familiar mythical names which forms part of the fascination of the Books, as when Los
> 'came down from Highgate thro' Hackney and Holloway towards London, Till he came to old Stratford, and then to Stepney and the Isle of Leutha's Dogs'.[84]

We catch just a resonance here with Williams' own 'mystical geography', celebrating, for instance, the 'ranged peaks of Caucasus' as 'the rounded bottom of the Emperor's glory', when 'The organic body sang together.'[85]

But it is the opposition of Urizen and Los that most attracts Williams' attention in reading the Prophetic Books, and so the status of reason within the human psyche. This is where lecture[5] offers us a leap forward not only into the character of Urizen, but into the Blakean myth itself. Williams comments:

> You will be told normally [that Urizen is] cold detached reason. Well, he is. But the main and important thing is that Urizen, this great shape, is the image of something that has insisted on being itself. It is not very different from *Paradise Lost* with the devil... 'Evil, be thou my good'... 'myself am Hell'; and Urizen has made for himself a kind of universe. It is the creation of the mind in separation [...] He is reason in one sense, he is a vegetable body in another; but still more, he is everything that closes and shuts up and confines within himself [...] Urizen is the closed and limited logic, the purely cold and the purely limited logic; it is the closing of the eyes and the shutting of the ears to everything but the concentration on the mere vegetable body.[86]

---

[81] Lecture[1],Wade CW/MS-190: 18–19.

[82] See Chapter 8, section 2; On the Kabbalistic cosmic man in Blake, see Sklar, *Blake's Jerusalem*, 62; Frye, *Fearful Symmetry*, 220–1.

[83] Lecture[5], Wade RH Notebooks 20: 3685.   [84] Williams, 'Blake and Wordsworth', 61–2.

[85] Williams, 'Vision of the Empire', *Taliessin*, 7.

[86] Williams, Lecture[5], Wade RH Notebooks 20: 3681.

Williams' reference to Satan in *Paradise Lost* is apt. For Blake, the 'Selfhood' can be symbolized as Satan, as well as the 'Spectre'. Williams does not, in his expositions, explore Blake's notion of Selfhood further than the need for it to be 'annihilated', but to understand Blake's mythology properly more needs to be said. The self becomes a 'Spectre' when it is in 'the state of Satan', divided from the eternal self, and this seems to be what Blake means by 'Selfhood'. Since the Satanic sphere is characterized by legalism, egocentricity, and self-righteousness, the spectrous self is dominated by the power of reason, which makes the laws that limit energy, desire, and forgiveness. Having entered the 'state of Satan', Urizen is 'Newton's Pantocrator, weaving the Woof of Locke'.[87] Thus the Spectre can be called Satan, and Satan can be identified with Urizen, but these are not simple equivalences.[88] The 'annihilation' of the Selfhood is really then a reclaiming of the *self*:

> ... Los embrac'd the Spectre, first as a brother,
> Then as another Self, astonish'd, humanizing & in tears,
> In Self abasement Giving up his Domineering lust.[89]

Blake perceives that, faced with our divided self, we must accept it and recognize it as our own, rather than trying to execute it legalistically, pretending it has nothing to with us. A power of self-justification cannot be dealt with self-righteously. While Williams does not examine this mythology of the self in Blake, showing in fact a definite impatience with it, he does allude to Blake's recognition of the divided self when he discerns the two states of innocence and experience in the human consciousness.

Williams also makes his own distinct contribution to understanding 'the state of Satan', and so the function of reason. Other critics have observed that Urizen is attempting to build a universe around himself,[90] but Williams brings in another dimension when the actual universe is conceived as a web of passionate relationships ('this web of simplicity and long suffering'),[91] that he has begun to call co-inherence. Reason with its own laws inhibits the expansion into the web, of which every soul should be the creative 'source'.[92] While Urizen is 'shut up', Los as imagination makes the 'effort to fling out, to produce something which is not

[87] Blake, *The Book of Urizen*, 20.8, K.234; *Milton*, 4.11, K.483.
[88] Cf. Blake, *Milton*, 40:33, K.533. Thomas J. Altizer has maintained that the 'Satan' is equivalent to the 'dead body' of an erstwhile transcendent God who has sacrificed himself for the created world: Altizer, *Gospel*, 91, 113–14; also Altizer, *New Apocalypse*, 71–3, 143–6. Against this theory, see Fiddes, *Freedom and Limit*, 92–3.
[89] Blake, *The Four Zoas*, 8.339, K.328.
[90] Rowland, *Blake*, 98–100, refers to Gnostic creation accounts.
[91] Williams, Lecture[5], Wade RH Notebooks 20: 3686.
[92] Williams, Lecture[5], Wade RH Notebooks 20: 3682.

one's own self, which is living, and fiery, and tremendous'.[93] Urizen is thus reason only in a particular sense, a reason in isolation, an intellect that does not enable the web of relations to proliferate. In the pre-lecture notes that Williams gave to Raymond Hunt, Williams writes:

'Rational power'—obviously Blake who drew out didactic arguments cannot have despised reason. We might perhaps think 'the feeling intellect' was what he wanted. Something dreadful has happened among these figures.[94]

Yet Wordsworth's term 'the feeling intellect'[95] does not actually appear in the lecture. Hunt wonders, in his editing, whether these notes of Blake were written for a different lecture altogether. In any case, by the time of his 'Blake and Wordsworth' essay, Williams has reinforced the 'perhaps' of his note; he is confident that Blake is indeed commending a 'feeling intellect', which brings him close to Wordsworth, 'whatever in his haste [Blake] sometimes implied'.[96] Quoting Wordsworth's line that imagination is 'Reason in its most exalted mood',[97] he remarks that 'The true Romantic, maintaining the importance of what Blake calls "the visionary Fancy or Imagination", admits and believes that the holy intellect is part of it.' Blake, he thinks, never failed this test of what it means to be a Romantic: echoing his lecture note earlier, he affirms that 'the Prophetic Books themselves break out continually into epigrams of philosophy, which pass it triumphantly'. He affirms that 'the feeling intellect' was the 'power which they [both] felt and believed', and this is 'neither incoherent nor boastful'.[98]

In lecture[1], as early as 1928, Williams had suggested that in his Lyric 'To the Muses', Blake had 'set out to say something intellectual, not the mere outbreak of emotional delight or sorrow which is often property of lyric'.[99] Now, in 1941, this holy intellect could be attributed to the figure of imagination, Los, and presumably to Urizen when he has been redeemed at the end of *Jerusalem*. It could, but Williams does not actually make this application to the 'giant figures' in his short essay where, as it proceeds, he turns to making a parallel between Wordsworth's 'feeling intellect' and his own 'forgiveness'. It seems, nevertheless, that Williams has put the notion of 'feeling intellect' (from Wordsworth) into the centre in order to answer the question: what will triumph over incoherence and bring co-inherence? The incoherence/co-inherence pairing has driven Blake closer to Wordsworth in Williams' mind, and opened up a significant dimension on both Urizen and Los—that a feeling intellect can unite these two faculties of imagination and reason.

---

[93] Williams, Lecture[5], Wade RH Notebooks 20: 3683.
[94] Williams' notes for Lecture[5], Wade RH Notebooks 20: 3689.
[95] For the 'feeling intellect', see Wordsworth, *Prelude* (1805), 13.205 (470).
[96] Williams, 'Blake and Wordsworth', 60.   [97] Wordsworth, *Prelude* (1805), 13.170 (468).
[98] Williams, 'Blake and Wordsworth', 61.   [99] Williams, Lecture[1], Wade MS/CW-190, 15.

We saw in section 9.2 that the pairing of 'co-inherence' with 'incoherence' prompt Williams to apply to forgiveness in Blake his own developing idea of the mutual exchange of pardon, as 'the nature of the co-inherence which is eternal life'.[100] In his early lectures, by contrast, Williams simply defined Blake's idea of forgiveness as 'not being vengeful'. Now we can see that it is the association of both imagination and forgiveness with co-inherence that leads to a view of reason in Blake that is not after all opposed to Wordsworth's kind of reason, blended as it is with imagination. Co-inherence is about living together in sympathetic relationships, and Williams affirms that Wordsworth saw the 'feeling intellect' as 'generative of all tenderness, of humblest cares and gentlest sympathies'.[101] Thus, Blake's 'holy imagination [...] is not far from 'the feeling intellect'. The intersection happens in the co-inherence of a 'covenant' of forgiveness that Williams speaks about in the same way as the web of relations of lecture[5]. This covenant is not just an agreement or a pact, but a sympathetic interweaving of relationships that stretch throughout the universe. That Williams thinks of the covenant like this is shown by his juxtaposing with it Wordsworth's vision of a universe whose grandeur 'subsists' entirely by love. Having quoted Blake's lines,

> Thus do Men in eternity,
> One for another to put off by forgiveness every sin,

Williams continues:

Anything else would be the destruction of the 'feeling intellect' and its tenderness; 'the Human Body' becomes sterile. But in this Covenant, what both poets demanded and declared, is declared in its full 'glory';
> the universe
> which moves with light and life informed
> Actual, divine, and true ...
>   By love subsists
> All lasting grandeur, by pervading love.[102]

Williams is finding in 'both poets', Wordsworth and Blake, a 'covenant' of love in the whole universe that is at the same time reasonable, moving 'with light and life *informed*'.

---

[100] Williams, 'Blake and Wordsworth', 65.   [101] Williams, 'Blake and Wordsworth', 65.
[102] Williams, 'Blake and Wordsworth', 67; Wordsworth, *Prelude* (1850), 14: 161–2, 168–9 (p. 467).

9.4 The Moment of Vision

In his first lecture on Blake, Williams recalls that at the age of eight Blake saw a tree filled with angels and the prophet Ezekiel sitting under a tree.[103] In the same lecture, he declares that the *Songs of Innocence* arose from 'a state conceived in Blake's mind which remained permanently there and could re-appear at any moment'. It was not a vision 'that could be argued about', but a vision of an archetypal world that was simply *there*.[104] Similarly, in lecture[2], Williams repeats what he had said earlier about Blake's childhood vision, and insists that 'it is not the Prophet Ezekiel or the heavenly host above which makes his poetry memorable: it is that he saw natural things, but—as most (not all) poets do—with a sudden freshness of sight'.[105]

In lecture[2], Williams celebrates 'this capacity for seeing things in all their virtue—the fierceness of the tiger, the inspiration of the lark...and so on'.[106] In lecture[3], Williams notes that 'This capacity for seeing animals for the first time lasted throughout his life' and judges that 'There is nothing so fresh from the early Elizabethans until Blake woke up and saw the animals'; among them he mentions 'the advent of that metaphysical animal, the Emmet [ant], in English poetry'.[107] But in lecture[2], Williams goes a stage further in explaining the nature of the vision. Vision is not only of *something* but of a *thought*: 'this capacity for staring straight at an object was combined with a capacity for staring straight at a thought'.[108] He addresses his audience, for instance, on the subject of Blake's *The Tyger*:

> You may think The Tiger a good poem or not; you may think it a silly poem. But you will agree, I hope, that in it Blake is simply staring at something. He is looking, in a kind of dreadful amazement, at this fierce and lovely & terrifying animal which is appearing, as it were, from the jungle. Who made it? What awful power invented the Tiger? For you will remark that in that poem the Tiger goes on being like a tiger; he is not turned into a pet lamb. Blake's mind is as startled at the vision of the beast as we should be if we met one casually any morning. Only he doesn't run away from his thought (which is a perfectly possible thing to do) as we should run from the appearance of the tiger. He is just admiring it, marvelling at it, gasping at it.[109]

This 'Tiger moment' appears to have some kinship with the 'Beatrician moment' when the lover marvels at the wonder of the beloved, as well as the 'ethical

103 Williams, Lecture[1], Wade CW/MS-190, 14.
104 Williams, Lecture[1], Wade CW/MS-190, 16.
105 Williams, Lecture[2], Wade CW/MS-190, 32.
106 Williams, Lecture[2], Wade CW/MS-190, 33.
107 Williams, Lecture[3], Wade RH Notebooks 1: 175.
108 Williams, Lecture[2], Wade CW/MS-190, 33.
109 Williams, Lecture[2], Wade CW/MS-190, 31.

moment' of confronting the absolute demand of love in Kierkegaard, and the 'crisis moment' described by Karl Barth as being seized by the infinite.[110] In a typescript of an address, Williams remarks that '[Blake's] Tiger becomes more and more infinite ... as the poem proceeds. In fact, by the time it got into the Prophetic Books it, and all other figures, had become so infinite that there is very little else.'[111] The Beatrician moment is the special vision of love, 'seeing' the lover in primeval glory, but here it seems to take its place among other moments of vision. Indeed, the Beatrician vision can be generalized into seeing 'your fellow creatures blazing with the eternal splendour of the original order of things'.[112] Williams assures us that 'what we call imagination is a world which is not something other than or less than this visible world—no, the one includes the other as the greater includes the less'.[113] The reflections of lecture[2], undated, on Blake's 'seeing' perhaps brings it close to the pages in *The English Poetic Mind*, where Williams writes that the 'power of awakening our capacity for seeing sanctity and inno-cence, and for seeing terror and anger, which was shown in the *Songs of Innocence and of Experience* was with Blake to the end'.[114]

Yet in lecture[5] from 1939, Williams suggests some failure in Blake to sustain the vision. 'Great images exist for a moment; there flashes across you this picture, the vision of the older, tight-bound Urizen; and the cities—they leap up for a moment and disappear.'[115] Williams seems to suggest that vision would have been more stable if Blake had been able to benefit from the positive images of the Christian tradition, and that here he 'suffered most from his severance' from it. Williams explains that in his mythology, Blake 'does seem to suggest that the physical and material universe is dangerous, that the leaping fire of Los will destroy this generating of things; and I think it was simply [...] because he had not come across the great tradition of the Affirmation of Images. He was a little sniffy of Wordsworth.'[116] But in his essay of 1941, Williams seems to have recovered his confidence in the visionary Blake. He quotes the passage from *Jerusalem* when England, 'a female shadow', cries out and wakens Albion from his deathly slumbers, and the lines are full of the imagery of seeing:

> The Breath Divine went forth upon the morning hills. Albion mov'd
> Upon the Rock: he open'd his eyelids in pain; in pain he mov'd
> His stony members: he saw England. Ah! Shall the Dead live again? [...]
> As the Sun and the Moon lead forward the Visions of Heaven and Earth,

[110] See Chapter 10, section 2. The 'Tiger moment' also has some affinity with the encounter of Anthony and Quentin with the archetypal lion in Williams' *Place of the Lion*, 14–15. For the pairing of the lion and the lamb in the same novel, see Chapter 11, section 3.

[111] 'The Alteration of Passion', Wade CW/MS-7, typescript address, n.d.

[112] Williams, Lecture[3], Wade RH Notebooks 1: 179.

[113] Williams, Lecture[2], Wade CW/MS-190, 35.   [114] Williams, *English Poetic Mind*, 186.

[115] Williams, Lecture[5], Wade RH Notebooks 20: 3685.

[116] Williams, Lecture[5], Wade RH Notebooks 20: 3686.

> England, who is Brittannia, entered Albion's bosom rejoicing [...]
> Then Jesus appeared, standing by Albion[.][117]

'From this point,' Williams declares, 'the theme of the Forgiveness of Sins advances, a *vision* of Heaven and Earth. It is the great fundamental covenant not only between man and man but between man and God.'[118] From the standpoint of the co-inherence in the covenant, the passionate relation between 'the absolute sublime inconceivable mind and the conceivable matter',[119] vision is possible.

In summary, the theme of co-inherence seems to have enabled Williams to find connections in Blake between the exchanges of forgiveness, the 'feeling intellect', and the capacity to 'see' with visionary eyes. Williams has not abandoned his critique of the mythical figures in the *Prophetic Books*, expressed consistently through the years, but his essay of 1941 recaptures the appreciation of Blake's vision that appears in one of the early drafts of a lecture:[120]

> There were the chimney-sweepers, there were the starving, the poor, the diseased. What had gone wrong? and what was to be done? It was to answer those two questions that Blake wrote the *Prophetic Books*—or rather, no, it was [...] to show the answer. The poets do not answer riddles; they present us with things happening. Blake proceeds to show the answer happening.

---

[117] Blake, *Jerusalem*, 4.95, lines 2–4, 21–2; 4.96, line 3 (K.742–3). The selection of lines and ellipses are Williams', designed to show the theme of vision.

[118] Williams, 'Blake and Wordsworth', 66. My italics.

[119] Williams, Lecture[5], Wade RH Notebooks 20: 3686.

[120] Williams, Lecture[2], Wade CW/MS-190, 36.

10

The Impossible Possibility

Charles Williams and Karl Barth

10.1 Approach to Barth: Co-inherence and the Impossibility

In the work of Charles Williams, the word 'co-inherence' suddenly made a first appearance in the opening paragraph of a lecture on Luther in January 1939. It had, he said 'occurred to me...as a single-word epigram', and we have already traced the story lying behind this innocent-looking statement.[1] 'Co-inherence' hovers in the air, though unspoken, in his lecture on Blake of Friday 3 March 1939. But it then made a dramatic entrance, occurring seven times, in a lecture that Williams gave on the Swiss theologian Karl Barth just three weeks later on Friday 24 March 1939, and it occupies a significant place in the argument. These lectures were part of a series on 'The Christian Idea in Literature' given under the auspices of the City Literary Institute. In the remainder of the series, 'co-inherence' fails to appear, and we do not meet it *in public* again until the publication of *The Descent of the Dove* in September 1939. This history might be thought curious enough in itself, but perhaps even more remarkable is the failure of any commentary on Charles Williams to mention that he gave a lecture on Karl Barth at all, or to comment on his view of Barth, beyond noting that he included many quotations from Barth in his anthology *The New Christian Year* (1941).[2]

The lecture appears to have been buried in the Raymond Hunt Notebooks, but it deserves to be unearthed, and particularly in this series of chapters (9–14) where we are exploring the impact that the idea of 'co-inherence' makes on diverse genres of writing by Williams and Lewis. In Williams' thought here, it produces an original theological argument that I judge should be of interest even to specialists in the work of Karl Barth in the present day.

Williams, however, manages to give the impression that Barth is hardly interesting at all, his initial approach to the theologian being a matter of damning with faint praise. He concedes that 'he has certain phrases and certain points which are perhaps worth developing', but he goes on, 'They are not new[3]...as Patmore

---

[1] See Chapter 4, section 1.
[2] Lindop, *Charles Williams*, 372; Cavaliero, *Charles Williams: Poet*, 174.
[3] Corrected by me; Hunt transcribes 'knew'.

Charles Williams and C.S. Lewis: Friends in Co-inherence. Paul S. Fiddes, Oxford University Press. © Paul S. Fiddes 2021.
DOI: 10.1093/oso/9780192845467.003.0010

said ... whatever one can say about Christian writers, one cannot say they were original.'[4] He informs his audience that

his reputation has grown fairly strong in England.—[chiefly based on] his *Commentary on the Epistle[5] to the Romans*. I am not certain it is altogether deserved,—I suspect because we're not yet sufficiently acquainted with Kierkegaard. Barth's feelings and presentation of the whole idea arise as a development of one side of that much more remarkable Danish writer.

In a somewhat patronizing tone he pronounces that:

I think a great deal of Barth does depend—like so many [things] in Germany—on the fact that though the poor darlings think they know everything, they don't know anything. They have never been properly trained. They have all the information and none of the manner. They have all the conviction but none of the style.

He allows that German writers share 'a sort of knowledge' that belongs to thinkers on the continent of Europe, but adds, 'I am not quite convinced that Barth has that.' Later in the lecture, he gives his opinion that 'he is primarily not a great theologian'.[6] To modern ears this sounds an extraordinary judgement of Karl Barth, and in fact Williams is going to applaud him for his insights as the lecture proceeds; he quotes extensively from his commentary on Romans, and seems to relish reading him at length to his audience. He does, moreover, include twenty quotations from Barth's *Epistle to the Romans* in his anthology *The New Christian Year*, completed in 1940.[7] This is in a context where, as he explains in the Preface, only 'a very few modern writers have been included'. While Barth is not named in the Preface, Kierkegaard is given explicit recognition as being among the 'two or three names which may seem to recur more often than others', although at twenty-seven he has not many more citations than Barth.

I suggest that behind Williams' cool assessment of Barth at the beginning of his lecture there lie significant personal reasons. Williams was a notable champion of the work of Kierkegaard in England, fostering and presiding over the project of the Oxford University Press to issue English translations of Kierkegaard's work by Walter Lowrie, Alexander Dru, and Robert Payne, as well as seeing Lowrie's own magisterial work on Kierkegaard (1938) through the press. Under Williams' oversight, the Oxford University Press published seven Kierkegaard books

---

[4] Williams, 'Karl Barth', Wade RH Notebooks 20: 3728 (3727–52), Friday 24 March 1939, CLI series 'The Christian Idea in Literature' 23. Henceforth = Williams, 'Karl Barth'.

[5] Hunt's text has 'Epistles' but this must be Hunt's error.   [6] Williams, 'Karl Barth', 3736.

[7] *New Christian Year*, Preface dated All Souls, 1940.

(including twenty separate works),[8] and it is the considered judgement of Michael Paulus that this 'laid the foundation for Princeton to continue publishing Kierkegaard into the present'.[9] Williams became an early and knowledgeable proponent of Kierkegaard in the English-speaking world, and one recipient of his enthusiasm was the poet W. H. Auden. According to Auden's own testimony, it was interactions with Williams' person and works that led the poet to read Kierkegaard and consequently find his way back to the Christian church.[10] At the time of Williams' lecture on Barth, Oxford at Amen House was publishing Kierkegaard's 'Dialectical Lyric' *Fear and Trembling*,[11] and Williams was involved in complex negotiations with Lowrie to secure further translations of Kierkegaard and in persuading his superior, Sir Humphrey Milford, to continue publication of them.[12] In addition to *Fear and Trembling*, Williams had already overseen the production, and probably read the proof-sheets, of Alexander Dru's selection from the *Journals* (1938), and was engaged with Lowrie's translations of *The Point of View for my Work as an Author* (1939) and *Christian Discourses* and *Three Discourses* (1939). It is from these works that all but two of the quotations come in his *New Christian Year*.

Further, he was engaged in writing a section on Kierkegaard for the final chapter of *The Descent of the Dove*.[13] It was these pages that brought Kierkegaard to Auden's attention, and especially Williams' exposition of the tragic attempt to live without a sense of the 'unconditional' in the modern age, which he largely drew from *The Point of View*. Auden consequently employed numerous phrases from Williams' book in the final 100 lines of his poem 'New Year Letter' (1940),[14] at the same time as showing the impact that Kierkegaard's 'existential' Christianity had made on him. The extent of Williams' continuing influence on Auden is demonstrated by a letter from Auden to Williams in January 1945, writing that 'The Co-inherence looks more invisible than ever, but now and again, as in your works, one hears its hymn a great way off, for which Laudamus.'[15]

In the light of his advocacy of Kierkegaard it is not surprising that Williams felt Barth had been given too much attention in England and Kierkegaard too little, especially since the 'dialectical theology' expressed in Barth's *Epistle to the Romans* did indeed owe much to Barth's own appreciative reading of Kierkegaard.[16] I suspect that there is also a personal reason why Williams begins by deprecating the tradition of knowledge within which Barth was working. He evidently found

---

[8] From 1940, however, the Oxford University Press used flat sheets of Kierkegaard translations that it purchased from Princeton University Press and published under its own imprint.

[9] Michael J. Paulus, Jr, 'From a Publisher's Point of View', 39.

[10] W. H. Auden, 'Preface' to *Descent of the Dove*, v; see Mendelson. *Later Auden*, 129.

[11] Kierkegaard, *Fear and Trembling*, trans. Robert Payne.

[12] See Paulus, 'From a Publisher's Point of View', 33–6.

[13] Williams, *Descent of the Dove*, 212–20.   [14] Mendelson, *Later Auden*, 124–7.

[15] Auden to Williams, 11 January 1945, Wade CWP 163.

[16] McCormack, *Karl Barth's Critically Realistic Dialectical Theology*, 235–40, thinks, however, that the debt has been exaggerated.

certain unexpected similarities between Barth's ideas and his own, as I intend to show in this chapter. Yet Barth showed no acquaintance with the tradition of English writing in which Williams' own thought was rooted; he was working in a different thought-world altogether, as an inheritor of nineteenth-century German theology and philosophy, and he did not make the same connections as Williams did instinctively. Williams' distance from Barth's particular Reformed tradition is, perhaps, shown by his comment in this lecture that 'Barth was a Lutheran, I think.'[17] It could only be a sense of finding himself in a strange environment with Barth that led Williams to remark so condescendingly that 'they think they know everything, [but] they don't know anything'.

Why, then, one may ask, did Williams choose to lecture to his class on Karl Barth at all? On the face of it, nothing seems less likely. The fact is that Williams seems to have been captivated by an epigram created by Barth, the 'impossible possibility', which Williams renders more rhythmically as 'the impossible possible'. Near the beginning of the lecture, Williams notes that Barth lays stress on 'evangelical conversion', describing it as 'the impact upon human experience' of 'this utterly other thing'. This momentous address to human life, together with human response, is—declares Williams—what Barth means by the 'impossible possible':

> Since Professor Otto became popular we do know about 'Otherness'.[18] We do know that God is something utterly other . . . this kind of thing has grown on us, and it is tending at the present time to become fashionable. But it is true that Barth was very full of this sense of something happening; and the phrase he constantly uses . . . for us is this kind of epigram about 'the impossible possible, the possible impossible.'[19]

The epigram looks as though it should have been produced by Kierkegaard with his theology of paradox, and Kierkegaard did indeed refer a number of times to the saying of Jesus that 'For humans it is impossible, but not for God: for God all things are possible.'[20] But Barth is actually the author of the memorable 'impossible possibility', which appears more than thirty times in his *Romans*. Williams seems to have also found the doublet 'impossible possible/possible impossible in

---

[17] Williams, 'Karl Barth', 3740.

[18] He is referring to Otto, *Idea of the Holy*; on the 'wholly Other', see 25–30. Williams may well have seen the volume through the Press.

[19] Williams, 'Karl Barth', 3727. Ellipses not marked with square brackets are as in Hunt's transcription.

[20] Mk 10:27; cf. Mt 19:26, Lk 18:27. See Kierkegaard, *Sickness Unto Death*, 38–40. On possibility and freedom in Kierkegaard and Barth, see Webster, *Barth's Moral Theology*, 115–17. Podmore, 'Holy & Wholly Other', 9–23, argues that Kierkegaard presents the 'impossible possibility' of forgiveness, but without locating the actual phrase.

Barth's text,[21] though it only occurs once. Williams' brief notes for this lecture show how much the epigram was intended to run through the entire lecture and give it a kind of structure, and I am intending to make this hint a little more systematic in the ordering of my present chapter. In the lecture as delivered, this structure is not quite so evident, probably owing to the largely extempore manner in which it was delivered.

We cannot be certain how Williams ran across Barth's expression, but the only Barth Williams knows is the author of the commentary on Romans, where it first appears. We are concerned here with the English translation of the sixth edition of Barth's *The Epistle to the Romans*, published in German in 1928, which itself is essentially a reprint of the second edition of 1922.[22] Williams' lecture is entirely concerned with this one work of Barth, although the ground-breaking first volume of Barth's *Church Dogmatics* had appeared in English translation in 1936. The English translation of *Romans* had in fact been published in 1933 by the Oxford University Press, from Amen House, and it is likely that Williams oversaw its publication. When discussing the Apostle Paul's view of the law and faith, in *The Descent of the Dove*, Williams gives an account that employs the impossibility-possibility pairing that Barth uses in traversing the same subject area. Williams writes in *Descent*:

> Yet the law was impossible, and it could not be modified, or it would become other than itself and that could not be. What then? How was man to find existence possible? By the impossibility doing its own impossible work on man's behalf, by the forgiveness (that is, the redemption) of sins, by faith.[23]

It would be natural for Williams, preparing to write a couple of pages on Paul to consult a book with which he was familiar and probably owned, since it appears on a booklist that Williams compiled in the early 1940s.[24] Writing *The Descent of the Dove* at the same time as his lectures for the CLI, much of its content is transferred into them, and Williams may have decided to take the Barthian theme of 'the impossible possible' for a lecture rather as a preacher selects a text for a sermon—and Williams' lecturing always had a sermonic tone. Be that as it may, Williams knows only the Barth of the 'negative way' of dialectical theology, of an awe before God as the infinite Other, insisting on the incapacity of human speech to speak about God. He does not know the Barth of the *Church Dogmatics*, who complements the *via negativa* with the *via positiva*, affirming the ability of human words to speak the truth about God *when* seized by God's own self-revelation in

---

[21] Barth, *Romans*, 344.

[22] The second edition was a heavily revised version of the first edition, published in 1919, and never translated into English.

[23] Williams, *Descent of the Dove*, 9.   [24] Williams, Wade CW/MS-95.

an 'analogy of faith'.[25] It would have been fascinating to see how Williams would have responded to this 'affirmation of images', which was so characteristic of his own work. But we only have Williams' reaction to *Romans*, and his jaundiced verdict that it is second-hand Kierkegaard.

Based on the fact that Williams extensively quoted Barth in his *New Christian Year*, Grevel Lindop suggests that Williams engaged with the 'crisis theology' of Karl Barth in the early 1940s as part of a dark mood of theology, when he was losing faith in established institutions.[26] But Williams' most extended recorded interaction with Barth, the lecture of early 1939, is in a positive mood (despite the faintness of the praise); it appreciates Barth's concern for Christians to remain a faithful part of the Christian church, despite its guilt and failings, and associates him with his newly discovered term 'co-inherence'. According to Williams' own record,[27] he started writing his promulgation of the 'Order of the Co-Inherence' on 25 March, the day after he gave his lecture on Karl Barth; if the scheme for the lay order were running in his head, it would explain the appearance of the term in his lecture, given its fairly extempore nature. The word does not appear in the notes he made for the lecture, but only as it was delivered. Thus, the two epigrams 'co-inherence' and 'the impossible possible' meet and mingle to produce an interesting perspective on Barth's commentary, which is totally unknown to Barth scholarship today.

10.2 The Impossible Possibility of the Divine Call

Having introduced the 'possible impossible', Williams suggest that Barth starts dealing with the theme when he considers St Paul's vocation, right at the beginning of the letter and the commentary: 'Paul, a servant of Jesus Christ, called to be an apostle.' Barth says quite correctly, observes Williams, that this call is 'something alien from his existence', and quotes accordingly from Barth:

'However good and important a man Paul may have been, the essential theme of his mission is not within him but above him—unapproachably distant and unutterably strange. His call to apostleship is not a familiar episode in his own personal history.'[28]

---

[25] Barth, *Church Dogmatics*, I/1, 243–6; III/3, 48–50. I indicate here that I am not entirely in agreement with the influential thesis of Eberhard Jüngel, that Barth moved in his thinking from dialectic to analogy: see Jüngel, 'Von der Dialektik zür Analogie', 127–79. However, against McCormack, *Karl Barth's Critically Realistic Dialectical Theology*, 40, I think there was a shift in emphasis.

[26] Lindop, *Charles Williams*, 372.   [27] In Wade CW/MS-77.   [28] Barth, *Romans*, 27.

Williams applauds this as 'a very good sentence', and expands it to: 'This call, this vocation, this impression and impact is not a familiar episode in his own personal history', going on to underline that it is not a mere 'episode' in the history of his daily life, but an 'impact of something different [which] imposes itself on the individual'.[29] Barth, he notes, borrows words from Kierkegaard to describe it: 'The call to be an apostle is a paradoxical occurrence, lying always beyond his personal self-identity.' Williams rubs in the paradox, suggesting that Kierkegaard—and Barth—are saying that 'you are the man upon whom this non-episodical thing happened. It is the moment at which something undefinable—it would be much more true to say, indescribable—imposes itself, attacks the human existence.'[30] Williams now lapses into a more colloquial and a little less coherent speech, to try and get this impact of the strange event across to his audience:

> That sort of moment is familiar to all of you. They are moments, as we have said so often, concerned in gazing at cows or missionaries... so what follows... You are then up against the apprehension of its meaning.[31]

On the face of it, claiming the event to be 'familiar to all of you' seems at odds with Barth's account that it is not a 'familiar episode'. Williams is speaking largely extempore, and so is prone to some contradictory speech. He seems to mean that the event is certainly exceptional and indescribable, and yet he believes those listening to him *have* experienced it. Looking at things around them, suddenly they have seen some reality that exceeds the everyday. That has led, he agrees with Barth, to the sense of being 'engaged in a strife with the whole, even with existence itself'. Williams had said something similar about Blake's 'seeing' things in his recent lecture on Blake; the poet's freshness of vision had led to a sense that the whole of human existence was dislocated, and he had expressed this mythologic-ally in the conflict between the 'great figures' of his *Prophetic Books*. However, Williams wants to add something to Barth's sense of being in strife with the whole; 'I would myself say', he demurs, that the person who receives this call 'is also for the moment reconciled with existence', that there is 'something completely satis-fying passing through the whole of existence'. The shorthand note-taker, Hunt, is evidently having difficulty catching Williams' excited speech, but we can get the gist of it:

> The moment that this consciousness, this peace, this satisfaction has this call, this conversion, this consciousness, this... You will remember that it comes not

---

[29] Williams, 'Karl Barth', 3729.

[30] In his introduction to Kierkegaard, *The Present Age*, Williams comments that 'Kierkegaard never claimed to be an Apostle; the most he claimed was to be capable of recognizing what an Apostle was, what a divine calling was. He claimed to recognize the unique.'

[31] Williams, 'Karl Barth', 3730.

merely with a crash from without but recognition from within. St Paul... 'I saw a light'... 'what would you have me do?' Without complete variation of the phrase 'What would you have me do?'... It is the complete change. That recognition is the non-episodical side of this happening.[32]

The word 'crash' here is surely an echo of Gerard Manley Hopkins' line about Paul's conversion, 'As once at a crash Paul.'[33] All this exegesis and expansion has been launched from Williams' claim that Barth's account of the divine call is an instance of the 'impossible possible'; that is, the 'crash' from outside and the 'recognition' from within are impossible, not part of 'episodic' life, and yet the impossible happens. Now, there is something familiar for readers of Williams about the way he picks up Barth's language about the 'strange' and 'non-episodic' event, and yet wants to say that this 'impossible' experience of being called or addressed is not only totally disruptive but 'completely satisfying'. It reminds us of Williams' constant theme of the 'Beatrician moment', when—as in Dante's vision of Beatrice—the lover suddenly 'sees' the beloved in glory and is shaken to the very core of his being. This experience, Williams wrote a year earlier, 'arouses a sense of intense significance, a sense that an explanation of the whole universe is being offered [...] only it cannot yet be defined'.[34] He reminds us here that Paul 'saw a light', and he has said of the 'Beatrician moment' that the beloved is seen as radiant, showing 'that portion of the divine light which is which, in the eternal creation of her in heaven, possesses her'.[35] Nor are we mistaken or being fanciful that this is in Williams' mind. Shortly afterwards in his lecture, he is to tell his audience:

> The testimony of man has continually repeated this suggestion that there are these moments when in fact something is intelligible only as an impossibility.[36] There are certain things—yes, you explain them; and when you've done all this you know you've changed the nature of the thing. It is only recognizable as impossible, it can only be defined by the word 'impossibility'. A great deal of the world's love poetry is filled with the whole clamour of the facts in the face of what seems to be impossible. Sometimes it is a satisfactory thing; sometimes it is an unsatisfactory thing. I do not think the Troilus crisis is less of the 'being called to be an apostle' than the first Beatrician crisis; but certainly it is this word 'impossibility' which can only define an experience of this kind.[37]

We shall come back to Troilus, and simply notice that here 'being called to be an apostle' and the 'Beatrician crisis' are placed in parallel. They are both instances of

---

[32] Williams, 'Karl Barth', 3731.   [33] Hopkins, 'The Wreck of the Deutschland', stanza 10.
[34] Williams, He Came Down, 92.   [35] Williams, He Came Down, 93.
[36] Here Williams is quoting from Barth, Romans, 59.   [37] Williams, 'Karl Barth', 3732–3.

'impossible' experiences, and clearly Williams thinks they are not the only moments in human life when the impossible becomes possible. In his notes for this lecture, Williams refers to the page in Barth's commentary where Barth uses the phrase 'intelligible only as a possibility'. On that page we read:

> [People] have met the incomprehensibility of God [...] felt the barrier of the judgement, the paradox of existence, and, hopeful in their distress, divined the meaning of life. They came to themselves in fear and awe and trembling and in— 'clarity of sight', In the presence of God they were compelled to stand still [...] When room is found for awe and humility in the presence of God, that is, when there arises the possibility of faith, this is intelligible only as impossibility.[38]

Williams' comment is: 'The continuation of the "impossibility". This is true on all levels. The "impossibility" is communicated: in ethics, in act even, *in lovers*.'[39] Lovers do not appear on *Barth's* page. Later in his lecture, Williams returns to the different visions that interrupt and 'bewilder' life, whether these are religious, ethical, or erotic:

> If only it had never happened, if we had none of us seen visions, if St. Paul had never had any vision, everything would be perfectly simple. Then we could fall back on the happy idea that we must do the best we can. But there is no best. It is all or nothing. It is the process of the whole thing which is so bewildering; but it is the very bewilderment which is a correspondence to the impossibility. It is natural that we should be bewildered; it is at least more consistent with the idea of the vocation, the call ... the whole development of the human race, except the process from death to death.[40]

The impossibility does indeed happen 'on all levels', in fact in 'the whole development of the human race'. The only exception is being trapped in a process that is deathly, wilfully closed against hearing any call at all.

10.3 The Impossible Possibility of Faith

In my account of Williams' lecture, I have leapt ahead a little to get a sense of what he means by the 'complete change' that comes with the 'impossible possible' of vocation, or the 'call' from beyond us. By 'impossible possibility', Barth was thinking of the act and life of faith, and Williams now develops his discussion

---

[38] Barth, *Romans*, 59.
[39] Wade RH Notebooks 20: 3750 (Williams' notes, as in Wade CW/MS-344).
[40] Williams, 'Karl Barth', 3739–40.

to consider Barth's understanding of faith more generally. I have already mentioned that he quotes Barth's claim that

> The man who apprehends its [the Gospel's] meaning is removed from all strife, because he is engaged in a strife with the whole, even with existence itself.[41]

Williams observes that the second half of the sentence is a rather surprising continuation from the first, but he affirms that 'Strife with the whole of existence is what roughly is meant by faith' and that 'The state you are in is, in fact, a state of hostility'—though we see that he wants to add the qualification that there are also moments of satisfaction. Barth himself probably means that we receive the Gospel message *when* we are engaged by nature in a strife with existence, and the result is that we are then removed from the conflict. As Barth goes on to say, 'By the Gospel the whole concrete world is dissolved and established.' Williams, however, reads Barth as defining the state of *faith* as being one of conflict with the whole world,[42] possibly because he is coming from the Kierkegaardian perspective that the act of faith 'suspends the ethical'.

In *Fear and Trembling*, Kierkegaard draws on the biblical story of Abraham, whose faith leads him to the scandalous act of being prepared to sacrifice his son Isaac. The 'knight of faith' thus 'exists as the Individual in contradiction to the universal',[43] since morality is a matter of universal consent to what appears right. Kierkegaard is reflecting, and accepting, Kant's view of ethics, that moral obligations are recognized by the reason as universal principles. 'When Abraham makes himself an exception to the universal rule, he has abandoned the ethical and moved into the realm of faith.'[44] He has set himself against the universal, and his faith is a 'paradox [which] consists in setting himself as the Individual in an absolute relationship to the absolute'.[45] On the very first day of the *New Christian Year*, Williams places a quotation from *Fear and Trembling*: 'God is that which demands absolute love.' This is indeed, we may say, a 'strife with the whole, even with existence itself'.

There is an echo of the Kierkegaardian position in Barth's reflection four pages later on the 'scandal' of faith. Williams quotes him as asserting that:

> 'Depth of feeling, strength of conviction, advance in perception and in moral behaviour, are no more things which accompany the birth of faith. Being of

---

[41] Barth, *Romans*, 35.

[42] In this same period, Williams, 'Theology of Crisis', 644, remarks that 'Existence itself is Christian; that is why we are at odds with it'; he also criticizes Barth for preaching 'the old doctrine of "total depravity"'.

[43] Kierkegaard, *Fear and Trembling*, 87.

[44] Arbaugh and Arbaugh, *Kierkegaard's Authorship*, 109.

[45] Kierkegaard, *Fear and Trembling*, 88.

this world, they are in themselves no more than unimportant signs of the occurrence of faith.'[46]

Williams underlines this depreciation of 'advance in moral behaviour', commenting that 'Morals are important, but they are not the important thing'.[47] With Kierkegaard in his mind, Williams is wanting to accentuate the 'paradox' of faith, even in excess of Barth.

On the same page of Barth's commentary, there appears what Williams hails as an 'important phrase', and which he believes gives the clue for faith's being an 'impossible possibility'; he quotes Barth's words 'Faith is awe in the presence of the divine incognito', and comments that 'There is everywhere a divine incognito... When room is found for awe and humility in the presence of God, that is, when there arises the possibility of faith, this is intelligible only as impossibility.'[48] Williams probably does not recognize that Barth's word 'incognito' (though not the phrase 'divine incognito') is actually drawn from Kierkegaard. Barth seems to have found it in Kierkegaard's *Practice (or 'Training') in Christianity*, which was one of three works of Kierkegaard that he owned in a German translation.[49] Lowrie's English translation of this work, which Williams was to shepherd through the Oxford University Press, did not appear until 1941 (and he quotes from it once in his *New Christian Year*).[50] Both Barth and Kierkegaard were using the word 'incognito' with regard to the incarnation, Kierkegaard writing, for example, 'it pleased God to wander here on earth in as strict an incognito as only an Almighty can wear [...] to teach people in the form of a lowly servant'.[51] Barth explains in this particular passage that it is through the incognito that God speaks a 'divine 'No' in Christ against the human condition. Williams, however, not only accentuates the 'impossible possibility', but also generalizes it. There is 'everywhere' the divine incognito, and he adds a biblical text that Barth does not use anywhere in *Romans*: 'Verily, he is a God that hideth himself'.[52]

For Williams, the source of the impossible possibility, wherever it is met, is the God who conceals the divine self everywhere in the world. This more expansive vision allows Williams to include among 'these moments' the experiences in human life that are like those of Dante meeting Beatrice and Troilus encountering a faithless Cressida.[53] I have already mentioned the Beatrician moment, but it is

---

[46] Barth, *Romans*, 39. Abbreviated by Williams.   [47] Williams, 'Karl Barth', 3732.

[48] Williams, 'Karl Barth', 3732.

[49] The others were a selection from the *Journals* and the collection of articles that Kierkegaard published under the title *The Moment*, referring to the intersection of eternity with time. See McCormack, *Karl Barth's Critically Realistic Dialectical Theology*, 235–6.

[50] The idea of the 'incognito' is not mentioned in Lowrie's treatment of *Training in Christianity* in his *Kierkegaard*, 525–37, which Williams knew well.

[51] Kierkegaard, *Practice in Christianity*, 125.

[52] Isaiah 45:15: 'Verily thou art a God that hidest thyself.' (KJV).

[53] Williams, 'Karl Barth', 3732–3.

worth dwelling for a moment on Troilus, whose experience Williams avers here is no less like a 'calling to be an Apostle'. In his *The English Poetic Mind* (1932), Williams devotes a good deal of attention to the scene where the Trojan Prince Troilus discovers that his beloved Cressida has (under pressure) transferred her affections to Diomedes, a commander among the Greeks besieging Troy. Troilus suffers an interior crisis, which Williams diagnoses as being common to all humankind, 'in which every nerve of the body, every consciousness of the mind, shrieks that something cannot be. Only it is.'[54] He finds himself in a conflict to which, Williams declares, Shakespeare has dedicated a line that is not just thrilling and beautiful, but 'a synthesis of experience, an achievement of a style': When Ulysses asks, 'What hath she done?' Troilus speaks the line: 'Nothing at all, unless this were she.' And yet it is, for 'This is, and is not, Cressid.'[55] This crisis in which we find suddenly that the world is not what we imagined it to be is, Williams tells us, also the experience of Wordsworth in *The Prelude*, who finds he is given up to 'a conflict of sensations without name'.[56]

All this is in Williams' mind when at this point in his lecture he invokes the event that befalls Troilus, though he does not expound it. The conflict he discerns there perhaps connects with his interpretation of Barth as defining faith as 'strife with all the world'. The 'unsatisfactory' moment of 'impossible possibility' can be an apostolic crisis, an opportunity for change and transformation, no less than can the more 'satisfactory' shattering of Dante's life by meeting Beatrice. As he says here, 'A great deal of the world's love poetry is filled with the whole clamour of the facts in the face of what seems to be impossible. Sometimes it is a satisfactory thing; sometimes it is an unsatisfactory thing.'[57] Here, Williams appears to be critical of Barth, commenting that:

> The impossibility has happened, it exists on different levels; and [...] I am not sure that one of Barth's weaknesses is not that he doesn't make it sufficiently clear that the thing has to be dealt with on different planes. He is inclined to say there is only this one thing that exists.[58]

It is hard to be sure what Williams means with 'only this one thing'. There is in fact a great variety of aspects of the 'impossible possibility' in Barth's commentary. Among more than thirty usages, the primary one is faith,[59] but Barth also uses 'impossible possibility' to describe many objects and orientations of faith, such as

---

[54] Williams, *English Poetic Mind*, 59.

[55] Shakespeare, *Troilus and Cressida* 5.2.140–1, 153; Williams, *English Poetic Mind*, 60. Heath-Stubbs, 'Figure of Cressida', 49–60, begins from Williams' appeal to Cressida, and then develops a study of the figure elsewhere.

[56] Wordsworth, *Prelude* (1850), 10.290 (373).   [57] Williams, 'Karl Barth', 3732.

[58] Williams, 'Karl Barth', 3733.

[59] Barth, *Romans*, 138, 148, 375, 376, 380, 381, 503, cf. 59, 121, 141.

a new world,[60] the new man,[61] the Kingdom,[62] the gospel,[63] redemption,[64] the faithfulness of God,[65] the crisis 'moment',[66] nearness to God,[67] grace,[68] exposure of reality,[69] life in Christ,[70] final human existence,[71] walking in the Spirit,[72] resurrection,[73] the faithfulness of the church,[74] the forgiveness of sins,[75] the mercy of God,[76] the word of promise,[77] fulfilling the law,[78]and simply 'God'.[79] These are surely 'different planes', except that they are all positive experiences, what Williams calls the 'satisfactory' nature of the crisis. Perhaps he is looking for the Troilus-type of crisis, and—unknown to Williams—Barth does later on find this kind of 'plane' of the impossible thing that is nevertheless possible. In the Second Volume of the Church Dogmatics, it is *sin*. Barth writes in 1940, in the midst of war:

> If [God] is the Creator and Lord of the world, this settles the fact that even in creation sin can only be the impossible possibility, the possibility rejected by his sustaining grace.[80]

The ambiguity of the impossible possibility relates in Williams' mind to the 'divine incognito'. While Troilus exclaims 'this is, and is not, Cressid', Williams has been frequently using the similar phrase 'This also is Thou, neither is this Thou' to express the negative and positive 'ways' by which we encounter God in the world, the rejection and the affirmation of images.[81] Thus, sometimes, as he says, the crisis of perception is 'satisfactory' and sometimes 'unsatisfactory'. We can see why Barth's epigram 'the impossible possibility' was so compelling to Williams in the light of his whole thought, and perhaps also why he pronounced that Barth did not 'know anything'. Clearly, for Williams, Barth had not been properly 'trained' in the tradition that Williams dubs the English poetic mind.

Four years later, Williams was to apply the term 'Impossibility' to another crisis in the life of faith, that undergone by the mystical writer Evelyn Underhill when confronted in 1907, as a Catholic postulant, by Pius X's encyclical condemning theological modernism. He comments:

> One is apparently left to live alone with an Impossibility. It is imperative, and in the end possible, to believe that the Impossibility does its own impossible work;

---

[60] Barth, *Romans*, 75.   [61] Barth, *Romans*, 196.   [62] Barth, *Romans*, 92.
[63] Barth, *Romans*, 92.   [64] Barth, *Romans*, 105, 467.   [65] Barth, *Romans*, 113.
[66] Barth, *Romans*, 137, 381.   [67] Barth, *Romans*, 206.   [68] Barth, *Romans*, 216.
[69] Barth, *Romans*, 207.   [70] Barth, *Romans*, 273.   [71] Barth, *Romans*, 229.
[72] Barth, *Romans*, 282.   [73] Barth, *Romans*, 381, 481.   [74] Barth, *Romans*, 368.
[75] Barth, *Romans*, 481.   [76] Barth, *Romans*, 515.   [77] Barth, *Romans*, 344.
[78] Barth, *Romans*, 497.   [79] Barth, *Romans*, 332, 374, 376, 494, 530.
[80] Barth, *Church Dogmatics*, CD II/1, 505. Cf. I/1, 154, 'He will sin against God's word...He will grasp, not a possibility, but an impossibility.'
[81] See Chapter 7, section 3.

to believe so, in whatever form the crisis takes, is of the substance of faith; especially if we add to it Kierkegaard's phrase that, in any resolution of the crisis, so far as the human spirit is concerned, 'before God man is always in the wrong.'[82]

Williams' debt to reading Barth here is obvious, although Glenn Cavaliero wrongly pronounces that Williams himself 'coins the phrase "The Impossibility" for a comparable crisis with his own'.[83] While not ascribing 'the Impossibility' to Kierkegaard, Williams associates with it Kierkegaard's saying that, 'before God man is always in the wrong',[84] a phrase that *is* central to Williams' interpretation of the human crisis according to Kierkegaard and which, through Williams, had a profound effect on W. H. Auden.[85]

Confronted by the 'impossible possibility', whether it is the call of love—human or divine—or the shock of a disordered world, Williams now observes in his account of Barth that 'You have the tendency to fall back on something very much like repentance.'[86] Driven to ask what we can do in the crisis, it seems a natural answer to say 'we must repent'. Williams is in fact reflecting on Barth's own reaction. He quotes Barth's call to repentance that occurs in the same section of his commentary as his statement that the possibility of faith 'is intelligible only as impossibility'.[87]

> What can He expect of me, that he has granted this unprecedented possibility TO ME? Nothing can be put forward to account for and explain this emphatic 'TO' and 'ME'; absolutely nothing. It all hangs in the air: it is a pure, absolute, vertical miracle. Every phrase descriptive of human experience is here irrelevant; for we cannot claim even to exist. We are once again faced by the undimensional line of intersection.[88]

Barth is commenting on Paul's question, 'Dost thou not perceive that the goodness of God leadeth thee to repentance?' (Romans 2:3–5), and his argument is that the crisis of 'awe and humility' in the presence of God can lead to a repentance in which the impossible (receiving 'the riches of God's goodness') becomes possible. Williams reflects that repentance is indeed necessary, and that the church needs to

---

[82] Williams, *Letters of Evelyn Underhill*, 15.

[83] Cavaliero, *Charles Williams: Poet*, 26; Cavaliero's mistaken belief that Williams coined the phrase leads him to find the theme pervasively through Williams' work, and it structures his own account of Williams, but he can find no instance of the actual word until Williams' introduction to the *Letters* of Underhill.

[84] See Williams, *Descent of the Dove*, 219. The wording appears to paraphrase sayings in Kierkegaard, *Either/Or*, 2: 348, which Williams doubtless found it in Lowrie, *Kierkegaard*, 271, and in Kierkegaard's *Journals*, 114.

[85] Mendelson, *Later Auden*, 130.   [86] Williams, 'Karl Barth', 3733.

[87] Barth, *Romans*, 59.   [88] Barth, *Romans*, 60, cit. Williams, 'Karl Barth', 3733.

become aware of its guilt—a theme he is to take up later—but that there is also a danger in repentance. It can become a focus on oneself, on the self that is doing the repenting: 'even faith, even repentance, tends to concentrate attention on the self, on the individual, on the person. "*I* believe" — "*I* have faith" — "*I* am sorry" — "*I*, I, I."' Here Williams compliments Barth, observing that:

> There is running all through the Commentary this sense that the real business of the human soul is always to be two steps ahead of the 'I'. When you say, as you must say, 'I believe'..., and you turn all those little phrases, still there should be some movement somewhere, perhaps unnoticed, that goes beyond the 'I'.[89]

This movement beyond the 'I' is, affirms Williams, exactly what is produced by the experience of the 'impossible possibility'. Without that, we begin to substitute what is 'possible' for us for the disturbance of the impossible. Williams admits that it is difficult to talk about this 'impossible', as does Barth,[90] and he is suitably a little incoherent in his own speech:

> This thing that is not 'I', this movement of the 'I'... yet [...] Just this is the result of the impossible thing happening. It is perhaps one of the great difficulties of any continuity of relation that the very talk of it makes it impossible. And secondly, that the possible is almost substituted for the impossible.

At this point he quotes Barth,[91] where Barth is commenting on the verse, 'Where there is no law there is no transgression' (Romans 4:15) and recognizing that even faith can be ego-centred. Barth writes, and Williams quotes him:

> There is, however, a justification of the Prophet and of the Pharisee [...] But this justifiable is by faith only. By faith—in so far as law, the whole concrete visibility of human behaviour, does not condition and control it. By faith—in so far as faith, as a positive or negative experience in this world, is rid of all arrogance and aware of its own emptiness[.][92]

Williams must have been attracted by the notion that faith, as the impossible possible, can be a 'positive or negative experience', given the duality of 'satisfactory' and 'unsatisfactory' he has noted. But he breaks off the last sentence, which Barth completes with the words 'before the pure 'No' of God'. Williams either fails to notice that Barth has his own kind of duality—or dialectic—of experience,

---

[89] Williams, 'Karl Barth', 3735.
[90] Barth, *Romans*, 273: 'we have no single word that we can make use of to define the impossible possibility of our lives (in Christ)'.
[91] Williams, 'Karl Barth', 3734–5.   [92] Barth, *Romans*, 137.

expressed in his own way, or does not wish to draw his audience's attention to it. For Barth, this is the theme that under the 'No' of God there is always hidden God's 'Yes' to humanity. 'In His "No", God utters His "Yes",'[93] affirms Barth, and 'the *krisis* of faith is a turning from the divine "No" to the divine "Yes"'.[94] He explains, 'It is his judgement and betterment, barrier and exit, end and beginning, "No" and "Yes".'[95] The sequence is one way: in the 'Moment' of crisis when the eternal enters time, '"Yes" proceeds from "No"',[96] and 'there is no subsequent reverse movement'.[97] Williams could hardly have missed this persistent theme, repeated dozens of times in *Romans*. Perhaps, however, he does not know what to do with it. This is not quite what Williams is looking for; the 'yes/no' experience of Troilus—'This is, and is not, Cressid'—cannot be 'dissolved'.[98] But how we should live in face of this conflict of experience will take us, at last, into the theme of co-inherence, which has not so far appeared in the lecture.

10.4 The Impossible Possibility of Communion with Christ

Having previously widened the sense of the 'divine incognito' from the event of Jesus Christ to a universal hiddenness of God in the world, Williams now turns to Christ as the 'impossible possibility' at the centre of faith. In his notes for the lecture, he refers to a passage in *Romans* where Barth writes:

> Jesus of Nazareth, Christ after the flesh, is one amongst other possibilities of history; but He is THE possibility which possesses all the marks of impossibility.[99]

Barth means that, regarded as a life in the framework of human history, Christ takes his place among all other possible things, but 'it is history pregnant with meaning [...] it is time awakened to the memory of Eternity; it is humanity filled with the voice of God'. Williams thinks he might have a higher assessment of the 'possibility' of Christ than Barth, but agrees that to *stress* the possibility 'has its great danger [...] just as Kierkegaard says, we have forgotten the scandal'.[100] The scandal is readily seen, he goes on, in the way that 'the highest, clearest and best minds in Palestine years ago', namely Caiaphas and Pilate, objected to what confronted them in Christ. Indignantly, if a little incoherently, Williams draws an analogy with modern times, when power faced 'scandalous' claims:

> A howling East End mob with the cavalry charging and cutting them to pieces. Let the cavalry loose! ... military moving against the unemployed. What is a riot

---

[93] Barth, *Romans*, 125.   [94] Barth, *Romans*, 177.   [95] Barth, *Romans*, 164.
[96] Barth, *Romans*, 112.   [97] Barth, *Romans*, 177.   [98] See Barth, *Romans*, 67.
[99] Barth, *Romans*, 103–4; Williams, 'Karl Barth', 3750.   [100] Williams, 'Karl Barth', 3735.

or two? [led by a person who] is either (a) a lunatic (b) pretending to be a god (c) an infernal nuisance to everybody. Half the point ... about this is that it was the right, the true, the just objecting to it ... It is an outrage against not only our decencies but our indecencies.[101]

The New Testament, goes on Williams, is 'chockful' of scandals, and the highest minds explain them away, saying 'Of course he did not really mean it was difficult for the rich man to get into the Kingdom of Heaven.' Williams comments, 'This is the impossibility which is yet to be so possible' (reflecting Jesus' own words),[102] and he now invokes what he clearly considers to be a fundamental impossible possibility about Christ: 'Closer is he than breathing, nearer than hands and feet.' With this quotation from Tennyson's poem 'The Higher Pantheism', Williams is suggesting that just as scandalous as the incarnation is the claim that believers can be united with Christ, who is 'the one breath, one life, one loveliness ... one–everything'. And *this* is where the word 'co-inherence' first appears, along with a criticism of Barth;

It is the Coinherence of one man in another![103] I do not know, I am not quite certain, that Barth explains how this is to happen. It was perhaps owing to the fact that he is not primarily a great theologian, and secondly that you cannot really explain how it does happen. Nobody has ever yet succeeded in explaining. This is the divine incognito. They would say things and their recognition like two friends meeting [would be] a flash here and a glance there ... It does not form a whole, and it cannot form a whole intense thing except by existence, except by the impossible becoming possible; and therefore it is not surprising that he could not explain the whole intense thing[.][104]

In this evidently extempore passage, Williams has packed in co-inherence, Barth, the divine incognito, and the impossible possibility. It is a little puzzling why Barth is suddenly attacked, and then at least partly excused, for not being able to explain the *communion* of the believer with Christ, which Williams calls co-inherence. Perhaps it is because Barth had written, in the passage about Christ as 'the possibility with all the marks of impossibility', that in Christ 'God himself wills to draw the whole world unto himself', affirming a communion with God. Perhaps it is because Williams is about to comment on Barth's attack on the claim of religion to be able to establish a 'direct communication' between human-ity and God. Williams does not disagree with Barth, but perhaps he is laying down

---

[101] Williams, 'Karl Barth', 3736.   [102] Mark 10:27, cf. v. 23.

[103] The word 'man' is inserted by Hunt above the line, possibly showing he had checked it with Williams. Hunt varies between the spelling of 'co-inherence' with and without the hyphen. I have preserved his spelling in every case.

[104] Williams, 'Karl Barth', 3736–7.

the challenge, 'in that case, *how would you* describe the communication or communion that believers find with God in Christ?'. Williams quotes Barth as saying:

> The religion which we are able to detect in ourselves and in others is that of human possibility, and, as such, it is a most precarious attempt to imitate the flight of a bird. And so, if religion be understood as a concrete, comprehensible, and historical phenomenon in the world of man and of sin and of death—it must be abandoned. All our respect and admiration for the part it plays in this world of ours must not prevent our recognizing that every claim to absolute and transcendent truth, every claim to direct relationship with God, made on its behalf, is utterly worthless.[105]

'Religion', then, as opposed to faith, seeks only what is possible and claims a direct relationship with God. Earlier, Barth had quoted Kierkegaard to the effect that 'Christ must be unknown, for to be known directly is the characteristic mark of an idol.'[106] Though Barth does not identify his source in Kierkegaard's work, he is drawing upon the long section in *Practice in Christianity* where Kierkegaard insists that nothing can be known directly about Christ, either by his contemporaries or by those at a distance in history, because he is God incognito and so unrecognizable:[107] 'About him nothing can be known; he can only be believed.'[108] Williams agrees with Barth (and so Kierkegaard), noting that 'You do not find that the great saints mention the direct relationship with God,' and suggesting that the present-day church makes too ambitious claims about knowing God because it is 'beginning to lose its adequate consciousness of guilt'. This is despite the ironic fact that 'In [its] rituals it is compelled to assent that it is of much the lowest kind of nastiness.'[109] However, Williams evidently thinks that there is a state of relationship with Christ that is adequately described *neither* as 'direct' communication *nor* a total lack of communion. In the situation existing between God and humanity there is 'this alteration, this re-transmutation of the whole thing'. It is, we are not surprised to learn, co-inherence:

> You will remember that Law said that what happened to the Blessed Virgin is supposed to happen to everybody: the notion that the real secret of humanity is the mortal maternity of the Blessed Virgin [...] All that is assented is that in some way every man, every woman, was intended to be the Mother of God. The coinherent soul of man, working through the community, held within itself the incredible maternity of deity. Matter is capable of salvation. It is matter which

---

[105] Barth, *Romans*, 184–5, cit. Williams, 'Karl Barth', 3737.   [106] Barth, *Romans*, 38.
[107] Kierkegaard, *Practice in Christianity*, 128–33.   [108] Kierkegaard, *Practice*, 26.
[109] Williams, 'Karl Barth', 3737–8.

was assented to partake of... sensuality and substance. They go on. *Here, here, here,* in this point, here is the thing happening.[110]

The co-inherence of God, Christ, and humanity means that the human soul can give 'birth' to Christ within itself and the community, just as the Virgin Mary gave birth to Christ biologically. 'Here' exclaims Williams in excitement, 'Here is the thing happening,' here among us today. William Law had written in his *Spirit of Love* that 'your whole heart is His dwelling-place and He lives and works in you as certainly as he lived in and governed that body and soul which He took from the Virgin Mary'.[111] Williams has made the image more graphic, in accord with his theology of romantic love, where 'the Divine Presence that accompanies her [the beloved one] is born of her',[112] and 'the Divine Child spiritually lives in the two... lovers'.[113] It was to be a tenet of the protocol for the Order of the Co-inherence, which Williams was writing at this time, that like the Virgin Mary, every Companion of the Order could be (in Dante's words) *figlia del tuo figlio,* 'the daughter of your son'—sons and daughters of the God to whom they had given birth.[114] The quotation from William Law, suitably coloured, was important to Williams: he had used it in his lecture on William Blake three weeks earlier in support of his claim that 'from every soul the whole web of creation springs',[115] and he includes it in his *New Christian Year.*[116]

Williams is always working towards an understanding of the world in which the impossible is possible, moving beyond a dialectical theology either of Kierkegaard or the Barth of the Commentary on Romans. As in his reading of Blake, the visionary crisis that prompts human transformation happens because there is a web of existence in which the immaterial and the material cohere. In short, the 'impossible possibility'—whether of a calling, faith, or communion with Christ— happens because there is co-inherence of God and humanity, centred on the birth of Christ in the human soul. Williams does his best, however, to make Barth fit. Immediately after saying 'The coinherent soul of man, working through the community, held within itself the incredible maternity of deity,' he claims: 'And so Barth carries on the tradition.'[117] Williams then quotes at length from Barth's comment on St Paul's command, 'therefore [present] also your members as weapons of righteousness unto God':

This presentation is an existential presentation unto God, which quite positively includes the limbs of our mortal body [...] through the creative word of forgiveness, through that 'And yet' with which God accepts us and reckons us

---

[110] Williams, 'Karl Barth', 3738–9.   [111] Law, *Spirit of Love,* Third Dialogue, 286–7.
[112] Williams, *Outlines,* 14.   [113] Williams, 'One Way of Love', 161.
[114] See Chapter 4, section 2.   [115] Williams, Lecture[5], Wade RH Notebooks 20: 3682.
[116] Williams, *New Christian Year,* 14.   [117] Williams, 'Karl Barth', 3739.

as His. Thus, in its questionableness and dereliction, our mortal body becomes a poem of love, a vessel of honour, and a weapon of the righteousness of God. [...] and we encounter the absolute demand that the impossible shall become possible.[118]

Williams is evidently reading the 'birthing' of Christ within the individual and the community ('the incredible maternity of deity') into Barth's phrase 'our mortal body becomes a poem of love, a vessel of honour'. His lecture notes, referring to this quotation from Barth, contain the comment that it is exactly the idea of being 'members' of the body of Christ that we object to as a 'possible impossibility'.[119]

10.5 The Impossible Possibility of the Church

In the final part of his lecture, Williams turns to the church, and the nature of its co-inherence within itself. His point of departure is what he rightly perceives to be Barth's commitment to the church. He remarks that 'What he was very keen on— and it is the thing, of course, upon which most of Christendom has been keen on—is the Church.' Williams finds 'a very odd fact' that 'the tendency has been for the wildest schismatics not to say "Oh, I am throwing over the Church", but to say "Oh, the whole thing has gone wrong there centuries ago, and I'm the only one upholding it; I, as a matter of fact, am maintaining the Church."'[120] It is not clear whether Williams counts Barth among these 'wildest schismatics', but he recognizes that 'you do find that in Barth very strongly', and he aptly quotes Barth as saying:

> However much he [the prophet] may be tempted to dislike the Church and pour scorn on it, he will never entertain the idea of leaving it or renouncing his orders, for that would be even less intelligent than if he were to take his own life. He knows the catastrophe of the Church to be inevitable; and he knows also that there is no friendly lifeboat into which he can clamber and row clear of the imminent disaster. He knows he must remain at his post in engine room or, maybe, on the bridge.[121]

Williams offers his audience seven long quotations from Barth on the nature of the church, six of which he has taken from the section of Barth significantly called 'Solidarity',[122] which is at least an aspect of co-inherence. Williams himself regards

---

[118] Barth, *Romans*, 211.   [119] Williams, 'Karl Barth', 3750.
[120] Williams, 'Karl Barth', 3740.   [121] Barth, *Romans*, 336; cit. Williams, 'Karl Barth', 3743.
[122] Barth, *Romans*, 330–9. Raymond Hunt has, however, apparently inserted these quotations from page references and notes (3741), so we cannot be sure whether Williams abbreviated some of them in delivery.

the church as an instance of the 'impossible possibility', remarking that the church has 'an incredible existence', that office in the church 'has a bearing on the "impossible-possible" business', and that 'It is all extremely absurd' with 'absurd hymns' and 'absurd people'.[123] Yet the impossible becomes possible through the co-inherence, as becomes clear when Jesus turns to look at the guilty disciple who had denied him:

> If the Christian Church is to do anything more, I think the Christians should be aware of the Co-inherence of Christendom in that moment which is summed up most peculiarly in that phrase: 'And He turned, and He looked on Peter',[124]—and in that moment the impossible became possible.[125]

It is surprising that Williams does not reference passages in Barth where he himself associates the church with the 'impossible possible'. Barth observes that 'when the Church is confronted by the impossible possibility of remaining true... to its proper theme, it selects rather the possible possibility of making humanity— religious humanity of course, its theme'.[126] Despite this, 'In the midst of the possibility of the Church lies the impossible possibility of God' so that 'the Church is enlightened by the light of eternity.'[127] Thus, this divine 'impossibility presses upon us, breaks over us, is indeed already present'. Set over against the possibility of the church, Barth affirms, is the 'impossible possibility of all possibilities', like 'an abyss' into which no man can apparently leap, and yet the church does leap into it—and the impossibility is threefold: the Lord, the Resurrection, and Faith.[128]

In his actual lengthy quotations from Barth on the theme of the church, Williams does, however, select passages where one can discern the impossible possibility of the church without the exact term being used. First, 'The Church is the place where the eternity of revelation is transformed into a temporal, concrete, directly visible thing in the world,'[129] placing the Kierkegaardian paradox of eternity and time in the life of the church. Then 'The Church is the endeavour to make the incomprehensible and unavoidable Way intelligible to man', but this is impossible since 'the gospel dissolves the Church and the Church dissolves the Gospel'.[130] The church indeed suffers under the divine incognito, so that it is impossible to speak directly about God: 'However clearly and precisely the Gospel is preached, the divine incognito remains,'[131] and St Paul, declares Barth, 'bows himself [. . .] under the pressure of the divine incognito, which is the characteristic

---

[123] Williams, 'Karl Barth', 3740, 3742, 3743, 3746.   [124] Luke 22:61.
[125] Williams, 'Karl Barth', 3746.   [126] Barth, *Romans*, 368.   [127] Barth, *Romans*, 374.
[128] Barth, *Romans*, 381.   [129] Barth, *Romans*, 332; cit. Williams, 'Karl Barth', 3741.
[130] Barth, *Romans*, 332–3; cit. Williams, 'Karl Barth', 3741.
[131] Barth, *Romans*, 333; cit. Williams, 'Karl Barth', 3741.

mark of the Church'.[132] Finally, all offices that people occupy in the church are 'lost posts', since 'the venturesome undertakings of ecclesiastical religion are an impossibility'.[133]

Williams selects another quotation from Barth in which he declares that what the church aims to be is, in human terms, impossible because of the guilt of the church in which all its members share:

> We must not, because we are aware of the eternal opposition between the Gospel and the Church, hold ourselves aloof from the Church or break up its solidarity; but rather, participating in its responsibility and sharing the guilt of its inevitable failure, we should accept and cling to it.[134]

Barth's view of the church as 'solidarity' in guilt becomes Williams' 'co-inherence' in guilt. Williams echoes Barth, while adding 'co-inherence', in saying here:

> The one thing that can't be considered for a moment is the abandonment of the Church. It is this thing which is full of guilt, is full of absurdity, but which is a coinherence of the thing full of guilt[.][135]

If in the church there is a co-inherence in Christ which makes the impossible a possibility, at the same time it is a co-inherence between people in which guilt is shared. Repeating the word 'co-inherence' three times in quick succession, Williams describes it as 'the new thing' that Christ brings into humanity, an 'other business' that nevertheless has to 'hold in itself' the fact of guilt:

> Church in this sense is not only the witness but the Co-inherence of men in guilt. The Co-inherence of our guilt does carry on into this thing; and it is the business of the Church, just exactly as Co-inherence, this movement of the new thing; but the new thing not merely as entirely free, but the new thing which holds both the guilt and the other business in itself. 'Sir, you cannot be saved alone'.[136]

Williams now gives an example of the guilty behaviour of the church and yet the presence of the 'new thing'. He quotes Barth as insisting that Christ 'is not the exalted and transformed ideal man. He is the new man.'[137] Nevertheless, continues Barth, the guilty church has turned the festival of his birth, Christmas, into a 'festival of mother-and child, with which we are so familiar, and which we find so attractive'. The festival celebrates human motherhood, thus implying that Christ is

---

[132] Barth, *Romans*, 335; cit. Williams, 'Karl Barth', 3742.
[133] Barth, *Romans*, 335; cit. Williams, 'Karl Barth', 3742.
[134] Barth, *Romans*, 334; cit. Williams, 'Karl Barth', 3742.   [135] Williams, 'Karl Barth', 3743.
[136] Williams, 'Karl Barth', 3744.   [137] Barth, *Romans*, 378; cit. Williams, 'Karl Barth', 3743–4.

an ideal example of the new-born human child. Williams agrees that Christmas is not a folk festival about the wonder of birth, but demurs a little from Barth. We must not forget, he says, that 'the Anthropos is indeed a thing so profound in man there is no bit of our hearts not related to the Divine Being'.[138] He is recalling what he has previously said about the call of human beings to give birth to Christ; a sentimental motherhood is to be rejected, but not the high vocation of being a mother to the Divine Presence in human hearts, so that *figlia del tuo figlio*, each is the offspring of their own holy Child.

It is with a sustained assertion of the guilt of the church that the lecture ends, in a sermonic flight that drifts away from Barth completely. Williams reminds his audience that according to the Gospel records the church's guilt is established right at its foundation, with Peter's denial of Christ:

> If you read the accounts of the Church before the Passion, you do find the whole thing regarded as a kind of guilt. We have talked often enough of St. Peter betraying Christ. But it is more than St. Peter. It is a question of the whole type, the whole existent Church then being precisely concerned one way or another with the destruction, with the Passion.[139]

Rather daringly, he claims that Judas when he betrays Jesus is one of the apostles of the church, so that 'It is not [just] a question of the Church existing accidentally round the Passion. It is the very means of the Passion.'[140] He paraphrases words of Jesus' prayer in Gethsemane to his heavenly father as 'Of them which thou gavest me I have lost none', omitting the qualification 'except one' (Judas). Judas is still one of the apostles and 'stood with them'. Peter, Judas, and all the apostles are guilty, since 'they all forsook him and fled'.[141] However, Williams now adds 'There is the other side.' When he concludes that 'Christians should be aware of the Co-inherence of Christendom in that moment which is summed up most peculiarly in that phrase, "And he turned and looked on Peter",' he does not only mean that we should be aware of co-inherence in guilt. He means that we should also be conscious of our co-inherence in the forgiving presence of Christ. In that very moment of Christ's judging and compassionate gaze, 'The impossible became possible.'[142]

So the lecture ends with a return to the language Williams has borrowed from Barth, that of the impossible possibility. He exhorts his audience:[143]

---

[138] Williams, 'Karl Barth', 3744.   [139] Williams, 'Karl Barth', 3744.
[140] Williams, 'Karl Barth', 3745.
[141] Williams paraphrases and compresses John 17:12, John 18:5, Mark 14:50.
[142] Williams, 'Karl Barth', 3746.
[143] Williams, 'Karl Barth', 747. I have slightly emended Hunt's punctuation to make better sense of this peroration.

Either we do the best we can and keep quiet, or we take up this incredible burden of the impossible. When someone says, 'Just on rare occasions I have not denied that the impossible could happen', I am not at all sure that any human being could say more—and even then he would be wrong if he says the 'I' too often.

10.6 Barth, Kierkegaard, and Williams: Negotiating the Impossible

Near the beginning of his lecture, Williams claims that Barth is simply developing some aspects of Kierkegaard. The influence of Barth's reading in Kierkegaard is certainly apparent in the commentary. Notably, there is the 'infinite qualitative distinction' between God and humanity, to which Barth first draws attention in his Preface to the second edition of *Romans*.[144] Other Kierkegaardian elements are Christ as 'the paradox', the incarnation as 'divine incognito', and the impossibility of 'direct communication'. However, Williams has made his structural theme a phrase that cannot be found in Kierkegaard in its epigrammatic form—the 'impossible possible (or possibility)'; Kierkegaard's affirmation that what is impossible to human beings is possible to God does not quite catch Barth's sense, since Barth also uses the phrase to speak of *'God's* impossibility'.[145] Moreover, Williams is attracted by the word 'incognito' and the phrase 'divine incognito', which he does not *recognize* as coming from Kierkegaard; this is clear when, in the discussion following the lecture, he attributes 'divine incognito' to Barth as 'a nice phrase'.[146] Williams does not at all mention Kierkegaard's stress on the 'unconditional' demand of God on human life, and the summons to humanity to 'live in the unconditional, inhaling only the unconditional', which is to be the main point in his exposition of Kierkegaard in *Descent of the Dove*;[147] this is despite the fact that Barth *does* mention it.

The way Williams responds to Barth's *Romans* is thus in line with the view of recent Barth scholarship that Barth's 'complementary dialectics', in which two terms stand over against each other in contradiction or antithesis (such as the 'impossible possible'), was already well developed before he read Kierkegaard.[148] Williams has been attracted by Barth's dialectical rhetoric irrespective of any connection he has actually found between him and Kierkegaard.

---

[144] Barth, *Romans*, 10; then 39, 50, 99, 202, 276, 355, 356, 365.

[145] Jüngel, *Karl Barth*, 66–70, argues that Barth's 'impossible possibility' exceeds Kierkegaard's notion of the inbreaking of eternity to time.

[146] Wade RH Notebooks 20: 3747. As noted earlier, Kierkegaard writes only of an 'incognito'; the phrase 'divine incognito' is indeed Barth's.

[147] Williams, *Descent of the Dove*, 218.

[148] See Fisher, *Revelatory Positivism?* 286–93; McCormack, *Karl Barth's Critically Realistic Dialectical Theology*, 237.

Barth and Kierkegaard actually conceive quite differently the problem to which they both bring a dialectic between eternity and time. Kierkegaard is opposing the metaphysic of Hegel in which the finite and infinite are overcome in the higher synthesis of Absolute Spirit, and his aim is to establish the authentic existence of the individual against mere absorption into this Absolute. Asserting the infinite difference between God and humanity, and affirming the striking of eternity into time in the 'Moment' of revelation, are designed to explain how one 'becomes a Christian' as a responsible individual.[149] Thus, as Bruce McCormack stresses, following Michael Beintker,[150] Kierkegaard's interest is in 'how revelation is subjectively appropriated by the individual'. On the other hand, 'Barth's central problem was that of the *divine* subjectivity in revelation', or the objectivity of revelation over against the human person. He was resisting Schleiermacher's view that God was the 'whence' of the human feeling of absolute dependence, which in Barth's view simply made God a projection of human subjectivity.[151] The established nineteenth-century German Protestant theology was taking 'a private road from the depths of human experience and consciousness to God'.[152] For Barth, the contraries experienced in human life (love/hate, birth/death, sorrow/joy) cannot be a *pre-condition* for the revelation-event. God can only be known to the human consciousness through God's word striking vertically into human existence. The dialectic of our 'Yes' and 'No' to God is only made possible by the dialectic of God's No and Yes to human beings, God's own wrath and acceptance.

Now, Williams stands with Kierkegaard in being concerned about the human, subjective response to revelation in the moment of crisis. Williams as a poet and novelist is interested in what happens in the human mind when it is confronted by the 'strange' and 'unfamiliar' event that disturbs life and makes an unconditional demand. As we have seen, he expands the apostolic 'call' of God to Paul into other human moments such as those of Beatrice and Troilus. He shows no interest in the divine 'No' and 'Yes' to human life. He does know that Barth is opposed to natural theology, or the attempt to find God as the final cause of human phenomena. In the discussion following the lecture, he relates the story of how Barth was invited to give the Gifford Lectures, which were founded—so Williams tells his audience—'to prove the existence of God by natural laws'. Barth accepted, he continues, but only by writing back (in Williams' jocular account), 'I strongly object to the whole idea, but I don't mind giving the lectures to show how wrong it is.'[153] However, Williams' turning of Barth's 'impossible possibility' into an

---

[149] However, Barth learnt from Kierkegaard that ethics is not *merely* an individual matter: see Biggar, *Hastening that Waits*, 74.
[150] McCormack, *Karl Barth's Critically Realistic Dialectical Theology*, 237–8; Michael Beintker, *Dialektik*, 233–4.
[151] Barth, *Theology of Schleiermacher*, 218–21.   [152] Torrance, *Karl Barth*, 46.
[153] Wade RH Notebooks 20: 3747.

aspect of human experience leaves us questioning whether he really shows an understanding of Barth's view of God's self-revelation.

Yet Williams is not essentially making a quasi-Kierkegaardian reading of Barth. It is not simply that Williams fails to apply Kierkegaard's categories or even to recognize Kierkegaard's ideas when they are present in the text. His interest in 'co-inherence' as a way of negotiating the impossible possibilities of life takes him beyond Kierkegaard and even against him. The co-inherence between divine life and human life expressed in the human 'mothering' of God would have surely appeared to Kierkegaard as the kind of synthesis between the finite and the infinite that he found so dangerous in Hegel. Nor, it seems at first sight, could this *perichoresis* between human and divine possibly be approved by Barth. But matters are not quite so simple, as long as God is not being *confused* with humanity. For Barth, God is not the infinite excluded from the finite, since this makes God only a negative projection of human experience.[154] God is the uncreated origin over against created beings, and there is no reason why God, in sovereign choice, should not have intended an intimate relationship with finite creation.

Here Beintker has pointed out the early influence on Barth of his brother Heinrich's philosophy, which envisaged an original 'synthesis' between God and what was created 'other' to God. This was not the situation generally in present, fallen human life, but it remained a possibility for the eschaton, which in Barth becomes the realized eschatology of the 'New Man'.[155] Beintker declares that Barth was making a 'clear distinction from Kierkegaard', when he brought into play 'the moment of synthesis as the protological-eschatological presupposition of the *diastasis*'.[156] He is claiming that in Barth's diastasis—that is, a dialectical relation between two members that cannot be resolved into a *higher* synthesis—the actual 'synthesis' is of a different kind from either a Hegelian synthesis or Kierkegaard's rejection of synthesis. It is one in which the partners, God and creation, remain themselves and yet mutually involved.

There are at least hints of this idea in the commentary on Romans, with positive references to the 'synthesis'. Of the church, Barth writes:

Fellowship is not an aggregate of individuals, nor is it an organism. In fact, Fellowship is no concrete thing at all. It is, rather, *that Primal synthesis and relationship and apprehension of all distinct concrete things* which is their final unobservable ONENESS. Fellowship is communion. It is, however, not a communion in which the 'otherness' of each particular individual is blurred or

---

[154] Barth, *Romans*, 231.

[155] For Barth's divergence from Kierkegaard in his eschatological Christology, see Roberts, 'Barth's Doctrine of Time', 94–9.

[156] Beintker, 234. Further on Heinrich Barth's influence on Karl, see Fisher, *Revelatory Positivism?* 266, 303, n.84.

limited or dissolved, but that ONENESS which both requires the 'otherness' of each individual and makes sense of it. Fellowship is the ONE which lies beyond every 'Other'. The ONE, the INDIVIDUAL, is therefore not one among others, not a cell in a larger organism, but simply the HOLY ONE—sanctus. In him is focused and summed up that OTHERNESS of the ONE which is contrasted with every other kind of 'Otherness'.[157]

The one individual in whom all hold communion is nothing other than the New Man, the Body of Christ, so that each single person 'must, in his particularity, put on the Lord Jesus Christ (xiii.14)'.[158] The 'Primal synthesis' and 'communion' in which all are held together in Christ, and thus in God, does not seem far from Williams' co-inherence in Christ. Barth is to develop this idea further in the *Church Dogmatics*, where he expounds the 'eternal covenant' that God makes with all humanity in the person of Christ, an act of covenant-making that is inseparable from God's eternal self-differentiation as Trinity. In that non-temporal event of God's free decision, when God chooses to be Another in God's own self (the eternal Son) he *also* determines that the Other in God should be identical with a human son, Jesus.[159] Thus, for the later Barth, God has 'placed Himself' in relation to humanity, 'a relationship outside of which God no longer wills to be, and no longer is, God'. God, affirms Barth, 'does stand in a definite relationship with the other', and 'we cannot go back on this decision if we would know God and speak accurately of God'.[160]

I do not mean that Williams holds such a developed theology. In fact, as I have suggested earlier in this book, his idea of co-inherence falters because he cannot carry it through into the kind of trinitarian theology we find in Barth's later thought. Nor am I suggesting that Barth would have accepted the colourful account of co-inherence that Williams expresses in the phrase *figlia del tuo figlio*. But Williams' conjunction of the 'impossible possibility' with co-inherence offers a perspective on Barth's *Romans* that continues to intrigue, long after his fairly extempore performance in a class one Friday evening in March 1939.

---

[157] Barth, *Romans*, 443, my italics. Cf. *Romans*, 147–8.   [158] Barth, *Romans*, 444.
[159] Barth, *Church Dogmatics*, II/2, 123–5, 161–5; cf. II/2, 6–9, 26; IV/1, 45–6.
[160] Barth, *Church Dogmatics*, II/2, 7, 6; cf. II/1, 281.

11

From Equilibrium to Exchange

The First Four Novels of Charles Williams

In an introduction to the novels of Charles Williams, one critic has written that
'Williams has coupled [the] idea of exchange with two other ideas, namely
substitution and "co-inherence", but they all come to the same thing.'[1] My
intention in this and Chapter 12 is to argue to the contrary: by no means do
they all come to the same thing. In his poem 'The Founding of the Company'
(1944), Williams registers a distinction between the three ideas, writing of the
members of the poet Taliessin's household that:

> In three degrees
> along the hazel they mounted the mathematics of the soul . . .

We have already seen how there is a progression from one 'degree' to the next in
Williams' thought, even where he has all three in mind at once, and although
he admits at times that the distinction may be an 'intellectual' exercise 'in the
common union'.[2] Exchange is the *general* basis for a *particular* calling to the
service of substitution in love for others, and both come to a climax in 'co-
inherence', which appears as a word in the novels only in the last, *All Hallows'
Eve*. Now I want to suggest that alertness to the idea of 'co-inherence' enables us to
see the path from one 'degree' of relationship to the other played out in the novels
of Williams from 1930 to 1945. While Williams conceived the idea of 'exchange'
no later than 1924, and 'substitution' no later than 1929, 'co-inherence', I have
already argued, does not appear anywhere in Williams' writings until 1939. It is as
if Williams in his novels is searching for the most adequate comprehensive term
for his vision of the world, trying out the candidates offered to his imagination.
The first candidate, we shall see, is not even one of the three just mentioned.
Travelling with him, through the development of his plots and characters, we
ourselves get a better sense of how he arrives at 'co-inherence' towards the end of
the process, and how it might have been developed further beyond the last novel,
had Williams only had 'world enough and time'.

---

[1] Howard, *Novels*, 26.   [2] Williams, *Region*, 37.

Charles Williams and C.S. Lewis: Friends in Co-inherence. Paul S. Fiddes, Oxford University Press. © Paul S. Fiddes 2021.
DOI: 10.1093/oso/9780192845467.003.0011

The seven novels of Williams defy classification. They are stories, certainly, but they also embody a whole range of symbols, esoteric and religious, and startle us by opening the everyday to realities of good and evil that transcend the merely material world. While I began by contesting a judgement of one critic, Thomas Howard, I am much more sympathetic to his view that 'we cannot read very far in Williams without becoming aware that almost every line summons the whole universe'.[3] T. S. Eliot thought highly of the novels, or at least of the *potential* of Williams as a novelist. Responding in 1934 to his reading of *The Place of the Lion* and *War in Heaven*, he writes to Williams that he is unable to assess his novels from a purely literary standpoint, because in them he is confronted by spiritual realities.[4] In an introduction to the next, and last, novel, issued after Williams had died, Eliot continues the theme that a strictly literary judgement would be inappropriate, concluding that 'What he had to say was beyond his resources, and probably beyond the resources of any language [...] Williams invented his own forms, [but] no form, if he had obeyed all its conventional laws, would have been satisfactory for what he wanted to say.'[5] My own account of the novels is shaped by my attempt to follow Williams in his search for these 'resources' of language.

11.1 Movement and Equilibrium: The Grail

In the first four of his novels, taken as a whole group, Williams' characteristic ideas of romantic love, exchange, and substitution are not entirely absent, but they do not take centre stage. The situation that really grips Williams is expressed by his character the Archdeacon of Castra Parvulorum, a hamlet in the English countryside:

The Archdeacon looked, and grew serious. His spirit felt its own unreasonable gaiety opening into a wider joy; its dance became a more vital but therefore a vaster thing. Faintly again he heard the sound of music, but now not from without, or indeed from within, from some non-spatial, non-temporal, non-personal existence. It was music, but not yet music, or if music, then the music of movement itself—sound produced, not by things, but in the nature of things. He looked, and looked again, and felt himself part of a moving river flowing towards some narrow channel on a ripple of which the Graal was as a gleam of supernatural light.[6]

---

[3] Howard, *Novels*, 19.   [4] T. S. Eliot to CW, 7 October 1934, Bod. MS Res. c. 321/XIII, 355–6.
[5] Eliot, 'Introduction', xi, xiii.   [6] Williams, *War in Heaven*, 117.

The Archdeacon is at ease with a universe *in motion*, hearing joyfully 'the music of movement itself', but others in the novel are not so comfortable at finding themselves engaged in a remorseless movement that can at times feel hostile. The passage comes from the first novel of Williams to be published, *War in Heaven*, which appeared in 1930, although written by Williams in 1926. The 'Graal' of which the Archdeacon is thinking is the 'Holy Grail' of Arthurian legend, which had been—long unrecognized—in the keeping of a church in his archdeaconry, and has now been stolen by the owner of a publishing house, Gregory Persimmons.

Persimmons is a practitioner of black magic, and aims to align himself by a magical use of the Grail to the 'flow' of the universe and so reach the satisfaction of his desires. He wants to be 'married to the whole universe', and, smeared with magic ointment, he experiences a 'Satanic' dance: 'the bridal dance was beginning; they and he and innumerable others were moving to the wild rhythm of that aboriginal longing' (75). This demonic dance is evidently a distorted version of the life-giving movement of the universe that the Archdeacon hears as music. Persimmons claims that 'I know the current of desire in which all things move, and I have guided it a little as I will' (212), but the will behind the movement of all things is going to thwart his will in the end. As the Archdeacon is to say, 'When the time comes He will dispose as He will, or rather He shall be as He will, as He is' (180).

To achieve his desires, Persimmons has already killed one man, whom he had used for evil purposes but who was about to confess his crimes to the police. The book opens with the discovery of his corpse in the publishing office by an editor, Lionel Rackstraw. Persimmon's plan is to manipulate the Grail to his own ends by means of the magical sacrifice of Rackstraw's child, Adrian, and he takes a step towards gaining control over him by applying the magic ointment to a prick he has made in the hand of his mother, Barbara. She falls into a feverish engagement with demonic movements in the universe, which are a parody of the Archdeacon's music:

> Suddenly Barbara moved and stood up. Her voice began again its despairing appeals to God and Lionel, but her limbs began to dispose themselves in the preliminary motions of a dance. Gently at first, then more and more swiftly, her feet leapt upon the carpet; her arms tossed themselves in time to unheard music. Lionel made an effort to stop her, throwing one arm round her waist and catching her hands with the other; before his movement was complete she broke his hold and sent him staggering across the room. Gregory's heart beat high; this then was the outer sign of the inner dance he had himself known: the ointment had helped him to seal his body while his soul entered ecstasy. But here the ointment gave the body helpless to the driving energy of the Adversary, and only through the screaming mouth a memory that was not conquered cried out to her lover and to her God. (161)

Persimmons also intends to misuse the Grail to unite ('wed') the soul of the murdered man to the body of the Archdeacon and so to create a living slave of evil. During the magical ritual of which he is the intended victim, the Archdeacon feels himself 'moving...passing to a pre-ordained tryst' (242). But a little earlier, we have heard the theme sounded that is to occupy the next three novels: 'It was not his business to display activity, but to wait on the Mover of all things' (234). When the Grail refuses to be manipulated, and turns its energies on those who thought they could master it, the Archdeacon is released from danger, and we read that 'he recovered his usual equilibrium' (248). In the midst of the movement of things, whether life-fostering or life-denying, what is needed is a quiet waiting and an 'equilibrium'.

This is a balance expressed in the complementary assertions 'Neither is this Thou' and 'Yet this also is Thou', which the Archdeacon recalls as he meditates before the Grail, and feels himself part of a universe in movement towards a point of stillness: '[He] was aware again of a general movement of all things towards a narrow channel...Sky, sea and land were moving, not towards that vessel, but towards all it symbolized and held' (137). He also repeats, 'as he so often said, "This also is Thou"' as he waits in desolation for the threatening magic ritual (240). When the pairing of the declarations occurs elsewhere (and many times) in Williams' work, it usually means a coming together of the negative and positive ways for knowing God, but here it expresses an equipoise in the midst of turmoil.

There is evidence elsewhere that Williams was fascinated by the idea of equilibrium in the period of the early 1930s. In 1930, the Oxford University Press issued a second edition of Robert Bridge's 1918 collection of the poetry of Gerard Manley Hopkins, in which Williams recollated the poems, adding others and providing a critical introduction; it was this edition rather than the first that resulted in the huge impact of Hopkins on modern poets. In fragmentary notes elsewhere for a lecture on Hopkins, Williams focuses on the poet's observation of a windhover, or kestrel, as it 'hangs' motionless upon the upward currents of air. Reflecting on the lines, 'the hurl and gliding / Rebuffed the big wind' he finds several areas of equilibrium. First there is the equilibrium of the verse: 'and what does it equilibriate? Itself against itself—lines, rhymes, or what not.' Behind this there is the poet: 'What then is GH's equilibrium? [...] the balance of a very intense poetic personality with a very intense poetic rejection of personality.' But further, there is a wider equilibrium, which for Hopkins is centred in Christ, whose presence he greets in the windhover: 'It is a continual reference to something—let us say, undefined—which is brought in as a continual balance [...] The something is called Christ.'[7]

[7] Wade CW/MS-214, 9–10.

Williams portrays this 'something' dramatically in the climax of *War in Heaven*, when mass is celebrated with the Grail by the legendary priest-king Prester John, who appears in the Arthurian tradition. He is not exactly Christ, but represents the human potential to be Christ, and he has already appeared several times in the story, speaking words of Christ from the Gospels in the first person, such as 'I will keep the Passover with my disciples' (203). There are three witnesses to the mass at the church in Fardles, just as Williams describes the mass in the chapel of Sarras in his version of the Arthurian legend. Replacing Galahad, Percivale, and Bors, they are the Archdeacon, the Duke of the North Ridings, who is also a poet, and the pair of lovers, Lionel and Barbara, who stand with linked hands. That the last are to be counted as one person is indicated by the liturgical reading from Genesis, 'in the image of God created he him, and male and female created he them', and by Williams' comment that those who watched were 'all separate beings, save where the hands of the lovers lingered in a final clasp' (254). Earlier in the novel, Lionel's fellow editor, Kenneth Mornington, had identified the Archdeacon, the poet-duke, and himself as Galahad, Percivale, and Bors (120), but now Lionel-Barbara replace him since he has been killed in an attempt to recover the Grail from Persimmons. The Archdeacon, like Galahad at Sarras, will shortly be assumed into the glory of the Grail as he dies before the altar. What these witnesses see is both dynamic movement and 'the continual balance',[8] summed up in the Christ through whom all things have been created. They

> were concentrated on that high motionless Figure—motionless, for in Him all motions awaited His movement to be loosed, and still He did not move. All sound ceased; all things entered into an intense suspension of being; nothing was anywhere at all but He. He stood; He moved His hands [...] All things began again to be. At a great distance Lionel and Barbara and the Duke saw beyond Him, as He lifted up the Graal, the moving universe of stars, and then one flying planet, and then fields and rooms and a thousand remembered places, and all in light and darkness and peace.   (254–5)

There is a foretaste here of the figure of the Juggler in *The Greater Trumps*, who is 'the beginning of all things—a show, a dexterity of balance, a flight and a falling'.[9] John is—as it were—keeping the balls in motion in the air, symbolized by the lifting up of the Grail, but only by being the centre of equipoise. Thus, 'silence succeeded to the flying music that had accompanied vision. Like the *centre* of that silence, they heard His voice calling...'(255).

The stress in this book lies, then, on equilibrium in movement. If it was published, unchanged, from the first draft of 1926, then we must suppose that

---

[8] This is Williams' phrase about Hopkins' Windhover/Christ: Wade CW/MS-214, 10.
[9] Williams, *Greater Trumps*, 98.

the idea of equilibrium or balance was already in Williams' mind before he re-edited Bridges' edition of Hopkins in 1929–30. But then, as Lindop suggests, Williams was probably involved in the production of the 1918 volume in the first place and had been reading Hopkins since that time.[10] He would have known 'The Windhover' much earlier than the 1930s, and the notes found among his papers cannot actually be dated. It is more surprising, given the date of the original composition of the novel, that there are no obvious marks of the theology of romantic love that was occupying Williams' mind in that period. Although there is renewal of love between Lionel and Barbara, they do not see each other in primal glory, even in the apotheosis of the mass. It is much less surprising that there is no hint of substitution in love. If this were a later novel, one would expect the conjunction between the despairing soul of the dead man and the living Archdeacon in the magic ritual to be an occasion for the vicarious bearing of burden. But here, as the Grail 'awoke in its own triumphant and blinding power', it (or rather the power it makes present) redeems the lost soul without assistance from any mortal mediator, so that the Archdeacon catches sight of a face that had been 'weak, anxious and harassed' and is now 'free and happy and adoring' (244–5). Prester John lifts the Grail, as he is to do later at Fardles, making the divine declaration, 'I am He that sent me',[11] and a great voice and an 'infinite chorus' sing what has been the Archdeacon's favourite saying, 'for His mercy endureth for ever'.

This mercy extends, unilaterally and without any human act of loving substitution, to Gregory Persimmons. The voice announces, 'there shall be agreement with you also in the end, for you have sought me and no other' (246). In seeking for delight in desire, it seems that Gregory has all the while been serving the good without knowing it. There is a curious echo of this mercy in the scene that C. S. Lewis portrays in The Last Battle, where Aslan accepts the Calormene warrior who has served the false god Tash all his life, assuring him that 'unless thy desire had been for me thou wouldst not have sought so long and so truly. For all find what they truly seek.'[12] This is entirely consonant with Lewis' view of the 'desire' that haunts all human life, but here we find a precursor in Williams.

After the shattering events of the elevation of the Grail during the magical ritual, it is typical that, when Prester John finally hands him this extraordinary Cup, 'the Archdeacon took the Graal with his usual sedateness' (246). He is a man who holds himself in balance, because he is held there by Another. However, the problem with stressing equilibrium as the key to living steadily in the currents of life is that Williams associates it strongly with a submission to the Will that is

---

[10] Lindop, Charles Williams, 71.

[11] Williams, War in Heaven, 245–6. This is not exactly a text from the Gospel of John. Prester John could be meaning (a) 'I am John, and I am Christ who sent me', or (b) 'I am John/Christ, and I am the God who sent me'. Cf. John 8:29, 42.

[12] Lewis, Last Battle, 166. For Lewis' inclusivism, see Ward, 'Church', 86–8.

finally driving all the movement of people and things in the world. Mornington is thus perplexed about the goodness of creation. In a mixed world, does God will evil as well as good? 'Does God will Gregory Persimmons?' he asks the Archdeacon, and receives the reply, 'Certainly he wills him [...] since He wills that Persimmons shall be whatever he seems to choose.' Mornington persists with the question, 'He wills evil then?' but he is only given a text from scripture in response: 'Shall there be evil in the City and I the Lord have not done it?'[13] We read that Mornington and the duke 'fell back on the simpler idea that agony and evil were displeasing to God, but that he permitted them' (180–1). The Archdeacon, and Williams with him, are hinting at something more difficult: that if there is a Will which is prior to human will, then we only 'seem' to choose to be evil, though the choice appears to the chooser to be a real one. Williams enters the Archdeacon's reservation, 'that is not technically correct, perhaps', and he offers another perspective on the question elsewhere in the novel:

> By long practice [the Archdeacon] had accustomed himself in any circumstances—at company or alone, at work or at rest, in speech or in silence—to withdraw into that place where action is created. The cause of all actions disposed itself according to that Will which was its nature, and, so disposing itself, moved him easily as part of its own accommodation to the changing wills of men, so that at any time and at all times its own perfection was maintained... (118)

The 'place where action is created' is the point of stillness that is later to be visualized in the mass at Fardles, and evokes once again a living in equilibrium. At that very point, Williams suggests here, there is a divine 'accommodation' to human wills. That seems more satisfactory than a mere 'seeming' of human will, but it is only a passing comment. A sentence or two later, the Archdeacon is reflecting that 'Nothing but Destiny could defy Destiny.' Williams was never able to solve the question as to whether evil was part of the 'Necessity' of creation, or its 'Destiny',[14] although his contemporary Reinhold Niebuhr was offering one answer in his book, *The Nature and Destiny of Man*, which Williams reviewed in 1942. Niebuhr suggests that evil might be seen as necessary in the sense of 'inevitable' in contingent reality, while not being necessary in strict logic, but while Williams recognized this view he did not adopt it.[15] As late as the last novel in 1945, he is playing with the idea that even corruption has its proper place in the good, as a dead soul, Lester, gazes upon the dirty waters of the Thames, full of sewage and rubbish, and reflects:

---

[13] Amos 3:6.   [14] See my essay 'Charles Williams and the Problem of Evil', 72–83.
[15] Williams, 'Image of Man', 143–5. See Niebuhr, *Nature and Destiny*, 1: 179–83, 194–6.

The evacuations of the City had their place in the City; how else could the City be the City? Corruption (so to call it) was tolerable, even adequate and proper, even glorious[.][16]

Perhaps Williams' uncertainty on the issue ('how else'?) was why the idea of 'equilibrium' could not ultimately succeed for him as a comprehensive term for coping with the human situation, since it was bound up with submission to an absolute Will.

Mornington had already raised his protest in an earlier conversation with the poet-duke. Stepping accidentally in a puddle, he had exclaimed 'Why was this bloody world created?' and received the unexpected answer, 'As a sewer for the stars [...] Alternatively, to know God and to glory him for ever.' The two then exuberantly compile a list of words with the prefix 'con-' for the way that the duke's two statements might co-exist, including consanguineous, contemporaneous, consubstantial, concomitant, consequential, congruous, and connectible.[17] If they are not just talking about a complementarity of ideas but realities, then the terms apply to the complexity of the world. Beyond these 'con-' terms, we thus seem to be on the verge of a significant 'co-' word: 'co-inherence'. But this is far too early for such a step. The playful conversation might well, however, hint at a world that is full of 'exchanges', since Williams was developing this idea as early as 1926. When the Order (or Company) of the Co-inherence is formed in 1939, the Companions' mantra of greeting is 'Under the Mercy', which seems to be a recollection of the Archdeacon's favourite exclamation, 'For His mercy endureth for ever', occurring no fewer than eleven times in the book.

11.2 Movement and Equilibrium: The Stone

In Williams' next novel, *Many Dimensions* (1931), the themes persist from *War in Heaven*. While the Grail is the central symbol of the previous novel, here it is a Stone, the Stone of Solomon, Son of David. This is a focus for all motion, since it makes possible 'movement in time, space and thought'.[18] Sir Giles Tumulty, who is an archaeologist, traveller, and student of the occult has got hold of the stone, once supposedly set in the crown of King Solomon, by bribing a member of the Islamic family that has been its guardian for many generations. He wants to use it to gain power, while his nephew, Reginald Montague, wants to use it for profit. It can be cut without diminishing it, and infinitely divided into 'types' or copies that all have the properties of the archetype. A large part of the plot consists of various attempts to misuse the stone, exploiting it to try and make money, to heal the sick,

---

[16] Williams, *All Hallows' Eve*, 197.   [17] Williams, *War in Heaven*, 95.
[18] Williams, *Many Dimensions*, 52.

improve the lot of the population in general, solve the transport problem, and even to pass examinations.

Hajji Ibrahim is a faithful descendant of the keepers of the stone, and explains that it was perhaps the first created thing, or 'First Matter', and that the whole universe came into being when the Shekinah of the Merciful One looked on it. All things, spiritual and material, were made through it, and its divisibility signifies the fragmentation of the created world. It is thus an object of great power. Hajji insists that the Stone must be recovered from the hands of those who are dishonouring it, and who are unknowingly harming themselves by abusing it, but it will not exert itself to return to the Unity unless someone, entirely uncon- ditionally, wills that both he or she and the stone should 'be with the Transcendence' (58). Chloe Burnett, the secretary of Hajji's acquaintance and collaborator, Lord Arglay, fulfils this task: the many images of the Stone 'rush swiftly together [...] in conjoining motion' into their original and the Stone sinks to 'its place in the order of the universe' (260, 262). In achieving this return of the Stone, Chloe is transfigured in glory—the Tetragrammaton, the four consonants of the Divine Name, appears on her forehead—but she also falls into a permanent comatose state, and finally dies in the loving care of Lord Arglay.

The Muslim scholar, Ibrahim, speaks like the Archdeacon in the previous novel, but rather more sternly. While the Archdeacon's favourite saying is 'For His mercy endureth for ever', Ibrahim repeats the phrase from the Qur'an, 'The Compassionate and the Merciful', finally blessing Arglay with the words, 'the Mercy of the Compassionate be with you' (266). He also uses the formula 'Under the Protection', which appears eleven times in the book, and which Lord Arglay and Chloe adopt to greet and bless each other (e.g. 137, 258). We only need to combine this phrase with 'His mercy endureth for ever' to produce 'Under the Mercy', the greeting that Williams provided for the Companions of the Co- inherence. While the Archdeacon urges obedience to the will of God, Ibrahim bids Chloe to foster a 'Resignation' within (45), and warns her: 'woe, woe, woe to you [...] if from this time forth for ever you forget that you gave your will to the Will of That which is behind the Stone' (228). The Archdeacon commands, 'Make yourselves paths for the Will of God' as he senses the attack beginning on the Grail,[19] and Ibrahim advises Chloe that 'as there is but one End, so there is now but one Stone with you, and it may be one path for the Stone' (232). Lord Arglay picks up the language of path and tells Chloe, 'if there is indeed a path for the Stone, in the name of God let us offer it that path, and let whatever Will moves justly in these things fulfil itself through us if that is its desire' (258).

Thus, as in *War in Heaven*, both the movement of things and equilibrium, or what both Ibrahim and Lord Arglay call 'repose' (45, 102), are associated with a

---

[19] Williams, *War in Heaven*, 139.

transcendent Will. On the one hand, the Will 'moves justly', and on the other, balance is kept by submission to the Will. Williams' tendency to value simple obedience to the divine Will here is in accord with the Islam ('submission') of which Ibrahim is a member. The Stone is the 'end of desire' (e.g. 45, 95), both in the sense of being the place *in which* to desire, and in putting an end to one's own desires.

The Stone is the intersection of all movement, which is why it is possible to travel anywhere in space and time by entering it. Chloe wants Lord Arglay to bid her to 'move in the stone' (257). This movement can be dangerous for those who do not enter it with a submissive will. This is exemplified by the hazard of moving backwards in time, which is achieved by an act of will directed towards the Stone; a return to the present will be an arrival at the point of willing to travel backwards, and so the whole process will be repeated, resulting in being trapped in an eternal recurrence, or perpetual motion. This terrible fate is demonstrated by the unfortunate young man on whom Tumulty experiments. Tumulty himself will finally experience the movements in the stone, and they will be his death:

> As he spoke the Stone seemed to open in his hand. He found himself looking into it, down coils of moving and alternated splendour and darkness. [...] [He] found himself close to what had by now become a nucleus of movement which passed outward from it into the very walls and furniture. They, so far as the mind which was now striving to steady itself, could discern, were themselves shifting and curving. [...] [The] awful change went on; it was as if the room itself, and he with it, were being sucked into the convolutions of the Stone [...]. Struggling and twisting, he was dragged down the curving spirals nearer to the illumination into which he was already plunged [...]; he saw himself gathered, a living soul, into the centre of the Stone.   (243–5)

Lord Arglay, on the other hand, can keep his balance in the currents of movement generated by the Stone:

> He looked out, and in the sky itself there was a change. There was movement between him and the heavens; the chimneys and clouds and sky took on the appearance of the Stone. He was looking into it, and the world was there, continents and cities, seas and their ships. The Stone was not these, yet these were the Stone—only there was movement within and beyond them, and from a point infinitely far a continual vibration mingled itself with the myriad actions of men.   (260)

Lord Arglay is not destroyed by the movement concentrated in the Stone because he has devoted his life to serving a principle of equilibrium or—to give it a legal name—equity. He is in fact the Lord Chief Justice of England, and his special study has been 'organic law'. Williams appears to be playing on the word 'organic', which in a legal sense properly means the law of organizations, such as governments, corporations, and other social groups. To this Williams adds the meaning of law that grows 'organically', in the human mind and in social relations. Lord Arglay is said by an admirer to understand law as 'the formal expression of increasing communal self-knowledge', and to have 'compared variations in law with the variations in poetic diction from age to age' (152). Williams has highlighted this notion of organic law with many references to it—Chloe was typing and annotating the script for Arglay's grand work on the topic—and by including it in two chapter headings. We gather that organic law is rooted in relationships, and gives stability in the midst of conflicting forces. Arglay claims that 'there is no dispute between men which cannot be resolved in equity. And in its nature equity is from those between whom it exists: it is passion acting in lucidity' (156). In older theological texts, 'equity' means 'moderation',[20] and so it stands close to what Ibrahim calls 'measure and degree in all things, even upon the Way' (45). We have an example of its use when Arglay finds himself caught in a conflict of emotions as he thinks about his brother-in-law, Giles Tumulty. On the one hand, he has a feeling of detestation; on the other, he intends to think generously about him:

> There ensued a moment's balance between those contending forces; they swung equal and then the effort ceased. His mind was aware of an ordered arrangement, as if in the outer world it had been considering the plan of a great city.   (61)

Later, this idea of 'measure' is to play a key role in Williams' vision of Byzantium. Reflecting on this, Lewis comments that Williams' sense of this realm has order and mathematical proportion within it: 'He started with a something in his experience, characterized by glory, but also by a strict or mathematic quality—something that meets him in the life of a great jurist (see *Many Dimensions*).'[21] With the 'equilibrium' possessed by the Archdeacon in *War in Heaven*, we may thus compare the 'equity' that characterizes Lord Arglay.

Although movement and balance or equity are the predominant themes in this novel, exchange and substitution are present, if slightly. The narrator comments that comparing her boyfriend (unfairly, one might think) with Lord Arglay 'did not make Frank less delightful in the exchanges discoverable by him and her together, but it threw into high relief the insufficiency of those exchanges as more than an occupation and a means of oblivion' (50). The 'exchanges' between them become even more insufficient when he tries emotional blackmail on her in an

---

[20] William Perkins' *Hepieíkeia* is an extended meditation on Philippians 4:5, 'Let your moderation be known to all men.'
[21] Lewis, 'A Sacred Poem', 131. On 'order' in Byzantium see Lewis, 'Williams and the Arthuriad', 105–6.

attempt to allow him to use her 'type' of the Stone to discover his examination questions ahead of time, and finally steals it (though it restores itself mysteriously to her). The relation of exchange becomes a kind of substitution when, in the moment of her union with the Stone,

> suddenly there came into her mind the memory of Frank Lindsay. 'Poor darling,' she felt with a renewed rush of pity and affection, 'he didn't, he couldn't, understand.' In her own understanding she offered his failure and his mischief to That which she held, and with him also [...] all those who for any purpose of good or evil had laid their hands or fixed their desires upon the Stone. Vague in image, but intense in appeal, her heart gathered all—from herself to Giles Tumulty—in a sudden presentation of them to the Mystery with which they had trafficked.   (259)

This is at least implicitly a substitution in love, though Williams is reserved in presenting it as such.[22] Indirectly, he confirms it when later he writes that 'On the same day when at Wandsworth the unhappy wreckage of a man passed into death'—that is, the victim of Tumulty's experimental use of the Stone to interrupt an execution—'the wreckage of his saviour was carried to a bed in the Chief Justice's house' (264).

11.3 Movement, Equilibrium, and Exchange: The Eagle

In Williams' third published novel, *The Place of the Lion* (1931), Hopkins' symbol of equilibrium, the hovering falcon, makes a dramatic entrance in the form of a gigantic eagle, riding the wind. Towards the middle of the novel, the hero, Anthony Durrant, enters the house of a man who has mysteriously fallen into a persistent coma, and on the landing outside the bedroom he has a frightening vision of standing above a deep pit or abyss, where the sky is in motion, continually passing into the wall of the abyss. Forced to the brink of the ledge by a strong wind, and shaken by 'coils of enormous movement', he senses that he is caught in the conflict of his own will. Then there comes a great winged form, an eagle, which hovers before him, and he finds himself held in the air over the abyss:

> He was riding in the void, flying without wings, securely existing by movement and balance among the dangers of that other world. He was poised in a vibration of peace, carried within some auguster passage [...]. [H]e moved now amid

---

[22] Watkins, 'Charles Williams', 232–4, draws parallels between the theme of substitution in Williams and in the earlier novels of R. H. Benson, but the instances in Benson do not make the same kind of association with romantic love.

sudden shapes and looming powers [...]. And as he adored those beautiful, serene and terrible manifestations, they vanished from around him. He was no more in movement; he was standing again on his ledge; a rush of mighty wings went outward from him.[23]

Unlike Anthony, we find ourselves on familiar ground. Amid the motion of the world, an equilibrium can be attained, for which this novel continually uses the term 'balance'. Anthony has 'rebuffed the big wind' and is 'riding' on the 'rolling level underneath him steady air'—as Hopkins puts it in the case of the windhover—and yet we sense he is not just being carried by an eagle; in some sense he *is* the eagle, or the eagle is within him. What is happening has been explained to Anthony and to us a little earlier by one of the devoted followers of the comatose man. The man in the mysterious house is Berringer, a mystical figure with a theory.

According to his fanatical disciple, Foster, the world was created by the entrance of 'certain great principles' or Powers into matter.[24] The human soul is composed of these principles in 'a just proportion', but in animals they are less mingled, so each power is shown in its own shape. The lion, for instance, makes visible strength or authority, the snake expresses subtlety, and the butterfly demonstrates beauty. Berringer apparently also believes that these Powers are equivalent to the 'Ideas' of Plato's philosophy, intellectual archetypes such as truth, beauty, and goodness of which this material world is a shadowy copy (23). The Powers are thus the originals of the animals, and there is a sympathy between them and the Powers. Then, if just one of the animals is brought within the influence of one particular Power through someone's intense concentration on that Power or Idea, the material body of the beast will be changed into an image of the Power. A breach will have been made between worlds, and in turn all animals and then all objects in this world will be drawn into the world of the Powers: 'More and more everything will be received into its original', and the world as we know it will be destroyed. With human persons the situation is more complex: some—like Foster himself—will welcome what is happening and can be 'joined to that Power which each of them best serves', singling out and exalting one principle from the human mix. Foster does not know what will happen to those who reject the process, 'except that they will be hunted. For nothing will escape.' (53–6) One disciple of Berringer, Miss Wilton, is consumed by the subtlety of the snake, the quality in her which she serves; Mr Tighe, an amateur lepidopterist, is consumed by the beauty of the butterfly. A giant snake and butterfly have thus manifested themselves in the locality. Anthony's eagle, as we shall see, fits into this scene.

---

[23] Williams, *Place of the Lion*, 113–16.
[24] For the following, see Williams, *Place of the Lion*, 53–5.

Berringer, thinks Foster, is the 'focus' of the movement between worlds: 'It's through him that this world is passing into that. He and his house are the centre.' (55) The novel begins with the escape of a lioness from a local zoo, and it transpires that Berringer met her while he was concentrating on the Power or Idea of authority and strength, so that through the mediation of his human consciousness the lioness changed into the archetypal Lion, the eternal image of this Power; henceforth, the Lion becomes the key archetype, the 'guardian' of the threshold between this world and the spiritual world of the Powers. The Lion is 'the place of entrance' (72), hence the title of the novel.

Anthony agrees with the theory, and determines to 'turn back the movement of the vast originals of all life', so saving the world. (74) This becomes the reality for which the readers of the novel suspend their disbelief. The belief is, however, complicated for the reader by two other conceptual schemes that are offered during the course of the drama. Damaris Tighe, daughter of the butterfly admirer, is a young scholar of medieval thought, working on a thesis in which she is arguing that the 'angels' of the Christian mystical scholar Pseudo-Dionysius correspond to the 'ideas' or 'forms' of Hellenic philosophy (24). Then Anthony comes across a text called *de Angelis*, written by the medieval Marcellus Victorinus of Bologna, which proposes that the 'Divine Celestials' or angels of Pseudo-Dionysius are the Universals that emanate from the transcendent Unity in the Neoplatonist cosmos. Though Williams has invented both the text and the scholar,[25] they make an important addition to a general equation of Powers, Ideas, and Angels that has been emerging. The thesis of Marcellus does not seem very different from that of Damaris, except that Marcellus holds that the Powers or Angels have become corrupted by worship offered by people to their 'energies' in the world, as distinct from their intellectual essences in heaven (90–1). This idea is actually quite close to scriptural notions of the fall of the angels, or the corruption of the 'Principalities and Powers' through idolatry,[26] and it allows Williams to present the movement between worlds as sinister, and the activity of the Powers as capable of being malevolent; both movement and activity are to be resisted.

Thus, not long after Anthony's conversation with Foster, Anthony confronts the Lion. In a scene that Eliot admired,[27] the landscape begins to move as the Lion treads through it, but Anthony is able to withstand the Lion because he has a strong element of authority in his own personality. Yet he has not, as has Foster, yielded himself to this one component of his nature, but maintains the balance between qualities that is truly human. He retains his conviction that 'every man— he himself—was a *pattern* of these powers' (71). Thus, walking on the rippling

---

[25] See McCoull, 'Woman Named Damaris', 118–22.
[26] Caird, *Principalities and Powers*, 2–8; Walter Wink, *Unmasking the Powers*, 87–92.
[27] T. S. Eliot to CW, 7 October 1934; see note 4 above.

road, the eagle appears to give him courage and strengthen his capacity for
balance:

> High above him some winged thing went through the air [...] the pure balance
> of that distant flight entered into him as if had been salvation. It was incredible
> that life should sustain itself by such equipoise, so lightly, so dangerously, but
> it did.   (65)

The word 'dangerously' evokes Hopkins' windhover, and 'the fire that breaks from
thee then, a billion/Times told lovelier, more dangerous'.[28] Anthony is going to
need the 'equipoise' inspired by the eagle as he comes up against the Lion: 'He felt
as if he were riding against some terrific wind; he was balancing upon the
instinctive powers of his spirit; he did not fight this awful opposition but poised
himself within and above it.' He refuses to fall, and 'as the striving force caught
him', he manages to overpass it 'by rising into the balance of adjusted movement'
(67–8).

Anthony also finds the eagle in Marcellus, who refers to four major celestial
powers, 'and *between* them is the Glory of the Eagle' (92). Its very function in the
heavenly hierarchy is that of holding a balance, an idea that really does come
from Pseudo-Dionysius.[29] Three of the four major Powers that make their
appearance in *The Place of the Lion* are the Lion, the Snake, and the Butterfly
(184). The fourth is probably the Unicorn, representing speed,[30] and like the Eagle
it is unmalevolent though disturbing (traditionally it is a symbol of Christ).[31] It is
seen by Richardson, the person who introduces Anthony to the manuscript of
Marcellus. He has determined to take the way of the 'negation of images', in
contrast to Anthony who prefers the 'affirmation of images': 'Not by images, or
symbols, or myths, did he himself follow [the way] [...] attempting always a
return to an interior nothingness' (139). Yet it is he who sees the 'Divine Unicorn'
during mass, showing that the negative and the positive ways always need each
other ('This also is Thou; neither is this Thou'). In his vision, he becomes aware 'of
a sensation of rushing speed passing through his being; it was not for him to adore
the unicorn; he was the unicorn [...] hastening to an end' (143–4). The speed
symbolized by the Unicorn is a motion that fosters life, moving people along the
'way' to the goal of life and the end of desire.

Authority is the strongest virtue within Anthony, although he keeps it in
balance with others. Unfortunately (or so it seems to the reader of the present
day), it is a quality that he intends to assert not only against the Lion, but against

---

[28] Gerard Manley Hopkins, 'The Windhover: to Christ our Lord', lines 10–11.
[29] Pseudo-Dionysius, *Celestial Hierarchy* 15.8 (188–9); See McCoull, 'Woman Named Damaris',
122. The eagle also appears in Dante, *Divine Comedy, Purgatory*, 9 and *Paradise*, 18–19.
[30] At one point Williams appears to count 'speed' as the fourth power rather than the Eagle: 183–4.
[31] For the unicorn in Williams' poetry, see Chapter 8, section 4.

the woman he wants to marry, who is no other than the woman scholar Damaris, his cousin. Reflecting on his capacity to exercise the dominion of Adam over the 'beasts of the field', he continues: 'if the proportion is in me let these others know it. Let me take dominion over them—I wish I had any prospect of exercising dominion over Damaris' (75). Williams is not making an entirely ironic criticism of his character here, as a major thread in the plot of the book is the coming of Damaris to recognize the proper ordering of Anthony's male authority over her. She finally repents of her own assumption of authority, discovering that she depends on the person who can exercise the 'balance' that she cannot:

> She permitted herself to savour, to enjoy, the sensation of trust and dependence, and was astonished to find how comforting it was. It was quite impossible for her to balance and equate great Ideas, but if there were among them one whose nature was precisely that balance, and therefore the freedom of assured move-ment, then she would give herself to it.   (72)

The 'one' here is an Idea, in fact the Idea of balance represented by the Eagle, but while it is 'impossible' for *her* to achieve the balance, we are constantly assured by the narrator that Antony *can*. When Anthony arrives to rescue her from the attack of a pterodactyl, a distinctly malevolent Power, she sees him with an eagle perched on his shoulder: 'he raised his hand, and as if in an august leniency it allowed itself to be caressed'. There went out from him 'a knowledge of safety would she but take it, and freely and humbly she let it enter her being'. We read that 'she longed to feel more closely the high protection of his power', and 'she was content to wait upon his will'. She makes a 'motion of assent' and apologizes, confessing that 'I've tried to make use of you' (134–5).

At this point, the critic Thomas Howard underlines the fact that Damaris finds salvation by putting herself under the protection of Anthony, but appears to find no problem with this subordination.[32] Nor, one suspects, would have C. S. Lewis, whose admiration of this novel initiated his friendship with Williams. The recog-nition of male authority also marked the relationship of Chloe to Lord Arglay in the previous novel, and will appear again in successive novels,[33] and in the relationship between the poet Taliessin and the slave-girl in 'The Ascent of the Spear'.[34] In Chapter 8, I have argued that Williams was not consistent in this view of male 'headship' over the woman, and (unlike Lewis) could conceive of a more flexible hierarchy. So, in the next novel, the saviour of the world and 'near enough'

---

[32] Howard, *Novels*, 164–6.
[33] In *Descent into Hell*, 124, Pauline regards Peter Stanhope as her 'master'.
[34] Williams, *Taliessin*, 48–50; 'assent' is punned with 'ascent'.

its Messiah,[35] will turn out to be a woman; yet even then it is from her male lover that the power 'still obscurely arose' and 'it was he who had given her that sovereignty'.[36] Here at least in *Place of the Lion* there is an unpleasant strain of patriarchy, where the desirable 'balance' in life is viewed as residing essentially in the male, as descendant of the male Adam. In the scene of the salvation of Damaris, Anthony in fact belittles her scholarship, lecturing her on merely making use for her own ends of the writings of the 'masters', turning their 'agonies and joys' into 'chatter [. . .], plottings and plannings and your little diagrams' (136). Clearly, this is a temptation that befalls all scholars, whatever their gender, but we also recall that earlier he had referred to her as 'a half-educated woman' (74), and later he is to permit her to continue with her work on Abelard, 'as long as you don't neglect me in order to do it' (196). He is, we feel, only half-joking.

The climax of the novel is Anthony's success in overcoming the invasion of this world by the Powers, through his assumption of the identity of Adam in the Garden of Eden, naming the animals. The 'lion and the lamb', with all the other animal-like qualities, must be led back into balance, and this is done by the act of authority of Adam, in whom 'there had been perfect balance, perfect proportion' (190). The Eagle sits once again on Anthony's shoulder as 'the image of Adam named the beasts, and naming ruled them [. . .]. [A]ll acts of peace that then had being through the world were deepened and knew their own nature more clearly' (204). Later that night, the house and body of Berringer are consumed in an intense fire, and the great shape of a lion is seen to leap into the flames.

At the centre of the book there is thus a balance or equilibrium in movement, whether the movement is life-giving (like that of the Unicorn) or life-destroying (like that of the Lion). As Anthony muses with Richardson,

> 'Isn't there an order', he said, 'in everything? If one has to find balance, and a kind of movement in balance [. . .] I mean to act here and now.'   (122)

Damaris is later to echo this phrasing of 'movement in balance' with her expression, 'balance and therefore the freedom of assured movement'. There is a brief mention of the doctrine of exchange, and this is interestingly associated with balance. When Anthony awakens from a sleep in which he has been dreaming of the birth of Eve from the side of Adam, he thinks that 'the knowledge of the name [of mankind] and its utterance was in the perpetual interchange of love' (191). His thoughts about exchange, however, have just occurred more extensively in his recalling of the male bonding between himself and his housemate Quentin. Reflecting on their close friendship, Anthony thinks that 'he had accepted those exchanges, so far as mortal frailty could, as being of the nature of final and eternal

---

[35] Williams, *Greater Trumps*, 230.   [36] Williams, *Greater Trumps*, 163.

being' (182). Though there is no indication that their love is sexual, some of the same language of the theology of romantic love is employed: 'He loved; yet not he, but love living in him' (187). Now he recognizes that this exchange between friends provides the essential balance, for 'No mind was so good that it did not need another mind to counter and equal it [...]. Only in such a balance could humility be found.' Drawing on the symbol of the eagle, he reflects that 'Balance— and movement in balance, as an eagle sails up on the wind—this was the truth of life, and beauty in life' (187). Using the word 'measure' that had been spoken by Ibrahim in *Many Dimensions*, he judges that 'the movement of the eagle was the measure of truth' (185).

The eagle symbolizes measure, moderation, or balance, while the movement of the universe has another bird for a symbol, the mythical phoenix that rises from fire and is consumed in fire: 'such was the inmost life of the universe, infinitely destroyed, infinitely recreated, breaking from its continual death into continual life, instinct with strength and subtlety and beauty and speed' (185). Stephen Dunning finds an echo of this bird of fire with the kabbalistic *Shekinah*, 'the glory of God, the visible presence of the immanent God of creation, the creative Logos'.[37] It is a representative, maintains Dunning, of 'Religion A' in Kierkegaard's classification of types of religion, and he finds this affirmation of 'immanent divinity', a religion of 'the accessibility of the divine to the self within the self', to be in conflict throughout all the novels with Kierkegaard's 'Religion B', or the Christian assertion of an infinite difference between God and the world.[38] Throughout this study, I have also been identifying a spirituality of divine immanence in Williams, showing that it sometimes (loosely) uses kabbalistic imagery, and contrasting this with Lewis' more dualistic view of the relation between God and the world. But it seems to be Dunning's own conviction about the nature of Christianity as a religion of transcendence and paradox that leads him to suppose there *must* be an inevitable contradiction between Williams' world view and Christian faith. Even on his own exegesis of the novels, it seems to be only in *Shadows of Ecstasy* that this tension becomes at all evident, though the other novels do show other tensions, and notably about the question of evil and necessity.

In this novel, there is no clear demonstration of Williams' theory of substitution in love, though the conditions are there for such an event to happen, in the generous action of Damaris. This concerns Quentin again, who had fled with terror before the remorseless pace of the Lion, and was lost to Anthony, hunted by the terrible creature that had once been Foster. Damaris sets out to rescue him, and having found his terrified form, she throws her body over his in the presence

[37] Dunning, *Crisis and the Quest*, 54–5. Cavaliero, *Charles Williams: Poet*, 73, also finds traces of the kabbalistic sephirotic tree.
[38] Dunning, *Crisis and the Quest*, 37–8, 47–8. For Religions A and B, immanent and paradoxical, see Kierkegaard, *Concluding Unscientific Postscript*, 493–8, 507.

of 'a solitary lamb', while the creature crept around them and 'across the meadow passed suddenly the shadow of the flying eagle, cast over her' (175). It is implied that its equilibrium passes into her, and she is able to resist the 'thing', so that 'repose' came back into the face of Quentin (177). In a later novel (such as *Descent into Hell* or *All Hallows' Eve*), we might expect such a scene to become an opportunity for substitution, where Damaris would have carried Quentin's burden of fear, but there is only the potential for this idea as it is. The stress is upon the equipoise of the eagle, which Foster lacks: the power of the Lion overcomes him 'in a great wind', and 'strangled and twisted, he was lifted and carried on the wind; he was flung into the air and carelessly dropped back on the earth' (178).

Williams as narrator comments on this scene that 'the place of the lamb [was] in the place of the lion' (177). Lion and lamb are to come together in the final scene of Anthony/Adam's naming of the animals, as he lays his hands on the head of the lamb while the lion 'paused by him' (204). Williams' referencing of the tiger and the lamb in Blake's 'contrary states' is apparent, as well as his invoking of the vision of the holy mountain in Isaiah 11:6–7, 'the wolf shall lie down with the lamb [...] the calf and the lion and the fatling together'. All the virtues and passions, symbolized in the animals, are to be held in balance, and we catch just a hint that this theme *could* give way to the deeper notes of exchange and substitution; but it is not yet so. Again, the problem of making equilibrium the large, comprehensive idea arises in this novel, because—as in the previous two—it tends to be equated with submission to some higher Will or Necessity. When Damaris asks, 'What is our necessity?', prompted by Anthony's use of the word, Anthony responds, 'If the pattern's arranged in me, what can I do but let myself be the pattern?', recalling his earlier characterization of every person as 'a pattern of the Powers'. He hastily adds, showing some discomfort with his own answer, 'Let's [...] talk of this another day' (196).

11.4 Movement, Equilibrium, and Exchange: The Dance

Exchange and substitution have still not replaced balance and equilibrium in the fourth of Williams' published novels, *The Greater Trumps* (1932), although I suggest that the tendency towards them grows stronger. In place of the symbol of the eagle there stands the image of the dance. In his first novel,, there appeared the grotesque dance of death, but here the dance of the cosmos contains within itself both movement and equilibrium, flow and poise. The situation is portrayed by a set of perpetually dancing golden figures, which are kept in the house of the aged magus, Aaron Lee. Early in the book, Aaron's grandson, Henry, views the figures, 'all in movement':

Gently and continuously they went, immingling, unresting—as if to some complicated measure, and as if of their own volition. There must have been nearly a
hundred of them, and from the golden plate on which they went came a slight
sound of music—more like an echo than a sound—sometimes quickening,
sometimes slowing, to which the golden figures kept a duteous rhythm[.]   (28)

The figures correspond to an ancient set of Tarot cards, consisting of four suits—
sceptres, swords, cups and coins—the fool, and 'the Greater Trumps', the latter
in a Tarot pack being additional to any usual set of playing cards, and consisting
of twenty-one extra picture cards. Aaron explains that the figures are the
'originals' of the particular pack that matches the dancers, and that this pack is
the 'original' of all Tarot cards. If the ancient cards and the figures can be
brought together, it will be possible to interpret the message of the dance, and
Aaron thinks that the interpreter will thus be able to predict the future. The cards
of the Greater Trumps are key here, for 'they are the meaning of all process and
the measure of the everlasting dance' (21). While nearly all the figures are in
motion, two embody a poise or equilibrium. First, the Fool in the middle of
the field:

It was still: it alone in the middle of all that curious dance did not move, though it
stood as if poised for running; the lynx or other great cat by its side was
motionless also [. . .]. And all about them, sliding, stepping, leaping, rolling,
the complex dance went on.   (30)

The phrase from T. S. Eliot comes to mind, 'The still point of the turning world',
and indeed Eliot once confessed that he got the idea from the figure of the Fool in
The Greater Trumps.[39] The second figure is the Juggler, who does move but still
maintains an equilibrium:

The Juggler [. . .] danced continuously round the edge of the circle, tossing little
balls up and catching them again; [. . .] a dexterity of balance, a flight and a
falling.   (29, cf. 98)

Henry has discovered that the crucial, ancient Tarot pack is owned by
Mr Coningsby, the father of the young woman to whom he is unofficially engaged,
Nancy. When he refuses to sell it, and is not convinced to give the pack up by
witnessing the golden dance, Henry plans to kill him in order to possess the cards.
His method of killing is to raise wind and snow while Coningsby is outside,

---

[39] In conversation with Helen Gardner: see Lindop, *Charles Williams*, 215.

making a storm by beating in the air with the Tarot cards, whose four suits represent the four elements. Nancy, however, sees the figures of the Tarot let loose and tries to stop him by holding his hands, out of love for both her father and for Henry; the result is that most of the cards are lost into the whirlwind, and natural and supernatural riot rule everywhere, threatening apocalypse on the whole world.

The advantage of the image of the dance is that it can express both movement and balance, and the relation between them. When the Coningsby family views the dancing figures in the house of Aaron, Mr Coningsby asks why the one in the middle (the Fool) does not dance, and Henry responds:

We imagine that its weight and position must make it a kind of counterpoise,'
[...] 'Just as the card of the Fool—which you'll see is the same figure—is numbered nought.   (73)

Yet Nancy's aunt Sybil sees the Fool move, commenting:

it's moving so quickly I can hardly see it—there—ah, it's gone again. Surely that's it, dancing with the rest; it seems as if it were always arranging itself in some place which was empty for it. [...] It certainly seems to me to be dancing everywhere.   (74)

Aaron is incredulous, exclaiming 'None [...] has ever seen the Fool move. [...] Why should this woman be able to see it?' (85). Henry's explanation is that, like the Fool, she lives serenely in a counterpoise of the spirit: 'She possesses herself entirely; [...] She's got some sort of a calm, some equanimity in her heart' (85–6). She has no desire, like Aaron, to know the future, since 'everything's complete for her in the moment'. Earlier he had commented that 'Nothing puts her out; nothing disturbs her' and she has 'found [her desire] and stands within it, possessing it perfectly'. This is why she 'can read the movements rightly' (35, 86).

In Chapter 13 of this book, I want to tease out the implications of this image of the dance for the Christian symbol of the Trinity, and for the possibilities of participating in the triune God. The Juggler seems to represent the *Primum Mobile* of medieval cosmology, the first reality to be moved, which then moves the other spheres (balls). The Fool thus represents God, or at least the divine principle at the origin of all things, who in traditional metaphysics—which Williams is challenging—remains unmoving but who is the cause of movement in everything. In this chapter, however, I want to follow the images of movement and equilibrium that, for the first three novels, have been the main linguistic resource for Williams' portrayal of human existence in the world. Sybil knows that the Fool, like the Juggler, perfectly combines motion and balance ('always arranging itself in some place which was empty for it'), though in different ways. It is not altogether clear whether Eliot, in his borrowing, grasps that the 'still point' is also moving, but he does indicate that 'arrest' does not sufficiently describe it:

> At the still point of the turning world. Neither flesh nor fleshless;
> Neither from nor towards; at the still point, there the dance is,
> But neither arrest nor movement. And do not call it fixity[...].
>   Except for the point, the still point,
> There would be no dance, and there is only the dance.[40]

Nancy shares something of Sybil's gift, for when Sybil sees the Fool move, she too has a sense of the same reality, though without such clear vision: 'it doesn't seem to be moving—not exactly moving. [...] In a way I feel as if I expected it to.' Henry retorts rather abruptly, 'Why should you expect it to?' (75). That is the key question: the expectation arises out of her nature, as does Sybil's sight. Later, Nancy does see the Fool moving, meeting the Juggler, and embracing (102). She is, crucially, going to show poise and counterpoise in the moment when she saves the world from dissolution in the apocalyptic storm. Using the remaining cards in the pack, she enters the 'golden cloud' of the dancing figures with Henry, to see what can be rescued from the disaster. Henry cannot combine movement with stillness, and having set the elements in chaotic and hostile motion with his beating hands is now simply immobilized, fixed rigidly in one place like the Tower of Babel portrayed on one of the Tarot cards. But Nancy is able to use her hands to hold back the storm and to balance the conflicting elements:

> [T]he warm hands of humanity in hers met the invasion and turned it. They moved gently over the storm; they moved as if in dancing ritual they answered the dancing monstrosities that opposed them. It was not a struggle but a harmony, yet a harmony that might at any moment have become a chaos. [...] She stood above the world, and her outstretched and down-turned palms felt the shocks, and she laughed aloud. [...] Danger itself was turned into some delight of love.   (104–6)

We may compare Hopkins' vision of Christ in the storm in 'The Wreck of the Deutschland': 'Thy unchancelling poising palms were weighing the worth / [...] Storm flakes were scroll-leaved flowers, lily showers.'[41] The hands that come out of the golden cloud (164–5),[42] which hold Henry static and work with Nancy's hands are not only a creative force, but also resemble Hopkins' 'poising palms'.

---

[40] T. S. Eliot, 'Burnt Norton' (1935), *Four Quartets*, in Ricks and McCue, *Poems of T. S. Eliot*, I, 181.

[41] Hopkins, 'Wreck of the Deutschland', stanza 21.

[42] In medieval art, the hand of God emerges from a cloud, as a reverent evasion of the portrayal of the whole divine figure; the earliest known example is in the murals of the mid-third-century Dura Europos Synagogue.

The conjunction of motion with equipoise has been felt earlier by the two women as they travelled in a car to visit the house of Aaron. For the men, comments the narrator, the movement of the car meant 'movement to something'. But for the women, 'it was much more like movement *in* something' (54):

> There was nowhere to go but to that in which they each existed, and the time they took to go was only the measure of delight changing into delight. In that enclosed space a quadruple movement of consciousness existed, and became, through the unnoticeable, infinitesimal movements of their bodies, involved and, to an extent, harmonized. Each set up against each of the others a peculiar strain; each was drawn back and controlled by the rest. Knowledge danced with knowledge, sometimes to trouble, sometimes to appease, the corporeal instruments of the days of their flesh.   (55)

Here we can detect the phenomenon of balance—'each was drawn back and controlled by the rest'—modulating towards the metaphysics of exchange: 'knowledge danced with knowledge'. And if this is true of something as banal as a car journey, it is even more the case in the dance itself. The image of dancing naturally lends itself to ideas of exchange, each partner taking from the other and giving in turn; and Henry has already stated that all beings participate in the dance ('everything is among the dancers'), while not everyone knows the dance from within.

There is a hint of the process of exchange, when Henry reflects, again early on in the story, that 'all things are held together by correspondence, image with image, movement with movement: without that there could be no relation and therefore no truth'. He therefore urges Nancy, 'It is our business—especially yours and mine—to take up the power of relation' (44). By this he means the relation between the figures and the cards, or between both and the elements of the world, but she takes it in a different sense, responding, 'Darling... How couldn't I know *that*? I didn't need the cards to tell me.' She understands the 'correspondence' and the 'power of relation' to be the love that is between them, and when she speaks 'he paused, arrested'. The narrator comments that 'it was as if she had immediately before her something which he sought far off'. (44) It is, in fact, surprising that Williams does not develop the image of the dance more in the direction of exchange, especially in love. The dance of the Tarot figures of the two lovers 'through and with all the other figures' has a 'joined beauty', and after separating for a period they meet again and 'mingle'; they approach the Fool who 'stood still as though he waited', and yet for all this the climax of the dance is not a blissful union but an encounter with the skeleton, death (102–3). Nevertheless, the Fool and the Juggler run towards each other to embrace, and 'the tossing balls fell over them in a shower of gold' (103).

We approach a clearer vision of exchange with the scene in church on Christmas morning, when Nancy feels its ethos of equipoise and balance. 'Strain and stress were everywhere; the very arch held itself together by extreme force' (106). As she kneels down she feels herself part of the cosmic dance, herself a 'conjunction of the images whose movement the cards symbolized', and she notices for the first time that an ordinary church service contains 'so much singing, so much *exchanging* of voices, so much summoning' (109, my italics). Among the 'dancing words', in affirming the Trinity in the Athanasian Creed, 'the men and boys of the choir *exchanged* metaphysical confidences', daring each other, 'in a kind of rapture' to deny the Trinity or the Unity. Yet for all this witness of exchange, she also recalls that in the last phase of the dance of the lovers, each had danced with the skeleton 'separately' (108). Her attention is caught by a line of a hymn, 'Rise to adore the mystery of love', but she asks Sybil, 'Is it true?'

Later, when Nancy discovers that Henry, whom she loves, has tried to kill her father, whom she also loves, Sybil speaks to her in her pain. Sybil bids her try the way of exchange: 'You've got to live in them or let them die in you' (142). There appears here for the first time a phrase that Williams is to use at least three more times in his works to express the reality of exchange, and which he attributes to Heracleitus: 'dying each other's life, living each other's death'.[43] She then bids Nancy, echoing the hymn line, to 'go and agonize to adore the truth of Love'. Sybil herself takes the hints of exchange to one definite moment of substitution in love, when, at the height of the apocalyptic storm, she heals Aaron's sprained ankle, 'loving and adoring' the Power that contained them both. 'Their eyes exchanged news' and 'his own fear passed through her being' (219).

In this novel, however, the emphasis has not yet tipped towards exchange and substitution, despite the potential of the image of the dance.[44] Sybil's act of substitution is not central to the plot of the novel; it happens in the storm, but it is not a means of calming it. Nancy's action in entering the dance is salvific, but— as in previous novels—there is no mention of substitution at a point when one might expect it. At the point when the storm has been turned, Nancy is pulled across the table of dancers by Joanna, the half-mad sister of Aaron, as if she were being laid on an altar. Joanna is frantic with grief because of the loss, years ago, of a child whom she believed to have been the expected Messiah who could have become the master of the dance. She has the fantasy that the child is hidden in Nancy, and as she savagely scratches Nancy's hand, to draw blood and 'let him out', Nancy takes the firm decision to 'adore the mystery of love' and to love her

---

[43] In 'Bors to Elayne: on the King's Coins', *Taliessin*, 45; *Forgiveness of Sins*, 120–1; 'The Founding of the Company', *Region*, 38.

[44] Cavaliero, *Charles Williams: Poet*, 78, finds the symbolism is not fully worked out, and suggests Williams was 'overwhelmed' by his material.

(198–200). But there is no hint that she has determined to bear the burden of the other's fear and pain, even when Sybil assures Joanna that 'all's well, the child's found' (226), and Joanna now regards Nancy herself as the lost Messiah.

Once again, as in the previous three novels, we can see why the stress on balance and equilibrium is going to prove insufficient. It is too much bound up with submission to the Necessity, with all its conceptual problems. Henry had instructed Nancy that the measure of the dance was remorseless, 'knowing nothing of joy or grief' (94). Yet the grief of Joanna registers a protest against this, with a 'wail that went up from the depths of the world [. . .] an antique misery was poised, and from the descent, from the house, from the earth, the sound of that universal distress misery beyond telling lamented and complained' (224–5). We recall Williams' own later complaint to Lewis, when he wrote about the dance of life: 'I do not want to be shown that pain is, or may be, a good, that (given our present state) its inevitability is a good.'[45] Williams recognizes that his emotions are in conflict with his reason—which tells him, instructed by Lewis, that suffering *is* a good—but the conflict remains to the last novel.

In each of the first four published novels of Williams, he has selected a symbol around which the action and characters are grouped—the Grail, the Stone, the Eagle (which is more central than the Lion), and the Dance. Perhaps, having begun with a powerful symbol, he was inclined to repeat the pattern. In seeking for what Eliot called linguistic 'resources' he has played variations on the motifs of movement and equilibrium, moving gradually towards the themes of exchange and substitution. The latter, which are to become so significant to Williams elsewhere in his work are as yet muted notes, and the issue of Necessity threatens discord. How Williams might resolve all this we shall discover in the next three novels.

---

[45] See Chapter 2, section 2.

12

From Exchange to Co-inherence

Three More Novels of Charles Williams

'If only he cd. be induced to write more fiction and less criticism!'[1] C. S. Lewis'
judgement of what was really valuable about Williams' authorship seems to have
been prompted by the slow progress of his novel-writing after the appearance of
the fourth novel in quick succession in 1932. It would take thirteen years for three
more to emerge, and while the first appeared within a year, it had already been
written in a first draft in 1925.[2] In Chapter 11, we traced Williams' search for
linguistic 'resources' of expression, bearing in mind Eliot's caution that 'What he
had to say was beyond his resources, and probably beyond the resources of any
language'.[3] I am considering the novel of 1933 and the final two novels of 1937 and
1945 as a group because none follows any longer the rather formulaic pattern of a
central symbol that characterizes the first four. The search for resources will
henceforth take a different form.

12.1 Transmuting Desire in a Parody of Romantic Love

The next published novel marks an interruption in the development of ideas of
balance and equilibrium towards exchange and substitution that we find in the
first four novels. As the earliest of the novels in origin, the first version of *Shadows
of Ecstasy* was drafted in 1925, was rejected by Faber, and was finally published in
revised form in 1933, Gollancz having been persuaded to consider it in the light of
sales of the previous novels. Although it was extensively revised by Williams in
1932, it was still refused by Gollancz in July 1932, but after further revision was
accepted in the autumn. It clearly bears the marks of the period of its first draft,
when Williams was preoccupied with developing his theology of romantic love,
and although it is something of an 'outlier', it provides a testing ground for
variations on the theme of exchange.

---

[1] CSL to T. S. Eliot, 10 March 1943, Lewis, *Letters* 2: 562.
[2] The first to appear, *War in Heaven*, had already been written in 1926.
[3] Eliot, 'Introduction', xi, xiii.

Charles Williams and C.S. Lewis: Friends in Co-inherence. Paul S. Fiddes, Oxford University Press. © Paul S. Fiddes 2021.
DOI: 10.1093/oso/9780192845467.003.0012

As a throwback (though revised) to 1925, it presents a puzzle. It is an unsettling and disturbing novel because the key figure, Nigel Considine, is promoting an ideology that appears to be a distortion—even a perversion—of Williams' theology of love, and yet the reader is left with the impression that the novel overall offers an essentially sympathetic account of him. This charismatic figure wins over to his cause another key character, Roger Ingram (a Professor of English literature), who—in his passion for poetry—seems to be a version of Williams himself. The novel ends with Ingram's reflection that, with the death of Considine, the world has 'subdued its fiercer desires to an alien government of sterile sayings', and that it could be 'delivered' (as well as 'threatened') by the second advent of Considine, restored to life as a Messianic figure of 'advancing humanity' and 'shining lucidity'.[4] The very last sentence of the novel offers us the wistful note, 'If, ah beyond, beyond belief!—but if he returned...', recalling Hopkin's exclamation about the energy of the Holy Spirit in the world: 'with ah! Bright wings'.[5] Thomas Howard judges that 'Williams is enthralled by Considine', and concludes that 'this leaves the reader with the suspicion that the author was not entirely in control of things'.[6] I suggest that teasing out the conundrum of this novel, out of time though it is, will throw some light on the journey Williams is taking through his novels in the 1930s, especially since this one was heavily revised in 1932.

Considine, who is 200 years old, has been overcoming death through a 'transmutation of energies', taking the passion evoked in him 'by poetry or love or any manner of ecstasy' and transforming it 'into the power of a greater ecstasy' (23). He is the 'High Command' of a group of African nations who have declared their freedom from the colonial rule of Europe, and who have threatened the European powers—especially London—with a coordinated attack if they refuse to liberate them. It transpires that Considine aims to use this emancipated territory to set up schools that will teach his method of 'transmutation'. The manifesto of the coalition, evidently written by Considine, condemns not only colonial oppression but also the bankrupt western intellectual and rational tradition, espousing instead the way of passion, art, poetry, and imagination, promising the 'conquest of death in the renewed ecstasy of vivid experience' (40). A key sentence in this document appeals for the support of all those who 'at this moment exist in the exchanged or unexchanged adoration of love' (41), which has obvious resonances with Williams' theology of romantic love. Swept up into the events of this movement are Roger Ingram, the explorer Sir Bernard Travers, Sir Bernard's son Philip, a Christian priest named Ian Caithness, and an exiled Zulu king, Inkamasi. They all, with the exception of Inkamasi, first meet Considine at a dinner where Ingram is

---

[4] Charles Williams, *Shadows of Ecstasy*, 223.   [5] Gerard Manley Hopkins, 'God's Grandeur'.
[6] Howard, *Novels*, 76. McLaren, Problem', 109–27, draws attention to the moral ambiguities in the portrayal of Considine; also see Borrow, 'Affirmation', 342–3.

giving a lecture, which Ingram ends with quoting from Shakespeare's Cleopatra, 'I will encounter darkness as a bride / And hug it my arms.'

Considine asks Ingram, 'And with what passion [. . .] do you yourself encounter darkness?' and this leads to his explanation of the way that he transforms passion into perpetual life. Despite his appeal to the notion of 'exchange' in love (the phrase is repeated twice more in quick succession),[7] his method of 'transmutation' seems to be the opposite of the exchange between partners that becomes characteristic of Williams' doctrine. In his *Outlines of Romantic Theology* (written in 1924), the word 'exchange' appears only once, in 'a mutual exchange of contemplative delight which we call love',[8] and Considine's reference to existing in the 'exchanged adoration of love' may owe something to Williams' development of romantic love in the later 1920s and early 1930s. Presumably the appeal to those who 'exist in the *unexchanged* adoration of love' refers to those who seek for such an exchange and have not yet received it. However, the 'transmutation of energies' in Considine's gospel undermines the act of 'exchange' altogether, whenever Williams developed the idea. For Considine, transmutation means turning this ecstatic experience inward, to reinforce the life of the individual rather than the life of the other. Transmutation means pouring the energy of love, poetry, and imagination into one's own life,[9] to build up a kind of Nietzschian 'superman' who can vanquish death, either by living on for hundreds of years or by returning to life after dying (a feat nobody actually achieves in the story). The ecstasy of the lover's vision is thus only a 'shadow' of true ecstasy (153, 155), and the very title of the novel announces this perspective. Joy and anguish alike are to be turned into 'strength and will' (180); adepts are to be 'lords of the spirit, postulants of eternity' (209).

In *Outlines of Romantic Theology*, Williams mentions the experience when the glow of glory fades from a lover, when he or she takes on a 'dull and uninteresting appearance', and yet one can still say of them, 'This also is He'—that is, 'the Love they serve', whose name is the Christ.[10] The phrase 'These too are He!' occurs in a poem in Williams' *Windows of Night* (1925), where lovers affirm the 'Love that is He and is ourselves / And all the bonds between!'.[11] 'This also is He' is shortly to be expanded into the often used coupling 'This also is Thou; neither is this Thou,' and in this form it appears in *War in Heaven* (1926).[12] In the Beatrician vision, 'This also is Thou' turns the lover outwards from himself to affirm the divine image in the other.[13] Yet Considine explains that the result of the transmutation of energy is that one can say 'This also is I.' A boy jilted by a girl can turn the

---

[7] Williams, *Shadows of Ecstasy*, 12, 41, 43, 44.   [8] Williams, *Outlines*, 33.
[9] Williams, *Shadows of Ecstasy*, 83, 203.   [10] Williams, *Outlines*, 53.
[11] Williams, 'Counsels of Perfection', *Windows of Night*, 62.
[12] Williams, *War in Heaven*, 137, 240.   [13] See, later, Williams, *Figure of Beatrice*, 8, 37, 111.

experience inwards and say 'This also is I—all this unutterable pain is I, and I grow everywhere through it into myself' (202). Ingram accepts this teaching, and reflects shortly afterwards that 'The great passions swept through him unrecognized till far off he saw the glory of their departure, and cried out, 'That was I!' (205).

 This gospel according to Considine is, however, deconstructed at several points in the text. One is the actual description of a Beatrician moment, which clearly shows the pattern of 'This also is He/Thee' and not 'This also is I.' Three of the previously published novels have included something like a moment when some-one beloved (not necessarily a sexual love) is seen in glory. In *Many Dimensions*, as Chloe is transfigured by aligning her will with that of the Stone, 'her eyes shone on her mortal master with an unchanged love and in the Glory that revealed itself there was nothing alien to their habitual and reciprocal joy'.[14] In *The Place of the Lion*, Damaris finds that 'a glory attended' Anthony when she sees him with the eagle on his shoulder,[15] and he later tells her that 'they will look in you as a mirror to see the Glory of God that is about them'.[16] He calls her an 'Image of sanctity', and in *The Greater Trumps*, Sybil remarks that Nancy is in a 'state of sanctity' because 'she's in love'.[17] However, it is in this novel, in the adoration of Philip for his fiancée Rosamond, that there is the clearest and most extended account of the vision of the beloved exalted in glory, however objectively unworthy she might be of sanctification. In Rosamond's case, that means very unworthy indeed, as she is presented as empty-headed, and more concerned with the image she presents to the world than with love itself.

But for Philip, her 'firmamental arm' (137) is a 'line, a curved beauty, a thing that spoke to both mind and heart; a thing that was there for ever' (56). In his Arthurian poetry, Williams is to give the same vision to Palomides when he sees Iseult's arm,[18] and to Bors viewing the 'channel' of Elayne's arm;[19] and he himself writes to one young woman about 'the movement of the light, of which your arms are the paths'.[20] The result for Philip is to turn his attention outwards from himself:

> Then as she stretched out her arm again he cried out that she was perfect, she was more than perfect; the movement of her arm was something frightfully import-ant, and now it was gone. He had seen the verge of a great conclusion of mortal things and then it had vanished. Over that white curve he had looked into incredible space; abysses of intelligence lay beyond it.   (56)

---

[14] Williams, *Many Dimensions*, 261–2.   [15] Williams, *Place of the Lion*, 134.
[16] Williams, *Place of the Lion*, 199.   [17] Williams, *Greater Trumps*, 41.
[18] Williams, 'The Coming of Palomides', *Taliessin*, 34. On women's arms as prompting the Beatrician vision, see Huttar, 'Arms and the Man', 61–97.
[19] Williams, 'Bors to Elayne; the Fish of Broceliande.', *Taliessin*, 24.
[20] Letter to Olive Speake ('Stella'), 10 July 1935, Wade CWP 78.

Rosamond's arm points him 'beyond', not within. Like God, she is a kind of centre whose circumference is nowhere, her eyes hold the secret origin of day and night, and the thing he had seen in Rosamond 'could not die' (36, 37, 99). There is an explicit parallel made with Dante's Beatrice in Philip's musings about his passion for Rosamond (46), where Beatrice is equated with theology as in the *Outlines of Romantic Theology* in 1924. But it is impossible to tell whether this passage dates from the first draft of the novel in 1925, or from Williams' renewal of interest in Dante in the early 1930s. The Beatrician vision is certainly given more emphasis in this novel than in the previous ones, and it stands against Considine's 'This also is I.' Philip, otherwise a prosaic and unimaginative young man, resonates with the phrase 'the exchanged adoration of love' in the African proclamation (47–8), as Roger's deep sense of the 'mystery of words' finds affinity with its affirmation of poetry, but in Considine's own mind these are energies to be respected and then turned to another purpose.

Other phrases in the novel underline this doubt thrown on Considine's 'gospel'. Isabel knows the secret of wanting what the beloved wants (163) and of suffering the beloved one's 'desolation' in 'vicarious grief' (218), thus hinting at a substitution in love for the other. In contrast to Considine's concern to foster the transhuman, there is mention several times of the Christian belief that victory only comes through the weakness of apparent defeat and despair. In preference to seeking 'a way of uniting yourself with God', Considine declares that human beings 'are themselves gods, if they will'.[21] But in mass at Lambeth, through which Inkamasi is wakened out of the slumber cast on him by Considine, there is a celebration of 'the formula by which Christendom has been defined'—that is, the 'resurrection of man [only] in God' (104). When Inkamasi chooses to die through taking a poisoned chalice offered to him by Considine, he does so to honour the 'high and holy office' of his kingship, which he thinks will never be recognized in a life in Europe. He explicitly rejects Considine's invitation to 'seek the way by which man descends living into the grave and returns', responding that 'I will not seek it [...] It has been opened once and it is enough' (182).

There are indications, also, that Considine is manipulating the imagination and the vision of love for his own ends. He appears to be 'using' the moment of ecstasy in love, beauty, and poetry (108), and such 'use' is heavily criticized in other novels, as in Henry Lee's attempt to use the cards and Nancy's sympathy with them. He exults in the self-sacrifice of his African troops, and seems to have little compunction in running them over in his car, declaring that 'they die for the Master of Death' (152). When he is finally shot dead by Colonel Mottreux, his closest military lieutenant and now his Judas, in a conspiracy with the Caiaphas figure of the Christian priest, many of his adepts 'abandon themselves' to a passion

---

[21] Williams, *Shadows of Ecstasy*, 180. Cf. Psalm 82:6, where 'gods' refers to the members of the heavenly court.

of greed. He had been teaching them to use passion, and even the experience of the death of another as a means of 'interior enlargement', and their inability to do so casts doubt in the effectiveness of his programme (215). He has utterly failed in his urging of Mottreux to transmute his desire for the jewels that are the cause of the murder (193).

Yet the narrator of the story never directly criticizes Considine, and through his character Roger he actually appears—at least partly—to approve of him. Considine's imaginative gospel is contrasted with the dogmatism of the priest, the pragmatic 'guessing' of the prime minister, the rationality of Sir Bernard, and the prosaic dullness of Philip's business occupation. Positive admiration of Considine is voiced through the consciousness of Ingram and his silent reflections. We are being called to make our own verdict upon the portrayal of Considine, and in the end this amounts to a judgement of Ingram himself; we are called to assess what Ingram, a poet like Williams, obviously believes to be Considine's contribution to the ineffable reality that poetry tries to describe with a phrase such as Milton's 'and thus the filial Godhead answering spake', a line that Ingram several times repeats as the quintessence of poetry (78, 79, 125, 204). All this makes reading the novel an ambiguous experience.

For instance, what are we to make of Ingram's version of exchange? Standing by King Inkamasi as he takes the deadly chalice, he evidently believes Considine's words that 'He dies for the sake of his kingship; we experience his death for the sake of making it part of our imaginations' (208). In Ingram's interior thoughts, 'he gave himself freely and wholly to the moment; he was to live the more completely through the king's death. [. . .] [H]is business was to live by it, as if necessary it would be the business of others to live by his death' (211). We catch an echo of the doctrine of exchange that Williams has been developing since 1924, and of the phrase 'dying each other's life, living each other's death' at the heart of it.[22] Yet it does not sound quite right: in the situation it is more a profiting by the experience of the other's death than a mutual exchange. It is certainly not yet a substitution in love.

The ambiguity of the narrator's attitude towards Considine perhaps derives from the closeness of his doctrine of 'the transmutation of energies' to William's own view of the sublimation of sexual desire in order to make poetry.[23] Considine is experimenting with the transmutation of many other energies and emotions beyond the sexual, including poetry and the witnessing of death, and this seems to echo the interest in 'transmutation' of passions that was circulating in the

---

[22] Williams, *Greater Trumps*, 121; 'Bors to Elayne: on the King's Coins', *Taliessin*, 45; *Forgiveness*, 120–1; 'Founding of the Company', *Region*, 38.

[23] See Chapter 1, section 4.

company around A. E. Waite in the aftermath of 'The Golden Dawn'.[24] It may be that Williams is trying out what a character would look like who lived by the *extremes* of transmutation. For Williams himself, the transmutation of desire in love coexisted with something more outward-looking—knowing a transcendent reality through the beloved, as in Dante's, and even Philip's, love-vision. An experiment in portraying an extreme practice of transmutation might, therefore, well lead to ambivalence.

But there is something else that Williams seems to want to experiment with in Considine, something that fits into the development of this thought towards exchange and substitution at this time, and places the revised text of *Shadows of Ecstasy* in the sequence of his novels. Standing with Inkamasi as he dies, Ingram remembers waiting for Isabel, his wife, to respond to him in the early days of their love, and of his passion for poetry that rises from 'the abyss' (96). Response to love and to poetry are both a matter of 'waiting upon necessity'; 'he had chosen necessity; so he had submitted his obedience to the authority of Milton or Wordsworth, waiting for the august plenitude of their poetry to be manifested within him' (211). With the issue of submission to Necessity we are on the familiar ground of the early novels, and the word 'waiting' evokes what was previously expressed by 'poise' and 'equipoise'. We have just witnessed Caithness struggling with the same theme of Necessity, though as a priest he examines it in terms of doctrine:

The most difficult texts for him to explain away had always been those that obscurely hint at the origin of evil in the Unnameable [...] [such as] the dark question of Isaiah, 'Shall there be evil in the city, and I the Lord have not done it?' He was always trying to avoid Dualism, and always falling back on the statement that Omnipotence might permit what it did not and could not originate, yet other origin (outside Omniscience) there be none. It is true he always added that it was a mystery, but a safer line was to insist that good and evil were facts, whatever the explanation was.   (196)

This is a virtual recapitulation of the conversation of the Archdeacon, Mornington, and the poet-duke from *War in Heaven*, even to the citing of the same text from the Book of Amos.[25] It surely belongs to the revisions of 1932, as do the reflections of Ingram. Howard makes the observation that 'This is a heavy burden for fiction to carry', and judges that 'the story sags under its weight'. He aptly judges that 'it plants in our mind the uneasy suggestion that room might be found in the

---

[24] Waite, *Hidden Church*, presents the 'transmutations' of alchemy, the Holy Grail and the Eucharist as symbols of the 'inward conversion' in the soul (545, 550, 663); the 'transmutations' of reason, motives, concupiscence, and self-interest, together with will, aspiration, and desire, will consequently prolong life in the body (547).

[25] Williams, *War in Heaven*, 180–1.

darkness of the Unnameable for Considine and his like'.[26] But his conclusion that 'the drama is in ruins' does not follow. Williams is precisely exploring the *ambiguities* of the origin of evil in 'the Necessity', and Considine, in his ambivalence, is a focus for them. But raising the doctrinal conundrum does make apparent once again, as in the first four novels, that a comprehensive vision is needed that does not imply a submission to Necessity.

In discussion after his lecture on Karl Barth, in March 1939, as recorded by Raymond Hunt, Williams appears to have returned spontaneously to the issue of Necessity.[27] On the one hand, he tells his audience that the view that 'the Fall was necessary' is 'erroneous doctrinally'. Although it might be allowed 'in the greatest writers' in the form of an epigram, such as Dante's *necesse est* and the church's *O felix culpa* ('O happy fault'), even this is 'very dangerous country'. But then, immediately afterwards, in dismissing the 'heresy of Dualism', he comments that the church was driven back on the notion of 'the Father as the source', presumably of both good and evil. This discussion, not obviously flowing from the lecture on Barth, shows that the matter was in Williams' mind as something unresolved. An 'equilibrium' that comes from mere submission to God, destiny, or Necessity would thus never be satisfactory for Williams, and I suggest that he would never be satisfied in portraying it in a novel.

12.2 Substitution and the Search for Something More

After a gap of four years from the last novel, there appeared *Descent into Hell* (1937). Williams returns in this novel to the image of finding an 'equilibrium' or poise within the movement of the world that he had worked out in the first four, but it is now subordinated to the themes of exchange and substitution in love that stand firmly in the centre of the plot. The stress has shifted. The most striking instance of substitution, which I have already recounted in Chapter 1 (section 6), is the recognition of Pauline Anstruther that she is carrying the burden of fear of a martyred ancestor, while the poet Peter Stanhope is carrying her own fear for her. It is hardly possible to consider the idea of substitution in Williams' writings without referring to this story, which sets out the meaning of substitution so graphically. Here I want to explore the way that this major substitution is put in the context of other substitutions, how substitution is presented in contrast to false 'equilibriums', and how there is the search for some reality that includes substitution and exchange and yet is even more comprehensive. This quest, I have been suggesting, finds its goal in the dawning of 'co-inherence' on Williams' consciousness in 1938–9.

---

[26] Howard, *Novels*, 61.   [27] Wade RH Notebooks 20: 3748.

For most of the novel, ideas of 'equilibrium' and its analogue 'peace' appear in a negative way, presented in either false or inadequate forms. The novel begins with an amateur dramatic society on a residential estate in the countryside, 30 miles from London, called Battle Hill, built on land that was once an ancient burial tumulus. The society is rehearsing a pastoral verse-play by a renowned local resident, Peter Stanhope, and a young woman with ambitions to be a professional actor has pronounced views on its production. The director has remarked that a play must establish 'equilibrium' with its audience, and Adela Hunt insists that 'the equilibrium's in the *play*,[...] a balance of masses. Surely that's what drama is—a symbolical contrast of masses' (14). Unfortunately, her view of 'balancing masses' means depriving the words of significance, so that 'she arranged whole groups of words in chunks, irrespective of line and meaning, but according to her own views of the emotional quality to be stressed' (92). Another false equilibrium is in the constant sound of 'footsteps pattering over the hill'; these belong to Mrs Sammile, a sinister aged woman, who is always offering to give people what they desire, and who turns out to be Lilith, the mythical first wife of Adam. Her continual walking is a sign of her 'haste of a search for or a flight from repose'; the two movements contend with each other, and 'the contention was the only equilibrium of that haunter of the Hill' (70).

Mrs Sammile, suspended between these motions of the spirit, offers Pauline Anstruther a 'peace' that is a freedom from having 'to do anything for others any more'. While initially seduced by the prospect of becoming a secure 'tower of peace', Pauline rejects the temptation to lose herself in the dream Mrs Sammile offers, because she has promised Peter to become part of a web of substitution: 'that she would carry someone's parcel as hers had been carried' (110–11). Another resident of the hill, Lawrence Wentworth, a middle-aged historian, does succumb to the dream. Obsessed by Adela, he creates out of his desires a succubus in her image, and thinks that in this incestuous relationship (she is actually the child of his own frustrated sexual urges) he is 'entirely at peace', shutting out the demands of the wider City: 'there was no City unless he' (131). Yet another character enjoying an unsatisfactory peace is the ghost of a dead workman, who hanged himself in despair from the scaffolding around Wentworth's house while it was being built. Harassed during his life by a complaining wife and a contemptuous foreman, he has been granted a period alone, walking the 'dead town' in an 'interior quiet' in recompense for the hurts he had suffered. The narrator comments that 'Exchange had been given; temporal justice, for what it is worth, done', but that now the Mercy was calling him to leave his illusory peace and 'choose love' (118). Finally, at the very end of the novel, after Wentworth has been steadily descending into his own self-made hell of frustrated desire and professional jealousy, he experiences a 'suspense', a 'silence', a 'pause' in which expectancy fails, and then 'nothing happened' (122).

In contrast to all these instances of failed equilibrium and empty peace, the novel presents exchange and substitutions in love. Not all instances of exchange become the deliberate act of substitution: there are references to 'interchanges' and 'exchanged memory' between lovers, even between Adela and Hugh in their somewhat shaky partnership (79), and Pauline thinks of the gift that comes from the 'glory of public exchange, law of the universe and herself a child of the universe' (110). It is this interchange that Wentworth rejects in favour of cultivating himself (102, 127), in what looks like a parody of Considine. Exchange, however, takes on new intensity in the act of substitution. Between the moment when Peter Stanhope carries Pauline's burden of fear, created by her seeing a counterpart of herself, and the moment when she takes the burden of her martyred ancestor on herself, another notable substitution happens. Margaret, the wise grandmother of Pauline, sees in her dying hours an apparition of the dead workman and offers him the gift of love: 'she said with a fresh spring of pure love, "My dear, how tired you look"' (121). At this moment, Pauline comes in to be with her grandmother, and offers herself as a substitute for her grandmother's suffering. In words almost identical to those that Stanhope had spoken to her, she says, 'Let me do something, let me carry it. Darling, do let me help' (124). The narrator comments that 'The three spirits were locked together', and the implication is that Pauline's carrying, or offer to carry, the burden of her grandmother is being transferred to the dead man through her grandmother's act of love. They are 'locked together' in one substitutionary act, and the ghost moans a little, with 'the first faint wellings of recognized obedience and love'. Its groan links the participants with another, greater act of substitution on another hill:

> That moan was not only his. As if the sound released something greater than itself, another moan answered it. The silence groaned. They heard it. The supernatural mountain on which they stood shook and there went through Battle Hill itself the slightest vibration from that other quaking [...] The groan was at once dereliction of power and creation of power. In it, far off, beyond vision in the depths of all worlds, a god, unamenable to death, awhile endured and died.   (124–5)

Wentworth, gradually descending into the abyss, suspended on the rope from which the workman hanged himself, hears the groan, but closes his ears while 'the pain of a god passed outwards from the mountain depths' as if 'from the cross that stood upon a hill that was also of skulls,' and 'united itself with all spiritual anguish that received and took part with it' (134). The ghost of the dead man does profit from the act of exchange, achieved by the anguish of the crucified one, and at least offered by Pauline, making his way to London to reach some kind of reconciliation with his wife. It is there that Pauline sees and directs him on his journey, and there that his figure merges with that of her ancestor, shortly to benefit from her act of substitutionary love as her other self cries to the one burdened with fear of the coming fire, 'Give it to me, Jon Struther.' The narrator comments, 'She had lived without joy that he might die in joy' (170–1).

One further offer of substitution is made later on by Pauline, to Adela, as she lies in delirium after rushing in terror from the graveyard on the hill when graves break open. In her mind she must keep on running, but she cries to Pauline, 'I want to stop,' and recalling her acting in Stanhope's play, now imbued with a deeper meaning, exclaims, 'I want to know my part' (202). Pauline responds, 'Let me run for you' and 'let me go and learn your part'. The narrator comments:

> She was not quite sure, as she said it, whether this came under the head of permissible interchanges. She had meant it but for the part in the play, but this new fashion of identities was too strong for her; the words were a definition of a substitution beyond her. Adela's past, Adela's identity, was Adela's own. A god rather than she, unless she were inhabited by a god, must carry Adela herself; the god to whom baptism for the dead was made, the lord of substitution, the origin and centre of substitution, and in the sides of the mountain of the power of substitution the hermitages of happy souls restored out of substitution.   (203)

There is a sense here that there is a limit to substitution; it cannot extend as far as Adela wants.[28] It requires a 'god' to carry the whole person of Adela, as distinct from some of her emotions. But an opening is made towards this possibility with the phrase, 'unless she were inhabited by a god'. Something like this might indeed be possible with what Williams is later to call 'co-inherence', but we are not there yet. Other reflections made in the course of the novel also hint at something more than substitution, or at least a larger context of relations in which substitution forms an element. Margaret is becoming aware of 'a slowly increasing mass of existence made from herself and all others with whom she had to do' (71). Reflecting on her experience of carrying Jan Struther's burden, Pauline felt 'the hint of a new organization of all things; a shape, of incredible difficulty in the finding, of incredible simplicity found, an infinitely alien arrangement of infinitely familiar things'. She has a sense of some reality that contains all substitutions, whether among the living or among the dead: 'perhaps everything was all at once, and interchanged devotion [...]. It lived; it intermingled; not among these living alone did the doctrine of substituted love bear rule' (150–1).[29]

A little earlier the narrator had reflected on what was happening to Lawrence Wentworth, on the effects of his rejection of relations with others, and of his unhealthy relation with himself:

---

[28]   Stanhope mentions another limit to human substitution: 'he endured her sensitiveness but not her sin. The substitution there [...] is hidden in the central mystery of Christendom' (101). The mystical writer, Evelyn Underhill, however, told Williams he was mistaken in thinking it impossible for one human being to take on the sins of another: see Lindop, *Charles Williams*, 369.

[29]   On the intersection of worlds here, see Shideler, *Theology of Romantic Love*, 96.

Yet, in the order of the single universe known to myriads of minds, the time and place that belongs to each of those myriads has relation to others; and though the measurement of their experiences may differ, there is something common to them all in the end. Sometimes where time varies place is stable; or where places intermingle time is secure, and sometimes the equilibrium of both, which is maintained in so many living minds, swings into the place of the dead.   (131)

Some context is being appealed to here for which the words 'exchange' and even 'substitution' do not appear adequate. There is something common to the experiences of all, and—significantly—this takes up 'equilibrium' (here between time and space) into itself (123). In hindsight, 'co-inherence' fits this common area of experience, but Williams has not yet found the term. The most extended reference to this state comes towards the end of the novel in Pauline's meditation on the impression that Peter Stanhope's verse-play makes on her as she takes her part in staging it, in the character of Periel.[30] A word is selected by Williams to describe this all-embracing reality, comprehending even substitution in itself, and this is 'stillness'. Pauline finds that the poetry of the play 'proclaimed the stillness—the harmony of motion and speech', and the narrator comments 'that living stillness had gathered the girl into her communion with the dead' (180). Stillness is named as the very basis for substitution:

So salvation lay everywhere in interchange: since, by an act only possible in the whole, Stanhope had substituted himself for her, and the moan of a God had carried the moan of the dead. She acted, and her acting was reality, for the stillness had taken it over.   (181)

She now sees all the relations she has had, 'with her ancestor and with that other man more lately dead and with her grandmother' as existing 'burningly in the stillness [...] and the stillness was the fire'. Most strikingly, this 'stillness' is now compared to the life of the triune God, in the 'eternal contemplation' of each other by the persons of the Trinity:

The words were no longer separated from the living stillness, they were themselves the life of the stillness, and though they sounded in it they no more broke it than the infinite particles of creation break the eternal contemplation of God in God. The stillness turned upon itself; the justice of the stillness drew all the flames

---

[30]   Kirstin Jeffrey Johnson, 'Conversing', 17–39, proposes that 'Periel' is associated with *perichoresis*, and so co-inherence, on the basis that Pauline is the leader of the (dancing) chorus, and that 'Stanhope has been teaching her what Williams called the law of Co-inherence'. But (a) Williams has not yet found the term co-inherence; and (b) *perichoresis* does not mean 'to dance around': see Chapter 13, section 3. For Periel, perhaps Williams has combined Phyllis (Jones) with Shakespeare's Ariel (for Ariel, see *Descent into Hell*, 178).

and leaves, the dead and living, the actors and spectators, into its power [...].
The dance of herself and all the others ceased.   (186)

It seems clear that Williams has deliberately chosen 'stillness' at this point as the most comprehensive term he can find for the reality that embraces and transcends exchange and substitution. The word has only occurred, in any significant sense, about eight times in total in the first five novels.[31] It now appears eighteen times in the account of the performance and impact of Stanhope's play over just eighteen pages (and twice more elsewhere),[32] Stanhope, of course, being a version of himself.[33] The reader is bound to ask, however, whether 'stillness' is the right word. It seems very close to the 'equilibrium' or the 'peace' that to this point have been shown in essentially negative forms.[34] We will not be surprised that Williams is to discover another term that is more capacious and convincing, and is not just comparable to the 'eternal contemplation' within the Trinity but actually descriptive of it. In stillness, the dance will come to an end,[35] but in what will be called 'co-inherence', the dance eternally goes on; the Fool, who is the 'still centre' of the dance, also moves. Looking forward, earlier on, to the last act of the play, Pauline had actually visualized it, not as stillness, but as movement like that portrayed in *The Greater Trumps*:

the act in which physical sensation, which is the play of love, and pardon, which is the speed of love, and action, which is the fact of love, and almighty love itself, all danced together.   (147)

We notice that the word and idea of 'stillness' does not appear once in *Descent of the Dove* or in *The Figure of Beatrice*, once 'co-inherence' has come into Williams' mind. It does appear in the final novel, but in ambivalent form, as we shall see.

Perhaps Williams is able to make 'stillness' the ultimate category in this novel, however inadequate it is, because he has avoided equating it with submission to an eternal Will or Necessity in the way he has associated equilibrium, balance, and poise in the previous novels. In fact, the note of Necessity is generally muted. Early on, Stanhope announces that goodness can be 'terrible' and 'terrifying' (16), and later he affirms that good 'contains terror, not terror good' (65). Pauline's

---

[31] I suggest *War in Heaven*, 76, 141; *Greater Trumps*, 76, 156, 192; *Shadows of Ecstasy*, 77, 103, 176.

[32] Williams, *Descent into Hell*, 178–86, and 124, 209.

[33] The title page of the first edition of Williams' play *Judgement at Chelmsford* lists 'Peter Stanhope' as author.

[34] However, the ghost of the suicide senses something that offers a 'peace ... of a different kind from the earlier revival of rest': *Descent into Hell*, 123.

[35] Urang, *Shadows of Heaven*, 92, finds that here eternity, or a 'supratemporal vision of the whole', overwhelms time and individuality.

grandmother concurs, declaring about their ancestor's dying cry, 'I have seen the salvation of my God', that 'Salvation is quite often a terrible thing—a frightening good' (55). There is, however, no suggestion that 'good contains evil'. A terrible good is not in itself an evil. With regard to the workman's suicide the narrator remarks that if the universe is good, 'its goodness is of another kind than ours' (28), but when Mrs Anstruther reflects that she had learned to accept 'what joys the universe offered', not trying to 'compel the universe to offer you joys of your own definition' (66), she does not add that one must accept *everything*. Moreover, some greater scope is given to human choice than in previous novels. After the dead workman has experienced love for the first time in the scene with Mrs Anstruther and Pauline, he begins a path towards London, and the narrator remarks that 'he knew he had already chosen, had come into obedience, and was no longer free'. Although he appears to have made a choice to obey the demand of love, the narrator qualifies this: 'In effect, the dead man's choice [...] had been less than it seemed. He could go, or he could wait to be driven' (152). Nevertheless, choice does matter. The narrator continues that the knowledge of what 'the end' is will be different according to whether someone hastens or delays their journey to it (153). All these are nuances that qualify a simple doctrine of Necessity, and make the injunction to 'be still' more tolerable.

While there are references to the 'exchange' between lovers, the outstanding instance of a Beatrician vision in this novel is linked not to these but to the act of substitution. When Pauline turns and views her counterpart, her other self, taking Jon Struther's burden of fear, she sees 'a glorious creature':

> It wore no supernatural splendour of aureole, but its rich nature burned and glowed before her, bright as if mortal flesh had indeed become what all lovers know it to be. [...] The glory of poetry could not outshine the clear glory of the certain fact... (171)

Shortly afterwards, as Stanhope meets Pauline, he sees her glory, quoting the biblical text 'Arise, shine; your light is come; the glory of the Lord is risen upon you' (173). The conjunction of the moment of glory with substitution makes clear that experiences of ecstasy in life are not intended, as Considine supposes, to be transmuted into the construction of one's own self, but belong to a self-sacrifice for the other. This lesson is rubbed home when Wentworth meets the ghost of the workman in his walk in the city of the dead under the hill, and gets an unwelcome jolt to his self-absorption, just like Beatrice disturbing Dante. The man was:

> inexorably advancing as the glory of truth that broke out of the very air itself upon the agonized Florentine in the Paradise of Eden: 'ben sem, ben sem, Beatrice' the other, the thing seen, the thing known in every fibre to be not the self, woman or beggar, the thing in the streets of the City. (88)

Wentworth protests, 'No, no; no canvassers, no beggars, no lovers.' But Williams as narrator makes clear that the 'glory of truth' is to give attention to the 'not the self'. This is the truth known by Stanhope and Pauline, who—while not lovers as the book ends—bid each other farewell with the words to be given in time to the Companions of the Co-Inherence, and now finally pieced together from earlier fragments: 'Under the Mercy.'[36]

12.3 The Context of Co-inherence

Given Williams' proclivity for repeating favourite words and phrases, it may seem puzzling that his final novel, *All Hallows' Eve* (1945), written in a period when he has been using the word 'co-inherence' freely, only contains the key word once. But Williams is *showing* something in this novel that depends upon his develop-ment of the idea of co-inherence, from *Descent of the Dove* (1939) through *The Forgiveness of Sins* (1942) to *The Figure of Beatrice* (1943) and *The Region of the Summer Stars* (1944). Co-inherence is the largely unspoken framework of plot, character, and theme, and the novel will not work without it. Williams has found the comprehensive concept and image for which he seems to be searching in *Descent into Hell*. Within this all-embracing context, earlier ideas of equilibrium, balance, glory, exchange, and substitution are held together and given new meaning. Williams moves naturally in the atmosphere of co-inherence; perhaps by now he feels that he has overworn the term itself, and intends to embody the idea without naming it.

At the dark centre of the novel, there is the attempt at a great reversal of all the realities that Williams' earlier favourite terms express. Considine might be seen as reversing the Beatrician vision of romantic love, by transmuting the ecstasy of lovers into an energy that builds up the self. Williams' attitude to him is, however, ambivalent. There is no ambiguity about the narrator's judgement of the Clerk Simon, a 'black' magician who self-consciously stands in the heritage of the Simon Magus mentioned in the Book of Acts (136; Acts 8: 9–24). By a ritual reversal of the Name of God, the Tetragrammaton, Simon intends to reverse all that Williams has previously meant by 'exchange'. As we shall see, this in turn can only be resisted by actions that rely on a co-inherence that exceeds even what has been previously affirmed about substitution in love. The exchange that Simon plans is the sending of his own daughter, Betty, into the world of the dead and the returning of a dead person into the world of the living: 'a balance must be preserved; where one was drawn in one must go out'(137).

---

[36] Williams, *Descent into Hell*, 78, 211. It is implied in CSL to Charles Williams, 23 September 1937, Lewis, *Letters*, 2: 219, that the formula was being used as a greeting by Williams by this time.

The time was very near, if his studies were true, at which a certain great exchange should be achieved. He would draw one from that world, but there must be no impropriety in numbers, either there or here; he would send one to that world. He would thus have a double magical link with infinity. He would begin to be worshipped there.   (100)

An exchange is indeed to be achieved, but not as Simon expects, for 'he knew nothing of the exchange of redeeming love that had taken place between those two' (Betty and her friend, Lester) (138). While the exchange of love is about self-giving for the sake of the other, Simon's exchange is a reversal of that; it is intended to give him power and domination in the worlds of the living and the dead.

The dead person whom Simon intends to exchange for the living is Lester Furnival, whom we meet at the beginning of the novel, suddenly transported into a silent and empty London through being killed by an aircraft crashing into the street where she was walking. Her relationship with her husband, Richard, had become uneasy through misunderstandings, but now, as they meet across the barrier of death, they experience a new 'interchanging joy' (164), and 'bodiless, she seemed to recall her body in the joy they exchanged' (152). In their exchange they experience the 'Beatrician vision' of each other; Lester remembers how, before her death, 'her heart had swelled for the glory and vigour of his coming' (123), and now, after her death, he wonders at 'the imperial otherness of her glory' and reflects that, like Dante meeting Beatrice, 'he must, it seemed, be born over again' (191). By contrast, the joyful exchanges of meeting are reversed by Simon. Together with Lester in the silent London of the dead is the spirit of Evelyn, a vindictive friend from school days who craves Lester's company and pity, and whose only satisfaction would be to make Betty as frightened of her as she used to make her at school. When Simon contacts Evelyn and decides to employ her in his schemes, they 'exchange' smiles of complicity in evil, and witnessing it, Richard is revolted:

> The exchanged smile, the mingling sound, was an outrage. [...] Yet there was only a smile—no pain, no outcry, no obscenity, except that something truly obscene was there. He saw, visibly before him, the breach of spiritual law.   (106)

A little later the narrator comments on 'the exchange of smiles—if that which had no thought of fair courtesy could be called exchange' (128).[37] As with exchange, substitution is also reversed by Simon from love into exploitation. He has been training Betty over the years to make visits into the country of the dead in order to

---

[37] Cf. 190, 'some remote frigid exchange between imbeciles'.

bring him news from the future: since the lands of the dead and the living continually intersect, she can walk through the one into the future of the other, and she does so as his 'substitute': 'up to now he had been content to send his daughter in her ghostly journeys as his messenger and in some sense his substitute' (136). Now she is to be sent without return, and this will require another substitution. While her body is to be retained by him as a continual point of contact with her released spirit, he will fashion a substitute body to be laid in a coffin and buried (137).

In contrast to these planned, perverted substitutions, a substitution in love thwarts his intentions. Lester and Betty have experienced the 'redeeming exchange' of forgiveness, Lester asking pardon for her thoughtless treatment of Betty at school and Betty gladly giving it, and so they are ready for Lester to take Betty's experience upon her during the magic ritual that Simon performs in order to send her permanently into the realm of the dead:

> Lester [...] was now incapable of any action except an unformulated putting of herself at Betty's disposal; she existed in that single act. It was then that she became aware that the Clerk was speaking to her.
>
> He did not think so. His intention and utterance were still limited to the woman on the bed. He was looking there and speaking there [...] [but] Lester felt the strange intoning call not to Betty but to her; it was she that was meant.   (142–3)

She feels herself being supported by something like a wooden frame, so that 'her arms, flung out on each side held on to a part of the frame, as along a beam of wood' (144). Her substitution is sharing in the great act of substitution by the crucified Christ. So far this account accords, movingly, with Williams' earlier thought about exchange and substitution, but he now takes a further step, consonant with his developed thought about co-inherence. Betty speaks her friend's name, and 'as the word left her lips, it was changed. It became—hardly the Name, but at least a tender mortal approximation to the Name.' It is this Name that contends with the sound of the reversed Tetragrammaton, the note striking out 'again and again, precisely in the exact middle of every magical repetition', and in this way 'it held just an equal balance, and made that exact balance a spectacular delight for any whose celestial concerns permitted them to behold the easy dancing grapple' (146). Into this account, Williams assumes his earlier images of balance and dance, but in a new context of analogy between the human name and the divine Name. It is the speaking, or singing, of the Name that 'makes the change' and causes Simon's magic to fail.

The Name might be the Tetragrammaton, but for any Christian writer mention of the divine 'Name' will always recall the 'Name of the Trinity'—the traditional formula in any Christian ritual being, 'In the Name of the Father, the Son and the

Holy Spirit'. For Williams, after his finding the term co-inherence, there is an analogy between human relations, such as that between Lester and Betty, and the internal relations of love within the triune God.[38] That Williams has this in mind becomes apparent when he goes on immediately afterwards to describe the way that Simon tries to rectify his failure, by enlisting the will of his lesser partner in magic, Lady Sara Wallingford, the mother of Betty. This was a mistake, comments the narrator, because she was merely subordinated to Simon, without also having 'exchanged that joyous smile of equality which marks all happy human or celestial governments, the lack of which had frightened Richard in Simon's own smile' (149). Then comes a comparison of Simon's relation to Lady Wallingford, embodied in the magic ritual, with that of the relations of the Trinity. The 'smile of equality' has

> existed because first the Omnipotence withdrew its omnipotence, and decreed that submission should be by living will, or perhaps because in the Omnipotence itself there is an equality which subordinates itself. The hierarchy of the abyss does not know anything of equality, nor of any lovely balance within itself, nor (if he indeed be) does the Lord of that hierarchy ever look up, subordinate to his subordinates, and see above him and transcending him the glory of his household. (149–50)

The 'equality which subordinates itself' within Omnipotence must refer to the eternal obedience of the Son to the Father within the Trinity, which nevertheless does not cancel out the equality of the three Persons. Radically, Williams works out this equality as a kind of reciprocal hierarchy, in which the one who subordinates others in one way is also subordinate to them in others ('subordinate to his subordinates'). While presumably this applies most obviously to the nature of human relations,[39] Williams is implying that it obtains within the 'celestial government' of God's own being.[40]

Williams raises exactly this point in the period of discussion at the end of his 1939 lecture on Karl Barth, as reported by Raymond Hunt.[41] Affirming the 'willing subordination of the Son, the willing subordination of the equal Person' in the Trinity, he quotes Milton's line, 'And thus the Filial Godhead answering spake.' Like his character Roger Ingram in Shadows of Ecstasy, he regards this as

---

[38] See Chapter 4, section 5.

[39] See Williams, 'Dialogue on Hierarchy', 129–30, and my discussion in Chapter 8, section 3. Lewis indexed this passage from All Hallows' Eve on the rear pastedown of his copy of the novel as 'Equality and hierarchy' (communication from Christine Murphy and Roger White at Azusa Pacific University, which holds the copy in its collection).

[40] In this concept of *mutual* subordination within the Trinity, Williams is even more daring than Karl Barth's statement of the eternal obedience of the Son to the Father, an 'above' and a 'below' in God: Church Dogmatics IV/1, 194–7.

[41] Wade RH Notebooks 20: 3749.

'one of the most marvellous phrases in the English Language', but here his appreciation is more than of the poetic cadence: it is a vision of the Trinity, confirming that this is indeed what Williams has in mind with his phrase 'an equality which subordinates itself'. Simon is defeated by the speaking of a human name (Lester) that is analogous to the divine Name, because there is a relation subsisting between the two girls that is analogous to the triune relations, or to what Williams has come to call the co-inherence.

The term itself occurs once, at the moment when Simon has fashioned magic-ally an endoplasmic body of a dwarfish woman as a 'refuge' to satisfy Evelyn who craves bodily form in the world of the living, and as a prison to 'trap' Lester, whom he wishes to prevent from interfering with any future attempt to kill Betty ritually. Lester consents to enter this misshapen body, but only as a generous gift to Evelyn who will not otherwise be allowed to have it. The narrator comments that 'The magical form which united them also separated; through it they co-hered to each other but they could not co-inhere' (196). Though the reference appears to be incidental, it is the tip that reveals the iceberg of an underlying mass of co-inherence, to which Lester consciously has allied herself, and which Evelyn is resisting.

The two images in which the mass—or better, web—reveals itself in the novel are the 'City' and the 'Waters'. The City had long been for Williams, even before 1939, an image for the network of exchanges that makes up human life.[42] Here, however, it exceeds in its complexity a sum total of separate exchanges. The City of London exists in many forms in the world of the dead, depending on the capacity of spirits for coexistence, and it also interpenetrates with all other cities in the realms of the living and the dead:

> There around her lay not only London but all cities—coincident yet each distinct; or else, in another mode, lying by each other as the districts of one city lie. She could, had she the time and her occasions permitted, have gone to any she chose—any time and place that men had occupied or would occupy [...]. For here citizenship meant relations and knew it.   (168)

This vision granted to Lester was only, the narrator stresses, 'a small part of the whole', since 'it was not for her yet to know the greater mystery. That waited her growth in grace...' Simon is said not to be 'able to enter that other world of pattern and equipoise' at all (169). Exceeding particular 'acts of exchange', there is the mystery of the sheer co-existence of all things. The *perichoresis* or co-inherence of the Trinity has been traditionally described as both *circumincessio*—a moving together, and a *circuminsessio*—a being 'seated' together. Each idea

---

[42] See Williams, *He Came Down*, 134–7.

illumines the other. 'Exchange' draws attention to movement (*circumincessio*), but a mutual interpenetration of *being* (*circuminsessio*) demands something like co-inherence. The integration of movement with being is even clearer with the second image Williams offers, that of flowing waters, a picture based on the river of the City, the Thames.

> Lester, looking down, saw in the river the sub-surface currents and streams. Below the exquisitely coloured and moving surface, the river by infinitesimal variations became lucid. [...] To her now all states of being were beginning to be of their own proper kind, each in itself and in its relationships [...]. So the Thames was still the Thames, but within it the infinite gradations of clarity deepened to something else. That other flow sustained and carried the layers of water above it; and as Lester saw it she felt a great desire to discover its source.   (197)

The flow of the river contains and yet unites 'infinite' streams of water, and the 'strong current beneath the surface' recalls to her the Name that she heard spoken during the magical ritual: 'the under-river sang as it flowed; all the streets of London were full of that sweet inflexible note—the single note she had heard in Betty's room'. (198) She is deeply saddened at this moment by the awareness that, as the streams of the river diverge, so she will shortly be parted from Richard, but she is also filled with the desire to find the source of this flow of life, where 'the lucid river flows into the earthly river' (198). When Evelyn finally rejects her and goes out into the dark night, Lester exclaims regretfully and generously that 'we might have found the waters together, she and I' (236). There is an interweaving movement of multiple 'states of being' depicted here that is more than 'exchange' can express, and again we hear between the lines the word of 'co-inherence'.[43] The image of water flowing through the city is connected with the triune Name and being of God through the 'lake' at the heart of the City from which Betty dreams several times about being lifted by a kindly woman; it transpires that her nurse had disobeyed Lady Wentworth when she was a baby by baptizing her herself, telling her that 'I marked you with [the water] and said the Holy Name'—which would have been the triune Name of God. In *Descent of the Dove*, Williams had written that a person is received into a state of 'supernatural co-inherence' through baptism, 'by the formula of The Trinity-in-Unity'.[44] Betty realizes immediately the meaning of the lake, and reflects, 'this then was what that strange rite called Baptism was—a state of being of which water was the material identity, a life

---

[43] St John of the Cross, 'Song of the Soul', in *Poems*, 43–5, describes the experience of the triune life of God as being immersed in water, feeling three currents or movements of 'delight', which intermingle and can nevertheless be distinguished from each other.

[44] Williams, *Descent of the Dove*, 234.

rippling and translucent with joy' (185). In the image of water there seems also, however, some resonance with Henri Bergson's theories of the 'flow' of life and time; Williams, we know, had recently read an essay by Jacques Maritain on Bergson and time.[45]

Jonathan Drayton, the artist who loves Betty, has had a similar vision of the City as Lester, and has made a painting of it that irritates Simon. Jonathan's art captures 'the massive radiance' of the city that 'flowed out towards [Richard] from the canvas', so that 'the inscape of the painting became central'—here the echo of Gerard Manley Hopkins' 'inscape' is unmistakable.[46] Jonathan thinks that the painting is changing before their eyes, and Richard finds that 'the shapes were more definite, that the mass of colour which had overwhelmed him before now organized itself more exactly, that the single unity was now also a multitudinous union'. For the 'multitudinous union' of distinct shapes we easily read 'co-inherence', and when Richard recognizes the 'weight' of the radiance, we recall the interest of both Williams and Lewis in 'the weight of glory'.[47]

The story comes to its climax with Simon's final attempt to send Betty permanently into the realm of the dead, though this time he resorts in desperation to more 'elementary' magic. Once again, we are presented with a reversed substitution as well as a genuine one. Simon fashions a doll from endoplasmic fluid as a substitute for Betty, and intends to kill her by stabbing it with a long needle. By accident, he stabs her mother's finger with the needle as she is holding the doll in the ritual, and as her blood seeps into the doll she realizes that she is, unintentionally, becoming a substitute for Betty. Wanting Betty dead, she wills him to stab her to death quickly, since 'she had a vague and terrible fear that the substitution might be so complete that Betty would not die' (217). However, she is finally to become a *willing* substitute. When Jonathan, Richard, Betty, and the dwarf-woman containing both Lester and Evelyn all burst in on Simon in the midst of the ritual, and when Simon tries to murder Betty with the needle, Sara Wentworth throws herself between them. She survives, but in a paralytic state, leaving her like a child to be cared for by Richard and Betty as long as she lives. The narrator comments that:

Since in that gift she had desired the good of another and not her own, since she had indeed willed to give herself, the City secluded her passion, and took her gift

---

[45] See Williams, 'The Jews', 161–3.

[46] Hopkins coins the term 'inscape' for the 'distinct form' of something. Williams refers to the term 'inscape' in his lecture notes on Hopkins, Wade CW/MS-214, 7, indicating that Hopkins uses it for 'opposition', followed by a note (possibly connected) on 'counterpointed morality and music=depth'. See Chapter 11, section 1, on 'balance' in Hopkins. As early as 1936, W. H. Gardner, 'Note on Hopkins', 326–30, had drawn attention to Hopkins' understanding of 'inscape' and its affinity to Duns Scotus' 'thisness' (*haecceitas*).

[47] See Chapter 2, section 3.

to its own divine self. [. . .] She was now almost in that state to which her master
had willed to reduce their child; the substitution was one of the Acts of the
City.   (238)

We notice that the City is a 'divine self', evoking co-inherence between the lines.
One of its Acts is said here to be substitution, and Betty continues this activity by
healing all the disciples of Simon whose diseases have savagely returned to them
now that their healer has perished miserably by his own magic, which has 'twisted'
against him. Her healing is an act in which she gives her energies for others, as the
'high heavenly power in her' was poured into these tormented beings, and 'so the
power, and still more quickly the joy of the power passed from her'. Significantly,
this is said to be possible because she has 'risen from the waters' (239).

The power of the 'Acts' of the City is presented in this novel in an ambiguous
way. On the one hand, the Acts are said to work unilaterally and to be finally
unevadable. As the night of All Hallows gives way to the day of All Saints, we read
that 'the Acts of the City took charge (228), and the return of the magical body to
its maker by breaking into Simon's house is said to be 'the operation of inflexible
law' (220). Looking at the rubbish floating on the surface of the Thames, Lester
reflects that 'corruption was tolerable' and 'all that happened . . . was good' (197).
On the other hand, when reflecting on the submission within the triune life of
God, the narrator declares that at the beginning of creation, 'the Omnipotence
withdrew its omnipotence, and decreed that submission [of creatures] should be
by living will' (149). In taking the dwarf-body to the crucial meeting with Jonathan
and Richard, we read about Lester that the Acts 'would, when the time came, see
that she spoke what she had to speak', but the narrator adds, 'for she was already
assenting to their will' (204). Assent, it seems, is needed, even by the Acts of
the City.

I have suggested earlier that equilibrium or balance as a desirable state of being
is associated in Williams' earlier novels with simple obedience to the divine Will,
but that Williams never resolves the question of whether this Will is an inexorable
Necessity, and so whether it is the ultimate origin of both good and evil. In *Descent
into Hell*, a refined version of equilibrium, stillness, is eventually presented as the
wider context for all exchange and substitution. But the last novel does not simply
continue this stop-gap solution. Stillness can be a positive value, as for example in
Richard's Beatrician vision when he sees Lester for the first time after her death; he
is held 'motionless', and 'the recognition was in her stillness'. The way she held her
hands in a 'stillness' that was natural shocked him into noticing her (47). When,
much later on, Lester generously shares the artificial body with Evelyn, she finds a
'new kind of silence, a sweet stillness' (196). But other references to 'stillness' carry
a sinister meaning, and especially the 'stillness' of the London that Lester finds
herself walking through immediately after dying. We read that Lester preferred
the 'immense' stillness to having to listen to Evelyn talking (19). The city lies in

stillness because Lester 'cared for the things people used rather than for people themselves' (14). It is a stillness that is static and lifeless. When Lester is later on redeemed from her previous self-enclosure, in her vision of the interpenetrating of London with all other cities, 'the dreadful silence she had known after death was no longer there' (167), but streets are bustling with the movement of their inhabitants.

In Williams' search for linguistic resources for what he wants to say, 'stillness' cannot be the final word that holds together the earlier 'equilibrium' and 'balance' with the now increasing sense of exchange and substitution. Williams has arrived at 'co-inherence', although this is *pictured* in the City and the Waters from which, and into which, Betty has been raised. Had Williams been able to write further novels, the association of these images with the triune, relational life of God would surely have been developed much further, reflecting Williams' portrayal of Taliessin's Company, which in this novel is parodied in Simon's household: 'its cult was the Trinity and the Flesh-taking'.[48] As it is, we are left at the end of this novel with the Waters pouring into Simon's hall of magic—water coming down from above in the form of rain, confusing Simon in his ritual, driving him down deeply into the enfolding petals of a rose of blood, melting the artificial body of Evelyn, and soaking and penetrating everything with life-giving energy. The blast of rain falls not only 'on', but 'through' them (234), embracing them with a flowing 'torrent' of water. 'Betty, still fresh from the lake of power, the wide waters of creation, lifted her face to it and felt it nourishing her' (234–5). In this moment, Lester bids them farewell, and enters a life that is full of co-inherent relations, with only the word missing:

[T]he approach of all the hallows possessed her, and she too, into the separations and unions which are indeed its approach, and into the end to which it is itself an approach, was wholly gone. The tremor of brightness received her.   (237)

---

[48] Williams, 'Founding of the Company', *Region*, 36.

13

The Great Dance in C. S. Lewis' *Perelandra*

'Lewis is becoming a mere disciple; he is now collecting the doctrine of exchange in the last chapter of the new novel. "That," he says, "is all yours".'[1] So Williams reported Lewis' admission of his debt in his novel *Perelandra*. I have several times, in the course of this book, had occasion to reflect on these semi-bitter words, and on the evidence that Lewis was influenced by Williams in his forming of the erratic block that the Great Dance of Perelandra embodies in the progress of Lewis' thought. However, I have also suggested that there are aspects in which Lewis 'out-dances' Williams. Reference to the Great Dance has formed a golden thread in the whole weave of my book, marking at a number of key points the impact of Williams' idea of co-inherence on Lewis and Lewis' development of 'co-inherence' beyond what Williams himself achieved, especially with regard to its trinitarian dimension.

In this chapter, I want to reflect more deeply on *why* Lewis' use of the image of the dance has this potential for expansion within it, as well as to situate the last chapter of *Perelandra* more clearly in the context of the whole novel and in its continuity with the first volume of the space trilogy, *Out of the Silent Planet*. As in other chapters in Part IV, being alert to the idea of 'co-inherence' helps us to see what we would otherwise miss. It will show us why the image of the dance is quite so extraordinary, and is such a pivotal point in the three novels. Beginning with a hymn of praise, and then culminating in the vision itself, this portrayal of the Great Dance is not the medieval commonplace that is often suggested—that is, just a picture of the universe as sharing in a dance around its centre, God. Something more startling is happening in Lewis' version of the Dance, something that shows the creativity of Lewis' thought, and the distance that he runs beyond Williams, so that the chapter is not after all merely 'all his', despite Lewis' generous admission.

13.1 The Two-Fold Centre

In line with his skilled use of metaphor, Lewis is bringing two images of a 'centre' together, merging them into one sharp focus, in a way that Williams has not. The

---

[1] CW to Anne Renwick, 13 May 1942; Bod. MS Eng. Lett. d. 452/4.

Charles Williams and C.S. Lewis: Friends in Co-inherence. Paul S. Fiddes, Oxford University Press. © Paul S. Fiddes 2021.
DOI: 10.1093/oso/9780192845467.003.0013

first is the image of a centre that is everywhere, so that—correlatively—'everything is at the centre'. In the dance, declare mysterious voices, *every* participant is at the centre (249), and the pattern of the dance can be seen as the movement of each entity becomes in turn 'the breaking into flower of the whole design' (250). This is because God is the centre and God is everywhere:

> Each grain is at the centre. The Dust is at the centre. The Worlds are at the centre. The beasts are at the centre. The ancient peoples are there. The race that sinned is there [...], the gods are there also. Blessed be He! Where Maleldil is, there is the centre. He is in every place. Not some of Him in one place and some on another, but in each place the whole Maleldil, even in the smallness beyond thought. [...] He is the centre. Because we are with him, each of us is at the centre.   (249)

> Set your eyes on one movement and it will lead you through all patterns [...]; there seems no centre because it is all centre.   (251)

We cannot miss the echo of the medieval saying that 'God is an intelligible sphere whose centre is everywhere and circumference nowhere.' We find this sentence in Bonaventure, who is quoting from Alan of Lille.[2] As I have observed already, Williams had already employed the idea that 'everything is at the centre' in a number of places, before Lewis' writing of *Perelandra*. The most obvious place that Lewis would have found it was in *He Came Down from Heaven*, which he read with care and appreciation:

> Bonaventura was writing that God was a circle whose centre was everywhere and its circumference nowhere. [...] The Love of the *New Life* is in the centre; to it all parts of the circumference, all times, all experiences, have this equal relation. [...] But beyond that is the state when there is, in effect, no circumference; or rather, every point of the circumference is at the centre, for the circumference itself is caritas, and the relation is only between the centre and the centre.[3]

'It is all centre', writes Lewis, and Williams had written, 'the relation is only between the centre and the centre'. Lewis could not have heard Williams' lecture on Blake in March 1939, but his expression there shows how easily Williams used the metaphor: 'Christianity involves the notion of every human being being the centre. If indeed [...] you regard every soul as the source of the web, then from every soul the whole web of creation springs.'[4]

---

[2] Bonaventure, *Itinerarium Mentis In Deum*, 5.8; Alan of Lille, *Theologiae Regulae*, rule 7. Jaime Vidal draws attention to Bonaventure in Vidal 'Ubiquitous Center', 1–6, but his argument is quite different from mine.

[3] Williams, *He Came Down*, 105–6.

[4] Williams, Wade RH Notebooks 20: 3682. For Williams, the notion of the 'centre' is also connected with the place of Christ at *tiphereth* in Christian Kabbalism: see Chapter 8, section 3.

Lewis is placing the image in the context of a question that Ransom is asking: who and what is at the centre of the presence and attention of Maleldil? (Maleldil is of course a name for God in Lewis' mythology.) Who is in the inner circle, the 'inner ring'?[5] The hymn and the vision are prompted by the disclosure to Ransom that his planet, earth, will be delivered from its bondage to dark powers as a preparation for a new beginning of creation. Far from being the 'last things', as earthly theologians name the event, this redemption of the earth from its Dark Lord will not even be the *beginning* of all things, but only the wiping out of a false start, mere prologue to the beginning.[6] Ransom is deeply troubled, because this perspective on time and space seems to him to thrust his world into a remote corner of the universe, when he was used to thinking that the coming down of Maleldil to earth as a man 'is the central happening of all that happens' (245). This disclosure seems to Ransom not only to displace the earth from the centre, but to open up a meaningless universe with no centre at all, but only millions of worlds that lead nowhere. Any hope of a plan or pattern seems to be an optical illusion, a trick of the eyes. The picture of the Great Dance counters this nihilism. In the dance, *every* participant is at the centre. Quite unlike Williams, the context of this image is thus a kind of 'space theology',[7] begun in *Out of the Silent Planet*, in which Lewis is creatively rethinking the particularity of Christian doctrines of incarnation and salvation in the new situation that modern science has revealed about the apparently insignificant place of humanity in the universe. The dance includes particularity and universality, time and eternity.

With this image of the 'centre' that is everywhere, Lewis now combines another. This is the ancient picture of the whole cosmos as a dance, moving around a centre that is God. In the Christian tradition, it is assumed that the Centre itself is *unmoving*, in accord with Aristotle's definition of the Unmoved Mover,[8] adopted (though with qualification) by Plotinus.[9] According to the traditional image of the dance, angels, planets, and other created beings circle around the still centre of God, moving around a God who is himself unmoving in a Neoplatonic stasis.[10] God moves all things, but himself remains motionless. As Lewis summarizes the medieval tradition in his book *The Discarded Image*, 'There must in the last resort be something which, *motionless itself*, initiates the motion of all other things.'[11] In

---

[5] Teresa Hooper makes an important contrast between the select 'inner ring' and the universal dance in Hooper, 'Playing by the Rules', 105–26.

[6] Lewis, *Perelandra*, 244; cf. Lewis, *Out of the Silent Planet*, 161–2.

[7] Cf. Lewis' appeal to 'super-cosmic reason' transcending merely human reason, in Lewis, 'De Futilitate', 65–8.

[8] Aristotle, *Physics*, 8.10; *Metaphysics*, 12.6–7.

[9] Plotinus, *Enneads*, V.2.1–2. Plotinus differs from Aristotle in that the unmoved Absolute Good or the One is not itself an intelligence; the principle of mind (*nous*) is an emanation from the Good (*Enneads* V.6.1–5).

[10] Plotinus, *Enneads*, II.2.1–2: 'the centre is a point of rest. [. . .] the Soul exists in revolution around God to whom it clings in love . . . '

[11] Lewis, *Discarded Image*, 113. My italics.

a Neoplatonist universe, indebted to both Aristotle and Plato, God or 'the One' as pure Being cannot share in the qualities of a world of becoming and change. Further, according to the image of the centre that is everywhere, God can be in all time and space just because God is eternal and unmoving. As Bonaventure puts it, pure and absolute Being 'comprises and enters all durations, as if existing at the same time as their centre and circumference, because it is eternal and most present'; quoting Boethius, he goes on to say 'Because it is most immutable, for that reason "remaining at rest [*stabilis manens*] it grants motion to everything else".'[12]

In *The Discarded Image*, Lewis sets out the medieval world order in which each planetary sphere, or something resident in it, is a conscious intelligence moved by intellectual love of God through the activity of the *Primum Mobile*, the First Moveable.[13] The *Primum Mobile* is moved by its love for God (the Primal Mover) and so communicates motion to the rest of the universe. God, while utterly motionless, initiates the motion of all other things, because they are moved by the object of their love. It is like, we may say, a beautiful woman or man setting a whole room of people in motion around him or her, while remaining stationary in the middle, toying with a glass of wine. Lewis himself opts for the image of a moth fluttering round a candle flame.[14] The first to be moved, and then to move others, is the *Primum Mobile*, and Lewis refers to 'one old picture' in which the intelligence of the First Moveable is represented as a girl dancing and playing with her sphere as a ball;[15] she is the leader of the dance, the swiftest mover and shaker. I want to return to this picture shortly. The key thing is that the dancers are the First Moveable and then the other spheres, but not God, who is the still centre of the turning world. Elsewhere in the *Discarded Image*, Lewis refers to the dance of the angels in Pseudo-Dionysius' treatise on *The Celestial Hierarchy*,[16] and notes that Dante has something similar.[17] Dionysius envisages a threefold hierarchy of dancing celestial choirs, moving in distinct patterns around God, providing a spiritual ladder of ascent for the soul to approach God.

In a moment, we shall see how Lewis is in fact dissatisfied with the traditional picture, but first we should notice that Williams has again preceded Lewis with the image of the whole cosmos as a dance revolving around an apparently still centre. The most obvious place is his novel *The Greater Trumps*, which is entirely structured by the idea of a cosmic dance; the set of nearly a hundred golden

---

[12] Bonaventure, *Itinerarium,* 5.8, citing Boethius, *De Consolatione Philosophiae,* 3.9 (poem).

[13] The *Primum Mobile* in Ptolemaic astronomy is the outermost concentric sphere of the universe: see Dante, *Divine Comedy, Paradise,* 27.97–148. Milton refers to the 'First-moved' in *Paradise Lost,* 3.482.

[14] Lewis, *Discarded Image,* 119.

[15] Lewis, *Discarded Image,* 119. The reference is to Seznec, *Survival of the Pagan Gods,* 80.

[16] Pseudo-Dionysius, *The Celestial Hierarchy,* 7.4 (209D–212B), cf. 7.1 (205B–C).

[17] Dante, *Divine Comedy, Paradise,* 28.121–9: but Dante does not explicitly mention a dance, only 'whirling'.

figures are moving in a perpetual and complex dance, reflecting the circulation of the cosmos and all the movements of people and nations in the world.[18] In a chapter called 'The Dance in the World', Henry explains this cosmic dance to Nancy:

> Imagine that everything which exists takes part in the movement of a great dance—everything, the electrons, all growing and decaying things, all that seems alive and doesn't seem alive, men and beasts, trees and stones, everything that changes, and there is nothing anywhere that does not change. That change— that's what we know of the immortal dance; the law in the nature of things— that's the measure of the dance, why one thing changes swiftly and another slowly.[19]

As the figures dance, and unite with the Tarot cards, Nancy and Henry have a vision of the world, and see into the movements of peoples, armies and civilizations:

> All earth had been gathered up: this was the truth of earth. The dance went on in the void; only even there she saw in the centre the motionless Fool, and about him in a circle the Juggler ran, forever tossing his balls.[20]

This scene focuses on two key images in the Tarot pack and among the golden figures. In the whirling, perpetual dance there is one figure, standing right in the middle, who appears to remain unmoving—the Fool; there is, says Henry, an unfathomable mystery about this figure. The Fool is the number zero in the Tarot pack, and so is the one who cannot be counted and numbered. By contrast, the most mobile figure is the Juggler, dancing and tossing his balls. He is the *Primum Mobile* of medieval cosmology, the first moved reality moving the other spheres (balls), and the Fool represents God, or at least the divine principle, who (traditionally) remains unmoving but who is cause of movement in everything. Emphasis is laid on the position of the Fool in 'the centre': '"It looks to me to be in the centre," [Nancy] said, "and it doesn't seem to be moving—not exactly moving".'[21]

Curiously, despite Williams' vivid portrayal of the cosmic dance in this novel, it is not an image to which he makes much more resort after 1932. Occasional references can be found. In *Descent into Hell*, Pauline has a mental picture in which 'physical sensation, which is the play of love, and pardon, which is the speed of love, and action, which is the fact of love, and almighty love itself, all danced

---

[18] On *Greater Trumps*, see Chapter 11, section 4.   [19] Williams, *Greater Trumps*, 94.
[20] Williams, *Greater Trumps*, 102.   [21] Williams, *Greater Trumps*, 75.

together'.[22] In *He Came Down from Heaven*, Williams remarks in passing that 'The "sweet reasonableness" of Christ is always there, but it is always in a dance and its dancing hall is from the topless heavens to the bottomless abyss.'[23] In *The Figure of Beatrice*, again in passing, Williams mentions that in Dante's vision, 'Paradise dances'.[24] Williams certainly does not associate the 'centre' of the dance as he portrays it in *The Greater Trumps* with his later imaging of the centre that is 'everywhere'. But this is precisely what Lewis is doing in the Great Dance of Perelandra. The centre of the cosmic dance *is* that centre where everything is 'at'. Lewis has fused the two kinds of centre together, in an imaginative vision that we cannot find in Williams.

13.2 The Moving Centre

The image of the cosmic dance traditionally relied upon the conviction that the centre of the dance does not move; but when Lewis brings them *together* here they make a different imaginative impact. The impression made on us is that the centre of the dance is itself dancing. We are not just witnessing a dance *around* God, but the dance *of* God. Admittedly, the hymn and the vision only *imply* that the primal dance is Maleldil himself. Lewis writes that 'His love and splendour flow forth like a strong river which [...] makes new channels',[25] so that the patterns of the dance are the passionate energies of God. But a divine dance is the imaginative effect of bringing together the cosmic dance and a centre that is everywhere in creation; the centre is everywhere, and everything is at the centre, because it moves everywhere. However, there is much else in Lewis that supports this understanding of the dance, so much else in fact that some commentators on Lewis simply assume that the Great Dance of Perelandra is led by Maleldil as master of the revels and the supreme Dancer,[26] and therefore miss the extraordinary reversal of thought and imagination that is going on.

In *The Discarded Image*, having expounded the cosmic dance of the spheres around God as the unmoving centre, Lewis adds that this picture generally failed to grip the imagination of Christian spiritual writers in the Middle Ages. In his view, this was because the image was too static; God, he urges, is not just the passive object of love but the active lover, the Good Shepherd who goes out to seek the lost sheep.[27] Lewis' version of the Great Dance, then, is not a medieval commonplace, and not even just an 'updated form of Christian Neoplatonism'.[28] While I have stressed that Lewis is working with a Christian Neoplatonist world

---

[22] Williams, *Descent into Hell*, 147.   [23] Williams, *He Came Down*, 69.
[24] Williams, *Figure of Beatrice*, 228.   [25] Lewis, *Perelandra*, 250.
[26] E.g. Kawano, 'C.S. Lewis and the Great Dance', 28.
[27] Lewis, *The Discarded Image*, 113–14, 120.   [28] Schwartz, 'Paradise Reframed', 592.

view, it is his own version. It relies on Neoplatonist hierarchy and dualism, but not on an unmoving origin of all things. Long before *The Discarded Image* (1964), and at about the same time as *Perelandra* (1943), Lewis had thus articulated a more dynamic understanding of the cosmic dance. The dance of heaven in which the creation participates is not merely that of the ranks of angels, but that of the triune God. In *Beyond Personality* (1944), he writes: 'In Christianity God is not a static thing—not even a person—but a dynamic, pulsating activity, a life, almost a kind of drama. Almost, if you will not think me irreverent, a kind of *dance*...'[29]

Once again, Williams had anticipated Lewis with the revolutionary proposal that the ultimate Reality in the 'centre' is in movement. In *The Greater Trumps*, Nancy's aunt Sybil, a kind of prophetess, has a moment of spiritual insight as she looks at the golden figures dancing: she sees the Fool move, though he is meant to stand motionless in the centre of the dance. She says, 'Surely that's it [the Fool], dancing with the rest; it seems as if it were always arranging itself in some place that was empty for it...' (74). Henry says in wonderment, 'No one has ever seen it move [...]. She saw it completing the measures, fulfilling the dance' (86). Later, in the storm that has been loosed by the Tarot cards that have slipped from Henry's hand, Nancy states, 'they say he doesn't move,' and Sybil replies, 'but I saw him move, [...] and there's no figure anywhere in heaven or earth that can slip from that partner. They are all his for ever.' 'Do you think the Tarots can ever escape while the Fool is there to hold them?' (139–40). Earlier, looking at the 'dance in the world', Nancy herself sees the Fool and the Juggler moving towards each other and embracing each other (103). At the climax of the book, it is the Fool who comes to rescue Nancy, who is to be the new Eve, coming at the call of love: 'he had come from all sides at once, yet he was but one. All-reconciling and perfect, he was there...' (228).

Williams' thought seems to be that if the Fool is love, then he must participate in a dance where a key measure is love. Lewis may well have been influenced by the images of *The Greater Trumps*, but he is arriving at the conviction through a different route—a combining of the two images of a centre that is everywhere, and the centre in the midst of a ring-dance. All things are at the centre just *because* the centre moves. Lewis had already set out the theory for this in *Out of the Silent Planet*. Ransom is instructed by the *sorn* that 'Body is movement', and so 'the thing at the top of all bodies' is 'so fast that it is at rest, so truly body that it has ceased being body at all'. The faster movement becomes, 'then that which moves is more nearly in two places at once', and with a body moving at infinite speed 'in the end the moving thing would be in all places at once'.[30] This discussion is prompted by Ransom's enquiry about the *eldila*, angelic powers whose bodies are made of

---

[29] Lewis, *Mere Christianity*, 138–9.   [30] Lewis, *Out of the Silent Planet*, 106.

light,[31] and so which move at the speed of light, but it leads to contemplation of 'the thing at the top of all bodies', which, through its movement, is omnipresent. In the Great Dance of Perelandra, this quasi-scientific theory becomes image:[32] the centre that is everywhere is the centre of a dance.

The result is not only to conceive that the centre moves, but also that there is a movement of mutual indwelling between all created things and the centre. If all things are at the centre because the centre is moving, there must be some kind of interpenetration. There is, in short, *perichoresis* or co-inherence, though Lewis does not use the word. While the *sorn* in *Out of the Silent Planet* declines to talk further to Ransom about the 'thing at the top of all bodies', there appears to be an analogy with the light-body of the *eldil*, who can 'go through' walls and rocks, not because he is 'thin [and] half-real', but 'because he is solid and firm and they are like cloud'. It may have been this kind of theory about the different motions of different realities that Lewis had in mind when he arrived in *Mere Christianity* at the idea of dwelling in a triune God, beyond the point that Williams had reached: 'The whole dance, or drama, or pattern of this three-Personal life is to be played out in each one of us: or (putting it the other way round) each one of us has got to enter that pattern, take his place in that dance.'[33] But we should notice that this picture of the dance is about *relationships* in movement, as it is later in the Great Dance of Perelandra. The image of a dance and a centre is giving Lewis the possibilities of expressing Trinity in a way that he did not have available earlier.

By speaking of God as 'beyond personality' but not as impersonal, Lewis is recognizing a necessary apophaticism or a negative way in all theological language. We might say that the very elusiveness of the picture of a *divine* dance at the heart of the Great Dance of *Perelandra*, implied as it is through the bringing together of two images, illustrates that the dance cannot be observed or even imagined but only participated in:

> 'He dwells (all of Him dwells) within the seed of the smallest flower and is not cramped: Deep Heaven is inside Him who is inside the seed and does not distend Him. Blessed be He!'.   (247)

This view of the relation of God to the world may be called panentheism—everything *in* God, which must not be confused with pantheism—everything *as* God. Similarly, Bonaventure follows his statement about God as the centre by declaring that God 'is within all things, but not as included in them, and outside of all things, but not as excluded from them'. However, Bonaventure bases this

---

[31] Lewis, *Letters to Malcolm*, 156, refers to Milton's concept of 'angelic creatures with bodies made of light who can achieve total interpenetration'.

[32] Perhaps Lewis is reflecting the theory of wave–particle duality, which holds that light and matter exhibit properties of both waves and of particles.

[33] Lewis, *Mere Christianity*, 139.

conviction on a notion of God as 'most perfect and immense', filling all space,[34] not as *moving* within all things, since he conceives of God as an unmoved mover.

13.3 The Dance and the Co-inherent Trinity

I have already mentioned that writers on Lewis fail to notice the breach with the medieval world picture that he makes with the picture of a dancing God, a moving centre. During the last thirty years or so the image of the divine life as a dance has become increasingly popular. It is common for religious writers of the present day to refer to the ancient notion of *perichoresis* or 'interweaving' of three persons in God with the image of the dance.[35] Some notice that there is a play on words taking place here: *perichoresis* derives from *perichoreo*, meaning to interpenetrate, which sounds similar to another verb, *perichoreuo* (to dance around). The mutual indwelling of the persons and movement in and through each other may thus be pictured as a kind of round dance. The pun is useful theologically as well as imaginatively, although there is no evidence that this association was made in theology of the Trinity until the modern period. Unfortunately, some writers simply assume that *perichoresis* can be translated as 'a dance', and so earlier theologians must have meant a dance when they used the term.[36] In fact, it has not been possible to this date to find any unambiguous reference to the Trinity as a dance in Christian thinking earlier than Lewis himself.[37]

Of course, the spheres, angels, and other beings dance around God, as we have seen. As well as envisaging all created intelligences as held together in a dance, Plotinus depicts the soul that has looked on the One as now dancing around Him, the fount of goodness.[38] In the Christian version, there is a 'never-ending dance' of the angels around the throne of God, in which Christians may aspire to participate in eternity; according to Basil the Great, Christians at worship here and now may imitate the ring-dance (*choreia*) of heaven in their prayers and hymns to the creator.[39] In addition to the dancing angels of Pseudo-Dionysius, we may mention the dance of the church Doctors in the sun that Dante sees in the *Paradiso*.[40] The picture persists from the Middle Ages to the Elizabethan era: in Sir John Davies' poem 'Orchestra', all everyday actions are included in the dance, including the

---

[34] Bonaventure, *Itinerarium* 5.8; in this he is probably following Hilary of Poitiers, *de Trinitate* 2.6.

[35] E.g. Hill, *Three-Personed God*, 272; LaCugna, *God For Us*, 271; Johnson, *She Who Is*, 220–1; Fiddes, *Participating in God*, 72–81.

[36] This error is made, for example, by Rohr, *Divine Dance*, *passim*, and Hastings, *Echoes of Coinherence*, 56–8.

[37] Brown and Loades, *The Sense of the Sacramental*, 13, claim that Dante's *Paradise* ends (33.115–45) with a vision of the three persons of the Trinity as 'three moving circles or spheres in a single orbit'. But the lines do not present these divine spheres as moving in themselves, but only as moving other things with their love.

[38] Plotinus, *Enneads* 4.4.33.   [39] Basil, *Hom. in Hexaemeron* 4.

[40] Dante, *Divine Comedy, Paradise*, 10.76–91.

fluttering of Penelope's eyelashes and the dancing of the point of a needle as she sews. When Antinous in the poem asks Penelope to dance, he invites her to participate in the heavenly dance, to

> Imitate heaven whose beauties excellent
> Are in continuall motion day and night.

The activity of *Christ* on earth is depicted as a dance in several texts, among them the Gnostic *Hymn of Jesus* from the second century,[41] when Jesus declares to his disciples at the Last Supper, 'I am the Word who did dance all things, 'Twas I who leapt and danced.' The medieval English carol 'Tomorrow will be my Dancing Day' depicts the birth, baptism, temptation, and passion of Christ as a dance, with the aim 'to call my true love [i.e. the human soul] to my dance'. But this does not exactly express the dance of God: the emphasis is strongly on the humanity of Christ, not on the eternal divine nature. It is Christ as man who dances:

> Then was I born of a virgin pure,
> Of her I took fleshly substance;
> Thus was I knit to man's nature
> To call my true love to my dance.[42]

It seems, then, that Lewis himself has converted the dance of Plotinus and Pseudo-Dionysius into a dance of the Trinity. This may be because—as he himself indicates—he has a strong sense of participation in God, and of the generous actions of God as *lover* of creation, not just the *beloved*. But other factors may well have influenced him. Among them there was perhaps his reading of Henri Bergson, for which Sanford Schwartz has made a strong case. Lewis commented that 'the Bergsonian critique of orthodox Darwinism is not easy to answer',[43] which has a particular bearing on the satire that *Out of the Silent Planet* offers on a materialistic reading of evolution and on social Darwinism. Schwartz writes of the 'inversion of Platonism' promoted by Bergson,[44] in which the world is no longer envisaged as a system of unchanging forms perceived by the intellect, but as a process of perpetual becoming, given to us in the stream of experience. Despite Lewis' negative judgements on Bergson, and his dismissal of the 'life-force philosophy' in *Mere Christianity*,[45] Schwartz demonstrates that the very landscape of Perelandra seems to be shaped by Bergson's dynamic naturalism. Lewis reverses the traditional concept of Paradise as an immutable state that precedes a lapse into

---

[41] *Hymn of Jesus*, set to music by Gustav Holst.
[42] 'Tomorrow shall be my dancing day', v.2, apparently first printed in Sandys, *Christmas Carols*.
[43] Lewis, 'Is Theology Poetry?', 163.   [44] Schwartz, 'Paradise Reframed,' 574.
[45] Lewis, *Mere Christianity*, 21.

time and change, and instead presents it as a perpetual flux.[46] The Green Lady rejoices in the distinctive character of each phase of the creation as it unfolds in time, greeting each wave of time and circumstance as it rolls towards her. The temptation she must resist is to stay on the fixed land, symbolizing the desire to control experience by fixing it into something she can possess.

Ransom's own experience on Perelandra begins with temptations to immobilize the flux. He overcomes the impulse to repeat a pleasurable experience, tasting the delicious fruit of Perelandra, or bathing in the bursting fruit of the bubble-tree. He reflects: 'the itch to have things over again, as if life were a film that could be unrolled twice, or even made to work backwards, [...] was it possibly the root of all evil'? (54). So Edward, in Narnia, finds that he always craves more of the White Witch's Turkish Delight.[47] In *Out of the Silent Planet*, the *hrossa* on Malacandra had already tried to teach Ransom that pleasures in love and poetry should be remembered rather than replicated.[48] Resisting the temptation to repeat a pleasure is partly a matter of obedience to God, a willingness to receive what God gives in each new moment, but it is also to live in accord with a world that—in a Bergsonian way—is always in process of development. The hymn that begins the Great Dance celebrates a vision of a kind of creative evolution that matches the need to throw oneself into the new wave that Maleldil sends:

> Never did He make two things the same; never did he utter one word twice. After earths, not better earths but beasts; after beasts, not better beasts but spirits. After a falling, not a recovery but a new creation. Out of the new creation, not a third but the mode of change itself is changed for ever. Blessed is He!   (146–7)

Schwarz does not suggest that this vision of continuous development in the created universe has implications in Lewis' mind for the very being of the Creator, as existing in some kind of state of becoming. Lewis clearly opposes Bergson's view that God is to be identified with the life-force, as a creative spirit that realizes itself progressively in the natural order. However, further to my suggestion that there is an imaginative effect when the omnipresent centre merges with the cosmic dance, we might say this is intensified when the dance itself is a continual process of becoming. The God who indwells a creation that is in a perpetual flux is even more likely to be a God who is mobile, not static, a God who joins the dance, or rather leads it onwards.

---

[46] Schwartz, 'Paradise Reframed,' 569–70, 580–1. See also Schwartz, *C.S. Lewis*, 55–73. Corey Latta similarly argues for the influence of Bergson's 'duration' on Lewis' *The Great Divorce*: Latta, *When the Eternal Can be Met*, 77–114.

[47] Lewis, *Lion, the Witch and the Wardrobe*, 39–41.   [48] Lewis, *Out of the Silent Planet*, 82–3.

The hymn that begins the Great Dance gives another clue to Lewis' thought about the moving centre, and his locating this within the context of Trinity. We hear the voices say:

'All things are by Him and for Him. He utters Himself also for his own delight and sees that He is good. He is his own begotten and what proceeds from Him is Himself. Blessed be He!'. (250–1)

This clearly refers to the Christian doctrine of the eternal generation of the Son from the Father, and in various places Lewis repeats the metaphors for this generation formulated by church Fathers such as Athanasius—the outshining of light from a lamp, the radiating of heat from a fire, or the speaking of a word from the mind. To these, however, Lewis adds the image of the dance. In *Perelandra*, the dance is only implicitly an image for divine generation, the association being made through the context of the opening hymn of praise, but the link is made explicitly elsewhere. In *The Problem of Pain* (1940), Lewis urges us not to hold on to our self, but to give it up, as players in a game pass on the ball to other players, a game that God plays with God's own self:

When [the ball] flies to and fro among the players too swift for the eye to follow, and the great Master himself leads the revelry, giving Himself eternally to his creatures in the generation, and back to Himself in the sacrifice, of the Word, then indeed the eternal dance 'makes heaven drowsy with the harmony.' All pains and pleasures we have known on earth are early intimations in the movements of that dance: but the dance itself is strictly incomparable with the sufferings of the present time. As we draw nearer to its uncreated rhythm, pain and pleasure sink almost out of sight, There is joy in the dance, but it does not exist for the sake of joy. It does not even exist for the sake of good, or of love. It [i.e. the dance] is Love Himself, and Good Himself.[49]

Here the ball-game played by the *Primum Mobile*, portrayed as the young girl in the picture to which Lewis refers,[50] or as the Juggler (tossing the spheres) in Williams' novel, is played by God himself. The cosmic dance is God's dance, and the rhythm is 'uncreated'; indeed, the dance is Love and so is God. The primal dance is the going out of the Son from the Father 'in the generation', and his return to the Father in obedient sacrifice.

In medieval theology, efforts were made to reconcile what appears to be divine movement in the eternal generation of the Son (and the *perichoresis* of the Trinity)

---

[49] Lewis, *Problem of Pain*, 141. There are many echoes of these final pages of *The Problem of Pain* in the Great Dance of Perelandra.
[50] See note 15.

with the cosmological belief that that the centre of all things is still and motionless. In Thomas Aquinas, the movement of the Son out from, and back to, the Father is explained as being entirely compatible with immobility; like the emission of light from the sun, or emanation of thought from the mind, says Thomas, there is a kind of motion (*kinesis*), but this is identical with rest (*stasis*), echoed in the stability to which—as we have seen—Bonaventure refers us. Thomas writes that 'The conception and birth of an intelligible word [...] involves neither motion nor succession.'[51] While dynamic images of light from the sun and the word from the mind might be accommodated to *stasis* in this paradoxical way, it is clear that the image of a dance cannot, and so Lewis' own image affirms the movement of God in self-begetting without equivocation in a way that would be disturbing to medieval cosmology.

13.4 The Moving Centre and Theodicy

The primordial dance between the Father and the Son is the basis for the dance of creation, all created beings emanating from God and returning to God according to the pattern of the Son. This picture enables Lewis to include the evil and suffering of the world within the dance: they disturb its measures, but finally they are overcome and transformed within its movement. Earlier, in *The Problem of Pain*, Lewis had appealed to the image of the dance:

> God saw the crucifixion in the act of creating the first nebula. The world is a dance in which good, descending from God, is disturbed by evil arising from the creatures, and the resulting conflict is resolved by God's own assumption of the suffering nature which evil produces.[52]

So in the Great Dance of Perelandra, we hear the voices say, 'In the Fallen World He prepared for Himself a body and was united with the Dust and made it glorious for ever. [...] The fountain that sprang with mingled blood and life in the Dark World, flows here with life only' (248). Lewis' approach to the problem of evil at this time was a mixture of several rational elements: to the so-called 'free will defence',[53] he added an assertion of the instrumental nature of suffering (pain is God's 'megaphone' to rouse a deaf world),[54] and the relativizing of suffering by

---

[51] Aquinas, *Summa Contra Gentiles*, 4, 11, n. 18. Similarly, Maximus the Confessor, *Quaestiones ad Thalassium*, PG90, 760A, ascribes to the Spirit a 'rest that is eternally in motion and constant motion that is at rest'. While Gregory of Nyssa writes that 'rest and motion are identical', he refers this not to God but to the soul that God has invited into his infinity (*Vita Moysis*, PG44.405BD). Earlier, Plotinus had ascribed 'simultaneous rest and motion' to the *nous*, circling in itself and returning to itself (*Enneads* II.3), but not to 'the One' that remains motionless.

[52] Lewis, *Problem of Pain*, 72.   [53] Lewis, *Problem of Pain*, 57.

[54] Lewis, *Problem of Pain*, 81.

final joy.[55] There are intellectual problems with all these elements, but I believe that Phillip Tallon is right to underline that Lewis' theodicy is finally not a rational argument but an *aesthetic* appeal to the universe as a work of art; the image of the dance draws us away from merely *intellectual* argument into seeing that God has the power to incorporate change, even rebellion and sin, into a beautiful whole.[56] This will only convince by participation in it, by joining in the measures of the dance, an art form that includes persons.

Nor is this a wholeness of beauty that suppresses the individual and the particular, as in a Hegelian synthesis. The image of the dance has room to honour all participants rather than subjecting them to the necessity of a process. In the hymn of praise, every world and its inhabitants is given significance. Echoing the speech of God in Job 38–9, the place of things in creation is not to be measured by whether they seem relevant to the development of the human spirit. God asks Job, 'Where were you when I laid the foundations of the earth [and] shut in the sea with doors?' (Job 38:4–8), and the voices here proclaim that 'the waters you have not floated on, the fruit you have not plucked, the caves into which you have not descended and the fire through which your bodies cannot pass, do not wait for you to put on perfection' (248). In the vision that follows, the dance appears to Ransom as an intertwining of

> many cords or bands of light, leaping over and under one another and mutually embraced in arabesques and flower-like subtleties. Each figure as he looked at it became the master-figure of focus of the whole spectacle.   (251)

These bands of light that weave together are all 'individual entities'. Ransom reflects:

> Some of the thinner and more delicate cords were beings that we call short-lived: flowers and insects, a fruit or a storm of rain, and once (he thought) a wave of the sea. Others were such things as we also think lasting: crystals, rivers, mountains, or even stars.   (252)

More luminous bands, flashing with colour were 'the lines of personal beings, different from one another in splendour'. Not all the cords were individual beings—some were 'universal truths or universal qualities'. But the point is this: the ribbons of light were to be contrasted with what Lewis calls 'mere generalities', or 'the secular generalities of which history tells—nations, institutions, climates of opinion, "civilizations, arts, sciences and the like"' The generalities, beloved of Hegelians, were merely tiny atoms of momentary brightness that appeared where

[55] Lewis, *Problem of Pain*, 132.   [56] Tallon, 'Evil and the Cosmic Dance', 208–10.

the cords intersected—'ephemeral coruscations that piped their short song and vanished'. Lewis' portrayal of the dance, this ever-moving work of art, might well convince us that everything can be included in God's generous love in a way that an abstract theodicy cannot.

If theodicy takes the form of an image in Perelandra, in *Out of the Silent Planet* it takes the form of a story. Both Perelandra and the Malacandra of the previous novel (Mars) are planets where the fall of rational beings away from the Good has, unlike earth (Thulcandra), not happened. But Malacandra is an older civilization, in which there has been time for God's original intention in creation to work itself out; in Perelandra, we are at the very springtime of life. The vision of co-inherence at the end of *Perelandra* has thus already been given a test bed. The whole of the first novel has the feel of a theodicy: is creation a project that could ever have worked? We are thus shown certain phenomena that we can recognize in our own world, but which—Lewis is claiming—would look and feel very different if there had been no disobedience to God on the part of created beings. First, Lewis intends to show how distinct rational species could have diversified through a kind of evolution in one environment (*hrossa*, *sorns*, and *pfifltriggi*—poets, intellectuals, and artists) without the competition for survival, emergence of a dominant species, and colonization of the 'other' that materialistic Darwinism assumes.[57] A great deal of the humour of the novel comes from the 'mismatch between terrestrial expectation and the realities of the alien world',[58] as Devine and Western enter Malacandra (carrying Ransom with them as a sacrifice that they think the *eldila* require) with the arrogance of a supposedly superior civilization and a contempt for the 'Other'.

Second, in the way that the *hrossa* conduct a hunt of an irrational beast (the *hnakra*) by the rational, Lewis intends to show us that even violence, which appears necessary for the development of life and virtues, can take the form of respect for a primordial bond between all life: 'the *hnakra* is our enemy, but he is also our beloved'.[59] Finally, Lewis is apparently on the side of those theologians who believe that death itself is part of creation and not the result of a 'fall', but that death would appear and be experienced quite differently in the context of continued obedience to God:[60] 'let us scatter the movements which were their bodies. So will Maleldil scatter all worlds when the first and feeble is worn.'[61] Lewis has thus made an attempt to answer some of the intellectual questions that might arise when viewing the vision of the dance, but the reader is left with the impression that if anything is to convince it will only be the artistry of the dance itself. Perhaps the apologetic approach fails because the story is too deeply embedded in Lewis'

---

[57] See Lewis, *Out of the Silent Planet*, 66, 78.

[58] Schwartz, *C. S. Lewis*, 26, suggests that Lewis is 'transfiguring' the evolutionary naturalism of H. G. Wells.

[59] Lewis, *Out of the Silent Planet*, 84.   [60] See, for example, Rahner, *Theology of Death*, 42.

[61] Lewis, *Out of the Silent Planet*, 149, cf. 85.

conviction that for creation to work there must be the hierarchy that we have seen is at the foundation of his world picture, and in which he includes—though subtly—the male–female relation:

> There must be rule, yet how can creatures rule themselves? Beasts must be ruled by *hnau* and *hnau* by *eldila* and *eldila* by Maleldil. These [earthly] creatures have no eldila. They are like one trying to lift himself by his own hair—or one trying to see over a whole country when he is on a level with it—like a female trying to beget young on herself.[62]

13.5 The Freedom of the Dance

This reflection brings us to the way that the Great Dance embodies the themes of the novel *Perelandra*. In this story of an unfallen world, and the temptation offered to its Eve, Lewis is working out a problem that perplexed Augustine in his account of the human Fall. Granted that humans are created with the freedom to disobey God, why would a person created in the bliss of communion with God *want* to fall away at all? Why would created beings *want* to turn away from the Good if they lived in unrestricted relation to the Good? Augustine himself found this to be an insoluble question that simply confirmed the nature of evil as 'non-being' and its origin as a mystery.[63] The same question has led some modern theologians to doubt whether it is at all coherent to think, as Augustine does, of a strict sequence of perfection followed by a fall at one point in time.[64] Lewis, however, wants to keep a primordial Paradise and comes up with his own solution. An unfallen being, enjoying full communion with God, could only be persuaded to disobey if she believed that this was in the service of a greater Good.[65]

The Enemy therefore puts it to the Lady that Maleldil really wants her to disobey his commandment not to spend the night on the fixed land. Such disobedience is the only way to growth and maturity, and God *wants* the Lady to develop in knowledge and experience. The Good of obedience, the Enemy urges, is outweighed by the Good of growth, of 'growing older' in wisdom. We know, as the Lady knows intuitively, that this is nonsense. Nothing can be better, more productive of joy, than obedience to Maleldil. In his study of Milton's *Paradise Lost*, Lewis had used the image of the dance precisely to express the joy of obedience to God, and the freedom this creates. He writes:

---

[62] Lewis, *Out of the Silent Planet*, 116.   [63] Augustine, *The City of God*, 12.7, 14.13.

[64] e.g. Schleiermacher, *Christian Faith*, 295; Hick, *Evil*, 75. Tillich, *Systematic Theology*, 2: 45–50, proposes that Creation and Fall coincide, though not as a logical necessity.

[65] This is portrayed in *Magician's Nephew*, 159–60, by Digory's being tempted to take a golden apple to heal his mother.

Discipline, while the world is yet unfallen, exists for the sake of what seems its very opposite—for freedom, almost for extravagance. The pattern hidden deep in the dance, hidden so deep that shallow spectators cannot see it, alone gives beauty to the wild, free gestures that fill it. [...] Without sin, the universe is a Solemn Game: and there is no good game without rules.[66]

Like a planet in the cosmic dance, the happy soul is a 'wandering star',[67] and yet in that very wandering she follows the invariable patterns of the dance. Lewis, however, moves just a little beyond the sheer paradox that obedience *is* perfect freedom, to hint that God might use this freedom to shape the very patterns of the dance itself. This is where the reversal of the tradition of the unmoving centre is finally leading us, even against Lewis' general world-view, to modify strict hierarchy. There is just a clue that through obedience we share in the creativity of God. Here Lewis' mood is very different from Williams, who finds the dance to be a symbol of cosmic necessity: Henry Lee tells Nancy that the dance

'is always perfect because it can't be anything else. It knows nothing of joy or grief [...]. If you cry, it's because the measure will have it so; if you laugh, it's because some gayer step *demands* it'.   (95)

It is because of this necessity that Henry thinks he can control the world around him; if only he can read the movements he can exploit them in his own actions. In his series of novels, Williams never entirely resolves the problem of Necessity and its implications for the existence of evil. Lewis takes the implications of freedom seriously. When Ransom first meets the Green Lady, something he says gives her a new perception. She had thought that Maleldil simply presented her with one good thing after another, one wave rolling in after another, but now she sees that she plays her own part: she exclaims:

I thought that I was carried in the will of Him I love, but now I see that I walk with it. [...] One's own self to be walking from one good to another, walking beside Him as Himself may walk. [...] I thought we went along paths—but it seems there are no paths. The going itself is the path.   (78)

As well as confirming that the Centre of all things does indeed move, *walking* in and through the world, she perceives that there are no pre-ordained paths: the obedient person creates them with God in the very going. After the vision of the dance, the king of Perelandra predicts that this freedom can only increase as beings grow and develop:

---

[66] Lewis, *Preface*, 79–80.   [67] Lewis, *Preface*, 80.

'I believe the waves of time will often change for us henceforward. We are coming to have our own choice whether we shall be above them and see many waves together or whether we shall reach them one by one as we used to'.   (254)

This perception illuminates what seems an obscure ending to the Hymn of Praise:

if we never met the dark, and the road that leads nowhither, and the question to which no answer is imaginable, we should have in our minds no likeness of the Abyss of the Father, into which if a creature drop down his thoughts for ever he shall hear no echo return to him.   (251)

It is just because the paths of the dance are not a predetermined necessity that we experience a need for courage in walking out into the dark.[68] So it is that 'the going itself is the path'. This is surely the point of the vision of the Great Dance, where the ribbons or cords of light, the patterns of the dance, *are* the myriad created things themselves. *They* are the pattern, just as Love *is* the Dance.

---

[68] Exactly the same image of the abyss of the Father occurs in the passage on the dance in *Problem of Pain*, 141–2. Perhaps there is an echo of Jacob Boehme, for whom the Abyss in God is both Non-Being and Absolute Freedom; see *De Signatura Rerum*, 2.7–10; Lewis writes of reading chapter 2 of *De Signatura Rerum* in 1930, recognizing that this is 'the most serious attempt ever to show the Many coming out the One', and, 'although I can't understand it', urges 'we must worry it out': CSL to Owen Barfield, 16 January 1930, Lewis, *Letters*, 3: 1515.

14

The Poetics of Desire in Thomas Traherne and C. S. Lewis

C. S. Lewis once wrote in a letter to his friend Arthur Greeves that 'At present I'm re-reading Traherne's *Centuries of Meditations* which I think almost the most beautiful book (in prose, I mean, excluding poets) in English.'[1] He thought it 'almost the most beautiful book', and yet it seems extraordinary that he never wrote so much as one whole page, let alone an essay, about Thomas Traherne. Perhaps this is why, in large reference books on C. S. Lewis, the reader will look in vain under the letter 'T' for Traherne.[2]

There are, in fact, fifteen references to Traherne in Lewis' books and essays, another twelve in his letters, and one in his diary.[3] Of these twenty-eight instances (all of which are referenced in this chapter), I believe that eleven have significant content, containing twelve separate direct quotations. Other references tend to be passing commendations of Traherne such as the one I began with; Lewis, it seems, was in the habit of enthusing about Traherne to those who wrote to him wanting to know what they should read among the Christian writers, and especially the devotional writers. Most of these endorsements tell us little more than that Lewis *did* think that *Centuries* was 'golden and genial',[4] and a 'beautiful book' with a 'Paradisial flavour',[5] and that he wanted others to share his appreciation.[6] But eleven of the references or quotations do go a long way to establishing the argument of this chapter that there is common ground between the idea of desire in Traherne and Lewis, and that this idea had a powerful effect on the shaping of their own creativity and their own poetics. Further, just as Williams' commentary

---

[1] CSL to Arthur Greeves, 23 December 1941, Lewis, *Letters*, 2: 505.

[2] There are, for instance, no references to Traherne in Duriez, *The A–Z of C.S. Lewis*; Schultz and West, *The C.S. Lewis Readers' Encyclopedia*; Goffar, *CS Lewis Index*; Edwards, *C.S. Lewis: Life, Works and Legacy*.

[3] The diary entry (Saturday, 24 May 1924, in Lewis, *All My Road Before Me*, 325) refers to a friend's plan to reprint Traherne's *Ethics*, while all the other instances refer to the *Centuries*.

[4] Lewis, *George MacDonald*, 20.

[5] C. S. Lewis, 'On the Reading of Old Books', 164. The whole phrase is 'mild, frightening, Paradisial flavour', and describes Vaughan, Boehme and Traherne. Cf. CSL to Arthur Greeves, 12 November 1961, Lewis, *Letters*, 3: 1295: 'there is all the gold and fragrance'.

[6] Other 'endorsements' are: letters of 29 July 1930 (to Arthur Greeves), 26 March 1940 (to Mary Neylan); August 19, 1942 (to H. Morland); April 22, 1945 (to Michael Thwaites); 3 November 1949 (to Rhona M. Bodle); 13 October 1958 (to Corbin S. Carnell); 9 May 1961 (to Margaret Gray). See Lewis, *Letters*, 1: 916; 2: 376; 2: 529; 2: 645; 2: 994; 3: 978; 3: 1264. Similarly, Traherne is included in listings of influential books in 'On the Reading of Old Books', 163, and in Lewis, *Preface*, 127.

Charles Williams and C.S. Lewis: Friends in Co-inherence. Paul S. Fiddes, Oxford University Press. © Paul S. Fiddes 2021.
DOI: 10.1093/oso/9780192845467.003.0014

on William Blake discloses much about his development of the idea of 'coinherence', so I suggest that Lewis' treatment of Traherne is revealing of his own approach to 'co-inherence' in the world and human life. Conversely, as with the other chapters in Part IV, being sensitive to the idea of co-inherence opens a fresh angle on the work of our two writers; here it alerts us to a more central place occupied by Traherne in Lewis' thinking than is usually perceived.

Why, then, has this place been missed or underplayed in studies of C. S. Lewis?[7] It is not, I suggest, because Lewis never wrote anything extensive about Traherne. I rather think it to be because the relation to Traherne is so *widespread* in everything Lewis wrote that critics have fallen into the age-long trap of missing the wood for the trees. To make clear that desire is the impulse behind poetics, or imaginative creation whether in prose or poetry, Lewis appeals quite naturally to Traherne. In *Surprised by Joy*, he recollects the time when—at the age of six, seven, and eight—he was inventing an animal-land. In retrospect, he admits 'that there was no poetry, even no romance, in it. It was almost astonishingly prosaic,' and 'in the highest sense of all, this invented world was not imaginative'.[8] However, he writes that there were other experiences that did truly touch his imagination, and proceeds to tell the story of early glimpses of something desired, commenting that 'The thing has been much better done by Traherne and Wordsworth.' What Lewis sees as making the difference, and turning the prosaic into poetry, is desire. The first glimpse of desire is the memory of 'when my brother had brought his toy garden into the nursery':

It is difficult to find words strong enough for the sensation which came over me; Milton's "enormous bliss" of Eden (giving the full, ancient meaning to "enormous") comes somewhere near it. It was a sensation, of course, of desire; but desire for what? [...] The second glimpse came through *Squirrel Nutkin* [...]. It troubled me with that I can only describe as the Idea of Autumn. It sounds fantastic to say that one can be enamoured of a season, but that is something like what happened; and, as before, the experience was one of intense desire [...]. The third glimpse came through poetry. I had become fond of Longfellow's *Saga of King Olaf* [...]. I was uplifted into huge regions of northern sky, I desired with almost sickening intensity something never to be described (except that it is cold, spacious, severe, pale, and remote).[9]

---

[7] McGrath, in his *Intellectual World of C.S. Lewis*, mentions Traherne only briefly, 108, 52, though he does use the phrase 'poetics of desire.' Price, 'Seventeenth Century', 154–5, associates Lewis with Traherne, citing seven references, but missing key examples I mention in this chapter. Three extracts from Traherne (1.80, 1.87, 1.53) are included in Bell, *From the Library of CS Lewis*, but none are actually from the passages to which Lewis himself refers. Barkman, *C. S. Lewis*, has five passing references to Traherne, and takes a little more interest in Lewis' failure to find enough fallenness in him (409, n.37).

[8] Lewis, *Surprised by Joy*, 22.   [9] Lewis, *Surprised by Joy*, 22–3.

Desire, then, is the impulse behind a poetics, and while he has not derived the idea of desire from Traherne, he associates it almost casually with him (and also with Wordsworth, but we will come to this in due course).

14.1 The Desire for Something Unknown

Having initially related 'desire' to Traherne, Lewis goes on to head one of his chapters in *Surprised by Joy* (chapter 5) with a quotation from Traherne, taken from the very beginning of his *Centuries*: 'So is there in us a world of love to somewhat, though we know not what in the world that should be' (1.2).[10] For Lewis, this encapsulates his life-long experience of desire for some reality transcending everyday life, a heavenly desire. Sometimes he calls it eros, sometimes a romantic yearning, and sometimes *Sehnsucht*, a longing for something sublime, or a happiness beyond the world not yet known. It is always associated with a sense of joy; as he writes, joy is 'an unsatisfied desire which is itself more desirable than any other satisfaction'.[11]

Traherne's phrase about a 'world of love to somewhat' is, in the *Centuries*, placed in the context of a reflection that:

> Things unknown have a Secret Influence on the Soul: and, like the Centre of the earth Unseen, violently Attract it. We lov we know not what: and therfore evry Thing allures us. [...] Do you not feel your self Drawn with the Expectation and Desire of som Great Thing?

This has strong resonance with Lewis' sense of desire, and yet for Traherne, the 'love to [a mysterious] somewhat' is a less strong motif than the sheer joy of living in God's world and sharing in the life of God *here and now*. The word 'joy' occurs on virtually every page of the *Centuries*, but it is not the joy of *unsatisfied* desire, as in Lewis, but of *satisfied* desire. As in God, so in humanity, 'Infinit Wants *Satisfied* Produce infinit *Joys*; And, in the Possession of those Joys, are infinit Joys themselvs' (1.43). The desire of human beings, which Traherne remarks is 'insatiable' (1.22), is properly directed to this world and to God who is known there. Traherne bids us: 'You never Enjoy the World aright, till you see all things in it so perfectly yours, that you cannot desire them any other Way' (1.38). Traherne does affirm

---

[10] This is Lewis' own text, reading from *Thomas Traherne, Centuries of Meditations*, edited by Bertram Dobell (1927), as with all Lewis' quotations in this chapter. When quoting directly from Traherne, I myself am using the text in *Traherne. Poems, Centuries and Three Thanksgivings*, edited by Anne Ridler.

[11] Lewis, *Surprised by Joy*, 23–4.

that *Eternity* is the object of every person's desire (5.3), but this is not a yearning for something beyond the world, because the world itself is the space where time and eternity interpenetrate. The human being is

> A seeming Intervall between Time and Eternity and the Inhabitant of both, the Golden link or Tie of the World, yea the Hymenaeus Marrying the Creator and his Creatures together.   (4:74)

I shall have more to say about this interweaving (*perichoresis*) of the spaces of time and eternity in a moment. There is nevertheless a kind of Lewisian *Sehnsucht* in Traherne, as witnessed in his opening observation about a 'love to somewhat'. This emerges most obviously in his search—together with all humanity—for Felicity or happiness, and he comments that we must 'believ that Felicity is a glorious tho an *unknown* Thing' (3.56).[12] Some of his references to joy also link it with an aspiration beyond present experience; for example, 'All Worlds [are] but a Silent Wilderness, without som living Thing, more Sweet and Blessed after which [the soul] Aspireth. [...] Lov in the End is the Glory of the World and the Soul of Joy ... ' (2.62).[13] Most graphically, desire as yearning for the unknown is depicted as longing for a 'far-off country'. He recalls:

> When I heard of any New Kingdom beyond the seas, the Light and Glory of it pleased me immediatly, enterd into me, it rose up within me, and I was Enlarged Wonderfully. [...] When I heard any News I received it with Greediness and Delight, becaus my Expectation was awakend with som Hope that My Happiness and the Thing I wanted was concealed in it. Glad Tidings, you know from a far Country brings us our Salvation.   (3.24–5)

The 'far country' is, literally, some distant and unvisited country in this world, and yet it evokes something more transcendent. Traherne is witnessing to a feeling, like that of Lewis, of having a home elsewhere that he desires. In following paragraphs, he recalls that 'Among other things, there befel me a most infinit Desire of a book from Heaven, for observing all things to be rude and superfluous here upon Earth, I thought the Ways of felicity to be known only among the Holy Angels: and that unless I could receiv information from them, I could never be Happy' (3.27). However, for Traherne he is swiftly brought back to the glory and grace that God gives in *this* world. He begins the poem that follows his childhood memory with his surmise that Felicity is absent from him because it dwells far away:

---

[12] My italics.   [13] Cf. Traherne, *Centuries*, 4.9.

> What Sacred Instinct did inspire
> My Soul in Childhood with a Hope so Strong?
> What Secret Force moved my Desire,
> To Expect my Joys beyond the Seas, so Yong?
> Felicity I knew
> Was out of View
> And being here alone,
> I saw that Happiness was gone
> From Me! For this
> I Thirsted Absent Bliss...

This has the Lewisian ring of desire about it, but he ends by exclaiming that (3.26):

> little did the Infant Dream
> That all the Treasures of the World were by:
> And that Himself was so the Cream
> And Crown of all, which round about did lie.

If we compare Lewis and Traherne, we thus find them both witnessing to a 'sacred instinct', a 'secret force', a 'desire' for the far-off country where there is true happiness.[14] It may well be that reading Traherne reinforced Lewis' own feeling of desire. But for Traherne, there is a decisive return to the world around him, where for Lewis something eschatological remains, something to be consummated in the future in resurrection from the dead.[15]

Traherne's recollection of childhood was not only of a yearning for far-off lands, but also a discovery that a glorious country was hidden beneath the surface of the everyday world. The vision of childhood made the earth paradise. He remembers:

All appeared New, and Strange at the first, inexpressibly rare and Delightfull and Beautifull. I was a little Stranger, which at my Enterance into the World was Saluted and Surrounded with innumerable Joys. My Knowledg was Divine [...]. I was Entertained like an Angel with the Works of GOD in their Splendor and Glory; I saw all in the Peace of Eden; Heaven and Earth did sing my Creators Praises, and could not make more Melody to Adam, then to me: All Time was Eternity, and a perpetual Sabbath.   (3.2)

The Corn was Orient and Immortal Wheat, which never should be reaped, nor was ever sown. I thought it had stood from Everlasting to Everlasting. The Dust

---

[14] Guite, 'Yearning', 114–17. stresses that for Lewis desire includes reason as well as imagination.
[15] On desire and eschatology in Lewis, see Wolfe, 'C. S. Lewis and the Eschatological Church', 107–10.

and Stones of the Street were as Precious as GOLD. The Gates were at first the End of the World. The Green Trees when I saw them first through one of the Gates Transported and Ravished me . . .   (3.3)

Lewis quotes from this very passage in *Letters to Malcolm*, commenting:

Traherne's 'orient and immortal wheat' or Wordsworth's landscape 'apparelled in celestial light' may not have been so radiant in the past when it was present as in the *remembered* past. That is the beginning of the glorification. One day they will be more radiant still. Thus in the sense-bodies of the redeemed the whole New Earth will arise. The same yet not the same as this.[16]

He is arguing that the intuitions of childhood, such as Traherne reports, become even more radiant in our *memory* of them than they were at the time. This is an anticipation of the resurrection, when our memory will recreate a glorified new earth. Again, then, his thought moves on to eschatology, to the last things. The visionary experiences of childhood are part of desire and joy, but they are orientated towards a *future* hope.

To use another significant phrase, desire is directed towards a future 'weight of glory'. In his famous sermon of this title, Lewis evokes the 'desire for our own far-off country', which he believes everyone knows as an 'inconsolable secret', and this is clearly orientated towards future fulfilment. It is 'a desire for something that has never actually appeared', a 'desire for our own proper place', a 'desire for Paradise', and 'a desire that no natural happiness will satisfy'.[17] More than twenty years before *Letters to Malcolm*, he makes in this sermon a similar reference to Wordsworth, whom he admits apparently identified the object of desire with certain moments in his own past; but these Lewis declares to be not 'the thing itself', but 'only the reminder of it', since 'what he remembered would turn out to be a remembering' of things *through* which the longing came:

These things—the beauty, the memory of our own past—are good images of what we really desire, but if they are mistaken for the thing itself they turn into dumb idols, breaking the hearts of their worshippers. For they are not the thing itself; they are only the scent of a flower we have not found, the echo of a tune we have not heard, news from a country we have never visited [. . .]. [T]hough I do not believe (I wish I did) that my desire for Paradise proves that I shall enjoy it, I think it a pretty good indication that such a thing exists.[18]

---

[16] Lewis, *Letters to Malcolm*, 156. My italics.   [17] Lewis, 'Weight of Glory', 200–1.
[18] Lewis, 'Weight of Glory', 200.

Just as Lewis differs from Charles Williams in conceiving of 'glory' essentially as an eschatological reality, where Williams finds it strongly present in the experience of lovers here and now, so he differs from Traherne in finding the object of the most piercing kind of desire to lie most evidently in the future. It is quite appropriate to associate Williams with Traherne here: in an unpublished address, Williams claims that Traherne is finding an 'appearance' of the infinite in the everyday, citing his experience that 'something infinite behind everything appeared which answered my expectation and *moved my desire*'.[19] Williams continues that, like Blake, Traherne looks 'at' the infinite; he 'observes' it as 'an objective fact':

> Suppose Traherne to be right; suppose that something infinite has appeared. What does one do about it? One of two things; you may look <u>at</u> it or you may look <u>into</u> it. You may prefer to acknowledge it merely or you may prefer to explore and to define it. The normal 18th century way was to look <u>at</u> it. They regarded the man who wished to explore it, to run a serious risk of losing himself in it, as an Enthusiast [...][Blake's] Tiger becomes more and more infinite ... as the poem proceeds.

But, rather than a desire arising from the 'objective' *appearance* of the infinite, in each of the key places in his writing over many years where Lewis reflects on desire in an intense sense, it is fundamentally a desire for 'heaven'. Of course, the term 'heaven' can only be a symbol of the future reality of that unknown country for which he feels a longing.[20] In the section on 'Hope' in his *Christian Behaviour* of 1943, he writes that 'if I find in myself a desire which no experience in this world can satisfy, the most probable explanation is that I was made for another world.'[21] In his 1943 Preface to his *Pilgrim's Regress*, in explaining what he means by 'romanticism' he writes similarly of a desire that indicates 'the human soul was made to enjoy some object that is never fully given—nay, cannot even be imagined as given—in our present mode of subjective and spatio-temporal experience'.[22] While Traherne and Williams would have agreed with the qualification 'fully', they would certainly have dissented from the more radical 'cannot even be imagined'. In *Surprised by Joy*, the feeling of desire is for 'something quite different from ordinary life', and 'in another dimension'.[23] The same desire is portrayed mythically in the *Narnia* stories in the voyage to the edge of the world, when the valiant mouse Reepicheep is presented with the challenge to 'go on into the utter east and never return into the world', and he responds 'That is my heart's desire.'[24]

---

[19] Williams, unpublished address 'The Alteration of Passion', Wade CW/MS-7, quoting from Traherne, *Centuries*, 3.3.

[20] Lewis, 'Weight of Glory', 202.   [21] Lewis, Christian Behaviour, 53 (*Mere Christianity*, 108).

[22] Lewis, *Pilgrim's Regress*, 10.   [23] Lewis, *Surprised by Joy*, 23.

[24] Lewis, *Voyage of the Dawn Treader*, 188.

Similarly, King Caspian 'has never forgotten that voyage to the world's end' and 'in his heart of hearts he wants to go there again'.[25]

In contesting the view that Lewis is developing a new form of the ontological argument for the existence of God based on this feeling of desire,[26] Arend Smilde argues first that Lewis is not formulating a proof but simply showing a probability, something that for him most economically explains a persistent phenomenon.[27] Second, and significantly here, he maintains that the 'desire' in Lewis is not primarily for God at all, but for a 'heavenly country'.[28] This accords with the basic contrast I have been pointing out that exists between Lewis on the one hand, and Traherne and Williams on the other, but the difference can only be an emphasis and not absolute. As Smilde himself admits, there is a relation between 'heaven' and God. Moreover, the picture in the Narnia stories of a 'desire' that various characters feel for Aslan blurs the edges. The Calormene warrior whom Aslan accepts in *The Last Battle* 'desires' to look upon the face of the divine in the form of Tash, and 'began to journey into the strange country and to seek him'. Aslan assures him that 'unless thy desire had been for me thou wouldst not have sought so long and so truly'.[29] In this case, desire is being fulfilled beyond death, but Aslan's presence in the everyday world of Narnia brings, at least by implication, the object of desire into the present. Lewis is, however, curiously oblique in portraying this. When the children, in *The Lion, the Witch and the Wardrobe*, hear that 'Aslan is on the move', Lewis as narrator observes:

> And now a very curious thing happened. None of the children knew who Aslan was any more than you do; but the moment the Beaver had spoken these words everyone felt quite different. [...] At the name of Aslan each one of the children felt something jump in its inside. Edmund felt a sensation of mysterious horror. Peter felt suddenly brave and adventurous. Susan felt as if some delicious smell or some delightful strain of music had just floated by her. And Lucy got the feeling you have when you wake up in the morning and realise that it is the beginning of the holidays or the beginning of summer.[30]

Aslan is shortly going to 'appear', as Traherne puts it, and these descriptions of what the name of Aslan feels like to the children are strikingly similar to what Lewis has recounted as instances of desire in his own childhood, triggered for example by the sight of a toy garden or the coming of autumn. Yet Lewis does not actually use the word 'desire' here; it is as if he wants to reserve 'desire' for the heavenly country that is to come, yet he cannot prevent attaching something like it

---

[25] Lewis, *Silver Chair*, 55.   [26] As first propounded by Beversluis, *C.S. Lewis*, 33–70.
[27] Smilde, 'Horrid Red Herrings', 38–50, 60–5.
[28] Smilde, 'Horrid Red Herrings', 72–3, 83–5. Also argued by McGrath, *Intellectual World*, 115–17 and Connelly, *Inklings of Heaven*, 46–96.
[29] Lewis, *Last Battle*, 164–6.   [30] Lewis, *Lion, the Witch and the Wardrobe*, 67.

to the presence of Aslan—who represents in some way, and however ambiguously, the divine. Indeed, the whole country of Narnia, reached through a wardrobe, might be seen as comparable to the country of 'immortal wheat' and golden dust that Traherne glimpses as a child. While Lewis does not make explicit reference to Traherne's observation that childhood vision is lost as one grows up and the 'first light' is 'eclipsed' (3.7),[31] the idea is surely present in his Narnia stories, since when the children reach adulthood they cannot return to their magical country. Aslan gently tells Edmund and Lucy: 'Dearest, [...] you and your brother will never come back to Narnia. [...] You are too old, children.'[32] They *will* return with the resurrection of the dead, as depicted in the final chronicle, *The Last Battle*, when Aslan tells them, 'The dream is ended: this is the morning.'[33] The final reality is eschatological, and the unicorn Jewell exults that this land beyond death is the 'real' Narnia: 'I have come home at last! This is my real country! [...] This is the land I have been looking for all my life, though I never knew it till now.'[34]

14.2 Desire as Enlargement of the Self: In-being and Co-inherence

Desire, then, in both Traherne and Lewis (for all their difference), takes the shape of the sensation of something unknown. In Traherne, it also has the effect of enlarging the self. In his *Preface to Paradise Lost*, Lewis heads a chapter with an epigram taken from Traherne: 'Men do mightily wrong themselves when they refuse to be present in all ages and neglect to see the beauty of all kingdoms.'[35] In this chapter, Lewis is contesting the view that there is some unchanging human heart to which different cultural forms are simply added on, as if the things that separate one age from another are artificial and that you can simply remove cultural accretions to find the same humanity underneath. Lewis is arguing that culture and the human heart are inseparable, so—and this is his point in a book on Milton—you cannot strip away the Christianity from Milton and still understand him. The result of this argument for poetics generally is that the maker and the reader of literature must be willing to live imaginatively in the lives of others. He goes on to write:

> To enjoy our full humanity we ought, so far as is possible, to contain within us potentially at all times, and on occasion to actualize, all the modes of feeling and thinking through which man has passed. You must, so far as in you lies, become

---

[31] See also Traherne, *Centuries*, 4.86.   [32] Lewis, *Voyage of the Dawn Treader*, 222.
[33] Lewis, *Last Battle*, 140, 183.   [34] Lewis, *Last Battle*, 172.
[35] Lewis, *Preface*, 61. The reference is to Traherne *Centuries* 1.85.

an Achaean chief while reading Homer, a medieval knight while reading Malory, and an Eighteenth-Century Londoner while reading Johnson.[36]

Similarly, in *The Abolition of Man*, in arguing for aesthetics as a preparation for moral growth, Lewis quotes Traherne's question, 'Can you be righteous unless you be just in rendering to things their due esteem? All things were made to be yours and you were made to prize them according to their value.'[37]

These phrases, 'all things were made to be yours' and being 'present in all ages and [...] all kingdoms', belong to a central perception of Traherne: that through love and desire the self expands to contain the whole created world. For Traherne, love enlarges the soul.[38] As he writes, through love, 'all Ages are present in my Soul, and all Kingdoms' (1.100). Indeed, the phrase 'all Ages and all kingdoms' becomes a kind of mantra in Traherne's *Centuries*, repeated at least a dozen times. The inner landscape of the self is the whole universe, embracing 'all things' in the physical world and even comprehending infinity. All space and time is compressed into the single life of the one who loves and desires to enjoy God. 'The World was more in me, then [than] I in it,' Traherne reflects.[39]

To be thoroughly inclusive, the self *expands* into 'infinite space', which Traherne calls the 'room of joys': 'There is a Space also wherin all Moments are infinitly Exhibited, and the Everlasting Duration of infinit Space is another Region and Room of Joys' (5:6). The soul both projects itself into this 'room' and at the same time embraces it within itself (4.73). Love is the means by which 'Thou Expandest and Enlargest thy self' (1.73), and 'The Soul without Extending, and living in its Object, is Dead with in it self' (2.56). True self-love is thus always love for the other.

Though Traherne does not use the precise word, there is a *perichoresis*, or co-inherence (a weaving together), of self, universe, infinity, and eternity. His own word is 'In-being' (1.100):

Wheras there are eight maners of In-being, the In-being of an Object in a Faculty is the Best of all [...]. The Pleasure of an Enjoyer, is the very End why things placed are in any Place [...]. And thus all Ages are present in my Soul, and all Kingdoms, and GOD Blessed forever. And thus Jesus Christ is seen in me and dwelleth in me, when I believ upon Him. And thus all Saints are in me, and I in them. And thus all Angels and the Eternity and Infinity of GOD are in me for evermore. I being the Living TEMPLE and Comprehensor of them. Since

---

[36] Lewis, *Preface*, 63.

[37] Lewis, *Abolition of Man*, 15. Lewis' argument is that value and beauty are inherent to objects, and not just in the subjectivity of the observer. The reference is to Traherne, *Centuries*, 1.12.

[38] Dickerson, 'Lanthorns Sides', 31–47, draws attention to images of boundary, such as the skin, between interior and exterior worlds.

[39] 'Silence' 81; in *Traherne* (ed. Ridler), 27.

therefore all other ways of In-being would be utterly vain, were it not for this: And the Kingdom of God (as our Savior saith, this Way) is within you.

Like Charles Williams three centuries later, Traherne believes that Christ's 'Concepcion Nativity Life and Death may be always within us'.[40] Traherne is thus frustrated when he feels cooped up: 'Creatures that are able to dart their Thoughts into all Spaces, can brook no Limit or Restraint' (5:3). The 'endless intellect' is the expanding 'eye' (3.42). Traherne is preoccupied by this idea, and he evinces a kind of physiological satisfaction at feeling strangely 'enlarged', 'extended', or 'expanded'.[41] Now we can see why joy for Traherne is a present experience, why eternity is in time, and why desire can be satisfied here and now.

Parallel to the enlargement of the self by love is the enlargement by desire. Love, desire, and joy are inseparable. Made in the image of God, a human person's 'Thoughts and Desires can run out to Everlasting. His Lov can extend to all Objects.' (2.23). While 'All Things in Heaven and Earth fall out after my Desire, I am the End and Soveraign of all' (2.55). We 'desire to hav Companions in our Enjoyments to tell our Joys and to spread abroad our Delights, and to be our selves The Joy and Delight of other Persons' (2.79). If human beings were not 'infinitly endebted to this illimited extent [...] there would be no room for their Imaginations; their Desires and Affections would be cooped up, and their Souls imprisoned' (5.3).

Moreover, God is the key part of this co-inherence in love and desire. God is infinite extension, occupying all space, so that nothing can exclude the presence of God.[42] The capacity of human beings to expand into everything and contain everything is because they share that divine state in relating to God. They share in the infinite extension of God because God is in them. God is pure 'Desire from which all things flow' (2.19). The human person is, says Traherne, capable of infinite 'Capacitie': as a circle whose centre is everywhere and whose circumference is nowhere, each human being is in exact spatial 'correspondence' to God. Traherne exclaims:

the whole Hemisphere and the Heavens magnifie your soul to the Wideness of the Heavens. All the Spaces abov the Heavens enlarg it Wider to their own Dimensions. And what is without Limit *maketh* your Conception illimited and Endless. The infinity of GOD [...] must be seen in you, or GOD will be Absent. (4.73)

---

[40]   See Williams on Dante's *figlia del tuo figlio*, Chapter 4, section 2.
[41]   See, for example, Traherne, *Centuries*, 1.73, 3.84.
[42]   Gorman, 'Thomas Traherne', 69–83, explores Traherne's conviction that 'God has focussed his whole Deitie into one small centre' of every atom.

It follows that every person 'is alone the Centre and Circumference of [infinity]. It is all his own, and so Glorious, that it is the Eternal and Incomprehensible Essence of the Deitie' (5.3).[43]

Further, because the expanding eye of the human person is love, and so is also *desire* for the other, the human soul is an image of God as a Trinity of love who also desires creatures for the satisfaction of God's own joy. The Trinity extends itself in love, both within itself (begetting and proceeding) and *beyond* itself. The human *eye* is a mirror for the love of God. (4.86), and love turns the world into multiple mirrors in which a person can 'liv again in other Persons' (2.70). Like the Trinity, the self extends itself through the act of love:[44] 'By Loving a Soul does Propogat and beget it self' (2.56, so also 2.48), writes Traherne. So 'in all love the Trinity is Clear [...]. Lov in the Bosom is the Parent of Lov, Lov in the Stream is the Effect of Lov, Lov seen, or Dwelling in the Object proceedeth from both' (2.40). Again, 'where Lov is the Lover, Lov streaming from the Lover, is the Lover; the Lover streaming from Himself; and Existing in another Person' (2.42).[45] Thus, Traherne's vision of co-inherence is not just imitating God, but participating in God.

The love and desire that expand the self shape the character of Traherne's poetics, which is about 'living again in other persons' or—as Lewis defines creative writing in the passage I quoted earlier—'to contain within us [...] all the modes of thinking and feeling through which man has passed'. One critic, Stanley Stewart, suggests that Traherne, the author, presents himself to us in the *Centuries* as a multiple personality with many voices.[46] Another critic, Robert Ellrodt, observes that Traherne's mind seeks to grasp a multiplicity of objects at one time, so that his poetic world is built out of these enumerations, and multiple phenomena. It is a matter of judgement whether Ellrodt is right that such a poetics may be tempted to resort to *mere* accumulation and repetition.[47]

Expressing his enthusiasm for Traherne in a letter to Arthur Greeves in 1930,[48] Lewis admires this poetics of expansion. 'What do you think of this?' he asks, quoting from Traherne:

'The world ... is the beautiful frontispiece to Eternity'[49] – 'You never enjoy the world aright till the sea itself floweth in your veins, till you are clothed with the

---

[43] Here we can discern the influence of the Cambridge Platonists: see Benjamin Whichcote, 'Sermon on Romans 1:18', in Patrides, *Cambridge Platonists*, 56: 'Every Creature is a line leading to God. God is every-where, in every thing.'

[44] See Stewart, *Expanded Voice*, 128, 130.

[45] See further Traherne, *Centuries* 2.46. Cf. Augustine, *de Trinitate*, 8.14, 9.2.

[46] Stewart, *Expanded Voice*, 131-3.

[47] Ellrodt, *Seven Metaphysical Poets*, 183. Lewis doubts that Traherne's style could be repeated in the modern world, in the face of a demand for 'functionalism'; see Lewis, *Screwtape Letters* (1961), Preface, 13.

[48] CSL to Arthur Greeves, 8 July 1930, Lewis, *Letters*, 1: 914.   [49] Traherne, *Centuries*, 1.20.

heavens and crowned with the stars ... till you can sing and rejoice and delight in God as misers do in gold'.[50]

He then links this with love, quoting once more from Traherne, who associates lack of love with the opposite of expansion—a contraction into isolation:

They [i.e. Souls] were made to lov and are Dark and Vain and Comfortless till they do it. Till they lov they are Idle, or misemployed. Till they lov they are Desolat[e].[51]

Traherne's perception that, because of their capacity for expansion, and because they are in God, every person 'is alone the Centre and Circumference' of infinity is echoed in Lewis' vision of the Great Dance of Perelandra, in which: 'Because we are with him, each of us is at the centre', and 'there seems no centre because it is all centre.'[52] Lewis is, as I have shown, more likely to have taken this idea from Williams than from Traherne, but it is a striking parallel. The interweaving movements of the dance, which is finally the dance of the Trinity, are a powerful image of what Traherne calls 'in-being' and what Lewis calls 'co-existing'.[53] As 'in all love the Trinity is clear [...] the Lover streaming from Himself; and Existing in another Person' (Traherne), so 'the whole dance, or drama, or pattern of this three-Personal life is to be played out in each one of us' (Lewis).[54] The dance ends with a drawing of Ransom into a transcendent desire: 'a simplicity beyond all comprehension, ancient and young as spring, illimitable, pellucid, drew him with cords of infinite desire into its own stillness'.[55]

The Chronicles of Narnia are full of dances—dances of Fauns, Dryads, dwarfs, and Maenads—but for the most part they picture a co-inherence of created beings with each other, rather than the co-inherence of the divine with creation. Notably in the 'Great Snow Dance' of Narnia, the intricate interweaving of the patterns of the dance exemplify the meaning of circumincessio: the point is not for the dancers to throw snowballs at each other, but to throw them 'through' the dance in such perfect time with the music that 'if all the dancers were in exactly the right places at the right moments, no-one would be hit'.[56] This illustrates, graphically, the perichoretic movement of the dance 'through' the dance. There are, however, dances of the children and Narnians with Aslan, such as the dance of the trees around a central open space where Aslan stands in Prince Caspian; just as the voices in the Great Dance of Perelandra proclaim 'Never did he make two things

---

[50] Traherne, Centuries, 1.29.   [51] Traherne, Centuries, 2.48. My italics.
[52] Lewis, Perelandra, 249, 251.
[53] E.g. Lewis, Problem of Pain, 18; also see Chapter 6, section 3.
[54] Lewis, Mere Christianity, 139.   [55] Lewis, Perelandra, 253.   [56] Lewis, Silver Chair, 195.

the same; never did He utter one word twice', so on this occasion Aslan warns Lucy that 'things never happen the same way twice'.[57]

Entering the stable that is to be the doorway to eternal life in *The Last Battle*, the Lord Digory remarks that 'its inside is bigger than its outside', and Lucy responds that 'In our world too, a Stable once had something inside it that was bigger than our whole world.'[58] The stable of Bethlehem and Narnia, like the dance, is a symbol of co-inherence, or Traherne's expansive 'in-being'; it represents the reality that 'all Ages are present in my Soul, and all Kingdoms, and GOD Blessed forever'. The scene in *The Last Battle* also exemplifies Traherne's point that without love for others, the soul contracts into itself and is 'dark and vain and comfortless'. The dwarfs' motto is 'the Dwarfs are for the Dwarfs', and they sit in 'very close together in a little circle', unable to see the 'sky and the trees and the flowers'. It seems to them that they are sitting in 'this pitch-black, poky, smelly little hole of a stable'.[59]

Part of the 'In-being' in Traherne is an interpenetration of the bodily senses with the life of the soul. In drinking wine as a gift of God's love, for example, there is a spiritual enjoyment by the senses: 'To consider it, is to Drink it Spiritualy [...]. And to take Pleasure in all the Benefits it doth to all is Heavenly' (1.27).[60] This image evidently stuck in Lewis' mind from his reading of Traherne; when complimenting Ruth Pitter on the vines grown on her farm in Essex, he slightly misquotes the phrase in the form, 'To consider it, is to *taste* it spiritually.'[61] Perhaps he had in mind also the verse from the Psalms, 'Taste and see that the Lord is good' (Psalm 34:8). However, like desire, for Lewis the *perichoresis* of body and soul is orientated eschatologically. In *Letters to Malcolm*, he draws on the idea that the life of the senses, involved as they are in the physical world, is contained within the soul, in order to suggest that in resurrection the soul can create a new material environment for itself and for fellowship with others: 'in the sense-bodies of the redeemed the whole new earth will arise'.[62]

Lewis, indeed, can be critical of Traherne. In his letter to Arthur Greeves of 1930, he quotes approvingly the sentence in which Traherne sees the human person as contracting into isolation from others, rather than expanding into them, when there is lack of love. Despite this, earlier in the same letter, he makes a criticism of Traherne's view of evil, writing that 'I think he suffers by making out everything much too easy and really shirking the problem of evil in all its forms.'

---

[57] Lewis, *Prince Caspian*, 127. © copyright C. S. Lewis Pte Ltd, 1951.
[58] Lewis, *Last Battle*, 143. Howard, *Narnia and Beyond*, 47–8, points out that the landscape of Narnia is internal and external at the same time.
[59] Lewis, *Last Battle*, 147.
[60] See also Traherne, 'Thanksgiving for the Body', 435–51, in *Traherne*, 386.
[61] CSL to Ruth Pitter, 17 March 1951, Lewis, *Letters*, 3: 1951.
[62] Lewis, *Letters to Malcolm*, 156.

In his *English Literature in the Sixteenth Century*, Lewis makes a similar criticism in writing about Hooker, commenting that in reading him 'we are reminded sometimes of Tyndale, often of Traherne's *Centuries*. Sometimes a suspicion crosses our mind that the doctrine of the Fall did not loom quite large enough in his universe.'[63] Perhaps he is also being critical of Traherne's view of original sin when he writes in *Studies in Words* that 'Traherne, wishing to suggest that example, rather than heredity, explains our corruption, says "it is not so much our parents' loins as our parents' lives that enthrals and blinds us".'[64] However, the context is about life as an ethical process, Lewis writing that 'A man's *life* in this sense is the general tenor of his conduct or behaviour,' and so he may be finding *support* in Traherne's reference to the example of parents' lives. Certainly he approves of Traherne's view of sin when he quotes him as an epigram to a chapter in the *Problem of Pain*:

> Love can forbear, and Love can forgive ... but Love can never be reconciled to an unlovely object - ... - He can never therefore be reconciled to your sin, because sin itself is incapable of being altered; but He may be reconciled to your person, because that may be restored.[65]

Traherne has in mind the possibility of 'alteration' in the sense of expansion towards God and others through love. *That* is why God cannot be reconciled to sin, but can be reconciled to a person who always has this potential. The context of the epigram in Traherne is that sin is hindrance to love, or despising the divine love, and since love is infinite, failure to love makes one 'infinitely deformed'. It is unclear whether Lewis was satisfied by this view of sin. In the chapter headed by the quotation from Traherne, Lewis understands sin not as the failure to love, but as a wilful abuse of freedom.[66] The main point of his chapter is that there is an analogy between the goodness of God and what *we* think to be goodness in human life, but Lewis here does not develop the same kind of analogy of love as in Traherne. I have suggested earlier in this book that Lewis shows some caution about Williams' understanding of co-inherence because he has a more acute sense of the need for nature to be transformed by Christ.[67] It seems, then, that Williams stands closer to Traherne's in-being than does Lewis, despite Lewis' real affinities with Traherne, especially in discerning the trinitarian nature of in-being.

---

[63] Lewis, *English Literature*, 461; there is a passing reference to Traherne, 536.
[64] Lewis, *Studies in Words*, 'Life', 273. The quotation is from Traherne, *Centuries*, 3.8.
[65] Lewis, *Problem of Pain*, 25. The quotation is from Traherne, *Centuries*, 2.30.
[66] See Lewis, *Problem of Pain*, 43; but, 55, he suggests that 'we all sin by needlessly disobeying the apostolic injunction to "rejoice"', which is more Trahernian.
[67] See Chapter 7, section 1.

14.3 Desire as Wanting

A poetics in which desire is the basic poetic impulse, and where desire enlarges the self, is also a creativity that reflects true wants. Desire *is* want. In his letter of 1930 to Greaves, Lewis explicitly quotes Traherne's promise that 'I must lead you out of this into another world to *learn your wants*. For till you find them you will never be happy' (1.43).[68] In his sermon on 'The Weight of Glory', Lewis repeats the idea: while in his desire he imagined that he wanted all kinds of things, he witnesses that since he heard of the 'glory' that is to come, 'I have begun to learn better what I really wanted.'[69]

The word 'want' includes ideas of dcsire, need, and lack, and Traherne plays on all three meanings. '*Be Sensible of your Wants*', he writes, '*that you maybe sensible of your Treasures* [...]. Did you not from all Eternity Want som one to give you a Being? Did you not Want one to give you a Glorious Being? [...] And at once present even like GOD with infinit Wants and infinit Treasures?' (1.45). It is this sense of want that is driving Traherne's rhetorical prose. In his Preface to *Pilgrim's Regress*, Lewis also reflects on the difference that desire makes to 'want': 'Sweet Desire cuts across our ordinary distinctions between wanting and having.' He explains that while having something normally means not wanting it any longer, having desire is by definition to want.[70] This is the 'old bitter-sweetness' that all writers in the romantic genre know.

Lewis' *Chronicles of Narnia* offer a number of illustrations of Traherne's admonition to 'learn your wants', which seems to have struck him so forcibly. Traherne bids us to 'Want like a God' (1.44), and Lewis believes that through our desires we can conform our wants to what God wants. In *Prince Caspian*, Lucy refers to the way the four children have been whisked out of their everyday life in England to the ruins of Cair Paravel in Narnia: 'But we want to be here, don't we,' said Lucy, 'if Aslan wants us?'[71] In a parable of faith, 'the evidence of things not seen',[72] for a while Lucy is the only one of the four who can see Aslan, and she tries to convince the others of his directions to her:

> 'I didn't think I saw him. I saw him.' [...]
> 'And he wanted us to go where he was—up there.'
> 'How do you know that was what he wanted?' asked Edmund.
> 'He—I—I—I just know,' said Lucy, 'by his face.'[73]

---

[68] See n. 48. Lewis' modernization.   [69] Lewis, 'Weight of Glory', 206.
[70] Lewis, *Pilgrim's Regress* (1943), 8.   [71] Lewis, *Prince Caspian*, 92.
[72] Hebrews 12:1. Lucy is evidently also playing the role of Mary Magdalen, who announces to the disciples of Jesus, 'I have seen the Lord' (John 20:18).
[73] Lewis, *Prince Caspian*, 112–13.

In *The Silver Chair*, Aslan assures King Caspian, who wants to see for a moment the world of the children, that 'You cannot want wrong things any more, now that you have died.'[74]

By learning to 'want like a God', Traherne, however, has something more radical in mind than Lewis. He means that 'want' is not a state confined to created beings; *we* want because we share in *God's* own wanting. God wants us from all eternity, and this gives us a kind of pre-existence in God. Because of God's want, Traherne asserts, from all eternity our being was with God. Want is the reason for God's own creativity, God's making of the universe and its creatures. Daringly, Traherne affirms that:

> He is from Eternity full of Want, or els He would not be full of Treasure. Infinit Want is the very Ground and Caus of infinit Treasure. It is Incridible, yet very Plain: Want is the Fountain of all His Fulness. Want in GOD is a Treasure to us. For had there been no Need He would not hav Created the World, nor Made us, nor Manifested His Wisdom, nor Exercised His Power, nor Beautified Eternity, nor prepared the Joys of Heaven. But he Wanted Angels and Men, Images, Companions: And these He had from all Eternitie.   (1.42)

This is not a want forced upon God by external necessity, but a want flowing from God's own overflowing desire. So, declares Traherne, 'Infinit Wants Satisfied Produce infinit Joys; and, in the Possession of those Joys, are infinit Joys themselvs' (1.43). This is the context of the saying that Lewis quotes directly, that we 'must learn what our wants are'. Traherne bids us: 'you must want like a God that you may be satisfied like God. Were you not made in His Image?' (1.44).

It is an ancient theological conundrum to ask why God created the world, and the classical answer has been that it could not be out of need, as this would seem to infringe the aseity (self-existence) of God.[75] Classical theology has insisted that no reason for creation can strictly be given, but that it must have been entirely an unmotivated act of the benevolence of God.[76] Lewis echoes this answer in *The Four Loves*, asserting that in our 'Need-love' we are 'least like God' whose love is Gift-love: 'For what can be more unlike than fullness and need, sovereignty and humility, righteousness and penitence, limitless power and a cry for help?'[77] Lewis, then, is not attending to the context of Traherne's saying that 'we must learn what our wants are', or deliberately ignoring it. Traherne is preserving God's aseity by a kind of pre-existence of all created beings with God, at least in God's mind: God is not affected or changed by having wants or needs because God had the objects of his wants with him 'from all eternity'. Here Traherne follows the Christian

---

[74] Lewis, *Silver Chair*, 214. © copyright C. S. Lewis Pte Ltd, 1953.

[75] On aseity, see Augustine, *Sermones* 7.7; Anselm, *Monologion* 24; Aquinas, *S.Th.* 1a. 9. 1.

[76] See e.g. Mascall, *He Who Is*, 112.   [77] Lewis, *Four Loves*, 12.

Platonist tradition, such as in the early Church Father Origen, of an eternal creation, an eternal existence of created images of God.[78] The result of this kind of theology is that God remains entirely unconditioned by the created world. While Lewis does not want to suggest that God has 'wants' in the sense of 'needs', he does think that human acts, and especially prayer, make a difference to God:

> Can we believe that God ever really modifies His action in response to the suggestions of men? [...] He allows soils and weather and animals and the muscles, minds, and wills of men to co-operate in the execution of His will [...].
> It is not really stranger, nor less strange, that my prayers should affect the course of events than that my other actions should do so. They have not advised or changed God's mind that is, His over-all purpose. But that purpose will be realized in different ways according to the actions, including the prayers, of His creatures.[79]

The efficacy of prayer has led Lewis, in *Letters to Malcolm*, to think that the classical insistence on the impassibility of God need not be maintained,[80] but he has not reached the point of thinking, with Traherne, that God has infinite wants. I suggest that it is possible to combine the insights of both Lewis and Traherne. Self-existence (aseity) need not mean self-sufficiency; God can freely desire to be in need;[81] God might will to have wants satisfied by created beings. As Karl Barth puts it, God 'ordains that He should not be entirely self-sufficient as He might be',[82] and 'God must not only be unconditioned but, in the absoluteness in which He sets up this fellowship [i.e. with mankind], He can and will also be conditioned.'[83]

14.4 Desire as Worship

In another letter written to Arthur Greaves in 1930, Lewis bids him:

> Remember too what Traherne says, that our appreciation of this world—and *this* becomes fully conscious only as we express it in art—is a real link in the universal chain. Beauty descends from God into nature: but there it would perish and does

---

[78] Origen, *De Principiis*, 2.9.1–3; this view was inherited by the Cambridge Platonists: see More, *Immortality of the Soul*, 2: 237–57. Scott, 'Platonic Recollection', 73–97, argues that the Cambridge Platonists, while accepting pre-existence and innate ideas, rejected Plato's doctrine of recollection; there is no trace of the power of recollection in Traherne.

[79] Lewis, 'Efficacy of Prayer', in Lewis, *The World's Last Night*, 8–9, © copyright C. S. Lewis Pte Ltd, 1960.

[80] Lewis, Letters to Malcolm, 72–5.

[81] For a fuller defence of this point, see Fiddes, *Creative Suffering*, 71–6.

[82] Barth, *Church Dogmatics*, II/2, 10.   [83] Barth, *Church Dogmatics*, II/1, 303.

except when a Man appreciates it with worship and thus as it were *sends it back to God*: so that through his consciousness what descended ascends again and the perfect circle is made.[84]

This is a close summary of Traherne's perception that human perception of the world is the 'golden link' (4.74) between creator and creatures, and that God loves creation *through* the creative mind of human beings. They are the means by which the love of God flows back to its source. Lewis also evidently has in mind the place where Traherne writes:

The World within you is an offering returned. Which is infinitly more Acceptable to GOD Almighty, since it came from him, that it might return unto Him. Wherin the Mysterie is Great. For GOD hath made you able to Creat Worlds in your own mind, which are more Precious unto Him than those which He Created: And to Give and offer up the World unto Him, which is very Delightfull in flowing from Him, but much more in Returning to Him. (2.90)

Traherne can even say, audaciously, that 'a Thought of the World, or the World in a Thought, is more Excellent than the World, becaus it is Spiritual and Nearer unto GOD'. Such appreciation of the world, comments Lewis, is expressed most fully in art. Several centuries later, the poet Coleridge was to define the primary imagination as an imitation of God's creative work, but the secondary imagination as even more powerful, as a creativity that, through poetic images, 'dissolves . . . in order to re-create', or in other words to make *new worlds* that God has not made.[85] Traherne anticipates this secondary imagination, or a co-creativity with God, in his perception that 'the Thought of the World wherby it is Enjoyed is Better then [than] the World. So is the Idea of it in the Soul of Man, better then [than] the World in the Esteem of God' (2.90).

It must be said that, although Lewis commends Traherne in this letter for his insight that art is worship, returning the beauty of the world to God, he is much less ready to follow his view of human creativity. His own poetics is—we may say—more like Coleridge's primary imagination, a matter of thinking the thoughts of God after God. He writes: 'We—poets and musicians and inventors—never in the ultimate sense, make. We only build. We always have materials to build from.'[86] This may well be because of a remnant in his mind of either Platonic

---

[84] CSL to Arthur Greaves, 28 August 1930, Lewis, *Letters*, 1: 933.

[85] Coleridge, *Biographia Literaria*, 1: 202.

[86] Lewis, *Letters to Malcolm*, 98. Cf. Lewis, 'Membership', 44: 'The pestilent notion [. . .] [that] to be original is the main end of life.'

ideas or the Absolute of idealist philosophy, of which images in this world are only shadows, relative forms, or pale reflections.

In understanding worship to be an offering of God's gifts of beauty back to God, Lewis stresses that this means praising persons and things in God's creation in a way that is appropriate to their worth.[87] It would, he thinks, be an 'absurd Deity' who needed our worship, although Traherne gets close to what Lewis considers an absurdity when he writes that 'He infinitly desires to be Admired and Beloved' (3.82) given Traherne's understanding that for God, desire is 'want'. For Lewis, we delight to praise what we enjoy and value, be this God or a lover, a poem, a game, or a mountain: 'the worthier the object, the more intense this delight would be'.[88] Here we catch a further echo of his quotation of *Traherne* in *The Abolition of Man* about 'rendering things their due esteem'.

14.5 Two Visions of Joy

Let us return, now we have come so far, to the enigma that, for all his references to Traherne and admiration of him, Lewis wrote not so much as a page about him. Lewis has two poetic visions of childhood available to him, two accounts of the openness of the growing mind of a child to joy. They are Traherne, especially in the third of the *Centuries*, and Wordsworth, in *The Prelude*. Lewis, in fact, simply links the two poets in several places: 'Traherne *and* Wordsworth'. For instance, in two essays, Lewis remarks that neither Traherne nor Wordsworth would have been permitted to cultivate the solitude that fosters 'long, long thoughts' if they had been born in the modern world.[89] On the surface, however, it seems to be Wordsworth who gets the weight of his attention: once, when asked to list the books that had influenced him most, he included Wordsworth's *Prelude* among ten he submitted, but not Traherne's *Centuries*,[90] though he went on pressing it upon his correspondents in book lists.

One commentator on Lewis, Mary Ritter,[91] argues that the semi-autobiographical *The Pilgrim's Regress* is modelled on *The Prelude*, both texts sharing the same thematic structure; in both the protagonist experiences a 'happy fall', and both receive back their reason and imagination in better forms. Lewis learned from the Romantics as a whole, and Wordsworth in particular, funda-mental ideas about the proper status and function of reason and imagination. He

---

[87] Lewis, *Reflections on the Psalms*, 93–6. Kallistos Ware, 'Sacramentalism', 54–5, 61–2, compares Lewis' appreciation of the beauty of the world to Traherne, and proposes that Traherne, Lewis, and Williams all affirm the 'sacramentality' of the world. I find this more appropriate for Williams and Traherne than for Lewis, given different world-views (see Chapter 6, section 2) and Lewis' understand-ing of desire (see section 1 of this chapter).

[88] Lewis, *Reflections on the Psalms*, 95–6.

[89] Lewis, 'Lilies that Fester', 42; Lewis, 'Membership', 35 (along with Augustine and Vaughan).

[90] See Werther and Werther, *C.S. Lewis' List*, xii.   [91] Ritter, 'William Wordsworth', 93–112.

could have learnt it from Blake, as Charles Williams did, but Blake seems to have had little appeal to him. Ritter urges that Lewis' understanding of 'joy' was particularly Wordsworthian and that he viewed his own pantheist stage, influenced by Wordsworth's pantheism, as an important stepping stone to his conversion. Wordsworth's poetry gave to Lewis, she argues, a way to understand his own history by documenting his moments of joy as Wordsworth does, and it gave to Lewis a language by which to express his own story.[92] Certainly, the title of Lewis' spiritual biography *Surprised by Joy* comes from Wordsworth's poem 'Surprised by Joy', a piece about his memory and intense longing for a love who is wholly other because she is dead.

Ritter thus concludes that Lewis was indebted to Wordsworth for both the concept and the term 'joy'.[93] For both, she affirms, joy is an experience of 'something behind the veil, of something spiritual that is immanent'. She discerns, however, a significant difference between them. For Wordsworth, joy was prompted by the pantheistic spirit that rolls through all things, while for Lewis, the desire at the heart of joy is ultimately the desire for God in response to God's calling. In other words, I suggest, it is a *Trahernian* understanding of joy, and a poetics of *desire*. As we have seen, in *Surprised by Joy*, Lewis compares his own story of a growing sense of joy to both Wordsworth *and* Traherne, modestly admitting that they have done it better.[94] Lewis was, however, critical of Wordsworth as one who had lost a sense of joy because he neglected to find its true source—namely in God.[95]

The term 'joy' itself is, of course, far more prevalent in Traherne than in Wordsworth. Ritter makes a lot of the statistical fact that there are forty-five occurrences of 'joy' or 'enjoyment' in *The Prelude*. If statistics matter, there are more than forty-five uses of these words in the first *Century* alone, and similar numbers in the other four. While Wordsworth supplies the title for *Surprised by Joy*, Traherne gets almost even honours by being chosen to supply the epigram to the key chapter 5.

However, the fact remains that Lewis included Wordsworth's *Prelude*, and not Traherne's *Centuries*, as one of the ten books that influenced him most.[96] We might find two reasons for this. First, Wordsworth stressed the note of fallenness in joy that Lewis missed in Traherne, so taking human sin seriously. Perhaps Lewis failed to register Traherne's confession about the loss of childhood joy through what he calls his 'Apostasy' (*Centuries* 3.2). Second, Lewis wanted to be a poet, and so perhaps found a kindred spirit in the growing story of a poet in Wordsworth, even a model. He thought Traherne's poetry poor stuff, and valued

---

[92] Ritter, 'William Wordsworth', 110.   [93] Ritter, 'William Wordsworth', 102.
[94] Lewis, *Surprised by Joy*, 22.
[95] Lewis, *The Four Loves*, 32; similarly, Lewis, *Surprised by Joy*, 166–7.
[96] Nevertheless, he apparently wrote no entire essay on Wordsworth.

him highly as a prose writer. Ironically, Lewis' own literary strength turned out to be Traherne's rather than Wordsworth's, and a poetics of desire drove his marvellous *prose*.

Perhaps reading Traherne sensitized Lewis to the theme of joy in Wordsworth, and then the two simply merged in his mind. The question is what Traherne may have distinctively given Lewis, and here we find the wedding of joy and *desire*, especially in the image of longing for a far country, and entering it in imagination. When Traherne writes of hearing about any new kingdom beyond the seas, he goes on to report that:

> I entered into it, I saw its Commodities, Rarities, Springs, Meadows Riches, Inhabitants, and became Possessor of that New Room, as if it had been prepared for me, so much was I Magnified and Delighted in it.   (3:24)

That seems much closer to 'Nothernness' and Narnia than Wordsworth's treatment of joy. In 'The Weight of Glory', Lewis refers to the far-off country of our desire and a 'far-off land', explicitly mentioning Wordsworth, but using the phrase 'news from a country we have never yet visited'.[97] This may be an echo of William Morris' 'news from nowhere',[98] or Yeats' 'land of heart's desire', but also surely of Traherne who witnesses:

> When I heard any News I receivd it with Greediness and Delight, because my Expectation was awakend with som Hope that My Happiness and the Thing I wanted was concealed in it. Glad Tidings, you know, from a far Country brings us our Salvation.   (3:25)[99]

So in *Till we have Faces*, Psyche tells Orual of her life-long desire 'to reach the mountain, to find the place where all the beauty came from—[...] my country, the place where I ought to have been born', and asks, 'Do you think it all meant nothing, all the longing? The longing for home?'[100] In *The Last Battle*, this country is clearly eschatological, a future new creation, and entering it Jewell the unicorn rejoices that 'I have come home at last! [...] This is the land I have been looking for all my life.'[101]

Might it be then that Traherne is a significant inspiration for the *Chronicles* of children visiting a 'far-off land of desire' and adults visiting far-off planets? I have been drawing on the *Chronicles* rather more extensively in this chapter than in others in order to give substance to my own suspicion that this is the case.

---

[97] Lewis, 'Weight of Glory', 200, 202.
[98] In 'Sagas and Modern Life', 409, Lewis writes about 'desire' and 'irrepressible thirst for immortality' in Morris; see also Lewis, 'William Morris', 225, 228.
[99] The reference is to Proverbs 25:25.   [100] Lewis, *Till We Have Faces*, 83–4.
[101] Lewis, *Last Battle*, 172.

Certainly, in the Narnian tales, a whole world is contained in a wardrobe or in a stable, just as for Traherne far-off countries are contained within his own soul, as he witnesses:

> This shewd me the Liveliness of interior presence, and that all Ages were for most Glorious Ends, Accessible to my Understanding, yea with it, yea within it. For without changing Place in my self I could behold and enjoy all those.   (3.24)

Differences certainly remain between the poetics of desire in Lewis and Traherne. For Lewis the emphasis is on wants *unsatisfied*, and for Traherne on wants *satisfied*. Lewis always looks towards future consummation, and the 'paradisial flavour' of a text leads us towards the last things (to the eschaton), though this will be a glorification of what we know now in the body. Traherne seems more satisfied with paradise here and now; everything can be fulfilled in the self in union with God. Perhaps this coheres with another difference: Lewis looks to art simply to reflect God's own creativity, while Traherne expects the human mind to create the world anew, new even to God.

Surely, a Christian poetics needs all these dimensions—a finding of hidden felicity in the everyday creation, and yet a sense of there always being something more with God, some overplus and excess such as late-modern critics find in the openness of a text. This paradox of satisfaction and lack of satisfaction is rooted in the reality of co-inherence or 'in-being' in the world that both Traherne and Lewis perceive. There is joy in the interweaving of all things in a triune God here and now, and joy in the anticipation of a still deeper participation or—as Lewis puts it—'farther up and farther in!'.[102]

---

[102] The title of the penultimate chapter of Lewis, *Last Battle*: see also 173, 175, 176, 177, 180.

PART V

THE THEOLOGY OF CO-INHERENCE

15

Co-inherence and Relations in the Trinity

15.1 Two World Views

At various points in this book I have made the suggestion that Lewis and Williams were writing from the perspective of two somewhat different world views. As a Christian Neoplatonist, despite making far-reaching changes to classical Neoplatonism owing to Christian beliefs, Lewis saw all things and persons as held within a rather strict hierarchy of higher and lower status in the order of being. Williams appears to have been influenced by a Christian Kabbalism, and despite the equally far-reaching changes he made to Jewish medieval Kabbalism by his orthodox Christian convictions, he saw the world as a place of divine immanence, where the eternal Logos of God was incarnate in far wider ways than in the historic person of Jesus of Nazareth and where the glory of God was instantiated in many places. He would surely have approved of the words that W. H. Auden put into the mouth of Simeon, that we may not 'limit the coinherence of the One and the Many to a special case'.[1] Indeed, *For the Time Being*, from which this meditation comes, owed much to the influence of Williams, as we shall see. When Lewis and Williams used, or deliberately resisted using, the word 'co-inherence', it was always these differing contexts within which they were writing.

In this last chapter, I want to consider the place of 'co-inherence' in the doctrine of God as Trinity from the viewpoint of modern theologians, beginning with more reflection on the context of the term 'co-inherence' in the study by G. L. Prestige entitled *God in Patristic Thought*, which Williams had read, and from which I have argued he took the unusual English word in the first place. In this reflection as a theologian, however, I shall be keeping in mind the implications for co-inherence that emerge from the different models of the created order held by Lewis and Williams.

It is at least of biographical interest that, until he ceased to supervise research students at the University of Cambridge in December 1962 owing to his increasing illness, Lewis was supervising a graduate student who was preparing an edition of the Latin text of *de Occulta Philosophia* by Heinrich Cornelius Agrippa of

[1] Auden, *For the Time Being*, in *Collected Poems*, 391–2.

Charles Williams and C.S. Lewis: Friends in Co-inherence. Paul S. Fiddes, Oxford University Press. © Paul S. Fiddes 2021.
DOI: 10.1093/oso/9780192845467.003.0015

Nettesheim.[2] Remarkably, Agrippa's three books fuse together Renaissance accounts of the two world views with which we are concerned,[3] compiling into one work the Christian Neoplatonism of Marsilio Ficino,[4] and the Christian Kabbalism contained in the writings of Pico Della Mirandola.[5] At first, Lewis had refused to supervise the student concerned, Francis Warner, because he thought that Warner wanted to study the impact of Agrippa on such twentieth-century writers as W. B. Yeats, who—like Williams—had been influenced by the modern hermetic movement originating in the Order of the Golden Dawn.[6] When Warner made clear that he was interested in an edited edition of Agrippa, Lewis agreed,[7] and met virtually weekly during term with Warner for sessions lasting more than two hours from 1959 to 1962,[8] in order to prepare the Latin text.

Lewis had in fact already showed interest in Agrippa. He had, just a few years before, referred to Agrippa's influence on English writers in his *English Literature in the Sixteenth Century* volume, quoting his claim that 'Once, by the iudgment of all olde philosophers Magick held the hyest place of honour', and that, although it has been unjustly forbidden and denounced by the church, it is 'a hye holy learning' (*sublimis sacraque disciplina*).[9] This clearly reflects Agrippa's kabbalistic interests, although Lewis also connects his 'high magic' with the 'characteristic' Platonic philosophy of the time.[10] Earlier, in the novel *That Hideous Strength*, Agrippa had appeared in kabbalistic guise as one of the Renaissance 'magicians' compared unfavourably with practitioners of the 'old magic' in ancient times, who are represented by the mythical figure of Merlin.[11] 'Magic' here means essentially the exploration of sympathetic connections between the natural world, celestial bodies in the heavens, and the human body on earth, and attempts to use these links to produce favourable outcomes for human life. In any case, Lewis greets Warner's proposal with enthusiasm 'if only for the selfish reason that I might then have a copy on my own shelves'.[12] He tells Warner that up to this point he has only had access to the Latin text of Agrippa in a volume in the library of University

---

[2] The full title of Warner's thesis was 'A Bibliographical Edition of the Latin Text of *De Occulta Philosophia* by H. Cornelius Agrippa [1533], edited together with a revision of the translation of the text published by J.F. in 1651'.

[3] See Yates, *Occult Philosophy*, 37–41.

[4] See Ficino, *Platonic Theology* on God, forms, and ideas: 11.3.22; 11.4.7–15; 12, 3, 5; 18.8.17.

[5] Pico della Mirandola, 'Seventy-One Cabalistic Conclusions'. Waite prints 49 of Pico's 'Conclusions' in his *Holy Kabbalah*, which Williams may have read.

[6] CSL to Francis Warner, 11 July 1959, Lewis, *Letters*, 3: 1065–6.

[7] CSL to Francis Warner, 15 July, 1959, Lewis, *Letters*, 3: 1067–8.

[8] For Warner's account, see Lewis, *Letters*, 3: 1727.

[9] Lewis, *English Literature*, 9, quoting the dedicatory epistle to Trithemius of *De Occulta Philosophia*; Lewis appears to be making his own translation from Latin in sixteenth-century English, since this does not correspond to the translation of J.F. (1651).

[10] Lewis, *English Literature*, 9, 13.   [11] Lewis, *That Hideous Strength*, 246.

[12] CSL to Francis Warner, 15 July, 1959, Lewis, *Letters*, 3: 1067.

College, Oxford, and from a much earlier letter we learn that he first discovered it there in 1917.[13]

Francis Warner was the last research student supervised by Lewis, and was himself to hold Fellowships at colleges in both Oxford and Cambridge,[14] as well as becoming a prolific and distinguished poet and playwright. Three years after his supervision by Lewis ended, he was appointed to a Tutorial Fellowship in English at St Peter's College, Oxford (where I was in his first batch of undergraduate students). He confirms that Lewis was content to be regarded as a Platonist of some kind at this late period of his life,[15] recalling that Lewis, Kathleen Raine, and others—with himself as a junior partner—dubbed themselves the 'Cambridge Platonists' of the modern day.[16] He also recalls that Lewis was more forthcoming in talking about the Neoplatonist elements in Agrippa, discoursing learnedly on Plotinus and the ancient 'Alexandrian Christian Platonists', than he was on the Kabbala. Warner's own view is that Lewis felt at ease with the Neoplatonist tradition since he could read its exponents in Greek, where he was unwilling to pronounce on kabbalistic elements since he had no Hebrew. Warner recalls that Lewis firmly refused to offer opinions about matters where he felt he had little academic grasp of a subject. Warner himself learned Hebrew (from the renowned Professor Winton Thomas) in order to understand at first hand Agrippa's quotations from the Jewish kabbalists.

Warner's recollections may well give a clue to one underlying reason for a difference of world view. Lewis was insecure academically about primary sources for Kabbalism, while he was familiar with the classical Greek tradition. It is, of course, highly unlikely that Williams could read Hebrew either, but then his own acquaintance with Kabbalism was through the works of A. E. Waite and his experience with the particular version that appeared in practical ritual in Waite's 'Fellowship of the Rosy Cross'. My case has not been that Williams had any academic expertise, or even academic interest, in Christian Kabbalism, but that a loose form of it offered him a resource for his imagination and for a poetic 'mythology'. Williams himself refers to Agrippa in *Witchcraft*, as someone 'concerned to discover a principle of operation in the universe'.[17]

With regard to Lewis, we might also speculate that working with ideas of divine immanence in the world in the Christian Kabbalism of Agrippa during weekly supervisory sessions with Warner could have had some slight effect in moving Lewis' mind towards the 'return to Williams' I have detected in his final writings.

---

[13] CSL to Arthur Greeves, 10 June 1917, Lewis, *Letters*, 1: 320.

[14] St Peter's College, Oxford (Tutorial Fellowship 1965, Honorary Fellowship 1999), St Catharine's College, Cambridge (Honorary Fellowship 1999).

[15] Personal conversation with Francis Warner, 21 December 2018.

[16] Perhaps Lewis is referring to this group in a puzzling comment to Raine that 'Yes, we are members of a pretty widely diffused secret society, who can usually recognise one another': CSL to Kathleen Raine, 8 August 1961, Lewis, *Letters*, 3: 1281.

[17] Williams, *Witchcraft*, 223, 232.

But I have no evidence for this supposition, and it remains for me an intriguing speculation.

15.2 Perichoresis and Co-inherence in the Thought of G. L. Prestige

In Chapter 4, I argued that Williams found the term 'co-inherence' in the book *God in Patristic Thought* by the distinguished Patristics scholar of his generation, G. Leonard Prestige. Prestige had used 'co-inherence' to translate the Greek term *perichoresis*, first in an article of 1928 headed '*Perichoreo* and *Perichoresis* in the Fathers',[18] and then in his book of 1936. In his article on *perichoresis* for the Lexicon of Patristic Greek,[19] he prefers, however, to use 'interpenetration' for the instances where *perichoresis* means what he elsewhere calls 'co-inherence'. I have been able to find no examples of the use of co-inherence in English writing after Cardinal Newman,[20] and before Prestige, but in any case it is sufficient to note that it was rare before Prestige used it so prominently in a volume that would become a standard and frequently quoted work for generations of students of Patristics students. I have already analysed what I believe to be Williams' debt to Prestige's chapter headed 'Co-inherence', but Prestige's treatment still has an interest for the wider question of the place of co-inherence in a doctrine of the Trinity for the present day, with which this last chapter is concerned.

In the first place, Prestige evidently found the term a useful one, not only as an English translation of *perichoresis*, but also because it gave him a way of referring neatly to *precursors* of *perichoresis* in the Greek and Latin Fathers, without implying that word *perichoresis* itself actually appeared where it did not. So he writes that 'the doctrine itself of the co-inherence of the three Persons in one another goes far back', suggesting that it is 'involved' in the very notion that one divine *ousia* (substance or essence) is 'expressed' in three divine persons (*hypostases*).[21]

Prestige thus relates a number of antecedents to *perichoresis* that he finds carry the idea of 'co-inherence'. Athanasius writes that Son 'is in' (*eneinai*) the Father and the Father 'in' the Son, while the Spirit is 'in' both. For Hilary, the divine Persons reciprocally 'contain' one another and so permanently 'envelop' and are enveloped by the other.[22] Cyril of Alexandria also uses the term 'contain', which is

---

[18] Prestige, '*ΠΕΡΙΧΩΡΕΩ* and *ΠΕΡΙΧΩΡΗΣΙΣ* in the Fathers', 242–52; see esp. 248, 249.

[19] *Perichoresis*, in Lampe, *Patristic Greek Lexicon*, 1077–8. According to the Preface, Prestige was working on entries for the Lexicon, including *perichoresis*, as early as the 1920s, and it may be assumed that it was his entry for *perichoresis* that was finally included.

[20] See Chapter 4, section 1.   [21] Prestige, *God*, 284.   [22] Prestige, *God*, 284.

Prestige, *God*, 284–5, citing Athanasius, *ad Serapionem* 2.4, 4.4, 4,12; Hilary, *de Trinitate* 3.1–4; cf. John 14:11, 'I am in the Father and the Father in me.'

denoted by the Greek verb *choreo* (to be highly significant later for the compound verb *perichoreo*); the Father, he states, is 'extended' in the Son, and the Son is *choretikos*, capable of containing the Perfect One. He also finds the Persons to be 'interwreathed' into a single godhead by means of the identity of *ousia*; the Father is 'in' the Son, not in the physical way that water is contained in a basin, but as the subject of an extremely accurate portrait might claim 'I am in this picture and this picture is in me',[23] an illustration borrowed from Athanasius.[24] Further useful images are that the Son 'indwells' the Father owing to identity of *ousia*, 'bearing' the Father entirely in himself. Gregory of Nyssa also takes up the image of 'containing', deliberately building on Hilary's language that the several persons mutually 'contain' each other (*chorein*) and so are 'enveloped' (*periechesthai*) in each other; the persons are *choretikos* of one another, which Prestige renders as 'permeative'.[25] Prestige notes that the word 'contain' had been accepted for centuries as a technical expression for the pervasion of all created things by God; God was thought to 'contain' the universe, and this picture was now extended to mutual relations of the divine Persons. Cyril of Alexandria argues that the Son can only 'fill all things' (Ephesians 1:23) because He is contained in the Father who fills all things.[26] This is a context to which I intend to return in developing a modern doctrine of the Trinity.

Prominent in this range of images, then, is that of mutual 'containment', though the passage in the Fourth Gospel where Jesus claims a mutual 'indwelling' with the Father (along with some kind of relation to the Spirit as 'Advocate') is evidently also influential. Prestige sums up:

> The fact, then, of the co-inherence of the divine Persons was well established, though no convenient term had as yet been invented to describe it, beyond the use of phrases indicative of mutual content, based on a rather crude, though expressive and not really misleading metaphor from the mensuration of physical capacity.[27]

The stage was set for the emergence of the 'convenient term' *perichoresis*, which appeared at first in Gregory Nazianzen and Maximus the Confessor as a way of describing the relation of the human and divine natures in Christ, and not as applied to the Trinity at all.[28] Prestige believes that the first application of *perichoresis* to the Trinity was made by the theologian he calls 'pseudo-Cyril',

---

[23] Prestige, *God*, 288, citing Cyril of Alexandria, *Commentary on John*, 28D.
[24] Athanasius, *contra Arianos*, 3.5.
[25] Prestige, *God*, 289, citing Gregory of Nyssa, *adv. Arianos et Sabellianos*, 12.
[26] Prestige, *God*, 290, citing Cyril of Alexandria, *dial. 3 de Trinitate*, 467C.
[27] Prestige, *God*, 290–1.
[28] Prestige, *God*, 291–3, citing Gregory Nazianzen, *Epistolae* 101, 87C, Maximus, *Ambigua* 112b.D, and Maximus, *disp. contra Pyrrhum* 187A.

about the middle of the seventh century, and that pseudo-Cyril's trinitarian text, *de Sacrosancta Trinitate*, was then adopted by John of Damascus in the eighth century, and copied almost entirely into his work on *The Orthodox Faith*.[29] *De Sacrosancta Trinitate* was in fact a manuscript bundled up with genuine works of Cyril dating from the fifth century, was soon recognized as being non-Cyrilline, and dubbed with the stop-gap name 'pseudo-Cyril'. It now seems clear that the work is a fourteenth-century manuscript, and that its contents are derived *from* John of Damascus rather than the other way around.[30] Pseudo-Cyril must, alas, disappear from scholarship, and all the plaudits bestowed on him for his original use of *perichoresis*, 'his greatest and wisest innovation',[31] must be transferred to John of Damascus.

What is more puzzling than the error over identity is, however, why Prestige refers to *perichoresis* as 'an admirable description of the union of the three Persons of God' and a 'simple and expressive term for the purpose',[32] when he has dismissed 'mutual containment' (based on *choreo*) as 'a rather crude' metaphor.[33] Prestige makes clear that while philologically *perichoresis* is 'a compound derivative' of *choreo*—which had been used 'time out of mind to express the "permeation" of matter by God': the philological link was 'a most felicitous accident'.[34] The etymology must not be pressed, therefore, but the association with 'containing' is—according to Prestige himself—apparently 'felicitous' as far as thought about the Trinity is concerned. One is thus left wondering why *choreo* as 'permeation' is 'crude', while *perichoreo*, also meaning 'permeation', is 'admirable'. Prestige hints that *perichoresis* is 'convenient' because it brings reciprocity and permeation together in one word, where otherwise it would need a phrase. He himself admits that *perichoresis* retains material connotations, but records that 'pseudo-Cyril' points out in a different connection that it is impossible to discuss God except by using symbols derived from physical experience.[35]

I suggest that, from the perspective of modern trinitarian theology, *perichoresis* is more felicitous than *chorein* because the verb *perichoreo* emphasizes the sense of movement. *Chorein* can certainly mean 'to go' as well as 'to contain', but *perichoreo* means 'to go round' or 'to rotate', as Prestige translates it in the Patristic Greek Lexicon.[36] This, indeed, is why he maintains that, when applied by Gregory and Maximus to the two natures of Christ, it means something like an interchange of *activities*; it is, he affirms, 'a metaphor of rotation', a moving backwards and forwards between various actions.

---

[29] Prestige, *God*, 294–9, citing 'Pseudo-Cyril', *de Sacrosancta Trinitate* 24; John of Damascus, *de Fide Orthodoxa*, 1.

[30] So, Conticello, 'Pseudo-Cyril's "De SS. Trinitate"'. *Orientalia Christiana Periodica*, 61 (1995): 117–29; accepted by Louth, 'Late Patristic Developments', 147–9.

[31] Prestige, *God*, 296.   [32] Prestige, *God*, 296–7.   [33] Prestige, *God*, 290–1.

[34] Prestige, *God*, 296.   [35] Prestige, *God*, 299, citing 'Pseudo-Cyril', *de Sanct. Trin.* 14.

[36] Prestige, 'περιχωρέω, περιχώρησις (perichoreo, perichoresis)' in Lampe, *Greek Patristic Lexicon*, 1077–8.

I suggest that unless this dynamism is kept in the idea of *perichoresis* when it is associated with the Trinity there will be a collapse into a static mutual containment, as may be happening when John of Damascus lays stress on the 'mansion and session' of the hypostases in each other.[37] *Perichoresis* has the potential of holding together what was to be later called in the West both *circuminsessio* (a being seated around together),[38] and *circumincessio* (a moving around together).[39] Here we are concerned with the usefulness of the English word 'co-inherence', and it has to be admitted that, taken in isolation, this tends to indicate a permeation that is more *circuminsessio* than *circumincessio*. Co-inherence is, literally, an abiding or belonging in each other. A doctrine of the Trinity, I will argue, requires an interpenetration that is a continual movement, an interweaving flow of relations of love. While 'dance' is not a translation of *perichoresis*, and I have argued earlier that the idea of a dancing Trinity is a modern innovation,[40] there is a play on words between dance (*choros*) and *perichoresis* that aptly maintains a dynamic meaning for co-inherence; if we use the synonym 'abiding in', we should give full force to the verbal noun 'abiding', as a *process* and not a static state.

A second major point that Prestige makes is that *perichoresis* in the sense of interpenetration is not, in his view, suitable for Christology. The story as he tells it is that when it is first used, to express the relation between the human and divine natures in Christ, as a verb in Gregory Nazianzen (*perichoreo*),[41] and then as a verb and a noun (*perichoresis*) in Maximus, it does not mean anything like co-inherence. Rather, it means a reciprocity, or interchange, between the actions and properties of the humanity and the divinity. One nature has *perichoresis* in its relation 'to' the other, but not 'in' or 'through' the other.[42] Prestige underlines that Maximus did not use the term 'in order to safeguard or explain the unity of Christ, but in order to express the singleness of result and effect which proceeded from the two natures that were united in his person'.[43] John of Damascus does, however, use *perichoresis* in the sense of interpenetration, or what Prestige is calling co-inherence, and so employs the word to describe the manner of union of the two natures. In this, comments Prestige, he 'entirely missed' the sense given to the word by Gregory and Maximus, 'being misled by the uncompounded verb *choreo* (= hold, contain) into thinking that they indicated a sort of penetration or permeation'.[44] In other words, he transferred to Christology 'a permeation or

---

[37] John of Damascus, *de Fid. Orth.*, 1.14.
[38] Preferred by Aquinas, *Summa Theologiae*, Ia. 42.5.
[39] Preferred by Bonaventure, *Sententiae in IV Libris Distinctae*, 1.19.1.1.4. concl.
[40] See Chapter 13, section 3.
[41] Gregory Nazianzen, *Epistolae* 101. He uses *perichoreo* in two more places, neither concerning the Trinity: *Orationes* 18.42 (the reciprocation of life with death), *Orationes* 22.4 (all things reciprocate into one another in the phenomenon of satiety).
[42] Prestige, '*ΠΕΡΙΧΩΡΕΩ* (Perichoreo)', 247; Prestige, *God*, 294.
[43] Prestige, '*ΠΕΡΙΧΩΡΕΩ* (Perichoreo)', 248; cf Prestige, *God*, 294.
[44] Prestige, '*ΠΕΡΙΧΩΡΕΩ* (Perichoreo)', 243–4.

co-inherence between the two natures similar to that which Gregory of Nyssa conceived between the Persons of the Trinity'.[45] John, continues Prestige, 'compensated for his Christological indiscretion' by the real advance of applying *perichoresis*, in the sense of co-inherence, to the triune God. Thus the shift was made from 'perichoresis to' in Gregory and Maximus to 'perichoresis in'. It is this contrast that I have claimed Charles Williams picked up from Prestige, underlining that co-inherence means not just 'sticking to' but 'abiding in'.[46]

Prestige considers *perichoresis*, and so co-inherence, to be unsuitable for Christology for two reasons. First, he thinks it must inevitably imply the fusion of two natures into one. With Trinity, there is no problem with the image of *perichoresis*, as the three Persons of God are affirmed to be one *ousia*. He maintains that John attempts to ward off a monophysite Christology by insisting that the two natures are not confused or changed into each other, and by presenting the permeation as a one-sided process: 'the divine nature, having once permeated through the flesh, bestows on the flesh an ineffable perichoresis with itself'.[47] Just as (in a time-honoured metaphor) heat penetrates through a red-hot sword in a forge, divine characteristics operate 'through' the human.[48] Second, *perichoresis*/co-inherence is unsuitable because 'it is impossible for the flesh to *perichorein* [penetrate] through the divinity'.[49] In actuality, John thinks that they interpenetrate only in so far as they both occupy the 'space' of the same divine hypostasis (person). In asserting that the created cannot 'permeate' the Uncreated, Prestige is not just reporting on the philosophical assumptions of the Church Fathers, deriving from a Platonist or Neoplatonist view of reality as hierarchical; he is clearly giving his own opinion on what *should* be Christian doctrine. Thus, the metaphor of *perichoresis*/co-inherence is—according to Prestige—'forced' for Christology, but entirely suitable for the mutual interpenetration of three Persons in the Trinity.

This is a conceptual framework for the relation between God and the world that, I suggest, a modern doctrine of the Trinity must challenge. In fact, Williams and Lewis in their own ways do challenge the assumption that the created cannot permeate the uncreated. Despite his debt to Prestige, Williams uses 'co-inherence' for the person of Christ; the fifth article of his Order of the Co-inherence 'recommends therefore the study, on the contemplative side, of the Co-inherence of the Holy and Blessed Trinity, of the Two Natures in the Single Person...'.[50] Even more daringly, he maintains not only that the human nature of Christ co-inheres with the divine, but that our own humanity 'co-inheres' in Christ in the same way as Christ 'co-inheres' in the Father within the life of the Trinity: 'The

---

[45] Prestige, *God*, 295.   [46] See Chapter 4, section 1.   [47] Prestige, *God*, 295.
[48] Prestige, '*ΠΕΡΙΧΩΡΕΩ* (*Perichoreo*)', 250–1.   [49] Prestige, *God*, 295.
[50] See Chapter 4, section 2. In this phrase 'Co-inherence' grammatically governs 'of the two natures', as it does the succeeding phrases 'of the Mother and Son, of the communicated Eucharist, and of the whole Catholic Church'.

Divine Word co-inheres in God the Father (as the Father in Him and the Spirit in Both). [...] In that sense he lives in us and we in Him, He and we co-inhere.'[51] While Williams does not explicitly draw the conclusion that human beings therefore co-inhere in the Persons of the Trinity, Lewis does suggest something like this—at least for those persons who have been transformed into 'sons and daughters' of God. He affirms that 'the whole dance, or drama, or pattern of this three-Personal life is to be played out in each one of us', while maintaining that we can put it 'the other way round—each one of us has got to *enter that pattern*, take his place in that dance'.[52] The language accords with the perception of Hilary and Gregory that God 'contains' and permeates all things,[53] but it also allows for the reverse, that the created when redeemed 'penetrates' the Uncreated, breaking a strict hierarchy. In the account of the Great Dance of Perelandra, where Lewis exceptionally comes onto Williams' ground, something like a *universal* mutual permeation also seems in view: 'Deep heaven is inside Him who is inside the seed and does not distend him.'[54]

As I have suggested, it is only in Lewis' latest work that he returns to this Williams-type of vision, when he has worked out a theological framework of different kinds of divine presence in the world. Until then, a difference of world view between Lewis and Williams means that Williams has a stronger view of the immanence of God in natural and human life. But the tendency of both of them to do doctrine through image means that they cannot be constrained within the tight conceptual bounds that cause Prestige to dismiss the Christological co-inherence of John of Damascus with short shrift: 'a term so meaningless, or alternatively so misleading as this [. .]. had far better been avoided altogether'.[55] For John's *trinitarian* co-inherence he has only praise, but any modern doctrine of the Trinity as co-inherent must, as Williams does, articulate the link between the two doctrines. To do this, however (as I intend to do before the end of this chapter), the language of 'nature' and 'essence', belonging as it does to the philosophy of the time, will need to be reviewed.

Co-inherence for Prestige is most useful in explaining how there can be one essence in God: this is why, for him, the word is 'meaningless' for the union of the divine and human in Christ. This one essence (*ousia*) can be conceived as a 'single objective being' and 'one centre of divine self-consciousness'.[56] A modern doctrine of the Trinity, I shall suggest, must get beyond talk of God as 'a being' and 'a self-consciousness', and it will be the very language of *perichoresis* or co-inherence that will assist us in doing so.

---

[51] Williams, 'Way of Exchange', 152.   [52] Lewis, *Mere Christianity*, 139; my italics.
[53] Hilary, *de Trinitate* 3.2, cf. 2.6, denies that God can be contained by anything, although God is both outside and within all things.
[54] Lewis, *Perelandra*, 247.   [55] Prestige, 'ΠΕΡΙΧΩΡΕΩ (Perichoreo)', 244.
[56] Prestige, *God*, 301.

15.3 'Co-inherence' in later English-Speaking Theology, 1952–1996

There is a certain lexical interest in tracing the use of the English term 'co-inherence' in English-speaking theology after Prestige's book of 1936, especially since the article on co-inherence (also co-inhere, co-inherent) in the magisterial *Oxford English Dictionary* only appears to have been slightly updated since the first edition of 1928, and the latest usage cited is from 1856. Neither 'co-inherence' nor 'coinherence' appear in the Merriam-Webster Online Dictionary (2020) of American English at all. But beyond lexical curiosity, the appearance of the term will, I believe, help us towards the end of creating a trinitarian theology.

After Prestige and Williams, the word 'coinherence' (without a hyphen) appears in *The Trinity in Contemporary Theology* by Claude Welch as early as 1953. He uses coinherence several times as an English translation of *perichoresis*, without any explanation, as if the word is self-explanatory. Of eleven page references to 'coinherence' in the index, four pages contain only the word *perichoresis*, showing that he is simply using the terms as synonyms. While there is no reference to G. L. Prestige in the bibliography, Welch appears to have gleaned the word 'co-inherence' from its use (once) by Charles Norris Cochrane, in his *Christianity and Classical Culture* (1940),[57] and Cochrane himself most probably found it in Prestige.[58] Like Prestige, Welch understands *perichoresis*, together with its translation 'coinherence', to be a way of expressing the unity of the three divine Persons in the 'one essence' of God. Although the term *implies* the diversity of Persons, its point is to affirm that the same divine essence permeates the three. He writes with approval, for example, of Barth's discussion of God's 'Three-in-Oneness', as if Barth is actually using the word 'coinherence':[59]

> The unity of God is further characterised (and emphasized!) by Barth in terms of the doctrine of coinherence [...]. The concept of *perichoresis* or coinherence is for Barth, as for Catholic theology, the completion of the dialectic of unity and trinity. [... *Quoting Barth*] '(None of [the persons] exists as a special individual, all three "inexist" in one another, they exist only in common as modes of

---

[57] Welch, *Trinity*, 244–7, discusses Cochrane's 'trinitarian philosophizing' extensively, and—while not citing co-inherence at this point—specifically refers to the page on which Cochrane declares that 'the Athanasian position is further emphasized in the doctrine of co-inherence (*perichoresis* [Greek characters]) among the "persons" of the Trinity': see Cochrane, *Christianity and Classical Culture*, 367.

[58] Cochrane does not feel obliged to provide references to many secondary sources, and there is no bibliography. There is thus no specific reference to Prestige, but Cochrane's single reference to co-inherence, when discussing Athanasius' use of the idea (Cochrane, *Christianity*, 367–8), has a striking verbal similarity to the account of Prestige, *God*, 284–5. Like Prestige, he spells co-inherence with a hyphen.

[59] Welch, *Trinity*, 188–9.

existence of the one God and Lord who posits himself from eternity to eternity).'[60]

Welch stresses that Barth understands 'the doctrine of coinherence as defining the unity of God'. While he hastens to clarify that 'this does not mean that the modes of existence are identical with each other', he does think that Barth agrees with Catholic theology in associating the concept of *perichoresis* with the doctrine of 'identity of essence', and quotes one instance where Barth writes of the *perichoresis* as being 'a further description of the *homoousia* [one-in-beingness] of the Father, Son and Holy Spirit'.[61] In his anxiety to oppose a social doctrine of the Trinity, according to which three consciousnesses are claimed to be so intensely inter-conscious that they make one God, Welch may be distorting Barth's affirmation of the one Being of God. Barth prefers 'three modes of being' to 'three persons', because 'person' carries today an inalienable connection with a psychological centre of consciousness. But Barth also stresses that the oneness of God is not a 'numerical unity' (as if God were a single being),[62] and that with God 'being' should always be understood as a 'happening', or 'event',[63] of three modes of being that are in relation.

Welch has learnt from Barth that the self-revelation of God in the world (the 'economic' Trinity) must lead us to a corresponding personal reality in the inner being of God (the immanent Trinity),[64] and he expresses this truth by what he calls a 'coinherence of Christian witness to the three Persons'.[65] The 'real ground of three-foldness is in revelation':[66] our three experiences of God, as Father, Son, and Holy Spirit are immanent in the other, each involved in the other, and in this experience to which we witness 'is the basis for the doctrine of coinherence' within God.[67] Welch, however, perhaps more firmly than Barth, tips co-inherence towards a way of confessing the One God, writing that co-inherence as 'mutual interpenetration of indwelling of the Persons' is certainly 'based on the divine processions or relations, but especially on identity of essence'.[68]

In 1958, J. N. D. Kelly published *Early Christian Doctrines*, which became an even more standard work in Patristics than Prestige's volume. Writing on the Cappadocians, like Prestige he uses the English word 'co-inherence' as a way of referring to a concept about God that had not yet been given the name 'perichoresis':[69]

---

[60] Barth, *Church Dogmatics*, I/1 (first English translation, 1936), 425.
[61] Barth, *Church Dogmatics*, I/1 (first English translation, 1936), 555.
[62] Barth, *Church Dogmatics*, I/1 (first English translation, 1936), 354.
[63] Barth, *Church Dogmatics*, II/1, 263.   [64] Barth, *Church Dogmatics*, II/1, 363.
[65] Welch, *Trinity*, 229.   [66] Welch, *Trinity*, 195.   [67] Welch, *Trinity*, 229.
[68] Welch, *Trinity*, 116.   [69] Kelly, *Early Christian Doctrines*, 264.

The essence of their doctrine is that the One Godhead exists simultaneously in three modes of being, or hypostases. So Basil remarks, '[...] The Son in his entirety abides in the Father, and in return possesses the Father in entirety in himself [...].'[70] Here we have the doctrine of the co-inherence, or as it was later called 'perichoresis', of the divine persons. The Godhead can be said to exist 'undivided [...] in divided Persons',[71] and there is an 'identity of nature'[72] in the three hypostases.

It seems that Kelly has found the word co-inherence in Prestige, since at the end of the chapter, Prestige's *God in Patristic Thought* is included among the five general works in the 'Note on Books'. Like Prestige, we notice that while 'co-inherence' implies the diversity of the Persons, its major work for Kelly is to affirm the unity of the Persons in one divine nature.

In William Hill's *Three-Personed God* (1982), the word 'co-inherence' does not appear, but the equivalent phrase that 'each hypostasis "inheres" in the other two' does,[73] with a reference to the page in Kelly's book (above) where he uses the word 'coinherence', and a repetition of Kelly's citation there from Gregory Nazianzen.[74] Like Kelly and Prestige before him, Hill finds *perichoresis* to be affirming that 'the unity of the Three' is 'a matter of ontological identity on the level of *ousia* (nature)'. Hill claims that *perichoresis* means 'literally "dancing around"' (missing the fact that a pun is involved here), and that 'The Greek Fathers made much of perichorēsis [...] to suggest this togetherness, this joyous sharing of divine life'.[75] It might be supposed that the image of dance would direct attention to the diversity of the persons, and Hill does in fact refer to the Persons as 'three centers of consciousness in community', but this is not a merely 'social' unity, as Hill affirms again a unity of essence: the Three 'are conscious by way of one essential consciousness' and 'the members of the Trinity are now seen as constituting a community of persons in pure reciprocity, as subjects and centres of one divine conscious life'.[76]

It is in another Hill, Edmund Hill, *The Mystery of the Trinity* (1985), that there is just a hint that *perichoresis* and co-inherence might be used to evoke the complex patterns of interweaving and interpenetration among the three Persons as a phenomenon worthy of attention in itself, rather than as a ground for the unity of nature. Edmund Hill uses the term 'co-inherence' when discussing the meaning of *perichoresis* as revolving or revolution. *Perichoresis*, he suggests, 'conjures up the rather lovely picture of an eternal divine round dance', while he recognizes that 'dance' is not the literal meaning of *perichoresis* but is a play on

---

[70] Citing Basil, *Epistolae* 38.8.   [71] Citing Gregory Nazianzen, *Orationes* 31.14.
[72] Citing Didymus, *de Trinitate*, 1.16.   [73] Hill, *Three-Personed God*, 49.
[74] Gregory Nazianzen, *Or.* 31.14. Hill, *Three-Personed God*, 36, does refer to Prestige, *God in Patristic Thought*, but in a different context from matters of *perichoresis*.
[75] Hill, *Three-Personed God*, 272.   [76] Hill, *Three-Personed God*, 272.

words between *perichōrēsis* and *perichoreuō*, meaning 'to "dance round" or "dance in a ring"'.[77] Augustine, he then notes, 'touches on this image' (he must mean *perichoresis*, not a dance) when he is working out the structure of the trinitarian image in human consciousness. A footnote at this point refers us to 'co-inherence' in Augustine's discussion of the 'trinity' of mind, self-love, and self-knowledge, and also in his later formulation of the trio of the three mental acts of self-memory, self-understanding, and self-will. Hill comments (twice) that the 'mutual co-inherence' of these faculties 'can easily be transferred to the divine persons' or to 'the divine three'.[78] Presumably he means that he (and the reader) can easily make this step. He appears to have derived the word 'co-inherence' from Prestige, as he has immediately beforehand referenced his book *God in Patristic Thought,*[79] and we note that he spells the word with a hyphen. What is significant for our discussion is that his consideration of *perichoresis* and co-inherence does not take the form of finding them to explain the one essence or nature of God, but belongs to an account of the divine relations, and to 'an eternal inter-communication of wisdom and love and glory between the three'.[80]

This emphasis is continued and expanded in a third study by a Catholic writer, *God For Us* (1991), in which Catherine Mowry LaCugna uses both the word 'co-inherence' and the verb 'inhere' in her discussion of *perichoresis*:

> in the eighth century the Greek theologian John Damascene used the term *perichōrēsis* to highlight the dynamic and vital character of each divine person, as well as the coinherence and immanence of each divine person in the other two. [...] [P]erichōrēsis expressed the idea that the three divine persons mutually inhere in each other, draw life from one another, 'are' what they are by relation to one another. *Perichōrēsis* means being-in-one-another, permeation without confusion.[81]

While she indicates elsewhere in the book that she has read both William Hill and Edmund Hill, at this point she cites the article by Prestige of 1928, in which he first uses the term 'co-inherence'.[82] Unlike Prestige, however, her thesis is that talk about God can only meaningfully be of the economic Trinity. It is a sheer speculation to conceive of either a unity of 'essence' or an 'immanent Trinity' behind the economy of salvation and the revelation of the concrete forms of human community proclaimed by Jesus as characteristic of the reign of God:

> The starting point in the economy of redemption, in contrast to the intradivine starting point, locates *perichōrēsis* not in God's inner life but in the mystery of the

---

[77] Hill, *Mystery*, 117.   [78] Hill, *Mystery*, 121, n.10.   [79] Hill, *Mystery*, 120, n.9.
[80] Hill, *Mystery*, 117.   [81] LaCugna, *God For Us*, 270–1.
[82] LaCugna, *God For Us*, 312, n.94.

one communion of all persons, divine as well as human. From this standpoint, 'the divine dance' is indeed an apt image of persons in communion: not for an intradivine communion but for divine life as all creatures partake and literally exist in it.[83]

The *perichoresis* of the divine persons is appropriately expressed by the image of dance; though she recognizes that there is 'scant' philological warrant for associating the two, she finds that 'the metaphor of dance is effective', and correspondingly she prefers the Latin *circumincessio* to *circuminsessio*.[84] *Perichoresis* for LaCugna is thus not an explanation of a single substance, or a single divine consciousness, but the description of the persons as centres of dynamic and creative energy in eternal and perpetual movement. 'To be a divine person is to be by nature in relation to the other persons', she writes, and:

> Perichōrēsis provides a dynamic model of persons in communion based on mutuality and interdependence. The model of perichōrēsis avoids the pitfalls of locating the divine unity either in the divine substance (Latin) or exclusively in the person of the Father (Greek) and locates unity in diversity, in a true communion of persons.'[85]

This is a kind of 'social' doctrine of the Trinity, locating the oneness of God in the intensity of relations between the divine persons, but it is unlike former versions,[86] as it restricts talk of unity to the interaction and communion of human persons with the Trinity in the world. This throws interest and attention onto *perichoresis* as a dynamic network of relations in which created beings can participate. The implication of this account, and in my view its weakness,[87] is that *perichoresis* is then supposedly a pattern of relationships *between* divine realities called 'persons', even though stress is laid upon the relational and intersubjective nature of the person. At one point, LaCugna appears to approve the view of the feminist theologian Patricia Wilson-Kastner, that the Persons in God are 'three centers of divine identity, self-aware and self-giving in love, self-possessed yet freely transcending the self in eternal trinitarian interconnectedness'.[88] Her approval may be qualified by an insistence that persons are an 'ineffable' and 'inexhaustible mystery', as 'a concrete, unique and unrepeatable ecstasis of nature', but she is applying this description to human persons 'created in the image of the relational God' as well as to Persons in God. Drawing such an analogy between human and

---

[83] LaCugna, *God For Us*, 274. [84] LaCugna, *God For Us*, 272, 274.
[85] LaCugna, *God For Us*, 271. [86] For Moltmann, *Trinity*, 171–2.
[87] See further section 4.
[88] LaCugna, *God For Us*, 270, citing Wilson-Kastner, *Faith, Feminism and the Christ*, 89.

divine persons is bound to imply that the Persons in divine *perichoresis* are subjects or agents of some kind.

To complete this group of four Catholic writers, Elizabeth Johnson published *She Who Is* in 1992, in which *perichoresis* plays a central part, and which she translates occasionally as coinherence. For instance, maintaining that the triune symbol 'calls for a differentiated unity of variety or manifoldness', she continues:

> Eastern theology points to it with the Greek term *perichōrēsis*, a word that signifies a cyclical movement, a revolving action such as in the revolution of a wheel. Secured in the theological lexicon by the usage of John Damascene, this term evokes a *coinherence* of the three divine persons, an encircling of each around the others.[89]

The meaning of coinherence as *circuminsessio* (seated in each other) is to be complemented by a more dynamic 'interweaving of things' in the sense of *circumincessio*, so that the net effect of the two metaphors is that 'each person encompasses the others, is coherent with the others in a joyous movement of shared life'. She continues by referring to Edmund Hill: 'In explaining the sense of *perichōrēsis* Edmund Hill muses that it conjures up the rather lovely picture of an eternal round dance', and goes on to recount his advocacy of the pun between *perichōrēsis* and *perichoreuō*. Johnson, then, does not follow William Hill (to whom she also refers) in his mistaken view that *perichoresis* means 'literally' a dance, though her phrase 'a joyous movement of shared life' does echo his 'joyous sharing of divine life'.[90]

Alongside her debt to Edmund Hill for the idea of *perichoresis* (and perhaps also for the word 'coinherence'), she refers to Brian Hebblethwaite's discussion of *perichoresis*,[91] which he translates as co-inherence, and where he reproduces Prestige's account of its development (featuring the wraith of pseudo-Cyril):

> the term 'perichoresis', from the Greek for 'encircling' or 'encompassing', acquired the technical sense in theology of 'mutual interpenetration'. Taken over from its less happy usage in Christology into trinitarian theology, it was used by Pseudo-Cyril and John of Damascus to refer to the co-inherence of the three persons in the one eternal God. In G. L. Prestige's words, 'it stands as a monument of inspired Christian rationalism'.[92]

It is worth a short diversion here to note that Hebblethwaite's essay reveals a fascinating convergence of usages of the word 'co-inherence', as I have been

---

[89] Johnson, *She Who Is*, 220; my italics.   [90] Hill, *Three-Personed* God, 272.
[91] Hebblethwaite, *Incarnation*, 11–12; reference in Johnson, *She Who Is*, 301, n.74.
[92] Here he footnotes Prestige, *God*, 299.

tracing them. He begins with lines from Auden's poem 'Compline' (1954), 'join the dance / As it moves in perichoresis',[93] marvelling that the technical word *perichoresis* can appear with such effect in a modern poem. He does not mention, or know, that this is a recollection by Auden, as Mendelson points out,[94] of Auden's earlier use of 'co-inherence' in Simeon's meditation in *For the Time Being* (1941–42), where it describes the interpenetration of divine and human natures in the Word made flesh.[95] As I have already mentioned, *For the Time Being* was written under the influence of Charles Williams' *The Descent of the Dove*, where Auden found the word 'co-inherence'. Another strong influence was Auden's reading of Cochrane's *Christianity and Classical Culture*,[96] in which the word 'coinherence' also appears,[97] as we have seen in discussing Welch. Both Williams and Cochrane appear to be indebted to Prestige, whom Hebblethwaite too is directly quoting.

But here we are concerned with Johnson, who is referring most immediately to Hebblethwaite (and less obviously to Edmund Hill) in her use of co-inherence, and more widely in her understanding of *perichoresis*. Using Edmund Hill's phrase, 'mutual coinherence',[98] she finds that there is a 'dancing around together of Spirit, Wisdom and Mother; or of mutual Love, Love from Love, and unoriginate Love; or of the three divine persons'.[99] Her book appears not long after La Cugna's, and so there is no opportunity for her to draw upon LaCugna's extended text, but she does employ several of LaCugna's shorter essays that lie behind her book.[100] She agrees with her that talk of the Trinity has 'lost its moorings' in experience,[101] and that the starting-point for talk about God as Trinity is the activity of the Trinity in the economy of salvation. The point of *perichoresis*/co-inherence is not to affirm unity of substance in the face of diversity of person, but to express the interweaving, dance-like movements of the 'persons' themselves. The *perichoresis is* the unity: 'being in communion constitutes God's very essence'. More concerned than La Cugna to renew vocabulary for God from a feminine perspective, she replaces the names Father, Son, and Holy Spirit, with 'Mother-Sophia', 'Jesus-Sophia', and 'Spirit-Sophia', working inductively from experience of the Spirit and believing that 'this starting point stems from the pattern of women's experience of birthing new life, caring for those they love, creating poetry and resisting constriction'.[102]

---

[93] Auden, *Horae Canonicae*, in *Collected Poems*, 639.   [94] Mendelson, *Later Auden*, 357.

[95] Auden, *For the Time Being*, in *Collected Poems*, 391–2.

[96] For the dual influence of Williams and Cochrane, see Auden, *For The Time* Being, edited by Jacobs, xiv–xix; Mendelson, *Later Auden*, 184–90.

[97] Mendelson stresses this fact: *The Later Auden*, 190: 'Auden found the word in Charles Williams … and also in Cochrane'.

[98] Hill, *Mystery*, 121, n.10.   [99] Johnson, *She Who Is*, 227.

[100] Particularly LaCugna, 'Reconceiving the Trinity', 1–23.   [101] Johnson, *She Who Is*, 199.

[102] Johnson, *She Who Is*, 123.

Johnson differs from LaCugna in still finding some point in attempting to speak about God's inner being, working back from the economic to the immanent Trinity; this is not to postulate a unity of essence or 'one divine conscious subject' that inheres in the three persons, but to find assurance that God's relation to the world is grounded in God's own being, as a power of love 'springing from all eternity'.[103] Johnson is also less specific than LaCugna in identifying three centres or agents of relation, stressing that 'the understanding of person in the trinitarian symbol escapes our grasp',[104] and—more significantly—that 'God is like a three-foldness of relation.'[105] Despite these differences from LaCugna, she continues her interest in exploring *perichoresis* as an image for interweaving patterns of relation in God, rather than as a supportive idea for the one essence of God.

Alongside these Catholic contributions, we may now place the *doyen* of modern Reformed Theology, Thomas F. Torrance. After occasional uses of the word after Welch, it is startling suddenly to find the word 'coinherence' or 'coinherent' some two dozen times in *The Trinitarian Faith* (1988). Of particular interest, as we shall see, are a number of instances of 'coinherent relations'. In addition we find such parallel expressions as 'inhering', 'co-indwelling', and 'reciprocal indwelling'. Correspondingly, his shorter *Trinitarian Perspectives* (1994) contains more than a dozen uses of 'coinherence', and it appears from this collection that Torrance was responsible for introducing the English term 'coinherence' into the historic Agreed Statement on the Holy Trinity reached between the Reformed and Orthodox Churches in 1991.[106] In what Torrance intended to be his definitive work on the Trinity, *The Christian Doctrine of God: One Being Three Persons* (1996), the words 'coinherent' or 'coinherence' appear over forty times, which still does not quite match the frequency of the word in Williams' *The Descent of the Dove*, but comes the closest of any book I know—with the exception of the present volume.

Like Prestige in his final chapter on 'Co-Inherence', Torrance evidently finds the term useful as a means of neatly denoting a vision of the relations of three Persons in one God before the word *perichoresis* became available, covering such images as 'indwelling', 'containing', 'enveloping', and mutual 'filling'. Thus, fourth-century theologians such as Athanasius, Hilary, Cyril of Alexandria, and Epiphanius are placed in continuity with those who later appealed to *perichoresis*, while those who speak English in the present day are also effectively included in the succession by his use of coinherence as a synonym for *perichoresis*. Torrance writes somewhat ambiguously, for instance, that 'While the actual term "coinherence" was not used by Athanasius, it was certainly he who developed the conception of coinhering relations in God.'[107] By the 'actual term' he must

---

[103] Johnson, *She Who Is*, 201.   [104] Johnson, *She Who Is*, 203.
[105] Johnson, *She Who Is*, 205.   [106] Torrance, *Trinitarian Perspectives*, 120.
[107] Torrance, *Trinitarian Faith*, 305, n.12; repeated in Torrance, *Perspectives*, 10.

mean *perichoresis*, for which coinherence is a modern synonym, while he finds the basic idea of 'coinhering relations' already in Athanasius. Thus, he declares both that Athanasius 'developed the doctrine of completely interpenetrating relations [...] which was later called the doctrine of divine coinherence',[108] and that 'Athanasius expounded his doctrine of the coinherent relations of the Spirit with the Father and the Son, along the same lines in which he had earlier worked out the mutually interpenetrating and indwelling relations between the Son and the Father.'[109] Other early theologians, such as Basil, 'shared the Athanasian doctrine of coinherence'.[110] In his *Doctrine of God* he makes clear that the actual term *perichoresis* is not employed for the Trinity as early as the Cappadocian Fathers,[111] ascribing its first use to the phantom pseudo-Cyril from where he declares it was 'lifted without acknowledgement' by John of Damascus. Here he makes explicit acknowledgement to Prestige's 'chapter on "coinherence"'.[112]

We are not surprised to find that Torrance refers to Prestige in all three of the books I have mentioned, and it seems likely that it was in his 'chapter on "coinherence"' that Torrance came across the useful word. Like Prestige (and unlike the developing trend in LaCugna and Johnson), he lays stress on coinherence as a way of expressing the inhering of the three persons in the *one being* of God. In *The Trinitarian Faith*, Torrance quotes Prestige approvingly to the effect that that Athanasius taught that 'in God one and the same identical "substance" or object, without any division, substitution, or differentiation of content, is permanently presented in three distinct objective forms'.[113] For Prestige, co-inherence reaffirms this 'crucial doctrine of "Substantial Identity"' from 'a fresh angle',[114] and Torrance makes the same link. Torrance believes that trinitarian faith must be based on the witness of the early theologians, for whom 'the one *ousia* [substance]' is manifested to us 'in the coinherent relations of the three divine Persons', and so is intensely personal in itself.[115] Several times, Torrance repeats that '*Homoousios* [of one substance] carried within it the conception of coinherent relations within the one being of God', adding that it was these 'to which the distinctions in the self-revelation of God in the "saving economy" pointed'.[116] In his commentary on the Approved Statement on the Holy Trinity,[117] he declares that 'This understanding of the One Monarchy, Trinity in Unity and Unity in Trinity, is reinforced by the conception of the mutual indwelling of the Father, the Son and the Spirit in one

---

[108] Torrance, *Trinitarian Perspectives*, 10.   [109] Torrance, *Trinitarian Faith*, 307.
[110] Torrance, *Trinitarian Faith*, 316.   [111] Torrance, *Christian Doctrine of God*, 170.
[112] Torrance, *Christian Doctrine of God*, 202, n.10.
[113] Prestige, *God*, xxix; cited Torrance, *Trinitarian Faith*, 310; *Trinitarian Perspectives*, 15.
[114] Prestige, *God*, xxxiii, cf. 284.   [115] Torrance, *Trinitarian Faith*, 311, cf. 123, n.47.
[116] Torrance, *Trinitarian Faith*, 199, 305; *Trinitarian Perspectives*, 10.
[117] From an ecumenical Colloquy of the Académie Internationale des Sciences Religieuses in Bethanien, Switzerland, 1975.

another,' so that the doctrine of God 'is wholly governed by the coinherent relations between the Three Persons of the Trinity.'[118]

A highly significant part of Torrance's thought in his first two books on the Trinity is his frequent use of the concept of subsistent relations and more than that—*coinherent* subsistent relations. The actual phrase 'subsistent relations' comes from Aquinas, who declares that '"divine person" signifies relation as something subsisting (*significat relationem ut subsistentem*) [...] "person" signifies relation directly and nature indirectly, yet relation is signified, not as relation, but as hypostasis'.[119] What Aquinas means by this is carefully unpacked by Eric Mascall, to whose discussion Torrance acknowledges himself indebted.[120] Mascall points to two meanings of 'subsisting'. First, it means that the category of relation has been 'elevated to the level of substance'.[121] The divine Person does not simply *have* relations, but exists *as* what we might call 'relational being'. That is, the Person *is* a relation which has as much reality as any substance one can think of. Augustine, as Mascall points out, thought of divine Persons like this, without the technical phrase 'subsistent relation'. He was being faced by the alternative presented to him by the Arians, that the Persons of the Trinity must be defined either as 'substances' (or three *ousiae*, hence ending in tritheism) or as 'accidents' (as contingent attributes, and hence as merely impermanent and mutable phenomena). He replies in an experimental, even playful, way, that 'the names, Father and Son, do not refer to the substance but to the relation, and the relation is no accident'.[122] Mascall maintains that Augustine, by a stroke of genius, has both located 'persons' in a third category of 'relation', evading the Arian cleft stick, and at the same time has given them substantial reality ('not an accident').

Mascall, however, also points to a second meaning of 'subsistent relation' in Aquinas, that the Persons as relations have substance as existing in the divine Being: these relations not only 'subsist' but 'subsist in'. Here he quotes Thomas:

> Distinction in God arises only through the relation of origin. However, a relation is in God not as an accident inhering in a subject, but it is the divine essence itself. Hence 'divine person' signifies a relation as subsisting. This means a relation in the manner of a substance which is a hypostasis subsisting in the divine nature.[123]

Mascall comments that 'it is fascinating to see the Angelic Doctor struggling to bring within the vocabulary of Aristotelianism this perplexing notion of a relation which has at the same time the character of a substance',[124] and he does so by making the relation subsist in the one divine substance.

[118] Torrance, *Trinitarian Perspectives*, 139–40.
[119] Aquinas, *Summa Theologiae* 1a.29.4: translation from Blackfriars Edition, vol. 6, 61.
[120] Torrance, *Trinitarian Faith*, 338.   [121] Mascall, *Triune God*, 12, 18.
[122] Augustine, *De Trinitate* 5.6; cited from Augustine, *The Trinity*, translated by McKenna, 180.
[123] Aquinas, 1a.29.4c, translated by Mascall, *Triune God*, 22.   [124] Mascall, *Triune God*, 21.

We (not Mascall) may observe that Aquinas helpfully begins his discussion with *actions* in God, that is with the two processions of 'begetting' and 'breathing forth'. Then he shows that two processions imply four kinds of 'real relations' (begetting, being begotten, breathing out, being breathed), which in turn imply three unique or 'real' relations: begetting (including breathing out), being begotten, and being breathed forth.[125] These are the subsistent relations that we call Father, Son, and Holy Spirit, and a key point is that Aquinas has begun with movements or actions within God rather than subjects who act in various ways. Unfortunately, the potential here for developing a dynamic concept of God based on action and relationship rather than agents is spoiled because Aquinas explains the self-existence or subsistence of the relationships by the fact that they are identical with the one essence of God; in his view, they subsist because they 'subsist in' the one divine substance that itself has self-existence.[126] This is effectively Mascall's second meaning, and the identity with 'one substance' gives inflammable fuel to the suspicion of Eastern theologians that talk of 'subsistent relations' is simply in aid of the typical Western stress on the unity of God's essence: the 'relations' seem to be swallowed up into the one essence with the loss of any real threeness and 'otherness' of persons within God. This is a point to which I intend to return in developing my own notion of subsistent relations.

Torrance, throughout his discussion, works in effect with the second sense of 'subsistent' from Mascall, as if it is the only one, although it is not a meaning we can find at all in Augustine's experimental thinking. Relations are 'enhypostatic in God, that is, having real, objective personal being in God and coinhering hypostatically in him'.[127] Moreover, as in this quotation, relations that subsist in God are in co-inherence with each other: 'In the Holy Trinity all subsistent relations are in eternal movement mutually containing and interpenetrating one another', and this is 'the Principle of the indivisible coinherence of eternally subsistent relations *in the one Being* of God'.[128] Torrance repeats several times the phrase 'the coinherence of subsistent relations in God',[129] and this stress on 'subsistence in' contributes to the sense that coinherence is a concept supporting the unity of God.

Reading Torrance, it seems that he wants to affirm two corresponding and linked realities: the coinherence of the Persons in God and the coinherence of subsistent relations in God. The Agreed Statement on the Holy Trinity, which he presumably helped to draft, states first that 'each Person dwells in or inheres in the Other', and then that 'The Three Divine Persons are *also* conjoined through their special relations.'[130] Perhaps Torrance himself felt his account was problematic, since in his *Doctrine of God* (1996), the term 'subsistent relation' does not appear

[125] Aquinas, *Summa Theologiae* 1a.27.1; 28.4.
[126] Aquinas, *Summa Theologiae* 1a.29.4; cf. 1a.3.6; 1a.27.4.
[127] Torrance, *Trinitarian Faith*, 135.   [128] Torrance, *Trinitarian Faith*, 33; my italics.
[129] For example, Torrance, *Trinitarian Faith*, 322, and *Trinitarian Perspectives*, 141.
[130] Torrance, *Trinitarian Perspectives*, 117–18.

once in the main text, let alone 'coinherent subsistent relationship', while he writes frequently about the 'coinherent relations' of the divine persons. I suggest that for Torrance what it means to say by 'the persons are subsistent relations' is that the persons subsist entirely in their relations, or that the Persons are entirely constituted by their relations. Thus, 'the Father *is* Father precisely in his indivisible ontic relation to the Son'. This is probably what Gregory Nazianzen means in saying that the term 'Father' is not a name for being (*ousia*) but for the relation (*schesis*) between the Father and the Son.[131]

With Torrance we are therefore still thinking of Persons who 'have' relations, although Persons can never be separated from a relational way of being, and are entirely characterized by relation. In the report of the *Colloquy towards an Ecumenical Consensus on the Trinity* (1975), written up and enlarged by its president, Torrance,[132] it is affirmed that 'coinherence applies fully to the three divine Persons as conscious of one another in their distinctive otherness and oneness'.[133] Any doctrine of the Trinity that stands within the Christian tradition must affirm the 'distinctive otherness' of the three Persons, but I suggest that we should look for a way of doing so that is compatible with the insight that the Person *is* relation, and not a subject with a distinctive consciousness who *has* relations, even if the Person entirely subsists in these relations. I have myself attempted, over the years, to set out an alternative way of understanding a perichoresis (or co-inherence) of relations. Such an account builds on Aquinas' perception that talk about Persons begins by thinking about dynamic actions and movements in God. In the context of this particular book, I believe that this vision of God is a proper theological context for what Williams and Lewis have wanted to express in imagination and image, and I will conclude by exploring it.

15.4 Co-inherence and 'Persons as Relations'

Tracing the use by trinitarian theologians of the word 'coinherence' becomes less easy after about 2005, when a plethora of articles and books began to be published that comment on Torrance's trinitarian theology, and inevitably therefore employ the word 'coinherence' as he does. He is almost solely responsible for a veritable explosion in occurrence of the word. Before this happened, however, two books appeared that mention 'co-inherence' as a synonym for *perichoresis*, and appeal to the notion of 'subsistent relation' in a different way from Torrance.[134] In 1998, David Cunningham published *These Three are One. The Practice of Trinitarian*

---

[131] Gregory Nazianzen, *Orationes*, 23.8.   [132] Torrance, *Trinitarian Perspectives*, 77, n.1.

[133] Interestingly, there is a note at this point, 97, n.45, to Welch's book, *Trinity*, 209.

[134] Neither book is in explicit dialogue with Torrance, though I reference his *Trinitarian Faith*.

Theology, and in 2000 I issued *Participating in God. A Pastoral Doctrine of the Trinity*.

Cunningham observes that the word *perichoresis* 'is not easy to translate', but suggests 'interpenetration is most commonly used today', and that 'coinherence ... comes fairly close to the "participatory" language' that he is using.[135] It is evident where he has come across the term 'coinherence', since he tells us that his treatment of 'the mutuality of divine participation', or *perichoresis*, 'follows that of G. L. Prestige, *God in Patristic Thought*', and he specifically names chapter 14 whose title is 'Co-inherence'.[136] *Perichoresis* also lies at the centre of my own study, and at one point I refer to coinherence and *perichoresis* together, writing that 'The term "perichoresis" thus expresses the permeation of each person by the other, their coinherence without confusion.'[137] I refer to previous work by LaCugna, Cunningham, and Torrance, but to the best of my recollection my use of the word 'coinherence' was not gleaned from any of these but came directly from reading Charles Williams.

Cunningham and I had both been developing, independently and unaware of each other, a more radical view of 'subsistent relations' than can be found in Torrance—that is, an insistence that 'Persons' in God are not subjects *exercising* relations, but simply *are* relations. Cunningham puts it that 'God is pure mutual participation—relation without remainder.'[138] I wrote that the idea of 'subsistent relations' indicates that:

> relations in God are as real and 'beingful' as anything which is created or uncreated, and that their ground of existence is in themselves. If we use the term *hypostasis* as the Fathers did for a 'distinct reality' which has being, then the relations *are* hypostases. There are no Persons 'at each end of a relation', but the 'Persons' are simply the relations.[139]

Both Cunningham and I appeal to Augustine and to Aquinas for precedents to this way of thinking, although I recognize that there is a jump of thought in modern theology to arrive at the kind of idea of 'person as relation' that I am commending. Although Aquinas has a significant strategy of beginning with processions (actions) in God, we need to put the idea of subsistent relations on quite a different basis from his own explanation of subsisting in the divine essence, and so also to take a step beyond Augustine's playfulness with language. Taking a clue from Karl Barth's insistence that 'with regard to the being of God, the word "event" or "act" is final',[140] we may speak of God as an event of relationships.

---

[135]   David Cunningham, *These Three are One*, 180–1.
[136]   Cunningham, *These Three are One*, 179: see esp. n.17.   [137]   Fiddes, *Participating in God*, 71.
[138]   Cunningham, *These Three are One*, 169.   [139]   Fiddes, *Participating in God*, 34.
[140]   Barth, *Church Dogmatics*, II/1, 263.

Barth's own definition of the persons as 'modes of being' fails to reflect his own perception of the dynamic nature of the being of God, even though he understood the modes as always being characterized by relationship.[141] It is better therefore to speak of movements of relationship, or perhaps three movements of relationship subsisting in one event. In 1988, in *The Creative of Suffering of God*, I had already promoted this idea of an 'event of relationships' and 'divine persons *as* relations', appealing to a precedent in the tradition of 'subsistent relations':

> the "persons" are really existing relationships, or movements of being character-
> ized by relationship. Augustine and Aquinas both spoke of the persons as
> relationships [...]. The divine personality can only be thought of as an event
> of relationships.[142]

Cunningham's own approach, some ten years later, is not to envisage an 'event of relationships', but to search for an analogy between human persons and divine persons that might approximate to the designation of 'person as relation', and inhibit us from thinking of a divine Person as any kind of individual who 'has' relations. Here he invokes a late-modern view of the self in which the human subject is radically decentred and viewed as the 'whence' and the 'whereto' of relationships, drawing attention to the thought of the philosopher Calvin Schrag about the self as a 'space of subjectivity'.[143]

I have myself aimed to take a more radical view of subsistent relations, making an analogy between relationships themselves, rather than between persons; so we can draw a comparison between relations in God and a wide range of relations in the world, such as those between a mother and the baby in her womb, between children and parents, between wife and husband, between humans and objects in their environment, and between members of various communities—not just religious communities such as churches but secular communities such as hospitals. Participating in God can be experienced as analogous to participating in these finite relationships; the analogy lies in the relationship itself, not with those who exercise it. This is a personal analogy, but not an analogy of persons. Talk about God as 'an event of relationships' is not therefore the language of a spectator, but the language of a *participant*. It only makes sense in terms of our involvement in the network of relationships in which God happens.[144]

Talk of 'divine persons as relations' is an experiment in speaking of God in a non-objectifying way, and has a strongly apophatic element, respecting the mystery of God who is unique and cannot be categorized among objects in the

---

[141] Barth, *Church Dogmatics*, I/1, 348.
[142] Fiddes, *Creative Suffering of God*, 139–40, 139, n.105, 141–3; cf. 10, 83, 123, 135, 196, 197, 201, 203. However, the term 'co-inherence' does not appear.
[143] Schrag, *Communicative Praxis*, 121, 1378, cited in Cunningham, *These Three are One*, 220–2.
[144] For what follows, see Fiddes, *Participating in God*, 34–46.

world.[145] It is not an observational but a participatory kind of speaking and knowing. We cannot 'see' three relationships (even in the mind) as objects; talk about them only makes sense as a witness that we find ourselves *participating* in movements of personal being that are like *relations* we know in the world. It is also a kind of God-talk that does not project God as a dominating subject, validating the pretensions of the human self to control the world and others, since God is being envisaged neither as one supreme subject nor three. Only divine Persons *are* relations, or using the traditional language, subsist as relations. In human life, relations must be 'between' persons, although finite persons always exist in relations, and should aim not to treat others as objects of their own subjectivity to be manipulated or dominated. God, however, is infinite and unclassifiable; we cannot insist that relations in God must be 'between' subjects called Persons.

The experience of Christian prayer, 'to the Father, through the Son and in the Spirit',[146] is one place where this kind of participation in divine relations comes alive. The cry of 'abba, Father' in prayer fits into a movement of speech that is like that between a son and a father; our response of 'yes' ('Amen') leans upon a movement that is like a filial 'yes' of humble obedience, glorifying the Father, a response that is already there before us. At the same time, in prayer and in moments of serving others, we find ourselves involved in a movement of self-giving like that of a father sending out a son on a journey, a movement that the early theologians called 'eternal generation' and has its outworking in the mission ('sending') of the Son by the Father in history to achieve the reconciliation of all things. In this moment of participation, we discover that these movements of response and mission are also undergirded by movements of suffering, like the painful longing of a forsaken son towards a father and of a desolate father towards a lost son. Here Jürgen Moltmann speaks of God as 'the event of Golgotha' and to the question 'can one pray to an event?' rightly answers that one can 'pray *in* this event'.[147] More, these two directions of movement, sending and response, are interwoven by a third, as we find that they are continually opened up to new depths of relationship and to the new possibilities of the future by a movement for which scripture offers impressionistic images—a wind blowing, breath stirring, wings beating, oil trickling, water flowing, fire burning. The traditional formulation that the Spirit 'proceeds from the Father through the Son' points to a movement that renews all relations from and to the other.

Thus, through our participation, we can identify three distinct movements that are all like speech, emotion, and action; they are like movements within relationships 'from father to son' and 'from son to father', together with a movement of

---

[145] So already Kant, *Critique of Pure Reason*, 87, 149.

[146] See e.g. Matthew 6.6, John 14.16, Hebrews 7.25, Ephesians 6.18. For prayer as participation in the Trinity, see Coakley, *God, Sexuality and the Self*, 100–51.

[147] Moltmann, *Crucified God*, 247.

'deepening relations'. They are mutual relationships of ecstatic, outward-going love, giving and receiving. Actively, they are such moments as originating, responding, and opening; passively, they are moments of being glorified, being sent, and being breathed. So far, in describing them, I have followed the form of address that Jesus himself taught his disciples, 'Abba, Father' (Matthew 6:9), offering the image 'from son to father' for the movement of response that we lean upon. But these movements of giving and receiving cannot in themselves be restricted to a particular gender, as is quite clear with the images for the movement of Spirit. They will also, in appropriate contexts, give rise to feminine images; for instance, the experience of our participation may require us to say that we are engaging in a flow of relationships like those originating in a mother (cf. Isaiah 49:14–15), or that are like the response of a daughter. Because we are thinking of divine persons as movements of giving and receiving in love, trinitarian language must be gendered in a variety of ways.

I am not ruling out the possibility that the names of God that have emerged in religious tradition may gesture to something 'more' than relations. With God, in the words of the theologian Jean-Luc Marion, there is always 'more, indeed immeasurably more' to be given to us.[148] All language about God must be metaphorical or analogous, and talk about God as an 'event of relationships' cannot be a literal description. My claim is simply that relations are the most *appropriate* analogy that we have, corresponding to experience, and that the word 'Person' or hypostasis (distinct reality) that has emerged in the reflection of church must therefore signify a relation, neither more nor less. Relations are appropriate language because God is encountered through relations of created beings; indeed, the divine relations cannot be found anywhere else. Through relations, there is not just imitation of the Trinity but participation in the Trinity. This embedding of talk about the interweaving, or *perichoresis*, of divine Persons in the complexities of human experience has been emphasized by LaCugna and Johnson; as an emphasis it stands in contrast to the making of *perichoresis* or co-inherence into a support for the oneness of divine essence as we have traced it in Prestige, Welch, Kelly, William Hill, and Torrance. But this mutual interweaving and interpenetration makes most sense when the 'Persons' are nothing other than relations.

In short, I am arguing for a 'relational' doctrine of the Trinity that is not 'social'.[149] Because the analogy is in relations and not in persons, talk about God can only make sense as participating in movements of relation, as known in such life-experiences as praying, suffering, exercising gifts of service, facing death, and sharing in the drama of the sacraments.[150] All relations in the created universe,

---

[148] Marion, *Being Given*, 196–9.
[149] For this distinction, see Fiddes, 'Relational Trinity', 159–85.
[150] I explore talk of Trinity in these areas of experience in Fiddes, *Participating in God*.

between not only animate but inanimate things, exist within the interweaving relations (*perichoresis*) of a triune God; God has made room for them within God's self in a humble act of self-limitation. Such a vision does not confuse the Creator with the created, because the divine relations are always inexhaustible in love, always more expansive, inclusive, and capacious than created relations can be. They are transcendent in the sense of always offering an excess, but can only be known in the immanence of bodily life. It is this excessiveness or moreness that will lead us, like Johnson and against LaCugna, to speak of an inner Trinity in God as well as an economic manifestation.

Among the images that arise in the poetic imagination for this experience of participation in divine *perichoresis*,[151] 'dance' appears in the writings of both Lewis and Williams. I have explored Williams' use of the image, especially in his novel *The Greater Trumps*, and Lewis' portrayal of the Great Dance in *Perelandra*. We have seen that, among those theologians that use the language of co-inherence, William Hill, Edmund Hill, LaCugna, and Johnson have all employed the image of dance. Cunningham notes the play on words between *perichōrēsis* and *perichoreuō*, and makes the shrewd point that that the image of the Trinity as a dance easily degenerates into the notion of three divine dancers, and so a relapse into 'three individual agents, each of whom is motivated by a relatively isolated will'.[152] He judges that the word 'coinherence' has the advantage of not immediately suggesting the picture of three agents, but the disadvantage of having a 'relatively static quality'. He prefers, then, to leave *perichoresis* untranslated.

However, the point of my advocacy of an 'event of relationships' is that created beings can find themselves, not dancing in the company of three divine dancers, but immersed into patterns and movements that are like a dance in their intricate rhythms.[153] The Trinity is not the dancers but the dance. As long as we use the active verb 'to coinhere', and the active gerund 'co-inhering' alongside the noun 'co-inherence', I believe that the word *can* evoke the kind of interweaving movements that we know in our various experiences. The word neatly brings together two metaphors: the dynamism of *circumincessio* and the sense of 'subsistence' (reality, beingfulness) in *circuminsessio*. Williams, I have suggested, uses the image of the waters of the Thames in this twofold way in *All Hallows' Eve*.[154]

---

[151] See Fiddes, *Seeing the World*, 291–2, for images of speaking, music and immersion in the fluidity of water.

[152] Cunningham, *These Three are One*, 180–1.

[153] For Trinity as rhythm, see Eikelboom, *Rhythm*, 136–43.   [154] See Chapter 12, section 3.

15.5 Conclusion: Analogy and Participation in C. S. Lewis and Charles Williams

This book has been the telling of the story of a literary relationship between Charles Williams and C. S. Lewis, in which the concept of co-inherence plays a central though often ambiguous part. In this final chapter, I have stepped back somewhat from that drama to trace the way that the word 'co-inherence' has been used, as a synonym for the Greek *perichoresis*, in developing a doctrine of the Trinity in modern theology. Neither story has been properly explored before, and a number of assumptions have needed to be exploded. The two stories are interconnected, at least in so far as the innovative use of the word 'co-inherence' by G. L. Prestige lies at the foundation of both of them. One recent study of the theologian T. F. Torrance has, for example, appealed to the idea of co-inherence in Torrance, Prestige, and Charles Williams, though without giving any account of Torrance's own debt to Prestige.[155] The image of dance also runs strongly through both stories, prompting resonances for readers of theology and literature. I now want to suggest, in conclusion, that the integration of analogy and participation for which I have been arguing in regarding 'Person' as 'relation' in God, may throw light on a long-standing difference between Lewis and Williams. It may even, in hindsight, provide a resolution.

From the beginning of their friendship, Lewis distanced himself from Williams with regard to the relation between human and divine love. For Lewis, there was an analogy (sometimes remote) between the two, while for Williams there was an actual participation of the human lover, in his or her erotic experience, in the eternal love of God, and especially in the glory of Christ. For Williams, the erotic love of lovers could even be seen as the Christ-child, born from their maternal relationship: 'the Divine Child spiritually lives in the two lovers'.[156] Curiously, when the image of the Trinity entered the scene with the term 'coinherence', Williams tended to stress an analogy between the triune relations and human relations of love, while Lewis was more ready to portray the participation of human beings in the actual interweaving life of divine Persons. However, whenever participation in God is in view, Williams is working on a universal level of what is available to all human persons, while—with the exception of the Great Dance of *Perelandra* and his final writings—Lewis is narrowing his focus to those who have received new life (*Zoe*) through faith in Christ. I have suggested that there are two different world views in play here, with Lewis indebted to a Christianized Neoplatonism and Williams to a Christianized Kabbalism. Neither Lewis nor Williams were wedded strictly to a philosophical or metaphysical scheme, but either Neoplatonism or Kabbalism offered a range of images to

---

[155] Hastings, *Echoes of Coinherence*; on Williams, see esp. 30–1.
[156] Williams, 'One Way of Love', 161.

their users, and a basic approach to the relation between the world and God. They shaped, in at least a general way, what Lewis felt to be different territories within the general landscape of Romanticism through which he and Williams were journeying on the 'secret road'.

Now, if the key analogy between human and divine life lies in relation rather than in 'Person', it is easier to see the way in which analogy and participation co-inhere, and how Lewis and Williams might have edged onto common ground. If the experiences of human relationships are all the time engaging (or co-inhering) in the divine *perichoresis*, then analogies will naturally arise between movements of love and justice in God and in the life of created beings. To take the rather startling image of Williams, the birthing of love in human life, when held in the triune dance of relations, is *like* the involvement of the triune God in the birth of Christ from Mary, behind which there lies an eternal movement of mission *like* the generation of a son from a father. Correspondingly, if the analogy lies in the *movement* of birthing (whether literal or metaphorical) rather than in any analogy between a human son and a supposedly divine 'Son', then participation in God is in view from the beginning. From the viewpoint of 'Person as relation', we can see how the positions of Lewis and Williams *might* converge. Indeed, with hindsight, I venture to say that we can see how they *are* converging.

Once we have a grasp on this process of participation, Christology itself is shaken free from a metaphysic of two natures. The classical co-inherence of human and divine natures, to which the language of *perichoresis* was first applied by Gregory Nazianzen, becomes a co-inhering of human and divine movements of life. For Christians, it is through the particular human sonship of Jesus of Nazareth expressed in his words, actions, and suffering, that we are drawn more deeply into the communion of God's being. The relationships in which this man lived were perfectly one with the dynamic of God's relations of love in a way that ours are not and never will be; in an early phrase of John Hick, he was 'homo-agape' with God with a numerical identity of love and not simply a generic sameness.[157] The Christian claim is that the human 'movement' of the life of Jesus fits more exactly into the movements in God than other finite lives do, but that all life shares to some extent in this same dynamic. So all the speech of Christ, all the ways he sees the world, all his bodily acts fit exactly into the movement in the Trinity that we recognize as being like a son relating to a father. The relation of the human person Christ to the one whom he calls his heavenly father can be mapped exactly onto the relation in God, which is like that between a son (or daughter) and a father (or mother). This human son is the same as a divine *sonship*, which is a relation analogous to that between a son and a father—or indeed, a relation like that between a daughter and a mother.

---

[157] John Hick, *God*, 156–9, 164. I differ from Hick in thinking, unlike him, that this function of identical loving has ontological consequences.

I am not, of course, suggesting that either Lewis or Williams would have ascribed to such a Christology. I doubt very much that they would; they show a firm fidelity to the classical language of two natures. I provide this brief sketch as a way of meeting the objection of Prestige that co-inherence is not suitable for Christology, and as a support to Williams' own use of the idea for both Christology and Trinity. I have already drawn attention to the discomfort that Williams felt with a dualism between soul and body, although he continued to hold to a dualism of 'natural' and 'supernatural' orders of being.[158] Lewis, from a more Neoplatonist perspective, works with the same duality more easily and naturally. But the disjunction between analogy and participation is more easily overcome when dualism between spirit and matter is entirely abandoned. Analogy is no longer then between two different areas of reality, but is a likeness between sets of relations that are participating in one reality.

The divine act of creation may thus be understood as the bringing of reality other than God into being *by* God to participate in God's life, which is then to be shaped through engagement in the interweaving relations of love and justice in God that we name in the Christian tradition as Father, Son, and Spirit. God acts in the universe in continuous creativity wholly as Trinity, not as separate persons in sequence. God acts through influence and persuasion on the created materials that are immersed into God. When we are involved in the dance of triune relations, we are moved to certain ends, caught up in their momentum. We are incited to follow patterns of love and sacrifice like relations between a father and a son, or between a mother and a daughter, and we are constantly opened up to new levels of being by the disturbance of Spirit. Everything participates in the triune God, but through Christ, who (in Christian thinking) participates more exactly than any other person, created beings can be drawn 'farther up and farther in'.[159]

Analogy thus constantly becomes participation, and we understand more of our participation through the forming of analogies, not least in poetry. As we accompany Lewis and Williams on the 'secret road' of their friendship, we want to affirm with Williams that 'Love is born in the soul; it may have its passion there; it may have its resurrection,'[160] and with Lewis that 'The whole dance, or drama, or pattern of this three-Personal life is to be played out in each one of us.'[161] Co-inherence is expressed in both sayings, in images of birth and dance. Those making the sayings are friends in the co-inherence, and so are we who read them.

---

[158] See Chapter 7, section 1, and Chapter 5, conclusion of section 1.

[159] I employ Lewis' phrase from *Last Battle*, 163–74, aware that I am making my own application of it.

[160] Williams, *He Came Down*, 113. I do not mean, of course, to subscribe to a dualistic understanding of the soul.

[161] Lewis, *Mere Christianity*, 139.

Bibliography

Altizer, Thomas J. *The Gospel of Christian Atheism* (London: 1967).

Altizer, Thomas J. *The New Apocalypse. The Radical Christian Vision of William Blake* (East Lansing: Michigan State University Press, 1967).

Anon. *The Dream of the Rood*, edited by Bruce Dickins and Alan C. Ross. Methuen's Old English Library (London: Methuen, 1963).

Anon. *The Gnostic Hymn of Jesus*, translated and edited by G. R. S. Mead (London and Benares: Theosophical Publishing Society, 1907).

Aquinas, Thomas. *Summa Theologiae*. Blackfriars edition (London: Eyre & Spottiswoode, 1964–81).

Arbaugh, George B. and George E. Arbaugh, *Kierkegaard's Authorship* (London: George Allen & Unwin, 1968).

Ashenden, Gavin. *Charles Williams: Alchemy and Integration* (Kent, OH: Kent State University Press, 2008).

Auden, W. H. *Collected Poems*, edited by Edward Mendelson (London: Faber and Faber, 1991).

Auden, W. H. *For The Time Being. A Christmas Oratorio*, edited by Alan Jacobs. Critical edition (Princeton, NJ: Princeton University Press, 2013).

Auden, W. H. 'Preface' to Charles Williams, *The Descent of the Dove*. Living Age edition (New York: Living Age, 1956).

Augustine, *The Trinity*, translated by S. McKenna. The Fathers of the Church (Washington, DC: Catholic University of America Press, 1963).

Aulén, Gustaf. *Christus Victor*, translated by A. G. Herbert (London: SPCK, 1937).

Baggett, David. 'Is Divine Iconoclast as Bad as Divine Sadist?', 2008. In Baggett et al., *C. S. Lewis as Philosopher*, 115–30.

Baggett, David, Gary R. Habermas, and Jerry L. Walls (eds). *C. S. Lewis as Philosopher. Truth, Goodness and Beauty* (Downers Grove, IL: IVP Academic, 2008).

Balthasar, Hans Urs von. *Theo-Drama. Theological Dramatic Theory*, Vol. II, *Dramatis Personae: Man in God*; Vol. IV, *The Action*, translated by G. Harrison (San Francisco, CA: Ignatius Press, 1990, 1994).

Barber, Stephen. 'Charles Williams and TS Eliot: Friends and Rivals', *Journal of Inklings Studies* 9.1 (2019): 1–18.

Barkman, Adam. *C. S. Lewis & Philosophy As a Way of Life. A Comprehensive Historical Examination of his Philosophical Thoughts* (Allentown, PA: Zossima Press, 2001).

Barrett, C. K. *A Commentary on the Second Epistle to the Corinthians* (London: Adam and Charles Black, 1973).

Barth, Karl. *Church Dogmatics*, translated and edited by G. W. Bromiley and T. F. Torrance. 14 volumes (Edinburgh: T. & T. Clark, 1936–1977).

Barth, Karl. *Church Dogmatics*, Vol. I, Part I, translated by G. T. Thompson (Edinburgh: T. & T. Clark, 1936).

Barth, Karl. *The Epistle to the Romans*, translated from the 6th edition by Edwyn C. Hoskyns (London: Oxford University Press, 1933).

Barth, Karl. *How I Changed My Mind*, translated by M. E. Bratcher (Edinburgh: St Andrew Press, 1969).

Barth, Karl. *No! Answer to Emil Brunner* (1934). In Karl Barth and Emil Brunner, *Natural Theology*, translated by Peter Fraenkel, 65–128. (London: Geoffrey Bles/Centenary Press, 1946).

Barth, Karl. *The Theology of Schleiermacher*, edited by Dietrich Ritschl, translated by Geoffrey W. Bromiley (Edinburgh: T. & T. Clark, 1982).

Beintker, Michael. *Die Dialektik in der 'dialektischen Theologie' Karl Barths* (Munich: Chr. Kaiser Verlag, 1987).

Bell, James Stuart. *From the Library of CS Lewis. Selections from Writers who Influenced his Spiritual Journey* (Colorado Springs, CO: Shawbooks, 2004).

Berkeley, George. *Three Dialogues between Hylas and Philonous*. In T. E. Jessop (ed.), *The Works of George Berkeley*, Vol. II, 171–262 (London: Thomas Nelson, 1949).

Best, Ernest. *One Body in Christ* (London: SPCK, 1955).

Beversluis, John. *C. S. Lewis and the Search for Rational Religion*. Revised and updated (Amherst, NY: Prometheus Books, 2007).

Bide, Peter. 'Marrying C. S. Lewis'. In White et al., *C. S. Lewis and His Circle*, 187–91.

Biggar, Nigel. *The Hastening that Waits. Karl Barth's Ethics*. 2nd edition (Oxford: Clarendon Press, 1995).

Blake, William. *Complete Writings*, edited by Geoffrey Keynes (London: Oxford University Press, 1966).

Blau, Joseph Leon. *The Christian Interpretation of the Cabala in the Renaissance* (New York: Columbia University Press, 1944).

Borrow, Anthony. 'The Affirmation of Images: An Examination of the Novels of Charles Williams'. *Nine* 3 (1952): 325–54.

Bradbury, J. G. 'Charles Williams' Arthuriad: Mythic Vision and the Possibilities of Belief'. *Journal of Inklings Studies* 1.1 (2011): 33–46.

Bradley, F. H. *Appearance and Reality. A Metaphysical Essay*, 6th edition (London: George, Allen and Unwin, 1916).

Bray, Suzanne and Richard Sturch (eds). *Charles Williams and his Contemporaries* (Cambridge; Cambridge Scholars, 2009).

Brewer, Elisabeth. 'Women in the Arthurian Poems of Charles Williams'. In Horne, *Charles Williams: A Celebration*, 98–115.

Brown, David and Ann Loades (eds). *The Sense of the Sacramental. Movement and Measure in Art and Music, Place and Time* (London: SPCK, 1995).

Budge, Wallis (ed). *The Paradise or Garden of the Holy Fathers: Being Histories of the Anchorites, Recluses, Monks, Coenobites, and Ascetic Fathers of the Deserts of Egypt between A.D. CCL and A.D. CCCC circiter, Compiled by the 7th Century 'Anân-Îshô', Translated and Edited by E. A. Wallis Budge*. 2 volumes (London: Chatto & Windus, 1907).

Caird, George B. *Principalities and Powers. A Study in Pauline Theology* (Oxford: Clarendon Press, 1956).

Carpenter, Humphrey, *The Inklings: C. C. Lewis, J. R. R. Tolkien, Charles Williams, and Their Friends* (London: George Allen & Unwin, 1978).

Cavaliero, Glen. 'Charles Williams and the Arthuriad: Poetry as Sacrament'. *The Charles Williams Quarterly* 108 (2003): 7–17.

Cavaliero, Glen. 'Charles Williams and Twentieth Century Verse Drama'. In Horne, *Charles Williams: A Celebration*, 194–205.

Cavaliero, Glen. *Charles Williams: Poet of Theology* (Grand Rapids, MI: Eerdmans, 1983).

Cavallo, Adolfo Salvatore. *The Unicorn Tapestries at the Metropolitan Museum of Art* (New York: Harry N. Abrahams, 1998).

Clark, Mary T. 'A Neoplatonic Commentary on the Christian Trinity: Marius Victorinus'. In O'Meara, *Neoplatonism and Christian Thought*, 24–33.

Clarke, Anthony. *A Cry in the Darkness. The Forsakenness of Jesus in Scripture, Theology, and Experience* (Macon, GA: Smyth and Helwys Publishing, 2002).

Coakley, Sarah. *God, Sexuality and the Self. An Essay 'On the Trinity'* (Cambridge: Cambridge University Press, 2013).

Cochrane, Charles Norris. *Christianity and Classical Culture. A Study of Thought and Action from Augustus to Augustine* (Oxford: Clarendon Press, 1940).

Coghill, Neville. 'The Approach to English'. In Jocelyn Gibb (ed.), *Light on C. S. Lewis*, 51–66 (London: Geoffrey Bles, 1965).

Coleridge, *Aids to Reflection* [1825], edited by John Beer. Bollingen Series (London: Routledge, 1993).

Coleridge, S. T. *Biographia Literia* [1817], edited by J. Shawcross. 2 volumes (London: Oxford University Press, 1907).

Coleridge, S. T. *Hints Towards the Formation of a More Comprehensive Theory of Life*, edited by Seth B. Watson (London: John Churchill, 1848).

Connelly, Sean. *Inklings of Heaven: C. S. Lewis and Eschatology* (London: Gracewing, 2007).

Conticello, V. L. 'Pseudo-Cyril's "De SS. Trinitate": A Compilation of Joseph the Philosopher', *Orientalia Christiana Periodica* 61 (1995): 117–29.

Cordovero, Moshe. *The Palm Tree of Devorah*, translated by Moshe Miller (Southfield, MI: Targum Press, 1993).

Cunningham, David. *These Three are One. The Practice of Trinitarian Theology* (Oxford: Blackwell, 1998).

Curtis, Jan. 'Byzantium and the Matter of Britain: The Narrative Framework of Charles Williams' Later Arthurian Poems'. *Quondam et Futurus: A Journal of Arthurian Interpretations* 2.1 (1992): 28–54.

Damon, Samuel Foster. *A Blake Dictionary: The Ideas and Symbols of William Blake* (Hanover, IN: Brown University Press, 1988).

Dante Alighieri. *The Divine Comedy*, translated by Dorothy Sayers and Barbara Reynolds. 3 volumes: 1. *Hell*. 2. *Purgatory*. 3. *Paradise* (Harmondsworth: Penguin, 1949–1962).

Dante Alighieri. *La Vita Nuova*, translated by Barbara Reynolds (Harmondsworth: Penguin, 1969).

Dickerson, Phoebe. '"The Lanthorns Sides": Skin, Soul and the Poetry of Thomas Traherne'. In Dodd and Gorman, *Thomas Traherne*, 31–47.

Dodd, Elizabeth S. and Cassandra Gorman (eds). *Thomas Traherne and Seventeenth-Century Thought* (Martlesham: Boydell and Brewer, 2016).

Dronke, Peter. *Medieval Latin and the Rise of European Love-Lyric*. 2 volumes. Revised edition (Oxford: Clarendon Press, 1968).

Dunning, Stephen M. *The Crisis and the Quest. A Kierkegaardian Reading of Charles Williams* (Carlisle: Paternoster, 2000).

Duriez, Colin, *The A-Z of C. S. Lewis. An Encyclopedia of his Life, Thought, and Writings* (Oxford: Lion, 2013).

Duriez, Colin. *The Oxford Inklings: Lewis, Tolkien and their Circle* (Oxford: Lion, 2015).

Edersheim, Alfred. *Life and Times of Jesus the Messiah*. 2 volumes. 2nd edition (London: Longmans/Green and Company, 1886).

Edwards, Bruce (ed). *C.S. Lewis: Life, Works and Legacy*. 4 volumes (Westport, CT: Praeger Publishers, 2007).

Edwards, Mark. 'C. S. Lewis and Early Christian Literature'. In Wolfe and Wolfe, *C. S. Lewis and the Church*, 23–39.

Eikelboom, Lexi. *Rhythm. A Theological Category* (Oxford: Oxford University Press, 2018).

Eliot, T. S. Introduction to Charles Williams, *All Hallows' Eve*, ix–xviii (New York: Pellegrini & Cudahy, 1948).

Eliot, T. S. 'A Lay Theologian'. *New Statesman & Nation*, Vol. 18, pp. 864, 866, 9 December 1939.

Ellrodt, Robert. *Seven Metaphysical Poets. A Structural Study of the Unchanging Self* (Oxford: Oxford University Press, 2000).

Emerton, J, A. 'The Interpretation of Psalm lxxxii in John x'. *Journal of Theological Studies* 11 n.s. (1960): 329–34.

Farmer, Stephen Alan. *Syncretism in the West: Pico's 900 Theses, 1486. With Text, Translation, and Commentary* (Tempe, AZ: Medieval and Renaissance Texts & Studies, 1998).

Feinendegen, Norbert. 'The Philosopher's Progress: CS Lewis' Intellectual Journey from Atheism to Theism'. *Journal of Inklings Studies* 8.2 (2018): 103–43.

Ficino, Marsilio. *Platonic Theology*, translated by Michael J. B. Allen with John Warden. 6 volumes (Cambridge, MA: Harvard University Press, 2001–6).

Fiddes, Paul S. 'C. S. Lewis: On Theology'. In MacSwain and Ward, *Cambridge Companion*, 89–104.

Fiddes, Paul S. 'Charles Williams and the Problem of Evil'. In White et al., *C. S. Lewis and His Circle*, 65–8.

Fiddes, Paul S. *The Creative Suffering of God* (Oxford: Clarendon Press, 1988).

Fiddes, Paul S. '"For the Dance All Things Were Made": The Great Dance in C. S. Lewis' Perelandra'. In Wolfe and Wolfe, *C. S. Lewis's Perelandra*, 33–49.

Fiddes, Paul S. *Freedom and Limit. A Dialogue between Literature and Christian Doctrine* (London: Macmillan, 1991).

Fiddes, Paul S. 'Lewis the Myth-Maker'. In Walker and Patrick, *Christian for All Christians*, 132–55.

Fiddes, Paul S. *Participating in God. A Pastoral Doctrine of the Trinity* (London: Darton, Longman and Todd, 2000).

Fiddes, Paul S. 'Relational Trinity: Radical Perspective'. In Stephen R. Holmes, Paul D. Molnar, Thomas H. McCall, and Paul S. Fiddes, *Two Views of the Doctrine of the Trinity*, 159–85 (Grand Rapids, MI: Zondervan, 2014).

Fiddes, Paul S. *Seeing the World and Knowing God. Hebrew Wisdom and Christian Doctrine in a Late-Modern Context* (Oxford: Oxford University Press, 2015).

Fisher, Simon. *Revelatory Positivism? Barth's Earliest Theology and the Marburg School* (Oxford: Oxford University Press, 1988).

Fleming, John V. 'Literary Critic'. In MacSwain and Ward, *Cambridge Companion*, 15–28.

Frye, Northrop. *Fearful Symmetry: A Study of William Blake* (Princeton, NJ: Princeton University Press, 1947).

Gardner, W.H. 'A Note on Hopkins and Duns Scotus'. *Scrutiny* 5.1 (1936): 61–70. Reprinted in Gerald Roberts (ed.), *Gerard Manley Hopkins, The Critical Heritage*, 337–344 (London: Routledge and Kegan Paul, 1987).

Goffar, Janine. *The CS Lewis Index: A Comprehensive Guide to Lewis's Writings and Ideas* (Wheaton, IL: Crossway, 1998).

Göller, Karl Heinz. 'From Logres to Carbonek: The Arthuriad of Charles Williams'. *Arthurian Literature* 1 (1981): 121–73.

Gore, Charles. *The Philosophy of the Good Life*. Reprint (London: Dent, 1954).

Gorman, Cassandra. 'Thomas Traherne and "Feeling inside the Atom"'. In Dodd and Gorman, *Thomas Traherne*, 69–83.

Green, Roger Lancelyn and Walter Hooper. *C. S. Lewis: A Biography* (London: Collins/Fount, 1979).

Guite, Malcolm. 'Yearning for a Far-Off Country', in White et al., *C. S. Lewis and His Circle*, 110–21.

Hadfield, Alice Mary. *Charles Williams: An Exploration of His Life and Work* (New York: Oxford University Press, 1983).

Hadfield, Alice Mary. *An Introduction to Charles Williams* (London: Robert Hale, 1959).

Hannay, Margaret. 'Arthurian and Cosmic Myth in That Hideous Strength'. *Mythlore* 2.2 (1970): article 3.

Hastings, Ross W. *Echoes of Coinherence: Trinitarian Theology and Science Together* (Eugene, OR: Wipf and Stock, 2017).

Heath-Stubbs, John. 'The Figure of Cressida'. In Horne, *Charles Williams: A Celebration*, 49–60.

Hebblethwaite, Brian. *The Incarnation: Collected Essays in Christology* (Cambridge: Cambridge University Press, 1987).

Hegel, G. W. F. *The Christian Religion. Lectures on the Philosophy of Religion. Part III*, edited and translated by Peter C. Hodgson (Missoula, MT: Scholars Press, 1979).

Hick, John. *Evil and the God of Love* (London: Fontana, Collins, 1968).

Hick, John. *God and the Universe of Faiths* (London: Collins/Fount, 1977).

Higgins, Sørina. 'Double Affirmation: Medievalism as Christian Apologetic in the Arthurian Poetry of Charles Williams'. *Journal of Inklings Studies* 3.2 (2013): 59–96.

Higgins, Sørina (ed). *The Inklings and King Arthur: J.R.R Tolkien, Charles Williams, C. S Lewis and Owen Barfield on the Matter of Britain* (Berkeley, CA: Apocryphile Press, 2017).

Hilder, Monika B. *Surprised by the Feminine. A Rereading of C.S. Lewis and Gender* (New York: Peter Lang, 2013).

Hill, Edmund. *The Mystery of the Trinity* (London: Geoffrey Chapman, 1985.

Hill, Geoffrey. *Collected Critical Writings*, edited by Kenneth Haynes (Oxford: Oxford University Press, 2008).

Hill, William. *The Three-Personed God* (Washington, DC: University of America Press, 1982).

Hooper, Teresa. 'Playing by the Rules: Kipling's "Great Game" vs. "the Great Dance" in C.S. Lewis' Space Trilogy'. *Mythlore* 25:1–2 (2006): 105–26.

Hooper, Walter. 'It All Began with a Picture. The Making of C. S. Lewis' Chronicles of Narnia'. In White et al., *C. S. Lewis and His Circle*, 150–63.

Hooper, Walter. *Past Watchful Dragons. The Narnian Chronicles of C.S. Lewis* (London: Collier Macmillan, 1979).

Hopkins, Gerard Manley. *Sermons and Spiritual Writings, Collected Works of Gerard Manley Hopkins*, Vol. V, edited by Jude V. Nixon and Noel Barber, SJ (Oxford: Oxford University Press, 2018).

Horne, Brian (ed). *Charles Williams: A Celebration* (Leominster: Gracewing, 1995).

Horne, Brian. 'From the Archives: The Recovery of Spiritual Initiative'. *Charles Williams Quarterly* 123 (2007): 12–24.

Horne, Brian. 'A Peculiar Debt. The Influence of Charles Williams on C. S. Lewis'. In Walker and Patrick, *Christian for All Christians*, 83–97.

Howard, Thomas. *Narnia and Beyond. A Guide to the Fiction of C.S. Lewis* (San Francisco, CA: Ignatius Press, 1987).

Howard, Thomas. *The Novels of Charles Williams* (Eugene, OR: Wipf and Stock, 2004).

Huttar, Charles. 'Arms and the Man: the Place of Beatrice in Charles Williams's Romantic Theology'. In Horne, *Charles Williams: A Celebration*, 61–97.

John, of the Cross. *The Poems of St. John of the Cross*, translated by John Frederick Nims (Chicago: Chicago University Press, 1979).

Johnson, Elizabeth A. *She Who Is. The Mystery of God in Feminist Theological Discourse* (New York: Crossroad, 1992).

Johnson, Kirstin Jeffrey. 'Conversing with Dante: Relational Assent in Williams and MacDonald'. *VII: An Anglo-American Literary Review* 26 (2009): 17–39.

Julian of Norwich. *Revelations of Divine Love*, translated by Elizabeth Spearing (London: Penguin, 1998).

Jüngel, Eberhard. 'Vom Tod des lebendigen Gottes. Ein Plakat'. *Zeitschrift für Theologie und Kirche* 65 (1968): 93–116.

Jüngel, Eberhard. 'Von der Dialektik zür Analogie: die Schule Kierkegaards und der Einspruch Petersons'. In Eberhard Jüngel, *Barth-Studien*, 127–79 (Zürich: Benziger Verlag/Gütersloh: Gerd Mohn, 1982).

Jüngel, Eberhard. *God's Being Is in Becoming*, translated by John Webster (Edinburgh: T. & T. Clark, 2001).

Jüngel, Eberhard. *Karl Barth. A Theological Legacy*, translated by Garrett Paul (Philadelphia, PA: Westminster Press, 1986).

Kant, Immanuel. *Critique of Pure Reason*, translated by N. Kemp Smith (London: Macmillan, 1933).

Kawano, Roland M. 'C. S. Lewis and the Great Dance'. *Christianity and Literature* 26.1 (1976): 20–38.

Kelly, J. N. D. *Early Christian Doctrines*. 4th edition (London: A. & C. Black, 1958).

Kierkegaard, Søren. *Concluding Unscientific Postscript*, translated by David F. Swenson and Walter Lowrie (Princeton, NJ: Princeton University Press, 1941).

Kierkegaard, Søren. *Either/Or*, translated by Walter Lowrie. 2 volumes (Princeton, NJ: Princeton University Press, 1971 [1944]).

Kierkegaard, Søren. *Fear and Trembling. A Dialectical Lyric* by Johannes de Silentio, translated by Robert Payne (London: Oxford University Press, 1939).

Kierkegaard, Søren. *Journals*, edited by Alexander Dru (London: Oxford University Press, 1938).

Kierkegaard, Søren. *Practice in Christianity*, edited and translated by Edna H. Hong and Howard V. Hong (Princeton, NJ: Princeton University Press, 1991).

Kierkegaard, Søren. *The Present Age*, translated by Alexander Dru and Walter Lowrie (London: Oxford University Press, 1940).

Kierkegaard, Søren. *The Sickness Unto Death*, edited and translated by Howard V. Hong and Edna H. Hong (Princeton, NJ: Princeton University Press, 1980).

Kierkegaard, Søren. *Training in Christianity*, translated by Walter Lowrie (London: Oxford University Press, 1941).

Kilby Clyde S. and Marjorie Lamp Mead (eds). *Brothers and Friends. The Diaries of Major Warren Hamilton Lewis* (San Francisco, CA: Harper and Row, 1982).

King, Roma A. Jr. *The Pattern in the Web, The Mythical Poetry of Charles Williams* (Kent, OH: Kent State University Press, 1990).

Knight, Gareth. *The Magical World of the Inklings: J. R. R. Tolkien, C. S. Lewis, Charles Williams, Owen Barfield* (Cheltenham: Skylight Press, 2010).

Kuhl, Rand. 'Owen Barfield in Southern California'. *Mythlore* 1.4 (1969): 8–10.

LaCugna, Catherine Mowry. *God For Us. The Trinity and Christian Life* (San Francisco, CA: Harper Collins, 1991).

LaCugna, Catherine Mowry. 'Reconceiving the Trinity as the Mystery of Salvation'. *Scottish Journal of Theology* 38 (1985): 1–23.

Lampe, W. G. H. (ed). *A Patristic Greek Lexicon* (Oxford: Clarendon Press, 1961).

Latta, Corey. *When the Eternal Can be Met. The Bergsonian Theology of Time in the Works of C. S. Lewis, T. S. Eliot and W. H. Auden* (Cambridge: Lutterworth Press, 2014).

Law, William. 'The Spirit of Love'. In Sidney Spencer (ed.), *The Spirit of Prayer and the Spirit of Love*, 164–295 (Cambridge: James Clarke, 1969).

Lawson, Penelope. *St. Athanasius on the Incarnation. The Treatise De Incarnatio Verbi*, translated and edited by A Religious of C.S.M.V. (London: Geoffrey Bles/Centenary Press, 1944).

Lewis, C. S. *The Abolition of Man. Reflections on Education with Special Reference to the Teaching of English in the Upper Forms of Schools*. Reprint (London: Geoffrey Bles, 1962 [1943]).

Lewis, C. S. *All My Road Before Me. The Diary of C.S. Lewis 1922–1927*, edited by Walter Hooper (London: HarperCollins, 1991).

Lewis, C. S. *The Allegory of Love: A Study in Medieval Tradition* (Oxford: Oxford University Press, 1979 [1936]).

Lewis, C. S. *Beyond Personality. The Christian Idea of God* (London: Geoffrey Bles/ Centenary Press, 1944). Reprinted in Lewis, *Mere Christianity*, 121–77.

Lewis, C. S. *Broadcast Talks* (London: Geoffrey Bles/Centenary Press, 1942). Reprinted in Lewis, *Mere Christianity*, 1–52.

Lewis, C. S. 'Charles Williams, *Taliessin Through Logres*'. *Oxford Magazine* 64 (14 March 1946): 248–50. Reprinted in Lewis, *Image and Imagination*, 137–46.

Lewis, C. S. *Christian Behaviour. A Further Series of Broadcast Talks* (London: Geoffrey Bles/ The Centenary Press, 1943). Reprinted in Lewis, *Mere Christianity*, 55–118.

Lewis, C. S. *Christian Reflections*, edited by Walter Hooper (London: Bles, 1967).

Lewis, C. S. *Clivi Hamiltonis Summae Metaphysices Contra Anthroposophos* Libri II. Unpublished document. The Marion E. Wade Centre, November 1928.

Lewis, C. S. 'Christianity and Culture (a letter)'. *Theology* 40 (1940): 356–66. Reprinted in Lewis, *Christian Reflections*, 25–7.

Lewis, C. S. 'Christianity and Culture'. *Theology* 40 (1940): 166–79. Reprinted in Lewis, *Christian Reflections*, 12–25.

Lewis, C. S. *Collected Letters*, edited by Walter Hooper. 3 volumes (New York: HarperCollins, 2004–6).

Lewis, C. S. 'De Futilitate'. In Walter Hooper (ed.), *Christian Reflections*, 57–71 (London: Geoffrey Bles, 1967).

Lewis, C. S. 'Denis de Rougement, Passion and Society'. *Theology* 40 (June 1940): 459–61. Reprinted in Lewis, *Image and Imagination*, 59–62.

Lewis, C. S. *The Discarded Image. An Introduction to Medieval and Renaissance Literature* (Cambridge: Cambridge University Press, 1964).

Lewis, C. S. 'The Efficacy of Prayer', in Lewis, *World's Last Night*, 3–12.

Lewis, C. S. *English Literature in the Sixteenth Century. Excluding Drama* (Oxford: Clarendon Press, 1954).

Lewis, C. S. 'The English Prose Morte'. In J. A. Bennett (ed.), *Essays on Malory*, 7–28 (Oxford: Clarendon Press, 1963).

Lewis, C. S. (ed). *Essays Presented to Charles Williams* (London: Oxford University Press, 1947).

Lewis, C. S. *The Four Loves* (London: Bles, 1960).

Lewis, C. S. *George MacDonald. An Anthology* (London: Bles, 1946).

Lewis, C. S. *The Great Divorce* (London: Geoffrey Bles/Centenary Press, 1945).

Lewis, C. S. as N. W. Clerk. *A Grief Observed* (Faber & Faber, 1961).

Lewis, C. S. *The Horse and His Boy* (London: Collins, 1974 [Bles, 1954]).

Lewis, C. S. *Image and Imagination. Essays and Reviews*, edited by Walter Hooper (Cambridge: Cambridge University Press, 2013).

Lewis, C. S. 'Imagination and Thought in the Middle Ages'. In Lewis, *Studies in Medieval & Renaissance Literature*, 41–63.

Lewis, C. S. 'Is Theology Poetry?'. In Lewis, *They Asked for a Paper*, 150–65.

Lewis, C. S. 'It All Began with a Picture'. In Lewis, *Of This and Other Worlds*, 78–79.

Lewis, C. S. 'The Language of Religion'. In Lewis, *Christian Reflections*, 129–41.

Lewis, C. S. *The Last Battle* (London: Bodley Head, 1972 [1956]).

Lewis, C. S. *The Letters of C. S. Lewis*, edited by W. H. Lewis (London: Geoffrey Bles, 1966).

Lewis, C. S. *Letters to Malcolm: Chiefly on Prayer* (London: Geoffrey Bles, 1964).

Lewis, C. S. 'Lilies that Fester'. In Lewis, *World's Last Night*, 31–50.

Lewis, C. S. *The Lion, the Witch and the Wardrobe* (London: Collins, 1974 [Bles, 1950]).

Lewis, C. S. *The Magician's Nephew* (London: Bodley Head, 1971 [1955]).

Lewis, C. S. 'Membership', in Lewis, *Transposition*, 34–44.

Lewis, C. S. *Mere Christianity* (London: Geoffrey Bles, 1952).

Lewis, C. S. *Miracles. A Preliminary Study* (London: Geoffrey Bles/Centenary Press, 1947).

Lewis, C. S. 'Neoplatonism in the Poetry of Spenser'. In Lewis, *Studies in Medieval & Renaissance Literature*, 149–63.

Lewis, C. S. 'The Novels of Charles Williams'. In Lewis, *Of This and Other Worlds*, 46–54.

Lewis, C. S. *Of This and Other Worlds*, edited by Walter Hooper (London: Collins, 1982).

Lewis, C. S. 'On the Reading of Old Books'. In Lewis, *Undeceptions*, 161–66.

Lewis, C. S. *Out of the Silent Planet* (London: Bodley Head, 1967 [1937]).

Lewis, C. S. 'The Pains of Animals. A Problem in Theology'. *The Month* 189 (February 1950): 95–104. Reprinted in Lewis, *Undeceptions*, 128–37.

Lewis, C. S. 'Peace Proposals for Brother Every and Mr Bethell'. *Theology* 41 (1940): 339–48. Reprinted in Lewis, *Christian Reflections*, 27–36.

Lewis, C. S. *Perelandra* (London: Bodley Head, 1967 [1943]).

Lewis, C. S. *The Pilgrim's Regress. An Allegorical Apology for Christianity Reason and Romanticism*. 3rd edition (London: Bles, 1943).

Lewis, C. S. *Poems*, edited by Walter Hooper (London: Bles, 1964).

Lewis, C. S. 'The Poison of Subjectivism'. In Lewis, *Christian Reflections*, 72–81.

Lewis, C. S. *A Preface to Paradise Lost* (London: Oxford University Press, 1942).

Lewis, C. S. 'Priestesses in the Church?'. In 'Notes on the Way'. *Time and Tide* 29 (14 August 1948): 830–1. Reprinted in Lewis, *Undeceptions*, 191–96.

Lewis, C. S. *Prince Caspian. The Return to Narnia* (London: Collins, 1974 [Bles, 1971])

Lewis, C. S. *The Problem of Pain* (London: Bles, 1940).

Lewis, C. S. *Reflections on the Psalms* (London: Bles, 1958).

Lewis, C. S. 'Rejoinder to Dr Pittenger' (1958), in Lewis, *Undeceptions*, 143–48.

Lewis, C. S. 'A Sacred Poem: Charles Williams, *Taliessin Through Logres*'. *Theology* 38 (1939): 268–76. Reprinted in Lewis, *Image and Imagination*, 125–36.

Lewis, C. S. 'The Sagas and Modern Life: Morris, Mr. Yeats and the Originals'. *The Times Literary Supplement*, 29 May 1937, 409.

Lewis, C. S. *The Screwtape Letters* (London: Geoffrey Bles/Centenary Press, 1942).

Lewis, C. S. *The Screwtape Letters and Screwtape Proposes a Toast*. New edition (London: Bles, 1961).

Lewis, C. S. *Screwtape Proposes a Toast and Other Pieces* (London: Collins/Fontana, 1965).

Lewis, C. S. *Selected Literary Essays*, edited by Walter Hooper (Cambridge: Cambridge University Press, 1969).

Lewis, C. S. *The Silver Chair* (London: Collins, 1974 [Bles, 1953]).

Lewis, C. S. *Spenser's Images of Life*, edited by Alastair Fowler (Cambridge: Cambridge University Press, 1967).

Lewis, C. S. *Studies in Medieval & Renaissance Literature*, collected by Walter Hooper (Cambridge: Cambridge University Press, 1966).

Lewis, C. S. *Studies in Words*. 2nd edition (Cambridge: Cambridge University Press, 1967).

Lewis, C. S. *Surprised by Joy. The Shape of My Early Life* (London: Bles, 1955).

Lewis, C. S. *That Hideous Strength* (London: John Lane/ Bodley Head, 1946).

Lewis, C. S. *They Asked for a Paper. Papers and Addresses* (London: Geoffrey Bles, 1962).

Lewis, C. S. *Till We Have Faces. A Myth Retold* (London: Geoffrey Bles, 1956).

Lewis, C. S. 'Transposition. A Sermon'. In Lewis, *Transposition and Other Addresses*, 9–20. Revised edition in Lewis, *They Asked for a Paper*, 166–82.

Lewis, C. S. *Transposition and Other Addresses* (London: Geoffrey Bles, 1949).

Lewis, C. S. *Undeceptions. Essays on Theology and Ethics*, edited by Walter Hooper (London: Geoffrey Bles, 1971).

Lewis, C. S. 'The Vision of John Bunyan'. In Lewis: *Selected Literary Essays*, 146–53.

Lewis, C. S. *The Voyage of the Dawn Treader* (London: Collins, 1968 [Bles, 1952]).

Lewis, C. S. 'The Weight of Glory'. *Theology* 43 (November 1941): 263–*. Reprinted in Lewis, *They Asked for a Paper*, 197–211.

Lewis, C. S. 'William Morris' (1937). In Lewis, *Selected Literary Essays*, 219–31.

Lewis, C. S. 'Williams and the Arthuriad'. In Williams and Lewis, *Arthurian Torso*, 93–200.

Lewis, C. S. *The World's Last Night and Other Essays* (New York: Harcourt, Brace and Co., 1960).

Lewis, C. S. and E. M. W. Tillyard. 'The Personal Heresy in Criticism'. *Essays and Studies by Members of the English Association* 19 (1934): 7–28.

Lillback, Peter A. *The Binding of God. Calvin's Role in the Development of Covenant Theology* (Grand Rapids, MI: Baker Academic, 2001).

Lindop, Grevel. *Charles Williams: The Third Inkling* (Oxford: Oxford University Press, 2015).

Link, H. G. 'Zur Kreuzestheologie; Gegenwärtige Probleme einer Kreuzestheologie. Ein Bericht'. *Evangelische Theologie* 33 (1973): 337–45.

Lois Lang-Sims (ed). *Letters to Lalage. The Letters of Charles Williams to Lois-Lang-Sims* (Kent, OH: Kent State University, 1989).

Louth, Andrew. 'Late Patristic Developments on the Trinity in the East'. In Gilles Emery and Matthew Levering (eds), *The Oxford Handbook of the Trinity*, 138–52 (Oxford: Oxford University Press, 2011).

Lowrie, Walter. *Kierkegaard* (London: Oxford University Press, 1938).

McClatchey, Joe H. 'Charles Williams and the Arthurian Tradition'. *VII: An Anglo-American Literary Review* 1 (1980): 51–62.

McCormack, Bruce L. *Karl Barth's Critically Realistic Dialectical Theology. Its Genesis and Development 1909–1936* (Oxford: Clarendon Press, 1995).

McCoull, L. S. B. '"A Woman Named Damaris": Pseudo-Dionysius' "Celestial Hierarch" in *The Place of the Lion*'. In Bray and Sturch, *Charles Williams and his Contemporaries*, 118–29.

McGrath, Alister. *C. S. Lewis: A Life, Eccentric Genius, Reluctant Prophet* (London: Hodder and Stoughton, 2013).

McGrath, Alister. *The Intellectual World of C. S. Lewis* (Oxford: Wiley-Blackwell, 2014).

McLaren, Scott. 'A Problem of Morality: Sacramentalism in the Early Novels of Charles Williams'. *Renascence* 56.2 (2004): 109–27.

MacSwain, Robert and Michael Ward (eds). *The Cambridge Companion to C. S. Lewis* (Cambridge: Cambridge University Press, 2010).

Mahan, David C. *An Unexpected Light. Theology and Witness in the Poetry and Thought of Charles Williams, Michael O'Siadhail, and Geoffrey Hill* (Cambridge: James Clark & Co., 2009).

Malory, Sir Thomas. *Works*, edited by Eugène Vinaver. 2nd edition (London: Oxford University Press, 1971).

Marion, Jean-Luc. *Being Given. Towards a Phenomenology of Givenness*, translated by Jeffrey L. Kossky (Stanford, CA: Stanford University Press, 2002).

Mascall, Eric. 'Charles Williams as I Knew Him'. In Horne, *Charles Williams: A Celebration*, 1–5.

Mascall, Eric. *He Who Is. A Study in Traditional Theism* (London: Longmans, Green & Co., 1958).

Mascall, Eric. *The Triune God. An Ecumenical Study* (London: Churchman Publishing, 1986).

Maynard, Theodore. 'The Poetry of Charles Williams'. *North American Review* 210.766 (1919): 401–11.

Medcalf, Stephen. 'Objections to Charles Williams'. In Horne, *Charles Williams: A Celebration*, 206–17.

Mendelson, Edward. *Later Auden* (London: Faber and Faber, 1999).

Mill, John Stuart. *A System Of Logic, Ratiocinative And Inductive*. 8th edition (New York: Harper and Brother, 1882).

Mirandola, Pico della. 'Seventy-One Cabalistic Conclusions According to My Own Opinion'. In Farmer, *Syncretism in the West*, 210–553.

Moltmann, Jürgen. *The Crucified God. The Cross of Christ as the Foundation and Criticism of Christian Theology*, translated by R. A. Wilson and J. Bowden (London: SCM Press, 1974).

Moltmann, Jürgen. *The Trinity and the Kingdom of God. The Doctrine of God*, translated by Margaret Kohl (London: SCM, 1981).

Moorman, Charles. *Arthurian Triptych: Mythic Materials in Charles Williams, C.S. Lewis, and T.S. Eliot* (Berkeley: University of California Press, 1960).

Moorman, Charles, *The Precincts of Felicity: The Augustinian City of the Oxford Christians* (Gainesville: University of Florida Press, 1966).

More, Henry. *The Immortality of the Soul. So farre forth as it is Demonstrable from the Knowledge of Nature and the Light of Reason* (London: J. Fletcher, 1659).

Moule, C. F. D. *An Idiom Book of New Testament Greek* (Cambridge: Cambridge University Press, 1963).

Newman, Barbara. 'Charles Williams and the Companions of the Co-inherence'. *Spiritus: A Journal of Christian Spirituality* 9.1 (2009): 1–26.

Newman, John Henry Cardinal, *The Arians of the Fourth Century* (London: J. G. & F. Rivington, 1833).

Niebuhr, Reinhold. *The Nature and Destiny of Man*. Vol. 1 (London: Nisbet, 1941).

Norris, R. A. *Manhood and Christ* (Oxford: Oxford University Press, 1963).

Noth, Martin. *Exodus. A Commentary*, translated by J. S. Bowden (London: SCM, 1962).

O'Donoghue, Bernard. *The Courtly Love Tradition* (Manchester: Manchester University Press, 1982).

O'Meara, Dominic J. *NeoPlatonism and Christian Thought* (Norfolk, VA: International Society for NeoPlatonic Studies, 1982).

Otto, Rudolph. *The Idea of the Holy. An Inquiry into the Non-Rational Factor in the Idea of the Divine and its Relation to the Rational* (London: Humphrey Milford/Oxford University Press, 1927).

Pannenberg, Wolfhart. *Anthropology in Theological Perspective*, translated by Matthew J. O'Connell (Edinburgh: T. & T. Clark, 1985).

Pannenberg, Wolfhart. *Systematic Theology*, translated by Geoffrey Bromiley. 3 volumes (Edinburgh: T. & T. Clark, 1991–98).

Patmore, Coventry. *Magna Moralia*, in *The Rod, the Root and the Flower* (London: George Bell, 1895).

Patmore, Coventry. *The Unknown Eros*, in *Poems*. 9th collective edition. 2 volumes (London: George Bell, 1906).

Patrick, James. 'Reason in Chesterton and Lewis'. *Chesterton Review* 17.3–4 (1991): 349–55.

Patrides, C. A. (ed). *The Cambridge Platonists* (Cambridge: Cambridge University Press, 1980).

Paulus, Michael J., Jr. 'From a Publisher's Point of View: Charles Williams' Role in Publishing Kierkegaard in English'. In Bray and Sturch, *Charles Williams and His Contemporaries*, 20–41.

Peirano, Robert. *Under the Mercy. Charles Williams and the Holy Graal* (Berkeley, CA: Apocryphile Press, 2014).

Perkins, William. *Hepieíkeia: or, a Treatise of Christian Equitie and Moderation* (Cambridge: John Legat, 1604).

Podmore, Simon D. 'The Holy & Wholly Other: Kierkegaard on the Alterity of God'. *The Heythrop Journal* 53.1 (2012): 9–23.

Poe, Harry Lee. *Becoming C. S. Lewis. A Biography of Young Jack Lewis (1898–1918)* (Wheaton, IL: Crossway, 2019).

Prestige, G. L. *God in Patristic Thought* (London: William Heinemann, 1936).

Prestige, Leonard. '*ΠΕΡΙΧΩΡΕΩ* and *ΠΕΡΙΧΩΡΗΣΙΣ* in the Fathers'. *Journal of Theological Studies* 115 (1928): 242–52.

Price, H. H. 'Survival and the Idea of "Another World"'. In John Donnelly (ed.), *Language, Metaphysics and Death*, 278–301 (New York: Fordham University Press, 1978).

Price, Michael W. 'The Seventeenth Century'. In Thomas L. Martin (ed.), *Reading the Classics with C.S. Lewis*, 140–61 (Grand Rapids, MI: Baker Academic/Paternoster, 2000).

'Pseudo-Dionysius'. 'The Celestial Hierarchy'. In *Pseudo-Dionysius: The Complete Works*, translated by Colm Luibheid, 143–92 (New York: Paulist Press, 1987).

Rahner, Karl. *On the Theology of Death*, translated by Charles Henkey (London: Burns and Oates, 1961).

Rahner, Karl. *The Trinity*, translated by Joseph Donceel (London: Burns and Oates, 1975).

Raine, Kathleen. *William Blake* (London: Thames and Hudson, 1970).

Reynolds, Barbara. *Dorothy L. Sayers. Her Life and Soul* (London: Hodder and Stoughton, 1993).

Ricks, Christopher and Jim McCue. *The Poems of T. S. Eliot*. 2 volumes (Faber & Faber, 2015).

Rist, John M. 'Forms of Individuals in Plotinus'. *The Classical Quarterly* 13.2 (1963): 223–31.

Ritter, Mary. 'William Wordsworth, *The Prelude*'. In Werther and Werther (eds), *C.S. Lewis' List*, 93–112.

Roberts, R. H. 'Barth's Doctrine of Time: Its Nature and Implications'. In Stephen Sykes (ed.), *Karl Barth—Studies of his Theological Methods* (Oxford: Clarendon Press, 1979).

Robertson, D. W. 'The Myth of Courtly Love'. In D. W. Robertson (ed.), *Speaking of Chaucer*, 154–63 (London: Athlone Press, 1970).

Rohr, Richard and Mike Morrell. *The Divine Dance. The Trinity and Your Transformation* (London: SPCK, 2016).

Rose, Mary Carman. 'The Christian Platonism of C. S. Lewis, J. R. R. Tolkien, and Charles Williams'. In O'Meara, *NeoPlatonism and Christian Thought*, 203–12.

Rougement, Denis de. *Passion and Society* (London: Faber & Faber, 1940).

Roukema, Aren. 'A Veil that Reveals: Charles Williams and the Fellowship of the Rosy Cross'. *Journal of Inklings Studies* 5.1 (2015): 22–71.

Rowland, Christopher. *Blake and the Bible* (New Haven, CT: Yale University Press, 2010).

Ruusbroec, Jan van. *The Spiritual Espousals*, translated by H. Rolfson (Collegeville, MN: Liturgical Press, 1995).

Sandys, William B. *Christmas Carols Ancient and Modern* (London: Richard Beckley, 1833).

Sayer, George. *Jack: A Life of C. C. Lewis* (London: Hodder and Stoughton, 1997).

Schakel, Peter J. 'Elusive Birds and Narrative Nets: The Appeal of Story in C. S. Lewis' Chronicles of Narnia'. In Walker and Patrick, *Christian for All Christians*, 116–31.

Schleiermacher, Friedrich. *The Christian Faith*, translated by H. R. Mackintosh and J. S. Stewart (T. & T. Clark, Edinburgh, 1928).

Schneider, Angelika. 'A Comparison of the Treatment of the Grail Legend in Tennyson's Idylls of the King and Williams'. Arthurian Cycle'. *The Charles Williams Quarterly* 125 (2007): 8–22.

Scholem, Gershom. *Kabbalah*. Library of Jewish Knowledge (Jerusalem: Keter Pub. House, 1974).

Schrag, Calvin O. *Communicative Praxis and the Space of Subjectivity* (Bloomington: Indiana University Press, 1986).

Schultz, Jeffrey D. and John G. West (eds). *The C.S. Lewis Readers' Encyclopedia* (Grand Rapids, MI: Zondervan, 1998).

Schwartz, Sanford. *C. S. Lewis on the Final Frontier. Science and the Supernatural in the Space Trilogy* (Oxford: Oxford University Press, 2009).

Schwartz, Sanford. 'Paradise Reframed: Lewis, Bergson, and Changing Times on Perelandra'. *Christianity and Literature* 51.4 (2002): 569–602.

Schwartz, Sanford. 'Perelandra in Its Own Time: A Modern View of the Space Trilogy'. In Wolfe and Wolfe, *C. S. Lewis's Perelandra*, 50–68.

Schweitzer, Albert. *The Mysticism of Paul the Apostle*, translated by W. Montgomery (New York: Henry Holt, 1931).

Scott (Renwick), Anne. 'Charles Williams as I Knew Him'. *Charles Williams Society Newsletter* 3 (Autumn 1976), 6–7.

Scott, Dominic. 'Platonic Recollection and Cambridge Platonism'. *Hermathena* 149 (1990): 73–97.

Seznec, Jean. *The Survival of the Pagan Gods. Mythological Tradition and its Place in Renaissance Humanism and Art*, translated by B. F. Sessions (New York: Pantheon, 1953).

Shepard, Odell. *The Lore of the Unicorn* (New York: Dover, 1993).

Shideler, Mary McDermott. *The Theology of Romantic Love: A Study in the Writings of Charles Williams* (Grand Rapids, MI: Eerdmans, 1966).

Sklar, Susanne M. *Blake's Jerusalem as Visionary Theatre. Entering the Divine Body* (Oxford: Oxford University Press, 2011).

Smilde, Arend. 'Horrid Red Herrings: A New Look at the "Lewisian Argument from Desire"—and Beyond'. *Journal of Inklings Studies* 4.1 (2014): 33–92.

Solovyov, Vladimir. *Russia and the Universal Church*, translated by Herbert Rees (London: Geoffrey Bles, 1948).

Stewart, Stanley. *The Expanded Voice. The Art of Thomas Traherne* (San Marino, CA: Huntingdon Library, 1970).

Strange, Steven K. 'Plotinus' Account of Participation in Ennead VI. 4-5'. *Journal of the History of Philosophy* 30.4 (1992): 479–96.

Tallon, Philip. 'Evil and the Cosmic Dance. C.S. Lewis and Beauty's Place in Theodicy'. In Baggett et al., *C.S. Lewis as Philosopher*, 195–210.

Tillich, Paul. *Systematic Theology*. Combined volume (Welwyn: Nisbet, 1968).

Tillyard, E. M. W. *Milton* (London: Chatto and Windus, 1930).

Tillyard, E. M. W. and C. S. Lewis. *The Personal Heresy. A Controversy*. Reprint (London: Oxford University Press, 1965).

Tishby, Isaiah. *La Kabbale. Anthologie de Zohar. Encyclopédie Juive* (Paris: Berg International, 1994).

Tolkien, J. R. R. *The Letters of J. R. R. Tolkien*, selected and edited by Humphrey Carpenter, with the assistance of Christopher Tolkien (Boston, MA: Houghton Mifflin Company, 1981).

Torrance, Thomas F. *The Christian Doctrine of God. One Being Three Persons*. 2nd edition (London: Bloomsbury, 2016 [T. & T. Clark, 1996]).

Torrance, Thomas F. *Karl Barth. An Introduction to his Early Theology, 1910-1931* (London: SCM Press, 1962).

Torrance, T. F. *The Trinitarian Faith. The Evangelical Theology of the Ancient Catholic Church* (Edinburgh: T. & T. Clark, 1988).

Torrance, Thomas F. *Trinitarian Perspectives. Toward Doctrinal Agreement* (Edinburgh: T. & T. Clark, 1994).

Traherne, Thomas. *Centuries of Meditations*, edited by Bertram Dobell (London: P.J. & A.E. Dobell, 1927).

Traherne, Thomas. *Poems, Centuries and Three Thanksgivings*, edited by Anne Ridler. Oxford Standard Authors (London: Oxford University Press, 1966).

Urang, Gunnar. *Shadows of Heaven: Religion and Fantasy in the Writing of C. S. Lewis, Charles Williams and J. R. R. Tolkien* (London: SCM Press, 1971).

Vidal, Jaime. 'The Ubiquitous Center in Bonaventure and Lewis: With Application to the Great Dance on Perelandra'. *CSL The Bulletin of the New York C.S. Lewis Society* 6 (March 1975): 1–6.

Waite, Arthur Edward. *The Hidden Church of the Holy Graal. Its Legends and Symbolism* (London: Rebman, 1909).

Waite, Arthur Edward. *The Holy Kabbalah. A Study of the Secret Tradition in Israel* (London: Williams and Norgate, 1929).

Waite, Arthur Edward. *The Secret Doctrine in Israel. A Study of the Zohar and Its Connections* (London: Rider, 1913).

Walker, Andrew and James Patrick. *A Christian for All Christians. Essays in Honour of C.S. Lewis* (London: Hodder and Stoughton, 1990).

Ward, Michael. 'The Church in C. S. Lewis' Fiction'. In Wolfe and Wolfe (eds), *C. S. Lewis and the Church*, 67–89.

Ward, Michael. *Planet Narnia. The Seven Heavens in the Imagination of C. S. Lewis* (Oxford: Oxford University Press, 2008).

Ware, Kallistos. 'C. S. Lewis, An "Anonymous Orthodox"?'. In Wolfe and Wolfe (eds), *C. S. Lewis and the Church*, 135–43.

Ware, Kallistos. 'Sacramentalism in C. S. Lewis and Charles Williams'. In White et al. (eds), *C. S. Lewis and His Circle*, 53–64.

Watkins, Gwen, 'Charles Williams and R. H. Benson'. In Horne (ed.), *Charles Williams: A Celebration*, 218–34.

Webster, John. *Barth's Moral Theology. Human Action in Barth's Thought* (Grand Rapids, MI: Eerdmans, 1998).

Welch, Claude. *The Trinity in Contemporary Theology* (London; SCM Press, 1953).

Wendling, Susan. 'Charles Williams: Priest of the Co-inherence'. *Published Colloquium Proceedings 1997–2016*: Vol. 5, Article 29. (2006). Available at: https://pillars.taylor.edu/inklings_forever/vol5/iss1/29/. Accessed 5/8/2021.

Werther, David and Susan Werther (eds). *C.S. Lewis' List. Ten Books that Influenced him Most* (London: Bloomsbury, 2015).

White, Roger, Judith Wolfe, and Brendan N. Wolfe (eds). *C. S. Lewis and His Circle. Essays and Memoirs from the Oxford C. S. Lewis Society* (Oxford: Oxford University Press, 2015).

Williams, Brian M. 'C. S. Lewis & John Hick on Theodicy: Superficially Similar but Significantly Different'. *Journal of Inklings Studies* 7.1 (2017): 3–28.

Williams, Charles. *All Hallows' Eve* (London: Faber & Faber, 1966 [1945]).

Williams, Charles. 'Blake and Wordsworth'. *Dublin Review* 208.417 (1941): 175–86. Reprinted in Williams, *Image of the City*, 59–67.

Williams, Charles. 'The Chances and Changes of Myth'. Review of F. C. Johnson (ed.), *La Grant Ystoire de Monsignor Tristan Li Bret*. *Time and Tide*, 23.29 (18 July 1942): 581–2. Reprinted in Williams, *Image of the City*, 183–85.

Williams, Charles. *Collected Plays*. Introduction by John Heath-Stubbs (London: Oxford University Press, 1963).

Williams, Charles. Critical Introduction to *Poems of Gerard Manley Hopkins*, edited with notes by Robert Bridges. 2nd edition, ix–xvi (London: Humphrey Milford/Oxford University Press, 1930).

Williams, Charles. 'The Cross'. In *What the Cross Means to Me: A Theological Symposium* (London: James Clarke & Co., 1943). Reprinted in Williams, *Image of the City*, 131–39.

Williams, Charles. *Descent into Hell* (London: Faber and Faber, 1961 [1937]).

Williams, Charles. *The Descent of the Dove. A Short History of the Holy Spirit in the Church* (London: Longmans, Green & Co, 1939).

Williams, Charles. 'A Dialogue on Hierarchy'. *Time and Tide* 24.40 (October 1943): 799. Reprinted in Williams, *Image of the City*, 127–30.

Williams, Charles. 'The Doctrine of Largesse', a Review of *Forgiveness and Reconciliation* by Vincent Taylor. *Time and Tide* 22.49 (6 December 1941): 1072. Reprinted in Williams, *Image of the City*, 140–1.

Williams, Charles. *The English Poetic Mind* (Oxford: Clarendon Press, 1932).

Williams, Charles. 'The Figure of Arthur'. In Williams and Lewis, *Arthurian Torso*, 5–90.

Williams, Charles. *The Figure of Beatrice* (London: Faber, 1943).

Williams, Charles. *The Forgiveness of Sins* (London: Geoffrey Bles/Centenary Press, 1942).

Williams, Charles. *The Greater Trumps* (London: Faber and Faber, 1965 [Gollancz, 1932]).

Williams, Charles. *He Came Down from Heaven* (London: William Heinemann, 1938).

Williams, Charles. *Heroes and Kings* (London: Henderson and Spalding, 1930; reprint Berkeley: Apocryphile Press, 2013).

Williams, Charles. *The House of the Octopus. A Play in Three Acts* (London: Edinburgh House Press, 1945). Reprinted in *Collected Plays of Charles Williams*, 245–324.

Williams, Charles. 'The Image of Man', review of *The Nature and Destiny of Man*. Volume I: *Human Nature* by Reinhold Niebuhr, *Time and Tide* 23.7 (14 February 1942): 136–137. Reprinted in Williams, *Image of the City*, 143–6.

Williams, Charles. *The Image of the City and Other Essays. Selected by Anne Ridler with a Critical Introduction* (London: Oxford University Press, 1958).

Williams, Charles. 'The Index of the Body'. *Dublin Review* 211.422 (July 1942): 13–20. Reprinted in Williams, *Image of the City*, 80–7.

Williams, Charles. 'The Jews', review of *Redeeming the Time* by Jacques Maritain, *Time and Tide* 24.33 (August 14, 1943):1066. Reprinted in Williams, *Image of the City*, 161–3.

Williams, Charles. 'John Milton'. Introduction, *The English Poems of John Milton*, edited by Charles Williams (London: Oxford University Press, 1940). Reprinted in Williams, *Image of the City*, 26–36.

Williams, Charles. *Judgement at Chelmsford* (Oxford: Oxford University Press, 1939).

Williams, Charles. 'Letters in Hell'. *Time and Tide* 23.12 (21 March 1942): 245–6.

Williams, Charles (ed). *The Letters of Evelyn Underhill* (London: Longmans, 1943).

Williams, Charles. 'The Making of Taliessin'. In Williams, *Image of the City*. Originally 'Charles Williams on *Taliessin through Logres*', *Poetry Review* 32 (1941): 77–81.

Williams, Charles. 'Malory and the Grail Legend'. *Dublin Review* 214.429 (April 1944): 144–153. Reprinted in Williams, *Image of the City*, 186–94.

Williams, Charles. *Many Dimensions* (Faber and Faber, 1947 [Gollancz, 1931]).

Williams, Charles. 'Natural Goodness'. *Theology* 43.256 (October 1941): 211–16. Reprinted in Williams, *Image of the City*, 75–80.

Williams, Charles. *The New Christian Year*. Chosen by Charles Williams (London: Oxford University Press, 1941).

Williams, Charles. 'Notes on the Arthurian Myth'. In Williams, *Image of the City*, 175–79.

Williams, Charles. 'Notes on the Way'. *Time and Tide* 23.10 (7 March 1942): 194–5.

Williams, Charles. 'One Way of Love'. *Time and Tide* 21.15 (13 April 1940): 394. Reprinted in Williams, *Image of the City*, 159–61.

Williams, Charles. *Outlines of Romantic Theology. With which is reprinted Religion and Love in Dante: The Theology of Romantic Love*, edited by Alice Mary Hadfield (Grand Rapids, MI: Eerdmans, 1990).

Williams, Charles. *The Place of the Lion* (London: Faber & Faber, 1962 [Gollancz, 1931]).

Williams, Charles. *Poems of Conformity* (London: Oxford University Press/Humphrey Milford, 1917).

Williams, Charles. 'The Problem of Pain'. *Theology* 42.247 (1941): 62–3.

Williams, Charles. *Reason and Beauty in the Poetic Mind* (Oxford; Clarendon Press, 1933).

Williams, Charles. 'The Redeemed City'. *Dublin Review* 209.419 (October 1941): 120–8. Reprinted in Williams, *Image of the City*, 102–10.

Williams, Charles. *The Region of the Summer Stars*. 2nd edition (London: Oxford University Press, 1950).

Williams, Charles. *Religion and Love in Dante* (London: Dacre Press/A. and C. Black, 1941).

Williams, Charles. 'St Anselm's Rabbit'. *Time and Tide* 24.41 (9 October 1943): 828.

Williams, Charles. 'The Screwtape Letters'. *Dublin Review* 211.423 (October 1942): 127–9.

Williams, Charles. 'Sensuality and Substance'. *Theology* 38.227 (May 1939): 352–60. Reprinted in Williams, *Image of the City*, 68–75.

Williams, Charles. *Shadows of Ecstasy* (London: Faber and Faber, 1968 [Gollancz, 1931]).

Williams, Charles. *The Silver Stair* (London: Herbert & Daniel, 1912).

Williams, Charles. 'The Society of Jesus'. *Time and Tide* 22.9 (1 March 1941): 176–7. Reprinted in Williams, *Image of the City*, 163–5.

Williams, Charles. *Taliessin through Logres*. Reprint (Oxford: Oxford University Press, 1969).

Williams, Charles. *The Terror of Light*. In Williams, *Collected Plays*, 325–74.

Williams, Charles. 'The Theology of Crisis'. *Time and Tide* 21.24 (15 June 1940): 644.

Williams, Charles. *To Michal from Serge, Letters from Charles Williams to His Wife, Florence, 1939-1945*, edited by Roma A. King, Jr (Kent, OH: Kent State University Press, 2002).

Williams, Charles. *War in Heaven* (London: Faber and Faber, 1957 [Gollancz, 1930].

Williams, Charles. *The Way of Exchange*. A Pamphlet (London: James Clarke, 1941). Reprinted in Williams, *Image of the City*, 147–54.

Williams, Charles. *Windows of Night* (London: Oxford University Press, n.d. [1925]).

Williams, Charles. *Witchcraft* (London: Faber and Faber, 1941).

Williams, Charles and C. S. Lewis. *Arthurian Torso. Containing the Posthumous Fragment of The Figure of Arthur by Charles Williams and a Commentary on the Arthurian Poems of Charles Williams by C. S. Lewis* (London: Oxford University Press, 1969 [1948]).

Williams, Rowan. 'Charles Williams'. *Journal of Inklings Studies* 6.1 (2016): 161–6.

Williams, Rowan. *The Lion's World. A Journey into the Heart of Narnia* (London: SPCK, 2012).

Williams, Rowan. 'That Hideous Strength: A Reassessment'. In White et al. (eds), *C. S. Lewis and His Circle*, 91–109.

Wilson, A. N. *C. S. Lewis: A Biography* (London: Collins, 1990).

Wilson-Kastner, Patricia. *Faith, Feminism and the Christ* (Philadelphia, PA: Fortress, 1983).

Wink, Walter. *Unmasking the Powers* (Philadelphia, PA: Fortress Press, 1986).

Wolfe, Brendan. 'A Note on the Date of C.S. Lewis' Conversion to Theism'. *Journal of Inklings Studies* 9.1 (2019): 68–9.

Wolfe, Judith. 'C. S. Lewis and the Eschatological Church'. In Wolfe and Wolfe (eds), *C. S. Lewis and the Church*, 103–16.

Wolfe, Judith and Brendan Wolfe (eds). *C. S. Lewis and the Church. Essays in Honour of Walter Hooper* (London: T & T Clark, 2011).

Wolfe, Judith and Brendan Wolfe (eds). *C. S. Lewis's Perelandra. Reshaping the Image of the Cosmos* (Kent, OH: Kent State University Press, 2013).

Woolf, Rosemary. 'Doctrinal Influences on The Dream of the Rood'. In Woolf, *Art and Doctrine. Essays on Medieval Literature*, edited by Heather O'Donoghue, 29–48 (London: Hambledon Press, 1986).

Wordsworth, William. *The Prelude 1799, 1805, 1850*, edited by Jonathan Wordsworth, M. H. Abrams, and Stephen Gill (New York: W. W. Norton, 1979).

Wright, N. T. 'Simply Lewis: Reflections on a Master Apologist after 60 Years'. *Touchstone* 20.2 (2007): 28–33.

Yates, Francis A. *The Occult Philosophy in the Elizabethan Age* (London: Routledge & Kegan Paul, 1979).

Yeats, W. B. *A Vision*. Reprint (London: Macmillan, 1981).

Zaleski, Philip and Carol Zaleski. *The Fellowship. The Literary Lives of the Inklings: J. R. R. Tolkien, C. S. Lewis, Owen Barfield, Charles Williams* (New York: Farrar, Strauss and Giroux, 2015).

Zizioulas, John D. *Being as Communion* (London: Dalton, Longman and Todd, 1985).

Index

3. Writings of Charles Williams